TIGERS BURNING BRIGHT
SOE HEROES IN THE FAR EAST

After a career including twelve years as an infantry officer with the Grenadier Guards and a long and enjoyable stint in international advertising and public relations, Alan Ogden decided to change direction and write about the history and culture of Eastern Europe. His books include *Romania Revisited*, *Fortresses of Faith*, *Revelations of Byzantium* and *Moons and Aurochs*. In 2010, *Through Hitler's Back Door*, his well-received study of SOE in Hungary, Bulgaria and Romania, broke new ground and *A Spur Called Courage* and *Sons of Odysseus* continued his coverage of the courage and heroism of SOE operatives.

TIGERS BURNING BRIGHT
SOE HEROES IN THE FAR EAST

Lieutenant Colonel Frank Chester [centre]

ALAN OGDEN
2013

By the same author

History

Sons of Odysseus: SOE Heroes in Greece

A Spur Called Courage: SOE Heroes in Italy

Through Hitler's Back Door: SOE operations in Hungary, Bulgaria and Romania

The Discontented: Love, War and Betrayal in Habsburg Hungary

Travel

Moons and Aurochs: Romanian Journeys

Winds of Sorrow: Journeys in and around Transylvania

Romania Revisited: On The Trail of English travellers 1602-1941

Art and Architecture

Revelations of Byzantium: The Monasteries and Painted Churches of Northern Moldavia

Fortresses of Faith: The Kirchenburgen of Transylvania

Tigers Burning Bright

SOE Heroes in the Far East

First published in 2013 by

Bene Factum Publishing Ltd

PO Box 58122

London

SW8 5WZ

Email: inquiries@bene-factum.co.uk

www.bene-factum.co.uk

ISBN: 978-1-903071-55-7

Text © Alan Ogden

The rights of Alan Ogden to be identified as the Author of this Work have been asserted by him in accordance with the Copyright, Designs and Patents Act, 1988.

All rights reserved. This book is sold under the condition that no part of it may be reproduced, copied, stored in a retrieval system or transmitted in any form or by any means, electronic, mechanical, photocopying, recording or otherwise without prior permission in writing of the publisher.

A CIP catalogue record of this is available from the British Library

Design and typesetting by Carnegie Publishing

Cover by Mousemat Design Ltd

Printed and bound in Malta on behalf of Latitude Press Ltd

Contents

	Introduction	1
Chapter One	Overview	7
PART ONE	SOE IN SOUTH EAST ASIA AND CHINA	31
Chapter Two	The Oriental Mission	32
Chapter Three	The India Mission and the Andaman Islands	63
Chapter Four	Burma	86
Chapter Five	Malaya	146
Chapter Six	Sumatra	207
Chapter Seven	China and Hong Kong	213
Chapter Eight	Thailand [Siam]	257
Chapter Nine	Operation Hainton / Heavy / Wolf	279
Chapter Ten	French Indo-China	287
PART TWO	SOE IN SOUTH WEST PACIFIC AREA	303
Chapter Eleven	SOE in Australia	304
Chapter Twelve	Jaywick and Rimau	319
Chapter Thirteen	Dutch East Indies	341
Chapter Fourteen	Borneo	349
Chapter Fifteen	Java, Lombok, Celebes and Molucca Islands	380
Chapter Sixteen	New Guinea	392
Chapter Seventeen	Timor	395
Chapter Eighteen	Epilogue	404
Annex A	Nixon's Memo to Taylor	406
Annex B	Natural Resources in Japanese Occupied Areas	408
Annex C	Tropical Diseases	412
Annex D	Mackenzie's 1945 Report on Force 136	415
Annex E	Notes on Force 136 Intelligence	421
Annex F	Summary of Force 136 Casualties in Burma	429
Annex G	Force 136 Establishment August 1945	431
Annex H	Notes on Use of JEDBURGHS	442
Annex I	HAINTON Supply Sorties	445
Annex J	V Force	447

Annex K	GSI[z]/Z Force	449
Annex L	Peter Fleming's Notes on China	451
Annex M	Allied Intelligence Agencies	457

Abbreviations	459
Glossary	462
Selected Bibliography	464
Index	468

To Robin Bieber

'War is the greatest curse of our age; the word which best describes it in my opinion, is waste: waste of time, money, friends, materials, chances, hopes – waste of everything. You would think, then, that those who take part in it would loathe every moment they were so engaged: and it is a tribute to the incredible ingenuity of the devil that it is not so. In war, many find the thrill, the excitement, and the sense of adventure they have failed to find in peacetime. I did. In danger, many find a wonderful comradeship with their fellow men – of all creeds and colours. I did. In war many people see interesting places they could never have seen but for war. I did. The worst part of war is not action. The worst things in war, in order, are the long separations from wives and families, and the deadly, soul-destroying, everlasting training, after which action becomes a pleasant and adventurous change. Yet that "pleasant and adventurous change" will be for the purpose of destroying as many of one's fellow creatures as possible at the smallest cost in lives to ourselves – what a fearful thought! I devoutly trust, therefore, that peace, as it can and as it should, will give to all soldiers who, like myself, are returning to civil life, the chances for adventure, comradeship and interest which we found in war, so that the great qualities of leadership, bravery, self-sacrifice and a host of others, which war brought forth, may be in future used for the rebuilding of the world and not for the waste and misery of war.'

Major John Hedley, DSO
Force 136

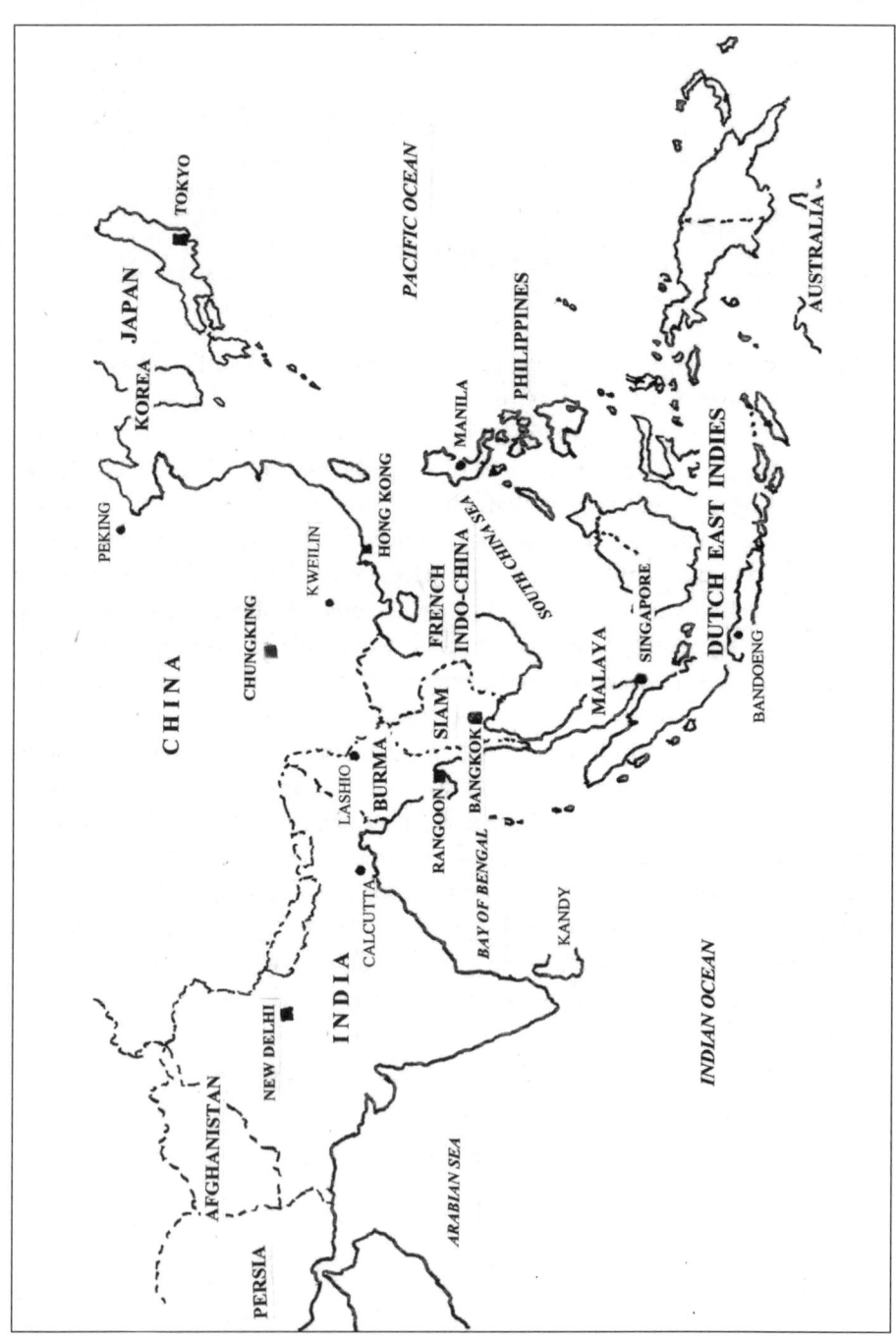

India and the Far East 1941-45

Introduction

Freddy Spencer Chapman's inspirational wartime SOE memoir was called *The Jungle is Neutral*. But Freddy's jungle was not neutral in the sense of harmless; indeed, for those who venture into its interior today, it is still not for tropical diseases and an antagonistic array of Mother Nature's creatures lie in wait for the unwary and ill-prepared. What Chapman implied was that the jungle provides an equally hostile hence impartial field of battle on which friend and foe fight out their differences. Both are exposed to its vicissitudes, limitations, hardships and dangers. For the men of SOE, who lived behind enemy lines, there was a host of additional threats from the implausibility of passing themselves off as natives, overextended lines of communications serviced by scant resources, the relentless vagaries of the weather dictating supply drops to the ruthless tactics of Japanese security forces and counter-intelligence agencies.

Soldiering in the jungle has its own set of obligations, almost the equivalent to those of a particularly ascetic monastic order. In the closed world of the jungle, where visibility rarely exceeds fifteen metres, where rivers mutate from slow running streams to raging torrents overnight, where often the only paths are those made by wild animals, silence is proverbially golden for the sound of an alarmed animal or bird, the crack of a broken branch and the echo of animated human voices all act as warnings of enemy troops. Add to those the tell-tale aroma of burning tobacco, the odours of cooking and camp fires, the scent of sweat and cosmetics like toothpaste, the litter of packaging on a jungle track, a give-away footprint, and ill-disciplined firing of weapons and it is hardly surprising that movement, at the best of times retarded by nature, becomes a silent sally in slow motion.

It was within this world of tropical forests, impenetrable mangrove swamps, steep mountain ranges, monsoon downpours, swollen rivers, terrorised and intimidated natives, anti-colonial nationalist bands and a determined and ruthless occupying power – Japan – that the officers and men of SOE operated, inserted either by submarine or Catalina flying boat or dropped from Hudson and Liberator bombers. They were literally hundreds of miles behind enemy lines, dependent on resupply either by air or sea or surviving in local communities by buying food. *In extremis*, they lived off the land. In the early days, many were recruited from the Colonial structures of police forces, forestry departments and the Civil Service for they knew the people, the languages and the land. Later this cadre was reinforced by experienced officers and NCOs who had already won their spurs with Jedburgh teams in occupied France or with SOE Missions in Greece and Yugoslavia. All were heroic. So in trying to put together a representative sample of SOE heroes in the Far East, I am only too conscious of doing an injustice to those whose stories I have not told.

*****

It would have been churlish to attempt to tell the stories of Freddy Spencer Chapman, Pat Noone and Tom Harrisson without delving into their pre-war careers. All were extraordinary young men, utterly fearless, highly intelligent and with that strong quirkiness and eccentricity so admired by the British. They were part of a generation that included Andrew Croft, Bill Tilman, Quentin Riley, Sandy Glen, Patrick Leigh Fermor and Peter Fleming who all had a passion for adventure and exploration and, not surprisingly, gravitated towards SOE and its ilk when it came to serving their country in the Second World War.

*****

Partisan and guerrilla warfare by definition extends way beyond the uniformed armies of nation states. In the Far East, the security and success of SOE depended on the loyalty and courage of a host of different constituencies, from the Chinese Communists and Malay resistance fighters in Malaya to serving officers in the Thai Armed Forces and patriotic Overseas Chinese scattered across the Western Pacific seaboard. One group which merits particular commendation for their bravery is the aboriginal people of South East Asia. Some like the Chins, Kachins and Karens in Burma were partially motivated by the promise of autonomy after the war but others like the Temiar people in the highlands of Malaya and the Kenyah and Kelabit tribes of Borneo had nothing to gain other than to honour their ancient customs of hospitality. These peoples willingly embraced the Allied cause and in doing so put their lives and those of their families and villages on the line for little or no reward. They are the unsung heroes.

*****

The geographical limits of SOE as a British wartime agency in the Far East were defined by the entrance of the United States as a belligerent power after the December 1941 Japanese attack on Pearl Harbour. Essentially, after that devastating shock, the vast theatre of war in the Far East was divided into three sectors. In the west, from 1943 onwards South East Asia Command [SEAC] under Admiral Lord Louis Mountbatten covered India, Burma, Malaya and Java and Sumatra; in the East, South West Pacific Command [SWPC], the preserve of US General Douglas MacArthur, took in New Guinea, Timor, Borneo, the Philippines and the myriad of islands that make up the intricate sprawl of the Dutch East Indies. To the north, Free China, an uneasy combination of Generalissimo Chiang Kai-shek's nationalists and Mao Tseng's Communists, fought against a common enemy in the Japanese. Allied support primarily took the form of Lend-Lease aid from the US and hence the senior military representative was a US General, initially Brigadier-General John Magruder, head of the American Mission to China [AMMISCA], and then from March 1942 General Vinegar Joe Stilwell, commander of the American Army Forces China Burma India Theatre [CBI].

There were some countries that lay outside these divisions – clandestine operations in French Indo-China belonged in the bailiwick of the Free French who operated within the structure of SOE but with their own coded signals traffic; Thailand, once the preserve of CBI, was transferred to SEAC, when both British and American special forces competed against each other in a game of one-upmanship overseen by their political masters. Australia put its own version of SOE, the Services Reconnaissance Department [SRD], at the disposal of both SEAC and SWPC. Although the SRD was an integral part of the Australian Military Forces and in that respect under the political control of Canberra and military control of SWPC, I have included a number of SRD Missions in which seconded SOE British and Dutch personnel took part. SOE worked hard at their relationship with their Australian counterparts and after an erratic start, it prospered.

*****

Sixty-eight years after the momentous events of the atomic bombing of Hiroshima and Nagasaki, it is easy to lose sight of where the Allies had reached in August 1945. SOE, having trained and armed substantial guerrilla forces in Malaya and Thailand, was gearing up to support fiercely contested invasions of both countries by working closely with the invasion forces as they sought to overcome anticipated fanatical Japanese resistance. In China, with the threat of civil war ever closer by the day, the objectives were the relief of Hong Kong and the interdiction of retreating Japanese armies as they made their way north. Although the Allies now enjoyed both air and maritime superiority, the prognostications were that it would be a long and bloody struggle. In this respect, the final chapter of the story of SOE in the Far East was providentially never written.

*****

The labour of deciding on correct spelling of place names and surnames on such a vast canvas has proved Herculean. As a general rule, I have used pre-war spellings of place names to match SOE and OSS historical reports e.g. Yenan rather than Yanan. Surnames of non-Europeans have a habit of varying from report to report, so I have tried to adopt those in general usage by other historians. Irrespective of my efforts, there will be for some people and places errors for which I readily apologise. In the instance of Thailand, there were at the time two schools of nomenclature. The Thai resistance movement in the US was known as the Free Thai Movement and in the UK as the Free Siam Movement. Since the name Thailand was officially adopted by Siam in 1939, I have used it throughout the Thailand chapter although I acknowledge the two names of the resistance movement to differentiate their separate political origins.

One particular phrase used by SOE in Malaya and Burma, 'left behind parties', struck me as ambiguous for it could convey a sense almost of accident or dereliction. So I have used 'stay behind parties' instead to describe a premeditated military strategy of establishing well organised small groups of trained men to remain behind enemy lines once an invading army has moved through them.

*****

Abbreviations and acronyms tended to proliferate in pre-war and wartime military and colonial circles and I have tried to keep them to a minimum. Many were intended to confuse for it must be remembered that SOE was a Top Secret organisation whose operatives had signed the Official Secrets Act, thereby acknowledging that their lips were sealed and like all servicemen their letters home censored. The idea was simple – the enemy were not to know of their existence. SOE adopted the cover name of Ministry of Economic Warfare and from 1944 onwards branded its Far East operations as 'Force 136' which replaced their original designator of GSI[k]; in the case of SIS – the Secret Intelligence Service – this Top Secret agency called itself in the Far East the

ISLD or the Inter Services Liaison Department. For the sake of clarity, I have used Force 136 and ISLD wherever possible in the Far East context.

*****

The structure of *Tigers Burning Bright* is designed to simplify what was a complex series of operations in several countries and embracing many different cultures across a four year time-frame. To accommodate the crucial distinction between British and US command, I have divided it into two parts: Part One embraces the ORIENTAL Mission, the INDIA Mission and Force 136 in SEAC; Part Two covers SOE activities in SEAC and SWPC which were in support of Special Operations Australia [SOA]. Within each part, each country in which SOE operated is discussed through the device of an introduction about politics, a summary of operations and then through the profiles of a number of outstandingly brave SOE officers and men. At the end of the book are a number of annexes supporting and illustrating some of the narrative in the main body of the text.

*****

As Clausewitz wrote, 'the end for which the soldier is recruited, clothed, armed and trained...is simply that he should fight at the right place and at the right time.' This may appear to be stating the obvious but the complexity of military organisation that underpins this tenet should never be underestimated. For SOE staff officers in London and in Meerut, Calcutta, Kandy and Melbourne, the intricacies and difficulties of 'battlefield delivery' were massive. Recruitment, training in all the various disciplines of Special Forces activities, procurement of equipment, logistics, planning, insertion/extraction, resupply, signals, medical care, intelligence acquisition and analysis, all these processes demanded extraordinary attention to detail, imagination in the sense that many operations had never been attempted before, perseverance to overcome obstructions and delays and an overall compliance to the highest standards: all represented huge challenges for an organisation started from scratch. The fact that, in the main, the execution of all these processes was little short of excellent is a testament to the brilliance and hard work of the SOE leadership and staff.

*****

My thanks to Dr Rod Bailey, Simon Keswick, Clive Lyon and Captain Jamie Lyon, Mrs Kirstie Phipps [née Mackenzie], John Trappes-Lomax, Mrs Jamie

Korner [née Julia Croft], the late Peter Goss formerly of Force 136, John Andrews of the Special Forces Club, Mrs Lois Watson, Dr Steven Kippax, Rich Duckett, Hugh and Gabriella Bullock [Major Billy Moss], Lord [James] Lindsay, Susan Lawrence, Jeremy Taylor, Anne Wedell-Wedellsborg, Henrik Wedell-Wedellsborg, the Imperial War Museum Collections, the National Archives, the British Library – and not forgetting, first, the memoirs of those many brave members of SOE who put pen to paper, thus enabling later generations to access their first-hand accounts of life behind enemy lines, and second, the rich historiography of post-war and contemporary historians which has thrown much needed light on a hitherto dark corner of clandestine warfare in the Far East.

Alan Ogden
London
April 2013

CHAPTER ONE

OVERVIEW

THE POLITICAL SPECTRUM

The European colonial empires in the Far East were far from peaceable backwaters in 1940. In fact, many colonies seethed with discontent. Strikes and revolts were ruthlessly suppressed in the 1930s by the British in Burma [suppression of Saya San rebellion], the Dutch in the Indonesian archipelago [suppression of all political parties] and the French in Vietnam [Yen Bay Uprising and the Nguh Tinh soviets]. Nationalist movements including fledgling Communist parties were banned, their leaders exiled or imprisoned.

The Japanese were quick to exploit the simmering dissatisfaction between the rulers and the ruled and explained how their concept of the Greater East Asia Sphere of Co-Prosperity would help the people they liberated to throw off the colonial yoke and take charge of their own destinies. It was not surprising therefore that in many areas they were welcomed, not unlike the warm reception afforded to invading German armies in the Ukraine. But Japan, like Germany, failed to capitalise on this goodwill and before long imposed a harsh economic regime on the occupied territories to serve her rapacious appetite for raw materials and food.

Colonial police forces were replaced by the Japanese Kempeitai, who used the same methods of intelligence gathering, this time executed with far more ruthlessness and with no civil accountability.

Although Great Britain and the United States were pursuing the same strategic goal of ultimately defeating Japan, Burma was still very much a permanent British possession in the eyes of Winston Churchill, who had no intention of presiding over the dissolution of the British Empire. Churchill saw the *status quo ante bellum* as a primary British war aim, with India, Malaya and Burma remaining colonies.

President Franklin D. Roosevelt had a rather different vision for a post-war Asia. Roosevelt believed that the European empires in the Far East were archaic and that their colonies would soon be independent countries, a view shared by the American liberal intelligentsia[1] and big business. He also wanted China treated as an equal Allied partner in the war against Japan in the hope that it would develop into a great power, friendly to the West.

The United States did of course have its own colonial possession in the South West Pacific, the Philippines. Taken from Spain in 1898 and incorporated as American territory under President McKinley's Proclamation of Benevolent Assimilation, Washington had deftly distanced itself from the European 'imperialists' by passing an act in 1935 giving the Philippines a ten year 'transitional period' to full independence. As far as Roosevelt was concerned, this set the standard for others to aspire to.

Throughout the war with Japan, these divergent views were to colour SOE policy, both in London and in the field.

SOE: EARLY DAYS

On 19 July 1940, after the last British troops had left mainland Europe, the Lord President of the Council [Neville Chamberlain] recorded that the Prime Minister [Winston Churchill] had decided that Section D [the sabotage service, a curious hybrid of SIS and the War Office], MI R [the War Office's irregular warfare wing] and Electra House [the propaganda arm of the Ministry of Information, formerly part of SIS] should all be amalgamated to form the Special Operations Executive [SOE] under the Minister for Economic Warfare [MEW]. On 22 July, the War cabinet formally approved these new arrangements.

When Hugh Dalton, the Old Etonian Labour MP and son of Queen Victoria's Chaplain, was given the task of running SOE by Churchill in July 1940, he first had to set out the scope of its activities. In *The Fateful Years*, he recalls:

> 'As to its scope, "sabotage" was a simple idea. It meant smashing things up. "Subversion" was a more complex conception. It meant the weakening, by whatever "covert" means, of the enemy's will and power to make war, and the strengthening of the will and power of his opponents, including in particular guerrilla and resistance movements.'

Subversion was indeed to prove a complex conception and just how it was

---

1 Pearl Buck, the best-selling author and Nobel Prize winner and arguably one of the most influential American women of her generation, campaigned for Indian independence throughout the war. She was vehemently opposed to Churchill's promotion of the British Empire and attacked him in the US media on numerous occasions. An expert on China, she sent General Donovan a fourteen page memo in 1943 on how the OSS should conduct itself in that theatre.

OVERVIEW

	CALICUT · COCHIN · QUILON · COLOMBO · CALCUTTA · SINGAPORE · PENANG · KUALA LUMPUR	

HARRISONS & CROSFIELD
LIMITED

1-4, Great Tower Street, London, E.C.3

With Branches and Associated Companies throughout the East, and in Canada, U.S.A., Australia and New Zealand.

Managing Agents of
Plantation, Mining and Industrial undertakings.
Secretaries of the following London Companies producing Rubber, Tea and other Produce :

	Issued Capital		Issued Capital
Allied Sumatra	£1,400,000	Malayalam	£1,812,021
Anglo-Malay	412,507	Malaysia	45,000
Ankola	46,250	Mendaris	430,862
Asahan	130,000	Namoe Tongan	337,500
Bah Lias	351,213	Pataling Rubber	305,146
Bajoe Kidoel	248,960	Pataling Royalties	22,503
Bikam	544,800	Prang Besar	85,400
Bila	171,343	Rubber Estates	
British Borneo		of Johore	188,444
Timber	180,000	Sandac	110,930
Central Sumatra	100,088	Seaport	187,500
Cluny	70,000	Sialang	300,000
Djasinga	448,126	Soengei Rampah	85,000
Golden Hope	364,490	Straits Plantations	526,692
Hoscote	166,378	Strathisla	80,000
Kasintoe	120,000	Sumatra Tea	439,250
Lanadron	360,000	Tai Tak	91,679
Langen	125,000	Tandjong	250,000
Ledbury	108,600	Toerangie	178,627
London Asiatic	929,928	United Serdang	1,423,272
Lumut	211,482	Wampoe	175,000
Lunuva	815,115	Rubber Trust	2,469,384

etc. etc.

Telegrams and Cables :
" Harricros, Bilgate,
London "

Telephone :
Mansion House 4333

	CHRISTCHURCH · PERTH · ADELAIDE · MELBOURNE · SYDNEY · BRISBANE · JOHANNESBURG	

Britain's overseas assets: advertisement in LSE Year Book 1939 meant to be applied in the Far East was from the very beginning far from clear.

After a period of inactivity, the terms of reference for an SOE group in Singapore were agreed by SOE HQ on 26 November 1940 and two months later the Governors of the Straits Settlements and Hong Kong were advised that the ORIENTAL Mission under Val Killery would be operating in their areas under the CinC Far East. It was the start of an extraordinary undertaking during which the courage and ingenuity of a small group of men would be tested to the extreme.

The scale of the task turned out to be enormous. The countries eventually covered by SOE in the Far East included India and Ceylon; Free and Occupied China; Korea; Manchuria; the Japanese Empire; Siberia; Afghanistan; Persia; French Indo-China [FIC]; Thailand; the Philippines; the Dutch East Indies [DEI]; Burma; Malaya; Hong Kong; Borneo; Sarawak and a host of smaller islands within the area of operations.

The initial senior intake of the ORIENTAL and INDIA Missions was nearly all distinguished businessmen. John Keswick was from Jardine Matheson, Val Killery from ICI, Colin Mackenzie from J&P Coats and Gavin Stewart from Stewart & Lloyds. The next level down was drawn from civil servants like Ritchie Gardiner and Innes Tremlett with extensive local knowledge and experience. Apart from a handful of energetic and adventurous young officers, the military was woefully under-represented. This emphasis reflected the view of SOE's first chief, Sir Frank Nelson[2] – and later the banker Sir Charles Hambro – that their brief included the destruction of the integrity of the enemy's financial and commercial infrastructure as well as his armies.

Sir John Lomax, a Foreign Office [FO] seconded to MEW, endorsed this when he wrote:

'That MEW achieved so much was a near miracle – largely the result of its inspired objectives and staffing. From the City and the law a truly remarkable collection of brains and experience was collected. Its top ranks were a cross section through the upper slice of the city solicitors, merchant banks and insurance, with a few of the more versatile members of the diplomatic service as a bridle upon lay enthusiasm'.

---

2   Nelson had started his career in India as an assistant in the firm of Symons, Barlow and Co, rising to be the senior partner. In 1922 and 1923 he was Chairman of the Bombay Chamber of Commerce and then President of the Associated Chambers of Commerce of India and Ceylon. From 1922 to 1924 Nelson was a member of the legislative council of Bombay. In 1924 he was knighted and returned to England, being elected Conservative MP for the Stroud division of Gloucestershire that year. He was re-elected in 1929 but resigned in May 1931 in order to go into business, being for some time joint managing director of the Lamson Paragon Supply Company.

OVERVIEW

At the heart of SOE's political objectives in the Far East was a desire to orchestrate a post-war world where British trade and investment could continue to flourish. Richard Aldrich in *Intelligence and the War against Japan* draws attention to a Department of Overseas Trade report to the Cabinet Far East Committee in which it refers to a report from SOE's John Keswick that 'the balance of British representation in Free China after the Japanese occupation of the coastal area could only be described as pathetic. He states that apart from Jardine Matheson, the Asiatic Petroleum Company, Butterfield and Swire, Barry and Dodwell, the British American Tobacco Company and a few others who maintain one man and a boy each, nothing remained.' The message was clear: ignore Britain's commercial and financial interests at the country's peril.

ALLOCATION OF BRITISH MILITARY ASSETS DECEMBER 1941

Formation	UK	Middle East	Persia and Iraq	Far East [Malaya][3]
British armoured divisions	6	3	none	none
British infantry divisions	21 excluding 9 'county' divisions for home defence	2	none	none
Dominion infantry divisions	2	6	none	1
Indian infantry divisions	none	2	3	2
Totals	29	13	3	3

A corollary of this line of thinking manifested itself in an underlying distrust of US post-war ambitions to dismantle the colonial possessions of the European powers and then install democratic government, in effect opening up their markets to US banks and business. The stark reality was that colonialism meant

---

3   On 2 August 1941 General Percival had asked the WO for reinforcements, insisting that he needed as a minimum a total of forty-eight battalions. One division was wanted to defend the Perlis-Kedah area; one for Kelantan-Trengganu-Pahang; one, with a tank regiment, for a reserve to III Indian Corps in northern Malaya; one for the defence of Johore; one and a tank regiment for Singapore Island. The Chiefs of Staff accepted this appreciation, but said that they could not provide the reinforcements required. In the event, the only substantial reinforcement to reach Singapore between August and December was the 28 Indian Brigade which arrived in September, poorly trained and incompletely equipped. Percival was still short of fifteen infantry battalions.

possession. The London Stock Exchange [LSE] Daily List of 9 September 1939 contains the names of hundreds of companies who traded in India and South East Asia from Indian Railway stocks like the Scinde, Punjab & Delhi Railway Company to the New Crocodile River [Selangor] Rubber Company in Malaya. And it was not just companies operating within the Dominions and Colonies for British capital had been widely invested in the Dutch East Indies [Allied Sumatra owned 44,205 acres of rubber plantations there and Anglo-Dutch Plantations of Java owned 215,607 acres in West Java] and China, e.g. The Shanghai Electric Construction Company Limited and The Oriental Telephone & Electric Company of Hong Kong.

Almost every aspects of commercial activity had been securitised. In Burma, for instance, one finds the Burma Railways Company, the Burma Electricity Supply Company, the Burma Oil Company [with refineries in Rangoon], the British Burma Petroleum Company [which owned the Yenangyaung oil fields], the Eastern Petroleum & Finance Company [majority shareholder in Salay Oil Lands Limited in Burma], the Rangoon Electric Tram and Supply Company, British & Burmese Steam Navigation Company Limited, and the quaintly named Irrawaddy Flotilla Company Limited. There were no less that eighty-seven quoted rubber stocks [with 455 unquoted rubber companies on the LSE Supplementary List] and fifty-four tea companies. All were customers of either The Chartered Bank of India, Australia and China or of the Hong Kong Shanghai Bank, today's HSBC.

It was ironic that when the physical security of the British Isles was threatened by the Germans, her principal financial and mercantile assets lay scattered across the globe from South America to New Zealand to such an extent that when the Japanese struck in December 1941 she was incapable of defending them.

*****

The first director of Overseas Groups and Missions, Colonel Brien Clarke, appointed Colonel Christopher Hudson in August 1941 as the head of the Far Eastern branch in London. Hudson sent a regular officer, Major A.B. O'Dwyer, to Singapore that September to inspect SOE field operations. He returned with a dismal report, concluding that too little had been done too late, not as a result of inertia on the part of SOE but due to the reluctance of both the FO and the War Office [WO] to appreciate the seriousness of the Japanese threat. The preparations and counter-measures proposed by SOE had fallen on stony ground.

OVERVIEW

After the surrender of Singapore in February 1942, together with Egerton Mott, Val Killery had managed to escape to Australia by boat. His report on the ORIENTAL Mission chronicled a series of disasters. The speed of the Japanese advance had been breathtaking with Malaya capitulating in January, Singapore, Timor and much of the DEI in February, Java in March, Borneo in April and Burma in May.

At around the same time that the ORIENTAL Mission was established, Colin Mackenzie of J&P Coats was appointed to set up SOE's INDIA Mission at

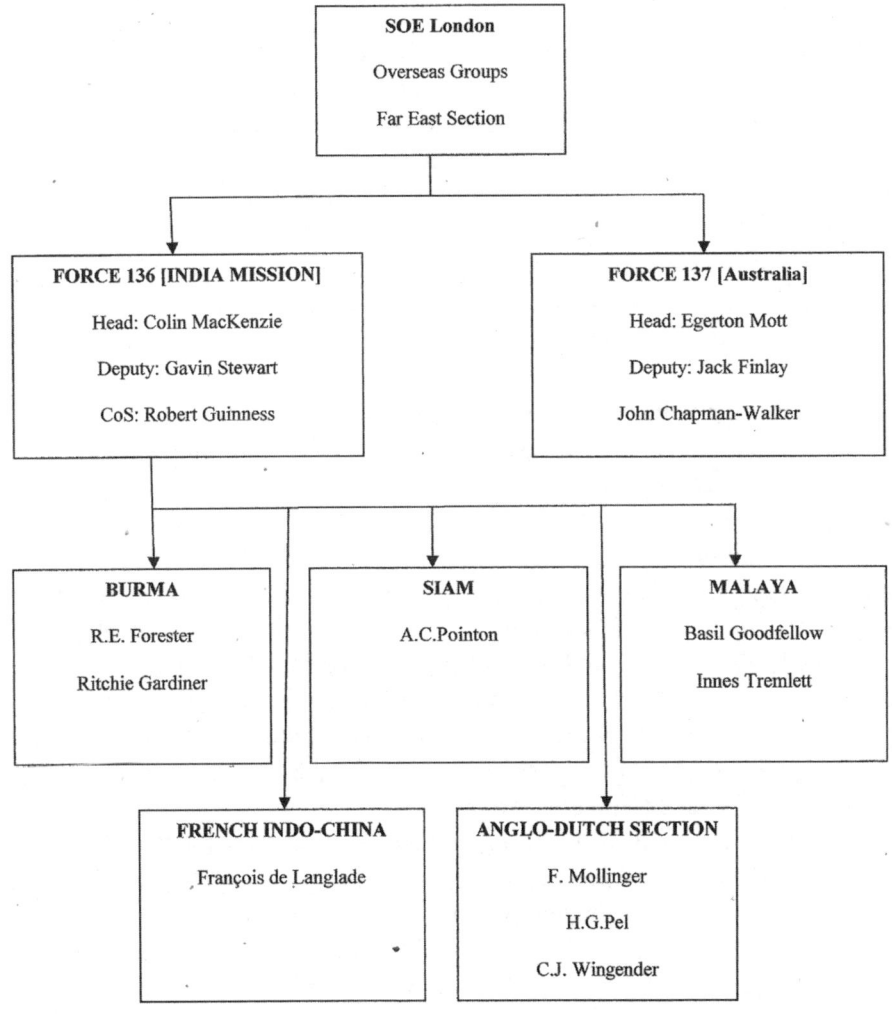

SOE Far East Organisation Chart 1942

Meerut. In 1944, renamed Force 136, the Mission moved to Kandy in Ceylon where Captain G.A. Garnons-Williams RN of P Division, reporting directly to Mountbatten, coordinated its activities in South East Asia with those of OSS and ISLD.

Before the end of the war, SOE operations had taken place in East Timor, Malaya, Singapore, British Borneo, Sarawak, Burma, Thailand, Dutch East Indies [Sumatra, Java and Dutch Borneo], French Indo-China, China [Chungking and Shanghai], Hong Kong, India, Goa, Andaman Islands, Labuan, the Moluccas and New Guinea.

THE CHANGING ROLE OF SOE

It was symptomatic of the haste in which SOE was established that the two senior operatives in the Far East, Colin Mackenzie in India and Val Killery in the 'Orient', were both civilians. This status affected Killery particularly as he was up against an unsympathetic CinC in Air Chief Marshal Sir Robert Brooke-Popham and an elitist and rather insular cadre of senior army officers who tended to reject the role of SOE on principle. Mackenzie, having served with the Scots Guards in the First World War, was fortunate enough to know the Viceroy well and also General Wavell. Even so, for the first year of the INDIA Mission's existence, little progress was made.

Nevertheless, prior to the Japanese invasion of Malaya and Burma, SOE's persistent advocacy of 'stay behind parties' [SBP] slowly won over the military. The idea was simple, namely to organise trained groups of volunteers to stay put in jungle hideouts where supplies of food, arms and explosives had been prepositioned. Once the enemy advance had begun, the SBPs could provide intelligence to the army, assist in demolitions, render industrial plant and equipment unserviceable and mount hit and run ambushes. Furthermore they would be the seed corn from which guerrilla forces would be raised. The European element of these parties needed to be familiar with both the terrain and the local languages; hence primarily they were planters, tin miners, forestry officials, traders and even regional bankers.

Such was the speed of the Japanese advance that most of the SBPs soon found themselves cut off and rendered ineffective, for resupply proved impossible and W/T [wireless transmitter and receiver] communications unworkable. Most personnel were captured or died of ill-health in the jungle. Some managed to escape and a handful remained in hiding, out of touch, presumed missing. SOE's options were now severely restricted because, first, the only method of inserting agents was by scant British or Dutch submarine forces whose primary role was to sink Japanese shipping and, second, the main effort of SOE was directed towards occupied Europe.

After the Japanese had completed their invasion of South East Asia, SOE were faced with a similar conundrum to the one they faced in Greece and Yugoslavia, namely that resistance fighters would most likely have to be drawn from the ranks of the Communists. However, in the Far East, the Communist parties were also anti-colonialists and their overriding political agenda was independence from their colonial masters after the war.

A further complication confronted SOE, for unlike in the European countries occupied by Nazi Germany, European soldiers could not blend with the local population in South East Asia. Whereas in Europe Tom Dunbabin and Patrick Leigh Fermor could masquerade as Cretan peasants, John Stevens walk around the streets of Turin under the noses of the Germans and Basil Davidson nonchalantly sit in a cafe in Hungary noting down the divisional signs of passing enemy traffic, in the Far East there was no possibility of such bravado[4]. So SOE had no choice other than to recruit and train indigenous operatives from within a relatively small pool of suitable candidates with all the attendant post-war political risks. As Roy Maclaren concluded in *Canadians Behind Enemy Lines*, 'SOE activities were [therefore] generally more rural than in Europe ... as a further consequence, the activities of Force 136 had a much more para-military air about them'.

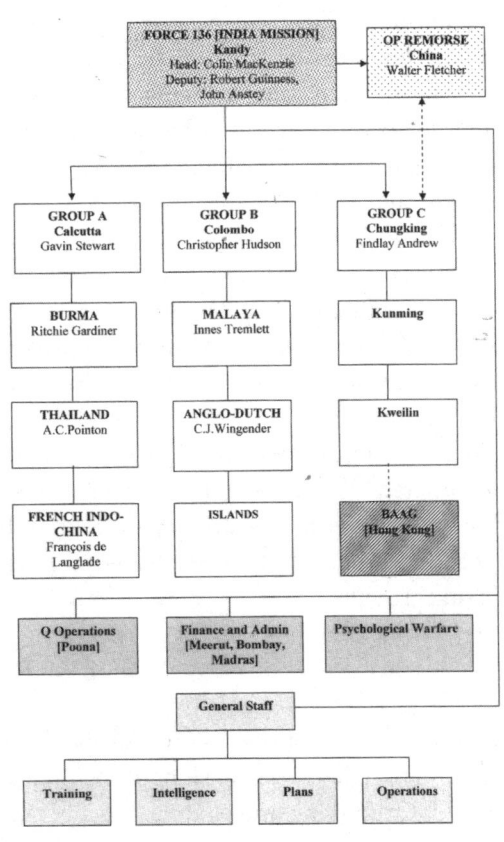

Force 136 Organisation Chart 1944

---

4 One exception was RAMC officer Cyril Dolly, an Indian-Canadian from Assam, who disguised as an Indian coolie, moved about freely in the Shan States of northern Burma, driving bullock carts – even occasionally for the Japanese – from March until August 1945.

Throughout 1943 and 1944, attempts were made to get W/T equipment and operators into Malaya by submarine. It was only towards the end of 1944 that long range Liberator bombers, converted to dropping stores and parachutists, enabled SOE to go on the offensive in Burma, this time working closely with the military commanders in the field. The lessons learnt from the SBPs were clear. SOE missions had to be integrated with the battle plan on the ground and report to field commanders. On this last point, General Slim of Fourteenth Army was insistent. It is instructive that General Alexander of Fifteenth Army in Italy, a former commander of the army in Burma, came to the same conclusion, at one stage in late 1944 controversially ordering the Italian partisans to lie low until the following spring when his exhausted formations would be ready to go back on the offensive. So SOE's role evolved into providing battlefield intelligence [everything from the movement and identification of enemy units to the state of the going on roads and the condition of bridges], identifying high value targets for the RAF to bomb and harassing the enemy's lines of communications by using local levies which had been armed and trained by SOE. The outcome was a spectacular improvement on the early days of 1941 and 1942.

In Burma, SOE missions accounted for over 16,000 enemy casualties during Fourteenth Army's advance to Rangoon. In Borneo, working hand in hand with the Australian 12th Division, SOE officers attached to the Services Reconnaissance Department [SRD] provided valuable intelligence on enemy troop dispositions and acted as a harassing force deep in the jungle as the Japanese attempted to regroup. In Malaya, over a dozen SOE missions were in place by August 1945 to support the long-awaited Allied invasion, an event fortunately curtailed by the sudden surrender of Japan after the two atomic bombs had devastated the Japanese mainland. The same situation applied in Thailand where SOE Missions were poised to act in support of an Allied breakthrough.

SOE AND SIS

At the outbreak of the war in Europe in 1939, SIS had five stations in the Far East – Shanghai, Peking, Hong Kong [2] and Singapore. In 1940 two more were added, Chungking and Manila. During the hectic days just before Malaya was overrun, SOE and SIS had worked closely together on the basis of all hands to the pump. However, once back in India, the two agencies found themselves competing for the same personnel, stores and transport, all from a limited pool. With a larger budget and greater political visibility in London, SOE tended to prevail and grew exponentially compared to SIS.

Even so, when SOE hooked a suitable fish in the personnel pond, it was another matter landing it. Take the case of Claude Fenner [see Chapter Five]. In September 1942, SOE had identified this up and coming young officer in the Malayan Police, fluent in Chinese, as a promising candidate for the Malayan Section. Located in Australia at the time, Fenner had been posted by the Colonial Office to Nigeria, and despite the strident request of the INDIA Mission, there he was destined to go for 'the need for competent policemen on the West Coast of Africa [was] acute'. Fenner himself had applied for a commission in the Australian Military Police. At the end of October, SOE tenaciously asked for his services 'with renewed importunity' until the issue was raised by the Secretary of State for the Colonies with the Governor of Nigeria in early November. The latter gave way with grace but by this time Fenner was already in Lagos, Nigeria, with his wife and new-born child. It was only in January 1943 that Fenner reached India; the debate about who was liable for the costs of his passage was finally resolved in March. Such tortuous extractions from the Colonial Office became routine staff work for SOE and SIS in the Far East.

In many respects, SIS and SOE operations were similar, involving the insertion and extraction of trained agents either by sea or air and maintaining W/T contact with them in the field. Both were under pressure from military commanders to deliver intelligence of the enemy's battlefield dispositions and intentions rather than garner information about a wider spectrum of political and economic perspectives, so inevitably there was duplication of effort[5] and on some occasions even a conflict of interest. Reluctance to share information could be dramatically counter-productive as in the case of Malaya where there were two SIS W/T stations in contact with Calcutta within a day or two's march from SOE's GUSTAVUS Mission which had been incommunicado for over two years. In Thailand, the Regent Pridi complained to SOE about the activities of SIS of which he had no prior knowledge until their operations went wrong.

Successive SIS Far East directors[6], in standing up to the military's demands, made it clear that SIS collected and distributed intelligence – it was not in the business of collating and analysing it[7].Furthermore, unlike SOE, it shied away from fermenting unrest and carrying out acts of sabotage which inevitably invited reprisals and meant losing valuable networks. It is worth remembering that SIS had indeed produced very accurate intelligence of Japanese troop

---

5   For instance, ISLD's BLOW operation in the Northern Shan States was mirrored by SOE's Operation HEATON.

6   All were soldiers – Colonel Leo Steveni, Colonel Reginald Heath and Brigadier Philip 'Bogey' Bowden-Smith.

7   In a report submitted to HMG after the war, Colin Mackenzie was very critical of this lack of 'added value' in SIS intelligence products.

movements in Thailand in late 1941 prior to the invasion of Malaya: it had been of little use since British defensive positions were in the wrong places. Gerald Wilkinson, the SIS officer in Manila, had passed on these same reports to the Americans.

It was not unusual for SIS and SOE teams to bump into each other in the field, leading to friendly if caustic rivalry. Major George Pennell of HAINTON met up with Lieutenant Zau Rip and five ORs who had been dropped to Major Butt [ISLD] in the area north of Takaw Ferry on the border of Burma and Thailand. Noting that most of the information they sent back 'came from our sources' as their own agents were 'poor types of persons', Pennell and his fellow officers considered it 'a hopeless show and [it] shouldn't have been sent in'. Doubtless similar opinions would have been expressed in ISLD about SOE.

The intelligence gathering activities of SOE and SIS in China were poorly co-ordinated and led to unnecessary tension over SOE's close contact with the Institute of International Relations and liaison with the Americans. Intelligence was eventually pooled but both agencies found the KMT Machiavellian to deal with and, according to official sources, neither succeeded in ingratiating themselves to the Chinese Communist Party [CCP] in Xian and accessing its extensive intelligence network in northern China. However, on the plus side, both agencies ran productive coast watching operations which yielded timely and accurate information about Japanese shipping movements for US pilots to attack.

In his 1946 report on SOE in Australia, Lieutenant Colonel Ambrose Trappes-Lomax [see ORIENTAL Mission] rated the achievement of SIS's Captain Roy Kendall as 'small' and noted that there was 'little co-operation between SOA and SIA'. This somewhat narrow view excludes the valuable service of Gerald Wilkinson who served as Liaison Officer [LO] to US General MacArthur, commander SWPA.

SOE AND OSS

American and British post-war aims were far from identical. They are best summed up in a *Life* magazine editorial of 12 October 1942:

'One thing we are sure we are not fighting for is to hold the British Empire together. We don't like to put the matter so bluntly, but we don't want you to have any illusions. If your strategists are planning a war to hold the British Empire together they will sooner or later find themselves strategizing alone'.

OVERVIEW

Contrast these words with Churchill's Mansion House speech of 10 November 1942:

> 'We mean to hold our own. I have not become the King's First Minister in order to preside over the liquidation of the British Empire. For that task, if ever it were prescribed, someone else would have to be found, and, under democracy, I suppose the nation would have to be consulted. I am proud to be a member of that vast commonwealth and society of nations and communities gathered in and around the ancient British monarchy, without which the good cause might well have perished from the face of the earth. Here we are, and here we stand, a veritable rock of salvation in this drifting world ... '

On the question of the post-war status of China, there were also widely divergent opinions between Britain and the US. Simplistically it could be argued that Britain wanted a relatively weak China to emerge after the war, thus posing a minimal threat to her Far East colonial possessions. The Americans on the other hand saw a strong China as a potentially valuable trading partner. The Chinese, be they KMT or CCP, played one off against the other. These contrasting attitudes were to colour the relationship between SOE and OSS throughout the war in the Far East. On its formation in 1943, SEAC was dubbed by the Americans as 'Save England's Asian colonies'.

In the early days, relations between SOE and the OSS in Burma were constructive if occasionally waspish. Detachment 101 won the approval of British commanders by conducting aggressive operations behind enemy lines that were well synchronised with military plans. To a degree, OSS largesse stole the clothes of SOE with local resistance movements. Writing to Commander Fourteenth Army in August 1944, Major Ian Fellowes-Gordon, commanding officer of the North Kachin Levies, despairingly noted that:

> 'British prestige in 1942, despite the severe setback of the Burma campaign, was high in the Kachin Hills. Unfortunately, since that time it has dwindled. The main reason for this has been beyond our control – the fact that this is an American combat theatre and all planes and the majority of troops and equipment are American. Another reason, it cannot be denied, is the niggardly support given by the British to this patriot movement. We have had contact with small groups of US recruited Kachins. All these receive higher pay, rations vastly superior in both quality and quantity and better clothing and equipment.'

SOE's Colonel Sweet Escott detected however that 'there was [accordingly] no conflict of interest between us [for] they were not primarily concerned with the recapture of Burma but with helping the Chinese'. This was not the case in other countries.

In Thailand, relations between SOE and OSS were particularly tense as a result of the different stances of the FO and US State Department. On the one hand, the FO, in consideration that Thailand had declared war against Great Britain in 1942 and had been openly collaborating with the Japanese since, felt that the Thais had to work their passage home if they were to join the community of free nations. The Americans, having chosen not to respond to the Thai declaration of war in 1942, took a more relaxed view and saw Thailand as a model friend in the new post-colonial nations of South East Asia where US influence and Christian values would predominate.

Doubtless they also had a slightly jaundiced view of the long-standing influence of the Bank of England which King Chulalongkorn had appointed as an adviser in the 1920s and of the tradition of Thai princes to be educated at English public schools. For Colin Mackenzie, this situation became untenable in late December 1944 when the OSS asked him not to inform the Free Siam Movement [FSM] that the British and Americans were working together. In his view, this would result in crossed lines in regard to intelligence and undermine the position of SEAC with the Thai resistance. A further stand-off occurred when the Americans refused to discuss with SOE sending their own senior operative into Thailand to liaise with the Free Thai resistance. This impasse reached into the upper echelons of the State Department and FO which, given that the officer in question, Major Nicol Smith, was both well-known to and well-liked by SOE, was all the more fatuous. In the end, OSS's ambitious plan to raise a force of 10,000 Thai guerrillas never came to fruition.

Relationships were often coloured by the individuals involved. In March 1944 the SOE War Diary recorded that Commander Davis Halliwell of the OSS had departed for Australia with some gadgets to show MacArthur and the Australians. 'He has been found very anti-British and difficult and had undoubtedly double-crossed SOE several times'.

Unwanted by General MacArthur [hence the Philippines and DEI were both out of bounds] and by Admiral Nimitz, who constrained them to an intelligence and liaison office in Honolulu, the OSS managed to cross swords with Force 136 and the French in Indo-China when their DEER Mission to the Viet Minh clumsily tried to enforce what they construed as the Roosevelt Doctrine of keeping France out of South East Asia after the war. Such was the acrimony between the two sides that, when three RAF Liberators on their way to drop supplies to Force 136 teams in Vietnam were supposedly shot down by

OVERVIEW

American fighters on the night of 22/23 January 1945, there was a real risk that the entire Anglo-US alliance would fracture. It was only the change of US Presidents in April 1945 that ameliorated the increasingly fractious stand-off between the Allies in French Indo-China.

Colonel Robert Park's 1945 report on the OSS contained an interesting conclusion: 'OSS is hopelessly compromised to foreign governments, particularly the British, rendering it useless as a prospective independent post-war espionage agency. Further questioning of British intelligence will evince nothing but praise because the OSS is like putty in their hands and they would be reluctant to forfeit a good tool.' While this overstates the OSS-British experience in the Far East, it emphasises that a country's intelligence service must be the servant of that country's self-interest and not the poodle of a close ally.

THE ENEMY

Once inserted behind enemy lines, SOE operatives often found themselves in a hostile security environment not on account of anti-colonial feelings – in most cases the local people were well-disposed towards them though invariably terrified – but because of the counter-intelligence activities of the Japanese Kempeitai and counter-guerrilla tactics used by the Japanese army.

The Kempeitai ['*ken*' meaning law and '*hei*' soldier] was the military police arm of the Imperial Japanese Army. It was composed of the Field Military Police and the Regular Military Police, each with its own personnel. Charged with the suppression of espionage and sabotage and for coordinating civil and military security in occupied countries, the Kempeitai made use of a network of spies and informers to identify persons suspected of being anti-Japanese. All the usual inducements and threats were used from financial rewards and wanted posters to burning down of villages and mass round-ups. Those arrested were routinely tortured until they revealed the information the Kempeitai required or 'confessed' to committing a crime or participating in anti-Japanese activities. Anyone who was identified as a subversive would be sentenced to death or imprisonment, including SOE personnel.

The rural nature of the campaign in the Far East and consequently the absence of roads gave the hunted an important advantage. It was almost impossible for Japanese counter-intelligence to pinpoint SOE W/T transmitters through vehicle-borne direction finding [DF] equipment. Likewise signal fires/torches in jungle clearings to mark dropping zones [DZs] were invisible to enemy troops even if stationed close by.

In the overall experience of SOE, the Japanese army was well trained and well disciplined in battle. In many cases the officers and NCOs were highly experienced for since the invasion of Manchuria in 1931, Japan had been involved in a prolonged insurgency there and after invading China in 1937, a state of all-out war existed between the two countries. That they were highly motivated, due to their adherence to the military code of *Bushido*, is a well-known fact. However, this goes much further than most people imagine. The *Kamikaze* role was not just limited to the Japanese Air Force, but every soldier was expected to die for his Emperor and never return home alive [the ultimate disgrace was for him to be taken prisoner]. To this one could add a gratuitous layer of brutality to the civilian populace.

Japanese army equipment was simple but well suited to its role. Tactics were well thought through, but the command structure was often unable to cope with changed circumstances. An outstanding example was the inability of Japanese units to adapt to the situation, whereby Allied Forces acquired air superiority, and instead of withdrawing units when cut-off, Allied commanders were able to order them to stand fast and re-supply and reinforce them by air, e.g. the battle for the besieged 7th Indian Division 'Admin Box' in the Arakan in February 1944.

THE JUNGLE ENVIRONMENT

Few descriptions of the jungle can match Joseph Conrad's in *The Heart of Darkness*:

'Going up that river was like travelling back to the earliest beginnings of the world, when vegetation rioted on the earth and the big trees were kings. An empty stream, a great silence, an impenetrable forest. The air was warm, thick, heavy, sluggish. There was no joy in the brilliance of sunshine. The long stretches of the waterway ran on, deserted, into the gloom of overshadowed distances. On silvery sandbanks hippos and alligators sunned themselves side by side. The broadening waters flowed through a mob of wooded islands; you lost your way on that river as you would in a desert, and butted all day long against shoals, trying to find the channel, till you thought yourself bewitched and cut off forever from everything you had known once – somewhere far away in another existence perhaps. There were moments when one's past came back to one, as it will sometimes when you have not a moment to spare to yourself; but it came in the shape of an unrestful and noisy dream, remembered with wonder amongst the overwhelming realities of this strange world of plants, and water, and silence. And this stillness of life did not in the least resemble a peace. It was the stillness of an implacable force brooding over an inscrutable intention. It looked at you with a vengeful aspect.'

Yet it is a misconception to think that all of South East Asia was covered with impenetrable jungle in 1941. In Malaya, tracts of jungle were often interspersed with rubber, coconut palm, pineapple and other plantations. Where there were village settlements, there were cultivated areas for crops and grazing animals. Even in the heart of Borneo, the Plain of Bah was well irrigated and fertile with fields of wet rice. Much of the south west of Timor was open country.

There are two types of jungle; primary, where nature has remained undisturbed, is characterised by a high and dense canopy of leaves, full of its own wildlife, audible but usually unseen for visibility is down to fifteen yards; and secondary, where man has slashed, cut and burnt and then moved on, leaving an almost impenetrable web of new growth. Some areas of secondary jungle have been taken over by sword or *lalang* grass where visibility is virtually nil. And then there are the bamboo thickets, in effect wooden walls, which proliferate near rivers and springs.

Owen Rutter, in his 1922 *Account of the History, Resources and Native Tribes of British North Borneo,* wrote of primary jungle:

> 'A philosopher might well find a world of symbols in a Borneo jungle. As in life itself, the law of the jungle is the survival of the fittest, and the struggle for existence which is the lot of humanity is repeated in the forest; there day after day, year after year, every wild green thing that grows fights desperately for life, battling for space and light and air. Each preys upon the other, and even the mightiest giant of today, rising superbly a sheer two hundred feet without a branch, tomorrow may be brought low by the parasites that are its deadly enemies; while the more defenceless may be strangled by creeping things that twine round their slender forms in an embrace which brings death at last. In the jungle there is never room for all.
>
> Yet it is a mistake to suppose that virgin jungle [so happily named] is a tangle of weeds and impenetrable vegetation; under foot are rotting branches and a carpet of dead leaves soft to tread upon, but in that shaded ground so seldom kissed by sunlight few weeds will grow. There are saplings, creepers and twisting coils of rattan, green as snakes; spiky palms and thorny briers to lay a detaining hand upon the passer-by; mantles of emerald moss and clumps of thick bamboo, but it is possible for a traveller to walk almost unimpeded, snicking now and then with a cutting knife at a branch or clinging hindrance that stays his steps. Thus

he may walk all day and scarcely feel the sun, of which he catches but fleeting glimpses through the matted branches far above, so locked and interlaced that the monkeys may journey days together without ever coming to the ground; for the denseness of the jungle is overhead, not underfoot. Save for the cicada's strident song the jungle is strangely silent; sometimes the ripple of a crystal stream, or a crashing, like a salvo of sixty pounders, of some great stricken tree disturbs its mysterious stillness, sometimes the hoarse cough of an orang utan or the crackle of dry twigs as a rhino gives a startled plunge and turns to flee. Except at the break of day few birds are heard; there are few butterflies, few flowers save here and there a wicked-looking scarlet blossom or an orchid bursting into bloom high up on a mighty tree trunk; but though it is rare to find a snake, yet in wet weather every leaf may harbour a leech that waits to attach itself unerringly to the passer-by.'

Within the jungle environment, there are extraordinary contrasts which defy descriptive generalisations. The moss-clad forests of the Malayan Highlands are in marked contrast to the dense mangrove and mud flats of its coastal periphery; the same contrasts can be applied to Burma, Thailand and Indo-China. Everywhere there is a constant hissing, chirping and croaking of insects that briefly abates during the oppressive midday heat. Any slight disturbance wakes the whole area into a frenzy of high-pitched ringing sounds. At night, the alarm mechanism reverses when the nocturnal boring beetles suddenly stop their drilling – usually signalling the onset of rain.

Movement is restricted by visibility, deadfalls [in primary jungle] and undergrowth like *wait-a-while* bush vines and stinging bushes and, in the monsoon, by rivers turned into torrents. Often the only way through the jungle is along animal tracks. Clothing is relentlessly ripped and torn, boots rot and socks disintegrate.

During the day, temperatures in the Malayan jungle can reach 27°C and at night can drop to 10° C. When you are wet and tired that can be very cold indeed. In the Cameron Highlands, the temperature at night can hover around zero.

An Australian officer recorded that 'learning to live in moist tropical heat at almost sea level on the Equator was a very different and easy matter compared to learning to know the jungle … the sentry in the jungle at night was more scared by his own imagination than by any denizens of the jungle itself.' Training was therefore all important. John Bowen of V Force spelt out the benefits of jungle warfare induction in *Undercover in the Jungle*:

OVERVIEW

'We were given practical experience of the jungle's usefulness to the knowledgeable soldier. By moving and living in it, we came to appreciate its value as cover. Dummy ambushes taught us how to achieve the element of surprise. We went out in small groups, patrolling by day and by night. We were sent out individually without provisions, so that we were compelled to exist on the jungle's natural resources. We learned how to carve out paths where no paths were, to fashion our own snug habitation, to extract drinking water from what looked like black slimy ooze, to eat strange fruit and even stranger flesh, to conceal ourselves so effectively that a man might approach to within a yard of our hiding-place without suspecting we were there. In time we could read the jungle like a book. Every tree, every creeper, every leaf had its message. We could interpret jungle sounds; we could identify jungle smells. We developed the quivering awareness of the beasts and reptiles of the jungle, for were we not sharing this tangled luxuriance with wild elephants, rhinoceroses, man-eating tigers, buffaloes, deer, monkeys, cobras, chameleons, and hamadryads twelve to fifteen feet long? We were still afraid in the jungle. The man without fear there is the man without caution and in the jungle it pays to be apprehensive. But our fear was no longer a vague, shapeless, illogical emotion. We had analysed it, reduced it to essentials, put it in its right perspective. Each combination of noises conveyed its appropriate message and we reacted accordingly. We knew when to relax and when to be on our guard.'

SOE jungle warfare instructors taught their students how to survive by collecting food such as edible tubers, leaves, fruits, and flowers; to catch fish by making traps; how to use bamboo as a spear, staff, water-carrier, mug, fuel, raft or house; to cook without pots and pans using sections of bamboo; to know where to look for dry firewood in dripping jungle and how to kindle a fire without matches by friction; to follow tracks and to conceal or mark one's own; to interpret bird warnings; to bridge streams and gorges; to make rafts and navigate them along rivers; to cope with leeches; to scare off snakes and animals.

In reality it was not that easy as CQMS John Cross, DCM, who spent three years behind enemy lines in Malaya, recalled: 'During the Malayan campaign one heard all sorts of twaddle talked, even by quite senior people, about parties being able to "live off the land" in the jungle. In fact, there was practically nothing edible except odd trees like *rambutan* and *lim bong*; wherever anything decent like durian or coconut was encountered the hand of man was in it somewhere.'

Lesson in raft building

Major Derek Headley stated the obvious when he reminisced that living off the land was 100 per cent time consuming. Even so, trapping deer, monkeys, monitor lizards and snakes was by no means guaranteed and apart from bamboo shoots, fern tips and a few fungi, there was little 'bulk' as hill rice and cassava were only cultivated in villages.

For those who linked up with the Chinese Communists in the Malayan jungle, food was still a problem. Jim Wright of the Norfolk Regiment who survived for three years behind enemy lines remembered at various times 'eating dogs, cats, bear and squirrel ... much of their protein was in the form of *belachan* [a fermented stinking fish paste] which he found nauseating in both taste and smell ... after a time he discovered fresh-water shrimps lived in the stream and they managed to catch them with flat baskets which the Chinese used to sift tin'.

JUNGLE HEALTH

The hot, damp and humid conditions of tropical jungles harbour one of the most difficult and dangerous environments for European expeditionary warfare. Among British troops in North Africa, for instance, the average number of admissions from sickness was 564 per thousand and the number of battle casualties only 60 per thousand. In north west Europe the sickness/casualty ratio was less marked, with an average of 151 admissions per thousand due to disease against 37 per thousand from hostile fire. The incidence of disease among British troops was highest in SEAC, with an admission rate of 811 per thousand from disease [mainly malaria] and 45 per thousand from wounds.

In tropical jungles, wounds turn to infected ulcers overnight, fungal skin infections are the norm, heat stroke common. In addition, the jungle is a breeding ground for disease carrying insects, malaria being the greatest threat. A list of tropical ailments and diseases suffered by Allied troops in South East Asia is laid out in ANNEX C.

INSERTION, RESUPPLY AND EXTRACTION

In 1942-43, the only way to insert SOE Missions into Malaya and the Dutch East Indies was by submarine from the naval base at Trincomalee in Ceylon where the RN 4th Submarine Flotilla was based. In the SWPC theatre, US submarines operated in DEI waters with the SRD from Freemantle in Western Australia As the primary role of a submarine was to attack and sink enemy shipping, SOE launched a charm offensive on the British and Dutch[8] Naval authorities to persuade them to take parties into enemy occupied territorial waters. It is a testament to inter-service co-operation that the submariners willingly agreed and, in doing so, took additional risks of navigating through shallow waters and tight channels and, once on the surface, exposing themselves to the threat of air or seaborne attack.

These were long and dangerous voyages for the SOE operatives, who were to all purposes passengers on hunting patrols. More than once, they were caught in anti-submarine attacks by Japanese surface vessels. Submarine commanders were at liberty to attack enemy shipping *en route* to the drop off point and in order to give a small window of normality in the area where the SOE/ISLD parties had landed reluctantly agreed not to launch any attacks in the area during the next twenty-four hours. The journey time into the target area could be anything up to fifteen days in hot cramped conditions. On one mission that was aborted, the SOE team spent three weeks at sea.

After successfully reaching the drop off area, the submarine would wait until darkness and then surface. Having assembled their folboats – and later on replaced by rubber boats with silenced outboard engines – and loaded their

---

[8] Submarine Divisions I, II and IV were placed under British operational control from November 1941 and based initially with 4th Flotilla in Colombo. Three modern O Class vessels were available for patrols as well as four much older K Class.

SOE underwater taxi

stores, the SOE party would paddle in over mud flats to the shore. This was a critical moment for in Malaya, for instance, the west coast plain was highly populated and any contact with local people would compromise the security of the mission. Japanese counter-intelligence was also alert to landings and ran an effective system of inducements backed by threats of retaliation to gather information of possible sightings. Once on shore, the parties instantly became the hunted.

On some occasions, the method of insertion involved the capture of a local fishing boat or junk, an additional complication to an already high risk operation.

To realise its plans to drop agents and stores behind enemy lines, SOE arranged with the RAF to draw on the services of a specialist unit, 1576 [Special Duties] Flight, which on 1 February 1944 became No. 357 [Special Duties] Squadron. Based in Digri and after September 1944 in Jessore and then

OVERVIEW

Mingaladon[9], initially it used Hudsons for supply drops to guerrilla forces in Burma, while the Liberators and Catalinas undertook long-range flights to Malaya and Sumatra, where the Catalinas landed agents and supplies on the coast. On 21 March 1944, the Catalinas became No. 628 Squadron, but the Liberators continued their supply flights until the end of the war. By January 1945, Dakotas had replaced the Hudsons, and C Flight was formed to operate Lysanders into strips in enemy controlled territory, mainly for picking up agents and supplying Force 136 teams operating behind Japanese lines.

These dedicated RAF crews flew in support of Force 136 in dangerous and demanding conditions. Different airfields were used such as Chittagong, Dum-Dum, Chabua, Alipore and Kunming with Cox's Bazaar available for emergency refuelling. The responsibility invested in the pilots included night navigation using primitive astral dead reckoning, identification of correct ground signals and finally manoeuvring the aircraft through tight approaches, usually at night and often in mountainous country, to drop bodies and stores on to pin-point locations. If the captain of the aircraft was not satisfied with the prevailing conditions, he had the authority to abort the mission.

The two aircraft which transformed the operational reach of SOE in the Far East were the Mark VI Liberator bomber and the PBY Catalina, both made by the Consolidated Aircraft Corporation of San Diego, California. The Liberator had a range of nearly 2,500 miles, depending on the amount of fuel and stores it was carrying, compared to the Mk III Hudson's 675 miles. With a cruising speed of 215 mph, these aircraft enabled SOE to mount long range operations at short notice and in quick time, especially in Malaya and Indo-China[10]. Even so, as Group Captain Leslie King of No. 160 Squadron pointed out, 'the major problem which coloured the whole operation was how to get the aircraft to the drop zone [DZ] and back without running out of fuel ... there was insufficient fuel to cater for a lengthy search of the DZ ... Enormous tropical storms, particularly in the Malacca Straits, interfered with several flights. It was impossible to go through them and there

The long-range Liberator which transformed SOE's reach

---

9 In August 1945, ten Liberators formed a detachment in China Bay, Ceylon, from where they resupplied Force 136 Missions on the ground in South East Asia.

10 Until Rangoon was recaptured in April 1945, Indo-China sorties had to take off from Degri or Jessore in Bengal and could only reach Laos and Tonkin, the northernmost part of Vietnam.

The ubiquitous and amazingly versatile PBY Catalina

was normally insufficient fuel to go over or round them'. Adding that the fuel gauges themselves were far from reliable, he concluded that running out of fuel was a far greater threat than enemy planes.

The most famous flying boat of the Second World War, the PBY Catalina, was built in large numbers and while it had a relatively slow cruising speed of 125 mph, it more than made up for its lack of speed with its reliability and great range of over 2,000 miles. Like the Liberator, the Catalina enabled SOE to insert and extract clandestine parties at night either offshore or in wide rivers, if necessary in fairly demanding weather conditions.

PART ONE

SOE IN SOUTH EAST ASIA AND CHINA

CHAPTER TWO

THE ORIENTAL MISSION

MAJOR VALENTINE KILLERY

Valentine Killery

In autumn of 1940, Sir Frank Nelson, the first head of SOE ['CD'], and Lieutenant Colonel Brien Clarke established the ORIENTAL Mission to introduce SOE into the Far East. Its effective life turned out to be about twelve months.

Following a Far East recce by A.E. Jones and F.H.B. Nixon in January 1941 when they identified 'significant opportunities'[11], 40-year-old Valentine Killery, a former managing director of ICI in China, was appointed the Mission's head and he left from Lisbon by the Boeing B-314 'clipper' via Washington, San Francisco and Manila, arriving in Singapore in May 1941, where together with Basil Goodfellow, also a former ICI executive, he set up SOE HQ in the Cathay Building. Joined by the immensely experienced Major Alan Warren RM of MI[R], the Mission set about establishing special operations in the region.

---

11 See Annex A.

Major Angus Rose, who soldiered with the Argyll and Sutherland Highlanders for two years in Malaya prior to the fall of Singapore in 1942, came up with a perspicacious and withering analysis of what awaited Killery:

'The main communities consisted of Europeans, Chinese, Malays and Indians. The European community was either there in an administrative capacity or else in search of wealth. The Chinese were there to exploit the country and the Indians to better their standard of living. The Malays were an easy-going, good-natured and peace-loving people, who were content to have their country run for them, provided they could continue their carefree existence. There was no common bond of love of country, or pride of race, but the whole four communities gave the impression of being loosely knit together by the ties of business interest. Money was the God. Nothing else mattered but money, and the ways in which money was acquired were, as often or not, scarcely in keeping with the accepted standards of honesty. On top of these business communities a military force of fair size was superimposed and this military structure sat very uneasily on its foundations. There was no unity of purpose embracing the whole resources of the States and colonies and including the military forces. There was neither strength nor power, nor greatness in the Government. There was never any serious effort to prepare the country mentally or materially for totalitarian war.'

The choice of Killery was far from random. When ICI was formed in 1926, one of its constituent companies was Brunner, Mond and Co, a company trading in industrial chemicals that had opened its first office in Shanghai in 1899. Such was its standing that its Chairman, Edward Selby Little, had presided at his home, 30 Gordon Road, over the formal proclamation of the first Chinese Republic when the Manchu dynasty abdicated in favour of Sun Yat-sen on 12 February 1912.

By 1932, ICI had 603 main Chinese agents, each of whom ran his own chain of sub-agents; in commercial terms a formidable sales and distribution network, in intelligence terms priceless access to the Chinese rumour mill. In 1933, Sir Harry McGowan, Chairman of ICI, expressed his dissatisfaction 'with our progress in that country [China] over the past two years' and personally appointed 'a brilliant young man', the 32-year-old Val Killery as vice-chairman and Managing Director of ICI [China]. The two travelled on the *SS Conte Rosso* from Venice to Hong Kong from where they set about reorganising the company.

Soon Killery found himself negotiating with Chiang Kai-shek and his wife for a proposed nitrogen fertiliser plant to be built and operated by ICI in China, a project eventually lost to the US-owned Nitrogen Engineering Corporation. Nevertheless, under Killery's leadership, which combined business acumen with social and political *savoir faire*, the company traded profitably and its relations with the Chinese flourished. In the middle of 1938, a year after the Japanese invasion of northern China, Killery reported to London that ICI China would probably need to be subsidised in the years ahead. This was over-cautious for it was still profitable in 1940 with a strong balance sheet. Sir Frank Nelson had been astute – Killery was clever, charismatic, successful and very well connected to the top echelons of the Far East political and commercial establishment.

In common with his contemporaries in the British Far East business community, Killery was under no illusions about the intentions of the Japanese government. Their record of aggressive expansion was blatant:

- 7 July 1937: Japan launched all-out war on China.
- 21 October 1938: Japanese troops occupied Canton, severing the main coastal supply route to Chiang Kai-shek's KMT.
- 4 November 1938: Chiang Kai-shek summoned HM Ambassador Sir Archibald Clark Kerr to clarify the British position in regard to assisting China in defending herself from the Japanese invasion.
- 10 February 1939: Japanese troops occupied Hainan Island, directly challenging British maritime interests in the South China Sea.
- 8 March 1939: HMG belatedly announced a £5 million credit to China to buy arms.

Killery doing the rounds

- 14 June 1939: Japan blockaded the British concession at Tianjin [Tientsin].
- 23 July 1939: Anglo-Japanese agreement signed.
- 18 July 1940: Britain closed Burma Road[12] for three months, shutting down main overland supply route to the KMT.
- August 1940: Japan forced Britain to withdraw its garrisons from Shanghai and North China.
- 26 September 1940: Japanese army entered French Indo-China and launched attack into China.
- 27 September 1940: Japan signed tripartite military pact with Germany and Italy, both of whom Britain was at war with.

*****

BAT in China

The multinational cigarette manufacturer British American Tobacco [BAT] had been active in China almost from the day of its incorporation in 1902. Under the direction of a remarkable businessman, James Thomas, the company had by 1919 established a comprehensive and extensive distribution network across the whole of China. He recruited salesmen from the US to introduce cigarettes into the farthest reaches of the Chinese Empire and paid bonuses to those who learnt to speak Chinese. Setting out on sales trips often lasting months, these salesmen built up BAT's business in every village, town and city and in the process they collected a mass of information. By default, BAT thus assembled a uniquely detailed and up-to-date picture of each region with an in-depth knowledge of personalities and politics. At a national level, the company had intimate contacts with all the key political players as a result of negotiating valuable tax and tariff arrangements.

The benefits of this ready-made nationwide intelligence network were not lost on SIS. The author and wartime SIS agent Graeme Greene remembered Archibald Rose, late of HM Diplomatic service and a director of BAT Co [China], as 'having the appearance of a senior army officer...he would have made a good intelligence officer, and I have little doubt now that he belonged, however distantly, to the Secret Service. A man in his position, recruiting and controlling men for the Chinese hinterland, could hardly have escaped contact with "the old firm" ... '

---

12 The 717 miles road running through rough mountain country was completed in 1938 and used to transport war materiel to China. Supplies were landed at Rangoon and moved by rail to Lashio, the road head in Burma.

In the chaotic days surrounding the rise of nationalist China, BAT forged its own links with influential Chinese officials by encouraging them to become shareholders in BAT Co [China] through discounted offers of shares. By the beginning of 1928, the company, already well known to the Soong family, had reached an agreement with General Chiang Kai-shek. During the next decade, tobacco goods emerged as the third most valuable source of income for the KMT government and by the mid-1930s, BAT had become its largest single taxpayer. Schwas the power of BAT that Sir Alexander Cadogan of the FO arranged for Rose to meet with Madame Chiang Kai-shek in 1934 to discuss KMT investment in a newly formed BAT subsidiary in China.

With the business in fine shape, there was however a dark cloud on the horizon: in the wake of Japan's military expansionism, the Japanese tobacco industry moved into the occupied territories. After the invasion of Manchuria in 1931, BAT's sales there had declined by 25 per cent within the year. Rose responded by visiting Japan in 1933 and talking to a number of senior political and military figures. It was a smart move and by 1935, sales of cigarettes in Manchuria accounted for 30 per cent of BAT Co [China] profits, up from 25 per cent. However, after Japan had invaded China proper in 1937, the company's manufacturing and distribution arms were severely disrupted and by 1941 Japanese firms controlled 40 per cent of the cigarette market in China. Nevertheless, up until the attack on Pearl Harbour in December 1941, BAT's market share was still 60 per cent. In 1942, the Japanese took control of all BAT assets in China and interned the company's expatriate staff. Ironically over 100 of them were interned at the BAT factory at Pootung which had been converted into an internment camp.

The story of BAT in China exemplifies the difference between diplomacy and business. With commercial tentacles covering the whole country, with political and financial contacts at the highest level in every region and with the ability to deliver major tax revenues to the government of the day, BAT was far more hands on than any government department or agency could ever hope to be. It was therefore entirely logical that SOE in establishing the ORIENTAL Mission sought to tap into this expertise and experience as it set about inventing itself in the Far East.

*****

Other early SOE officers included S.C. Miskin, A.B. Butler, C. Nicholl, Sir George Sansom [who had oversight for all non-military covert operations in the Far East], P.R.C. Wren and G. Wint. They were later joined by Egerton Mott [a partner in the McLean Watson trading company], John Galvin and L.D. Reeve.

Steve Cumming

ISLD was represented on the ORIENTAL Mission by Wing Commander Pile. Steven Cumming, a bright young Scot from the Butterfield and Swire trading house, took on the Burma and Chinese country sections. Likewise, Freddy Spencer Chapman set up the Thailand and Indo-China desks before heading for Australia to set up a Special Training School [STS] in Victoria.

From the beginning there were problems with bureaucracy – there were no less than nine different government agencies e.g. The Dominions, Colonies and India Offices as well as the FO. Sir Josiah Crosby, HM Ambassador to Thailand, virtually went to war with Killery. On 12 November 1941, he sent a closely typed five page whinge to Sir Alexander Cadogan, the Permanent Undersecretary at the FO, with a copy to Duff Cooper, the Resident Cabinet Minister in Singapore, complaining about every aspect of SOE's work.

The attitude of the FO was understandable. Britain was not at war with Japan and the idea of a 'third front' opening up after Japan signed a tripartite pact with Germany and Italy in September 1940 – Britain herself was engulfed in the Battle of Britain and, in the words of Air Vice Marshal Keith Park, 'holding her own ... just' – was anathema to many. The policy of appeasement towards Japan which had so infuriated Chiang Kai-shek after the Japanese invasion of Canton in October 1938 was replaced by one of expediency and Sir Robert Craigie signed a statement in Tokyo on behalf of HMG in which the

British recognised that 'the Japanese forces in China have special requirements for the purposes of safeguarding their own security and maintaining public order in regions under their control, and that they have to suppress or remove any such acts or causes as will obstruct them or benefit their enemies'. Even when a limited attack on Thailand to deny the Rai Isthmus to the Japanese was proposed [Operation MATADOR] in August 1941 and considered eminently sensible in terms of military strategy, the attendant risks of provoking Japan were gauged unacceptable despite the doomsday scenario of an alliance between Germany, Russia and Japan which had seemed very real in early 1941 no longer being valid. Furthermore, the Americans took the line of strict observance of Thai neutrality.

Some like Sir John Lomax thought that the attitude of the FO was more parochial for '[it] above all, regarded its [MEW] existence and activities with suspicion and throughout the war hindered its work by inertia, jealousy and outright opposition'.

Surprisingly, the attitude of the military, particularly Lieutenant General Arthur Percival, the CinC Malaya, who was backed by Air Chief Marshal Sir Robert Brooke-Popham, the CinC Far East, towards special operations and SBPs was almost entirely negative. It was the old story of turf wars. Worse was to come as the SOE War Diary recounts: 'When General Wavell assumed Supreme Command of the South West Pacific the situation [had] altered radically for the worse. Wavell [had] expressed his distrust of SOE based on his experience in the Middle East and his LO with SOE, Brigadier Field, held the same views.'

Nevertheless, Operation SCAPULA, the Far East Mission recruited in London, arrived in Singapore at the end of July 1941, bringing the total strength of STS 101 run by Major Jim Gavin at Tanjong Bolai to 150. In its short history, STS 101 directing staff included Majors Gavin and Spencer Chapman, Captains Trappes-Lomax, Knott, Low, Cumming, Williamson, Le Seelleur, and Lieutenants McGarry, Corkran, Passmore [RNVR] and Heath. Between them they trained students from the Burma Frontier Force and Burma levies and civilians from Hong Kong, Thailand, and Burma including Swedes, French, Dutch and a lone American.

The sheer size of the footprint of Killery's Mission was daunting and progress proved laborious. Goodfellow visited Saigon on 4 November 1941 and discovered that the pro-German Vichy authorities knew all about SOE's nascent resistance plans. In Thailand, Crosby's opposition remained implacable and in the Dutch East Indies, Brooke-Popham refused to let Killery get involved, so all that SOE achieved was the provision of seven W/T sets and some money to Captain

Laurens van der Post's[13] 43 Special Mission in Java. The Mission itself, put together by Military Intelligence, was tasked to collect British and Commonwealth stragglers and then attempt to exfiltrate them to Colombo 'by native craft'.

Major O'Dwyer, sent out by SOE London to assess what was going on, was unimpressed by what he found.

> 'In my opinion, your Far Eastern Mission has achieved [apart from Propaganda and the Tin Denial scheme] little or nothing.
>
> I have tried to appreciate all the difficulties encountered and I fully recognise the hard work, good will and honesty of purpose Killery has put into his task. He was, however, in my opinion, saddled from the very start with an incubus – the Charter of the Far Eastern Mission.
>
> This Charter was utterly unworkable – especially so in the hands of a man of Killery's character. He interpreted its clauses to the letter and endeavoured with the best will and enormous industry to make the best of a bad job and to stave off admitting defeat.
>
> After my arrival I was very soon disturbed by the conclusion I was forming as I went through the Mission. The major efforts seemed to be on too high a plane and in high circles and the real objective, i.e. detailed planning of subversive operations and realistic thinking in the form of recruitment of personnel seemed very obscure. Moreover, I was very unimpressed by Killery's staff. Killery himself is not, I consider, subversive-minded and his staff are ill-chosen and unsuitable [with one fine exception] to give him real assistance. Also his organisation has lacked throughout any military staff branch and a really efficient one is a necessity to any such headquarters.'

In Malaya, the idea was to train SBPs and create caches of arms and explosives in well-stocked jungle hideouts in order to harass extended Japanese lines of communication. Due to the swift advance of the Japanese which began on 8 December 1941, little was achieved in the chaos which followed. Both SIS and SOE improvised and formed SBPs, each led by a graduate of STS 101, but, forced deep into the jungle, with no radios, there was little they could do. Of the forty-five Europeans in the SOE network, only four evaded death or capture. As to denying commercial assets to the enemy, only three out of thirty-four mines earmarked for sabotage were put out of action[14]. However, it is important to

---

13 Van der Post was captured at the end of June and the remainder of his men were all forced to surrender in September [including W/T operator Lieutenant Cooper RNVR].

14 SOE did well to sabotage the smelting works in Penang, the power station at Prai and the airfield at Kuala Lumpur.

remember that responsibility for denying industrial assets to the enemy was never solely entrusted to SOE; the civil authorities in Malaya were charged with responsibility for denying tin and rubber, the military and civil authorities in Burma for mines and oil fields, the Dutch authorities in the DEI likewise, and the Royal Navy for oil installations in British Borneo.

A sense of the chaos encountered by the SBPs is given by Boris Hembry in a letter he wrote to Colin Mackenzie of Force 136 in January 1984:

'Frank Vanrenan and Ronald Graham [two planters] ... for sheer guts and initiative, stand out head and shoulders above all we others. Vanrenan and Graham were the first to volunteer, together with Chapman, to go with Angus Rose on his first sortie behind the lines. Shortly afterwards they volunteered to join Chapman's first SBP at Slim River. They roped me in for this one. The three of us went into the jungle at Slim River about 5 January 1942 and were to be joined by Freddy, Sartin and others on or by 6 January. In the event they failed to join us ... All our stores, arms, ammunition, radio, food supplies were subsequently looted by Chinese so we three plus a Chinese W/T op were left high and dry, without a leader, without stores, without plans or maps and without any idea of other parties infiltrating into the jungle. We decided to catch up with the British army. What a hope. They were in lorries, we were on our flat feet and behind the lines. After about four hazardous weeks, with many close brushes with the enemy and by then with over twenty British soldiers whom we had picked up en route, we made the Selangor coast. But not before Vanrenan, while on a recce, was captured by Japanese and placed in a police station. Fortunately they were no cells and he was kept under guard in the charge room by two Japanese. At about 8pm, the RAF raided Kuala Lumpur and the guards took their eye off Frank and went to the door to watch the fireworks. Whereupon, Vanrenan, seizing a hurricane lamp crashed it on the back of the head of one guard, laid out the other with his fists and made his escape into the darkened village ... the following morning he found us where he had left us.'

One story that only came to light in October 1944 concerned the exploits of eighty volunteers of the DEI Marechaussee Division [a military and civil gendarmerie]. Flown from Medan to Singapore on 13/14 January 1942, this special force under command of two Dutch officers, Captain Supheert and Lieutenant Kroon, was directed by Colonel Warren and Major Campbell to infiltrate into the jungle in the Paloh area in Johore to ambush and harass the approaching Japanese army. In a series of highly effective engagements, the Marechaussee volunteers killed several hundred enemy soldiers before withdrawing in late March to Bengkalis in Sumatra where they donned civilian attire and dispersed to their various homes.

In China, W.J. Gande, SOE's man in Shanghai, and his close associates were arrested and imprisoned. Killery and Warren flew up to Chungking to set up a second STS in January 1942, this time using Danish citizens under Erik Nyholm, an idea originally put forward in 1941 by Sir Alexander Clark Kerr, the British Ambassador to China, as a way round not upsetting the Japanese with whom Britain was not yet at war. Chiang Kai-shek agreed that 'the China Commando Group' could be a self-contained unit within the Chinese Special Operations Section but the commander of the latter, General Zhou Wei-Lung, although making a favourable impression on Killery had another agenda.

John Keswick of the Jardine Matheson trading house, and a leading advocate of Britain's China lobby before the war, was now working at the MEW with Sir Frederick Leith-Ross whom he had got to know well on Leith-Ross's year-long China Mission in 1935-36. As MEW's representative in Chungking and hence *de facto* the senior SOE officer, Keswick took charge of the China Commando Group but despite having the support of Madame Chiang Kai-shek, he found Wei-Lung determined to prevent the group from becoming operational and after refusing to be commanded by the Chinese General, Keswick left in April 1942.

Killery visited Burma in August 1941 to work out a modus operandi with Sir Reginald Dorman-Smith, the Governor. He delegated the task to the GOC Burma, Lieutenant General DK McLeod who was unhelpful. Finally when it was obvious that the Japanese were going to invade, the Burmese authorities insisted that they should have operational control of all SBPs. W.D.R. Eve, Killery's representative, protested but it was academic since it was too late to get the scheme off the ground.

On 19 January 1942 Killery left for Java, leaving Goodfellow in charge of Malayan operations. Major Ambrose Trappes-Lomax commandeered the 856 ton SS *Krain* of the Straits Steamship Company and most of STS 101 left with him on 5 February. After Singapore fell on 15 February 1942, SOE's ORIENTAL Mission HQ was knocked out. Gavin escaped to Trincomalee on the SS *Krain*, Killery and Egerton Mott reached Batavia in Java and from there made it to Australia. When Killery signalled London that he was going to Australia to reorganise his Mission, Baker Street replied with a short signal 'presume you are going at your own expense'.

Goodfellow's journey was an epic. After instructing Boris Hembry and Sergeant Lamb to set up an escape route between Singapore and Sumatra using a Straits Steamship Company boat, he had joined them with Captain Morgan and two Straits Steamship Company officers and after establishing dumps on three islands, reached Jambi where he planned to set up a shuttle service. When their ship was sunk in an air raid, Goodfellow's party drove to Padang where they managed to embark on the destroyer HMS *Encounter* and sailed for Batavia in Java. Here they were given a choice to make their way either to Australia or India. Goodfellow chose the latter and with Sergeant Lamb and Hembry went down to the docks to look for a suitable boat. There they met three Straits Steamship officers who had discovered the *Pierrot*, a fully victualed boat but condemned as unseaworthy. They were confident that they could reach India in it, so after collecting thirty passengers including women, the party left harbour and headed for Colombo where they made landfall after ten days at sea.

There was no blame attached to SOE for the disaster of the fall of Singapore. As Richard Aldrich points out in *Intelligence and the War against Japan*, the briefings by the Joint Intelligence Committee in London had been uncannily accurate; the problem was 'a stubborn failure of command at several levels to accept warnings'.

ISLD's efforts in Malaya were marginally more successful. Between January and February 1942, John Davis [a senior policeman] and Dick Broome [civil servant] managed to insert 163 members of the Malayan Communist Party [CPM] into Japanese-held territory with seven arms and food dumps before the British collapse. Davis, Broome, Lyon, Passmore and Campbell all reached Calcutta after sailing across the Indian Ocean on the *Sederhana Djohannes*, a native Malayan *prahu*. After thirty-four days at sea they sighted land and were eventually picked up by a freighter, the SS *Anglo Canadian*.

Other ISLD members were less fortunate. Sergeant John Cross, Lance Corporal Fred Wagstaff and Signalman Doug Morter spent three years in the jungle until finally evacuated on 31 May 1945. Their commanding officer, Captain Louis Cauvin [cover name Major James Barry], tormented by failure, committed suicide, and Sergeant Meldrum died of illness.

The CinC Far East, Air Chief Marshal Sir Robert Brooke-Popham[15], submitted a despatch to the British Chiefs of Staff on 21 May 1942:

'A branch of the Ministry of Economic Warfare known as the

---

15 Brooke-Popham was an immensely experienced soldier and administrator. He had originally joined the Army and seen service with the Oxfordshire Light Infantry in the Boer War. After passing Staff College, he joined the Air Battalion of the RE and went on to become one of the founding fathers of the RAF after wartime service with the RFC. Prior to coming out of retirement to take on the role of CinC Far East, Brooke-Popham was Governor of Kenya.

ORIENTAL Mission was started on the arrival of Mr. Killery at Singapore in May 1941. He and his staff were keen and capable, but they had no experience and very little knowledge of how to set about their work. Further, as in the case of intelligence, this is work that requires a great deal of preparation. In consequence of this, but through no fault of Mr. Killery or his staff, the ORIENTAL Mission activities really never got functioning properly by the time that war with Japan broke out. There was also a curious reluctance on the part of many people to have anything to do with these activities, or to help on the work. This was particularly noticeable in the case of intended activities in Thailand.'

Brigadier Field, Wavell's LO, penned a damning critique of the ORIENTAL Mission. Accusing the staff of being 'ill-chosen, unsuitable and over-paid', he concluded that 'the former Mission had collapsed, leaving no useful foundation on which to build'. Killery vigorously rebutted this last statement, pointing out that, far from collapsing, the Mission had been able to arrange that its work should be carried on in Burma and China and continued to function to the last possible moment in Malaya and Sumatra.

Sir George Moss, SOE's adviser on Chinese affairs, disagreed with Field:

'It is clear that the British Colonial administration, British officialdom in the Far East and the British SIS had failed to make adequate preparations in time of peace for internal organisation in time of war ... Sir Josiah Crosby virtually expelled the Oriental Mission from Thailand two weeks before war was declared, the Free French organisation in Indo-China proven a broken reed ... The military failed to give orders for demolition in time, and crowning misfortune, failed to hold Singapore long enough to enable his [Killery's] stay behind parties to operate in favourable circumstances ... It is a story of military ineptitude.'

Bickham Sweet Escott who served as a senior staff officer at SOE throughout the war agreed with Sir George:

'The lesson of Killery's ill-fated ORIENTAL Mission at Singapore was of great importance. For months it had had to contend with obstruction and frustration. Our ambassador in Bangkok had flatly forbidden us to make any preparations in Siam. In Malaya, the British commanders had refused to allow us to train Malays or Chinese to leave behind if the country should be overrun ... It was not the Mission's fault that its contribution to the Far East was so small or that its only real achievement was on the day in January 1942, when, with the temperature at 103 degrees, Freddy Spencer Chapman pushed off into the jungle to create a left-behind party of his own.'

MAJOR GENERAL JIM GAVIN, CB, CBE

Jim Gavin

Jim Gavin was born in Chile in 1911, and educated first at St Peter's school in Santiago, and then Uppingham School in the UK. After passing out of the Royal Military Academy Woolwich with a commission in the Royal Engineers, he read mechanical engineering at Trinity College, Cambridge, where he took up climbing with the university mountaineering club.

One of his climbing companions was Frank Smythe, who suggested to Hugh Ruttledge, leader of the 1936 Everest expedition, that Gavin would be a useful man to take along with them although he had no Himalayan experience. Smythe's judgment proved correct and the two of them opened the route to the north col, raising hopes of an early summit attempt. Sadly, these were thwarted by the arrival of the monsoon.

In 1940, Gavin joined the 5th Battalion [skiing] Scots Guards which was training in Chamonix. All were volunteers and many had resigned their commission in order to join, including Gavin. The plan was to enter and support Finland – then at war with the Soviet Union – via neutral Sweden; in the event, it came to nothing, and the skiers left in a hurry as the Germans took control of France.

Recruited by SOE in early 1941, Gavin then embarked on a sabotage mission to Norway, but after his submarine HMS *Truant* was damaged in a minefield, the expedition was abandoned and Gavin moved to the mountain warfare school at Lochailort in Scotland run by Bill and David Stirling. Here he set up the first SOE STS and after six months was sent to Singapore to open STS 101, SOE's first attempt to set up an overseas training school.

After recruiting a team in London, his establishment was approved on 4 April 1941 and Gavin flew via the United States to Singapore where he was met on 28 May by Killery, Goodfellow and Warren. After looking for a suitable location, Gavin chose the former home of an Armenian tin millionaire at Tanjong Balai, a headland connected to Singapore by a long, narrow causeway at the mouth of the Jurong River. With Cumming as his 2 i/c, Lieutenant McGarry as QM, Captain Michael Low and Sergeant John Sartin as explosives instructors, on 14 July Gavin opened STS 101 for the business of training SBPs for SOE and ISLD.

When Freddy Spencer Chapman arrived back in September from Australia where he had been setting up an STS and took over as 2 i/c, Gavin was sent up to Hong Kong where in the space of a few weeks, he helped to form The Reconnaissance Unit, in the process constructing six hideouts in the New Territories and establishing a secret training centre and a covert HQ. He was then sent to Lashio on the borders of North Burma and China where he met up with Warren and Killery coming back from Chungking. He arrived back in Singapore at the end of November 1942 to find most of STS 101 staff suffering from dengue fever.

The next few weeks saw Gavin in Fortress Penang with Trappes-Lomax, Brian Passmore RNVR and ten other ranks in a desperate attempt to deny it to the Japanese. On 19 December he reappeared at STS 101 where Spencer Chapman was and then headed up to Kuala Lumpur in January 1942 to help ISLD's Major Rosher in his frantic efforts to train and supply fifteen CPM SBPs.

In February, Gavin, with his girlfriend Barbara Murray, managed to catch a plane in Singapore heading to Rangoon but it was diverted to Bandung in Java. Here they announced their decision to get married as only wives were allowed to accompany departing officers. The Japanese had destroyed much of the local Sumatra shipping, and Gavin and Barbara at first found themselves marooned. But as an engineer and a keen sailor, who had once participated in the Fastnet race, he was able to rig up a tug, and, despite suffering from diphtheria, he skippered it to Ceylon before embarking by train for northern India.

It was during a riot on that train that Gavin suffered the heart attack that was to seriously impair his health, and leave him considerably weaker for the rest of his life. After recuperating in Kashmir, he returned to England in March 1943 and was employed by SOE [Scientific Research] to design equipment suitable for sabotage in occupied Europe. He was then sent out to the Middle East in January 1944 where he served as GSO1 [RE] with Force 133 through to September that year when he returned to the UK and rejoined his parent corps, the Royal Engineers, as a senior staff officer in SHAEF.

LIEUTENANT COLONEL ALAN FERGUSON-WARREN, RM, CBE, DSC

Alan Warren

Commissioned in the Royal Marines [RM] in 1919, Alan Warren joined the Fleet Air Arm in April 1925 along with nineteen other RM officers. Having qualified in Fleet Spotter, he served in 441 Flight on the aircraft carriers HMS *Hermes* and HMS *Eagle* and was in the Fighter/Seaplane Flight at Kai Tak airfield at Hong Kong in 1926 during the trouble between North and South China.

On return to Corps Duty he qualified as an Adjutant and was appointed to the Royal Marine Depot at Chatham in 1930. After this posting, he passed into Staff College and on gaining his psc, he was Assistant Military Instructor at Deal. Then, after a tour in Shanghai spent chasing pirates, in 1938 he was seconded to D Section, the hybrid sabotage and propaganda organisation run by SIS and the WO.

Tasked to destroy iron ore mines in Sweden, his mission was cancelled when news of it leaked to the King of Sweden. He was then sent to France to set up an underground organisation. On his return to England, he was employed to put sabotage groups ashore in Norway; unfortunately HMS *Truant*, the submarine carrying Warren and his saboteurs, was damaged in a minefield and had to return to Rosyth. On 20 June 1040, he was posted to MI[R] as GSO2.

Now ordered back into occupied France to round up stragglers and to form them into commando units, Warren landed in France with three French speaking officer cadets. After three fruitless weeks, he decided to withdraw and having found an abandoned ten-foot rowing boat, set off across the English Channel. Eventually, after fourteen hours, the bedraggled party was spotted and hauled on board the Dungeness Point Lightship. The MI[R] War Diary noted that although the 'scheme could not be called a success', it 'showed that the idea of mosquito raids into enemy territory by small bands of picked men was possible'.

In August 1940, Warren joined Brigadier Gubbins's stay behind companies in Kent. Meanwhile, word of his escapade had reached Admiral Sir Roger Keyes, chief of the new Combined Operations directorate, who appointed Warren his GSO2 [intelligence] and told him to plan a Commando raid on Guernsey. His recce party landed by submarine on 7 July but pick-up arrangements went wrong and some of the party were left stranded. Ten days later a motor boat [MB] went in to collect them but two had already given themselves up and had been sent to Germany as POWs. After several more recces on the German-occupied French mainland, Keyes put Warren up as Chief of Operations for the newly formed SOE but he was sidetracked as military LO with the Inter Service Research Bureau. For the time being, the war for Warren was a long way away.

Then, in January 1941, as GSO1 Special Operations Far East, Warren sailed to Singapore on HMS *Nestor*. After playing a key role with Valentine Killery in setting up the SOE ORIENTAL Mission including a trip to Chungking with Killery to establish the ill-fated Chinese Commando Group, he went up to Penang on a fact finding mission where he met up with Major Gavin and Brigadier Lyons RA and ended up running the evacuation from the fortress stronghold off the north west coast of Malaya.

An RAF Fairmile crash boat 1941

Under constant attack from the air and with scant resources, Warren and Commander Alex Alexander, the Senior Naval officer, set about trying to impose some sort of order on the mounting chaos. There were no lists of Europeans or Asians to refer to, bodies lay unburied in the streets and typhus had broken out. Their first priority was the evacuation of women and children, their second the destruction of secret documents and the demolition of naval shore batteries and key installations around the harbour. Their last act before they left the island on 16 December was to sink the ferry, an action which later came in for criticism by CinC Far East for being 'insufficient' in denying maritime assets to the invaders. It was an unfair observation, for the two officers, through brilliant improvisation, had turned adversity into triumph; not a single European casualty had been incurred during the evacuation. However, this statistic must be qualified in that nearly 3,000 Asian people were killed or injured during the ferocious Japanese bombing and strafing of the island.

Attached to III Indian Corps as GSO1, Warren then took on the responsibility for all behind the lines activities and taking Freddy Spencer Chapman with him to Kuala Lumpur, on 22 December the two of them set about recruiting planters for SBPs in Malaya and establishing a second STS at the Chinese School in Kuala Lumpur. Warren then linked up with Major Angus Rose of the 2nd Battalion, Argyll and Sutherland Highlanders, who had been given by GHQ an independent raiding unit ROSEFORCE and who helped him plan a raid against the Japanese forces on the estuary of the Trong River[16]. It was a qualified success, including the killing of a Japanese Major General in an ambush, but by now events were moving too quickly to repeat it, so arriving back in Singapore on the last train from Kuala Lumpur [the city fell to the enemy on 11 January], in tandem with Major Ivan Lyon and Major Jock Campbell, a former rubber planter, he initiated, planned and organised a supply/escape route from Singapore to Sumatra.

Major Angus Rose, who had commanded ROSEFORCE on the raid with Warren, wrote of him: 'Warren himself had so many characteristics that it is hard to say which predominated. In the first place he was incredibly ubiquitous; a master of time and space. He was fearless, but too intelligent to be foolhardy. In manner, he was upright, downright, and straightforward, and in appearance he was hard, handsome and immaculate.'

On 8 February 1942, Warren left Singapore and made for Padang in Java where thousands of civilians and troops had congregated after the fall of Singapore. When he arrived there, he was appalled at the chaos and

---

16 According to Rose, Warren was on his way up the Bernam River in an RAF Fairmile crashboat to one of the Sembilan Islands to eliminate a Japanese W/T station.

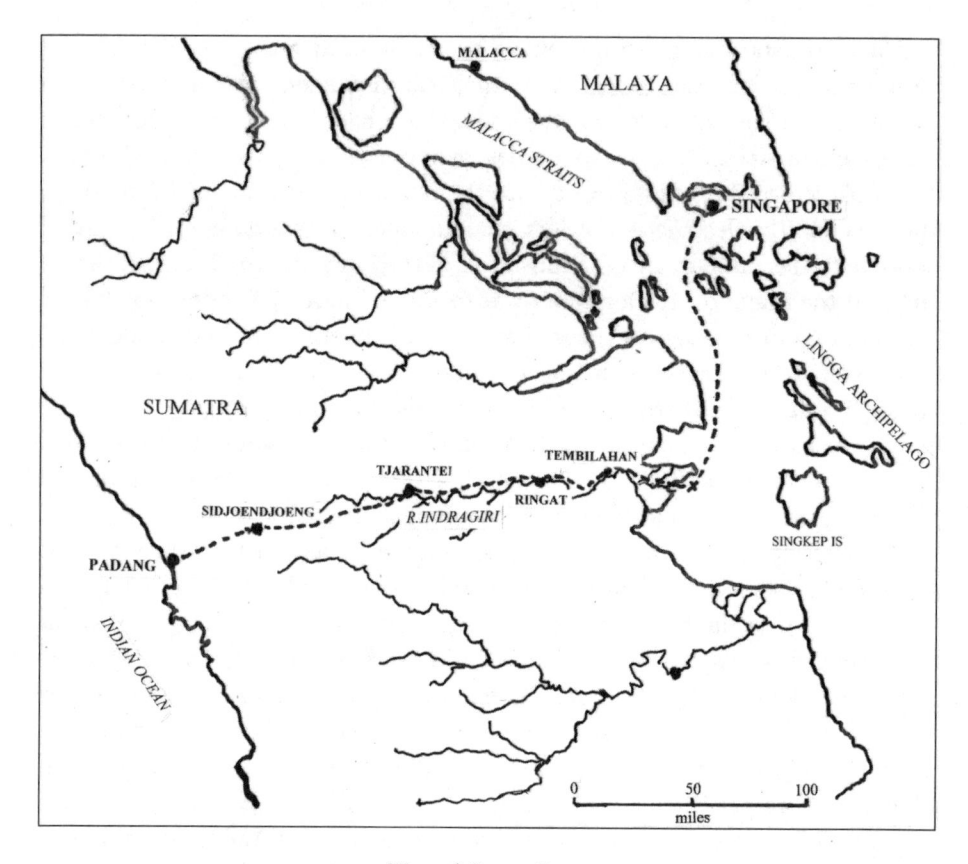

Warren's Escape Route

ill-discipline of the troops and as Senior British Officer [SBO], having supervised the evacuation, made decision to remain, giving up his slot on a boat to a Royal Artillery [RA] officer.

Ian Skidmore in his biography of Warren sums up the dilemma facing Warren at this moment:

'It was not an easy decision to make. Capture was inevitable and he knew he faced years of privation, and possibly, if the Japanese found out he was SOE, of torture or death. He knew, too, that he was throwing away his career. If he escaped from Sumatra and joined a fighting command, his record and talents would inevitably bring him to the highest rank. But he stayed because any other course would have been unthinkable.

He had the means to escape. Lind had bought a native *prahu* ... and stocked her with stores of food and water, enough to take him and his men, under sail, to Ceylon. In fact she did successfully cross the Bay of Bengal under a single mainsail with Warren's party. But Warren was not with them. At the last moment he gave his place to a young RA Major, Geoffrey Rowley-Conwy, and he stayed.'

When the Japanese entered the town, he officially surrendered the remains of the British army in Sumatra to them on 16 March. In the three and a half years that followed, he was a prisoner of the Japanese in the slave labour camps built to construct the Burma-Thailand railway. Had the Kempeitai discovered his identity he would have been shot; there had been a price on his head since the early days in Malaya.

An Australian surgeon Lieutenant Colonel 'Weary' Dunlop[17], who worked alongside Warren on the Burma Railway, wrote of him: 'His was a life of a man who at the crucial point turned his back on what he was supremely equipped to be, a highly successful soldier, and chose instead the gesture of compassion towards the wounded and battered debris in Sumatra.'

After the surrender of the Japanese in August 1945, Warren was appointed Chief Staff Officer of an international HQ, set up to clear the POW and internment camps. He located 13,000 British prisoners, 11,000 Dutch and 5,000 Australians. Of the 60,000 who had worked on the railway, 15,000 had died. The estimate of the death toll of native labourers was put at 100,000.

Warren's is indeed an extraordinary story of devotion to duty, courage and self-sacrifice. His decision to remain behind when he had the chance to escape was a true act of heroism, his motives honour and duty to his country and, above all, to his fellow men.

---

17 Later Sir Ernest Edward Dunlop, AC, CMG, OBE.

LIEUTENANT COLONEL PETER LINDSAY, DSO

Peter Lindsay

Educated at Eton and a contemporary of Colin Mackenzie, in the 1920s Peter Lindsay started an estate agency business in England and then founded a land development company in France, specializing in ski resorts. On the outbreak of war, he joined the Irish Guards aged 39. After serving with the Second Battalion in Holland and France, he requested a transfer to SOE. His commanding officer supported his application, commenting 'this officer distinguished himself in Boulogne and is of an adventurous and enterprising temperament. He desires to serve in a unit which is likely to see Active Service sooner than this battalion'. In the meantime, in October 1940 Lindsay married Jane Kenyon-Slaney, whose sister Vivien was married to the Viceroy of India's heir, the Earl of Hopetoun. It was to prove a useful connection.

Recruited by SOE London as an Overseas Liaison Officer, Lindsay was sent to Killery's ORIENTAL Mission in Singapore via the USA and from there to Burma where he met up with Colin Mackenzie, the head of the INDIAN Mission who had come to see for himself the conditions at Lashio. By now it was too late to organise SBPs but working with Noel Stevenson of the Burma Frontier Service, Lindsay recruited Noel Boyt, a forest manager with Steel Brothers, and Cecil Smith, the Conservator of Forests, and dispatched them to the Karenni Hills to raise levies. Boyt recalled 'in the short space of three weeks we[18] had 3,000 Levies on the ground, doing first class work, patrolling; gathering intelligence; decimation of Burmese spies; hiding of supply caches; successful attacks on villages held by the enemy; helping stragglers...back to our lines.' Poorly equipped and with only a fraction armed with modern rifles, the Levies managed to help 13 Brigade and the Chinese Sixth Army to delay the Japanese advance for two critical days as British troops retreated up the Sittang Valley. Boyt wrote that 'we undoubtedly were able to put in some excellent work in Burma during the last few weeks. Unfortunately time was always against us otherwise more could have been done.'

Moving north, the ORIENTAL Mission together with an assortment of Levy officers under Major Stevenson managed to blow up between 5 and 12 May most of the bridges from Myitkyina to Sumprabum and then from Sumprabum to Fort Hertz. In the process, many civilians were 'ferried to safety – at one point Stevenson had three women and eighteen children in his jeep. This was in marked contrast to previous failures by the Mission to blow up the Shweli Bridge thus allowing the Japanese to push quickly on to Bhamo. On 14 May 1942 after an eighty mile journey in five days, Lindsay's party approached Fort Hertz where they were met by the Assistant District Commissioner for Sumprabum. He had arrived a few hours earlier with the Government party led by the 60-year-old Sir John Rowland, the Chief Railways Commissioner, who had left Myitkyina by road on 4 May with a party of nineteen. Along the way he had been joined by Captain Noel Boyt and five men from the North Burma levies, including Jardine, McCrindle and Gardiner, and E.W. Rossiter of the Burma Frontier Service together with the Assistant Superintendent of Putao and a group of twenty-five civilians. All along the border between Burma and India a mass exodus of refugees was underway, primarily Indians who had flocked to Burma to pre-empt imminent immigration restrictions. The Assam Tea Planters Association was mobilised as the principal relief agency to deal with an influx of over 150,000 refugees[19], many of whom were suffering from malnutrition and exhaustion.

When Lindsay discussed the situation with Sir John, he discovered that the Government party intended to walk to India. The route Sir John proposed to take had been walked by only five previous European explorers – none in the last fifty years. The only map showed large unsurveyed areas indicating that for some 200 miles the journey would be through

---

18 Boyt, Smith, Seagrim and McCrindle. They were later joined by Captain Thompson and a company of Burma rifles.
19 Bayley and Harper use a revised total of 600,000 that fled from Burma to India either by sea or land and a figure of 80,000 dead of exhaustion, disease or malnutrition.

uninhabited mountains and unexplored forests. The muleteers and elephant mahouts had all been paid off, for conditions ahead were too bad for them to continue and in any case their fodder had run out. Some ninety porters had agreed to go with the party as far as the Chaukan Pass[20] but then would return to Fort Hertz, leaving the main party to make their way to India the best way they could. Lindsay's W/T operator, Sergeant Benson, got through to the SOE W/T station at Chungking, giving details of the Government party's intended trek and seeking orders from Calcutta. Later that day, the reply came that they were to close the W/T station down, bury their equipment and join the Government party[21].

Having sent a small party of John Leyden, an Extra Deputy Commissioner of Myitkyina, and G.D.L. Millar, a former tea planter, ahead with thirteen Nung porters and Millar's elephant tracker, Goal Miri, to mark the trail on 17 May[22], Sir John and the main body set off in a long straggling Indian file. The going through tangled forests and across fast flowing streams, spanned by swaying bamboo bridges, was very slow and after covering only twelve miles in two days, they camped for three days to allow the porters to go back to the fort and bring out more supplies. By the end of the first week the van of the party was again on the move, following the markers.

Recounting the story to Major Jim Gavin some months later, Cumming recollected the first part of the journey to the Chaukan Pass was through thick jungle, over innumerable hills, anything from 1,500 feet to 6,000 feet high. On a good day they would march some five miles in ten hours. The monsoon had broken early and the ground had become a quagmire. Some members of the party sank up to their thighs in red mud as they pulled themselves, step by step, up the mountains or scrambled down rock faces. It rained continuously and every night they cut bamboo and small trees to build shelters. They often went days without a fire and invariably went to bed wet and hungry. At first light, Cumming and Lindsay would go round the makeshift camp urging everyone to get on their feet and continue the march. The rains and melting snows turned passable streams into raging rivers, some waded chest deep, others crossed by

---

20 This mountain pass, at an altitude of about 5000 ft [the Chaukan Bum or hill is 8000ft high], is situated exactly on the border between India and Burma, respectively in the neighbouring states of Arunachal Pradesh and Kachin.
21 Mackenzie wrote that he was trying to organise the extraction of Lindsay's party by air. When he failed to get through to him on the W/T, he assumed that they had set off across the Chaukan pass and immediately asked the Assam Tea Planters Association to set off and try and meet them half way.
22 Rowland says in his diary that he never heard of them again which is incorrect. They did indeed get through and were responsible for organizing the rescue effort of the Rossiter and Rowland parties.

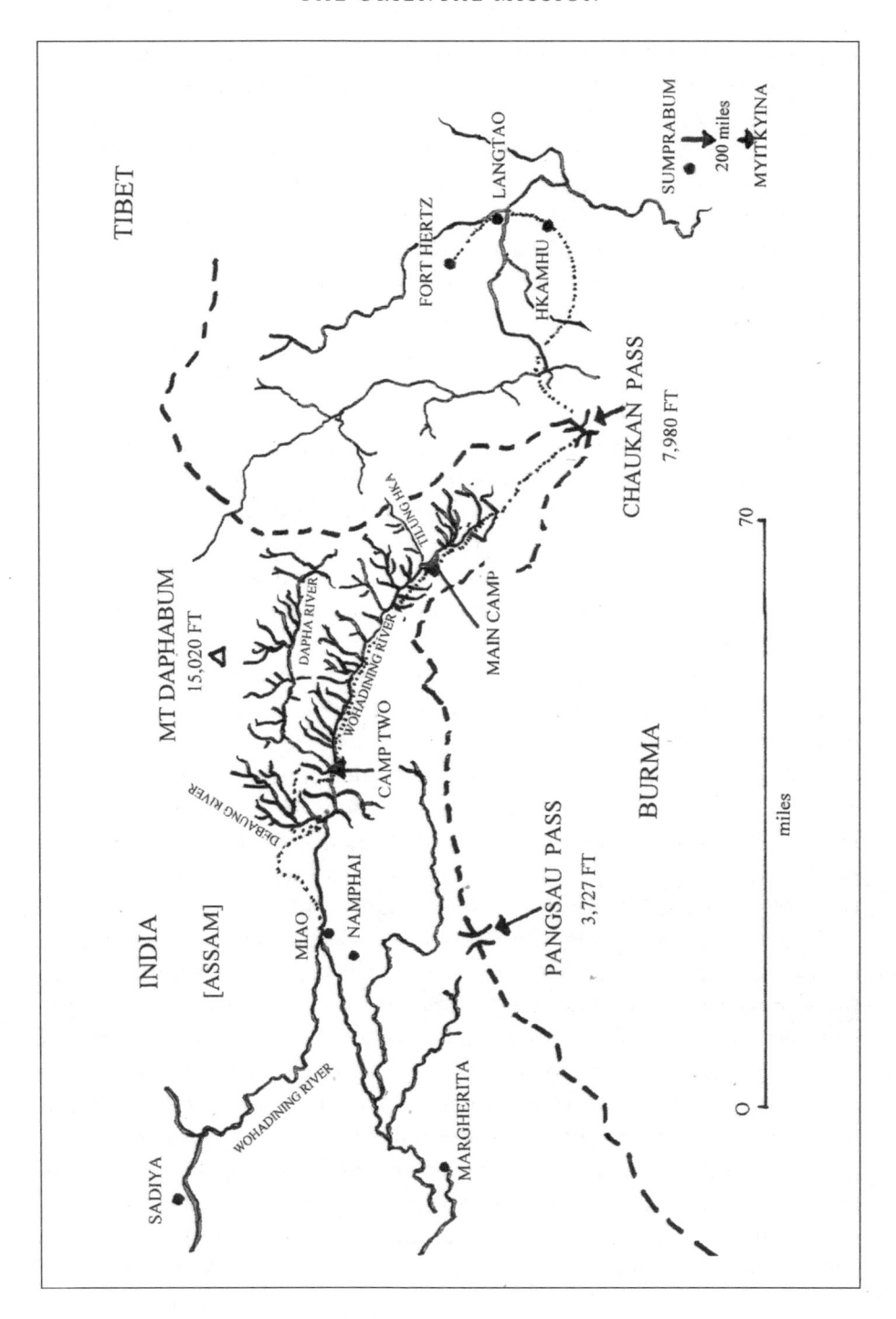

Rowland's Route to India

hacking down large trees on the river banks to span the torrent. On other occasions, tree trunks were lashed together with ropes and bamboo enabling the party to be rafted across.

Apart from the signs left by the markers, there were no paths other than animal tracks. Often the terrain was so impossible that the party had to spend days wading along the river bed to make progress. Eventually, after climbing some 6,000 feet, they reached the Chaukan Pass[23]. By now they were covering less than three miles a day and everyone was exhausted.

On the 23 May, Cumming was surprised to see Corporal Sawyer and two Burma Levy officers, Captains Jardine and Gardiner. They had walked across the mountains from Sumprabum when Rowland's porters had arrived back with the news that the *Sahibs* had left Fort Hertz for India: Sawyer decided there was nothing left other than to follow Lindsay and Cumming and walk to India. Almost everyone in the Government party expected to be rescued any day and was so convinced that the planes flying overhead were looking for them that two large bonfires were lit to attract attention. The planes in fact were on regular supply runs to China and took no notice of the beacons.

On 28 May, all thirty-three porters refused to go on for fear of being stranded up country by the heavy monsoon rains. They all left. According to Rowland, two days later Captain Fraser and Sergeant Pratt arrived with 102 Punjabi ORs.

The monsoon rains continued without a break and everyone huddled in makeshift, leaky, bamboo shelters. On 29 May, Boyt and Gardiner set off with a civilian, aptly named Moses, to try and make contact with the relief party and were soon lost from view in the mist. Two days later Corporal Sawyer also left with a small party made up of two escaped POWs, Captain Fraser and Sergeant Pratt from the Hussars, and two other officers, McCrindle and Howe, a former rice trader with the Anglo Burmese Rice Company Ltd.

A party of forty-five Ghurkhas and twenty Garwahlis under command of Jemadar Rattan Singh had stumbled on the main camp and sheltered there for a few days. They now volunteered to help carry the food and baggage in exchange for rations and payment. On 2 June the party moved off into country worse than that already covered. In one day alone they criss-crossed rivers some fifteen times, hacking their way through bamboo and climbing hill after hill. The column had by now broken up into small groups. The stronger members were in the lead and, depending on their state of exhaustion, the survivors attached themselves to others in similar condition. The infirm were carried on improvised stretchers made from bamboo, army webbing and blankets and the walking sick took turns as

---

23 Rowland writes that it was here that he met Lindsay and Cumming.

stretcher bearers. The Ghurkhas, concerned at the slow pace the party was making, were becoming impatient and asked permission to strike out on their own. Progress was indeed slow – Rowland recorded covering four miles in four and a half hours on 4 June, five in nine and a half hours on 5 June, and four in seven hours on 6 June. The weather remained atrocious.

Unknown to Rowland, Leyden and Millar had stumbled across three Mishmis tribesmen on 3 June who had led them to Bishi village where they had been able to contact the tea planter in charge of the rescue effort, Gyles Mackrell[24] who had eighty-four elephants at Namphai Camp a few miles away. He immediately set off with twenty of his best animals to the River Dapha to attempt a rescue. This was the start of an extraordinary story of courage and determination by both man and beast as they braved the appalling monsoon conditions, fording swollen rivers and seeking safe passage along slippery muddy banks. First to be rescued on 9 June was a group of sixty-eight Ghurkhas from a piece of land that had become an island surrounding by foaming torrents. Then twenty-seven Sikhs and a mixed party of thirty-eight Ghurkhas and Sikhs were ferried to safety on the backs of Mackrell's elephants.

But for Rowland's group, the outlook was bleak. It was three weeks since the first party had left to fetch help and since then at least three other parties had gone ahead searching for rescue parties. Nothing had been heard from any of these and it was assumed that some if not all had perished. When the main party arrived at a river in full flood, in the absence of any tracks along the bank they waded through the water until they discovered Corporal Sawyer's party, exhausted and starving, waiting for the river [Tilung Hka] level to drop before they could ford it. As the stragglers gradually stumbled in, Lindsay and Cumming urged everyone to build shelters for themselves.

The party was trapped by this unfordable river for about twelve days, all the time gradually eating into the food stocks. About 12 June the SOE party decided to try and ford the river. There was now only two weeks' food left and unless help reached them soon everyone would die of starvation. There had been some talk of building rafts but eventually the party waded diagonally across the Tilung Hka torrent; joined by the Ghurkhas

---

24 Mackrell was born on 9 October 1888, and educated at Epsom College. Prior to the Great War, he had worked as a tea planter at Sylhet, India. Granted a commission in the Royal Flying Corps [Special Reserve of Officers], he was appointed Flying Officer on 21 August 1916 and served in France and England before taking command of B Flight No. 114 Squadron in Lahore, where he was engaged in operations on the North-West Frontier. Decorated with the DFC in June 1919, Mackrell returned to civilian life in Assam, where he worked as an area supervisor for Steel Brothers, the tea exporters.

and the three civilians, Jardine, Kendal and Moses, they formed a human chain. Finally reaching the far bank, Cumming clung to its steep sides and looked around in time to see Corporal Sawyer being swept away. Captain Fraser, who had decided to join them, was also swept down-stream and trapped by his webbing against a tree. Eventually the rest of the party managed to free him, more dead than alive, and dragged him ashore[25].

After some hours resting it was agreed that the SOE party consisting of Lindsay, Cumming, and Kendal would move on with the Jemadar and the Ghurkhas to make best possible speed to find the rescuers.

Describing the rest of the journey to Major Jim Gavin, Cumming recalled that Lindsay had badly bruised himself crossing the river and Jardine was also very ill and needed treatment. Finally on 19 June, after carrying them across the flooded River Dapha, Cumming left both exhausted men on a sandy beach alongside the river and headed off on his own. His condition was desperate. He was both mentally and physically exhausted, his uniform was in rags held together by bits of rattan. All he had to eat was two ounces of rice. He had only the vaguest idea of where he was but assumed he was some fifty miles from the nearest habitation – in India – a prospect of some ten days' march. Stumbling in the rain through the trees along game tracks, he bumped into a column of elephants coming towards him in single file. Suddenly brown-skinned soldiers crowded around him and in their midst appeared Mackrell[26]. This was the search party that Colin Mackenzie had sent in from Assam. Cumming was sufficiently coherent to give general directions where to find his two companions. A search party immediately set off to find them while the rescue team bivouacked for the night. Steve Cumming's mumbled directions were sufficient and Kendal and Lindsay were brought in later that day. Mackrell noted that 'Lindsay had a terrible leg – big abscess from a bruise – and Kendal looks desperately ill'.

The following day, after explaining that more groups were close behind and giving instructions where to find the Government party, Lindsay and Cumming rode off on two elephants and eventually reached the local military headquarters at Margherita. Here Lindsay insisted on telephoning the Viceroy's private office so that the RAF could be alerted to make supply drops to the main party. Captain Fraser's team reached Mackrell on 21 June.

---

25 Ritchie Gardiner was awarded a George Medal for this action.
26 Mackrell had been joined on 17 June by another Assam tea planter, Captain Reg Wilson, with sixty men. He stayed with him for the next month, making repeated crossings of the river to rescue and supply others making the dangerous crossing.

Boyt was unstinting in his praise for Lindsay: 'After the fall of Lashio I cannot speak too highly of the help and the great example of devotion to duty we received from Major Peter Lindsay. He was an inspiration to us all during those extremely difficult days and his heroic dash ahead, accompanied by Captain Cumming, into Assam to get help laid on for the Rossiter/Rowland... was a superb example of unselfish "guts" and determination to see that help came to others before himself.'

Meanwhile, from 12 to 30 June, the Government party, now twenty-five strong, had remained static at their makeshift camp. Rossiter had let the Sepoys walk off with all of his party's rice rations leaving them with only six days full rations left. Accordingly everyone was put on quarter rations. Supplemented with fern fronds and tree hearts to form bulk, it was hoped to spin out the rations for twenty-four days. On 1 July, an RAF plane dropped food to them, prompting Rowland to note in his diary 'so ended the first day of July 1942, truly a day of miracles.' Another drop followed on 6 July. Rowland now decided to move on with the fitter members of the party, leaving Rossiter with the sick but it was not until the rescue team headed by Captain Street found them on 31 July that they reached safety.

In the weeks that followed Mackrell established a camp on the banks of the river, where he gave help to the steady stream of refugees that struggled out of the Burmese jungle. By mid-July, however, sickness had descended on the camp and Mackrell and many of his men were struck down with fever. Reluctantly he was forced to return to Assam to recover but vowed to return to continue his rescue work. Whilst convalescing he conducted an aerial survey of the River

Mackrell's elephants braving the Dapha

Dapha area and was convinced that a second expedition should be mounted using both elephants and boats.

This second expedition formed up at the riverside camp on 21 August and Mackrell pushed forward with his boats and elephants to go in search of Rossiter. On 4 September they came across some more of the party who had by now left the camp in search of help. They carried urgent messages informing that food supplies were now reduced to little more than a week and that help must come immediately if disaster was to be averted. At the same time Mackrell received two letters from the British authorities in Assam ordering him to immediately desist from any further attempts to rescue this party. However, deciding that it was impossible to withdraw in the existing circumstances, Mackrell decided to push on once more.

Progress was becoming so slow that, on 7 September, Mackrell sent forward a striking party of his best elephants and fittest men with a supply of rations in a last desperate attempt to reach the camp. On 10 September, a team he had earlier dispatched by boat now arrived and Mackrell was able to make further progress, but still he could not get close enough. The striking party was now the only hope that remained and all he could do was wait for news. On 20 September, by which time they had all but given up hope, a runner from the striking party arrived in camp with news of their success and, later that evening, the elephants arrived in camp bearing their weak and emaciated cargo of refugees. By the end of September 1942, when operations finally ceased, about 200 people had been saved.

Rowland calculated that by the time he reached Simla, he had travelled 2,798 miles from Lashio, including 225 miles on foot across the Chaukan Pass and 232 miles without seeing a single villager. In a letter to his wife dated 13 August 1942, Rowland wrote that he crossed 'the most appalling country I have ever struck in my life – mountains 2,000 feet high to climb and the descent down slopes almost like the side of a house – no footholds, only wet mud and slush, with the rain coming down in torrents, morning, noon and night'. Only when the rescue was fully underway did Lindsay and Cumming make their way to Delhi and report to Colin Mackenzie. Steve Cumming became Operations Officer [G II] Group A[27] and Ritchie Gardiner head of Burma country section. Lindsay, whose health had been severely affected by the 'walk' to India, went on sick leave and then

---

27 In April 1944, Cumming became GSO I Group A and in August 1945 took over from Gavin Stewart as Commander Group A with the rank of Colonel. He was awarded an MBE and Mentioned in Dispatches. Stewart thought very highly of him: 'Has an almost infinite capacity for intelligent and hard work. Makes courageous decisions and does not suffer fools gladly. Observant and shrewd, with a sense of humour.'

returned to SOE India as LO to General Zhou Wei-lung in Chungking. Apart from a few specific missions to China, he remained in Meerut as a senior staff officer until he was sent to Kandy in March 1944 to establish Advanced HQ for the INDIAN Mission. He was then sent to New York by SACSEA when he became very ill and spent the three months in hospital, finally having a hernia operated on in Vancouver. From there he returned to London and after a month's sick leave, joined the SOE staff at Baker Street as a GSO1.

When Lindsay's death was announced in *The Times* in 1971, his first cousin wrote to the Irish Guards to tell them that this was the first time the family realised he had a DSO.

31 July 1944 [resubmitted 23 January 1946]: Recommendation for DSO.

This officer, who was in charge of the Oriental Mission in Burma, was responsible for organizing denial projects during the Japanese advance, and for initiating and subsequently cooperating with the Burma levies. When all organised resistance in the north of Burma had ceased, Major, now Lieutenant Colonel Lindsay, was responsible by his personal example of energy and tenacity of purpose for extricating a substantial quantity of arms and explosives which were transported from Lashio to Bhamo and thence to Myitkyina. It was with these explosives that a] the Namtu mines were denied to the enemy and b] the levies and Oriental Mission officers destroyed the five main bridges between Sumprabum and Myitkyina. The arms formed the basis of arms distribution to the force which later became the Northern Kachin levies. The civil authorities having left, Lieutenant Colonel Lindsay took over temporarily the administration of Sumprabum and assisted thereby the orderly evacuation of several mixed civil and military parties.

He again displayed similar high qualities of determination and endurance by crossing the hitherto rarely traversed Chaukan Pass in May 1942 and thereby was instrumental in bringing assistance to a stranded party of refugees, who might otherwise have not escaped. Throughout the campaign in Burma, Lieutenant Colonel Lindsay showed commendable devotion to duty and untiring zeal in the face of most difficult and discouraging circumstances.

Awarded

29 January 1943: Gyles Mackrell; citation for George Medal

Mr. Mackrell, while in charge of the elephant transport, heard that a number of refugees were attempting to reach Assam over the Chaukan pass. In appalling weather he led his elephants by forced marches over a route hitherto considered impracticable. At great personal risk and after several vain

Exhausted members of the Chaukan Pass trek

attempts he took them across the flooded river, the bed of which consisted of shifting boulders. He thus rescued 68 sepoys and 33 other persons who were facing starvation. Without medical assistance he fed and doctored them until they were fit to proceed. He fell ill with severe fever, but remained behind and was responsible for saving the lives of over 200 persons. Mr. Mackrell showed the highest initiative and personal courage, and risked hardships which might easily have proved fatal.

Awarded

CHAPTER THREE

THE INDIA MISSION and the ANDAMAN ISLANDS

The Secretary of State for India, Leo Amery MP, sent Colonel Joyce of the Indian Political Service to Singapore in May 1941 to talk with Valentine Killery. The subject of their discussion was the best way to broaden the ORIENTAL Mission to incorporate India. They concluded that a new Mission should be formed and Colin Mackenzie, a friend of the Viceroy Lord Linlithgow[28] and a decorated First World War soldier who had lost a leg during the war, was appointed to command it.

The new Mission, known as GSI [k], was to be wholly responsible for Afghanistan, Tibet, possibly Persia and of course India. In March 1942 General Wavell directed the Mission to organise irregular forces from local tribesmen to defend the East Persia Road. Connor Green was despatched to Afghanistan to report on conditions among the tribes as to their suitability for harassing a German advance. This scheme was wound up in 1943 when the threat of a German invasion through the Caucasus had receded.

*****

Afghanistan

Primarily on account of the Fakir of Ipi's border disturbances in Waziristan, the British government decided not to provide weapons to the Afghan armed forces for national defence. So, not surprisingly, in 1935 Kabul turned to Germany and soon the Nazis began to increase arms exports to Afghanistan and the Todt Organisation undertook major infrastructure projects. German officers instigated a program designed to equip and train the Afghan armed forces to Western standards. In two years, German trade with Afghanistan increased tenfold. Undoubtedly London had lost the initiative on its vulnerable north west Indian colonial border.

---

28 Both were also directors of J&P Coats Ltd. Linlithgow put Mackenzie's name forward to Amery.

When France surrendered in 1940, Abdul Majid, the Afghan Minister of National Economy, indicated that his country was ready to support the Axis cause, including incitement of the frontier tribes to take up arms against the British. Germany immediately stepped up the flow of pro-Axis, anti-British propaganda directed toward the Afghan population as well as across the border into India.

The headache for the British was that among the Todt Organisation personnel in Afghanistan were a number of German secret service operatives. In April 1940 the Abwehr's Hauptmann Morlock arrived with two tons of diplomatic baggage including small arms, and a 20mm canon and ammunition. Under cover of a research group studying leprosy, more Abwehr operatives entered Afghanistan and concentrated on the Indian border in preparation for a campaign of sabotage and insurrection. A number of incidents occurred, none of any consequence except the shooting of two German 'scientists' while attempting to make contact with the Fakir of Ipi.

On 1 February 1941, Subhas Chandra Bose, the Indian nationalist leader, arrived in Afghanistan after escaping British custody in India with the help of the Abwehr. From Kabul, he then travelled to Berlin via the Soviet Union where he spent the next three years engaged on anti-British propaganda beamed into Central Asia and the Indian subcontinent.

When Germany invaded Russia in June 1941, the Afghan government had no choice but to accede to the joint Anglo-Soviet demand in October 1941 for the expulsion of all Germans and Italians. For once, they knew that there were no other options.

*****

By the summer of 1942, the fortunes of the INDIA Mission were at a low ebb. After ten months, there was very little to show for, as long as Germany threatened the Caucasus and the Japanese remained bent on invading India, the Mission was on the back foot. Its primary role was defensive, organising SBPs in Assam, Madras and Calcutta responsible for demolitions. 150 members of the Indian Communist Party from Madras were trained on a special course at Kohima to lead these parties.

Training, the very essence of the making of a Special Forces operative, was high on Mackenzie's agenda. A training establishment was therefore created from scratch to indoctrinate recruits into the black arts and military skills they would require once in the field. Major Alfred Le Seelleur RE, who had originally been recruited by Jim Gavin to help run the ORIENTAL Mission's STS 101 in Singapore, started the Demolition Wing of the Infantry Training

School at Saugor and then in March 1943 set up ME 25 at Trincomalee, later known as the Allied School of Jungle Warfare. Here recruits were given advanced training in demolitions, weapons, jungle craft and small boat handling. Major George Ingham-Clark, a TA officer in the Argyll and Sutherland Highlanders and a former director of the international paint company Messrs Pinchin, Johnson and Company Ltd, was appointed commandant of the Eastern Warfare School at Poona in December 1942. In the autumn of 1943, Major Oliver Windle, an officer in the India Police Service with over thirty-four years of service, was transferred from running SOE's Madras office to become commandant of the School of Eastern Interpreters where students were taught agent handling and propaganda techniques. To coordinate these three distinct and separate schools, Major John Bush arrived in September 1943 as GSO1 training. A pre-war marketing executive with Lever Brothers commissioned in the Independent Companies in June 1940, Bush had helped Colonel John Munn start the very first STS at Arisaig in Scotland in December 1940. On balance, it was a strong team which had to engage with mainly Asiatic students who were somewhat different in outlook compared to their European counterparts. Tact and patience prevailed over the usual British army gambit of blunt and direct criticism.

SOE Far East Training Establishment September 1943

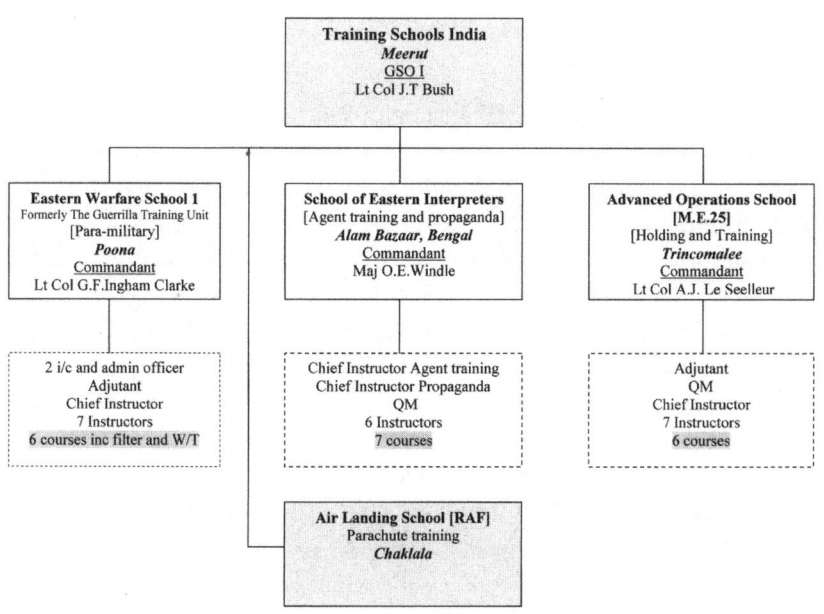

Training Schools India
Meerut
GSO I
Lt Col J.T Bush

Eastern Warfare School 1
Formerly The Guerrilla Training Unit
[Para-military]
Poona
Commandant
Lt Col G.F.Ingham Clarke

- 2 i/c and admin officer
- Adjutant
- Chief Instructor
- 7 Instructors
- 6 courses inc filter and W/T

School of Eastern Interpreters
[Agent training and propaganda]
Alam Bazaar, Bengal
Commandant
Maj O.E.Windle

- Chief Instructor Agent training
- Chief Instructor Propaganda
- QM
- 6 Instructors
- 7 courses

Advanced Operations School
[M.E.25]
[Holding and Training]
Trincomalee
Commandant
Lt Col A.J. Le Seelleur

- Adjutant
- QM
- Chief Instructor
- 7 Instructors
- 6 courses

Air Landing School [RAF]
Parachute training
Chaklala

V Force, a stay-behind guerrilla force raised by Wavell in April 1942 along the 800 mile Indian-Burmese border to harass enemy lines of communication and to provide intelligence from behind enemy lines in the event of a Japanese invasion of India, was also administered by the SOE military representative but this decision was reversed when all guerrillas came under the command of the army except those actually operating behind enemy lines.

A new directive in August 1942, after the demise of the ORIENTAL Mission which had relocated to India after the fall of Singapore, authorised the Mission to operate in Thailand, Indo-China and Malaya. The structure of the INDIA Mission now assumed the following shape:

- Delhi – Liaison office with the Viceroy
- Meerut – Mission HQ [four divisions – Finance and Administration/Operations and Training/Political Warfare/Country Sections] and W/T centre
- Bombay – new arrivals reception

THE INDIA MISSION and the ANDAMAN ISLANDS

- Calcutta – Group A: Burma, Thailand and Indo-China
- Colombo – Group B: Malaya, Anglo-Dutch and Islands
- Chalala – Parachuting school [then Jessore]
- Poona – Demolitions school
- Chungking and Kunming – Chinese sub-missions

Given the distances involved, this structure was far from efficient, yet there were few alternatives given the scarcity of resources, most of which were devoured by the military.

In September 1942 Colonel Christopher Hudson flew to Ceylon to set up new base for the INDIA Mission and appointed former Malayan policeman Innes Tremlett, the leading authority on the CPM, to run it. This was important for two reasons. Firstly, all submarine operations were based out of Trincomalee and secondly, Ceylon was the nearest staging post for the Andaman Islands, the target for the Mission's first insertions into enemy held territory. Operation BUNKUM and Operation BALDHEAD duly took place and both were successful. However all was to little purpose since no invasion of the islands took place and hence all the intelligence gathered was superfluous.

*****

COLONEL GEORGE TAYLOR, CBE

George Taylor

The INDIA Mission was fortunate to have Colonel George Taylor as their champion in London. Born in Australia in 1903, Taylor had gained a double first in Philosophy and History at Melbourne University before being accepted by Oxford for a doctorate in Tudor Papal relationships. However when his father suddenly became ill, he returned to Australia where, after a stint as a foreign correspondent on the Melbourne Age and then being called to the Victorian bar after completing a law degree, he joined Shell, first as General Manager New Zealand, and then Assistant General Manager Australia. Aware of the potential of their high flier, Shell sent him in 1933 on a round the world trip to London where he became the Personal Assistant to the Chairman, Viscount Bearsted. Taylor family memory has it that at a dinner at the Tower of London in 1938 he was invited to join Section D, the hybrid guerrilla warfare organisation attached to SIS, and, on acceptance, was appointed head of its Balkan network. His oil expertise initially took him to Romania to plan sabotage attacks on the oil fields and distribution systems there. When Section D was merged into SOE in the summer of 1940, Sir Frank Nelson despatched him back to the Balkans, and in the hectic days following the German invasion of Yugoslavia in March 1941 he was captured by the Italians in Montenegro along with his great friend Sandy Glen after the submarine sent to pick them up at Kotor failed to arrive. As they were accredited diplomats, the two men were interned in a castle on the Italian mainland and after two months regained

THE INDIA MISSION and the ANDAMAN ISLANDS

their freedom when they were exchanged for two senior Italian diplomats held by the British.

Back in London, Bickham Sweet Escot's 'brilliant but ruthless Australian with a mind of limpid clarity' was made up to full colonel as Chief Assistant to CD. As 'one of SOE's strongest formative characters' as Professor William Mackenzie dubbed him, Taylor became Director of Overseas Groups and Missions [with Tony Keswick reporting to him as i/c Far East] in March 1942 and then, after briefly serving as Chief of Staff to Sir Charles Hambro, in May 1943 he was appointed Director of the Far East Group, a post he held until the end of the war. The last chief under whom he served, Major General Sir Colin Gubbins, regarded him as 'a very able, quick-thinking officer, of great energy and persistence, who at times presses his points too hard'.

*****

When South East Asia Command [SEAC] was established in Ceylon in November 1943, its commander Admiral Lord Louis Mountbatten ruled that all special operations should report to P Division, headed by Captain G.A. Garnons-Williams RN who was accredited to SIS. The military would route all its requests to 'P' and that way there could be no confusion. In March 1944, the designation of the India Mission was changed to Force 136.

The story of the activities of the Mission's Country Sections is told in the chapters on Burma, Malaya, Thailand, China, French Indo-China and Dutch East Indies.

In close co-operation with SOA, the INDIA Mission's most successful sabotage operation was JAYWICK, Major Ivan Lyon's spectacular raid on Singapore which sank 50,000 tons of enemy shipping. Sadly, it was followed by the complete failure of Operation RIMAU when all members were killed or captured.

An altogether different operation was REMORSE, run by Walter Fletcher, ably assisted by Edward Wharton-Tiger [formerly of SOE's Gibraltar section]. They ran the currency black market in China and engaged in a number of other lucrative trading activities such as smuggling diamonds [provided by De Beers] and Swiss watches [sourced by Jock McCafferty, SOE's man in Berne] into China. Operation REMORSE netted SOE about £950m.

The activities of Section N, the Mission's para-naval group, came to nought due to problems in finding serviceable native craft and adapting them to special operations. From the beginning, when fast launches were requested for the insertion of parties along the coast of Burma, there was opposition by the RN establishment to the idea of 'a private navy'. In June 1943, SOE could boast four

SEAC Theatre of Operations

dhows, six small junks and one sloop but discussions with the Admiralty as to who would man the Bengal Auxiliary Flotilla were still in progress a year later. By the end of the war, only one Force 136 vessel, the *Anwari*, had successfully put to sea and completed the round trip of 3,000 miles to the Coco Islands from Ceylon.

At the time of the Japanese surrender in August 1945, Force 136 was gearing up to help SEAC implement the Directive of the Combined Chiefs of Staff issued at the Potsdam Conference in June:

- To open the Straits of Malacca at the earliest possible moment.
- To take part in the main operations against Japan [Operation CORONET] in the spring of 1946 [a contribution of three to five divisions and a small tactical air force].
- To complete the liberation of Malaya.

- To maintain pressure on the Japanese across the Burma-Thailand frontier.
- To capture key areas of Thailand.
- To establish bridgeheads in Java and/or Sumatra.
- To include the part of FIC south of the 60th Parallel, thee Celebes and Borneo within SEAC boundaries.

It promised to be an enormous undertaking which would stretch SOE's resources and logistics as never before. It was not to be.

COLIN MACKENZIE, CMG,
Officier Légion d'Honneur and Dutch Resistance Cross

Colin Mackenzie

The son of General Sir Colin Mackenzie KCB, 43-year-old Colin Mackenzie was appointed on 17 July 1941 to run SOE's INDIA Mission at the suggestion of his friend, Lord Linlithgow, Viceroy of India. Despite the fact he had never been to India, it was an inspired choice and over the next four years he presided over an organisation which grew from literally a handful of men to well over 6,000.

A King's Scholar [KS] at Eton College, in February 1917 Colin joined the 3rd [Reserve] Battalion, Scots Guards, in London where, in between courses at Clapham Common [bombing] and Esher [pioneering], he enjoyed the glamorous and hectic social life that carried on in the capital, irrespective of the war across the Channel. Posted to France in April 1918, he served with B Company 1st Battalion, Scots Guards, in France where, in August 1918, he was hit by 'whizz bangs' and seriously wounded in his left thigh and back, resulting in the loss of his left leg below the hip. His father, commanding the 61st Division, was wounded in the line around the same time. Shot through the jaw by a German sniper when inspecting the trenches, he refused to go for treatment beyond the Casualty Clearing Station as he had just been gazetted to command a Corps. Unfortunately despite this courageous determination to soldier on, the wound flared up and he had to be evacuated for treatment in London. Young Mackenzie was also evacuated to England at the end of October and placed on the retired list in 1920 'on account of ill-health caused by wounds'.

After the war, Mackenzie went up to King's College Cambridge where he read economics under John Maynard Keynes and graduated in 1922 with First Class Honours. He had also showed great promise as a poet and won the Chancellor's Medal for English verse. By his own admission, he did not enjoy Cambridge as much as he had Eton but he met a wide group of people including Bloomsbury group luminaries such as Duncan Grant and Roger Fry who were close friends of Keynes. Francis Partridge became a lifelong friend.

Since childhood, Mackenzie had known the Coats family of J&P Coats, the Glasgow-based thread manufactures, and although Tom Coats[29] was five years older, the two had become close friends, spending holidays together at Glen Tanar in Aberdeenshire. In 1922 he joined J&P Coats in Italy where he worked for their Milan subsidiary and for the next fifteen years travelled extensively in the Americas and in Europe, gamely coping with his prosthetic leg and the periodic intense pain associated with it.

Listed on the London Stock Exchange since the 1890s, Coats was one of the pioneer British multinational companies along with the likes of British American Tobacco. In the 1930s, it built a knitting yarn mill in Toronto, constructed its first mill in the United States in Georgia, and started manufacturing thread in Sao Paulo, Brazil and in Buenos Aires, Argentina. Mackenzie had been a driving force during this period of expansion and by the beginning of the war he had risen to the position of Managing Director.

He chose as his 2 i/c Colonel Gavin Stewart[30], a director of the Corby-based iron and steel company, Stewart and Lloyds, to whom Lord Bearsted had introduced him in SOE's Baker Street HQ. The two men sailed to India on 2 September 1941. Frustrated by the 'dead time' at sea, Mackenzie managed to go ashore when their convoy reached Freetown and arranged for them both to be flown from Lagos to India via Cairo. It saved several weeks which were now gainfully spent in Delhi setting up the Mission from scratch.

Having experienced the 'greatest difficulties in getting a brief' before he left London, his original terms of reference were somewhat vague in that he was to be attached to the Viceroy as 'head of a special operations Mission'. As to where he would operate, his instructions were equally vague although he was responsible for Afghanistan, Tibet, Persia if called on and maybe Russia and China. The threat in 1941 lay to the west where the Germans had to be stopped 'coming down the East Persia road'. After the Japanese advances of 1941 and 1942, the

---

29 Later the second Baron Glentanar, 1894-1971.
30 Stewart had previously spent three years in the Calcutta area.

emphasis switched to the East and his new directive included all the territory which fell under the remit of the Viceroy and CinC India and from 1943 onwards South East Asia Command [SEAC].

As soon as they arrived in India, Mackenzie and Stewart reported to the Viceroy and introduced themselves to Denys Pilditch, Director of Central Intelligence [Home Department, Government of India] and the Director of Military Intelligence [DMI], Major General R. Cawthorne[31]. With the strength of only two men – they were still waiting for Charles Neil, the chief clerk of one of J&P Coats's selling departments, to join them – the first request from Baker Street to look for potential recruits among Italian POWs held in India proved testing. Dividing up the camps between them, Mackenzie and Stewart did the rounds and 'managed to recruit a limited number' who were duly shipped off to SOE's ME HQ in Cairo.

After setting up their base in Meerut forty miles outside Delhi, the Mission took on two new members of staff, Lieutenant Colonel Basil Ivory and Baron Bror Wedell-Wedellsborg. Ivory, a chartered accountant by training and former managing director of the £7 million British Assets Trust Ltd set up by his father James Ivory, was an excellent choice as his financial and business experience made him ideally suited for the post of Chief of Administration and Finance. Commissioned in the RA in 1939, Ivory had been on active service in the Middle East when Mackenzie tracked him down and was extracted in a matter of weeks to Meerut where he took up his post in May. Logistics and stores were the bread and butter of the Far East trading houses with their go-downs and cargo ships, so it was fortuitous that Baron 'Bror' Hannibal Wedell-Wedellsborg, who had set up an import-export company in San Francisco, volunteered to take on the role of Director of Supplies [Finance and Stores Officer] in May 1942. Two of his brothers were working for the Danish resistance. A third new member of staff, Michael Nethersole, DSO, was appointed Political Director of the Mission in July. Unfortunately for Mackenzie, he had to leave almost immediately to take up a senior civil service position as Commissioner of Benares.

In November 1941 the territories of Iraq and Iran were transferred from SOE Cairo to the INDIA Mission. Mackenzie flew down to Baghdad with Major Ronald Critchley MC, his new Staff officer who had come from SOE in Ethiopia, to visit Adrian Bishop [another Old Etonian KS who had been a year ahead of Mackenzie at school] who was running the show. He was away in Jerusalem when they landed so Mackenzie drove up to Tehran[32] through the snow, fortifying himself with vodka to keep warm as he had left his coat

---

31 Later founded the Pakistan ISI in 1948.
32 Iran had been invaded by a joint British-Russian force in August 1941 and Tehran occupied in September.

behind in Baghdad. Staying with HM Minister Sir Reader Bullard, that legendary figure of British imperialism in the Middle East, Mackenzie oversaw a propaganda exercise by dropping off anti-German leaflets in overnight stopping places for long distance lorry drivers. After driving back to Baghdad, news came through of the Japanese attack on Pearl Harbour. A rushed meeting with Bishop[33] followed before Mackenzie hurried back to Delhi, only to find more bad news of the sinking of HMS *Prince of Wales* and HMS *Repulse* waiting for him.

The difficulties in starting up SOE in India in wartime conditions were considerable. The distances were enormous, recruitment competitive [with ISLD and various Indian intelligence agencies] and transport, be it submarines or aircraft, hard to come by. As Colonel Bickham Sweet Escott drolly recalled 'this far flung but loosely-knit empire was connected, if that is the word, by a telephone network on which it was almost impossible to have any coherent conversation, even if you and the man at the other end remembered the elaborate code system you were supposed to use ... because of the innumerable exchanges through which the land line passed'. As a civilian, Mackenzie ran the Indian Mission more or less as a business with himself as Chairman, a deputy Chairman [Colonel Gavin Stewart till 1943, then Brigadier Bobby Guinness RE followed by Brigadier John Anstey of Imperial Tobacco] and four Controllers – Finance and Administration, Operations and Training, Political Warfare and Country Sections – who acted as divisional Directors.

The attitude towards SOE of some senior army officers is summed up by SAS officer John Verney in *Going to the Wars*:

'A general in the War Office, one of the rugged sort, whose co-operation I was seeking to include two pretty ATS sergeants on an Establishment, once told me that in his opinion all irregular formations and private armies like Bomfrey's Boys contributed precisely nothing to Allied victory. All they did was to offer a too-easy, because romanticised, form of gallantry to a few anti-social irresponsible individualists, who sought a more personal satisfaction from the war than that of standing their chance, like proper soldiers, of being bayoneted in a slit trench or burnt alive in a tank. He went so far as to hint that Bomfrey's Boys in particular had caused more dislocation to its own side than it ever had to the enemy.'

---

33 Bishop, a rather large man, shortly afterwards came to a sad end in Tehran when the banister on a hotel balcony gave way causing him to fall to his death.

The year 1942 in India was characterised by General Wavell as 'full and eventful'. India Command had been 'rudely awakened ... by the shock of Japan's aggression and the wholly unexpected disasters in Malaya and then Burma'. He reminded the Chiefs of Staffs that in March 1942 India had not a single fully-trained division, that the Air Force was 'similarly ineffective' and that the Eastern Fleet was 'unable to control Indian waters'. Transport facilities to north east India were diabolical, made the more so by a particularly heavy monsoon and unusually high occurrences of malaria in the workforce. Against this background, the achievements of Mackenzie and Gavin in getting SOE off the ground were all the more remarkable.

After a slow start when Mackenzie battled to preserve the operational function of SOE rather than allow it to become just another intelligence gathering organisation, the INDIA Mission went on the offensive in the summer of 1943 with a raid on Goa. For some time, SOE had suspected that information about Allied shipping movements in the Indian Ocean had been reaching the German U-boat command through an agent in Goa, a small enclave on the Indian mainland belonging to Portugal, at that time a neutral country. Furthermore, it was likely that the information was being transmitted from the radio room of the *Ehrenfels,* a 7,752 tons German freighter which had sought shelter in Marmagoa harbour along with three other Axis ships. After kidnapping the suspected agent [codename TROMPETA] and his wife, it was clear that information was still leaking out, so SOE put together a scratch force of twenty-five of their own men and volunteers from the Calcutta Light Horse and the Calcutta Scottish to board the *Ehrenfels* and, having overcome the crew, tow her out to sea with the assistance of a tug [actually a Hopper Barge from the Hooghli River]. The Axis captains had anticipated such a move and as soon as the SOE raiders opened fire, all four ships were scuttled. Four crew members of the *Ehrenfels* were killed by the raiders, thereby compromising Portuguese neutrality. On 9 March 1943 Mackenzie signalled London that the attempt had failed.

Irrespective of the fact that German U-boats in the Arabian Sea and Indian Ocean had been cut off from their prime source of shipping intelligence, Eden and the FO in London were furious, for keeping Portugal out of the war was one of Britain's key diplomatic objectives. However they could not claim ignorance for they had been kept in the loop from the very beginning. Indeed in December 1942, the FO had agreed to the operation being carried out by bribery and confirmed it in writing providing that the words 'trickery' and 'chicanery' in SOE's plan meant 'bribery pure and simple and nothing else'.

Although Mackenzie had discussed the operation as a concept with SOE London, he had not informed them of his decision to proceed, so he had little option other than to offer his resignation to placate the FO. Lord Selborne, by

THE INDIA MISSION and the ANDAMAN ISLANDS

now the political head of SOE, 'took a most serious view' and noted that 'it is impossible to work SOE unless officers throughout the world conform to instructions, otherwise we may have a Jameson Raid at any time'. However he refused to accept Mackenzie's resignation and instead sent him a 'letter of reproof' though it was accompanied by a stern warning from Sir Charles Hambro: 'I want to impress on you that this experience must be a lesson to us both to be very particular that we understand each other in regards any operation where neutral Powers are concerned ... I wish you to realise how very serious the matter nearly became and we cannot possibly afford to have another misunderstanding of this nature'.

In hindsight, Mackenzie admitted that 'we were rather desperate – we had been there for two years and nothing had happened.' Indeed he confessed that there were moments when he and Stewart had both considered resigning as there was so little for them to do. Nothing had been achieved in China, there was no W/T contact with Burma or Malaya and the Dutch and French country sections were marking time. A Mission had been inserted into the Andaman Islands, 'because they were there' as Mackenzie later put it. 'I wouldn't say that it yielded anything very much.'

It was the arrival of the long-range Liberators in 1944 that enabled the INDIA Mission to up its game and begin to drop small parties and stores into Japanese occupied areas and thereby avoid the heavily patrolled coastlines. Mackenzie was quite clear about what direction he wanted to take the newly christened Force 136, namely to raise, arm and train guerrilla bands to work in coordination with Allied invasion forces. Sabotage was never a priority; the more so since it invariably triggered disproportionate retaliation from the Japanese as was evident after Operation JAYWICK[34]. The collection of military intelligence was also a priority as it greatly helped army commanders in planning their attacks and contributed to target acquisition for the Allied air forces.

One of the more unusual requests Mackenzie received was when fellow SOE officer John Keswick, who had been appointed Mountbatten's Political Advisor/Director of Psychological Warfare at SEAC, asked him to recruit Peter Murphy, a left-wing Cambridge bookseller. Mountbatten had confided in Keswick that he needed Murphy, an old friend of his who had lost an eye serving with the Irish Guards in the First World War, to bounce his ideas off but given his left-wing connections the FO was unlikely to countenance his presence in SEAC HQ in Kandy. Sure enough, Murphy arrived in Ceylon as an SOE operative and installed himself next to Mountbatten's office[35].

---

34 Launched from Australia, Major Ivan Lyon's astonishing sabotage mission sank 40,000 tons of enemy shipping in Singapore.
35 Mountbatten minuted 'have seen Mackenzie and Guinness who run SOE here and they are delighted to fall in with this proposal' [SEAC War Diary].

A classic SOE operation, GRENVILLE, was the long running saga of forging Japanese currency, involving plates, printing presses and distribution. The attractions were obvious in that forged notes would devalue the military yen banknotes issued by the Japanese in occupied territories and moreover bankroll SOE and resistance activities for free. But there was a hierarchy of permissions to pander to, from HM Treasury, the Bank of England and the India Office. Furthermore one of the main customers was Chiang Kai-shek's KMT. As the SOE War Diary noted in August 1943, 'the politics of GRENVILLE in China were indeed confusing'. SIS was also an interested party, in effect more of a competitor than customer, and frequent squabbles erupted as to which agency should control the printing and issuance of forged bank notes. Add to that the American interest either through the Miles Mission or the OSS and at best the picture remained murky.

Colonel George Taylor, SOE's head of Overseas Missions in London, wrote in his 1944 report: 'No one can visit India without being impressed by Colin Mackenzie; by his exceptional grip on the working and personnel of his group; by his capacity to simplify and without delay go to the root of any problem; and by his remarkable sense of timing and diplomacy. The high regard in which he is held in SEAC, in GHQ India and in the Viceroy's Department is obvious. Not less impressive is the respect which all members of his group, scattered as it is all over India and China, have for his judgment; the faith they have in his capacity to produce the right solution for all problems; and the personal affection in which he is held.'

Another senior SOE staff officer, Colonel John Beevor, wrote: 'He [Mackenzie] remained at the head of it from start to finish. This was both a tribute to his effectiveness, his sound judgment and to the quality of his relations with the authorities, British, American and Dutch, with whom he had to deal.' Bickham Sweet Escott echoed this when he wrote that Mackenzie 'was immensely well read, and combined unusual gifts of imagination and good judgment with a personality of great charm'.

In a characteristically amiable and modest note, Mackenzie wrote to all members of Force 136 on 14 November 1945:

> 'It is a common and justifiable habit to put circular letters in the wastepaper basket. I hope, however, that you will not do it to this one until you have read it, as it is the only way I have of saying goodbye to most of the members of the organisation.
>
> Force 136 ceases on 15 November 1945 as an operational unit and on the same day I am handing over to Brigadier John Anstey who as Commander will continue to deal with the problems of the liquidation

of the Force with which we have both been mainly concerned since shortly after VJ Day. During my recent tours I was able to see many of you individually but I now wish to express to all members of the organisation my most grateful thanks for the loyalty and consistent support which has made the Commander's task possible and has been responsible for the success the organisation has achieved.

My best wishes naturally go out particularly to the old hands who have served with the organisation since the early days, but it has been I think remarkable, considering the speed with which the organisation grew during the last twelve months of the war, how well and quickly new members achieved and developed the right 'esprit de corps' and took their place in the organisation.

We suffered many delays, disappointments and set-backs but through your tenacity of purpose we ended the war with a respectable record of achievement ...

Good luck to you all.'

Mackenzie relinquished command of Force 136 to Brigadier John Anstey in November 1945. He received many letters of thanks and appreciation but one stood out:

'My dear Mackenzie

As you are now leaving SEAC and as Force 136 operational commitments now come under my command I would like to take this opportunity of expressing to you my appreciation of the very real contribution which you and your Force have made towards the defeat of the Japanese.

I know that in the early days of the war there were great difficulties in establishing and organizing resistance movements and I consider it is a great tribute to your personal endeavours that resistance forces have been built up and successfully operated in all countries in SEAC.

The contribution which your Force has made towards the killing of the Japanese, the gathering of Intelligence, the aid to RAPWI, has been of considerable assistance to the Forces under my command.

Everywhere your parties were first in the field and thereby established most valuable political contacts and relieved much suffering.

I would like to express to you and all ranks under your command my deep appreciation of your fine achievements over a prolonged period of operations.

W.J. Slim'

The award of a CMG in January 1946 came as a great disappointment to those who had worked closely with Mackenzie. In a personal letter to him, Mountbatten was 'shocked and grieved not to see your name among the knighthoods in the New Year Honours list of 1946'. He went on to refer to the 'unwarranted down-grading of my original recommendation to the FO'.

The following year he was a member of the British Economic Mission to Greece under Major General John Clark, tasked with assisting in the reconstruction of the war torn Greek economy and in providing aid to its impoverished population. He then resumed his duties as director at J&P Coats until his retirement in 1958 when he settled in Skye. He was Chairman of the Scottish Arts Council from 1962 to 1970.

Mackenzie was extremely proud of his service with the Scots Guards. On his appointment as commander of the India Mission, he had been given a wartime commission on the General List, something with irked him considerably and on his first leave back to the UK in August 1944, he wrote to the Military Secretary requesting to be transferred to the Scots Guards. He followed this up with a letter to Colonel Eric Mackenzie of the Scots Guards explaining that as he dressed as a civilian the question of rank did not apply although he believed he was technically a Lieutenant. He was only anxious that 'having taken up service which is as near to military service as my physical category allows, I should be permitted to have this service related to the Regiment'. His wish was granted.

SOE strength August 1945

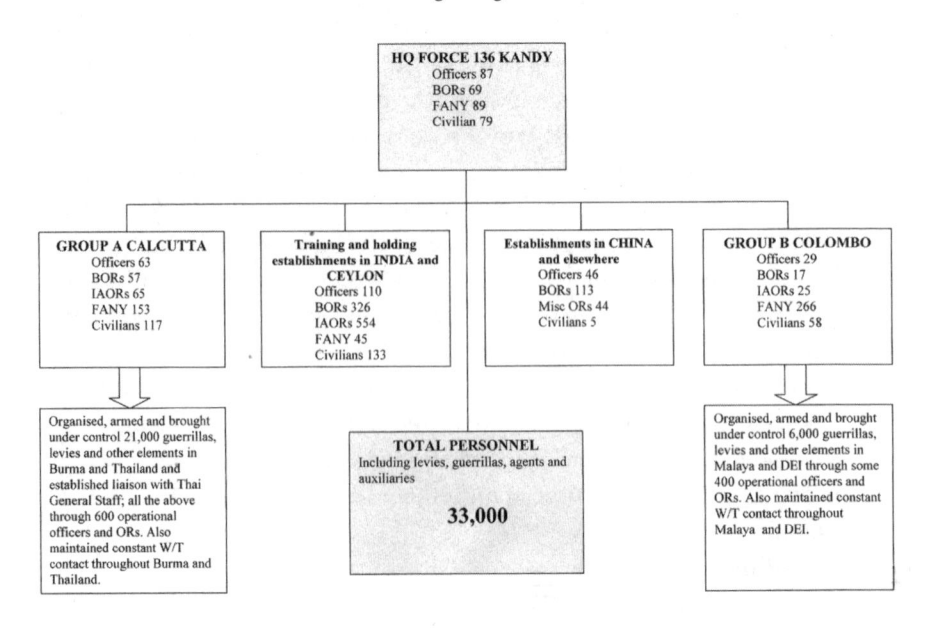

HQ FORCE 136 KANDY
Officers 87
BORs 69
FANY 89
Civilian 79

GROUP A CALCUTTA
Officers 63
BORs 57
IAORs 65
FANY 153
Civilians 117

Training and holding establishments in INDIA and CEYLON
Officers 110
BORs 326
IAORs 554
FANY 45
Civilians 133

Establishments in CHINA and elsewhere
Officers 46
BORs 113
Misc ORs 44
Civilians 5

GROUP B COLOMBO
Officers 29
BORs 17
IAORs 25
FANY 266
Civilians 58

Organised, armed and brought under control 21,000 guerrillas, levies and other elements in Burma and Thailand and established liaison with Thai General Staff; all the above through 600 operational officers and ORs. Also maintained constant W/T contact throughout Burma and Thailand.

TOTAL PERSONNEL
Including levies, guerrillas, agents and auxiliaries
33,000

Organised, armed and brought under control 6,000 guerrillas, levies and other elements in Malaya and DEI through some 400 operational officers and ORs. Also maintained constant W/T contact throughout Malaya and DEI.

THE INDIA MISSION and the ANDAMAN ISLANDS

Mackenzie's Progress

FORCE 136 Field Stations in contact

1943

Country	Jan	Feb	Mar	Apr	May	Jun	Jul	Aug	Sep	Oct	Nov	Dec
Siam												
Burma										3	3	6
FIC												
Malaya												
Andamans												
Cocos		1	1	1								1
Sumatra												
Total		1	1	1						3	3	7

1944

Country	Jan	Feb	Mar	Apr	May	Jun	Jul	Aug	Sep	Oct	Nov	Dec
Siam								3	4	4	4	4
Burma	7	7	7	4	4	2	1	1	1	1	2	13
FIC							2	2	2	7	8	14
Malaya										1	2	3
Andamans	1	1	1	1								1
Cocos												
Sumatra												
Total	8	8	8	5	4	2	3	6	7	13	16	35

1945

Country	Jan	Feb	Mar	Apr	May	Jun	Jul	Aug	Sep	Oct	Nov	Dec
Siam	6	8	8	9	13	16	23	28				
Burma	20	25	27	34	35	32	32	30				
FIC	17	21	30	26	24	24	28	23				
Malaya	3	5	9	11	16	25	42	48				
Andamans	1	1	1									
Cocos							1	1				
Sumatra							8	8				
Total	47	60	75	80	88	97	134	138				

PETER MURPHY

Peter Murphy

Peter Murphy was born in 1897 in Portslade, a village between Brighton and Shoreham in Sussex, and spent his childhood in France to where his parents had moved. After completing his studies at Harrow, he was commissioned in the Irish Guards and was invalided out in the spring of 1918. He went up to Cambridge in 1919 where he read Economics. It was here he became friends with Lord Louis Mountbatten when the young naval officer spent two terms at St John's College reading engineering. They were to remain lifelong friends and confidants.

Murphy, who described himself as an anthropologist, was excellent company. Fluent in French, he was a peripatetic traveller, often seen in Paris and along the Mediterranean coast from Marseille to Rapallo, a lover of jazz [for a short time he had earned a living as a professional jazz pianist] and an avid reader. His German was passable.

After joining Brendan Bracken's Political Warfare Executive [PWE] in 1942, Mountbatten asked for him to act as Liaison between PWE and the CCO [Chief of Combined Operations]. He excelled in this role and warned of the dangers of replicating Dieppe before D-Day proper for public opinion was prone to disaster fatigue. PWE gave him a good report: 'He has been with us for two years and had been in possession of very secret information. We have never had the slightest cause for complaint against him or for imagining that he had disclosed any secrets or had allowed his political views, if he still held them, to influence his work.'

On 20 January 1944, he left for India in his new role of LO between SOE's General Gubbins and Mountbatten. His cover was 'a civilian Personal Staff Officer to Lord Louis'. Although Murphy was known to the Security Service as a Communist sympathiser, their main concern was his relationship with George Pavett, his former valet and a paid up member of the Communist Party of Great Britain. During the years 1936-38 Murphy had financed a left-wing bookshop in Cambridge and had put Pavett in to manage it. It was this 'close and rather unsavoury' relationship that exercised MI5, the later adjective referring to Murphy's brazen homosexuality.

Perhaps it is fitting that the last word on this curious appointment should come from Mountbatten's son-in-law, Lord Brabourne:

'Few people actually know what Murphy's role was in Dickie's life, but his real position was a sounding board. He was brilliant at spotting mistakes in something that Dickie was planning, and he wasn't afraid to speak up. Dickie would show him a letter he had drafted and Peter would read it and say what he thought the reaction of the recipient would be.'

It should also be added that Murphy's fluency in French and extensive knowledge and love of that country was of considerable value to Mountbatten in his dealings with French Indo-China.

THE ANDAMAN ISLANDS

Almost 1,000 miles to the east of Colombo, the Andaman Islands, which had been part of British India since the eighteenth century, were evacuated on 12 March 1942[36]. Once SOE had reorganised itself after the fall of Singapore and the loss of Burma and Malaya, the islands were an obvious target to probe forward Japanese positions and at the same time to develop sound tactical doctrine in inserting and extracting parties in and out of enemy occupied territory.

Operation BUNKUM was therefore designed as a recce of Japanese-occupied Andaman Islands and to establish a relay station for Far East W/T traffic to Calcutta and Colombo.

On 19 January 1943, Major Denis McCarthy [formerly Commandant Military Police Battalion and District Superintendent of Police in Port Blair], together with Sergeant Dickens as W/T Operator and four others were inserted by the Dutch submarine *O 24* and set up their base camp in the jungle on the west coast of Middle Andaman. From here, a three man recce team led by McCarthy, travelling in two folboats and by foot, reached the outskirts of Port Blair, the capital and centre of the Andaman redwood industry, on South Andaman where they contacted a potential resistance leader, the Headman of Ferrarganj village. Avoiding frequent Japanese patrols, after thirty-two days on the move, they returned to their jungle base on the North Island. One of the team was killed by an accidental discharge of his Sten gun when he fell into a dry river bed.

Operation BALDHEAD 2, conducted by Colonel Beyts, arrived by submarine on 21 March 1943 and established a cache of 6,000lbs of stores near Tan Maguta on the west coast of South Andaman Island as well as clearing up all traces of BUNKUM. McCarthy, who was ill with malnutrition and suffering from anaemia, and the rest of his party were safely extracted.

In December 1943, a larger group – Operation BALDHEAD 3 – consisting of Major C.L. Greig, Captain K.J. Falconar, two British W/T operators, Sergeants Dickens and Allen, and ten Indian NCOs were inserted by submarine on the west coast of South Andaman. The original plan, to find a base as part of preparations for a full scale assault on the islands [Operation BUCCANEER],

---

36 On 23 March, the Japanese landed on Andaman Island with one Battalion from the 18th Infantry Division. There was no resistance as white flags had been posted. Port Blair was occupied and the local militia [23 British officers and 300 Indian Sikhs] were disarmed. The Japanese Army set about releasing 425 penal prisoners as a gesture to the local populace. The British Officers were sent to Outram Prison in Singapore, while the Sikhs were interned with an option to enlist in the INA, which most of them did.

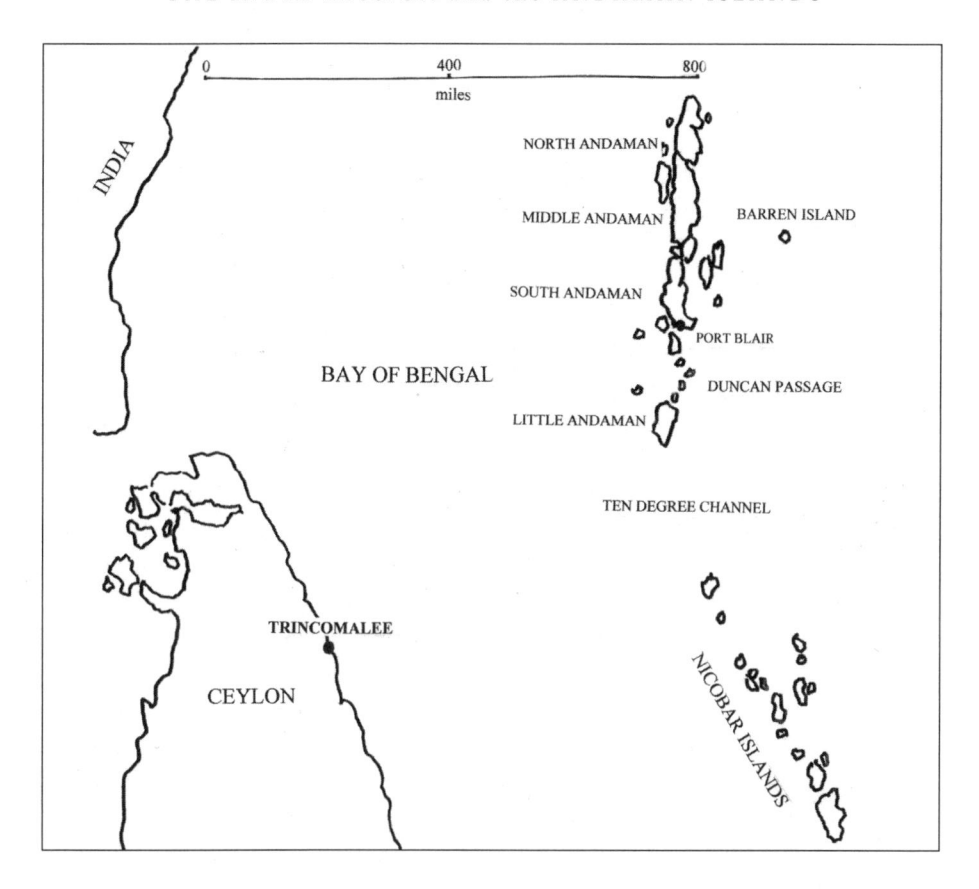

was changed when they landed and they were told to survey strategically important areas, collect intelligence and identify suitable inlets for motor launches [MLs].

On 23 January 1944, Operation BALDHEAD 4 under Major T.V. Croley arrived to reinforce Greig and Croley took command of the combined force. Both parties were extracted by HMS *Taurus* the next month. Greig returned by submarine on 21/23 December 1944 – Operation HATCH – with a seventeen strong party and 30,000 lbs of stores. All personnel were subsequently withdrawn by HMS *Taurus* on 24/5 March 1945 and returned safely to Trincomalee.

Operations BUNKUM, BALDHEAD and HATCH had demonstrated it was possible to successfully insert personnel and sufficient stores by submarine in enemy occupied territory, extract them safely and, crucially, for the parties to maintain W/T contact with Calcutta.

CHAPTER FOUR

BURMA

POLITICAL BACKGROUND

In the nineteenth century, the Burmese empire which had waxed and waned across South East Asia over the centuries was dismantled step by step by the British: it lost Arakan, Manipur, Assam and Tenasserim in the First Anglo-Burmese War [1824–1826], Lower Burma in 1852 in the Second Anglo-Burmese War and the Karenni States in 1875. Alarmed by the consolidation of French Indo-China, the British annexed the remainder of the country in the Third Anglo-Burmese War of 1885. The last Burmese monarch, King Thibaw Min, abdicated and Burma became a province of British India.

Rangoon became the capital of British Burma and an important naval and trading port between Calcutta and Singapore. The attraction for the British was Burma's natural resources; tin, tungsten, jade and rubies; five per cent of the world's petroleum; and an abundant rice harvest which enabled the Empire to export rice to India, Europe and America. By 1920, Burma was the world's largest exporter of rice with nearly 3 million tons. Between 1 April and 30 November 1938, out of a total export index of 30, rice accounted for 12.3, kerosene 4.79 and wood and timber 2.34.

Burmese resentment against British rule festered, with occasional riots caused by British insensitivity to the predominant Buddhist culture and propensity for high taxation. The Burmese were incensed by the whole scale importation by the British of Indian labour: by 1931, Indians accounted for one million of the estimated 14.5 million inhabitants of Burma. Anti-Indian riots broke out in 1930 and 1938.

A more serious disturbance had occurred in 1930-32. Known as the Saya San rebellion, it was a curious blend between a peasants' revolt against taxation, a British ban on the cutting down of trees and a Buddhist monarchical revival. 10,000 British troops were used to suppress it with over 3,000 rebels killed or wounded and 8,000 incarcerated.

On 1 April 1937, Burma became a separate colony of Great Britain – previously it had been administered by the India Office – and Dr Ba Maw made the first Prime Minister and Premier of Burma. Yet the country was far from united as the Frontier Areas in the north remained nominal sovereign states under the

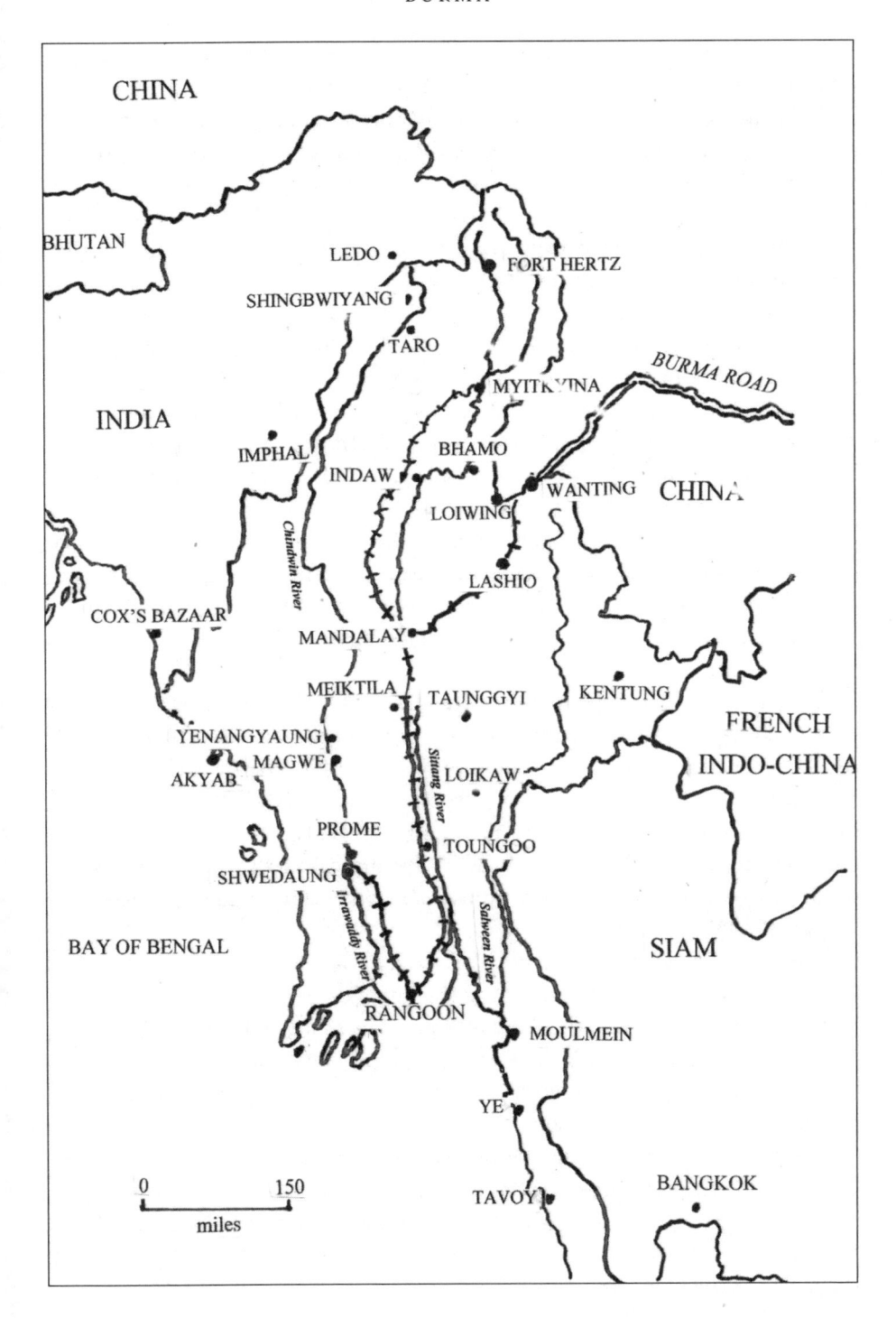

BURMA

rule of hereditary chiefs – Shan, Karreni, Kachins – and administered by a Governor assisted by forty Burma Frontier Service officers.

1938, dubbed The Year of Revolution by Burmese nationalists, began with a series of marches and strikes, reflecting the grievances of poorly paid labourers in the oil fields and the resentment of peasants against their landlords. Communal violence broke out between Burmans and Indians, particularly Muslims. A riot in August triggered a State of Emergency. Students went on strike in November and clashed with British troops who had been called in to support the civil authorities.

An outspoken advocate for Burmese self-rule, Ba Maw opposed the partic10ipation of Great Britain, and by extension Burma, in the war with Germany. He resigned from the Legislative Assembly and was arrested for sedition. In November 1940, before Japan formally entered the Second World War, Aung San, an ardent supporter of self-rule and a founder member of the Thakin nationalist movement [We Burmans Association] and the Communist Party of Burma [CPB], had met Colonel Suzuki, a senior Japanese intelligence officer, in Tokyo. Out of that meeting came the formation of the Burma Independence Army [BIA], a liberation force that would revive the Burmese warrior tradition and expel the British colonialists. Ominously it was under Japanese command.

By March 1942, within months of entering the war, Japanese troops had captured Rangoon and the British administration collapsed. The 18,000 strong BIA, which had not only carried out unprovoked ethnic attacks on the Christian Karens and Indian communities but also mutated into a quasi-criminal organisation, was reconstructed by the Japanese as the Burma Defence Army [BDA] and run along strictly military lines. A Burmese Executive Administration headed by Ba Maw, now released from prison, was established by the Japanese in August 1942.

The geography of Burma effectively produces two Burmas, the great central plain of thirteen million Burmans and then the horseshoe of mountains to the north with non-Burmans: the Arakan Yonas, the Chin and Naga Hills inhabited by 50,000 Chins, the Kachin range with 150,000 Kachin tribesmen, the Shan Plateau with a million ethnic Thais, and the Karenni hills with 500,000 people of Thai/Chinese ancestry.

Despite its wealth of natural resources, the communications infrastructure in 1942 was fairly primitive with a one-metre gauge railway running south to north, a single all weather road and a reasonable road system on the Shan Plateau. From May to October, all travel and the movement of freight were at the mercy of the monsoon.

THE ORIENTAL MISSION IN BURMA

Val Killery visited Burma in August 1941 to work out a modus operandi with Sir Reginald Dorman-Smith, the Governor. He in turn delegated the task to the GOC Burma, Lieutenant General D.K. McLeod who was unhelpful. Finally, when it was obvious that the Japanese were going to invade, the Burmese authorities insisted that they should have operational control of all SBPs.

In early 1942, Killery's ORIENTAL Mission began to recruit officers to form SBPs and to delay the Japanese advance by sabotaging transport infrastructure. An equally important task was to destroy the British-owned oil fields and mines.

With the support of Major Jim Gavin of STS 101 and Major Michael Calvert of the Maymyo STS, Noel Stevenson of the Burma Forestry Service formed a network of SBPs using Karens, Shans, Chins and Kachins. Gavin then sent Steve Cumming and Lieutenant Heath to join him. The first SBP organised by Major Hugh Seagrim and Heath was located at Papun. There Seagrim with Lieutenant Ronald Harvey planned how to deny British-owned assets to the Japanese.

SOE India was rightly concerned by the speed of the Japanese advance and sent Major Peter Lindsay to Lashio in March 1942 to report; he was followed by Colin Mackenzie himself – the two met briefly at Maymyo – but the rout of the British was almost complete. Rangoon was abandoned. Finally General Alexander, the new GOC Burma, agreed to a proposal from Lindsay and Stevenson to deploy their force of Karens, who by now numbered nearly 2,000. Once deployed, they fought well and provided accurate and timely intelligence.

Lindsay formed a second SBP at Mawchi under Captain Boyt, a timber manager for Steele Brothers. Nearly 3,000 volunteers came forward but there were only 250 rifles to go round. Cecil Smith of the Burma Forestry Service raised a band of eighty Kachins and, with Lieutenant Thompson and a company of untrained Kachins, valiantly went to assist the Chinese defenders of Toungoo, which fell on 30 March.

Meanwhile Lindsay with Lieutenant Heath and Corporal Sawyer conducted a number of demolitions before pulling out of Mawchi with Boyt and Smith. Meeting up with Captain Cumming in Lashio, the party made its way to Myitkyina, Sumprabum and finally Fort Hertz. There they joined Sir John Rowland's party and crossed the Chaukan Pass into India. Their only casualty was Corporal Sawyer, who was swept away when crossing a river.

Another officer recruited by SOE, Colonel 'Elephant Bill' Williams, made his way to India with forty-five elephants and their ninety mahouts and attendants together with forty Karens and sixty-four European women and children, including his own wife and child.

By the end of the British withdrawal, only Major Hugh Seagrim remained in Burma with his Karens.

From SOE's perspective, as in Malaya, it was a question of too few resources and too little time for their plans to be effectively implemented. The oil fields were effectively put out of action, e.g. oil wells at Yenangyaung were blown in mid-April but few demolitions of mines and plant were carried out. According to a report in *The Melbourne Argus* of 7 May 1942, 'the smelting works and all technical equipment, also the powerhouse, were completely destroyed' at the Burma Corporation's Namtu Bawdwin silver and lead mine[37]. However, the Mawchi wolfram mine and Tenasserim tin mines were hardly damaged except for their power supplies, leaving the bulk of Burma's industrial and mining assets intact for the Japanese.

THE OSS IN BURMA

Detachment 101 of the OSS arrived in the Burma theatre in July 1942 with a vague directive to gather intelligence and conduct guerrilla warfare behind enemy lines. Under the overall command of General Stilwell, commander of all US forces in CBI as well as chief of staff of Allied forces in China under Chiang Kai-shek, Detachment 101 led by Major Carl Eifler set about recruiting Anglo-Burmese volunteers and training them at Nazira in Assam from where he planned to send them over the border. In early 1943, Group A of Detachment 101 parachuted into the Kaukkwe valley with the aim of cutting the Mogaung-Katha railroad to coincide with a planned Allied offensive. Despite the cancellation of the offensive, Group A went ahead with its mission and managed to put one railway bridge out of action before hurriedly withdrawing to Fort Hertz[38].

Initially suspicious of the OSS, Stilwell was sufficiently impressed to allow them to start recruiting from the Kachin tribes and by the end of the year they had six operational bases in northern Burma, three on both sides of the

---

37 See under Lindsay in ORIENTAL MISSION.
38 Group B consisting of six Anglo-Burmans was not so lucky. When it dropped in the Lashio area, three were killed and three captured. The Anglo-Burmans of Group W were also all killed or captured in the Arakan.

Irrawaddy River, with nearly 1,800 guerrillas under arms[39]. Altogether Detachment 101 had eleven W/T stations reporting from behind enemy lines in Burma by December 1943. This was in marked contrast to SOE which had none.

Although on General Wavell's directive of June 1942 Major Edmund Leach and Colonel Gamble had set up the Northern Kachin levies at Fort Hertz in September 1942, it was Stilwell's Detachment 101 who flew there in April 1943 to develop and expand their guerrilla warfare capabilities. SOE had no choice other than to live with the OSS in Burma given the political clout of Stilwell but it was not without some loss of face, for to cede the Kachin hills to the Americans stuck in the British gullet. Mackenzie, who wanted the OSS to report to him, rued that 'Eifler, while genuinely co-operative, is even for an American difficult to control. He has no conception of higher policy ... ' Unfortunately for SOE, Sir Reginald Dorman-Smith, the Simla-based Governor of Burma, was a great admirer of the OSS and their achievements.

Ironically, the original members of Detachment 101 included a number of British officers.

---

39 FORWARD under command Captain Wilkinson/Lieutenant Commander Luce operating from Fort Hertz; KNOTHEAD under command Major Curl operating with Zhing Htaw Naw in the Hukawng valley; PAT under command Lieutenant Quinn in Myitkyina area; RED under command Captain Maddox at Taro.

LIEUTENANT COLONEL PATRICK 'RED' MADDOX, MC
Legion of Merit

Patrick 'Red' Maddox

Patrick 'Red' Maddox was born in Burma in 1913 and brought up in the Tenasserim area. Commissioned in the Burma Levies on 6 January 1942, he was immediately recruited by SOE and joined the ORIENTAL Mission in Burma.

Major Noel Stevenson of the Burma Levies ordered Maddox 'to go to Namtu and make certain that the very well equipped machine shop in particular and power plants in general were adequately destroyed' which had not been the case during the retreat from Burma. This task successfully completed, Maddox then destroyed the five main bridges between Myitkyina and Sumprabum where he rejoined Stevenson and accompanied him to Ningma. Here they met with the Kachin chiefs to persuade them to fight on. However, knowing that Myitkyina had fallen to the Japanese without a shot being fired, the chiefs understandably demurred. Chaotic days followed in Sumprabum with disheartened Kachin Levies and Indian soldiers wandering aimlessly about, after looting what little was left in the houses. After blowing up their bungalow and ammunition stores, the Levy officers reached Fort Hertz on 25 May. Maddox along with Milton then left on foot for China with Brigadier Norman Upton's party.

In September 1942, while on sick leave recovering from a crash in a Lysander, Maddox's former commanding officer, Noel Stevenson, wrote in his report:

> 'The whole railway system from Naba to Myitkyina, the Irrawaddy from Katha to Myitkyina, the road from Bhamo to Shwelui bridge, the railway and the road from Maymyo to Lashio – all these lie in densely forested country and are wide open to the saboteur ... provided that there are British officers and small British wrecking gangs sharing their troubles, there will always be plenty of willing guerrillas in Burma.'

These were to be prophetic words with one exception. For British, read American. In 1942, having reached India, Maddox was seconded to the US army as a fluent Burmese speaker and became part of the Office of Strategic Services Detachment 101.

Detachment A: Maddox [standing fifth from right with cigarette]

As Deputy Group Leader of Group A of Detachment 101, Maddox commanded the TRAMP Mission, one of three OSS groups operating behind enemy lines in Burma in 1943. Together with Anglo-Burmese officer, Lieutenant Francis, he blew up a main railway bridge north of Namhkwin.

In 1944, with another Anglo-Burmese officer, a Burmese W/T operator and three Kachins, he went back into the jungle to command Area IV to the west of the Hukawng Road. His tasks were to establish a base in the Chindwin River valley and then to raise a force of 300 guerrillas. They operated in support of Merrill's Marauders [Operation GALAHAD] in the Myitkyina area.

He was then given command of the 3rdBattalion at the end of April 1945 and was engaged in heavy fighting around Lawksawk and Pangtara where his guerrillas killed over 600 of the enemy.

He was awarded the Military Cross and the US Legion of Merit [Officer] [26 November 1947]

21 July 1943: Recommendation for MC

On 24 April 1942 he successfully carried out the destruction of the Namtu mines, so denying their effective use to the Japanese. Between 6 and 9 May 1942 he supervised and set off charges destroying the five main bridges between Myitkyina and Sumprabum. On 8 February 1943 he was dropped by parachute 250 miles behind the Japanese lines in Northern Burma, since which date he has assisted in bridge and railway destruction and the passing back of valuable intelligence. Throughout all the above operations this officer has displayed high qualities of endurance, courage and resourcefulness.

Awarded

CAPTAIN OLIVER MILTON, MC

Born in Devon in 1916, Milton worked for Steel Brothers for eight years as a Forest Assistant. Originally commissioned in the Burma Levies where he commanded an Animal Transport Company, he joined the OSS in November 1942 and dropped behind enemy lines in February 1943. He remained with the OSS until the end of the war. A character reference read: 'Very good linguist, quite mad, but has found his feet in this war whereas Steel Brothers had to dispense with his services for being too unstable for forest administration'.

21 July 1943: Recommendation for MC

This officer has acted as 2 i/c of a party of twelve mainly composed of Anglo-Burmans dropped by parachute 250 miles behind the Japanese lines in Northern Burma in February 1943. This party has destroyed one bridge and twenty-one other objectives along the railway a distance thirty miles north of Hopin. The unit continued to operate behind the Japanese lines and pass back information of value until the end of May 1943. This British officer has shown qualities of courage, endurance and resourcefulness over a period of four months deep in enemy territory.

Awarded

MAJOR JACK BARNARD, MC

Born in Mogaung, Upper Burma, in 1910 of Anglo-Burmese parentage, Jack Barnard was educated at Marlborough College before joining Steel Brothers where he was a Forest Assistant for thirteen years. Originally commissioned in the Kachin Levies in March 1942, he distinguished himself by blowing up the main bridge along the Myitkyina and Sumprabum road. On reaching Fort Hertz he was made the Political Officer by Brigadier Upton before withdrawing to China with the 96th Division. He was then attached to the OSS in November 1942 and dropped behind enemy lines in February 1943. A fluent linguist in Burmese and Kachin [Chingpaw], he joined SOE's China Section in August 1943 and was sent to join Munro Faure in Kokang.

21 July 1943: Recommendation for MC

This officer on 7 February 1943 accompanied by one rating of the Burma navy dropped by parachute 250 miles behind the Japanese lines in Northern Burma. He was joined the following day by the rest of his party and since that date maintained a group of twelve men operating behind enemy lines. This party has destroyed one bridge and twenty-one other objectives along the railway a distance thirty miles north of Hopin. He remained in W/T contact throughout and continued to pass information of value for four months. This officer has shown high qualities of leadership under considerable danger and uninterrupted strain.

Awarded

*****

The OSS tactical doctrine was to use the native Kachin levies in support of conventional ground offensives and to sabotage Japanese lines of communication, a decision which won plaudits from British military commanders on the front line. By March 1945, with a total of 10,800 guerrillas in the field, the OSS accounted for over 5,400 Japanese soldiers killed, an estimated 10,000 wounded, and almost eighty captured. In the performance of its intelligence gathering task, Detachment 101 provided seventy-five per cent of all the intelligence from which the 10th Air Force chose its targets and eighty-five per cent of all the intelligence received by Stilwell's Northern Combat Area Command. In addition Detachment 101 infiltrated 162 native agent and W/T teams into Burma: between them, these agents and guerrilla bands demolished fifty-seven bridges, derailed nine trains, destroyed or captured 272 enemy vehicles, and destroyed 15,000 tons of Japanese supplies.

THE BURMA COUNTRY SECTION

After the ORIENTAL Mission had been absorbed into the India Mission and country heads selected, Major R.E. Forester and Lieutenant Colonel Ritchie Gardiner [a survivor of the Chaukan Pass exodus] came up with a number of initiatives for SOE, which was now known as GS1[k]. Essentially, Gardiner's strategy was to try to contact the different ethnic groups that comprised the rural population and ascertain what their capability and aptitude was for resisting the Japanese and aiding the Allies.

Operation MAHOUT was designed to create unrest among Indian dockers and railway workers. Sunil Datta Gupta, a member of the Indian Communist Party [ICP], dropped into Burma in June 1943. Two more ICP members were dropped in October. Nothing was heard until Gupta finally turned up in 1945 after being arrested in September 1944 and then tortured. Attempts were also made to contact the Chinese community but came to nothing since the first operative dropped without a W/T set and the next two were killed on landing.

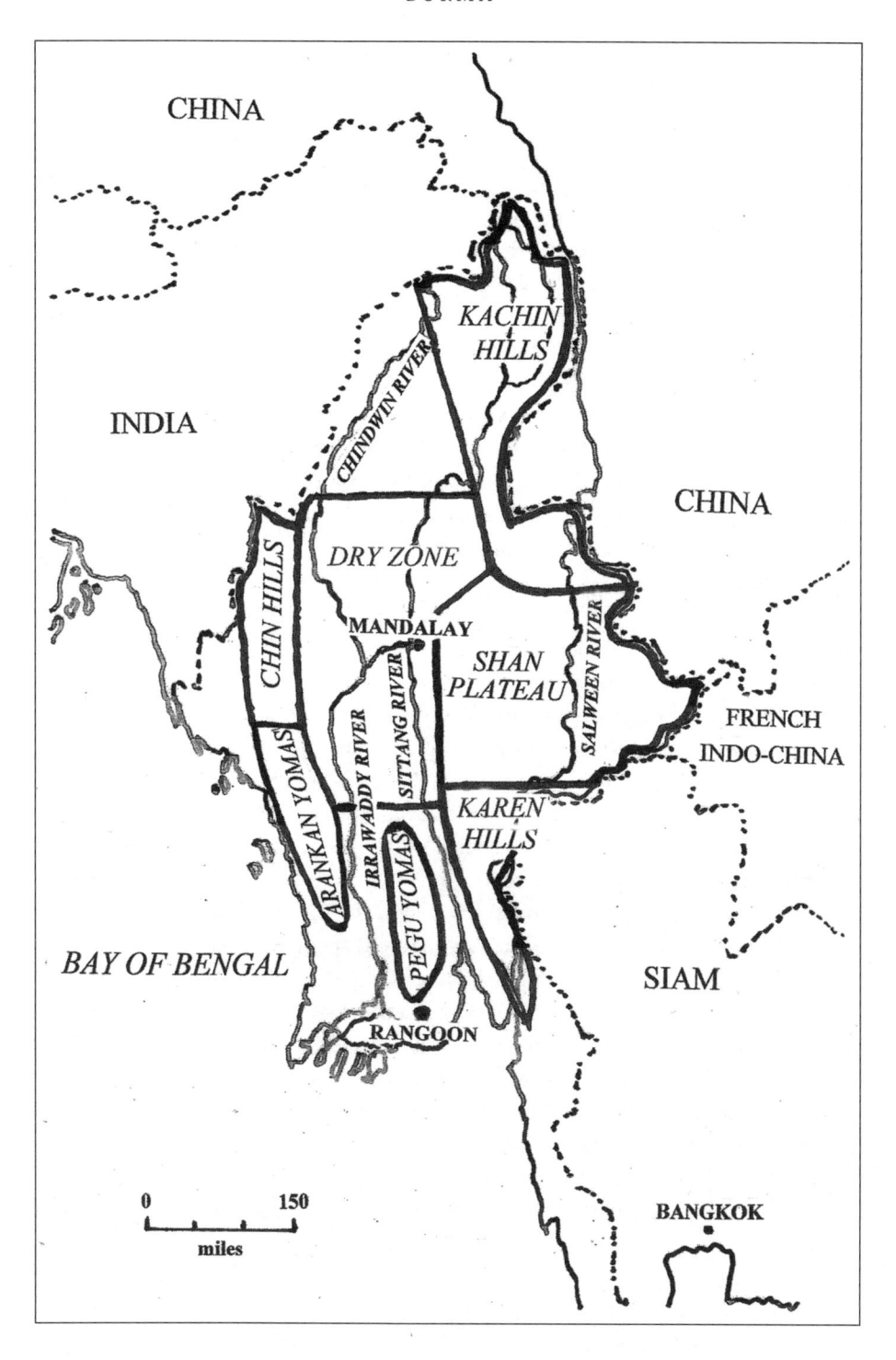

BURMA

Major C.B. Jones established a forward operating base [Operation HAINTON] along the Burma/China border to the north of Kengtung from where he planned to rally the Shans.

Operation HARLINGTON was planned to make contact with the resistance movement in the Karenni Hills. In February 1943, Lieutenant Ba Gyaw and three SOE trained Karens dropped near Shwegyin. Their W/T station was scheduled to follow on the next drop. For a variety of reasons, the W/T station drop never materialised and it was only on 12 October 1943 that Major Jimmy Nimmo[40] managed to parachute in with a set. Two days later he linked up with Ba Gyaw and Seagrim. He was able to confirm to SOE India that the Karens were looking forward to the return of the British. An attempt to contact the Delta Karens in February 1943, Operation FLIMWELL, failed when the agent landed on the roof of a house and was promptly arrested.

On 9 December, Captain E.J. McCrindle dropped to join HARLINGTON. Later, SOE were convinced that because the ISLD dropped three agents at the same time, the Japanese undertook a sweep which resulted in Nimmo and McCrindle both being captured and executed. Soon after, Hugh Seagrim surrendered to prevent further atrocities on the villagers by the Kempeitai. He, together with Ba Gyaw and five others, was executed in Rangoon.

In March 1943, Operation DILWYN 1 commanded by Captain Kumje Taung dropped with four Kachin ORs near Myitkyina to set up an 'underground railway' to infiltrate stores and agents into the Upper Irrawaddy valley. After two months had passed, there was still no news from the party, so Major Shan Lone, another Kachin officer, this time inserted overland at Fort Hertz, set off with twenty-six coolies and a small W/T party. Four months later, after a gruelling cross-country march, 'reduced to mere bones and covered with jungle sores from head to foot' Lone's party arrived in the Myitkyina area on 3 October where it found DILWYN 1 safe and well. Here it set about raising Kachin levies and collecting intelligence about Japanese activities in the Myitkyina and Bhamo areas. His journey had been nothing short of epic for 'marching with no shoes, disguised as locals and moving only at night under guides, we managed often to pass through Japanese outposts unnoticed'.

Meanwhile SOE discovered that Brigadier Orde Wingate proposed to send a glider-borne expedition to the Kachin Hills – DAHFORCE[41] [Knife Force] – which threatened to compromise the security of all SOE's work to date. After discussions between the two organisations, it was agreed that DILWYN would

---

40 Both Nimmo and McCrindle had been forest assistants with MacGregor & Co Ltd.
41 Not to be confused with the 2,000-strong Singapore Overseas Chinese Volunteer Army under Special Branch officer John Dalley – known as DALFORCE – which valiantly fought against the Japanese in the battle for Singapore.

provide the reception for DAHFORCE. When Major Percy Lovett-Campbell sent the signal that the reception party was ready, Wingate misunderstood the timing and DAHFORCE under Lieutenant Colonel Dennis Herring arrived by Dakota aircraft 100 miles south of DILWYN which by this time had been waiting for three days. At best it was a catalogue of errors, at worst incompetence. However, once the Chindits had arrived, DILWYN swung into action, harassing, ambushing and attacking the Japanese lines of communication.

In Burma proper, politics dictated events. The anti-colonial Communist Thakin party [Master Party] led by Thakin Soe had decided to work with the Allies after Russia's entry into the war in the hope of post-war independence. Another party, Our Burma League under Thakin Aung San, opted to collaborate with the Japanese and founded the Japanese Burma Independence Army [commanded by Thakin Aung San]. The Japanese cottoned on to the notion that the Our Burma League also wanted post-war independence and reformed the BIA as the Burma Defence Army and then, on 1 August 1943, formally gave Burma its independence under Dr Ba Maw and consolidated all pro-Japanese forces into the Burma National Army [BNA].

Two prominent members of the CPB well known to the Burma Defence Bureau, Thein Pe and Tin Shwe, had arrived in India in July 1942. Thein Pe who had studied in Calcutta for two years before the war was also well known to the ICP. When he had returned to Burma in 1938, he became the Upper Burma organiser for the People's Revolution Party. As war loomed, unlike General Aung San, he argued that there should be no compromise with either the British or the Japanese. The true task was to kick the imperialist British out of Burma.

With the Japanese occupation a fait accompli, Thein Pe set off on 1 May to India with Tin Shwe. After an epic journey by car, raft and mostly on foot, the two men arrived there in July 1942. After being interrogated by S.D. Jupp, Deputy Director of the Government of Burma's Intelligence Bureau, both were held under house arrest in the Punjab Hotel in Delhi. Thein Pe was sent to work with the Far East Bureau, a propaganda agency of the Ministry of Information in India.

Their relationship coloured by a mutual dislike, Dorman-Smith remained intensely suspicious of Thein Pe's motives and it was only when Mackenzie intervened on 5 December 1942, urging him to release Thein Pe and Tin Shwe to General Wang Ping-shen, Chiang Kai-shek's principal expert on Japanese affairs, that the Governor relented[42]. Arriving in Chungking on 18 January

---

42 General Wang had suggested to Dorman-Smith on 18 April 1942 that he should take Thein Pe and Tin Shwe with him to Chungking but the Governor demurred, distrusting both the Chinese as to their intentions towards Burma and the reliability of the two Burmese Communists.

1943, the two Burmese Communists spent the next seven months in China where they became increasingly disillusioned. As Thein Pe later recalled, 'politically we found Chungking as discouraging as we had found India.'

Although good intelligence networks had been established by SOE with the hill tribes and minorities in North Burma, there was a vacuum about political and military conditions in the centre and south of the country. It was therefore crucial to establish contacts with the Communist-led underground in Burma. Mackenzie shrewdly extricated Thein Pe and Tin Shwe from China and re-engaged them in India on anti-Japanese propaganda work. The ace up his sleeve was to despatch Tin Shwe to Rangoon where he arrived on 4 December 1943. After meetings with other underground resistance leaders at which the seed of the Anti-Fascist Organisation [AFO] or the Anti-Fascist People's Freedom League [AFPFL] was sown, Tin Shwe returned to India in May 1944, once again to be interrogated by Jupp. His report was nothing less than a cornucopia of military, political and economic intelligence. It was on the basis of this that SOE was able to make progress in mapping the structure of the resistance networks and when firm word of the formation of AFO was received in September 1944, it was able to draw up concrete resistance plans. The CPB and BDA established the Burmese National Army in August 1944, this time directed at evicting the Japanese.

To SOE, who had previously dropped Captain Sein Tun [Operation EYEMOUTH] with no results, it was now clear that there was potential for a genuine resistance party. Thakin Soe sent five men out for training at the School for Eastern Interpreters, the first batch of a final total of seventy. One of the five, Tun Kyaw, who held a key intelligence post in the Japanese army, was sent back and was followed by Ba Thein who dropped into the Rangoon area. Both his W/T operators were killed when their parachutes failed to open and it was only in November 1944 after several mishaps that a W/T operator and set were successfully dropped to him [Operation DONKEY]. Now, for the first time, there was a radio link with the official Burmese resistance.

Between September 1944 and January 1945, there was a critical debate led by Lieutenant General Slim of Fourteenth Army as to the purpose of Force 136 in Burma. Although it now had LOs with formation commanders [Fourteenth Army, XV Corps and NCAC], its role remained unclear. Various solutions were discussed including the merger of Z Force[43] and SOE's Force 136, amalgamating SOE and SIS [a course advanced by Slim's Chief of Staff Major General Walsh] and then subjugating them to the OSS who would take over all clandes-

---

43 A behind-enemy-lines intelligence gathering unit reporting to Fourteenth Army. See Annex I.

tine forces in Burma. The end result was a change of emphasis on SOE's role. Intelligence gathering became the number one priority with reports to be delivered directly to Fourteenth Army HQ.

Throughout 1944, ISLD was conducting parallel operations inside Burma and on its borders. BANTAM [Kokang], BITTERN [Northern Shan States], BULLFINCH [Rangoon], BUG [Bassein], BUFFIN [Bhamo], BLOODHOUND [Monghika], BOTTOM [Tilin, Gangaw], BANDIT [Loikaw], BAFFLE [Shwebo], BLAST [Pwin U Lwin] and BULGE [Maymyo] all dropped bodies and stores between April and December 1944.

SOE IN SUPPORT OF NORTH CHINESE AREA COMMAND [NCAC]

After the defeat of the Japanese at Kohima and Imphal, the Allies slowly advanced east. With the approval of the Americans, DILWYN was reinserted to operate in Northern Burma in support of the NCAC offensive against Lashio launched by the Chinese 38th Division in November 1944. To the north of the town, in the area between Wanting and Hsenwi, an advanced party, MONKEY [Captain Hkun Nawng], was dropped on 28 November at Monghawng. Once a firm base had been established, Major William Howe was dropped in to take over command and on 25 January 1945 CHEETAH [Major Hood and Captain RubInstein] arrived as reinforcements. The two Missions provided intelligence and orchestrated harassing attacks until 7 March when the First Chinese Army captured Lashio.

Three other Missions – BADGER [Major Zau June], SQUIRREL [Captain Khun Nawng],and BEAR [Captains Beamish, Bulman, Hunter and Wakelin] – under the command of former French Jedburgh Lieutenant Colonel 'Bing' Crosby were dropped between 29 November 1944 and 28 January 1945 to the north east of Lashio, the HQ of the Thirty Third Japanese Army. Their task was to raise levies and then harass the Japanese lines of communication south of Lashio and then Mongyai. By the end of June 1945 when US levies of 101 Detachment arrived in the area, all had made useful contributions to the NCAC advance to Kyaukme. One example of intelligence collection was the insertion of a Subadar by Major Shan Lone into the Japanese 56th Division HQ north of Hsenwi. Disguised as a coolie, he managed to obtain the complete order of battle of the Division and sent it by W/T link to Calcutta. Close cooperation by Force 136 with the 10th USAF resulted in the destruction and damage of a number of prime targets like food and POL dumps. By October 1945, Crosby and his teams had travelled over 250 miles on foot and liberated eight of the Shan States.

Crosby's war in Burma had its moments of theatricality and poignancy as well as savagery; from the rescue of the Sawbwa of Mong Yai whose entourage, led by his two pretty teenage daughters on horses, emerged from the jungle 'like the children of Israel leaving Egypt', negotiating with the uncle of the Kyemaing of Mong Hsu who looked exactly like a bandit chief in a musical comedy, complete with a straggly moustache, and stumbling across the household of the Sawbwa of Laikha, 'a small pocket edition of Hitler complete with small moustache', consisting of his fourteen wives and fourteen concubines together with a photograph album of them making love with the Sawbwa, to the need to provide his Wa head-hunters with buffalo meat once a week and a modest supply of opium without which they lost their desire to kill. With his unfailing sense of humour, cultural sensitivity and sound military judgment, Crosby stands out in many respects as the ideal SOE officer, self-reliant, practical and above all determined. After nine months behind enemy lines, within two days of returning to Calcutta he was asked to produce his Mission's financial accounts, a chore he cheerfully completed without a murmur of complaint.

SOE IN SUPPORT OF FOURTEENTH ARMY

SOE's capability in the field had commensurately increased with the arrival of additional aircraft. In December 1944 ten B24 Liberators and ten C47 Dakotas were followed by sixteen B24 Liberators in January 1945. Coupled with Allied air superiority, this additional lift capacity made a huge difference to operations on the ground.

Operation ELEPHANT dropped to Shwebo to provide intelligence for Fourteenth Army. It failed to provide any but it did get involved with a local revolt by the BNA.

Operation BISON operating between Mandalay and Kyaukme was given five tasks:
- Establish communications with base
- Report on road and railway traffic
- Report possible bombing targets
- Harass enemy convoys
- Save key installations from destruction by Japanese.

The last two were only to be actioned on orders from Fourteenth Army.

In support of XV Corps' advance to Akyab, SOE launched Operation MANUAL to provide battlefield intelligence. Two two-man teams, HOUND and LION, were dropped and quickly established communications. They reported on Japanese positions and indicated bombing targets. The teams were reinforced on 27 December 1944 by Operation CAMEL [Major TA Carew, Captain JH Cox and Sergeant Sharpe], a mission modelled on the JEDBURGH concept which had proved so effective during the run-up to D-Day [See ANNEX H]. Eight Arakanese dropped with them to spread diversionary rumours. Carew found little evidence of any support and on 1 January 1945 signalled India that it was pointless to carry on. As luck would have it, the next day he spotted a concentration of nearly 1,000 Japanese troops and called in the RAF to take them out. As a result Carew's standing with the villagers rocketed and he was able to raise a band of local guerrillas. CAMEL was overrun by advancing Allied troops on 22 January 1945 and its 200 guerrillas paid off with cash and sarongs [*longyi*]. There was a hiccup – the Civil Affairs Service Burma [CASB], tasked with taking over the administration of the country, began to arrest CAMEL's guerrillas for being in league with Nyo Tun who was on their black list as a Communist agitator.

XV Corps also asked SOE to provide intelligence south east of CAMEL's area where the terrain was hard to interpret by air. Operation MOUSE – Major Kemball, Major Blathwayt and three Arakenese – dropped blind and, despite being pursued by Japanese for the next three months, they managed to provide regular reports to XV Corps about road traffic which resulted in twenty air strikes. They also recruited a band of 100 guerrillas and succeeded in killing fifty Japanese.

It was now that a long simmering row broke out between SOE, CAS[B] and Fourteenth Army. Mackenzie had consistently argued that the AFO and the BNA should be armed for if weapons were denied to the Burmese on the plains but given to the hill tribes, it would inevitably sow the seeds of post-war grievances. Furthermore if the AFO and BNA were snubbed, then the equivalent organisation in Malaya, the AJUF, would see SOE as a Judas. CAS[B] protested loudly and in February 1945 Lieutenant General Sir Oliver Leese banned the issue of arms to AFO. It took an appeal by Mackenzie to Mountbatten to get the order rescinded and for SOE to continue as planned.

Then the issue of the BNA erupted again when Aung San announced he was off to fight the enemy, i.e. the Japanese. Slim liked the idea of a rising and from 24 March members of the BNA defected in increasing numbers. Despite a further outcry by CAS[B] who wanted Aung San tried as a war criminal, on 16 May he arrived at Meiktila for a meeting with Slim, who accepted his offer of help on the understanding that his forces would take their orders from local British commanders.

Stung by the criticism of Mountbatten by the Chiefs of Staff who considered that he had been too political, Mackenzie reminded Gubbins that:

'it has only been SAC's action in overruling CAS[B] that has prevented serious trouble and probably a rebellion. CAS [B] specifically proposed that the BNA should be outlawed. If the Civil Affairs ruling had been announced, it would have thrown the Patriotic Burmese Forces immediately into opposition, and, as stated by ALFSEA, this would have required at least two divisions to suppress, while the effect on Burma as a whole would have been deplorable. Similarly, decisions have been taken by the Supreme Commander overruling the decisions and recommendations of Civil Affairs on such items as the death penalty and the attendance of the Patriotic Burmese Forces at the Victory Parade. Finally the whole treatment of the difficult question of Major General Aung San which has required very careful handling has been mainly due to SAC's personal intervention. In view of the fact that Force 136 has sponsored the AFO and has acted as liaison between the British Command and the BNA and Major General Aung San, we have had a direct and indeed vital interest in the way the various questions concerning these organisations have been handled. If you consider that there is any chance of being given an opportunity to speak to General Ismay on the above subjects, I feel it would be useful, both in equity, and in order to clear away misunderstandings.'

*****

The 'NATION' series of Jedburgh-style operations[44], starting with TERRIER in late January 1945, dropped near Toungoo; ELK [later YAK] dropped blind in Tharrawaddy district; WEASEL [Major Carew, Captain Brown and Sergeant Sharpe] soon had their hands full dealing with the temperamental and touchy Than Tun, the acting head of the AFO once Thakin Soe had gone underground; REINDEER [Major Britton] by 12 April had assembled 300 men under arms due west of Toungoo and called in a series of highly successful air strikes on a variety of targets; Operation PIG under Major Cox dropped on 30 March and ran into a platoon of rebel soldiers of the Indian National Army [INA] – Captain Brown was captured but later escaped; Operation CHIMP dropped on 10 April near Pyinmana where Major Rubinstein raised 200 guerrillas until they were overrun by advancing British troops on 19 April when he moved to REINDEER whose leader had been killed and continued his task of providing a first class

---

44 By 2 May 1945, Jedburgh teams in Burma comprised 62 British officers and 32 British W/T operators. The French had a similar number for operations in Indochina.

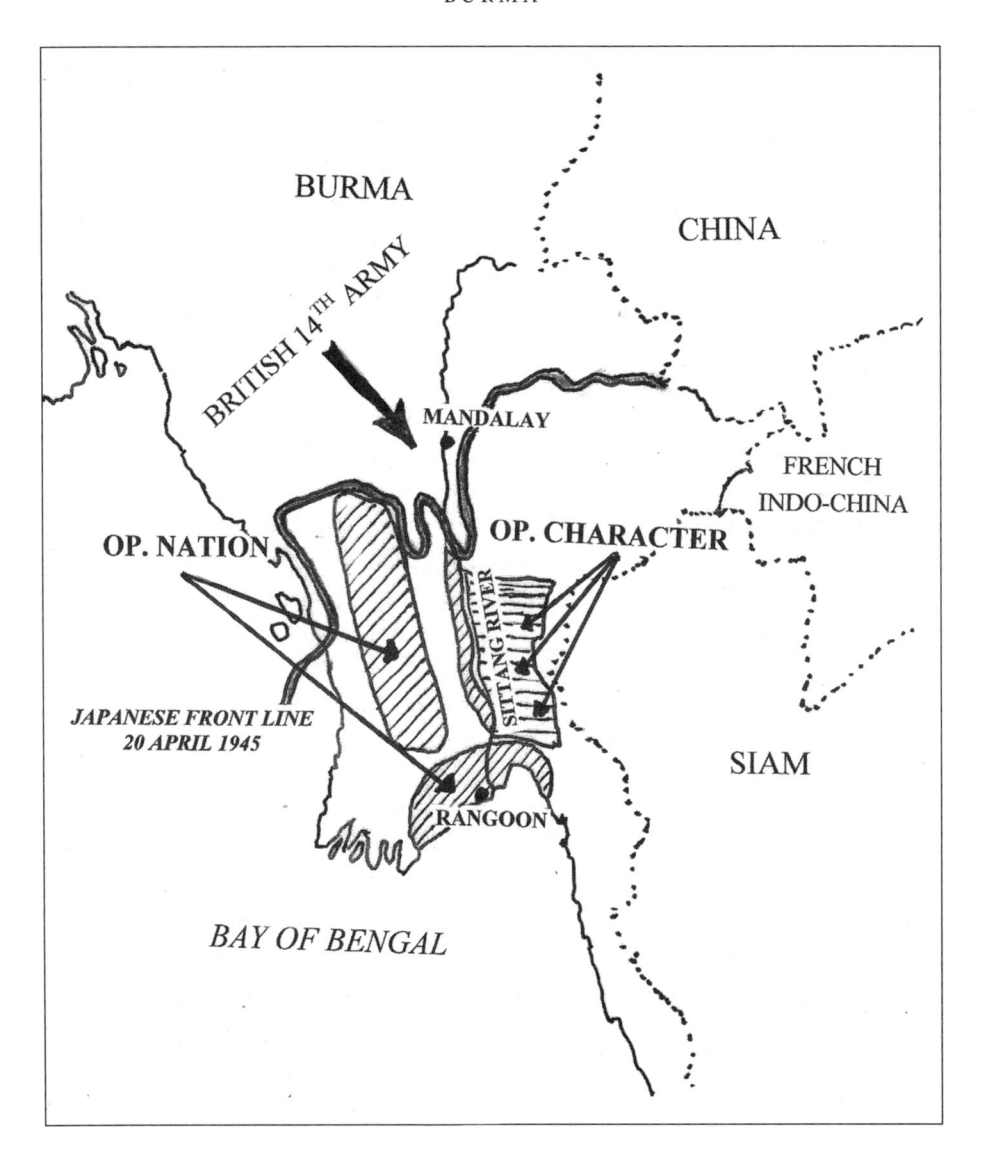

intelligence screen; other drops included ZEBRA [Major Hood], JACKAL [Major Harrington, Captain Pierre Meunier], GIRAFFE [Major Macadam], and COW [Major McCoull].

NATION operations accounted for 3,381 Japanese killed, 201 wounded and 156 POWs. Allied losses were 13 killed and 52 wounded. The AFO came in for high praise from the SOE officers unlike the BNA who were considered a bunch of military prima donnas.

It is worth mentioning at this stage the role of the Indian Field Broadcasting Units [IFBUs] formed by SOE in response to a request by the DMI India for combat propaganda in the field. Under command of Major George Steer, five IFBUs were deployed, four on the Assam/Burma front and one between Mandalay and Kalewa. The idea was to lower the morale of frontline Japanese troops through conveying to them the certainty of defeat, either by broadcasting through an array of loudspeakers or in writing by leaflets delivered from mortars or aircraft. Another aspect of the work of IFBUs was termed 'consolidation' propaganda, or 'Hearts and Minds' campaigns, and was carried out behind enemy lines by patrol groups led by a British captain with up to seventy Assam Riflemen, usually Ghurkhas, under command. Their role varied from the collection of battlefield intelligence to establishing local markets where essential foodstuffs and clothing could be dropped by Dakota and sold at pre-war prices in exchange for pre-war currencies. Medical treatment of villagers also played a major part in bringing local people over to the Allied side. Captain Peter Goss remembers how, after completing his training at the Psychological Warfare Camp near Darjeeling on the Sikkim border, his party, No. 2 IFBU, was infiltrated at Myingyan near the junction of the Chindwin and Irrawaddy Rivers some fifty miles ahead of 20th Indian Division[45]. His experience of trying to get the Japanese to defect through propaganda messages showed it was 'not a very good idea as the Japanese could be relied upon not to surrender'. On more than one occasion he had to extricate a Psyops team from a firefight, both side incurring casualties.

One such occasion was on the morning of 13 March, when Goss and a dozen of his men followed Captain Bacon and the Field Propaganda group to within 200 yards of a strong Japanese position. Oblivious to two appeals to surrender, the last one from only seventy yards away, the Japanese opened fire with small arms, wounding Bacon and a sepoy. Both men were rescued by Goss who twice ran forward under fire to carry them individually to safety.

*****

Similar to NATION but inserted into the Karenni Hills, Operation CHARACTER was designed to meet Slim's specific SOE requirements which were firstly for it to maintain surveillance on the roads running between Pyinmana and Pegu and from Toungoo in the Sittang Valley through the Karenni Hills to Bawlake and Loikaw and on to the Thai border; second, to

---

45   Operation BARGE, January to May 1945. No. 2 IFBU was the first unit to enter Rangoon on 2 May.

prevent Japanese moving forces [there were three Japanese divisions in the Shan States] south from Northern and Central Burma; and third, to oppose reinforcements coming in from Moulmein into the Sittang valley or Rangoon area. As Ian Morrison wrote, 'it was a curious reversal of history. In 1942 Karen troops and levies tried to stop the Japanese coming up the road from Toungoo into the Shan States, in 1945 *down* the road to Toungoo *from* the Shan States'. To ensure optimal coordination, Force 136, at Slim's request, set up a Tac HQ at Fourteenth Army HQ. SOE were learning fast that operational independence, however desirable, did not fit into the complex battlefield geometry of Burma.

CHARACTER's area of operations necessitated thee separate commands[46]. In the north, Operation WALRUS was commanded by Colonel 'Pop' Cromarty Tulloch. His twenty-strong force took off from Jessore on 24 March and after initial difficulties, was forced to choose a new landing ground from the air where they dropped blind from 400 feet. One was killed and several were injured. A second wave dropped on 28 March – three Majors, three Captains and two Sergeants[47] – together with sufficient arms for 1,000 levies. By 13 April, Tulloch had 2,000 men under arms. On that day, WALRUS was warned that the Japanese 15th Division was coming south to reinforce Toungoo. Combining their efforts with OTTER [see below] WALRUS held the Japanese up for a week, thereby allowing Fourteenth Army to establish itself at Toungoo and block the exits from the hills. A force of nearly 7,000 levies had been raised and armed by the middle of April. One reason for the unexpected speed of the recruiting drive was the rapid RAF response to targets indicated by the SOE teams. Seeing the accurate bombing and strafing attacks persuaded the Karens that they were fighting on the winning side and that from now on they would not be subjected to reprisals.

In the centre, Operation OTTER, commanded by Lieutenant Colonel Peacock [ex Burma Forestry Service and a fluent speaker of native languages] dropped with a group of British, Burmese and Karen parachutists on night of February 23/24 at Pyagawpu and then moved north to Mawchi road.

In the south, near Pyagawpu, Operation HYENA under Major Turrall had been the first to drop on 20 February. Later it divided into two with Lieutenant Colonel Critchley and MONGOOSE taking over the other half. HYENA maintained thirty-three ambushes on the main track from Kemapyu to Papun.

Slim was unequivocal about the effectiveness of CHARACTER:

---

46 By the end, there were six, including FERRET I, FERRET II and MONGOOSE.
47 Majors Denning, Cockle and Campbell; Captains Wilson, Steele and Troward; Sergeants Smith and Gibbs.

Levies and mentors

'I gave the word "Up the Karens" on 13 April. The Japanese, driving hard through the night, ran into ambush after ambush. Bridges were blown ahead of them, their foraging parties massacred, their sentries stalked, their staff cars shot up. They fought their way slowly forward, losing men and machines, until about forty miles east of Toungoo and there they were held up for several days by roadblocks, demolitions and ambuscades. They lost the race for Toungoo.'

Critically, Rangoon was captured before the monsoon rains started.

*****

When Fourteenth Army reached Rangoon on 3 May, there was a hiatus. The Japanese now concentrated on building up their forces in Mawchi/Kemapyu area and with 50,000 troops in the Karenni Hills they took counter-measures against Force 136 and the levies. WALRUS was forced to cede the Bawlake-Mawchi road, OTTER was limited to minor hit and run attacks and both MONGOOSE and HYENA forced to give ground.

The last major action by SOE in Burma was at end of July when the Twenty-Eighth Japanese Army attempted to cross the Sittang River from the west and break through to Moulmein. MONGOOSE had a party of 750 guerrillas waiting for 3,000 Japanese south east of Shwegyin. The Japanese built rafts but pinned down by MONGOOSE forces on the other bank they were sitting ducks for RAF. This battle went on till 8 September, well after the surrender of Japan. Sergeant Roger Leney, the MONGOOSE W/T operator, remembered how

> 'Every time they tried to cross, the Karens just knocked them off. They always tried to cross at night and it was a question of shooting at anything you saw coming down the river, because they would try hanging on to bamboo, branches or anything. Anything you saw moving in the river, branches or debris, anything got shot at. Down at Shwegyin they were more or less counting the bodies as they were floating down. I think, in total, there were about three thousand Japanese killed on the Shwegyin river.'

Japanese losses attributed to SOE's CHARACTER Missions and its levies were 11,000 killed, 644 wounded and 18 POWs – excluding any casualties caused by airstrikes called up by Force 136.

Summing up the activities of SOE in Burma, Lieutenant Colonel Ritchie Gardiner, the officer who had run the Burma desk since 1943, wrote a remarkably honest appraisal:

> 'On the ultimate success of operations in Burma there should be no need to elaborate. What must be emphasised however is that this only took place ONCE THE TIDE HAD TURNED [his emphasis]. By early 1945 the people of Burma to a greater or lesser degree were beginning to realise that the Allies were coming back, and they were prepared to risk something to help them. For all practical purposes we achieved nothing until this time and it brings out once again the truth of the principle that for success in SOE work the active support of at least an influential section of the populace is a sine qua non.

> In a protracted campaign, as was the case in Burma, this inevitably means a long and disheartening period of preparation, when there is nothing to show in the way of results to justify the necessarily large organisation. At first we did plan certain operations to produce quick results, and we also planned a campaign of industrial sabotage, such as was successful in certain European countries. They came to nothing

and the writer does not consider that, even with better personnel and facilities, anything in the way of a protracted sabotage campaign could have succeeded in Burma. The fact is that people have neither the necessary fire and patriotism [nor the necessary toughness] to carry it through for any length of time, especially in the face of a determined, efficient and quite ruthless enemy. On the other hand, such a campaign might have had a considerable degree of success if the masters [Thakins] adopted the kid gloves methods generally associated with the British rather than the iron hand of the Japanese.

The lesson to be derived from this is the necessity to foster during the build-up period an atmosphere of understanding with the forces who will ultimately be the beneficiaries of SOE's efforts i.e. the Army, RAF and possibly Navy.

There is little doubt that there will not be in the future the same suspicion of SOE as there was in the past, since its success has inevitably made its aims [and to a certain extent its methods] widely known in army circles. There is equally little doubt, however, that had the Supreme Allied Commander not been sufficiently far seeing to appreciate the possibilities of SOE – and therefore to support us during the build-up period – Force 136 would either have been thrown out of the theatre, or would have been at best a useless appendage of SEAC – something in the nature of ISLD. There was hardly a single commander of note who spontaneously gave us his support until it became obvious to everyone that we had something very valuable to offer.'

For several SOE officers, the war in Burma left a bitter taste, for the hill tribes which had so loyally and unconditionally given their alliance to the British found their own post-war political aspirations for autonomy frustrated. For Lieutenant Colonel Ronnie Kaulback, the issue was clear:

'Early in 1945, when I was OC Tac HQ Force 136 at Fourteenth Army Headquarters [then in Meiktila], Force 136 had some 15,000 Karens fighting for them in the Karenni Hills as guerrillas under British officers. At this time, the Japanese were making a big effort to stamp out these guerrillas and were destroying crops and villages and slaughtering the women, children and old men wherever they could. The Karens said that they were prepared to put up with all their sacrifice and would continue to fight for the British as loyally as ever; but what was going to happen to them after the war was over? ... I was in no position to answer the Karens, so I referred the question to the headquarters of Force 136 in Calcutta, who referred it, in their turn, to the Supreme Allied Commander South East Asia [Admiral Lord Mountbatten]. The reply was as clear as daylight – that under no circumstances would the Karens be handed over to the Burmese after the war. I passed that on to the Karens, who continued to fight with us as courageously as ever until the war ended. And then the British handed them over to the Burmese.'

A Karen Goodwill Mission consisting of four Karen Christian lawyers arrived in London in 1946 hoping to gain a hearing from the Attlee government for a separate state under British protection, free of Burmese domination. They were given a cocktail party and then sent on their way in December. HMG's policy to integrate the Frontier Areas with Burma Proper was formalised in the Aung San-Attlee agreement the next month. There was no consultation with the Karens and hence no consent by them.

In 1948 Lieutenant Colonel Pop Cromarty Tulloch wrote that 'those of us who love Burma and her peoples and have fought for her liberation from the bondage of foreign occupation and its relentless and untold miseries during the war, cannot but be greatly distressed to learn that our friends, the loyal Burmese, Karens, Shans, Kachins and other Hill people are again suffering the same fate under the present political situation in the country'. Roundly accused of plotting with the Karens to overthrow the Burmese government with the aid of Alex Campbell of *The Daily Mail*, Tulloch found himself in hot water with the FO 'for stirring up the Frontier Areas people against the Government'. There is no question that he was up to his neck in encouraging the Karens to declare UDI but there is little evidence that he could have provided the means and ways. Independently from Tulloch, the Karens managed to gain military control of much of their proposed state but in January 1949, after arresting most of the Karen leaders, Rangoon declared the Karen National Defence Organisation unlawful. It was the beginning of a long drawn out insurrection that continues to the present day.

MAJOR HUGH SEAGRIM, GC, DSO, MBE

Hugh Seagrim

Hugh Seagrim was born on 24 March 1909, one of five sons[48] of the Reverend Charles Seagrim. When his father was the rector of Whissonsett, Hugh attended Norwich Grammar as a boarder in the Lower School towards the end of the First World War and then King Edward VI School, Norwich. After RMA Sandhurst, Hugh joined the Indian Army in 1931, going to Cawnpore, where he was attached to the Highland Light Infantry. During the first year he spent his leave on expeditions in the Himalayas. He later joined the 1st /20th Battalion, the Burma Rifles, then in Taiping, where he commanded a Karen company and began his life-long love affair with these remarkable hill people who live to this day on the southern borders of Burma and Thailand. At six foot four inches, the lofty Seagrim was nicknamed 'Stooky', a pun on the notorious Rector of Stiffkey. Remembered by his contemporaries as 'highly unconventional' although all agreed that he did not set out deliberately to create this impression, he loved music, motorbikes and above all his adopted tribe of Karens. He was

---

48 All five fought in the Second World War: Charles [commissioned into the Royal Artillery], Cyril [commissioned into the Royal Engineers], Derek [commissioned into the Green Howards], Jack [commissioned into the Indian Army] and Hugh [also commissioned into the Indian Army].

then posted to 19th Hyderabad Regiment, later the Kumaon Regiment, in effect a paper entry, for he never left his Karens.

As soon as war was declared by the Japanese, a number of British soldiers were sent from Singapore to Rangoon to prepare Burma's defences against Japanese attack and, in the event that Burma fell, they were to ensure that all industrial assets be denied. Meanwhile H.N.C. Stevenson, Assistant Superintendent at Kutkai in the Northern Shan States, who had had some success training Chin and Kachin tribesmen to become guerrilla fighters, was appointed by Burma's Governor, Reginald Dorman-Smith, to raise a country-wide levy force to stem the impending invasion[49].

Stevenson promptly sent for Seagrim, who was at the time in Quetta, to help organise the Karen levies. He immediately flew back to Rangoon and went to Papun, only twenty miles away from the Thai border, to form what would become the first of the Karen Levy Corps.

Seagrim decided to move his base of operations away from Papun to Pyagawpu, three days march north west from Papun and surrounded by a number of small Karen villages. By this time he had obtained 470 volunteers and deployed them on patrols. Only 360 had weapons. He divided his levies into sections of ten to twelve men and into areas. Saw Willie Saw, a forest ranger, was responsible for the areas around Kadaingti; Saw Darlington, a former teacher and carpenter at a Wesleyan mission school was responsible for the Papun area, while Pyagawpu fell under the jurisdiction of Saw Digay, an influential lumber contractor. Seagrim had managed to obtain some arms and ammunition from Noel Boyt, the commander of the Karen Volunteers at Mawchi, but they did not amount to much – around 150 twelve bore shotguns, fifty .410 shotguns, five .303 rifles with fifty rounds of ammunition each and two boxes of grenades.

At the beginning of March 1942, the Burma Independence Army [BIA][50] entered Papun to take over its administration on behalf of the Japanese. Seagrim countered this by sending fifty men to take up positions around the town and shoot at the BIA whenever a target presented itself. At around that time, Saw Willie Saw attacked a 500 strong BIA foraging party in broad daylight and drove them back to their base at Kawkayet. Realizing that little progress could be made without arms and money, Seagrim, taking a few ex-Burma Rifles soldiers with him marched north to Mawchi to link up with

---

49 He was later joined by the young anthropologist Edmund Leach whose wartime adventures with the Kachins later formed the basis of his academic work.

50 While many Burmans supported the BIA – the Karens, long time enemies, continued to support the British, and as past racial animosities once more rose to the fore the Karens were to find themselves the victims of a rampaging ill-trained militia bent on ethnic destruction.

Noel Boyt and then to head to either Mandalay or India to arrange supplies. From June to October, Seagrim remained in Mawtudo village in the Mawchi area, organizing harassing patrols against Japanese foraging parties near the main road. In November, suffering from malaria, he returned to the Pyagawpu area, encouraging the Karens to hold out against the Japanese and their Burmese cohorts. Relations between the BIA and the Karens had gone from bad to worse with many instances of ethnically inspired atrocities. This prompted Seagrim to send parties of his irregulars to stay in villages to protect them against the BIA.

Late in 1942, a plan had been approved by the Indian Mission to drop four Karen parachutists east of Shwegyin near the Karenni Hills to assess the chances of dropping two British officers, Major Jimmy Nimmo and Captain Eric McCrindle, and a team of Karen radio operators into the Salween area so that they could link up with Seagrim and set up an intelligence and sabotage network. On the night of 18 February 1943, Lieutenant Ba Kyaw and three comrades dropped into the hills; in dreadful weather conditions their W/T set was smashed on landing.

In February 1943, a seventy-strong Japanese patrol arrived at Pyagawpu looking for British soldiers. Fortunately, the Karens had been forewarned and had been able to send Seagrim by elephant into the jungle at Payasedo, some twenty-three miles west of the village. Ordering his men to lie low, this did not stop him from travelling around the country to retain control of his organisation and to give encouragement. As Duncan Guthrie wrote:

> 'Gradually he discarded his khaki drill uniform. He put on instead the red and white shirt of the Karens and the wide Shan trousers. He walked abroad with a red Karen bag over his shoulder and in it the little round Karen box with tobacco and betel nut which he chewed as the Karens chew. He said that if he could have a Bible and a Shakespeare, he would have all that man would possibly need. The Karens brought him a Bible and a Shakespeare and he would sit for hours reading or re-reading one or other of his books.'

After no fewer than nine more attempts to drop a W/T set to Ba Kyaw, it was eventually decided that Nimmo and five other Karens should parachute into the hills bringing a new W/T set with them [Operation HARLINGTON]. On 12 October 1943, after two attempts both aborted by bad weather, they successfully dropped and two days later made contact with Seagrim and Ba Gyaw who had by now joined him. By 15 October they were in W/T contact with India.

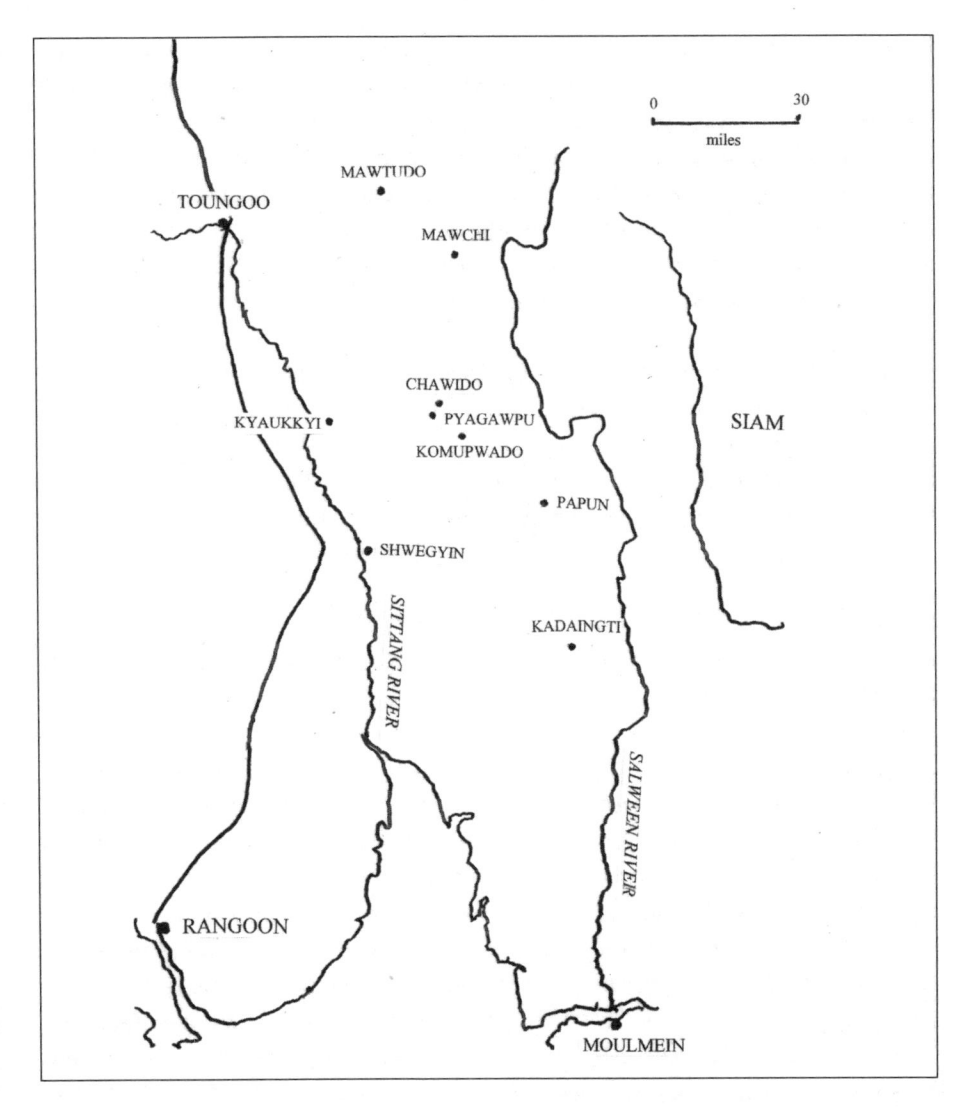

For the most part Seagrim relied on receiving his intelligence from Saw Po Hla, a delta Karen born near Myaungmya. Po Hla had been educated at Rangoon University and graduated with degrees in Religion and Philosophy. After working for the Irrawaddy Flotilla Company he joined the 11th Battalion, Burma Rifles. When the Japanese started searching for ex-Burma Rifles soldiers he escaped and, after an informer reported him to the Kempeitai, he found his way to Seagrim in the summer of 1943. Po Hla was responsible for travelling through the hills conveying messages and receiving information. On one trip to Rangoon Po Hla had also been able to meet two Karen leaders working with the Burmese government, Henson Kya Doe and San Po Thin, and from them he learnt that there was much discontent within the Burma Defence Army, renamed in 1943 the Burma National Army [BNA], and that Aung San and it leaders were already planning to revolt against the Japanese.

By early 1944 Seagrim had been joined by another SOE officer, Captain Eric McCrindle[51]. His first act was to hold a conference to introduce the two new British arrivals to his Karen network. McCrindle had brought certificates signed by Mountbatten, Lieutenant General Pownall, his CoS, and General Auchinleck for the Karen people. The one from Auchinleck read:

> 'The loyal attitude of the Karens has been reported to me by my officers. Loyalty through so long a time in your difficult and dangerous circumstances is worthy of the highest praise. I know that many of you have borne arms in defence of your country and will bear them again to ensure final victory. In the meantime my officers and I do not forget you and the loyalty of Karenni.'

Seagrim wisely decided to keep these certificates himself until the main body of British troops arrived; their discovery in a Karen home would have meant instant death for the occupants.

Major Nimmo and three of his Karen operatives then left to set up their own camp north of the Mawchi road. The number of SOE parachutists dropping into the Salween area had not gone unnoticed by the Japanese and soon seventeen Japanese soldiers, claiming to be from a goods distribution unit, arrived in Papun. Suspicious that they were Kempeitai, Seagrim moved his camp near to the village of Komupwado about ten miles south west of Pyagawgpu.

For Po Hla there was worse news. The Japanese had heard about his trip to Rangoon and his meeting with San Po Thin. The Kempeitai had arrested his parents, his fiancée, some relatives and some of his contacts in Rangoon. Fearing for the welfare of his relatives Po Hla planned to deceive the Japanese by spinning them a bogus story concocted by Seagrim and McCrindle and surrendered to the Japanese on 18 January after which, believing his story, the Japanese treated him well and asked him to help them get the support of the Karen community.

However, while Po Hla was being dined in Rangoon, a Kempeitai detachment, under the command of Captain Motoichi Inoue, arrived in Kyuakkyi. At the same time as they were putting on cinema shows for the villagers and giving sweets to children, the Kempeitai also set about brutally interrogating the locals as to the whereabouts of Seagrim and the Karens fighting for him. One

---

51 Dropped 9 December 1943.

man, an ex-Burma Rifles Jemadar called Maung Wah[52], was brutally beaten for three days, until the Japanese, realising he was not going to give them any information, gave him an ultimatum. He was to go to the hills and return with the whereabouts of Seagrim and a map of his camp and sentry posts. If he did not return in one week, action would be taken against his family.

On arriving at Seagrim's camp, Maung Wah told Seagrim everything that had happened. Seagrim told the old man to go back and tell the Japanese what he knew. By the time he returned, he discovered that the Japanese already had the information they sought for a young levy had been tortured to disclose the information after the Kempeitai had discovered the village's hidden arms cache. The next day a Japanese Infantry regiment arrived and they set off into the hills.

The Kempeitai and Japanese infantry arrived in Pyagawpu and arrested a number of Seagrim's elders including Saw Ta Roe, the *thugyi* of Pyagawpu area. They forced them to lead them to Komupwado which they found deserted as Seagrim, after being contacted by Maung Wah, had decided it was best for his own safety to keep moving. They burnt the camp down.

For Seagrim time was running out. On 4 February he signalled India that the Japanese had knowledge of his party and he estimated he had about ten days grace. He asked for the immediate drop of arms for 1,000 men at Papun in the hope of starting a fight and creating a diversion. He was advised that arms could not be dropped at such short notice and that his plan was unsound anyway. It was best that he headed for China with Nimmo and McCrindle. On their return to Pyagawpu, the Japanese captured a young Karen, Saw Yay, who had run away when he saw them and subsequently tortured him into revealing the whereabouts of the camp. The Japanese once more headed into the hills, on the way meeting a number of Karen Police, who led them to where the British party was camping, close to Komupwado.

On 15 February 1944, the Japanese surrounded the camp and a fire fight ensued in which McCrindle was fatally shot. Seagrim and the rest of the party were able to escape into the thick jungle. The next day, Nimmo, who had set up his own camp in the north not far from Komupwado, was to face a similar fate to that of McCrindle. Using information probably found in Komupwado, a detachment of Kempeitai from Toungoo arrived and began torturing the local Karen villagers in the area: information as to the whereabouts of the British was finally beaten out of one of the locals and the Kempeitai soon surrounded Nimmo's camp. Nimmo was killed instantly as he emerged from his tent, revolver in hand; a number of Karen levies were wounded though a larger group were able to escape.

---

52 Aka Maung Mlo Lwe.

It was fortuitous that Nimmo had already been recommended for a DSO and the citation was in due course sent to his widow:

> 'On 12 October 1943 this officer was dropped by parachute 380 miles inside Burma for the purposes of establishing W/T communication with India and contacting personnel who remained after the Japanese invasion and who were believed still to exist under the leadership of major Seagrim. Major Nimmo has since succeeded in both these tasks, which represent an earnest of British intentions to re-conquer Burma, until which time he is committed to remain within it. The fact that this officer has had to undergo the strain of preparing himself to carry out this hazardous mission each moon period since February 1943 owing to bad climatic conditions with the skill with which he has fulfilled his task, reflects determination, courage and devotion to duty of a very high order.'

Life for the Karen villagers worsened. The Japanese stationed detachments in the larger villages and the local people were forced to search the hills – all the time suffering the brutal ill-treatment and beatings meted out by the Kempeitai[53]. If Seagrim should escape, they declared, every house in the Papun district would be burnt and anyone found to be in contact with him would be imprisoned and sent to work on the Burma railway. Seagrim's location in a mountain paddy hut eventually became known when one of the survivors from the attack on his camp surrendered and unwittingly gave information to a Japanese informer. Captain Inoue arrived in Komupwado and immediately had the headman deliver a message to Seagrim warning him that if he did not surrender the entire village would be burnt down and its occupants arrested.

Seagrim sent a message back to Captain Inoue that he would surrender at Komupwado and, despite the sores on his feet, walked out of the jungle on 14 March. He had not eaten for twenty days. Saw Lin Gyaw recalled that he 'last saw Major Seagrim in [Second Lieutenant] Kurkata's car with red tapes on his neck and wrists. He gave me a farewell wink just before the car started'. Along with fourteen Karens, he was sent to Rangoon where he was imprisoned in the New Law Courts. Despite assurances from Inoue that those Karens who had helped him would be left alone, he was joined by Digay, Darlington, Willie Saw, Po Hla and the old man Maung Wah among many others. They were soon moved six miles outside of Rangoon to the main Jail at Insein.

---

53 About 200 were tortured, many of whom died.

Sentence was passed on 1 September 1944. Among the Karens given eight years imprisonment for helping Seagrim and the British were Saw Po Hla, Saw Ta Roe, Saw Digay, Thara May Sha, Thra Kyaw Lay, Saw Rupert, Saw Henry, Saw Po Myin, Saw Tha Say and Saw Yay. For Seagrim, along with a number of his Karen friends – Lt. Ba Gyaw, Saw He Be, Saw Tun Lin, Saw Sunny, Saw Pe, Saw Peter and Saw Ah Din – the sentence was death.

As soon as the sentences were announced, Seagrim stood before the Court and addressed the President, saying that he had been in command and anything the others had done had been done on his orders. He was quite ready to die but asked that the others should be spared. His pleas were ignored and all the men were returned to prison to await execution. That night he told his fellow captive Saw Ta Roe, 'Don't worry, Ta Roe, we are Christians and must have faith in God and trust him. Christ came down to earth and suffered on a cross. We must suffer like him'. He quoted him the passage from St Paul's epistle to Timothy: '... for if we be dead with him, we shall also live with him.'

Arms tied behind their backs, they were taken by truck to the execution ground at Kemmendine cemetery, shot by firing squad, and dumped in an unmarked communal grave. Duncan Guthrie paid tribute to Seagrim: 'He never had any doubt what the Japs would do to him. Many of the Karens are Christians, but whether they are Christian, Buddhist or animist, they all know what Seagrim did for them. There has not been – there could not be – a more heroic act during this war. Major Seagrim was a very great Englishman.'

In a faint echo of Freddy Spencer Chapman's 1946 outburst to the *Daily Mail*, Saw Kan Nyun remembered Hugh Seagrim once saying to him 'the British government is always slow to begin. Had the volunteer organisation been formed a month earlier, things would have been quite different'.

News of Seagrim's capture reached Ritchie Gardiner on 26 August through Captain D. Anderson of ISLD. Four of their agents had returned to India with information that four W/T sets had been captured in the Papun area and that two British officers had been killed. Furthermore Seagrim was being held in the Law Court Buildings in Rangoon.

23 November 1943: Recommendation for DSO

> This officer has remained 380 miles within enemy-held territory ever since its occupation by Japanese forces in April 1942. During this period he has sustained the loyalty of the local inhabitants of a very wide area, and thereby has provided the foundation of a pro-British force whenever occupying forces arrive in that area. This officer has now been contacted by Major Nimmo, ABRO, and is passing valuable military intelligence by wireless. The fact that he has remained there in constant danger and has maintained pro-British

sympathies in such adverse circumstances has proved his determination, courage and devotion to duty to be of the highest order.

Awarded

28 June 1945: Recommendation for George Cross

Major Seagrim was the leader of a party, which included two other British and one Karen officer, operating in the Karenni Hills [Burma] from February 1943 to February 1944. Towards the end of 1943 the presence of this party became known to the Japanese who commenced a widespread campaign of arrests and torture in order to discover their whereabouts. In February 1944 the other two British officers with Major Seagrim were located, ambushed and killed but major Seagrim and the Karen officer escaped.

The capture of the other two British officers' equipment furnished the enemy with all the information they required of Major Seagrim's activities and they accordingly redoubled their efforts to locate him. Captured documents show that the Japanese arrested at least 270 people including elders and headmen. Many of these were tortured and killed in the most brutal fashion.

In spite of this the Karens continued to assist and shelter Major Seagrim, but the enemy managed to convey a message to him that if he surrendered they would cease reprisals. Major Seagrim accordingly did so about 15 March 1944. He was immediately conveyed to Rangoon along with some other members of his party. On 2 September, he along with eight others was sentenced to death. On hearing the sentence Major Seagrim pled that the others be excused since they had to obey his orders and that he alone deserved the death sentence. The degree to which he inspired his men may be realised from the fact that they all expressed their willingness to die with him. The death sentence was carried out shortly afterwards.

There can hardly be a finer example of self-sacrifice and bravery than that exhibited by this officer who, in cold blood, deliberately gave himself up to save others, knowing well what his fate was likely to be at the hands of the enemy.

Throughout his sojourn in jail he made every effort to comfort his men and sustain their courage by his Christian example. Finally when sentence was pronounced, he again displayed that supreme degree of self-sacrifice when he pled that he only should be executed.

I count it a privilege to recommend this very gallant officer for the award of the George Cross.

Awarded

His brother, Lieutenant Colonel Derek Seagrim, was awarded the Victoria Cross for gallantry in Tunisia on 20-21 March 1943, and died of wounds shortly afterwards. This is the only instance of one family being awarded the Victoria and George Crosses.

MAJOR GUY TURRALL, DSO, MC

Educated at Queen Elizabeth's Grammar in Crediton, Devon, and then at Trinity Hall Cambridge, where he read engineering, Guy Turrall had started his military career as an RE officer in 1914, serving in the Dardanelles with the 1st NZ Division and then in the Balkans with the 22nd Division from 1916-19. He was twice mentioned in despatches and ended the war commanding an RE field company as a temporary major.

He returned to Cambridge in 1919 to study geology and astronomy and took a BSc at London University. In 1921 he was a member of an expedition to report on the mineral resources of British Somaliland which covered 2,700 miles and then, after studying under the German geophysicist Sehweydar in The Hague and Potsdam, for the next four years he prospected for gold in Texas, Oklahoma and Louisiana. After trips to Greece and Serbia in 1926-7, he spent a year in Budapest studying under Dr Pekar at the Hungarian department of Geophysics. The next five years were spent in Venezuela, London, Germany, Hungary and Holland.

In 1934, Turrall 'investigated gold mineralisation in East Africa' and worked with the prominent Australian geologist, Sir Edmund Teale, on the Tanganyika Geological Survey.

He rejoined the army in 1939 [by now a married man with two young children] and was posted to Ethiopia where he joined the 101 Mission under Colonel Terence Airey and served with Colonel Hugh Boustead's 3rd Infantry Battalion, Frontier Force, from February to September 1941. He was wounded at Gulit Fort in April 1941 by a splinter from an Italian hand grenade which lodged in his skull and awarded an MC.

After attending various sabotage courses, on 11 January 1942 he was 'lent' by Boustead to SOE and landed in Crete with Xan Fielding to reinforce Christopher Woodhouse, an ill-starred adventure during which he infuriated his fellow officers by advertising his Britishness and personal idiosyncrasies like plant collecting to the point of foolhardiness. His inability to speak Greek did not help. A note in his file of August 1942 notes that 'he worked in Crete and was absent without leave for a considerable period. Lt Col Pembroke [said] that he had been found ill in a pension in Cairo'. A court of enquiry was therefore cancelled. A further note states that 'there had been some disagreement in Crete and he was dissatisfied with the whole position and returned [on 16 April 1942 by submarine] to Cairo'.

He then rejoined Hugh Boustead's Frontier Force in October 1942 and remained with it until the following October when he underwent parachute training before being posted to Imphal on 13 February 1944 on the orders of

Brigadier Orde Wingate for Operation THURSDAY, the Second Chindit Expedition. Here he joined BLADET Detachment, a raiding unit formed by Wingate under command of Major Blain, Brigadier Mike Calvert's former sergeant-major in the 1943 First Chindit Expedition. The idea was for a glider full of specially trained troops to land, carry out a demolition or a raid and then erect the snatching gear for a Dakota to hook up with their glider and take them safely home. Consisting of six officers and sixty men, it operated for six weeks behind enemy lines before being withdrawn and then disbanded.

Turrall led a BLADET deep penetration patrol into Singhkaling-Hkamti-Man Pang area. A second patrol was cancelled as the Japanese approached Imphal and Turrall was appointed Officer commanding Hong Kong Volunteers.

After an interview with General Lentaigne on 12 May 1944 in which Turrall pointed out he was kicking his heels in the BLADET Special Force, Brigadier Mike Calvert, the commander of 77 Independent Infantry Brigade, wrote to HQ Special Forces in August 1944, recommending that Turrall take command of BLADET. If not, then he felt he should be released to SOE which he duly was on 19 September 1944.

Turrall was given command of Operation HYENA[54], one of the three elements of Operation CHARACTER, and was the first to drop on 20 February 1945. For a 54-year-old man, it was a considerable achievement and despite being wounded in the leg and lumbar region on 15 April at Kyaukkyi by a Japanese hand grenade, his stamina, courage and determination never left him.

On 16 August, Turrall walked into the Japanese lines to tell them that the war was over. He was immediately detained, tied up and then marched south for two days, for his captors, without W/T communications, refused to believe him. Turrall had been in the field for over six months and soon the strain began to tell on him, causing momentary blackouts which provoked his guards to slap him around the head and remove his boots. The Karen who had gone with him to the Japanese lines was shot in the back one night. After five days of captivity, he managed to work his ropes loose and made a dash for freedom, only to be caught and clubbed about the head with rifle butts. It was only when some leaflets were dropped by the RAF with the text of the Emperor's surrender speech that the Japanese were convinced. They released Turrall and he reached Allied lines at Kyaukkyi on 24 August, having been in Japanese hands for a week and, at times, certain that he was going to die.

---

54 Until 24 March 1945 when Major Howell took over. Turrall then led HYENA RED, one of seven HYENA colours.

6 September 1945: Recommendation for DSO

This officer, who, at the age of 54, commanded the original 'blind' parachute jump of Force 136 personnel to Pyagawpu on 25 February 1945, organised the reception of operations OTTER and FERRETS a few nights later in spite of Japanese forces having arrived in the area from Papun. He also organised and trained several hundred levies who eventually became the hard core of Operation HYENA. On 15 April 1945, he personally led the successful attack on Kyaukkyi which resulted in enemy supplies, spare arms and a W/T set being destroyed. Later he operated in the area east of Kyaukkyi and with his levies killed over 500 Japanese and gave intelligence for air strikes and artillery which resulted in 924 estimated enemy casualties. For his outstanding powers of leadership and great gallantry shown on numerous occasions I recommend very strongly that this officer be awarded the DSO.

Awarded

BURMA

LIEUTENANT COLONEL EDGAR PEACOCK, DSO, MC and Bar

Peacock with his Levies

Peacock, 'a solid square chunk of a man, bristly moustache', was a 44-year-old Indian-born Rhodesian farmer[55] who had enlisted in July 1940 in East Africa and after being commissioned in the Royal Artillery in October 1941, went to Ceylon with 21 Brigade the following year. He had previously spent sixteen years in the Burma Forestry Service, at one point Deputy Conservator of Forests in charge of Upper Chindwin Forest Division and Game Warden of Burma and well-known for his book, *Game Book for Burma and Adjoining Territories* published in 1934, two years after he returned home to England. There was little Peacock did not know about Burma, being fluent in Burmese and Urdu. As Terence O'Brien said in *Moonlight War* 'he seemed to know every creature in Burma that walked, crawled, flew or swam'. He had taken part in suppressing Saya San's Burmese Rebellion of 1930-32.

His Indian Intelligence School report writes that he was 'a very capable, active, popular and efficient officer who has extensive experience of Burma and a good knowledge of the languages used in that country. He is capable of shouldering great responsibility and is suitable for an active intelligence appointment

---

55 On leave in 1922, Peacock had visited Zebedelia in the Transvaal and bought some land there. In 1934, having retired from the Burma Forestry Service, he built a house there and moved his family out from England. In 1937, the family moved to Bulawayo in Rhodesia to farm.

in a specialist capacity in connection with Burma. He would be very suitable as divisional Intelligence Officer [IO] in a forward formation or for organising guerrilla warfare'. It was this recommendation that brought about him being loaned to the Indian Army and Force 136 in March 1943 when he commanded guerrilla and Deep Penetration Troops in the Chindwin and Manipur campaigns in 1943-44.

Following SOE parachute training, Peacock was put in command of the OTTER mission, one of the three Missions earmarked for Operation CHARACTER which was designed to prevent Japanese reinforcements coming south to stop Fourteenth Army reaching Rangoon before the monsoon. On 13 April, OTTER was informed that the Japanese were beginning to send their 15th Division down from the Shan States. Fourteenth Army was then at Pyinmana, so the race to reach Toungoo looked fairly even. This was to be Peacock's moment of glory and over the next seven days, his levies made countless attacks against the Japanese by ambushes, road blocks and demolitions. By the time the forward battalions of the Japanese 15th Division emerged from the hills onto the plain, Fourteenth Army had taken Toungoo.

In his post-operational reports, Peacock explained how he managed to stop the enemy so successfully by using a cortex[56] explosive trap which he had devised on operations in the Chindwin valley. This was used to great effect on the Mawchi road as witnessed by the hundred-odd smashed Japanese trucks. The same trap played havoc with enemy personnel following jungle tracks. 'The explosions and terrible effects of one hundred or more yards of cortex laid with grenades and heavy charges of explosive raises the morale of one side as much as it reduces that of the other. We used many hundreds of pounds of explosive and thousands of yards of cortex as an offensive weapon … these traps do not fall under the category of 'booby traps' because they are usually and most effectively operated by pull switches and lengths of cord pulled by hand at the right moment.'

When its mission in support of Fourteenth Army's advance to Rangoon had come to an end in May, OTTER continued to face a determined and aggressive enemy although it was forced to adopt a lower profile, engaging in limited hit and run operations designed not to provoke the Japanese into mass retaliation against the Karen villages. By the time the Japanese had crossed the Sittang River, OTTER had killed over 2,800 Japanese troops and destroyed ninety-five vehicles.

---

56 Cortex is a detonating cord about the thickness of electrical extension cord with an explosive core inside a plastic coating. It 'burns' at 2 km per second. It is used to daisy chain a sequence of explosives together.

Peacock had shown himself to be a highly capable and courageous officer, something he was determined to do having been disallowed from serving in the First World War on the grounds that his job in Burma was deemed an important Reserved Occupation. However, he also deserves credit for his intellectual grasp of irregular warfare and the contribution he made to its application in the field. He understood the need to recalibrate infantry training so that field craft and minor tactics not only matched but outperformed those of the enemy. Core to this was the ability of troops to be able to carry their own food for periods of a week or more. With few preconceived ideas about military strategy, Peacock was also able to see opportunity where others saw problems. For instance, when army officers told him that the Japanese defences on the Mawchi road were almost impregnable owing to the steepness and general difficulty of moving across the terrain, he countered that the defence of jungle roads which the Japanese had been tasked with was 'one of the hardest tasks that any enemy could have been given'. He was very ably supported by his 2 i/c, Captain Bill Poles[57].

May 1944: Recommendation for MC

Major E.H. Peacock was in command of a special force of Burmans and Karens which, shortly before the Japanese advance started, was sent on 13 March 1944 to watch the approaches from Yuwa into the Kabaw valley.

On 23 March, the day before this long-distance patrol was due to withdraw, one of his officers, Captain J Gibson, a very heavy man, was very seriously injured by a grenade and had to be carried back over very difficult country by slow stages. On arrival at his old camp site at the Yu River crossing, Major Peacock, whose wireless had failed to function for several days, discovered that the enemy were in possession of Tamu and Hesin and between him and Moreh and was uncertain how far our own troops had withdrawn. It was imperative to get assistance quickly for Captain Gibson who was left hidden at the Yu River crossing with food and water, while Major Peacock and his party, by now considerably exhausted, made their way through the jungle via the northern flank of Moreh to Sibong where he

---

57 41-year-old Bill Poles had joined SOE from the 2nd Battalion Rhodesia Regiment in April 1943. He was recommended for an MC in September 1945: 'This officer who parachuted into the central Karen country in February 1945 has shown consistent gallantry and qualities of leadership worthy of high commendation. In spite of lack of supplies, he has kept the morale and fighting efficiency of his force of Levies at a high level. In July, with only five Levies, he stalked a party of fifteen Japanese, killing them all, and since February his force operating west of Thandaung has inflicted nearly 600 casualties on the enemy. I recommend him strongly for an award of the Military Cross.'

contacted our forces again. In spite of his considerable exhaustion and the effects of heatstroke from which he was suffering, Major Peacock's sole concern was the safety and rescue of Captain Gibson. He wasted no time in going to Moreh and after consultation with the commander of the Moreh garrison, left Moreh the next night with an escort of Ghurkhas and two Karens to fetch Captain Gibson. At this time, considerable enemy forces, including tanks and guns, were in the Nakala, Tamu and Hesin areas, but no exact information was available. Without thought for his personal safety and knowing that speed was vital to Captain Gibson's safety, he took this party successfully under cover of darkness straight towards Tamu and Hesin villages to the Yu River crossing, and safely brought back Captain Gibson who was still alive, the same night.

It was entirely due to Major Peacock's dogged determination, drive, unselfishness and great courage that Captain Gibson's life was saved.

Awarded

18 May 1945: Recommendation for bar to MC

In March 1945, Lieutenant Colonel Peacock after having been parachuted into enemy territory, raised and commanded a group of Karen guerrillas operating in the country north east of Pegu. On 13 April he was warned that a Japanese division was moving along an axis running close to his base. The enemy's objective was to link up with the main enemy forces in order to deny us a vital airfield and communications centre. Within twenty-four hours, Colonel Peacock had established a number of road blocks. During the following ten days, by skilful handling of his guerrillas, and a nicely timed series of demolitions, he succeeded in preventing the link up of the Japanese forces. The objective is now in our hands. In this short period his guerrillas killed 114 of the enemy, destroyed a large amount of transport and blew six bridges.

Credit for this outstanding performance must go largely to Colonel Peacock whose gallant leadership and sound tactical judgment have formed an important contributory factor in the success of the main operations.

Awarded

14 September 1945: Recommendation for DSO

During the period under review this officer who parachuted with a party into the Pyagawpu 63 area in February 1945 has been in command of Operation OTTER operating on the Toungoo-Mawchi Road which has raised local levies who have killed 2,743 enemy troops and destroyed 94 W/T besides giving much intelligence of great value to Fourteenth and Twelfth Army HQ.

BURMA

Lieutenant Colonel Peacock has displayed leadership, organising ability and tact in handling the locals, worthy of very high commendation. The outstanding courage and resource of this officer within two months turned a small hunted party into the controlling force over a wide area.

I strongly recommend him for the award of the DSO.

Awarded

LIEUTENANT COLONEL RONALD CRITCHLEY, DSO, MC

Karen static guards, young and old

Born in 1905 in Edinburgh, Ronald Critchley grew up as one of six children at Stapleton Tower, a sixteenth century fortified manor house overlooking the Solway Firth near Annan. Educated at Wellington College, he attended the RMAS and was commissioned into 13/18 Hussars which had recently moved to Edinburgh in September 1925. Four years later, the regiment embarked for Cairo where it was to spend two years as part of the Cairo Cavalry Brigade before posting to Sialkot and later Risalpur in India. The regimental history noted that 'Captains Butler, Critchley and Harrap, Major Hirsch and Lieutenant Cordy-Simpson were probably the best five [polo] players' and 'what with the demands of soldiering, regimental games, polo and hunting, there were few idle hours, and officers and other ranks found that their time abroad seldom hung heavily on their hands'. In 1937, Critchley married Violet Hirsch and took on a 6-year-old step son Nicholas.

Ordered to return to England in autumn 1938, the 13/18 Hussars found themselves in Brest with the BEF the following year. Critchley had by now left the regiment and spent two months as a language student in Slovenia learning Serbo-Croat. He attended an MI[R] course during July and August 1939 before joining the Balkan Section of the Middle East Intelligence Centre [MEIC] in Cairo which had just been established to collect and collate intelligence for the WO. The FO refused to share diplomatic intelligence with MEIC which only served to duplicate those activities and the centre processed both military and diplomatic material. A pressing concern to Middle East Command at the time was the activities and intentions of the Italians who had been in Ethiopia since 1936. Now that Italy had declared war against Britain, there was a very real threat to British maritime lines of communication in the Red Sea. At some stage Critchley and MEIC parted company for the MI[R] War Diary recorded on 2 May 1940 that 'Captain R.A. Critchley turned up from Egypt asking for an exciting job'.

General Wavell instructed Colonel Dan Sandford, a former adviser to the Emperor Hailie Selassie, to draw up a plan to engage, arm and train the tribes still loyal to the Emperor with a view to mounting guerrilla operations against Mussolini's troops. Although instigated by MI[R], the operation known as Mission 101 was handed over to SOE to control and on 15 August 1940, Critchley with Captain Tim Foley RE, Captain Drew [Medical Officer] and W/T operator CSM Grey crossed the border into Ethiopia to raise levies in the Gojjam area. By early 1941, Mission 101 had to all extents coalesced with GIDEON FORCE run by Major Orde Wingate and its irregular levies went into action against the Italians up until their surrender in May. For the Mission 101 officers like Critchley, Ethiopia marked the beginning of a wartime career with SOE.

After spending the summer of 1941 with the Yugoslav POWs Commission in Kenya, Critchley was appointed Military Staff Officer to Colin Mackenzie [G1 to GSI[k]] with the India Mission in New Delhi in January 1942. It was an important role for a weakness of SOE in India to date had been its lack of know-how of how to interface with the British Indian military colossus. One of Critchley's tasks was to organise SBPs which in turn led to contact with V force, the organisation set up by General Wavell to harass Japanese lines of communications along the frontier between India and Burma, and to provide intelligence from behind enemy lines in the event of a Japanese invasion of India. In August 1942, released by Mackenzie, Critchley took command of V Force in the Assam Zone. The Japanese did not invade India that year as had been feared, so taking the chance of home leave after fourteen years overseas, he returned to England to see his family.

Anxious to use his Serbo-Croat, Critchley lobbied Cairo for a slot in Yugoslavia. Twice his application was turned down although rated 'obviously capable and tough though possibly inclined to be over-confident'. He may have been tainted through his association with Wingate with whom SOE Cairo had never seen eye to eye or it may have been that he had made some enemies in the highly charged political atmosphere of Rustem Buildings along the way. The outcome was that he returned to India and took command of the 2nd Battalion, Burma Rifles, the principal unit of DAHFORCE, which had distinguished itself on the first Chindit operation in March 1943. When it had crossed back into

India in May, its casualties told the story of the severity of the expedition: three British Officers [including the Commanding Officer], seven other ranks killed and 180 missing, of whom 120 had been allowed to shed their uniforms and stay in Burma. 2nd Burma Rifles joined 3rd Indian Infantry Division [Special Force] at Jhansi in August 1943, and underwent an increase in size to provide reconnaissance sections for each of the new Chindit columns currently being formed. In February, the sections moved with the Chindits to Assam before embarking on Operation THURSDAY, the second Chindit expedition, on 5 March 1944.

Wingate's task for DAHFORCE was for it to organise a Kachin rebellion behind enemy lines in conjunction with the advancing Chindit columns. This was later scaled down to conducting guerrilla operations to the north of the Taiping River, for SOE, which viewed the business of raising irregular forces as their prerogative, was concerned that an uprising of the Kachins without a permanent British military presence on the ground would inevitably lead to their wholesale slaughter by the Japanese once the Chindits had withdrawn. It was SOE who had responsibility for the reception of DAHFORCE which was to be inserted by gliders but when Lieutenant Colonel Herring overflew the landing zone [LZ] in a light aircraft and saw no sign of the signalling arrangements, he had no option other than to change his plan. DAHFORCE subsequently flew into the Broadway airstrip and walked into their area of operations where they finally met up with the SOE reception team. From 10 March to June 1944, DAHFORCE killed about 300 enemy soldiers, wounded many more, destroyed twelve trucks and tied down an unknown number of troops to protect the Bhamo-Myitkyina lines of communication.

In 1945, Critchley rejoined SOE as a Jedburgh team commander and on the night of 20/21 February was dropped 'blind' with his 2 i/c, Captain 'Trof' Trofimov, along with Major Guy Turrall's Special HYENA Group, into the dense jungle of the Karenni Mountains at Pyagawpu. His job was to organise an intelligence network that covered the group's area of operations and to recruit, train and arm the levies. Trofimov landed with a crash among the trees, took a step forward in the darkness and pitched thirty feet into a ravine. He crawled his way back up and found that he had lost his torch. There was no sign of the rest of the Jedburgh, but having taken note of the location of the DZ as he was coming down, he managed to find his way to it by dawn. Sergeant Little turned up several days later.

At the end of the month, Critchley headed south, establishing his main training camp at Lekawdo and within a short time had about 100 levies under training, necessitating a move to Kaumudo to be nearer the DZ. W/T communications with Calcutta had proven difficult but once a reliable link was

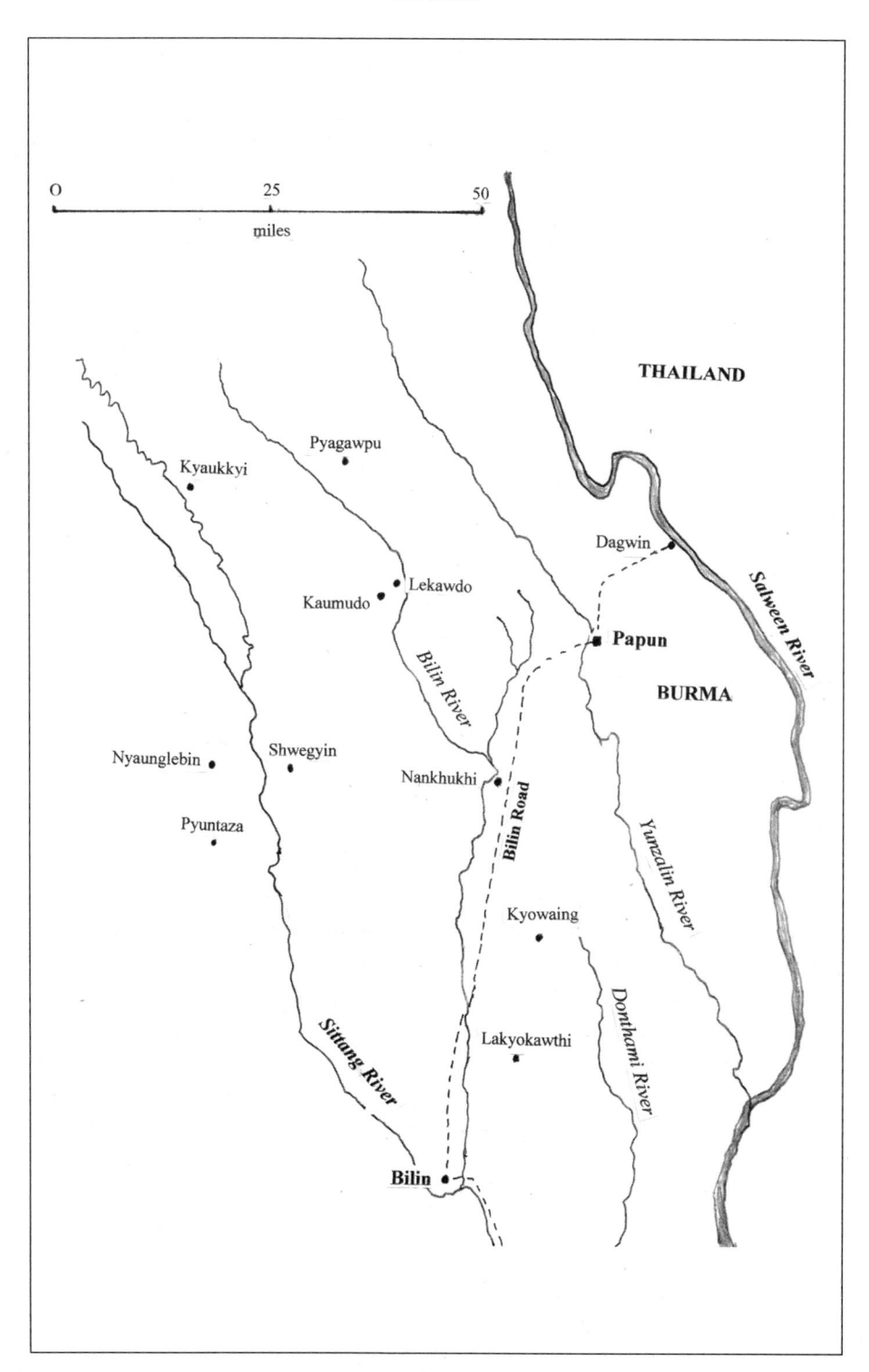

BURMA

established on 28 March, Group A announced the formation of MONGOOSE with Critchley, at the time suffering from a badly poisoned foot and eye infection, as the Area Commander with the rank of Lieutenant Colonel.

The mission was quickly brought up to strength with Major Lucas dropping on the night of 24/25 March, Captain Woolf [IO] and Lieutenant Van Kett [signals officer] on 5 April and Captains Byrne [2 i/c] and Williams on 9 April. Critchley now set up his advanced HQ at Mekyita where arming and training of the guerrillas could be carried out on a large scale.

After tasking Woolf and Byrne to block the Bilin Road and having split the levies into two platoons of fifty, Critchley gave the order to attack the 300 strong Japanese garrison in Papun. Following a strafing and bombing attack by six Spitfires at 06.35 hrs on 28 April, the platoons attacked the town from different directions. However the Japanese had been forewarned, not least because the town's Burmese officials had unexpectedly and rather obviously made themselves scarce, so Trofimov's platoon, most of whom had never seen action, almost immediately came under intense machine-gun fire. Some Karens took to their heels, but most held firm. After a furious battle which raged for nearly three hours, MONGOOSE withdrew with one KIA and two wounded, leaving an estimated thirty-six enemy dead behind including five officers. 'Trif' felt that it had all been rather too hasty and that if they had waited for Major Milner and his three inch mortars, 'Papun would have been ours'. Nonetheless, he was awarded an immediate MC for his part in the battle.

Three sub-teams Red [Captains Ford and Williams and Sergeant Dallow], White [Major Milner, Captain Bourne and Sergeant Leney] and Blue [Major Lucas and Captain Clark, operating with the BNA] now began systematically ambushing and mining the roads in and out of Papun with their levies. At one point, a 1,000-strong Japanese force descended on Nankhukhi to clear the area where Major Trofimov was with MONGOOSE GREEN.

On 20 May, Critchley called a conference for all his officers at Lakyokho in the Kyowaing area. The enemy was now too well organised along the main supply routes [MSRs], so the decision was taken to rest the levies and to regroup on 22 June in the Mewaing area. Over the course of the following eight weeks, the MONGOOSE patrols relentlessly harassed the Japanese using hit and run tactics, ambushes and mines.

Official figures show that MONGOOSE accounted for 1,420 enemy killed, eighty-two wounded and one captured at a cost of three killed and one wounded.

Critchley left Burma in October 1945.

24 August 1945: Recommendation for DSO

During the period under review, this officer, who parachuted with a party for which there was no reception into the Pyagawpu area in February 1945, has been in command of Operation MONGOOSE operating in the southern Karen area which has raised local levies, who have killed 1,390 enemy troops. Besides giving much intelligence of great value to Fourteenth and Twelfth Army HQs, Lieutenant Colonel Critchley has displayed leadership, organising ability and tact in handling the locals worthy of very high commendation and I strongly recommend him for the DSO.

Awarded

MAJOR JOHN 'BATH' HEDLEY, DSO

John Hedley

Born in 1908, John Hedley was educated at Eton and King's College Cambridge. On coming down, he joined the Bombay Burmah Trading Corporation and when war broke out in 1939, immediately volunteered for the army. Commissioned in the 4th Burma Rifles in November, he in turn became Signals Officer, Mortar Officer and by July 1941 Adjutant and Signals Officer. The battalion moved to the Eastern frontier at Kawkareik at the foot of the Dawnas Hills where it bore the brunt of the main Japanese thrust when they attacked on 20 January 1942.

In March 1942 Hedley was posted as a Burmese language interpreter to 63 Brigade when it arrived in Rangoon. On the first brigade recce, the brigadier and brigade major were both wounded and two commanding officers killed in an ambush. Hedley now found himself in charge of the brigade defence platoon during the battle of Taukkyan. After a long withdrawal the brigade arrived in Kohima in June 1942 where Hedley became Brigade Intelligence Officer to the new brigade commander, Brigadier Lentaigne. A year later, he was posted as IO to 111 Brigade in Ghatera in India, where he again met up with Brigadier Lentaigne and his brigade major, John Masters. The brigade flew into Burma with the second Chindit expedition on 9 March 1944. Wounded in the knee by a Japanese grenade, he was evacuated towards the end of the expedition and as soon as he was fit again, transferred to SOE.

After selecting and training a team of Kachins, Hedley dropped into Japanese occupied Burma on 22 January 1945. With three captains including Bill Nimmo as 2 i/c, three sergeants and sixteen Kachins, Operation BISON's mission was to observe the road and rail links between Maymyo and Mandalay, indicating suitable targets for the RAF to bomb and preparing to harass Japanese lines of communication when ordered. An additional task was to prevent the destruction of key points by the enemy. Dropped fourteen miles to the south of the correct DZ and on the wrong side of the Namtu River, Hedley then discovered his W/T set had been damaged beyond repair during the drop. A week later, resupplied with two new W/Ts, the Mission moved off to the upper reaches of the Lema Chaung where they established their main cache of stores. The point finally selected as a base from which to observe the MSRs was on a hill called Kyaing Taung. From there, Hedley was able to construct a hide for his patrols – typically one officer, one NCO and two Kachin riflemen – just ten yards from the side of the main Mandalay-Maymyo road.

For the next seven weeks, they watched the road by night when it was used by the Japanese and twice a day sent back detailed intelligence reports. The main railway line was within hearing distance, so the patrols were able to report how many trains went up and down the line every twenty-four hours. Moving their camp from time to time for security, the Mission continued to send its daily reports until ordered to march to Maymyo which had been retaken by the British. It was around this time that Hedley witnessed the horror on the ground caused by RAF fighters strafing two innocent villages and the tragic loss of life of some of their inhabitants. They had been behind enemy lines for fifty-four days.

John Masters in *The Road past Mandalay* wrote of him at this time:

'John Hedley, pale and sweat-stained as always, swung into camp with huge strides at the head of six of the most exhausted men I have ever seen. He was carrying three of their rifles as well as his own. I offered him a tot of rum but he refused – he had sworn not to drink until he was back in Mandalay.'

With Operation BISON now completed, Hedley was briefed to act as LO between two combined Ghurkha parachute battalions and local guerrillas trained by SOE. The aim was to seize Elephant Point at the entrance of the Hlaing River near Rangoon. Although SOE information indicated that the area was unoccupied, the airborne assault went ahead and the operation succeeded in capturing the Point with minimal casualties. Twenty-five Japanese troops had been in the area and taken shelter in a single bunker which was destroyed by ground attack aircraft. On 29 May 1945, Hedley flew home to England on leave. It took sixty hours to get from Ceylon to Godalming in Surrey, which Hedley considered 'not bad going'

After the war, he rejoined the Bombay Burmah Trading Corporation until he retired in 1953. He later became a housemaster at Gordonstoun.

CAPTAIN DAVID BRITTON, MC

David Britton

Educated at Queen Elizabeth's Grammar School Wimborne, Dorset and UCL where he read Economics, French and Geography, 31-year-old David Britton joined SOE in 1943 and after numerous abortive missions to France and Belgium, finally arrived in Paris on 25 September 1944. Told to hang around for two weeks, he attached himself to a Liaison Mission under command of Captain Soual which was heading for Carcassonne. On arrival the only need for his services was as a chauffeur, so once again Britton used his initiative and went first to Bordeaux to help negotiate the terms of the German surrender and then on to the Pyrenees and Spain on general intelligence gathering missions. He turned to England on 18 October. All in all it had not been a very unsatisfactory three weeks.

His next mission was to head a Jedburgh team [REINDEER] for Force 136 in Burma. After two aborted attempts, he dropped with Captain Jock Waller and Sergeant Brierley in March 1945 in the area due west of Toungoo and by 12 April he had over 300 men under arms and an intelligence network covering a radius of some twenty miles. Between 19 and 27 April, REINDEER, in the words of SOE historian Charles Cruikshank, 'made a remarkable contribution' to the advance of the Fourteenth Army, directing RAF airstrikes on to ammunition dumps and motor transport concentrations, cutting the railway in several places, sinking river boats and capturing or destroying stores, as well as carrying out innumerable attacks on enemy soldiers. On the arrival of Fourteenth Army, Britton was asked to stay on and help clear out the pockets of Japanese troops who had escaped to the hills.

On the evening of 2 June, a force of some 300 Japanese had been reported in the area of Shanywa and although harassed by Britton's levies and the Royal Berkshires, it had managed to reach Yeozin and by dawn more than half had made it across the Sittang River. Taking some levies and a section of Assam Rifles, Britton decided to cross the river and attack the Japanese on the east bank. With his force now numbering some 100 men, Britton engaged the enemy and succeeded in driving them out of a small village into the cover of a large clump of trees. Here they prepared to stand and fight. Britton now led his men forward through close country where visibility in the long grass rarely exceeded twenty yards. Personally firing a Bren gun from the standing position, he knocked out at least one Japanese machine gun. As he advanced across a small clearing, a concealed enemy MG opened up and he was hit in the chest and went down. The fire was so heavy that his men were unable to reach his body, although one managed to get a water bottle to him, although he was probably dead. Later he was hit again, this time in the thigh but by now ammunition was running short and the guerrillas had to withdraw, fighting all the way. A message was passed to the Royal Berkshire's 3 inch mortar line and accurate fire came down on the wood, causing a large number of enemy casualties. That evening an attempt was made to retrieve Britton's body but it was not until the next morning that it was recovered. He was buried in the Toungoo military cemetery on 4 June.

In writing to his widow in August 1945, Major C.B. Jones said of him:

'His unfailing cheerfulness and happy disposition made him popular wherever he went. The men of his guerrilla force would follow him anywhere and I do not think I can better finish this letter than by quoting a remark made by one of his party – "We deeply mourn a great loss, but we are proud to have served and fought under such a great and courageous leader".' The brigadier of 98 Independent Infantry Brigade noted that "the assistance offered by REINDEER to troops under my command has extended over a very wide field and has been of the greatest possible value".'

Sergeant Brierley, MM, the W/T operator for the REINDEER Mission, later wrote:

'The loss of such a fine leader as Captain Britton is a grievous one to us all. At all times during this operation his leadership and personality have been dynamic and infectious. He has at all times gone out with the guerrillas and personally led many successful attacks. He had absolutely no regard for his own personal safety. The men of this guerrilla force would follow him anywhere and worshipped him. He was fair with them in all things –military and civil. All military commanders with whom he came into contact were greatly impressed with his great work and the help he gave to them at all times and in all things.'

28 June 1945: Recommendation for DSO

This officer was the leader of a party dropped by parachute behind the enemy lines south of Toungoo during March 1945. He rapidly organised a most efficient force of Burmese guerrillas which provided intelligence of great value to Army. Besides this intelligence they carried out numerous offensive actions in the course of which they killed over 200 of the enemy before being overrun by our own troops. Thereafter at Fourteenth Army's request Captain Britton's group carried out their role of the flanks of the Lines of Communications Toungoo-Pegu and continued to provide intelligence of great value besides increasing their roll of enemy up to 600 killed and 28 POWs. Captain Britton was only one of several groups which were organised and launched by Force 136 in this area but his was by far the most successful and this must be attributed to his outstanding powers of leadership and personal bravery. He led his men in a number of actions and it was his example which inspired them to a degree of bravery and perseverance far beyond the usual of men of their elementary training and discipline. I most strongly recommend this officer be awarded the DSO for his outstanding services and bravery in the field.

Downgraded to MC

David Britton was married with two young sons. Mrs Britton with her 7-year-old son Peter received her husband's posthumous MC from the King on 5 November 1945.

LIEUTENANT COLONEL HUGO HOOD, DSO, CROIX DE GUERRE

Hugo Hood

Hugo Hood was born in August 1915, a month before his father was killed on the Western Front. Educated at Wellington, he became a schoolmaster, an occupation that allowed him to play sport, at which he excelled.

Hugo Hood joined SOE in August 1943 and after a frustrating wait in Cairo to be dropped into the Balkans, he volunteered to lead a Jedburgh team into France where he parachuted with PAUL in August 1944. After four months in the Jura, the team was withdrawn and once more Hood volunteered, this time for Burma, where he arrived in early 1945. On 25 January, he was given command of CHEETAH and then in early April took command of ZEBRA. In August 1945, he took over MONGOOSE.

14 September 1945: Recommendation for an immediate DSO

This officer landed by parachute behind the enemy lines in January 1945 and by his personal example and devotion to duty contributed very materially to the organisation and efficiency of the guerrilla forces then operating in the Kuteai area.

On returning from this task he immediately volunteered for further operations and was again dropped by parachute behind enemy lines south of Toungoo at the end of March 1945. On landing he and a small party of guerrillas went on an extremely arduous march over a hundred and twenty miles over the Pegu Yoma [mountain range] to contact and organise local resistance forces in the Tharrawaddy district. Major Hood covered this distance in six days in order to keep to the time limit laid down, and he set about his task with such initiative and drive that from mid-April to the end of May the forces under his command inflicted over 800 casualties on the enemy.

On a number of occasions Major Hood led his men in action against the enemy. Throughout the operation he furnished intelligence of the greatest value to our troops advancing south down the Irrawaddy Valley.

During this whole period his courage, determination and leadership were of the highest order and his initiative and personal example were an inspiration to his men, resulting in a most successful operation.

Awarded

MAJOR RICHARD RUBINSTEIN, MC

Richard Rubinstein was born in London in 1921, and after attending University College School, won a place at Imperial College to read aeronautical engineering. A member of the TA Royal Engineers, he was commissioned in the RA and commanded a searchlight troop in Norfolk. By 1943 he was a Searchlight Battery Training Captain in Wiltshire but wanting to take a more active role in the fighting war, volunteered for SOE. After passing selection and training, on 6/7 August 1944 he dropped into Brittany as the leader of a three-man Jedburgh team, DOUGLAS I. Six weeks later, he dropped for a second time in the Jura area with DOUGLAS II to assist the Maquis in harassing the German lines of communication as the Allied forces advanced north after the invasion of southern France. For his work in France, Rubinstein was mentioned in Despatches and awarded the Croix de Guerre.

Recalled to SOE in London, Rubinstein was posted to Force 136 and on 25 January 1945 dropped with Major Hugo Hood and W/T operator Ken Brown to assist an SOE intelligence group led by Bill Howe and his resistance group of 200 Kachins in the Kutkai area. After distributing the arms which had been dropped with them, Hood and his team started training the guerrillas who by the end of January numbered about 350. Within days, the Kachins were ready for action and the two SOE officers set about organising and supervising attacks on Japanese military targets, mining and shooting up convoys on roads and ambushing jungle tracks. By 7 February, six actions had been fought in which 109 Japanese had been killed, 31 wounded and 42 POW. It was a promising start. In March, after inflicting more casualties on the Japanese, Hood's Jedburgh was ordered out after almost two months behind enemy lines.

Arriving back in Calcutta, Rubinstein, by now a 24-year-old major, was made a team leader and with Dick 'Doc' Livingston, a Rhodesian, who had been with SOE in Greece, and Ken Brown again as W/T operator, dropped [Operation CHIMP] on 9 April 1945 some twenty miles north of Pyinmana. The objective of the team was to report on all Japanese troop movements in order to call in air strikes, contact and arm the local Burman Defence Army resistance, and prepare a drop zone for arms. Within ten days Rubinstein's men had ambushed, captured and killed as many as forty-eight Japanese, including a major general and his staff of six officers; a large amount of documents were also captured and sent to Major Boyt who was the 5th Indian Division's liaison with SOE. By 8 May, after several more successful ambushes, the area was free of enemy and Rubinstein was ordered to withdraw some seventy miles south to the river crossing near Toungoo, where it was expected the Japanese would try to break across and retreat further into Thailand. Here they were to meet another team, Operation REINDEER, and put themselves at their disposal.

Within minutes of arriving at Toungoo, Rubinstein learnt from a runner that REINDEER's commander, Major Dave Britton, had been killed in a firefight whilst scouting along the bank of the Sittang River. He quickly reorganised his forces, taking over REINDEER's mission to collect intelligence on Japanese attempts to cross the Sittang in order to set up air strikes and artillery harassing fire. Keeping Sergeant Brierley, Britton's W/T operator, with him, he sent Livingston with W/T operator Brown to operate CHIMP on the eastern river bank in co-ordination with REINDEER.

During the next two months, Rubinstein's force reported on the troop movements of two Japanese divisions as they concentrated for the breakout across the Sittang. By June, the British had prepared a trap along a twenty mile front of the river and road, waiting for the 10-15,000 strong Japanese force to make their move to cross. When the battle came, it lasted for a week and the Japanese were annihilated; bodies littered the river and its banks and the stench of death was everywhere. Rubinstein estimated in his report that up to 2,500 Japanese were killed by his group of fighters alone, as well as taking over 200 prisoners. Eventually the Japanese surrendered.

7 November 1946: Recommendation for MC

Major Rubinstein was landed by parachute behind the enemy lines in January 1945 and by his initiative, determination and efficiency, contributed materially to the effectiveness of the guerrilla forces then operating in the Kutkai area [of Burma]. On returning in March 1945, he immediately volunteered for further operations, and early in April 1945 was dropped by parachute near Pyinmana. Here, in an area through which large numbers of Japanese troops were passing daily, he quickly organised the local Burmese resistance forces with such success that ten days after landing, he and his forces ambushed a party of the enemy, killing one major general, six officers and seventeen other ranks, the majority of whom were NCOs. From the period 8 April to 8 June, Major Rubinstein's party of guerrillas, operating firstly in the Pyinmana area and later south of Toungoo, inflicted over 400 casualties on the enemy.

The success of the operation was entirely due to Major Rubinstein's initiative, determination and personal courage.

Awarded

CHAPTER FIVE

MALAYA

Political Background

In 1939, the population of Malaya broke down into 2.3m Malays, 2.4m Chinese, 0.75m Indians and about 100,000 British and other Europeans. The Chinese were concentrated mainly in the towns while the Malays were farmers and coastal fishermen.

The epithet 'British Malaya' in 1939 described a set of states on the Malay Peninsula and the Island of Singapore that were brought together under British control between the eighteenth and the twentieth centuries. It included the Straits Settlements, the Federated Malay States and the Unfederated Malay States.

Under British rule, Malaya was one of the most profitable territories of the Empire, being the world's largest producer of tin and rubber.

The Straits Settlements

After securing Singapore from the Dutch through the Anglo-Dutch Treaty of 1824, the British determined to centralise the administration of Penang, Malacca and Singapore. To this end, in 1826, a framework known as the Straits Settlements was established with Penang as its capital. Later, in 1832, the capital was moved to Singapore. While these three holdings formed the core components of the Straits Settlements, Christmas Island, the Cocos Islands, Labuan and Dinding of Perak were all later placed under its authority.

In 1867 the Straits Settlements was declared a crown colony and placed under the Colonial Office in London.

The Federated Malay States

The Federated Malay States – Selangor, Perak, Negeri Sembilan and Pahang – were still ruled by their Sultans but were advised by a State Council, made up of the Resident [or in certain cases by the Secretary to the Resident], native chiefs, and representative[s] of the Chinese community nominated by the Sultan. The council discussed matters of interest for each respective state such as legislative

MALAYA

and administrative issues while the Resident and his staff [mostly consisting of Europeans and Malays] carried out day to day administration.

Along with Perak and Selangor, Negeri Sembilan was a major producer of tin in Malaya.

The Unfederated Malay States

The states of Kedah, Terengganu, Perlis, Kelantan and Johore collectively constituted the Unfederated Malay States and were under indirect British control, having become British protectorates between 1885 and 1909. Britain was responsible for Foreign Policy and defence while the states had control over their domestic affairs. There was no legal commonality.

Labour unrest

In *The British and Rubber in Malaya, c 1890–1940,* Hagan and Wells write: 'Malayan rubber plantations were not only a source of considerable wealth for British companies and their shareholders; they provided the British Government with a strategically essential product in times of war, and in times of peace one which earned valuable overseas credits[58]. The good health of Britain's balance of payments depended in no small measure on exports of Malayan rubber'. In 1940, rubber and tin accounted for eighty per cent of Malayan exports of which fifty-two per cent went to the US, which, paid for in dollars, helped prop up Britain's declining dollar balances.

But all was not well in British administered Malaya. By 1927 the colonial authorities were seriously worried about the subversive potential of the Chinese population. They were right to be so, for the aim of the Communist Party of Malaya [CPM], formed in 1930 by the Comintern representative in South East Asia, Ho Chi Minh, was to overthrow British colonialism, abolish Malay feudalism and set up a Malayan People's Republic. The CPM adopted a multi-ethnic outlook by attempting to recruit Malays, Chinese and Indians, the three major ethnic groups in Malaya, but by 1939 it was mainly Chinese.

The planters and the colonial government in Malaya had to contend with a wave of strikes orchestrated in large part by the CPM through its General Labour Union [GLU]. The strikes began in March 1937 on rubber estates in Selangor and Negri Sambilan and spread to the collieries at Batu Arang. The authorities responded by a massive police presence in the strike areas supported

---

58 By 1913 British capital investments in Malaysia amounted to 40 million Straits dollars and by 1923 it had risen to more than a 100 million. The area under rubber cultivation grew from 20,200 hectares in 1900 to 219,000 in 1919 and 1,320,000 hectares in 1938.

MALAYA

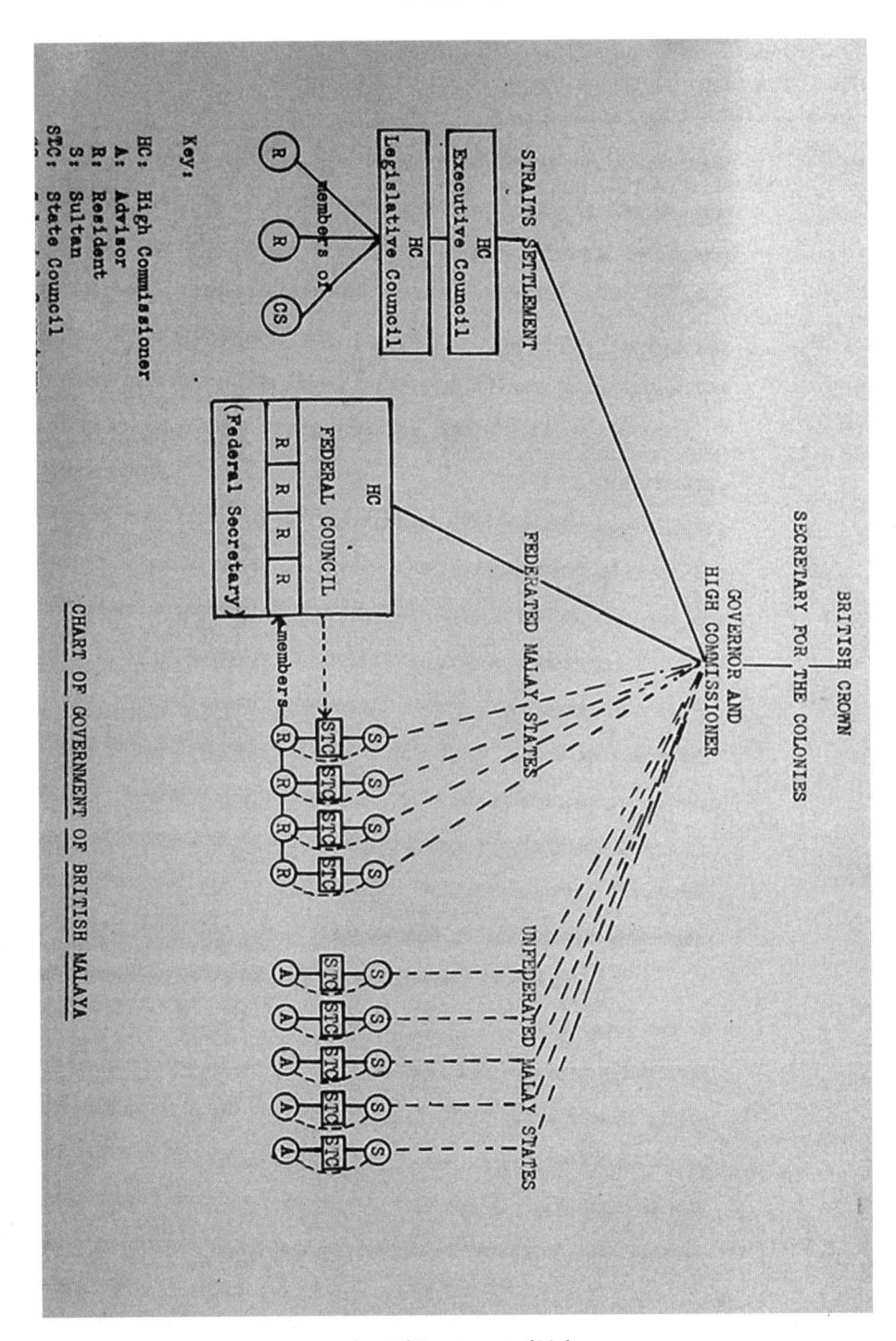

oss chart of Government of Malaya

by armed soldiers from the Punjab Regiment and the Malay Rifles. At one stage, the workers decided to march on Kuala Lumpur to present their grievances directly to the colonial government.

Another wave of unrest followed in 1940, with fifty-seven strikes in the Selangor province alone. The unrest spread to the rubber factories in Singapore and culminated in the occupation of the Firestone plant, when police shot dead two demonstrators and wounded another two. A sit-down strike at the Firestone plant lasted for two months until, on 1 July 1940, the police stormed the factory and ended the occupation. A Colonial Office official calculated that there had been 130 strikes in Singapore alone since the outbreak of the Second World War, hardly surprising given that trade unions were not legalised in Malaya until the eve of the Japanese invasion of 1942 and hence there was no forum for collective bargaining and the arbitration of legitimate grievances.

The ORIENTAL Mission

Once the Japanese had completed their occupation of Malaya in February 1942, little was heard of the ORIENTAL Mission's SBPs other than the news garnered by Davis and Broome when they visited Selangar in February 1942. It later transpired that most of the Europeans had been killed or captured. Only four had evaded capture – Spencer Chapman, Frank Quayle, Robert Chrystal and William Robertson. Some of the other Europeans managed to remain free including J.K. Freer and Pat Noone although the latter died in the jungle in 1944. Cotterill, who had led the Pahang party, which was separate from the stay behind parties, also survived and finally met up with Major A.C. Campbell-Miles's TIDEWAY Mission in September 1945.

MALAYA

Breakdown:

Stay behind party	Area	Composition	Outcome
One Inserted 8 January 1942	Tanjong Malim and Tras	Leader: Major F.S. Chapman	Survived and remained free.
		Frank Vanrenan Planter Lewin Estate FMSVR	Initially escaped to Sumatra, then made way back to Singapore. Returned to Malaya via Sumatra. 15 March 1942 captured, imprisoned Kuala Lumpur, escaped, recaptured at Bentong 2 September and executed 18 September.
		Boris Hembry Planter FMSVR	Initially escaped to Sumatra, then made way back to Singapore. Reached Java with Killery. Returned as ISLD member.
		Ronald Graham Planter Reawood Tin & Rubber Estate FMSVR	Same as Frank Vanrenan
		All the above save FSC initially escaped by fishing boat to Sumatra and then went to Singapore. They then sailed with Warren, Davis and Broome to Bagansiapiapi on east coast of Sumatra to establish a base. Vanrenan and Graham crossed to Selangor hoping to get in touch with Spencer Chapman. Then both were captured.	
		Bill Harvey Planter Gapis Estate FMSVR	Captured, escaped, recaptured and then executed 18 September
		Sgt John Sartin RE [later Lt] demolitions instructor	Captured. Survived war
		An Lam W/T op – STS 101 trained	Not known

Two Inserted 8 January 1942	Benta	Leader: Lt Bill Stubbington Surveyor North Perak	Killed 17 March 1942
		2/Lt Guy Rand Planter	Killed 17 March 1942
		2/Lt Cyril Pearson	Survived as POW
		2/Lt Oliver Darby Planter	Killed 17 March 1942
		2/Lt Edward Elkin, Mining engineer	Survived as POW
		Shukor Bin Uda	Not known
Three Inserted 9 January 1942	Selangor Bentong	2/Lt William Robinson Planter	Died in guerrilla camp in Perak September 1943
		Leader: James 'Pat' Garden NZ Tin miner	Captured. Survived war
		Capt Frank T. Quale I Corps NZ Engineer	Survived in jungle to 1945
		Lt Clark Haywood RNR Engineer	Killed 11 July 1942
		2/Lt Robert Chrystal Planter	Survived. Awarded MC

MALAYA

Four Inserted 14 January 1942	Seremban in Negri Sembilan	Leader: 2/Lt Alfred Wynne Irrigation engineer	All captured
		2/Lt Thomas Cubitt Civil engineer	
		2/Lt Foster Pelton Irrigation engineer	
		2/Lt James Wilson Civil engineer	
		2/Lt William Hardy Engineer	
		2/Lt Edward Berwick Agricultural officer	
		2/Lt Leslie Brown Planter	
		2/Lt Leonard Morrison Civil servant	
Five Inserted 20 January 1942	South east of Labis	Captain Tom Smyllie former OCPD Kedah	Died of illness 21 March 1943
		Lt A.E. 'Scotty' Scott-Skovso [Danish]	Executed 8 July 1943
		2/Lt Leslie Taylor Mining engineer	Died 17 July 1945
		2/Lt Morley Barlow Planter Johol Estate	
Six Inserted 24 January 1942 Later joined by Brian Smith and Jim Wright, escaped POWs Joined Major Johnny Hart's MINT party on 17 April 1945	Near Kluang: ISLD Johore stay behind party tasked to run a secret W/T Station	2/Lt John Reid	
		Major James Barry [Captain Louis Cauvin]	Died 13 July 1944
		Sgt John Cross [later CQMS] DCM	Taken off by submarine 31 May 1945
		Liu Ching Hung	
		Lee Boon, interpreter	
		L/Cpl Wagstaff [later Sgt]	Taken off by submarine 31 May 1945
		Sgn Morter [later Sgt]	Taken off by submarine 31 May 1945

Seven Inserted 27 January 1942	Off road between Kota Tinggi and Mersing	Lt Thomas Mackay Planter	
		2/Lt F.G. Brown Forests	
		2/Lt Roland Thompson Planter	
		2/Lt James Cumming	
		2/Lt R.H. Brown Planter	
		2/Lt H.R. Crawford	
Eight Inserted 29 January 1942	North east Johore Bahru	Lt Dudley 'Jesse' Mathews	Captured in Sumatra. Taken to Padang
		2/Lt James Matheson	See above
		2/Lt Fred Tallant Malayan Prison Service	Captured in Sumatra. Taken to Padang, then Burma
		2/Lt David Thompson	See above
		2/Lt Harold Villiers aka Villars	See above
		2/Lt Ernest McGlashon Tin miner	See above
		2/Lt George Brockman	Captured. Died of dysentery 1943
Nine	Pahang: Kuala Reman rubber estate	J.M. Cotterill Tea planter	Survived.
		B.F. Tyson Tin miner	Died Jan 1943
		J.W. Smith	
		Chinese W/T op	
		Indian soldier	

MALAYA

THE MALAYAN COUNTRY SECTION

In January 1943 Lieutenant Colonel Christopher J.P. Hudson[59] RASC was sent by the INDIA Mission as LO to the Dutch Forces in Ceylon where he set up and directed Group B operations. Innes Tremlett[60] had taken over from Basil Goodfellow as Country Head with Davis, a former policeman, and Broome, a senior civil servant, remaining as advisors.

In 1943, the INDIA Mission began to plan for guerrilla warfare, small scale industrial disruption, and attacks on oil installations and shipping, mindful that at the time Malaya was out of range of its aircraft and the sea approaches extremely dangerous for surface craft. Any operation therefore had to be transported to and from Malaya by submarine. Not surprisingly, keen competition developed between ISLD and SOE for scarce RN submarine resources, on occasions leading to friction.

It was also clear that the Malayan Communist Party [CPM], a hitherto illegal organisation as far as the British were concerned, now constituted the only viable partner in forming a credible resistance movement, particularly since the CPM had aligned itself with the Allies after the German invasion of Russia. The Malays and Tamils had shown little interest in fighting the Japanese and had no underground organisation to speak of.

The first operation by SOE planners – GUSTAVUS – had four elements to it:
- To establish a submarine link between Ceylon and Malaya
- To create an intelligence system
- To contact guerrilla forces
- To find survivors of the 1942 stay behind parties

John Davis came ashore in a folboat launched from a Dutch submarine on 24 May 1943 at Tanjong [cape] Hantu in the Pangkor-Lumut area with five Chinese agents. As Trenowden writes, 'it was, in fact, the first Allied landing since the British had been kicked out of Malaya only fifteen months before'. He acquired a junk and successfully rendezvoused offshore with GUSTAVUS 2 on 25 June which was bringing Dick Broome and Claude Fenner, a former Assistant Superintendent in the Straits Settlement Police, to join him. As Davis considered that more time was needed to prepare for the infiltration of agents, they all returned on the submarine to Ceylon, leaving the junk in the hands of a Chinese.

---

59 Like Mackenzie, the Oxford educated 36-year-old Hudson was a former employee of J&P Coats, having been Executive Director of The Central Agency Ltd, its selling company.
60 Later killed in an air crash in 1945 together with staff officer Lt Col Dan Norton MC. Bickham Sweet-Escott viewed it as a disaster for he would have been 'invaluable to those who had to deal with Malaya in the subsequent emergency'.

Davis returned on 4 August with Fenner as conducting officer on GUSTAVUS 3, making a second successful rendezvous with the junk.

The political situation had changed. The original CPM grouping of left-wing parties, The Anti-Enemy Backing-Up Society [AEBUS] had been replaced by the Anti-Japanese Army [AJA] which operated from camps deep in the jungle and was supplied by the Anti-Japanese Union with money and food. Together the two organisations were known as The Anti-Japanese Union and Forces [AJUF].

Davis was now joined by Broome on GUSTAVUS 4 in late September and they moved with Chen Ping to a camp at Blantan in the jungle east of Bidor in the Perak Hills for better security and closer proximity to the guerrillas. On Christmas Day, they were joined by Spencer Chapman just in time for the first AJUF conference, held on 31 December. Chang Hung representing the AJUF and CPM[61] confirmed that when the invasion came they would take their orders from the Allied CinC. He then went on to give the SOE party details of the strength and dispositions of guerrilla units throughout the Peninsula. Although Lim[62] Bo Seng had arrived in early November on GUSTAVUS 5 to accelerate the construction of the intelligence network, GUSTAVUS 6 – Major Harrison – had been aborted in December when the shore party could find no sign of the post box, and the Emergency GUSTAVUS 6 [Claude Fenner and Jim Hannah] which successfully picked up a Chinese agent on 5 January 1945 – the later notorious Chin Peng – was premature to collect Chang Hung's information.

The six GUSTAVUS operations had in fact achieved very little other than to land two British officers on the mainland of Malaya and in the later stages provide them with two B Mark II W/T sets.

So while two objectives had been met – the submarine link proven and contact established with guerrilla groups – the intelligence network was still being set up by Wu Chye Sin [Codename Ah Ng]. Having recruited a ring of agents and placed them in strategic areas, disaster overtook Ah Ng when a key member of the network was arrested in Ipoh and then, soon after, the agent who managed the submarine rendezvous was also picked up. From here on the network was compromised and effectively out of action.

On 13 April 1944, Spencer Chapman left to go in search of Pat Noone. It turned out to be a fruitless and dangerous journey and he returned to the GUSTAVUS Mission on 25 July after 103 tormenting days in the jungle.

---

61 And it later turned out also the Japanese!
62 Lim was the head of wealthy family with brick and biscuit manufacturing firms in Singapore. Known for his anti-Japanese views, he arrived in India in late 1942. With his excellent KMT connections, he was able to recruit Malayan Chinese from Chungking.

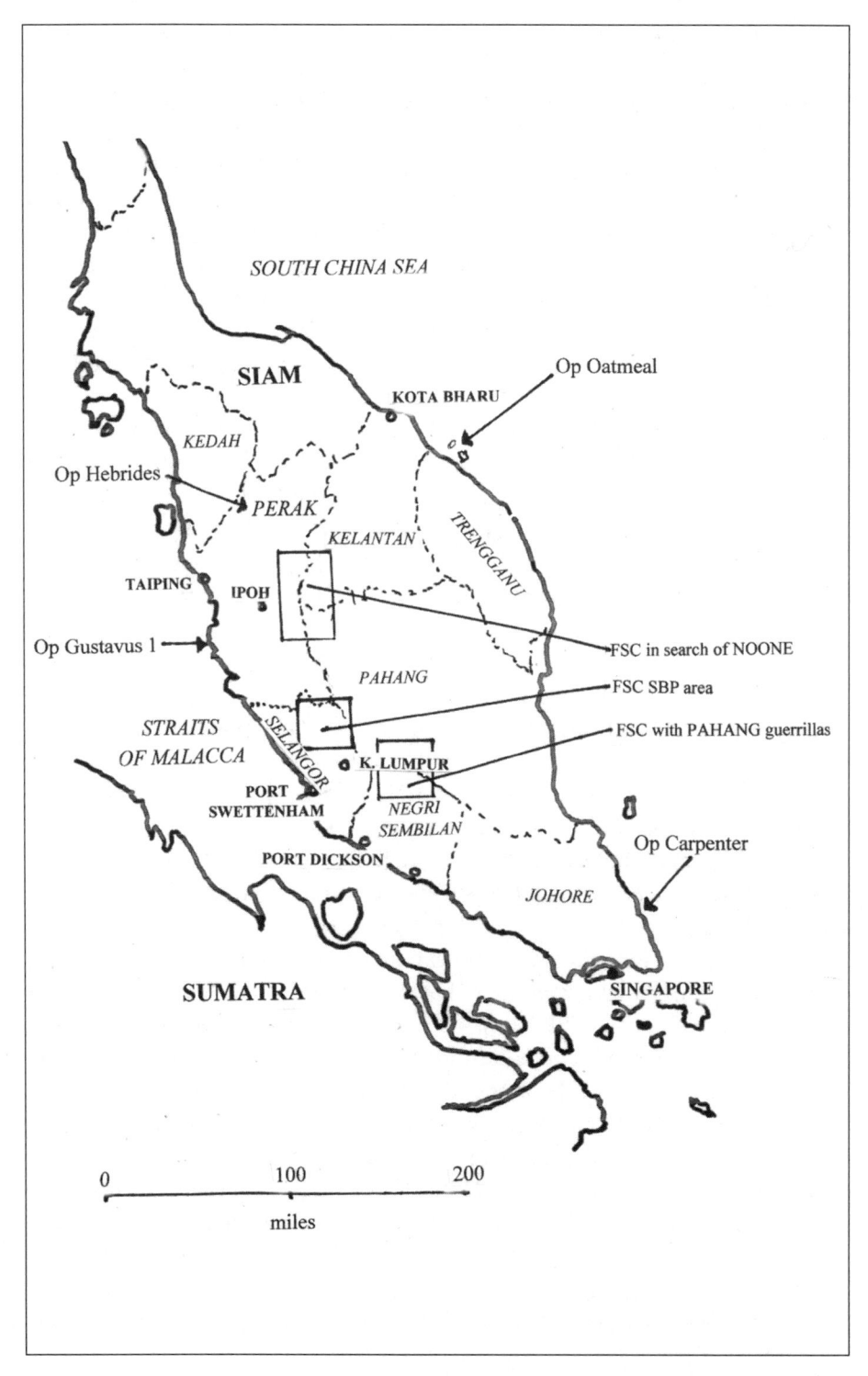

MALAYA

W/T communications had still not been established with the INDIA Mission. No one knew whether Davis and Broome were even alive. REMARKABLE 1 [Capt PG Dobrée and a Chinese W/T operator] and REMARKABLE 2 [Fenner and Hannah], both submarine-borne missions with W/T equipment and other stores, had both returned to Ceylon after failing to identify any recognition signals at the RVs; REMARKABLE 3 in April had a similar experience and only managed to put two Chinese agents ashore by folboat in what was a blind landing. In June REMARKABLE 4, which included the head of Malaya Country Section, Ian Tremlett, attempted to RV with these two, but yet again no recognition signals were seen. SOE now decided to suspend the REMARKABLE series and to try and infiltrate agents overland. This came to nothing.

In May, Davis and Broome managed to collect some W/T equipment that had been earlier hidden and found two W/T sets in good working order but no batteries or charging engine. It was not until 1 February 1945 that Colombo picked up the first GUSTAVUS transmission officially confirming its existence, although the CARPENTER Mission in South Johore had told the Malayan Country Section on 16 December that Davis and Broome were safe.

*****

Within a few weeks, Major Jim Hannah's FUNNEL Mission dropped to GUSTAVUS. Davis summoned a second conference with Chang Hung once more representing AJUF. It was agreed that AJUF 'regiments' would each receive a British Liaison Officer [BLO] and each patrol a Patrol Liaison Team. AJUF would remain independent but after D-Day, act on orders of the Allied CinC through Group Liaison officers. Finance and medical arrangements were also discussed.

Access to the comparatively secure east coast of Malaya was best facilitated from Australia and it was from there that the submarine HMS *Telemachus* had sailed with the CARPENTER Mission[63], a large mission of five British officers including Majors Reddish and Sime and seven agents led by Major W.B. 'Paddy' Martin, to the coast of South Johore. After landing on 5 October 1944, the ferry party did not manage to make it back to the RV, so the size of the Mission exponentially increased. Although able to provide useful coast watching intelligence on Japanese shipping movements, CARPENTER was a long way from the main AJUF force. After Martin was killed on 25 January when the Japanese attacked

---

63 CARPENTER had caused quite a rumpus with the OSS who wanted to send their own parties JUKEBOX I and JUKEBOX II to the east coast of Malaya. SOE had to lean on P Division to postpone them indefinitely.

his camp at Kambau [Johore] after an airdrop the previous evening, CARPENTER 2 [Major J.V. Hart] arrived to reinforce the Mission in February 1945; likewise, CARPENTER 3 arrived in May with three more officers and sixteen Royal Marines. From now on it was able to continue its tasks of coast watching and organizing local levies to prepare for the invasion.

PONTOON under Major George Leonard, together with Captain Leslie Chapman and Captain Noel Robinson, parachuted into Pahang on 24 February 1945 to make contact with the Sixth Regiment of Chinese Guerrillas. This involved a 250 miles trek across some of the most rugged and inhospitable country in Malaya. Leonard was ideally suited for this demanding role. Born in Conoor in India in 1909, he had joined the India Police aged twenty and then transferred to the Malaya Game Department where he was a warden for five years. In 1939, he was commissioned in the FMSVF and attached to 9th Indian Division. Still at peace, he left Kota Bharu on leave to Australia where by the time he arrived war had broken out. He immediately enlisted in the Australian Military Forces [AMF] and after a stint with Z Special Unit had joined Force 136 in August 1944.

Although the Chinese represented by far the largest component of the anti-Japanese resistance, SOE recognised that the Malays must not be seen to have been excluded by the Allies from playing their part and so the LIKEWISE Mission was sent in by submarine in August 1944 commanded by Captain Dobrée with Captain Ibrahim bin Ismail and four Malays. It failed to make land, so it was reconstituted as LIKEWISE 2 [Dobrée] and OATMEAL [Ibrahim]. Inserted by Catalina, OATMEAL was subsequently captured and from then on, a cat and mouse game was played out between the Japanese, who had Ibrahim [codename VIOLIN] 'under control', and D Division [Lieutenant Colonel Peter Fleming], who knew he was operating his W/T set under duress. By the time of the Japanese surrender, it was not clear whether either side had gained a decisive advantage but Ibrahim[64] was recognised by the British with a MBE.

SOE had not given up trying to establish a link with the Malay resistance and Dobrée was dropped blind with the HEBRIDES Mission[65] east of Grik in North Perak. W/T communications were immediately established and soon Dobrée had thirty agents operating, some as far away as Singapore. Volunteers proved easy and plentiful to recruit and after selecting 100 of the best, Dobrée formed the Loyal Malay Army. Three other SOE Missions went in to recruit more Malays – FIGHTER under Major G.A. Hasler in Kedah; BEACON under

---

64 Later General Ibrahim bin Ismail Chief of the Armed Forces Staff of Malaysia.
65 An OSS Mission – CAIRNGORN – had tried to drop in the same area on 27 November 1944 but the aircraft had to turn back due to low fuel. On 6 December, the four-man Mission dropped successfully.

Major 'Doug' J.A. Richardson in Pahang; and MULTIPLE under Major Derek Headley to the east of Raub [in Pahang].

Meanwhile Broome and Spencer Chapman were finally extracted by the submarine HMS *Statesman* on 13 May 1945.

The conundrum of whether to arm the AJUF exercised SOE London and SEAC as well as the Malayan Country Desk. On balance, SEAC believed that the military advantages outweighed the political risks and once this was tacitly endorsed by the Chiefs of Staff in London, Operation ZIPPER, the invasion of Malaya, was brought forward from December to August 1945. Suddenly, SOE were under intense pressure to train and arm its guerrilla bands that would be sent into action at the time of the invasion.

Experienced Group Liaison Officers as promised by Davis to the AJUF were now dropped. The SOE support to the Malayan People's Anti-Japanese Army [MPAJA] in August 1945 was as follows:

Area	Group Leader	AJA Leader	Patrol Liaison Officers
Group 1 Selangar	Lt Col D.K. Broadhurst Dropped 30 May 1945	Ay Yau aka Po Lui	Major Hunter Major Thomson Walker Major Maxwell Captain MacDonald Captain Heine
Group 2 Negri Sembilan	Major C.R. Fenner Dropped 18 June 1945	Teng Fook Loong	Major Olsen [A.S.] Major Olsen [P.A.] Captain White Major Gibson
Group 3 North Johore	Major A.C. Campbell-Miles Dropped 26 June 1945	Lee Sang	Major MacKenzie Captain Wilkinson Major Benoit
Group 4 South Johore	Lt Col I.S. Wylie		Major Trevaldwyn Major Reddish Major Sime Captain Newell Captain Wright

MALAYA

Group 5 Perai	Major J. Hannah Dropped 26 February 1945	ITU	Major Harrison Captain Greet Major Owen Major Alexander Major Wilson
Group 6 West Pehang	Major G.R. Leonard Dropped 24 February 1945	Wu Ling Ming	Captain Robinson Captain Chapman
Group 7 East Pehang	Lt Col F.S. Chapman		
Group 8 Kedah	Major J.R. Hislop	Long Fu, Chen Lo and Lee Mint	Major Latham Captain Wight Major Landes Major Chassé
Operation HEBRIDES Lenggong, Kg Habi and Kg Jeli	Lt Col P.G. Dobrée	Hong Ghee, Tai Man, Lee Fong Sam, Wong Shin, Ah Weng	Major Clifford Captain Creer
	Col R. Musgrove		

These men would have control of more than 4,000 armed AJUF fighters and several thousand auxiliaries[66]. At the time of the Japanese surrender, Force 136 had over ninety British officers and forty-eight W/T sets in the field, together with six Ghurkha Special Groups, consisting of two British officers and sixteen Ghurkha ORs[67].

Operation ZIPPER, the invasion of Malaya, finally took place on 9 September one week after VJ Day. It was unopposed and British troops were in Kuala Lumpur by 13 September 1945.

The strength of Group B HQ in Colombo at the war end was 29 officers, 17 ORs, 25 Indian ORs, 266 FANY and 58 civilians.

SOE's sister organisation in Australia, the Services Reconnaissance Department, although it reported to the CinC SWPA and not SEAC, was allowed to launch two operations against the Japanese in Malaya. On 9 August

---

66 Colin Mackenzie gave a figure of 2,800 armed and trained by the time of VJ Day, leaving another 700 to meet the planning target. Ian Tremlett calculated 2,481. A total of 4,601 small arms were dropped.
67 Ian Trenowden gives a total of 371 people infiltrated into Malaya of which 120 were British officers, 56 British ORs, 9 Canadian Chinese, 70 Asiatics and 134 Ghurkha all ranks.

1943 Operation JAYWICK [Captain Ivan Lyon and Lieutenant Duncan Davidson with two officers and ten ORs] sailed 2,000 miles to Singapore where the assault group in three two-man folboats sank seven Japanese ships with Limpet mines. All made it back to Australia with no casualties after forty-seven days at sea. In September 1944, a repeat attack codenamed Operation RIMAU was launched, when Lyon and twenty-three men were infiltrated into the target area on a converted mine laying submarine. It was a highly complex operation, depending on the capture of an ocean-going junk and the use of new Sleeping Beauty submersible canoes to approach the harbour defences. A chance encounter with an enemy patrol boat compromised the operation and all participants were either killed or captured and subsequently executed.

LIEUTENANT COLONEL FREDDY SPENCER CHAPMAN, DSO and Bar

Freddy Chapman

Freddy Spencer Chapman, destined to become SOE's best known Far East warrior, got off to a bad start in life: his mother died a month after he was born and his father, after being defrauded by his clerk, became an undischarged bankrupt solicitor. Leaving his two small sons in the care of elderly relatives in the Lake District, Frank Spencer Chapman left for a new life in Canada. Fortunately for Freddy, his guardians were both kind and erudite, allowing him the freedom of the hills tempered by a strict religious upbringing. In 1915, Frank, who at the age of forty-two had enlisted as a private in the Canadian army, paid a brief visit to see his sons in the Lakes; it was to be his last for he was killed at Ypres in October the following year. Thanks to a legacy left by his mother, Freddy was sent to Clevedon House Preparatory School in Yorkshire and then to Sedburgh School in Cumbria, where despite his unconventional behaviour of eschewing team sports and roaming the woods and fells whenever he had a chance, he was allowed to thrive as an individual. In 1926 he went up to Cambridge to read Natural Sciences and Mathematics at St John's.

After an unremarkable undergraduate career save for some high jinks climbs around the buttresses of chapels and colleges as befitted a member of the Cambridge Mountaineering Club, he came down in 1929 and joined an expedition to Iceland to study plants and bird life for Kew Gardens and the National History Museum respectively. Ironically, given his later wartime experience, it was funded by the Japanese Prince, Hashisuka, a keen ornithologist. With his love of nature, self-reliance and sense of adventure, Chapman set off from Leith with two fellow students and after a memorable month spent in the wild north west of the island, he returned home to consider his future. Mulling over the options of either teaching or entering the Sudan Civil Service, he went skiing in Davos in November 1929 where fate decided his future. On the ski slopes he met an old Cambridge friend, Gino Watkins, who had led the Cambridge expedition to Spitzbergen two years before. Asked whether he would like to go to Greenland, Chapman replied: 'Right you are. Why?' The answer was the 1930 British Arctic Air Route Expedition to discover whether the future of transatlantic flying lay in an Arctic route.

In July 1930, the expedition sailed into Angmagssalik on the east coast of Greenland to start its ground surveys and most important to set up a weather station on the highest point of the Greenland ice cap. No British expedition had wintered in the Arctic for the last fifty years. Chapman teamed up with Augustine Courtauld and the two set off by whaleboat to survey the coast to the north. He was soon in his element as navigator and hunter, shooting two aggressive polar bears during the trip. After returning to Angmagssalik, Chapman set off on 26 October with a five man team to the weather station, 150 miles away. The idea was to leave Courtauld and another team member, Lawrence Wager, to man it for the duration of the winter. Atrocious weather almost forced them to abandon their journey, but after thirty-nine gruelling days they reached the station in time to relieve the two men who had spent the last eight weeks there. Courtauld insisted on being left on his own; he considered it too hazardous to risk two lives. Leaving him with enough supplies to last until April, Chapman led the team back, again through treacherous weather, and delivered them safely to Angmagssalik after a round trip of fifty-four days.

The relief team which had set off in mid-February to take over from Courtauld had been on the ice cap for forty days, unable to find the weather station which had been completely snowed under by storms, effectively entombing its occupant. Finally driven back by the weather, their supplies exhausted, they returned to Angmagssalik to sound the alarm. Watkins having radioed the expedition committee in England with a report, immediately set off with Chapman and John Rymill with enough supplies for five weeks. After twelve days of sledging fourteen hours a day, they finally located the weather station on 5 May and found Courtauld alive and well in a nine foot hole. Little did they know that the fate of Courtauld had been the leading story in *The Times* and when they returned to England, Watkins asked Chapman to write the official account of the expedition, later published as *Northern Lights*.

The following summer, in July 1932, Chapman again headed for Greenland on Gino Watkins's new Arctic air route expedition funded by Pan-Am, the

Royal Geographical Society and *The Times*, confident in making his mark through expedition writing and photography with a part-time job at Cambridge or the British Museum. For someone with no personal financial means at all, it was a modest and attainable way of life to make ends meet while living dangerously. The four-man expedition, Watkins, Chapman, Rymill and Quentin Riley, reached Angmagssalik on 2 August where to his surprise and delight Chapman discovered he was a father to a small boy, courtesy of his Eskimo girlfriend Gertrude. Dropped off at Lake Fjord with enough supplies to last them through the winter, the expedition was overtaken by tragedy when Gino Watkins drowned while out hunting for seals alone in his kayak. After returning to Angmagssalik to break the news to the world, the remaining three expedition members set off again to Lake Fjord. With Eskimo guides, they survived till May with a mid-winter replenishment trip by Chapman and Rymill to Angmagssalik for more dogs. Then Chapman was left on his own, entirely self-sufficient and living off wild plants and any animals he could shoot or catch. He was in his element and it was not until late September 1933 that he finally sailed for England.

A well received new book, *Watkins' Last Expedition*, allowed Chapman to buy a Lagonda and drive to the Alps for a summer climbing season. Then he began a teaching job at Aysgarth preparatory school in Yorkshire. In the spring of 1934, he went with a friend[68] to Lapland intending to drive a reindeer sledge on a cross country compass bearing for 150 miles. It was a typically rugged and uncomfortable expedition which perfectly matched Chapman's expectations. In a letter to fellow Arctic explorer Sandy Glen, he wrote 'we had no tracks sometimes and bad weather; we slept in a tent, were hungry – in fact we had all the discomforts we had hoped for!' That summer, when climbing in the Lake District, he bumped into an old Cambridge friend, Marco Pallis, who asked him to join him in a Himalayan expedition. An unequivocal Yes saw Chapman sail from England in February 1936 and by 8 April, having selected their porters, the expedition left Gangtok for Lachen twenty miles to the north west on 8 April. Their objective was the Simvu Massif where there were two unclimbed peaks: Pyramid Peak at 23,750 feet and, on the same ridge, The Sphinx at 22,890 feet. Ten miles to the east was another peak, The Flute, which they planned to climb if they had time.

On their way up to the Massif, they had met Jock Harrison, a subaltern in the Punjabis who had set out on a climbing trip with another officer who had since fallen ill. Chapman and Jake Cooke welcomed him into their team but it was not

---

68 He asked Andrew Croft to join them but he was already committed to Sandy Glen's expedition to Spitzbergen.

until 5 June that they were able to make their assault on the summit of the Sphinx which they reached at 11.00 hrs that day. From it, they could see Everest, Lhotse and Makalu above the clouds in the west, a magnificent view to reward the first men on the summit. They then set off for the Flute on 11 June which they conquered, albeit briefly due to bad weather. Descending to Lachen, Chapman found instructions waiting for him to join Basil Gould, the Resident for the Indian Government's relations with Sikkim, Bhutan and Tibet, in Gangtok for a Mission to Tibet to mediate the return of the Tashi, the ruling lama who had fled to China. In less than eighteen hours, Chapman covered fifty miles, dropping 7,000 feet and climbing 5,000 feet. The trek normally took four days.

Gould had employed Freddy as a general factotum for the Mission, acting as secretary, cipher clerk, photographer, naturalist and surveyor. The other principal member, Brigadier Neame VC, was there to advise the Tibetans on general military matters. Supported by two signal lieutenants, they set out for Lhasa at the end of July 1936 but on arrival Chapman soon became bored and decided to accompany an army officer on his return journey to India and to turn around when they had met up with his replacement who was already on his way. The new officer, Major Finch, instantly took to Chapman and the two greatly enjoyed each other's company on the way back to Lhasa which they reached in time for the Tibetan New Year on 12 February 1937.

The mission returned to India the same month but when he reached Calcutta, Chapman found himself hankering after the unclimbed 24,000 feet Chomolhari which he has passed on the road to Lhasa. As luck would have it, he met Charles Crawford, who had taught at Sedburgh and was now working for ICI in India. Although not an experienced mountaineer, Crawford was fit and easily persuaded; the two reached Kalimpong on 6 May and eight days later set up base camp at 17,500 feet, just below the snowline. As they approached the summit, Crawford declared he was all 'used up', so Chapman carried on alone with one Sherpa, Pasang. Bad weather forced them to bivouac at 21,500 feet, but the next day, in perfect sunshine, they reached the summit. Their descent was perilous, both falling 500 feet at one stage, and after an epic journey through appalling conditions they finally reached Phari and an extremely worried Crawford. The ascent of Chomolhari was later written up by Chapman in *Memoirs of a Mountaineer*. He left India for England in June and, after a winter with the Courtaulds on their yacht *Virginia* in the Far East, found a post at Gordonstoun, the progressive Scottish school founded by the educationalist Kurt Hahn. In charge of expeditions as well as teaching geography and history, close to the mountains and the sea, it was the perfect job for Chapman with one exception – war intervened.

*****

With his Arctic credentials, he was posted to the 5th Scots Guards and sent to Chamonix for winter warfare training with the Chasseurs Alpines. The intended deployment to Finland was overtaken by events and after another sojourn in Chamonix, this time to recce a training area for a mountain division earmarked for Norway, Chapman ended up at the STS in Lochailort as a fieldcraft instructor. With unusual foresight, the decision was made to set up a Lochailort clone in Australia and Chapman, together with Major Mike Calvert RE, were despatched to Wilson's Promontory training area in Victoria as demolitions and fieldcraft instructors. Major Jim Gavin, who knew Chapman from Lochailort had meanwhile been posted from Australia to Singapore to set up STS 101 in May 1941 and as soon as he had it up and running, he requested Chapman to be posted in as his 2 i/c. He arrived on 8 September 1941, the beginning of an uninterrupted tour of duty which lasted to 19 May 1945.

The ORIENTAL Mission's priority was to train SBPs to be positioned throughout the Malayan peninsula to harass Japanese lines of communication should they invade the country and buy time until 'Fortress Singapore' could be reinforced. Chapman thought that six was the ideal number for such parties; the party could be divided into two groups of three and stage snap ambushes at night with the ability to withdraw quickly and almost invisibly.

Soon theory was turned into practice. Chapman was ordered north with Sergeant Sartin RE to Kuala Lumpur to organise SBPs. With Colonel Alan Warren, they reached Kuala Lumpur on 22 December where they found that all the Chinese anti-Japanese societies were united under CPM leadership as in Singapore. At a conference convened by Dally, the head of Special Branch FMS Police and attended by John Davis and Chapman as the SOE representatives, fifteen areas were chosen to insert parties of ten Chinese guerrillas, each under two CPM members who were to be trained in a new STS [102] at the old Chunjin Chinese school. Although open for business on 3 January, STS 102 was disbanded before even the first course had completed its training.

In Kuala Lumpur, Chapman was introduced to Frank Vanrenan and Bill Harvey, both rubber planters, who had been recruited by Colonel Alan Warren together with two more planters, Ronald Graham and Boris Hembry. With the party now at full complement, two stores dumps were established on either side of the main range of mountains which separated Pahang in the east from Selangor in the west, one at an old gold mining camp at Sungei Sempan near Raub and the other at a tin mining camp on the Behrang estate. On 3 January 1942, with the Japanese fast closing, Chapman ordered Graham and Hembry to join Vanrenan at the tin mining camp; en route they collected two more recruits, Bob Chrystal and Bill Robinson, both veterans of the First World War. Gavin was rushing around organising more groups under Pat Garden and Captain Stubbington, delivering stores of weapons, ammunition and explosives to jungle hideouts. At this critical moment, Chapman went down with benign tertiary malaria and all Gavin could do was drop him off at Sungei Sempan before returning to Kuala Lumpur to supervise last minute demolitions.

Now began a trek which was to become almost a daily feature for Chapman over the next three years. The distance between the gold mining camp and Vanrenan's group at the tin mine was fifteen miles as the crow flies, albeit divided by a 6,000-foot ridge of primary jungle. Loaded with Tommy guns and ammunition, Chapman, Harvey and Sartin set off on what they had reckoned to be a five day journey. Twelve days later they straggled into Vanrenan's camp only to find that his group had gone[69]. Now they were down to three men, all exhausted and weakened by their recent arduous cross-country march. Fortunately the two Chinese who had helped Chapman establish the camp in the first place were still in the vicinity and one of them, Leu Kim, recognised Chapman and put his house and victuals at his disposal. It was now time to go on the offensive.

With blackened faces and dressed in white shirts with sarongs around their waists and a dirty white cloth wrapped round their heads, the three Englishman managed to pass as Tamils as they approached their targets. On 3 February they laid charges on two railway bridges, wrecking one locomotive and two days later repeated the exercise, this time putting two locomotives out of action. Chapman then switched his attention to laying ambushes and booby traps on Route One which went from Singapore to the Thai border. Over the next ten days, using more than 1,000lbs of explosive and over 100 hand grenades, Chapman's best guess was that they cut the railway line in sixty places, destroyed forty vehicles and killed or wounded between 500 and 1,500 Japanese troops. It was quite a tally for three men. On 15 February, Chapman decided to withdraw back across the Main Range to the gold mining camp. When they arrived, they were greeted by the news of the fall of Singapore. From now on, they were on their own, the whole of the Malayan peninsula now behind enemy lines. With no W/T set, there was no hope of rescue or resupply: soon, Chapman was posted 'missing, believed killed'.

The first objective for Chapman was to get to India where he intended to raise a larger and better trained force to return to Malaya when the time came.

---

69 Graham, Vanrenen and Hembry met up with a well-disciplined sub-unit of Argyll & Sutherland Highlanders and escaped on a fishing boat to Fort Bagansiapiapi in Sumatra from where they made their way to Singapore. Vanrenen and Graham returned to Malaya to look for Spencer Chapman but were captured.

While his group was resting up, preparing themselves for the dangerous journey to the coast, they were joined by Pat Garden and Clarke Haywood, part of another SBP which had come to look for them. Chapman agreed to go back to Sungei Gow with them to collect the rest of their group and after brazenly cycling dressed in British army uniforms through Japanese controlled towns and villages, they reached the camp where Chapman met the rubber planters, Chrystal and Robinson, for the first time. They now set off on bicycles with food and ammunition strapped to the handlebars back to Sungei Sempan where Chapman divided the party into two; he would go first with Haywood, Chrystal and Robinson: Harvey, Garden, Quayle and Sartin would follow two nights later.

Luck, which so far had been on the side of the SBPs, now deserted them. Mechanical breakdowns meant that Chapman's party split in two, he and Haywood going ahead. In the ensuing delays, the second party lost touch and, with the exception of Quayle, were all captured and taken to Pudu jail in Kuala Lumpur where they found Vanrenan, Graham, Elkin and Pearson. Vanrenan later organised a breakout but all were recaptured including Harvey and Graham. They were executed on 18 September 1942. Meanwhile Chapman and Haywood, after meeting local Communist guerrillas, had moved to the Ulu Slim Communist base run by Chin Peng, completing a twenty mile trip in a week. Chrystal, Robinson and Quayle arrived there on 6 April. Somehow, five members of Chapman's group had managed to reunite, this time under the protection of the CPM. Within days, Chapman received an invitation to meet the head of the CPM at the Batu Caves camp fifty miles away. Accompanied by Haywood it took him a fortnight to get there and on arrival Chapman was introduced to six British soldiers, four privates and two sergeants[70], all acutely suffering from beriberi. No sooner had they settled in, the camp was attacked by the Japanese, forcing them to disperse and build a new camp. By now it was May and Chapman decided to return to the Sungei Gow dump to retrieve a W/T set and also the stack of ammunition and explosive.

The fifty-mile journey by bicycle ended in disaster when Chapman was shot in the calf by a Malayan police patrol and by the time he reached Sungei Gow with Haywood and their two Chinese guides, he was showing the symptoms of acute pneumonia. Haywood then went down with a fever and it was only after five weeks that the two were strong enough to travel, this time by car to an

---

70 Sergeants Regan and Meldrum who had been sent by SOE to watch the east coast railway at Kuala Krai. Meldrum soon died of sickness. The four privates were two gunners, one called Baker, and two Argyll and Sutherland Highlanders, Docherty and Scott, both of whom had VD. Chapman established that Regan died of exposure in September 1942, Baker died of malaria and the three others died soon after.

CPM camp at Menchis, twenty-five miles south of Karak. Once more, disaster struck when they almost ran into an approaching Japanese truck. Both vehicles stopped and in the ensuing melee, Haywood was killed and Chapman shot in his left arm. After a desperate fourteen-mile march, all the time suffering from amoebic dysentery – at one stage it took him nine hours to cover three miles – he finally made it on 13 June to the CPM camp, the home of No. 6 Independent Anti-Japanese Regiment.

With his injured leg still weak and the gunshot wound in his arm not yet healed, still ill with dysentery, he was in no fit state to continue his journey and settled down to daily camp life with its lectures and training periods. But life was never safe as he discovered when out hunting one day when he was peppered in his right thigh and buttock by a shotgun blast. It transpired that it was a planned attempt to kill him; three Chinese traitors were brought into the camp and two disposed of with bayonets. The third managed to escape, which meant they had to move camp immediately six miles to the north west and then again in November, this time twelve miles north east to Mentakab.

In October 1942, Chapman had received a letter by courier from Chrystal, saying that Robinson and Quayle had been very ill and that he had met the anthropologist Pat Noone and was planning to move north with him. He also got word of two Englishmen, Cotterrill and Tyson, living with 'bandits' near Segamat to the south of the state border with Johore. Fortuitously his CPM hosts asked him to move south in November to train two patrols at Triang but when he arrived there, his legs were a mass of ulcers caused by swamp grass and thorns. 'I had about twenty stinking and suppurating sores the size of a shilling and a quarter of an inch deep'. It was six weeks before Chapman could walk properly and it was not until New Year's Day 1943 that he met up with Cotterrill and Tyson in Johore. Much to his sorrow, Tyson died a week later.

The 'bandits' or non-CPM guerrillas implored Chapman to stay on and train them to fight the Japanese but he had already undertaken to train the next 200-strong cadre at Mentakab, so left on 9 January to return to Triang. Yet again, ulcers on his legs laid him low for a month and it was only when he had recovered in March, that he was asked by the CPM leader in Negri Sembilan to visit his camp where an Argyll sergeant had asked to see him. Andy Young had been on the run since January 1941 and had been with the Communists for about a year, most of the time suffering from one jungle illness or another. However, in the intervals when he was fit, he had trained the guerrillas in minor tactics and personally led several attacks against the Japanese. After a four day march, Chapman reached Young[71] who perked up considerably, just in

---

71 Young died of fever in early 1944.

time, for they were then chased around the jungle by the Japanese for a week. Then came a message from the CPM in Perak; Chapman was required to proceed immediately to their main camp to meet 'someone of importance'. It took him four months to reach the camp on the Seroi River during which time he suffered incessantly from recurring malaria.

The 'someone of importance' was Chin Peng, who told him on Christmas Eve that Majors Davis and Broome who had landed that autumn by submarine, were waiting for him at the Blantan camp less than three hours march away. Brought up to speed on Force 136 and the world situation, Chapman then found himself sitting down in January 1944 with Broome and Davis at a meeting with Lai Tek, the Secretary General of the CPM, to thrash out the niceties of a post-war Malaya where somehow the British and CPM would co-exist peacefully. This was something of a non-event since the British officers did not have access to a W/T set, although two B Mark IIs had been cached on the coast. It was a question of waiting, made even more frustrating by the news that Davis's intelligence network had been rolled up by the Japanese and the April submarine RV programme compromised.

Eager to get out and about, Chapman jumped at the opportunity to search for Pat Noone and Bob Chrystal when Frank Quayle arrived at the camp and said that no one had heard from either of them for over a year. It was the sort of challenge Chapman yearned for, a one-man expedition through the high jungles of the Main Range of central Malaya in the wild country of the Orang Asli, described by Peter Dobrée as 'people of the forest who lived their lives ... untouched by the laws of the land or the religion of the village people'. He left on 13 April 1944 and, as he approached Grik, found himself in the company of pro-Japanese Chinese determined to betray him. Making a quick getaway, he then ran into a hunter force of 200 Japanese troops and was taken prisoner. Asked whether he knew a Colonel Chapman, he replied he was his elder brother and that he had heard he had been killed near Pahang. Chapman played his captors to a tee and lulled by the lowly status of their prisoner, they failed to spot him stealing out of the camp at 01.00 hrs. For the next eighty-five hours he was constantly on the move, only resting for an hour or two to get the measure of his pursuers. From then on, helped by the Orang Asli and Chinese, both civilians and AJA, he made his way back to Blantan where he finally arrived in July, 103 days after he had set out. He never found Noone.

To his amazement, W/T contact had still not been established with Ceylon and as long as this problem continued, camp life proved to be dull and monotonous with everyone getting on each other's nerves. Aside from hunting with the Orang Asli when he felt elated at the freedom he had come to associate with the jungle, Chapman went down with tick typhus and it was not until 1 February

1945 that W/T contact was finally made. Drops by Liberators of personnel and stores followed, including reading material, which Chapman craved for after his three year literary famine. He was still far from well and it was opportune when SOE Colombo asked for two British officers to be exfiltrated to assist with detailed planning of Operation ZIPPER, the planned invasion of Malaya. Taken off by submarine in enemy controlled waters, Chapman and Broome arrived in Ceylon on 19 May. After he had finished his report on conditions in Malaya, he was flown to England for three weeks leave.

When the atomic bomb dropped on Hiroshima on 6 August, Chapman was back in Ceylon and he volunteered to drop into Pahang to assist the BLO there who was having difficulties with the guerrillas, Chapman's old comrades in arms. It was his first ever parachute jump and he landed awkwardly. The Liberator crew were relieved to see him stand up and wave. He was the first British officer into Raub and on 5 September he reached the provincial capital Kuala Lipis. On 30 September, Chapman took the Japanese surrender at Kuantan on the east coast; it was the end of their war and the end of his. And an extraordinary war it had been by any measure.

Chapman was not the only British soldier to remain at large behind the Japanese lines in Malaya. Mention must be made of three brave and resourceful members of the Royal Signals, CQMS John Cross DCM, Sergeant Fred Wagstaff MM and Sergeant Douglas Morter MM. All three had been recruited by Major Rosher of ISLD as W/T operators for SBPs in late 1941 and survived the next three years in the jungle living with Communist guerrillas. It was at times an endless ordeal for them, particularly when their officer, Major Cauvin, committed suicide. Yet at no time did they give in to despair or defeatism.

In October 1945, Chapman incurred the wrath of the WO for what was deemed an ill-considered interview with the *Daily Mail*. The headline read 'Explorer tricked Japs for years; the man who might have saved Malaya'. Chapman was quoted as saying that:

> 'I maintain that Malaya would never have fallen had I been allowed to go ahead with my scheme when I first put it forward. My guerrillas, if their numbers had been strong enough, could so completely have disorganised the Jap attack that time would have been gained to allow our reinforcements to arrive from Australia.'

The article went on to state that Chapman had told his superior officers in Singapore that Malaya would soon be invaded. He was laughed at, he declared, and told he was talking nonsense. He insisted that his summing-up was correct. He claimed that he was requested 'to keep his nose out of things that could be handled perfectly by highly trained officers whose profession it was to learn the art of war'. He received no encouragement until Singapore was bombed. Then, according to Chapman, he was called in by the people who had been ridiculing his plans a few months before, and told to go ahead.

21 April 1944: Recommendation for DSO

This officer was last known to be operating against the enemy lines of communication during the Japanese campaign in Malaya in December 1941, a hazardous undertaking for which he had volunteered and was not heard of after the Japanese occupation.

He has now been contacted and it has been learnt that for the last two years he has been visiting and instructing guerrilla bands in Malaya, having visited some twenty-five different camps, and has undoubtedly been personally responsible to a great extent for the continued resistance made by these guerrillas to the enemy.

He has displayed outstanding qualities of endurance, courage and leadership over a very long period of existence under the most difficult and arduous conditions, living in a tropical and malarious jungle country.

Major Chapman has kept himself physically fit and his morale is high. He has now stated his wish to stay on in the country in order to lead and fight with the bands he has trained.

This officer has displayed outstanding qualities of endurance, courage and leadership and his conduct is deserving of the highest praise.

Awarded

Recommendation for Bar to DSO

Lieutenant Colonel Chapman was awarded the DSO on 21 April 1944 for his service and courage behind the enemy lines during the period December 1941 to February 1944.

From that date until 13 May 1945 when he was evacuated by submarine he remained with the guerrillas in the jungle. He was continually travelling from camp to camp instructing in weapons and demolitions and on one occasion made a hazardous journey from central Perak to Kelantan in an endeavour to contact Creer and Chrystal who had also stayed behind in 1942. It was on his return from this expedition that he was captured by the Japanese. However, by a superb piece of bluff he managed to escape the following night.

After a ten day forced march with practically no food he returned to base camp where he resumed his previous occupation of training the guerrillas.

Throughout the whole period, Lieutenant Colonel Chapman suffered from frequent bouts of malaria and on one occasion contracted blackwater fever.

In April 1945 it was decided to exfiltrate Colonel Chapman and Major Broome by submarine, both for reasons of health and to give the officers planning the invasion and Force 136 the benefit of their experience. A submarine was accordingly detailed to pick them up off the coast of Perak. The journey from the hills near Bidor to the coast was difficult and hazardous and on arrival they found that they had to swim to the submarine.

Shortly after the surrender and before the arrival of British troops in Malaya, the situation in Pahang was developing badly and the guerrillas were showing signs of taking independent action. Lieutenant Colonel Chapman immediately volunteered to be dropped in and use his influence to bring about increased control. He had no previous parachute training and time was too short to allow it. He therefore dropped into Malaya within two days of his volunteering after half an hour's instruction on the airfield.

His administrative work after the surrender was excellent.

Awarded

LIEUTENANT PAT NOONE

Pat Noone

The son of a successful businessman who had worked for the East Indies merchants, Shaw Wallace and Company, Pat Noone lived a peripatetic childhood following his father's early retirement, first in London, then Dymchurch in Kent followed by the Brittany coast until the family finally settled near St Jean de Luz by the Spanish border. H.V., as his father was known, immersed himself in the study of Buddhism with diversions into prehistory which included expedition to Les Eyzies to the west of Bordeaux. So, after finishing a glittering school career at Aldenham in Hertfordshire, it came as no surprise that Pat chose to read history and anthropology at Cambridge. He came down in 1930 with a double-first and promptly accepted the post of field ethnographer at the prestigious Perak Museum which had been established at Taiping in Malaya in 1886. It was a wonderful opportunity to do original field work among the tribes in the Peninsula.

In the remote jungles between the Cameron Highlands and the Upper Perak was one of the remaining blank spaces on the map of Malaya, with mountains shrouded in clinging mist, their steep slopes plunging into narrow valleys. Here there lived a tribe called the Temiars whose existence was still based on rumour and fanciful reports. No anthropologist had penetrated this remote interior and after receiving formal permission to undertake an expedition, Noone set off in May 1931, following the aboriginal paths along the river lines in search of the Temiars along the crest of ridges and peaks that divided the states of Pahang and Kelantan. He finally found a longhouse on the banks of the River Relong, with eight families living there, but after a week of taking notes, he returned to Taiping, writing that 'he had not been able to find the magic password to unlock their hearts'.

Almost immediately, he set off again and by mid-July was camped along the banks of the River Telom, hoping that news of his arrival would lead to further contact. It was not to be and quite fortuitously the breakthrough came when he chanced across a sickly young girl, her body covered with sores. After nursing her back to health, it turned out she was the daughter of a Semai headman called Batu. From here on, Noone was welcomed in all the Semai settlements in the area and when he returned in March the following year, this time accompanied by a young planter on leave, Bellamy-Brown, the long awaited breakthrough came when he was introduced to his first Temiar warriors. 'As they stepped out of the gloom of the jungle into the sunlit clearing, [they were confronted by] a line of braves led by a man in his thirties wearing a leafy headdress and carrying a long blowpipe lightly against his shoulder. He was Along, chief of the group at the headwaters of the Rening, with Andor, his son-in-law, and some of their kinsmen.' Noone soon developed a great affection for Along, for they were the first true Temiars he had met and it was from them that he gleaned the first hint of the phenomenal psyche of the tribe.

In June 1932, Noone was promoted as curator of the Perak Museum and, with this post, he was able to lobby for a Temiar reserve and the appointment of Along as its *Dato* or chief. His next expedition almost ended in disaster when he and his Malayan porters went down with malaria and it was only when the Temiars came to look for him that he was able to send a runner to the District Officer at Tanah Rata for some quinine. That October, Noone settled down to a systematic study of the Temiars and within the next three years, between spells of museum duty, he visited most of their settlements and carried out a census of every group, a programme that involved fifteen separate river journeys to various sources and five crossings of the main mountain range. By now, the 26-year-old Noone was becoming an academic celebrity and in 1934 he addressed the Oxford and Cambridge Joint Faculty of Anthropology and the Musée d'Ethnographie du Trocadéro in Paris where he received resounding applause. After turning down an offer of the chair of anthropology at Cambridge, Noone returned to Malaya and completed his survey of the Temiars just before Christmas 1935. It was at around this time that he confided to his younger brother that he had married a beautiful Temiar girl, Anjang.

If his standing with the Temiar was high, the same was not true of his relations with colonial society in Malaya and he was never fully accepted. For Noone this could not have mattered less; his house in Taiping usually had twenty or thirty aborigines staying in it and he was always in financial difficulties as a result of spending three quarters of his salary on funding the Temiar and associated schemes. As he began to spend more time as an advisor on aboriginal affairs to the government, Noone found himself more often than not in towns and cities rather than the jungle. So he travelled with a small entourage or *maison* as he called it, consisting of Anjang, Puteh his French-trained cook and Uda, a young Temiar brave, who acted both as jungle guide and tribal PR man with the status of a blood brother. In Temiar tribal lore, this relationship included certain rights and obligations, including sexual intercourse with a brother's wife if he was away. By necessity Anjang would sleep in the servants' quarters whenever they stayed in hotels or government guest houses for Noone's detractors would have pounced if he flaunted her as his wife. The end result of this arrangement was a *ménage à trois* which was to lead to disaster.

In 1938 Noone returned to Cambridge where he completed his thesis in the dream psychology of the Temiars. In December 1939, by now back in Taiping, he became the first Protector of Aborigines in the Perak reservation, which had recently been enacted in a law which he himself had drafted. It was an extraordinary achievement and a fitting tribute to the energy, brilliance and integrity of a young man who had devoted his entire life to date to the wellbeing of the jungle tribes of Malaya. *Tata*, or grandfather as the Temiar affectionately called him, continued his eccentric lifestyle, presiding over a chaotic commune of tribal visitors and conscientiously carrying out his duties as Protector of the entire aborigine population of the Perak.

*****

When the Japanese occupied Indo-China in January 1941, the British Malayan Command set up an intelligence gathering organisation along the Thai border to recce jungle routes and to watch for any suspicious moves by the Japanese or their proxies. Called the Frontier Patrol, it was 'hidden' in the Game Department and headed by E.O. Shebbeare[72], the chief game warden of Malaya; among the European sector officers under command were Pat Noone, his brother Richard and Eric Robertson of the British Forest Service. One unfortunate officer, W.F. Baldock of the East African Forestry Service, was found by his cousin Major

---

72 Edward Shebbeare ['Shebby'] acted as transport officer on the 1924 and 1933 Everest expeditions, and was also appointed Deputy Leader by Ruttledge in 1933. Although not himself a climber, he reached the North Col that year at the age of nearly fifty.

J.P.A. Wildey crucified on a makeshift cross in December 1941. Each sector officer was left to recruit his own men and organise his own set up. Predictably, Pat Noone used Temiars.

On 6 December 1941 orders were received by the sector officers to disband the Frontier Patrol and to report to the nearest infantry battalion. In Noone's case, this was the Argyll and Sutherlands Highlanders[73] and at the head of a twenty-four strong platoon, together with two *dayaks*, Noone reached Grik where he sent up the Kroh road on a recce patrol. Attacked by the Japanese during the night, the platoon withdrew back to Grik where they found that the battalion has left along with all its transport. They decided to split in two; the main body including two wounded soldiers boarded the ferry and pushed off downstream, using it as a raft. Later it was reported that it had capsized in the rapids south of Grik and all on board perished. Meanwhile Noone, with four of the Highlanders including the platoon sergeant and the two *dayaks*, set off for a kampong a few miles upstream from Grik. The plan was to march through the jungle in a wide detour and to come out south of the British lines. Noone and Anjang led the way, followed by Sergeant Conolly, Privates Westhead, Richardson and Boult, then the *dayaks* and lastly, thirty Temiar including two children. The trek took them up the Perak River, then up the Jemheng River, over the high shoulder of Gunong Besar and down a steep track on the other side. Finally after reaching the Gambir River, they climbed into the longhouse above Kampong Lasah and literally dropped on the floor, their feet torn, legs swollen with leech bites and boots split. But there was no time to rest as news came of more Japanese advances and it was a dispirited party that spent Christmas 1941 at a house in Tanjong Rambutan.

Worn out by the speed of the Japanese advance, Noone decided that the best course was for the party to stay put and recover their strength and so they moved to a concealed position up a tributary of the Korbu River where they built a small bamboo house. Sergeant Connolly was by now restless, so taking the two *dayaks* with him, he set off for the Cameron Highlands. Westhead and Richardson, both of whom had malaria, died within three days of each other toward the end of January; Boult then contracted it, at which

---

[73] The 2nd Battalion arrived in Singapore in August 1939. After two years intensive training, its first contact with the Japanese was on 15 December 1941, at Baling, a week after the Japanese landed at Kota Bahru in north east Malaya. It was then in almost continuous action as it retired through north and central Malaya, until the fall of Singapore in February, 1942. In all 60 Officers and 880 Other Ranks served with the 2nd Battalion in Malaya and Singapore, of whom 17 Officers and 227 Other Ranks were killed in action. The remainder became prisoners of the Japanese: 5 Officers and 182 Other Ranks died in captivity whilst working on the infamous Burma Railway.

point Noone also decided to head up to the Cameron Highlands in search of quinine. Taking Anjang, Uda and Boult with him, he hired some local guides and started the journey to the Rening River. On 3 March, Boult died and six days later, on reaching a longhouse on the river, they learnt that Sergeant Connolly and another British party, Private Driscoll and Dolman of the Game Department, were living at the house of a Christian missionary a few miles away.

By the time Noone reached the house, it was too late, for the three Europeans had just left to give themselves up. However he learnt that two others were in the area, John Creer, the Kuala Tregganu DO, and a game warden called Hubback. Much to his surprise, when he returned to his longhouse on 25 March, Noone found Creer, barefoot and dressed only in shorts, waiting for him. He had bad news – a large force of Japanese was coming down the River Telom looking for Noone. It turned out to be a false alarm. Nevertheless they left the area and settled in Kuala Rening where Siantoeri, the missionary, supplied them with quinine, blankets, clothing, shoes, books and writing materials. Considering the circumstances, they were relatively well off, although Creer's funds were running low. At one stage, Creer recalled how the Orang Asli saved his life 'by invoking friendly spirits and removing about two catties of an invisible and intangible cotton-wool-like substance which ... was choking my lungs'. Altogether the two men stayed put for four and a half months, uneventful save for 'a bad cut on [Creer's] scalp inflicted accidentally with a *kukri* by the unskilful Noone, busy about the household chores'.

Maybe as a result of his childhood wanderings, Noone was unable to stay put and persuaded Creer[74] to come with him to Pulai on the River Galas where a group of KMT guerrillas, mainly Hakka farmers, were operating. After a month, Noone became bored and leaving Creer, a fluent Chinese speaker behind, returned to the Telom when he got wind of another two Europeans, Robert Chrystal, the manager of the vast Kamunting rubber estate in Perak, and a planter called Robinson, who were living with a 100-strong band of Chinese Communists, grandiloquently known as the V Corps of the Malaysian People's Anti-Japanese Army. A meeting was duly arranged when the two men witnessed the extraordinary spectacle of Noone at the head of half a dozen Temiar braves emerging from the jungle in a pair of brief shorts with a gleaming *parang* thrust through a black cummerbund round his waist.

Initially intrigued by the idiosyncrasies of Communist dogma and the discipline of camp routine, Noone was quickly accepted by Lai Foo, the V Corps

---

74 In his account, Creer says he left Noone on 5 August to go to Pulai to get in touch with Chinese guerrillas.

commander, and sent on a tour of aboriginal villages to extol the virtues of the Communist guerrillas while at the same time establishing a network of aboriginal intelligence agents to warn of Japanese incursions into the area. Chrystal however had had enough of listening to non-stop anti-British propaganda and set off to join Creer and his band of KMT guerrillas, a venture that almost immediately went awry when Communists gained control of the district and forced the two men to flee over the Pahang divide in July 1943. When they reached the Telom River, they found Noone living near Kuala Betram; he too had fallen out with the Communists over their rabid anti-Englishness and vowed never to have anything to do with them again. The three men built a small house on the south bank of the Telom where they were looked after by Anjang and Ula. It was a strange coexistence, made even harder by the underlying animosity between Creer and Noone.

At the end of August, Noone accepted an invitation from the Chinese Communists at Pulai to join them and he accepted, probably to get away from Creer. It was while he was in Pulai that he came up with the idea of founding a jungle settlement of his own in a beautiful valley of the Upper Korbu. Still suffering from recurrent bouts of malaria, Noone returned via Jalong to collect an old supply of quinine and to procure some salt, arriving back at the Telom at the end of October. Very weak and wracked by malarial attacks, he left within a week and was last seen by Chrystal on 7 November heading up the Telom River path with Anjang, Uda and Busu, a friend of Uda.

The story of the last days of Noone has been painstakingly put together by his brother Richard. A Temiar, Akob, recounted how he had met Noone in a little house near Ngah's *ladang* together with Anjang, Uda and Busu. A week later, when he passed by the house again, he enquired where the *Tata* was but no one would tell him. Confronting Busu, whom he found hiding in a little hut, Akob discovered that Uda and Buzu had both conspired to murder Noone so that Uda could have Anjang all to himself. The deed itself was done by Uda who used his blowpipe to fire poison darts at Noone, one of which struck him in the eye, the rest in his right thigh. After running for some distance, he had fallen to the ground vomiting, raging at Uda who then killed him outright with a stroke of his *parang*. So in the end, it was not the Japanese who were responsible for the death of this gallant Englishman; unlikely though it sounds, it was a crime of passion.

COLONEL JOHN DAVIS, CBE, DSO, and COLONEL DICK BROOME, OBE, MC

L to R: Fenner, Davis, Broome and Goodfellow

Known as Dum and Dee, John Davis and Dick Broome worked hand in hand behind enemy lines in Malaya to organise resistance against the Japanese. Their contrasting attributes made them a formidable team, Davis the man of action, Broome the strategist and diplomat. Both were independent-minded and to a degree surprisingly unconventional in their attitudes.

The son of a Barclays Bank manager in the City of London, Davis was born in Sutton in 1911 and grew up in the Home Counties. After leaving Tonbridge School and eager to sample colonial life, he was selected as a probationer to serve in the Federated Malay States and the Straits Settlement Police. After six months training in Kuala Lumpur, he was posted to Pahang as Officer in charge of Police District [OCPD] Kuantan and then to Pekan in the Sultanate of Pahang. In 1933, he was sent on a two year course to learn Chinese in Canton and on his return was posted first to Ipoh with the CID and then as OCPD Taiping and Matang.

Now fluent in Malay and Chinese, there was little that Davis did not know about policing the Malayan countryside. However, as an obvious high flier, there were more demanding jobs in the pipeline for him and in December 1940 he was posted to the Criminal Investigation Department [CID] in Singapore and put in charge of bribery and corruption cases which involved completing the enquiry of the Loveday case in which Captain Loveday RE was found guilty of corruption in awarding defence contracts. Within months Davis was promoted to Assistant Superintendent in charge of Investigations but as the international situation deteriorated, the Inspector General of Police, Arthur Dickinson, saw in Davis the perfect candidate for the role of Services Liaison Officer for Police in the Defence Security Office, in effect a Special Branch cover to work with the various military intelligence and counter-intelligence agencies and to improve liaison between the fragmented police departments within Malaya.

Within a short time, Davis was much in demand with approaches for assistance by Basil Goodfellow, Jim Gavin and Freddy Spencer Chapman of the ORIENTAL Mission, Colonel Alan Warren of MI[R] and Major Jimmy Green of the ISLD. Almost the first joint action was to arrange a meeting with Lai Tek, the head of the CPM in Singapore, to discuss the recruitment and training of Communist Chinese for SBPs[75]. On 22 December 1941, Davis flew up to Kuala Lumpur with a Malayan Civil Servant Mervyn Sheppard, at the request of ISLD and quickly started preparing such parties with Warren and ISLD's Major Rosher. The next two weeks involved a hectic schedule of assembling stores, sourcing serviceable W/T equipment and dropping off SBPs and it was an exhausted Davis who returned to Singapore on 3 January 1942. He was far from convinced that anything worthwhile had been achieved.

Returning to the north, Davis bumped into Richard Broome, an old friend from Chinese Language School days in Canton. A Malayan Civil Servant, Broome had been ordered as a fluent Chinese speaker to report to Singapore for 'special duties'. At his ISLD interview, it was explained how they wanted him to stay behind to look after agents in the event of a Japanese invasion. By coincidence, he bumped into Basil Goodfellow who made the same pitch and persuaded him that the SOE plan to use CPM Chinese volunteers already in training at STS 101 was better. From then on, Broome had been involved in taking CPM volunteers from 101 STS to their dropping off point at Serendah. He was about to set off with a second group, this time to Tampin, and asked for Davis to come along. Feeling that he had more than discharged his duties to ISLD, Davis agreed and the two of them headed off together. At Tampin, they met up with Warren and from then on every day was spent frantically getting Chinese guerrillas into the field as the military situation worsened. Over 300 were inserted in seven separate batches with Davis managing to position fifty-eight in the Kota Tinggi area before the Singapore causeway was blown. The two friends then put their heads together to work out how best to stay in touch with the SBPs, for access across the Johore Straits was now out of the question. Meeting up with Basil Goodfellow on 2 February, they put forward a plan to

---

75 Confusingly this was arranged by a Special Branch policeman, also called Davis.

use the east coast of Sumatra as a springboard from which to re-enter Malaya and contact the SBPs.

By chance, two European members of an SBP, Frank Vanrenan and Ronald Graham, who had escaped to Sumatra having failed to make contact with their OC Freddy Spencer Chapman, arrived to see Goodfellow in Singapore at the same time[76]. They were also keen to return, so Goodfellow and Warren approved a two-part plan; Vanrenan and Graham would go in to locate Spencer Chapman and Davis and Broome would undertake an intelligence gathering mission. In due course, they set off from Singapore in a Chinese motor *tong-kaung* called the *Hin Lee*, and reached Fort Bagansiapiapi on the Sumatran coast on 10 February. Here the party split into two, each hiring its own junk to sail to the Malayan mainland.

After an uneventful journey, Broome and Davis's junk reached the Sepang River where they landed on 15 February and, after making contact with Chinese Communists, set about collecting intelligence on the deployment of Japanese troops and nascent resistance movements. By the 19th they were back in Sumatra where they learnt from Warren of the fall of Singapore. Davis was told to stay put in Labuan Bilik to await news of Vanrenan's party while Warren and Broome headed for Padang. It was not long in coming and the Chinese crew members of their junk told him that, after dropping them off and waiting six days in the area for their return, there was no further contact so they sailed back. It was a bitter disappointment for Davis that SOE now had no means of contact with any of the SBGs in Malaya. Broome returned to collect him and on the night of 8 March, the two officers sailed on the *Sederhana Djohanis*, a sixty-five foot traditional Malay sailing ship, along with sixteen other British officers including Ivan Lyon, reaching Bombay on 19 March after being taken aboard the Anglo-Canadian, a 5,000 ton Welsh freighter off the coast of Ceylon some five days earlier. It had been an epic voyage and a tribute to Lyon's and Broome's seamanship and leadership that, despite being machine gunned by a Japanese fighter, alternatively becalmed then battered by squalls and storms, everyone had survived the 1,700 mile journey across the Bay of Bengal.

SOE in India was still in its infancy. The ORIENTAL Mission was widely and unfairly seen to be a failure; the INDIA Mission was focussed on the threat of a German advance in the West. When Colin Mackenzie, the head of the INDIA Mission, met Davis and Broome, he was unable to offer them any Malayan project and sent them to Calcutta to await employment. However, he

---

76 They had been separately flown by a member of the Malayan Auxiliary Air Force in a Tiger Moth from Sumatra.

agreed that Davis could keep an eye on Malaya and soon this concession had mutated into the Malayan Country Section comprised of Goodfellow, Davis and Broome. Their first priority was to re-establish communication with the SBPs and other intelligence assets and the only way this could be done was by landing a party with a W/T set on the mainland. It would be fraught with risk, involving a 'blind' landing. Since Davis was a single man and the fittest of the three, it was agreed that he should lead it. If successful, Broome would follow. Now they had to put a Malayan Country Section team together and, through the good offices of Lim Bo Seng, a young Chinese industrialist who had escaped from Singapore, managed to source a bodyguard for Davis [Ah Piu] and a number of high quality Malay speaking KMT Chinese recruits from the Chungking Overseas school, subsequently known as 'the Dragons'[77]. Both Davis and Broome were immensely impressed by Lim Bo Seng and treated him as 'the third member of the team'. Training facilities were sourced, first at the Eastern Warfare School at Khrakvaslanear Poona and then in Ceylon. All this took time and it was not until the spring of 1943 that all the elements of the operation were in place.

The plan was by necessity ambitious, for as Broome put it, 'we were totally out of touch ... no intelligence of any useful kind was coming out of Malaya'. Davis was to take a group of five Dragons to the Port Swettenham area to try and contact the CPM guerrillas there. A second objective was to establish a direct submarine link between Malaya and Ceylon, involving secure reception arrangements and W/T communications. Another goal was to set up an intelligence network run by Chinese agents and finally, the last task was to ascertain what had happened to the SBPs. Clearly there needed to be more than one insertion to fulfil this multiplicity of objectives, so a number of sequential landings were envisaged under the codename GUSTAVUS. If things went wrong at any time, backup plans were in place to extract personnel or indeed to cancel future landings.

On 11 May 1943, fifteen months after he and Broome had left Malaya, Davis left Ceylon on the Dutch submarine *024* commanded by Lieutenant Commander de Vries. On board were the Mission's stores, folboats and W/T equipment, and the five Chinese Dragons. It was to be the first of many such voyages for the Malayan Country Section. After stalking a junk and then boarding it with a view to being put ashore, Davis was uneasy about the trustworthiness of the Hailam crew and returned to *024*. They finally went ashore by folboat near Segari under cover of darkness on the night of 24/25 May and

---

[77] The Country Section initially tried to recruit from the Chinese seafaring population in Calcutta but had difficulty in finding any volunteers with sufficient educational qualifications.

rapidly moving inland away from the exposed beaches, struck camp at Bukit Segari. Davis's overriding need was to establish contact with the local people, for at this stage he had no idea as to whether there was any formal or indeed informal resistance to the occupying Japanese power. Keeping Ah Piu with him as his bodyguard, he despatched Ah Ng, his senior agent, to secure food for the group and bring news of conditions outside the jungle. Ah Han and Ah Ying were sent to Ipoh and Segari respectively to start collecting intelligence. The fifth Dragon, Ah Tsing, was given the all-important task of setting up a secure link for the reception of the GUSTAVUS 2 submarine scheduled to bring in Broome and additional supplies.

A month later, a junk arranged by Ah Tsing collected Davis and his bodyguard from Segari beach and successfully rendezvoused with the GUSTAVUS 2 submarine. Broome, with three more Dragons, was waiting eagerly to come ashore[78] but Davis was adamant that this was not the right time for a second landing as he felt it was imperative that he returned to Colombo to personally brief Goodfellow on what he had ascertained. On their return, they found that Goodfellow had moved on but were relieved that his replacement, Innes Tremlett, was their old colleague from the Canton Chinese language course. Davis reported how the STS 101 Chinese guerrillas had built up a large, overwhelmingly Communist force, the MPAJA, logistically supported by the AJU. From the British point of view, Davis stressed it was essential to make contact with the AJA/MCP at the highest level to reach agreement on how they could co-operate in the fight against the Japanese. Without such an agreement, it would be a waste of time and resources to proceed. Davis proposed that he should therefore return to Malaya on GUSTAVUS 3, taking with him Broome's three Dragons to reinforce those whom he had left in situ.

After a very rushed departure, GUSTAVUS 3 reached the rendezvous with Ah Tsing's junk off the coast of Pangkor on 4 August and made a safe landing not far from their first beach landing at Segari. After caching their heavy Mark III W/T sets, Davis and his party made their way by a circuitous route to his old camp where Ah Ng had arranged a meeting with the 23-year-old Communist Acting Secretary of State for Penang, known as Chin Peng. After establishing Davis's bona fide, he confirmed that the MPAJA was now a countrywide resistance movement and also told Davis that both Freddy Spencer Chapman and Pat Noone were alive, being well looked after by Communist guerrillas.

However, Chin Peng warned Davis that the security situation in the area of Segari had deteriorated and as soon as Broome [GUSTAVUS 4] had been

---

78 GUSTAVUS II spent three weeks in the submarine, hardly conducive to good health, as Broome quipped.

safely landed by submarine near Segari beach on 23 September, the SOE mission prepared to move. It was none too soon for unknown to them the Japanese had been unsettled by Operation JAYWICK's attack against shipping in Singapore on the night of 26/27 September and patrolling and counter-intelligence operations had commensurately increased. Chin Peng organised the move to the rainforests of eastern Perak and after a dangerous and punishing journey by sea, river and jungle track, they reached their new camp near the 2,000-foot summit of Blantan Hill. Broome, down with fever, insisted on returning to the coast to rendezvous with Lim Bo Seng who was coming in on GUSTAVUS 5 on 6 November but was overruled on security reasons by Chin Peng who went in his place. At the rendezvous, he briefed Lim Bo Seng about the intense level of Japanese activity and, on the basis of this information, Lim Bo Seng refused to let his companion, Captain Harrison[79], land on the grounds that it was far too risky for a European to attempt the journey to Blantan. After caching Harrison's stores and W/T sets, the two Chinese set off back to Perak and rejoined the SOE party.

Lim Bo Seng had brought with him an important official document signed by Admiral Lord Louis Mountbatten on behalf of SEAC. It confirmed Davis's authority to negotiate an agreement with the CPM 'for the purposes of aiding and strengthening all those elements who can be counted on to assist in the preparations for the final ejection of the Japanese from Malayan territory'. On 30 December, the long awaited Communist 'plenipotentiary' arrived at Blantan to start negotiations. To Davis's surprise, it was Lai Tek, the double agent Special Branch had handled in Singapore from 1934 onwards. With Davis, Broome and Lim Bo Seng representing the SEAC and Lai Tek the CPM, AJA and AJU – neither Chapman[80] nor Chin Peng who were both present were accredited – the Blantan Agreement was hammered out. Lai Tek accepted that 'the Communist Party will follow the instructions of the Allied CinC in so far as military operations in Malaya are concerned' but neatly avoided extending the agreement beyond the expulsion of the Japanese. With no W/T set in operation and having passed the deadline to send the news out on GUSTAVUS 6, which had made a successful rendezvous on 5 January but found it too dangerous to land Claude Fenner and Jim Hannah with their eight Chinese agents, Davis and Broome, although elated by the success of their negotiations, were only too aware of their isolation.

---

79 Harrison returned on GUSTAVUS VI, an operation designed to either reinforce Davis's party or extract a member of it in the event of illness. However, it failed to make the rendezvous with the reception junk and, after checking the GUSTAVUS emergency post-box on Pulau Lalang South Island on 9 December, the Mission returned home to Ceylon.
80 To their delight, Freddy Spencer Chapman had arrived at the camp on Christmas night.

MALAYA

Lim Bo Seng

Increased enemy air activity dictated another move and the Mission moved to a small clearing above the confluence of the River Woh – one of the five tributaries of the Batang Padang River – and its own tributary the Ayer Busok. Here they were joined in March by Frank Quayle, one of the survivors of the original SBPs. In their secluded jungle base, events conspired to prolong their isolation: Operation REMARKABLE 1 was unable to make contact with its reception party during 17 to 19 February, and in mid-March, REMARKABLE 2, with Fenner and Hannah, experienced identical difficulties. Frustrated by the continuing difficulties of moving the heavy W/T sets cached at Jenderata on the coast up through enemy held territory into the highlands, and the consequent inability to arrange drops of weapons, money and stores to honour their commitment to the CPM, the SOE Mission then received the news from an exhausted Ah Tsing who stumbled into their camp that Lim Bo Seng's intelligence networks had been penetrated up by the Japanese Kempeitai. Within days, Ah Lim, Shek Fu, Ah Ng, Mo Ching and worst of all Lim Bo Seng himself had all been arrested. The boatmen from the SOE junk, so vital to manning the submarine rendezvous, were later picked up and forced to reveal the details of the rendezvous. Finally the original arms and W/T cache at Segari was uncovered by the Japanese. It had been an unmitigated disaster alleviated only by the arrival of two new Dragons from REMARKABLE 3 who had landed blind on Pangkor on 25 April and made their way to the River Woh camp, bringing much needed gold and new submarine rendezvous instructions.

Ill with suspected leptospirosis, Davis forced himself to travel to Blantan with Broome where Chin Peng had finally managed to move the Jenderata W/T sets to. It transpired that only two batteries and a hand generator were available on their arrival, so sending them on to the River Woh camp, the two officers stayed on in Blantan to discuss the next submarine rendezvous with Chin Peng. Although two Dragons were despatched to set up a reception committee, intense enemy patrolling make it impossible to reach the rendezvous and REMARKABLE 4 returned home. On 30 May, Davis and Broome left for their River Woh base, only to find that it had been discovered by the Japanese and totally destroyed. Worse, the batteries and hand generator which had safely arrived had been found by the enemy together with the security bag containing money, the signals plan, Chinese codes and the all-important life-saving supply of quinine. The only good news was that the SOE party in the camp had all escaped and they regrouped at an aboriginal house at Juit above the Kuala Telom. With the devastating news that Lim Bo Seng had died in Batu Gajah Gaol on 29 June, the morale of the SOE officers, weak from malnutrition and fever, hit rock bottom. The only one unaware of these disasters was Chapman who had gone off in search of Pat Noone.

In July, Chin Peng moved the SOE camp to Gurun in the primary jungle, about 2,500 feet on the shoulder of Gunong Batu Puteh. The four officers, Davis, Broome, Quayle and Chapman who was back after a fruitless search for Noone, now faced a prolonged period of inactivity for there was still no means of contacting SOE HQ. Dick Broome later recalled that:

> 'It wasn't an ideal life exactly. One was slightly under-fed all the time, bored stiff most of the time and very anxious to get back to comparative civilisation and get in touch with one's relatives. We made a dartboard. We cut a board out of the roots of a large tree, buttress roots. We had some difficulty in remembering how the numbers went round the board. Darts we made from nails. I also made a chess set out of bamboo, slats of bamboo stuck together, and carved the pieces. Our Chinese made a chess set but they also made *mah jong* and that was rather an achievement if you think of the number of tiles in a *mah jong* set. They had a high old time playing *mah jong* and we, in reply, made a Monopoly set. It was a bit wild to see these Chinese sitting in the middle of the Malayan jungle, buying and selling Piccadilly and Leicester Square.'

Although the two Mark II W/T sets were serviceable, they had no way of powering them up and it was not until November that two car batteries and a pedal generator were finally procured and rigged up by Quayle. Lee Choon, the W/T operator, was then able to receive transmissions, albeit limited to All India Radio broadcasts.

At least the party now had news of the outside world and when, on 20 December, a message arrived from Chin Peng that he had been in contact with Operation CARPENTER, an SOE Mission headed by Major Paddy Martin which had been inserted into Malaya from Australia in late October, and had arranged for news of them to be sent through CARPENTER's W/T set to SEAC, morale started to recover. The quick thinking and ever optimistic Davis sent a return message to Martin asking him to alert SOE in Ceylon of the imminent arrival of GUSTAVUS back on the airwaves. It was sent on 19 January, a week before Martin was killed in a Japanese ambush on his DZ. When a second-hand car dynamo arrived in Gurun in the New Year, Quayle and Lee Choon set to work and by 1 February 1945 Colombo received their first transmission. For the first time, Davis was able to tell them about the 1943 Blantan Agreement and the urgent need to start honouring its commitments, especially the supply of arms, ammunition, food and medicines.

With the arrival of the long range Liberator bombers, SOE was now able to parachute in bodies and stores, and the relief/reinforcement mission Operation FUNNEL was given to Major Jim Hannah and Major Harrison[81], both of whom had been conducting officers for GUSTAVUS. Dropped on the night of 26/27 February 1945, the reinforcements all landed safely as did the long awaited supplies. Hannah brought news of Operation HEBRIDES, SOE's new all-Malay Malayan Resistance policy, launched towards the end of 1944, which came as a surprise to Davis. Concerned that it could undermine the Blantan Agreement, he quickly re-established his authority with Colombo and was put in command of the Group Liaison Team attached to CPM HQ; in effect, he was the link between SOE's MALT network and the AJUF in the run-up to Operation ZIPPER, the Allied invasion of Malaya.

Chin Peng had been down with typhoid but reappeared on 1 April at Gurun to organise a meeting between the MCP and SOE to update the Blantan Agreement and make concrete plans to assist the Allied invasion. Two weeks later the two sides met in the jungle seven hours walk from Gurun. Davis, Broome and Hannah represented the British, Chin Peng, Lai Tek and Colonel Itu of 5th [Perak] Regiment of the MPAJA, the CPM. The agenda was simple: how best to get on with the business of fighting the war. Some 3,300 AJUF guerrillas were envisaged to be under arms within the next three months with

---

81 Harrison and another officer, Captain John Davidson, had joined Force 136 after completing the JAMPUFF Mission in Bulgaria.

Chin Peng as acting commander of the MPAJA, a role that would involve keeping 'in constant personal touch with Davis'. Each AJUF regiment would have a British Group Liaison Team headed by a Group Liaison Officer attached to it and each patrol a British Patrol Liaison Officer. The Teams would all have their own W/T station reporting to Colombo. A quota of guns, ammunition and explosives was agreed with a similar undertaking in respect of finance and food. Once the invasion was underway, the AJUF regiments agreed that they would accept orders from the Allied Task Force Commander via the Group Liaison officers. Finally, Davis and Broome's cherished plans for an CPM resistance army were falling into place.

Ill health had dogged Broome throughout his two year stay in the jungle and so after the conference, together with Chapman, he made his way down to Pangkor for extraction to Ceylon by submarine. It had been an extraordinary partnership with both men dedicated to the common goal of organizing resistance against the Japanese irrespective of the hardships and disappointments along the way.

By August, the British had dropped arms and ammunition sufficient for 5,000 guerrillas along the length and breadth of Malaya and over ninety SOE officers, who with various support personnel brought the total deployed to around 400. On 2 August Davis set off on a ten day trek to Selangor in order to be closer to the new CPM Central HQ. Unbeknown to him since he was out of W/T contact, SEAC had signalled all the SOE teams with news of the two atomic bombs dropped on Japan and advised them to wait for the declaration of the Japanese surrender. The Teams were to take no action other than to ensure that Japanese arms did not fall into the hands of the AJA. For Davis and the Malayan Country Section it was an unexpected anti-climax to all the hard work they had put into the training and preparation of the AJUF regiments. Now it was a matter of winding down their organisation and after successfully disarming and disbanding the MPAJA, an astonishing achievement due almost entirely to Davis's superb relationship with Chin Peng, by November 1945 Force 136 in Malaya ceased to function as an operational unit.

MALAYA

MAJOR PETER DOBRÉE, OBE

Peter Dobrée

Educated at Westminster School with a Diploma in Agriculture from Reading University, Peter Dobrée had been a rubber planter for two years on an estate to the south of Johore before moving to the Malayan Agricultural Department in 1937 where he remained for the next five years. In 1942, he enlisted as a Volunteer in the Light Battery and after escaping in a small boat and reaching India via Sumatra, he then transferred to 3rd Ghurkha Rifles until he moved to Force 136 in October. Working for the Malayan Country Section, as a fluent Malay speaker he had been conducting officer for various Malay parties. His one and only mission, REMARKABLE 1, was aborted on 4 March 1944 when HMS *Tally Ho*'s commander after patrolling off the landing point for three days considered it too dangerous and Dobrée and his Chinese W/T operator returned to base in Ceylon.

On 16 December 1944 he was dropped blind into Malaya with four Malay agents – Lieutenant Nor Rani, W/T operator Imram, W/T operator Hussein bin Sidek and Jamal, a former policeman – to the east of Grik in North Perak. As leader of Operation HEBRIDES, his task was to open up communications with the hill area of northern Kedah and if possible to find Pat Noone[82]. After establishing communications with Ceylon, he quickly set about establishing an

---

82 Dobrée did meet up with Bob Crystal and John Creer, neither 'in robust health' after two years in the jungle. They regaled him with stories including the time they had been offered the brains of a spy to eat.

intelligence network and in creating a resistance movement which he christened the Loyal Malay Army. It was a gruelling assignment with very little food about, large numbers of Japanese informers and tricky relations with KMT bands and the AJUF. In all, Dobrée's team transmitted 954 items of intelligence to SOE HQ in Kandy. Towards the end of his mission, he was joined by Doug Richardson and then John Clifford.

28 April 1945: Recommendation for DSO

In December 1944 it was decided to drop a British officer and a small party of Malays into Malaya with the object of contacting friendly natives and building up a] an intelligence network and b] a resistance movement. Major Dobrée was selected for this difficult and dangerous task in a country from which there was no possibility of withdrawal until its liberation. His was the first party ever to drop into Malaya which was done in daylight on 16 December 1944 after a previous aborted attempt by night.

On 21 December after a week of incredible hardship he made W/T contact with Ceylon, briefed and sent out his agents and before long established excellent contacts amongst responsible Malays in the area. By the end of March 1945 he had recruited, armed and trained 100 Malays and 80 Chinese and had started a Malay resistance Movement which is still growing. He organised an intelligence network which included the main garrison towns of North Malaya and from which a great deal of extremely valuable information of enemy forces and dispositions has been and continues to be reported. He organised the reception in Malaya of four other British-led parties, supplying them with guides, contacts and porterage which ensured success attained in other areas.

In April 1945 the Japanese attacked his jungle base in strength. Major Dobrée personally laid a series of ambushes which forced the Japanese to withdraw. Following up he again personally led his local resistance forces into the attack and took the village used by the enemy as a base and three Japanese transport elephants. Japanese casualties included the head of the Kempeitai in the area who was killed. Major Dobrée himself was shot and wounded in the leg, but this did not prevent him from re-grouping his forces and organizing their withdrawal to a new and more secret base.

He has since continued to organise and direct his resistance and intelligence forces. His influence now extends over north of Malaya from coast to coast and he controls more than 300 armed men and an uncalculated number of unarmed reserves who wait word to concentrate for arming and training. Major Dobrée has now been in Malaya seven months, 1,500 miles from the nearest British supply base, and has shown unexcelled leadership, determination and courage in the heart of enemy occupied territory, and in one of the most difficult and unhealthy places in the world.

Awarded OBE [19 April 1946]

CAPTAIN ROBERT CHRYSTAL, MC

Born in Glasgow in 1894 and married with two teenage children, Robert Chrystal was one of SOE's oldest recruits. A rubber planter working on the Kamuning Estate for the old established firm of Guthrie FCO Ltd since he was 24, Chrystal had some military experience from his army service in the First World War when, after enlisting as a private in the 6th Cameron Highlanders, he was commissioned into the East Yorkshire Regiment and served with the 2nd and 3rd battalions in France, Belgium, Macedonia and Egypt. After contracting malaria in Salonika, he was invalided out of the army in November 1917.

With war approaching, he joined the Kedah Volunteers as a Corporal in the Pioneer Section and by 1941 was a Sergeant in the Local Defence Force of Perak. On 22 December he was attached to 11th Division as LO. When the division moved a few miles above Kuala Lumpur, Chrystal and fellow planter William Robinson bumped into Boris Hembry and Ronald Graham, who recounted how they were on their way to a jungle hide-out as part of an SBP. Inspired and excited, the two men immediately volunteered for similar duties and, after being vetted by Colonel Alan Warren, were commissioned on 8 January 1942 into the General List for service in stay behind party No. 3 [STS 101] commanded by Lieutenant Pat Garden, a mining engineer and fully trained by STS 101 in the dark arts of guerrilla warfare.

No. 2 SBP, now composed of Garden, Chrystal, Robinson, Frank Quayle and Clark Haywood, entered the jungle on 11 January near Karak in the Pahang/Kurah road area and after weeks of lying low met up in early March with Freddy Spencer Chapman who Garden and Haywood had found near a reserve dump near the village of Tras. On 13 March, encouraged by Chapman, the party set off on bicycles, hoping to reach the coast and make their way to India by boat.

From here on, the story of Bob Crystal is best told by following his extraordinary progress over the next three years.

The bicycle escapade ended in mild chaos and on 6 April 1942, with Quayle and Robinson, Crystal found himself at the Chinese guerrilla HQ Perak at a camp in the Ulu Slim area. Here he was appointed Chief Instructor by Chapman; Chrystal and Robinson took the young Communist recruits in drill, small arms and jungle warfare, Quayle took them in grenades, PT and unarmed combat. Ten student leaders were given an intensive leadership training programme as well.

After their camp was attacked by a strong Japanese fighting patrol, in July 1942 Chrystal and his companions went to a new camp by Slim village with the Chinese guerrillas who were now known as V Corps AJA [No. 4 Coy]. It was here that they heard that Haywood had been killed, although miraculously Chapman had managed to get away.

In September 1942, once again their camp was compromised, this time unwittingly by Chrystal who had taken a wrong turning and been challenged by some Chinese when he inadvertently strayed onto a rubber estate. Leaving Quayle at Beda, who was down with a virulent attack of malaria, Chrystal and Robinson trekked through the jungle for seven days until they reached their new base at Simpang Pulai. In October 1942, the two men were summoned to yet another new camp in the Ipoh area which they reached on 7 November 1942. Here they found the Jalong area camp of V Perak Corps HQ and No.1 Coy. From a rocky ledge above the camp, Chrystal could pick out through binoculars the town of Sungei Siput and even see his old bungalow and garden on the Kamuning Estate. At Corps HQ, Chrystal and Robinson were mainly employed by their Communist hosts on writing propaganda leaflets and drawing up a training manual which included sketches of weapons for use by both guerrilla leaders and their students. The latter was well received though his propaganda efforts fell well short of the post-colonial revolutionary scenario the CPM had in mind.

On 1 December 1942, Chrystal was overjoyed when the young anthropologist Pat Noone of Shebbeare Frontier Force visited Jalong Camp. He described his arrival to Dennis Holman in *The Green Torture* thus:

'The entertainment was proceeding apace when it was suddenly interrupted by a shout from a guerrilla sentry. The singing stopped, and all turned to gape at a bearded European with his hair cropped short, naked save for a pair of brief shorts and black cummerbund tied with the end hanging loose in the Temiar style, and armed with a gleaming *parang* thrust through it on one side. It was Pat Noone and he was followed by a personal bodyguard of half a dozen aboriginal braves armed with *parangs*, blowpipes and quivers full of poisoned darts.'

Noone brought news of another European, John Creer also of Shebbeare Frontier Force, at Pulai in Kelantan and of a W/T set there.

As 1942 drew to a close, Crystal was one of the few survivors of the ORIENTAL Mission's SBGs. He had had the good luck to be put in touch by Freddy Spencer Chapman with the Chinese Communist guerrillas and the good sense to co-operate with them. For it was only by moving from camp to camp under their auspices that he had evaded Japanese patrols to date.

After four months of mounting irritation and disillusionment with his Communist hosts, Chrystal proposed that he should join up with John Creer at

Pulai and try and activate the W/T link. Somewhat to his disappointment Robinson and Noone both elected to stay on at Perak Corps HQ. So on 6 March 1943, he left for Kelantan with Noone, who had agreed to escort him over the main range. Dropped off at a *Sakai* settlement to wait for guides, he 'stayed there a week and enjoyed every moment of it. I bathed and fished in the river and went out hunting with my *Sakai* hosts ... They were altogether a most delightful people, with a keen sense of humour, so different from the phlegmatic Chinese with whom I had been living. I had a wonderful sense of freedom away from the constant Communist propaganda, away at last from the feeling that I must keep apologising for my existence ... '

After a long trek with his three aboriginal guides which included spending a week at a long-house in a Temiar *ladang* – 'most nights there would be dancing in the long-house' – he encountered a band of KMT guerrillas heading for Pulai and joining forces with them. When, on 30 March 1943, he reached the settlement which lay in a secluded valley on the upper reaches of the River Galas, he found many houses burnt down following an attack the previous January by the Japanese in reprisal for a KMT raid on a Japanese post.

John Creer, a 35-year-old Malaysian civil servant, had been in the area for nearly a year and when he met Chrystal at a *kampong* just to the south of Pulai, he told him how in the intervening time a vicious confrontation between the KMT and CPM guerrillas had broken out, resulting in a frail armed truce. The much vaunted W/T set was unobtainable on account of the Chinese dresser fleeing during the reprisal raid.

For the next few weeks, the two British officers tried to be as even-handed as possible, fraternising with the KMT as well as the CPM bands. However, one day, it was all too much for Ah Loy, the Communist guerrilla leader, who disarmed them after a struggle and put them under village arrest with strict orders never to visit the KMT again. With their personal rifles and ammunition confiscated, there was little they could do other than comply and it was only after a Japanese attack on Kundor on 13 July 1943, that the two men managed to slip away and, on the initiative of Creer, headed for the Telom River where he had once lived with Noone.

To their delight, after crossing over into Pahang, an aborigine took them to Noone's long-house where he was in residence. Chrystal recalled: 'I shall never forget Pat's surprise when he peered out across the floor as we approached and then recognised us. He was always warm and spontaneous and friendly and he jumped down off the dais and embraced us. For us it was the end of our long and nerve-racking journey. It was good, wonderful, to be among friends again'. Noone, weak from malaria, told of his gradual realisation that the anti-British propaganda put out by the CPM was poisoning the minds of the Sakai, the very people he had introduced to them. He was in no doubt that the Communists planned to seize power after the war had finished.

When his strength returned, Noone went over to Pulai at the invitation of the Chinese Communists there and on his return, reported that the strife between the different guerrilla bands was still ongoing though the Japanese had withdrawn to Gua Musang. Still weak and with an enlarged spleen, Noone insisted on setting off again and on 11 November 1943, left for Sungei Siput in Perak with a letter from Chrystal requesting medicines and cash from his agents there. Noone did not return at the end of the month and both Creer and Chrystal set off in search of him, but to no avail. When a group of Cantonese merchants passed through with a consignment of rock salt for Kelantan, Creer opted to go with them, leaving Chrystal to maintain a vigil for Pat Noone.

It had been another extraordinary year for Chrystal, this time finding him at the year-end alone in a small hut on the Telom River. Once more, his cheerfulness and resilience, his almost easy-going nature, had held him in good stead although there were times when his relationship with Creer, an austere and icy intellectual, had been under considerable strain.

Early in the New Year, Chrystal received the devastating news that Noone had been murdered by his Sapai companions. Initially he refused to believe it but over time there were other confirmations. A letter arrived by courier from Lai Foo of the Perak Communist guerrillas inviting him to return to them and link up with Freddy Spencer Chapman and Frank Quayle who were with them. Foo also gave him the sad news that Bill Robinson had died from malaria. Soon after another letter arrived, this time from Creer, who had established himself with a KMT band at Kuala Betis. Still determined to solve the mystery of Noone's disappearance, Chrystal stayed put. It was an unselfish act that nearly ended in disaster, for unknown to Chrystal, his vitamin-deficient diet had brought on severe beriberi, resulting in grotesquely swollen legs, a raging fever and hallucinations. It was only the timely appearance of a Chinese neighbour and his swift diagnosis and care that saved his life.

On 20 August 1944, after nearly nine months of living alone in the jungle, Chrystal left for Kuchon Kelantan to rejoin Creer. A group of Communist guerrillas had earlier passed by his camp and told him that neither they nor Spencer Chapman had been able to find any trace of Noone. After a seven day journey by foot and raft, he found Creer with a KMT band at Kundor in the middle of what was to all extents a Chinese civil war. Creer related how one night, a captured Communist leader, Ah Loy, whom he had known in Pulai, was brought into their camp and butchered alive, his liver and heart being thrown into the communal cooking pot.

The next few months were spent in various KMT camps and it was in March 1945 that the first rumours reached them that 'men from the skies' had dropped in early January. Soon this was confirmed by a letter from Major Peter Dobrée, urging Chrystal and Creer to join him as soon as they could manage the journey. They needed no further encouragement and after crossing into the Grik area found Major Geoffrey Hasler with some Malay levies.

'We got the thrill of our lives as they approached, and, laughingly, we stood to attention and gave them what we considered a smart salute. I was bare headed and John was wearing his old, felt hat shaped like a cone with a gaping hole at the top. The party stopped a few yards from us and the officer gaped for a second. Then he burst out laughing. When he could speak, he said, "You two look like a pair of scarecrows. Really it is the funniest sight I've yet seen".'

On 27 March 1945, Creer and Chrystal became part of Dobrée's Operation HEBRIDES in Upper Perak. At the main camp, they met Major Desmond Wilson of the ISLD who gave Chrystal news of Boris Hembry, by now chief of ISLD's Malayan desk in India. After filing their reports, it became clear that the British had little idea of the anti-Japanese activities neither of the KMT bands in Kelantan, Upper Perak and Pahang, nor of the true nature of the civil war waged against them by the Communist controlled 5th Regiment MPAJA detachments and the 10th MPAJA of Pulau Kelantan. Consequently, both men were needed in Ceylon to be debriefed by the DMI. The extraction plan was simple yet extremely risky. They were to make their way across the peninsula to one of the islands off the east coast where they would be picked up by a Catalina on 30 April, the date of the next full moon. This involved crossing into Japanese-controlled Trengganu where there were no KMT contacts and the risky business of procuring a fishing boat to take them across to the island.

Leaving Dobrée's camp on the afternoon of 7 April with their KMT escort, they soon ran into difficulties as their Malay porters could not cope with the heavy loads Dobrée insisted they travelled with and Creer, who had been suffering from severe heart palpitations, could not keep up. Leaving him at Belum, the most northerly Malay village on the River Perak, Chrystal pushed on with the W/T set, reaching Dabong on the night of 20 April. In spite of intense enemy activity, he nearly reached the coast. It was the failure to raise Dobrée on the W/T set – the cranking handle broke – that forced him to turn round and trek back over the mountains into Kelantan to avoid capture. Playing cat and mouse with Japanese patrols, Chrystal's party made good progress until he woke one morning to find that his Malay W/T operator and assistant had vanished, taking with them all the team's food and gold sovereigns.

Now without food or money, in an epic tale of survival in enemy held territory, Chrystal made his own way back over the jungle clad mountains, by animal tracks and rafting on bamboo down rivers until he finally reached Belum where he had left Creer. Here he found Dobrée and his parachute group installed in a new HQ and to his amazement, far from welcoming him, Dobrée 'looked up and said, "Good God!" With that, he got up and very pointedly strode out of the door.' It transpired that Dobrée had debriefed Chrystal's Malay W/T operator [who incidentally he had trained in Ceylon] and believed his story that they had had to leave Chrystal behind as he had refused to leave the Kuala Gris area for fear of being captured by the Japanese. Deeply hurt by the disbelief shown by his CO in his own version of events, Chrystal had no choice than to let the matter drop and continued working with HEBRIDES until the end of the war. Early in October 1945, he handed over his duties as a civil affairs officer and went down to Kuala Lumpur where he met up first with Creer– 'we half expected to wake suddenly and find ourselves back on a bamboo sleeping platform in some *atap* hut' – and then with Boris Hembry, who was astonished how little he had changed after three and a half years in the *ulu*.

November 1945: Recommendation for MC

Captain [then Second Lieutenant] Chrystal, although forty-eight years old at the time, volunteered to remain behind enemy lines in Malaya when the Japanese were over-running the country in 1941-42.

Eight 'stay behind parties' were organised by Lieutenant Colonel Warren RM for the purpose of harassing enemy communications and so forcing dispersal of their troops. Chrystal was a member of No. 3 Party which assembled in Kuala Lumpur and went into the field on 9 January 1942 to operate south west of Bentong. A large proportion of the party's stores were lost at the start and it was decided to try and join up with Lieutenant Colonel [the Major] F.S. Chapman, leader of No. 1 Party in the Tras area. This was achieved late February 1942.

After further separations and narrow escapes from the Japanese, Chrystal, with Captain [then Second Lieutenant] and Second Lieutenant Robinson [who later died], rejoined Chapman in the Ulu slim area at the Perak Guerrilla HQ. Here Chapman appointed him i/c training before he left for other areas. Chrystal remained until March 1943 when he decided he would be better employed if he joined Noone [who has disappeared] and Creer in Kelantan. There he and Creer played a lone hand with various guerrilla bands and eventually joined Lieutenant Colonel Dobrée of Force 136 who was operating with the Malay resistance Movement in North Perak. The knowledge and intelligence of his varied experiences were of great value to Dobrée.

The courage, endurance and perseverance of Captain Chrystal during three years of jungle life which enabled him to survive incredible hardships and dangers deserves high recognition.

Awarded

MALAYA

LIEUTENANT COLONEL DOUGLAS BROADHURST, DSO

Born in London in 1910, Douglas Broadhurst joined the Malayan Police when he left school. During the Japanese invasion of Malaya, he assisted the ORIENTAL Mission and then managed to escape to Australia where he joined the ISD and was commissioned on the General List. A WO memo described him as 'one of the Officers of the Malayan Police, and during the Malayan campaign he did a very good job there. He is a most valuable officer ... '

Prior to Malaya, Broadhurst had completed no less than three highly dangerous operations in the South West Pacific Area. In July 1942, he had accompanied Captain Ian Wylie on Operation LIZARD 1 into Portuguese Timor where they had made contact with the Australian SPARROW FORCE before being withdrawn after thirty days. The two officers then returned to Timor in September on Operation LIZARD 2 to assist the Portuguese governor as best they could by relaying his messages to Australia and to make arrangements for resistance in the event of a Japanese takeover. Despite a last minute appeal by the Governor to General MacArthur 'to assist us to prevent utter loss of Portuguese sovereignty', the Allies simply did not have the resources to mount an invasion of the island, even though LIZARD estimated that there was potential for a 50,000 strong guerrilla army. In October Broadhurst took over from Wylie who had been evacuated by sea suffering from malaria, and although reinforced by the four-man LIZARD 3, the political and military situation could no longer justify the ISD team's presence on the island and after dodging Japanese patrols for six weeks, they were evacuated by submarine on 10 February 1943. Six months later, as a member of Operation PYTHON, Broadhurst landed by submarine on the east coast of British North Borneo near Labuan Point. From October 1943 to March 1944, Broadhurst conducted recces of Japanese defences and troop dispositions as well as making contact with native people to assess their fighting potential. When it became apparent that there were Allied commandos in the area, the Japanese committed over 500 troops and twenty launches to a relentless search, and it was on his second attempt to be evacuated that Broadhurst was safely recovered by US submarine.

29 November 1945: Recommendation for DSO

Lieutenant Colonel Broadhurst who had previously undertaken operations behind the lines in the South West Pacific was dropped blind by parachute into Selangor on 30 May 1945 with a small team of officers and W/T operators. The same night he was attacked by the Japanese and his party was split. He made early W/T contact with Ceylon and within a few days had contacted resistance forces and had started to organise them. With difficulty he was able to reform his party and then organised the reception of four more liaison teams for other areas.

Lieutenant Colonel Broadhurst was appointed Force 136 Group Liaison officer for the State of Selangor and by his leadership and great determination in the face of constant dangers and within a few miles of strong enemy garrisons, built up within a short time five guerrilla patrols which by mid-August were ready to take offensive action when called on, and were so disposed that there is little doubt that, although he was naturally unaware of the time and place of the operation, his contribution to the success of an opposed landing would have been out of all proportion to the size of his forces.

He was particularly successful in collecting and transmitting intelligence and reported enemy defences, identifications and strengths in great detail. Throughout he was constantly harassed by strong Japanese patrols which he regularly outwitted.

His courage, tact and patience combined to overcome the many difficulties of reorganising the Selangor guerrillas who prior to his arrival had been broken by persistent Japanese attacks.

Awarded

CAPTAIN IBRAHIM BIN ISMAIL, OBE

Ibrahim Ismail was born on 19 October 1922 in Johore. After attending the Dehra Dun military academy he was commissioned into the Indian Army following the Japanese invasion of Malaya. From there he was recruited into SOE and was in charge of the only all-Malay team in Force 136. Colonel Christopher Hudson considered him so 'extraordinarily keen' to get into action that they agreed to send him on a mission about which most had grave doubts. His 2 i/c was Mohamed Zin bin Haji Jaffar.

Operation OATMEAL was designed to infiltrate a sabotage and observation team by Catalina on to the western coast of Trengganu, some fourteen hours flying time from Ceylon. The first attempt was made on 28 October when the two Catalinas took off from Trincomalee with the four-man team, which included two W/T operators Ahmad bin Nayan and Yahya bin Haji Mohamed, and landed just off the Prehentian Islands and began to taxi towards the mainland. The idea was to split the mission into two pairs and for them to make for the area north of the Semerak River to Ayer Tawar. However after spotting some vessels heading in a northerly direction, the OC of the Catalina party decided to abort the mission and they returned to Trincomalee after twenty-nine hours of flying. W/T operator Nyan was promptly hospitalised with severe air sickness. Well aware that they may have compromised their security during the aborted landing, time was of the essence as the window before the monsoon was getting smaller by the day. So it was decided to make a second attempt and the Catalinas took off again on 31 October, this time without Nyan, and landed just off the Prehentian Islands at about 23.30 hrs. In twenty minutes, when the kayaks and rubber dinghies had been assembled and stores loaded, the Mission set off and made landfall at Prehentian Kechil. After unloading the stores and caching them in the thick undergrowth, Ismail decided that the best course of action was to contact the *batin* or *penghulu* and enlist his help to ferry them and their stores over to the mainland. Zain was despatched to find him and on his return reported that he was not too sure about the *penghulu* despite his assurances to help OATMEAL in any way he could. The mission then tried to raise Calcutta on the W/T but did not succeed.

The next morning, good as his word, the *penghulu* had a *prahu* waiting ready to take them across to Besut. He advised them to report to the Customs Office in order to keep up their cover story that they were rice smugglers from Tumpat whose craft had capsized during the night. They duly followed his instructions and were arrested on arrival by a Japanese military police NCO. It was clear that they had been betrayed.

Ibrahim was on the end of 'some slaps and kicks' and, after being questioned by the Kempeitai at Kota Bahru, was taken back to the island and made to reveal the cache of stores. At this stage, much against his will, he had to show the Japanese how to work the ciphers and the signals plan in order to get on air and let base know by reading their messages that OATMEAL had been caught.

During a month of interrogations, the three gradually managed to convince their captors that they were not trusted by the British and had been given only the vaguest of instructions. On 7 November a Japanese Military Police Major arrived and, apparently satisfied by their stories, told them to get in contact with their HQ over the W/T link [codename VIOLIN]. After initial transmission problems, the first message was sent on 13 November. Although the Japanese were in possession of the security check details, Ibrahim still knew the verbal check which had not been written down and was therefore able to alert Calcutta that they were transmitting under duress.

The Japanese now began a double-cross operation, taking Ismail round the coastal area of Kelantan and to Kampong Lembah where the Kempeitai had decided to 'base' OATMEAL. In Ceylon, meanwhile, SOE was aware that they now had a perfect conduit for feeding the Japanese misinformation[83] and on 15 December sent a signal asking OATMEAL to relocate on the west coast in the Province Wellesley area to obtain military intelligence and then rendezvous with a contact who would be inserted into the area. Before they left, they were asked to send their route. Concerned that they could be compromised if they went by land or rail, the Japanese flew OATMEAL to the west coast and installed them in a house on a hill near Kemunting close to Taiping. On arrival another message came in from Ceylon saying that the contact had been delayed and they were to lie low until the spring. Somewhat disappointed by this turn of events, their captors nevertheless continued the deception and 'installed' Zain in the Penang area with Ismail and the W/T operator 'living' in a village on a rubber estate near Jarak where the set was 'kept'.

By May, the Japanese were beginning to get impatient and told Ismail to send a message asking for contacts and stores and money to be dropped. He explained that this was totally out of order and it would only serve to alert HQ that something was suspicious. His bluff worked and after a dicey moment when Yayha was recognised by an old acquaintance in the street in Kemunting, another message came through proposing to send another W/T set if Ismail could recruit a local operator. This was manna to the Japanese who immediately began training up one of their own operators in British Morse code.

---

83 This triple-cross was masterminded from India by a group of intelligence officers that included Colonel Peter Fleming of D Division.

Ceylon also promised to drop the set and other stores during the July moon period. In quick succession, DZs were recced, changed and confirmed, dates postponed and drops cancelled. On one occasion, a Japanese officer failed to notice a ten-foot pig trap near the drop zone and fell in to it.

Finally at 20.45 hrs on 7 August, the Japanese reception party along with OATMEAL manned the DZ near Kebun Kopi. A perfect drop followed and the next day all the stores were on display at the Kempeitai HQ in Taiping. Ismail was congratulated in helping to fool the British and urged to keep up the good work. All though was far from satisfactory for there were a number of deficiencies in the five containers according to the packing list. Where were the money, crystals, signals plan and codes and why was there soap, rice and .22 ammunition which were not on the manifest? Ismail immediately sent a signal informing Ceylon of the errors and an apologetic reply was received, arranging another drop on 19 August. In the event, OATMEAL received a message on 17 August, before Operation ZIPPER was put into action, confirming Japan's unconditional surrender following the dropping of the atom bombs on Hiroshima and Nagasaki.

Ismail was immediately concerned that 'the Japs might just bump us off', and regretfully informed his Kempeitai captors that his religion would not permit him to commit *hara-kiri* with them. Eventually the OATMEAL members were released and made contact with British forces which had landed without opposition in early September.

In his post-operational report of 19 November 1945, Ismail summarised that:

'although we were caught, we were determined then to put up some sort of fight and when we decided to collaborate with the Japanese our only aim was to sabotage their time and energy for nothing. We knew that we were running much greater risks by doing that but we were prepared to suffer the consequences if things did not work out well for us. Providence helped us right through and we succeeded in what we set out to do.'

MAJOR 'PADDY' MARTIN

Born in Batu Gajah Malaya, Paddy Martin had worked as a rubber planter and member of the SSVC until the Japanese invasion when he was recruited by HQ Singapore [Army] to undertake intelligence work in south east Johore in the last two weeks of the campaign. He joined SOE in May 1943 from The Sappers and Miners [Madras] in Bangalore and spent his first year training Malays in small boat handling, jungle warfare and demolitions. In May 1944, he started to prepare for Operation CARPENTER and, on 21 September, was parachuted into Malaya with two Australian SRD officers, Major Durward Sime [2/4 Australian Cavalry Commando Squadron, then Z Force] and Captain Neville Reddish [2/7 Australian Commando Squadron]. On 25 January 1945, Japanese troops attacked their camp and Martin was killed by the first burst of fire. Sime took over command and successfully raised a band of guerrillas as did Reddish. Sime, a former Johore planter, was awarded an MBE and Reddish an MC.

CHAPTER SIX

SUMATRA

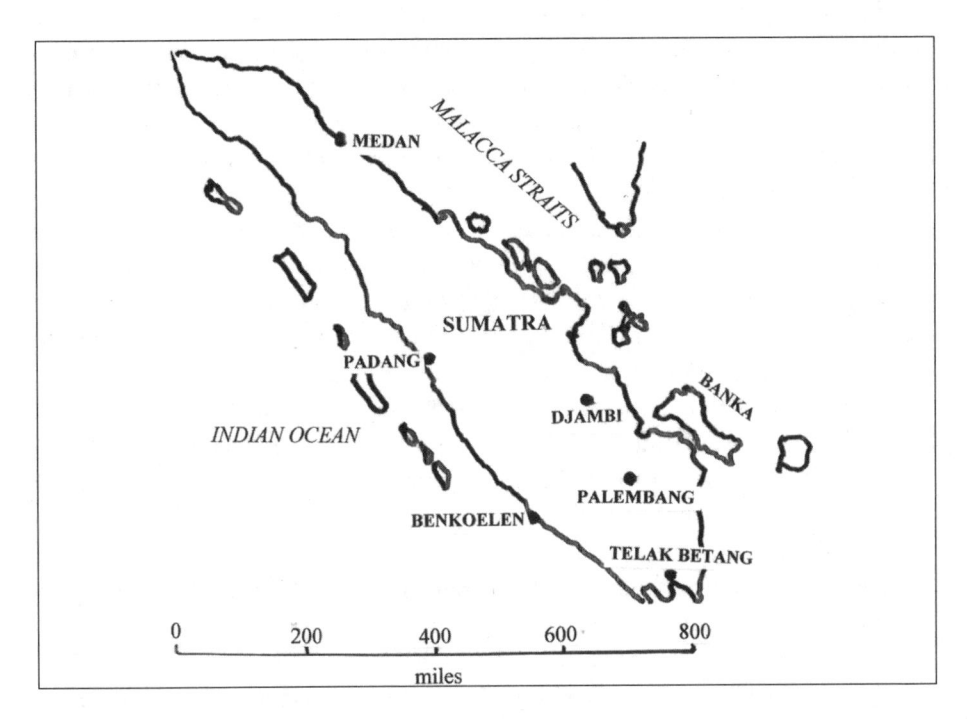

For political background, see *Chapter Thirteen: Dutch East Indies*

14 February 1942: 360 paratroopers of Japanese 1st Airborne Division landed at Pangkalanbenteng airfield near Palembang. The next day they are reinforced with 100 additional paratroopers, helping with the securing the oil refineries and other facilities.

12 March 1942: Japanese troops landed in north east Sumatra at Sabang at 02.35 hrs, Koetaradja at 03.30 hrs, Idi at 05.40 hrs, and Laboehanroekoe at 07.00 hrs. They captured the airfield at Medan that morning.

28 March 1942: Dutch Major General Roelof T. Overakker surrendered his 2,000 troops at Blangkedjeren, marking the end of resistance on Sumatra.

With the surrender at Blangkedjeren organised resistance on Sumatra ended. A number of small guerrilla groups continued to fight on, but hostile natives made it impossible for them to continue for long. One by one, they either surrendered or were tracked down and killed by the Japanese. The last group finally surrendered in March 1943, a year after the Japanese landed.

The possibility of establishing a viable resistance movement was remote from the very beginning. SOE faced several difficulties, the distance from Ceylon, traditional hostility of the Acehnese people to outsiders, the Japanese 'post-colonial offer', strained relations with the Dutch in Ceylon and London and lastly, the Dutch special forces chief, Admiral Helfrich, who had a preference for commando raids.

Major Christopher Hudson was appointed head of the Anglo-Dutch Country Section with Major Mollinger as his 2 i/c. Mollinger had undergone training at Arisaig and brought forty men from the Korps Insulinde [Dutch Commandos] with him to Ceylon. Almost immediately there was friction since SOE did not want the Korps as commando raids were contrary to their operational doctrine. Captain H.G.C. Pel and Lieutenant Jan Scheepens were then flown to Ceylon from Britain as team leaders, the former described by Boris Hembry as 'thoroughly dislikeable and distrustful of anything British'. In contrast, Hembry held Scheepens who hailed from a distinguished Dutch military family in the highest esteem.

The following operations were all launched from Ceylon by the Anglo-Dutch Country Section of Force 136:

- In May 1942 Lieutenant H.A. Wijnmalen was inserted by submarine *K15* at Bungus Bay, south of Padang. He was captured, tortured, and executed.
- In December 1942 Major Pel, Captain Scheepens, Lieutenant Baron van Truyll van Seroskerke, Lieutenant de Bruine, Lieutenant Sisselar and six ORs were inserted by submarine *O24* at Trumon off the west coast. All were recovered.
- In February 1943 Captain Scheepens and a party of seven were prevented from landing by rough seas.
- In April 1943 Major Pel[84] planned Operation MATRIARCH to land Captain Scheepens, Lieutenant van Eek, Lieutenant de Roo, Lieutenant Witkamp and six ORs by submarine at Lho Seumawe on the east coast. The final party consisting of Captain Scheepens, Lieutenant de Jonge, Lieutenant de Roo, seven Dutch other ranks, and two British ISLD officers – Captain Boris Hembry and Major Laurie Brittain – landed by submarine *O24* at Trumon and Meulabeuh, on the west coast over 17-19

---

84 Wing Commander C.J. Wingender took over from Pel around this time.

April 1943. In effect it was a large recce patrol and it ran into an ambush, its members narrowly escaping with their lives. They found that the villagers did not want to be associated with them and after abducting two Acehnese farmers and taking them on board the recovering submarine, they returned to Ceylon.

The next operations were in support of Operation FIRST CULVERIN, Churchill's cherished plan to invade northern Sumatra. SOE was tasked to recce sites for landing strips on the west coast of Sumatra and on the island of Simalur.

- RESIDENCY and SUGARLOAF left Trincomalee on 26 April 1944 and between 30 April – 5 May 1944, Captain J.G.D. Lowe's recce group which included Royal Engineer airfield experts Captains A.F.S. Wright and W.R. Annan and the main group of Captain Scheepens, Lieutenant Sisselar and six ORs were inserted by HMS *Templar* on the coast of north west Sumatra. Altogether they made five landings. On the last landing, despite 'strong advice' from Scheepens that the area had been compromised, Lowe insisted on completing his mission. With Scheepens providing a ferry party, Lowe, Annan and Sepoy Mehar Beg swam ashore from their dinghy. An exchange of gunfire followed by long bursts of MG fire on the beach indicated that the shore party had been ambushed. There was no option other than for the ferry party to return to the submarine and sail without delay.
- On 3 May 1944 SUGERLOAF 2 commanded by Lieutenant Peer USNR sailed from Trincomalee on HMS *Truculent* to recce possible air strips on Simalur Island, 100 miles to the west of Sumatra. Flight Lieutenant Bunting and Lieutenant Donald Lowe, escorted by an OSS shore party under Lieutenant Peterson, made a chaotic landing in fifteen feet high surf on 7 May – 'one boat was disembowelled and another capsized'. The party, having gone ashore naked, immediately retrieved their rubber boats and dragged them to the edge of the jungle, where they put on their kit and cocked their weapons. They reached their recce target – the Bangkala airfield – in heavy rain on 10 May. According to the plan, the exit route should have been along a well defined jungle track. It turned out that it was non-existent and a dreadful seven day walk out through atrocious country ensued. Rations ran out and feet became 'like lumps of raw meat'. One member of the party arrived at the beach RV literally on his hands and knees. All were safely picked up.

Operations RETALIATE 1-3 were launched to make contact with Overseas Chinese in north east Sumatra and then to organise sabotage groups. One idea was to recruit Chinese agents to sail junks armed with 40mm canons in

Sumatran waters.
- RETALIATE I under Lieutenant van Eck sailed on 12 June from Ceylon on HMS *Truculent*. Van Eck and his group managed to abduct some Javanese policemen from the Padang River and also a Chinese fisherman en route back to Ceylon which they reached on 28 June.

So far little of any value had been achieved. By the beginning of 1945, Sumatra was the only territory where SOE had no agents on the ground. The tempo of landings was therefore stepped up in 1945:
- In March 1945 Operation CARRIAGE [Captain Scheepens and Major Lodge [British] with four Chinese agents] landed from HMS *Clyde*. They were immediately spotted by the Japanese who opened fire and returned in haste to the submarine. On their return journey, they captured a small vessel and its nine man crew as a consolation prize.
- In May 1945, Lieutenant de Jongh and Corporal Bruynster with four Chinese agents were inserted by HMS *Torbay* off the east coast. They returned safely.
- In June 1945, Operation TETHER [a four man team led by Lieutenant Sisselar] dropped blind in the Hoeta-Baroe area of northern Sumatra where it successfully established a base and 'produced intelligence of considerable value'.
- On 1 July 1945 Lieutenant Commander Lefrandt was dropped by air on Operation SWEEP.
- On 3 July 1945 Operation STEEL/GLOVE [Major Lodge [British] and three Chinese agents] landed by HMS *Torbay* near Soengai Tengah, west of Bagansiapiapi and later operated in the Pakanbaroe area.
- In July 1945 Operation SWEEP/STUD [WO Lefrandt] dropped by parachute into the Sigli area on the north coast of Atjeh and successfully made contact with the local population, providing timely and accurate intelligence. Later reinforced by Major Knottenbelt and Captain Burton [BLO], who made contact with Dr Soekarno, the leader of the Nationalist Party.
- On 16 August 1945 a parachute landing was made by Lieutenant Brondgeest, Ensign Classens and three others [Operation STATUS/BUTTON] in the Medan area where it provided assistance to POWs and useful political intelligence. It was one of the few operations which produced sufficient evidence of war crimes to indict those responsible.
- After the Japanese surrender, a number of missions were dropped in early September to collect political and military intelligence – ARREST/POCKET, BLUNT/PLEAT, ASPECT/HANDBAG, ANIMAL/COLLAR, SYMPATHY/LOOP, JANITOR/BUCKLE.

MAJOR ERNEST LODGE, MBE

Ernest Lodge

Born in Normanton, Yorkshire in 1906, Ernie Lodge graduated from Leeds University with a BSc Hons Physics in 1929. After three years gold mining and prospecting in Australia, he became a rubber and oil palm planter on the east coast of Sumatra where he learnt Malay, Javanese and passable Dutch. He enlisted in the Royal Tank Regiment in June 1940 and served in the Middle East with 32 Anti Tank Brigade where he was wounded and taken prisoner in June 1942. He escaped from Italy in October 1943.

Recruited by SOE in February 1944, his SOE report of May 1944 described him as 'a good solid type of Yorkshireman. A somewhat slow and deliberate thinker, but painstaking and efficient'.

By the beginning of 1945, Sumatra was the only enemy occupied territory where SOE did not have any agents on the ground. In February that year, Captain Scheepens of the Indian Mission's Dutch Section and Lodge took a party of four Chinese agents on Operation CARRIAGE to the north west coast where they planned to observe traffic on the main road and also make contact with the local Acehnese. Landing by submarine on 1 March, they were almost immediately spotted and withdrew under fire back to the beach where the ferry party was still waiting and all returned to the submarine safely. A second attempt to land 140 miles further up the coast was considered too dangerous and after capturing and then sinking a small coastal vessel, their submarine commander returned to Ceylon.

On 3 July 1945, Lodge went in again with three Chinese agents on Operation STEEL, this time landing by submarine on the east coast north of Bagansiapiapi. The war ended before he could accomplish anything.

TIGERS BURNING BRIGHT

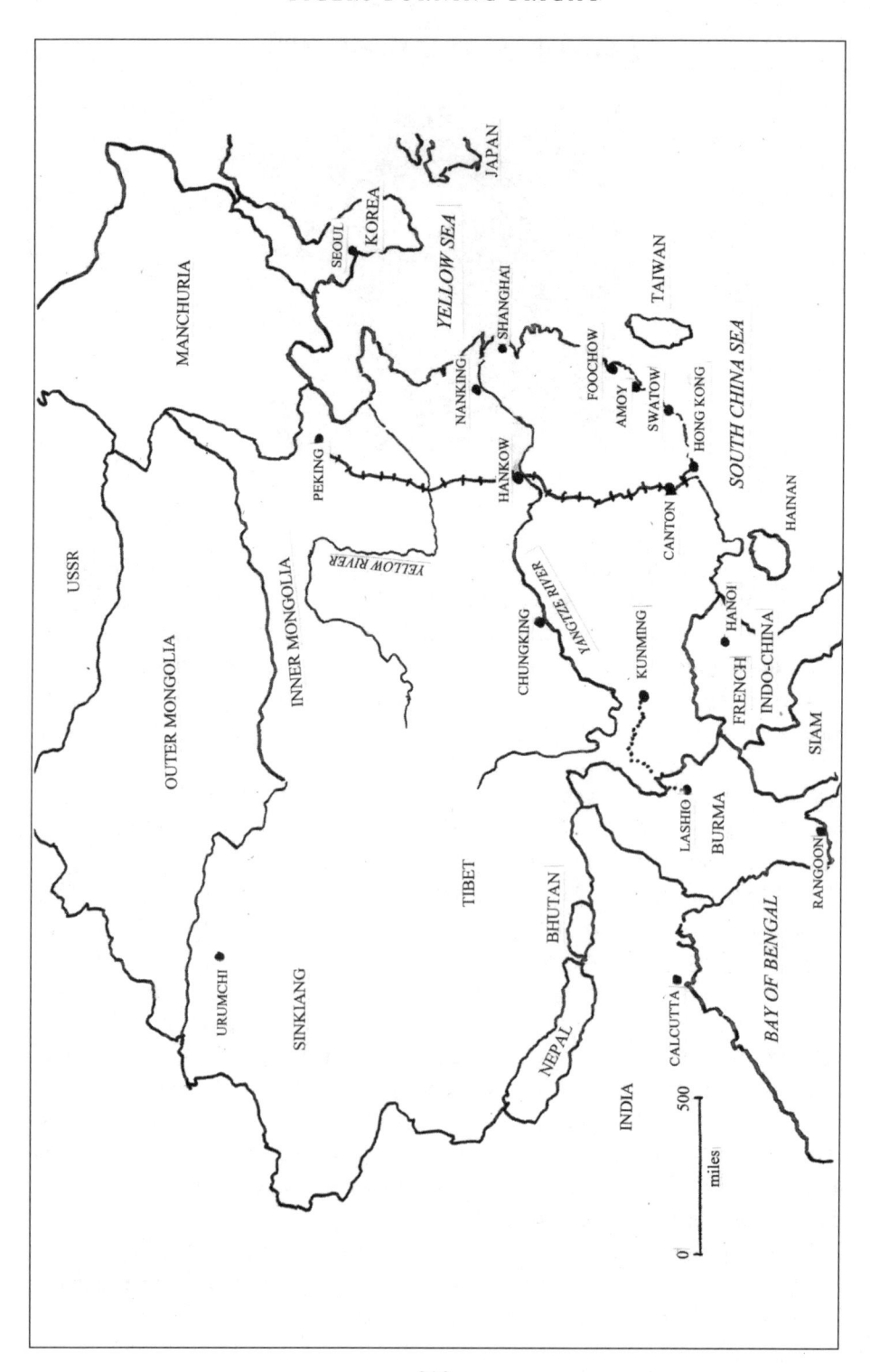

CHAPTER SEVEN

CHINA and HONG KONG

POLITICAL BACKGROUND

On 1 January 1912 the Republic of China was established, heralding the end of Imperial Manchu China. Sun Yat-sen of the Kuomintang [the KMT or Nationalist Party] was proclaimed provisional president of the new republic but real political power remained embedded with the regional warlords.

When the First World War broke out in 1914, Japan fought on the Allied side and seized German holdings in Shandong Province. In 1917 China declared war on Germany in the hope of recovering this lost province, then under Japanese control. When the Treaty of Versailles confirmed the Japanese claim to Shandong, a violent nationalist reaction swept through China and helped revive the flagging republican revolution. The territorial dispute was eventually settled at the Washington Naval Conference in 1922 when, after securing a favourable naval treaty with the US and Great Britain, Japan returned Shandong to Chinese control.

It was only in the late 1920s that the KMT under Generalissimo Chiang Kai-shek managed to reunify the country on his famous Northern Expedition, though not entirely since the CCP[85], at war with the KMT since 1927, refused to kow-tow to the government in Nanjing, Chiang's new capital.

Tension between Japan and Nationalist China had been growing since the Japanese invasion of Manchuria in 1931 and the subsequent creation of a nominally independent state, Manchukuo, with Puyi, the last monarch of the Qing Dynasty, as its sovereign. At the end of 1932 the Japanese army invaded Rehe Province and annexed it to Manchukuo. Then, in 1935, Japan officially established the East Hebei Autonomous Council, turning the Chinese provinces of Hebei and Chahar into a puppet state. By early 1937 all the areas north, east and west of Peking were controlled by Japan. Whereas the intentions of Japan were starkly clear to both the CCP and the KMT, their priorities were diametrically different. The CCP needed a war with China to escape defeat at the hands of Chiang; the KMT needed to defeat the CCP and solidify their political and military position before they took on the Japanese.

---

85 Supported in Britain in the 1930s by the League against Imperialism and the Friends of the Chinese People.

Just as a KMT victory looked in sight as the Communists retreated north to Shaanxi Province on their Long March, one event changed the entire picture. On 12 December, 1936, Chiang Kai-shek was visiting the city of Xi'an to encourage 'the Young Marshal' Zhang Xueliang, leader of the 400,000-strong Northern Border Defence Army, to intensify his military offensive against the Communists. Instead, Zhang put Chiang under house arrest and only released him when he agreed to terminate the KMT's war against the Communists and join forces with them in a war against Japan.

When a clash occurred between Chinese and Japanese troops outside Beijing near the Marco Polo Bridge in July 1937, the looming military confrontation became a reality and the horror of a full-scale invasion was unleashed on China. A disastrous defeat for Chiang followed at Shanghai in October when he lost over half of his professional officer corps and then the world watched the fall of Nanjing in December 1937 with its gruesome mass killings and rape of civilians when an estimated 200,000 Chinese were massacred.

China still had about 3,820,000 men under arms. Of these, 2,920,000 were formed into 246 divisions classed by the Chinese as 'front-line' troops, plus forty-four 'brigades'. In rear areas there were another seventy divisions and three brigades. Except for the Generalissimo's personal troops, estimated at about thirty divisions, the loyalties of China's troops tended to lie with their war area commanders.

Having lost his ports and access to the sea, Chiang needed a supply route to the rest of the world, so he ordered a road built from Kunming to Lashio in Burma. The 681-mile road was built by tens of thousands of Chinese labourers in a year and a half, and was opened to traffic in mid-1939. Supplies for Chiang's government and troops were shipped by sea to Rangoon, then by rail to Lashio, and finally by road to Kunming. It was aptly called the Burma Road, and it was Nationalist China's main source of supply from the outside world for two and a half years – from mid-1939 to 8 March 1942, the day Rangoon fell to the Japanese.

*****

Throughout the 1930s, the British had been playing it safe in trying to protect their Far East investments and yet not alienate Japan. Steering a middle course through the invasion of Manchuria, where British interests were easily outweighed by her need to maintain cordial relations with Japan, the Government despatched its chief economic adviser, Sir Frederick Leith-Ross, to Tokyo in September 1935 with the idea of promoting economic co-operation between the two countries in China. Little resulted from this bold initiative to bring Japan back into the international fold but talks were revived when a Federation of Japanese Economic Organisations Mission came to London in July 1937 to meet with UK industrialists and bankers. Unfortunately the Marco Polo bridge incident happened the same week as a result of which discussions were curtailed.

In a House of Lords debate in February 1938, Viscount Elibank outlined British interests in China:

' ... Here [in Shanghai] is situated probably the largest entrepôt for international trade in the world and here is the centre for the investment of many millions of pounds of capital in various undertakings in Shanghai and other parts of China. This country holds the largest share of those investments, aggregating something like £150,000,000 ... Any single Power having Shanghai in its control would be able to injure the business interests of other nations far beyond the boundaries of Shanghai right into the centre of China.

If the Customs in Shanghai were dominated by Japanese there is little doubt that it would be run principally in Japanese interests ... What have the Japanese done with regard to the revenue which they have taken over elsewhere, in Tientsin, Tsingtao and other places? They have paid this revenue into the Yokohama Specie Bank. What guarantee is there, if they do the same with the Customs revenue in Shanghai, that they will not, as time goes on and their funds for war purposes get lower and lower, appropriate to their own purposes the amount which is required to pay the services of the foreign loans?

Finally, I should like to know what is to become of Sir Frederick Maze, the present Inspector-General? If he were to leave that post, what is to become of British prestige; or, if I might put it in this way, if he is to leave that post and no British Inspector-General is to be appointed in his place, what is to become of British prestige in China?

I should also like to ask what is the position with regard to Canton, for if Canton were taken by Japan communications between Hong Kong and probably the whole of the South China field would be blocked to British trade, and this is where British trade largely lies in China.'

Despite these major investments and trade flows, Britain had to remain on the sidelines when it came to military support for the KMT simply because she was in the process of rearming herself and there were no weapons or munitions to spare. Prior to the outbreak of the Second World War, Chiang was supported by

Chinese troops: now you see them, now you don't

Germany[86] and then the Soviet Union, the latter providing aircraft, military supplies, and advisors. However Britain allowed Hong Kong to be used as the main entry port for shipments of arms to the KMT until this channel was cut by the Japanese capture of Canton and the closure of the Kowloon-Canton railway.

Sir Archibald Clark Kerr, HM Ambassador to China, was under no illusions about the state of affairs in China. Writing to the Foreign Secretary in January 1941, he drew attention to the review of China in 1940 by Sir Arthur Blackburn, the Embassy Counsellor in Chungking.

---

86 In 1935, the trading organisation HARPO [Handelsgesellschaft zur Verwertung industrieller Produkte] was established. Its goal was to funnel German military goods to Chiang Kai-Shek through commercial cover. Trade to China not only contained items such as uniforms, guns, munitions, and tanks but it also included items such as manufacturing know-how, railroad technologies, munitions plants, and communications technologies. In return, China delivered a number of strategic raw materials such as wolfram to Germany. When Germany recognised Manchukuo in early 1938, Göring officially called a halt to German military export shipments through HARPO to China – regardless of contractual obligations. By the summer of 1938, most of the German military advisors in China had been recalled to Germany.

'While Japan has been free to draw upon the outside world, China has seen nearly all sources dry up. Of late the Japanese military effort has been almost entirely designed to bring this about. The blocking of the ports of Fukien and Chekiang and of the hinterlands of Hong Kong and Macao, and the seizure of Tonkin have barred routes by which a regular and considerable flow of imports entered China, while the loss of Ichang has dislocated her internal system of distribution. The effect has been to leave China in poor case. Her large armies have been deprived of nearly all of their offensive power and reduced to an inactivity from which they cannot emerge unless by some supreme effort, it may prove impossible to keep them supplied by the Burma Road. Nevertheless, by the sheer weight of numbers, they continue to contain in China very large enemy forces which Japan would now like to set free for use elsewhere.

In October the Generalissimo, departing from the buoyancy and serenity which have characterised him in the past, drew a gloomy picture of the situation. China was feeling the full effects of three years of war. The will to resist remained unabated, but the means were becoming dangerously meagre. His difficulties were economic rather than military, for the morale of the army was high and it still had reserves upon which to draw. With some material help from outside he could not only prolong resistance indefinitely; he could also usefully take the offensive. Without such help he must confess that he could not hold out.'

Subsequently the British government helped finance the construction of the Burma Road from Lashio to the Chinese border and established air services between Burma, India and China.

Financially Britain did its best in 1939. British banks under a Treasury guarantee provided half of a £10 million currency stabilisation fund to thwart Japanese attempts to undermine the Chinese currency and replace it with one under their own control. A further £5 million was added to the fund in December 1940 and a £5 million credit for use in the sterling area granted in June 1941 [in 1939 exports credits worth £3 million were granted]. In 1942, the Government made available a loan of £50 million. As Sir John Pratt, the FO's Adviser on Far Eastern Affairs, wrote in *War and Politics in China* [1942], 'this assistance was enough to keep Chinese resistance alive but not enough to enable her to drive the invader from her soil'.

*****

Being less exposed to the threat of Japanese militarism, the American stance towards China was markedly more overtly supportive in contrast to the British. When hostilities commenced in 1937, President Roosevelt did not invoke the 1937 Neutrality Act on the grounds that neither party had formally declared war. This enabled American supplies to reach the KMT albeit in British 'bottoms'. In two loans in 1939, the American Export-Import Bank lent the Chinese-owned Universal Trading Corporation $45 million, although their use was restricted to the purchase of civilian supplies. In June 1940 Chiang Kai-shek's brother-in-law, T.V. Soong, visited the United States to ask for arms and more credits, resulting in a third credit of $25 million[87].

In November 1940 the Generalissimo sent another mission under General Mao Pang-tzo, of the Chinese Air Force, to the United States. With him was the retired American Army Air Corps flier, Captain Claire Chennault. The Mao mission presented a request for 500 combat planes to be flown by American volunteers [AVG] to the President's Liaison Committee. The extension of a $100 million credit duly followed on 1 December 1940. Of the total sum, twenty-five per cent could be used to purchase arms.

DEPLOYMENT OF JAPANESE INFANTRY DIVISIONS IN THE FAR EAST: CHINA AND MANCHURIA DEVOURED MOST OF THEM.

Country	December 1941	Comments	August 1943
Manchuria	13		15
China	22		26
Formosa and Palau Is.	2	14th Army: Philippines invasion force	2 in Philippines
China and FIC	2	15th Army: Burma invasion force	6 in Burma
China and FIC	4	25th Army: Malaya, Borneo and Sumatra invasion force	1 in Malaya and Sumatra
Japan and Palau Is.	1	16th Army: Dutch Borneo, Celebes, S. Sumatra, Timor and Java invasion force	2 in E.New Guinea, Celebes and Timor 2 in Java
Korea			2
Solomons and W.New Guinea			6
Thailand			1
FIC			1
Total	**44**		**64**

---

87 The United States also continued its silver purchases, which gave China US $252 million in cash.

With the available $25 million, the State Department hinted that military aid to China would start with aircraft and that no objection would be raised to the formation of the AVG. On 19 December 1940 President Roosevelt approved military aid for China and asked the relevant departments to find ways of implementing a program. Because of the pending exhaustion of British dollar resources, President Roosevelt proposed that same month the device of removing the 'dollar sign' by lending or leasing arms to Great Britain and any other nation whose defence was thought vital to American security.

The Lend-Lease bill went before Congress on 6 January 1941 and was signed off by the President on 11 March 1941. In May, the first Lend-Lease equipment for China left New York for Rangoon. By late spring an additional $100 million of Lend-Lease funds was allocated to Soong's communications and air force projects. Although the AVG was not supported by Lend-Lease funds, both the War and Navy Departments extended facilities for recruiting agents and released pilots and crews for service in China's Air Force. When the first volunteers arrived on 28 July, they were sent to the RAF airfield at Toungoo, with the proviso that the Burmese airfields would not be used as a base to attack the Japanese.

In mid-May 1941 the Secretary of War agreed that the Chinese might begin their rearmament with $50 million of Lend-Lease funds and that $23 million worth could be from U.S. army stockpiles or current production.

On 3 July 1941 General Marshall approved the American Military Mission to China [AMMISCA]. Its head, Brigadier General John Magruder, was told to:

1. Advise and assist the Chinese Government in all phases of procurement, transport, and maintenance of materials, equipment, and munitions requisite to the prosecution of its military effort.
2. Advise and assist the Chinese Government in the training of Chinese personnel in the use and maintenance of materials, equipment, and munitions supplied as defence aid material by the United States.
3. When requested, assist personnel of other Departments of the [United States] Government in carrying out their respective duties in furtherance of the objectives of the Lend-Lease Act pertaining to China.
4. Assist the Chinese Government in obtaining prompt and co-ordinated administrative action by the United States authorities necessary to insure the orderly flow of materials and munitions from Lend-Lease agencies to the Chinese military forces.
5. Explore the vital port, road, and railroad facilities with a view to the establishment and maintenance of an adequate line of communications.

The War Department released its first shipment of ammunition to the Chinese at the end of August 1941. On 13 September 1941 the first group of AMMISCA personnel flew to Chungking via Manila and Hong Kong.

After the Japanese attack on Pearl Harbour in December 1941, the US saw its main role in China as keeping it in the war, for as long as it stayed in the war, hundreds of thousands of Japanese soldiers could be tied down on the Asian mainland instead of being used to fight on other fronts. To that end, the aim was to deliver sufficient equipment, weapons, and munitions to build thirty well-equipped and trained Chinese divisions.

Deployment of Japanese divisions in China and SEAC

Country	Dec 1942/Mar 1942	Aug 1943	Aug 1945
Manchuria [Kwantung]	13	15	11
China	22	25	25
Burma	2	6	10
Malaya, Borneo, Sumatra	3	1	10
Total	40	47	56

Source: John Ellis, World War Two Databook

The British, with a far smaller cheque book, were in a somewhat weaker position, for as Madame Chiang Kai-shek told the *New York Times* in April 1942, 'we cannot see why the West, with its vaunted prescience, could not see that each passing hour gave Japan added opportunity to prepare to strike more deadly blows while the powers contented themselves with fortifying their positions with paper bullets'. For the West, read Britain.

Therefore the British had to be more circumspect. While the defeat of Japan was a strategic imperative, they were well aware of the tendency of the Chinese to nibble at the northern borders of Burma and Thailand and also fearful of losing their valuable commercial enclaves on mainland China after the war. Unlike the Americans, they neither had the money nor the materials to support Chiang, so had to rely on guile, diplomacy and charm.

MI[R] IN CHINA

In mid-September 1939, MI[R] planned to send Peter Fleming, Michael Lindsay and John Keswick to see how they could help China against the Japanese. The

FO vetoed the idea. Fleming, who as a Special Correspondent of *The Times* had travelled from Moscow to Peking via Central Asia [written up in *To Peking: A Forgotten Journey from Moscow to Manchuria* and *One's Company: a journey to China*] had made an overland journey in 1935 from China to India, described in *News from Tartary* [1936]. While not for a moment passing himself off as a Sinologist, he had amassed in a relatively short time sufficient experience and insight to prepare a perspicacious and realistic plan for British military assistance to the Chinese. His appreciation [see ANNEX L] formed the foundation of SOE's Chinese strategy and indeed that of the OSS.

Michael Lindsay had arrived in Japanese-occupied Peking in January 1938 to teach at Yenching University, an American missionary university with extra-territorial status, where his job was to help introduce the Oxford University tutorial system. On his first spring vacation, Lindsay and two Yenching colleagues decided to venture into Chinese-controlled territory outside Peking, and stumbled upon the Chinese Communists' Eighth Route Army, which had just started to move into the area. Lindsay returned to Communist-controlled areas in the summer of 1938, and again in the summer of 1939. Accounts of these journeys were published in *The Times*. During the 1939 trip, the Communists asked Lindsay to serve as a purchasing agent for their troops, taking advantage of his status as a British citizen who could move relatively freely in Japanese-controlled Peking. Not being a fluent Chinese speaker, he recruited one of his students, 23-year-old Li Hsiao Li, to help him re-label in Chinese the medical supplies, radio parts, chemicals and other supplies intended for the Eighth Route Army.

In April 1940, when funding for his position at Yenching temporarily dried up, Lindsay's brother-in-law, Robert Scott[88], arranged for Lindsay to be seconded to the British Embassy as 'Press attaché' to the Ambassador, Sir Archibald Clarke Kerr. He started in Shanghai and Hong Kong, and then moved to Chungking where the incumbent Press attaché was Walter Gordon Harmon, the SIS officer tasked with liaising with the KMT. After six months he returned to Yenching where he resumed smuggling supplies to the Communist army. He married his student accomplice, Li Hsiao Li, in June 1941 and the two just managed to escape the clutches of the Japanese secret police on 8 December as they fled the city. For the next two years Lindsay worked as a radio technology instructor and technical adviser to the Jinchaji Military Region, moving between various radio departments in sub-district HQs.

---

88 Robert Scott was the brother of Ian Scott, the husband of Michael's younger sister Drusilla. After the war, he served as Commissioner General of Singapore and then Permanent Secretary of the Ministry of Defence.

Eager to draw the attention of the outside world to the real situation in northern China and to the pressing need to supply the CCP with sufficient arms and equipment to take on the Japanese, in May 1943 Lindsay tried to establish a W/T link with British intelligence in Chungking but the Americans had arranged for his signals to be routed through a Chinese KMT station manned by Tai Li's secret police. Not surprisingly, given that the KMT was blockading the Communist areas, they did not reply to Lindsay's signals and told the Americans that they could not hear him calling. An earlier attempt by Lindsay to send a report on 'The North China Front' to the British Embassy in Chungking had also failed. When the courier, Grey Martel Hall, the former manager of the National City Bank of New York in Peking, reached Chungking, he handed Lindsay's report over to the American authorities, who promptly classified it and did not pass it on to the British. Hall's original plan of placing the report as an article in the influential magazine *Foreign Affairs* had come to nought and it was to be another two years before it finally saw the light of day in *Amerasia*.

Frustrated by this, Lindsay decided to move to the Communist army HQ at Yenan where he had a better chance of contacting British and American

Michael Lindsay and family in China 1945

organisations in Chungking and set off on a 500-mile trek with his wife and new born daughter on 8 March 1944. After safely reaching Yenan at the end of May having crossed the Japanese lines no less than three times, Lindsay and his family were installed in a cave and he started to build a high powered transmitter to establish a link with India and North America, one which could bypass the KMT in Chungking. Now the 'Wireless Communications Advisor' to the Third Department of Eighteenth Group Army, he was busily constructing the transmitter when the US Army DIXIE Mission arrived in July. With an air link subsequently established to Chungking, Lindsay prepared a report on the situation in North China for Lieutenant Colonel Gordon Harmon, the SIS chief in Chungking, and gave it to a US officer who was flying out. Included in it was an invitation from Eighth Route Army HQ for Harmon to visit Yenan. No acknowledgment from Harmon was ever received and several years later it transpired that certain American officers had decided not to pass it on.

With the transmitter completed by August, Lindsay transferred his attention to the New China News agency, advising the CCP how to best present their information to the outside world. After nearly eight years in Japanese occupied China and in the intervening time the father of two children, he finally left Yenan in November 1945 and returned to England where his father, the Master of Balliol College, was now a peer, an ennoblement which conferred on Hsiao Li the distinction of being Britain's first Chinese peeress when her father-in-law died in 1952.

THE ORIENTAL MISSION

SOE's initial efforts in Shanghai proved disastrous. A.E. Jones, a former Shanghai policeman, who had arrived in Singapore in January 1941 with the ORIENTAL Mission advanced party, had recruited W.J. Gande, a 55-year-old wholesale liquor merchant, to head up operations in Shanghai. He in turn created his own network of agents, mainly ex-pats, including the 65-year-old H.G. Clarke, a retired Deputy Commissioner of the Shanghai Municipal police. From the beginning, SOE found itself up against the implacable opposition of both the Ambassador and the SIS representative and worse, unbeknown to the cell, Gande's long-serving book-keeper, a Romanian called Kaman, was selling to the Japanese every piece of incriminating paperwork he came across in the offices of Gande, Price & Co to the Japanese. However, some progress was made when one of Gande's men, Mr Brand, went to Singapore in August to do a short course at STS 101. On his return, he began to organise a course for the Shanghai cell in anticipation of a visit by Major Jim Gavin. It was never to happen.

On 17 December, Clarke was arrested and tortured; ten days later Gande and two other members of the network, Brand and Brister, were rounded up[89]. Kept in medieval conditions – at one stage on a freezing winter's night they found themselves thrown into a 27 feet by 12 feet cage with twenty-nine other prisoners already in it – they were all tried before a Japanese Military Tribunal in April 1942 and sentenced to imprisonment. Gande spent the next four years in Ward Road jail; others were repatriated in prisoner swaps.

In February 1941, Major General L.E. Dennys[90], Military Attaché in Chungking, discussed military assistance to China with Chiang Kai-shek and General Ho Yaozhu, which included taking a Chinese military delegation to India, Burma and Malaya. These discussions ended with a proposal from Dennys to set up an elite guerrilla force, under command of the Chinese but officered and equipped by the British, to attack Japanese lines of communication. The Chinese responded favourably and Detachment 204 was born; the Chinese agreed to raise six battalions and the British to provide officers[91] and ORs skilled in demolitions. Training began almost immediately at the STS at Maymyo in Burma, with volunteers from Australian and British units. Under the watchful eye of Major Mike Calvert RE, students learnt the art of 'blowing things up' and how to fight and survive behind enemy lines. In London, news of this thoroughly alarmed the FO, which immediately sent word that under no circumstances could British personnel fight alongside the Chinese until war had been officially declared between England and Japan. This was the situation Killery inherited when he arrived in Singapore in May 1941 to set up the ORIENTAL Mission.

It was Clark Kerr who ingeniously found a way around this impasse by suggesting that non-British Europeans should be used to man a China Commando Group [CCG], although Britain would pay the costs of their expenses and all equipment and materials. Operation ANTIPODES was a neat solution and warmly welcomed by Chiang Kai-shek, who asked General Tai Li, his secret service chief[92], to implement it on the Chinese side. Choosing to use a long spoon to sup with the British, Tai Li delegated the task a subordinate,

---

89 Three others were arrested in February 1942 – Elias [an Iraqi], Jack and Riggs. It is Riggs's report that tells the story of their capture, interrogation and treatment.

90 Killed in an air crash in China on 14 March 1942, Dennys was replaced by Brigadier J.G. Bruce.

91 204 Military Mission included Colonel Munro-Faure as COS and Lieutenant Colonel Gill-Davies and Captain Ananand as instructors.

92 Tai Li was head of The Military Investigation and Statistics Bureau, known as the *juntong* and abbreviated to either BIS or MSB. In June 1940, Tai Li had flown to Hong Kong in pursuit of Y.C. Wen, the head of OSTR, the Chinese cryptographic centre, who had gone to the colony for medical tests. British airport police arrested him and held him overnight in jail, a humiliation that coloured his attitude to the British from then on.

General Zhou Weilong[93], and in August 1941 the project got underway, the British being represented by Jardine Matheson's John Keswick, who arrived in Chungking in December as head of MEW. Keswick understood the politics from the start. He told the WO that 'the scheme can be worked in such a way that it is of defensive benefit to British interests without prejudicing in any way our political relations with Japan and I see no reason why it should when organised through the Chinese'.

The man chosen by Killery to head up the CCG was a Dane called Erik Nyholm, a contractor and an agent for the Madsen Arms Company[94]. After a brief period of preparation in Malaya, the Group moved to Lashio in Burma and began training the Chinese recruits who started to arrive from October onwards. All went well until, following the Japanese attack on Pearl Harbour, Keswick told Tai Li that SOE, who had all along been the real sponsors of the Group, intended to take it over and that from now on he would be in charge. This was construed by the Chinese as contrary to the spirit if not the letter of Dennys and Clark Kerr's original proposal for Chiang Kai-shek had agreed that the CCG should be a self-contained unit within General Zhou's Chinese Special Operations Section. From here on suspicion ranked over trust.

Nevertheless, Keswick now took over and by April 1942 a considerable amount of stores including explosives had been stockpiled at Kweiyang under Nyholm's supervision. Contact was made with Chinese resistance forces in several provinces, not all loyal members of the KMT, and the surviving members of Detachment 204 crossed into Yunnan Province, apparently without General Zhou's knowledge[95]. When Keswick merged the remnants of Major Kendall's Hong Kong Z Force with the CCG, it immediately led to rumours that the CCG was to be used to recapture Hong Kong where of course the Jardine Matheson HQ was. It was therefore not surprising when Zhou instructed Nyholm to hand over all of his war stores on 20 March 1942 and even less when Chiang refused to meet Keswick. The demarche which Clark Kerr received on 4 April referred to 'bad reports' of the CCG and 'improper dealings' with provincial governors.

It was clear to Keswick that these accusations of intrigue were merely the excuse to disband the CCG, not the reason. The Chinese had hoped they could sit back and 'wait while the Allies blasted Japan from the map' but 'the disasters which had befallen the Allies gave rise first to a sense of keen disappointment followed by a feeling of resentment, particularly strong against the British who

---

93 In charge of sabotage and secret activities in Japanese occupied areas.
94 His 2 i/c was Hans Tofte aka Tufts.
95 In 1943, Major General Gordon Grimsdale, the British Military Attaché in Chungking, took control of it with a sabotage school at Pihu and officer training establishment at Chiki.

are blamed for the loss of Singapore and Hong Kong[96]. The vitally important failure of the Americans at Pearl Harbour is largely overlooked ... The Chinese government has no intention in present circumstances of undertaking any offensive operations against Japan nor of actively stirring up trouble against the Japanese... [so] the dissolution of the CCG on orders from General Chiang Kai-shek is not surprising.' He had harsh words for General Zhou who was 'inefficient, jealous and unaccustomed to dealing with foreigners' and for the 'complete incompetence' of his organisation. Nevertheless, an important lesson had been learnt, namely 'that China in her present mood will not allow foreigners to play with her guerrillas, she will take any equipment we like to give and will hang on to it for her own use in her own time and until the Far Eastern situation changes we cannot expect anything better for this "octopus" ally'.

Before John Keswick left at the beginning of July 1942, he took some satisfaction in bringing Operation CONWAY, the SOE plan to blow up the Kailan coal mines to a conclusion. The Kailan Mining Administration [KMA] was the largest coal mining operation in Japanese-occupied China. Its output in 1939-40, produced by a 47,000 strong labour force, was 6.5 million tons of which 2 million tons went to Shanghai to supply forty per cent of its power generation. It was also the largest single supplier of coal to Japan. If KMA could be put out of action, the impact would be a fifty per cent reduction in Shanghai's iron production with serious consequences for the Japanese steel industry, let alone Shanghai's power generation capability. The extraordinary twist was that this massive strategic natural resource was controlled by the Chinese Mining and Engineering Company headquartered in the City of London. Furthermore, the Japanese had left the KMA management in situ, including over seventy British personnel. For a variety of reasons, the ORIENTAL Mission had failed to carry out any sabotage operations against the KMA, and it was through Keswick's efforts that the US 10th Air Force bombed the plant in October 1942. Initial damage reports were encouraging though later on it was evident that production had only been marginally interfered with.

Meanwhile, Detachment 204 which had been sitting at Maymyo, was finally loaded into trucks at Lashio and driven over the Hump to Kunming where they were transferred to Chinese army lorries, finally reaching the Guerrilla School at Liu Chiu Ping outside Kiyang after twenty-five days on the road. Here, after a welcoming reception hosted by General Li Mo-an to toasts of 'together we will dismay Japanese imperialism with lead bullets', they began training with the Chinese battalions, and on 20 April 1942 orders were received to make their

---

96 In a message to London in April 1942, Keswick wrote that 'it is only here [in Chungking] that one realises how sad and how bitter is the feeling about Hong Kong where all the Chinese that count had their money, their wives and quite a few of them their sweethearts'.

CHINA and HONG KONG

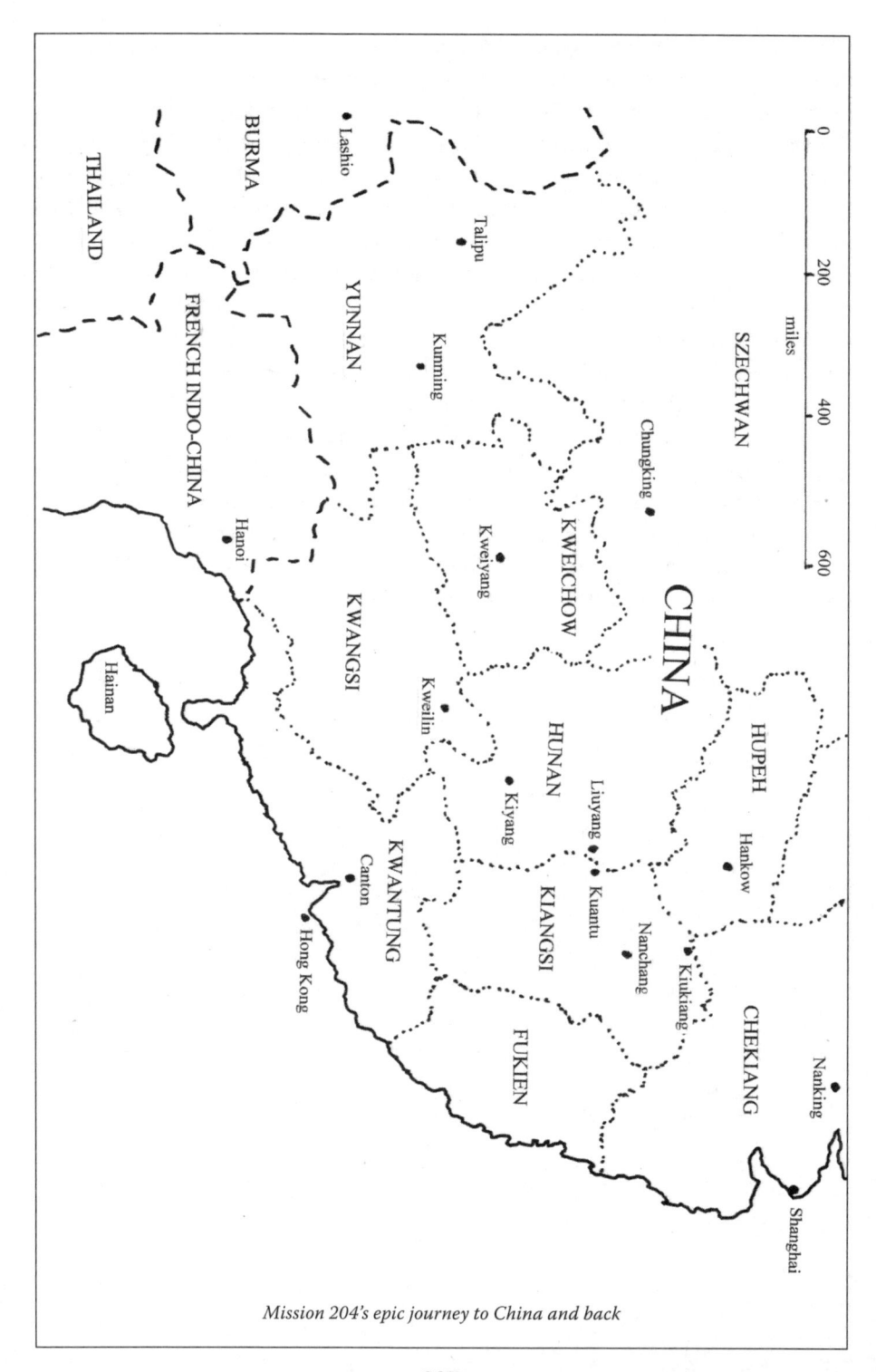

Mission 204's epic journey to China and back

way by rail and foot to Kweiyang in Kweichow Province and from there by truck back to Lashio to commence guerrilla operations in Burma. The Detachment set out on 2 May, only to be recalled and told by Brigadier Bruce and Sir Frederick Eggleston, the Australian Minister in Chungking, that they would be operating in northern Kiangsi as originally planned. So the force went by rail to Hengyang and then by river *sampans* to Kuantu where they disembarked and unloaded their stores. From here, with a baggage train of eighty coolies, they set off in heavy rain to the area west of Nanchang-Kiukiang railway and after a miserable and unproductive four months, with most men suffering at one time or other from malaria or dysentery, the three Detachment 204 contingents moved back to Kunming during October and November. They had never once been allowed by the Chinese to attack the Japanese.

Back in India, as the Australian contingent prepared to embark for home, Colonel Miller, 2 i/c of Detachment 204, read aloud a cable from Wavell: 'On leaving my command I wish to convey to you, your officers and men, my sincere thanks and congratulations on your gallant work carried out under the most trying circumstances and difficult conditions. Good luck to you all'. To those on parade it resonated with the truth.

*****

CHINA and HONG KONG

THE KESWICKS

L to R: Tony, David and John Keswick

Scions of the great Far East trading, financial and industrial conglomerate Jardine Matheson which before the Second World War employed over 100,000 workers in textile mills, factories and go-downs and boasted a fleet of over thirty merchant and passengers ships, the three sons of Major Henry Keswick collectively made a most valuable and unique family contribution to SOE.

The eldest son, David, was born in 1901 and after finishing his education embarked on a career as a banker in the City of London. Recruited by SOE at its inception, his first mission was with fellow banker, Louis Franck, to Lagos in West Africa for the West African Governors' Conference, their cover for assessing sabotage and intelligence targets. Returning to London, he became Regional Director i/c France and the Low Countries and then to coordinate SOE's activities with the Allied invasion of North Africa, he helped establish the MASSINGHAM Mission in Algiers from November 1942 to April 1943. In April 1944, David was promoted to Director Mediterranean Group and as such became a member of the Council of SOE in London. He finished the war with the rank of Colonel and was awarded the CMG. After the war he returned to the City of London as a director of Samuel Montagu & Co along with fellow SOE officer Colonel Louis Franck CBE.

William Keswick, the second son known as Tony, was born in Yokohama in 1903. Educated at Winchester and Trinity College Cambridge, he joined Jardine Matheson in Manchuria in 1925 as soon as he came down. At the relatively young age of 31, he became *Tai Pan* in Hong Kong from 1934-35 and then *Tai Pan* in Shanghai from 1935-41. Married to the daughter of Sir Francis Lindley, HM Ambassador to Japan 1931-34, Tony was elected chairman of the municipal council of the Foreign Settlement in Shanghai in 1941. As he stood up on the dais to give his opening speech, he was shot three times by Hayashi Yukichi, the 70-year-old chairman of the Japanese Ratepayers Association in response to the abject failure of the Japanese community to win seats on the council. Fortunately it was a bitterly cold day and the bullets lost some of their momentum penetrating Keswick's fur-lined overcoat. Nevertheless, as he wrote to his mother on 5 February 1941, 'to have two bullets through one's body without any ill effect is miraculous'.

With the Battle of the Atlantic now underway, Churchill commissioned Sir John Salter MP, the Parliamentary Secretary to the Ministry of Shipping, to go to Washington in March 1941, sending him on his way with the words: '... Of all our needs none is more pressing than that of obtaining from the United States the assistance which we require in the matter of merchant shipping'. The Mission's chief tasks were to secure a large allocation of American tonnage for British services, an increase in American shipbuilding, help in repair facilities, together with defensive equipment from United States yards and administrative co-operation in general shipping problems. Tony Keswick became a member of the mission and can undoubtedly share some of the credit for its success. By December 1941 – before the entry of Japan and the US into the war – the American shipbuilding programme had been raised to eight million deadweight tons for 1942, a figure which, with British and Canadian building, would more than cover probable losses.

Tony then joined the Duff Cooper Mission to Singapore in August 1941[97]. Previously Minister of Information, Duff Cooper had been given cabinet rank [Chancellor of the Duchy of Lancaster] by Churchill to go to the Far East and prepare its disparate institutions for war. Mission security was lax by modern standards, for the playwright and journalist Clare Booth was on the same Pan Am Clipper as the Duff Coopers out of San Francisco and filed for *Life* magazine that 'the handsome husky six-footer with the high-bridge nose is Mr Anthony Keswick, one of their two secretaries'. The Mission lasted for just twenty-one days when its terms of reference were overtaken by the appointment of General Wavell as Supreme Commander, South West Pacific, ABDA Command.

When he left Shanghai, Tony had moved with his family to England where he now returned and joined SOE as a senior executive in December 1941[98].

---

97 Duff Cooper in *Old Men Forget*: 'I spent some of that time in Washington, where I attended a large press luncheon with the Ambassador and was the principal speaker. I also acquired in Washington the services of Tony Keswick, a director of Jardine Matheson & Co. and a specialist in Far Eastern affairs, who accompanied me to Singapore as my chief adviser, and whose services proved invaluable'.

98 In typical SOE style of the time, he was both 'recommended' and 'interviewed' by Colonel George Taylor.

Described in his interview notes as 'very much the big business executive but rather a good fellow all the same', almost immediately he was sent back to Washington by Sir Charles Hambro in February 1942 as the Far East expert on Colonel Louis Franck's team attached to British Security Coordination run by William Stephenson. Other SOE members included Colonel Tom Masterton as the Balkans expert, Mostyn Davis [West Africa and South America] and Bickham Sweet Escott [Western Europe]. In Issue No. 11 of the Matheson &Co newsletter, he pithily described his experience there as, 'I can tell you nothing of my work in Washington except that it was largely warming a chair in a very large building which itself was extremely warm...'

Returning to the UK on 13 April 1942, he was allocated the symbol A/DU, and in his new role as London-based Director of Missions Area C [India and Far East; North and South America], he recruited some exceptional talents, including Godfrey Philips, the former Secretary and Commissioner-General of the Shanghai Municipal Council, who went on after the war to become chairman of Lazard Brothers in London, and G. Findlay Andrew from Butterfield and Swire. He finished his service with SOE on 26 April 1943. He was later asked by PM Clement Attlee to join the Royal Commission on the Taxation of Profits and Income 1951-1955 and in June 1972 was knighted for his services to the UK.

Henry Keswick's youngest son, John, was born in 1906 and, like Tony, on completing his education he had joined the family business in Hong Kong. When he was over in London in 1939, he was invited to join the MEW and accepted, writing in a letter to Ingram of MEW that 'I feel that there should be some useful work to be done regarding China and Japan'. His appointment was confirmed on 4 December. When Tony left Shanghai in 1941, John took over as *Tai Pan* but on the outbreak of war with Japan in December 1941 he immediately flew from London to Chungking as the senior MEW representative and de facto head of SOE in China. Under the cover of a counsellor at the British Embassy, he ran the China Commando Group [see pages 224-226] until ordered out of the country by Chiang Kai-shek.

Leaving for London in July 1942[99], he worked for Military Operations 1 [Special Plans], War Office – yet another innocuous cover name for SOE – and in June 1943 wrote a critical paper on *China: Politics and Trade*. In it, he drew attention to the fact that 'everyone in Chungking ... is interested in post-war reconstruction' and given that the Americans 'see themselves as liberators of the Far East from Japanese conquest and the initiators of a new era of enlight-

---

99 Moachun Yu says JK became the SOE LO in Donovan's New York HQ and shipped in Petro Pavlovski as his No. 2, a combination which deeply troubled Tai Li!

ened exploitation', urged the British Government to develop a strategy at Cabinet level to protect and promote British interests in the Far East after the war. Keswick himself was never short of ideas, proposing in December 1942 that the British should form a joint-venture with the Bank of China to buy out Lufthansa's dormant stake in the Eurasia Corporation[100], then purchase British or American aircraft and extend the airline's routes. The proposal went the rounds in Whitehall where despite support from Tony Keswick, it eventually ran aground on the rocks of Anglo-American sensitivity.

In April 1943, Sir Charles Hambro asked Keswick to return to Chungking to report on the situation there. Carrying a letter to General Wang Ping-shen from Hambro and a fountain pen –'I have chosen a pen as my token gift as it is mightier in the field of subversive propaganda and intelligence than the sword' – Keswick emphasised the importance of IIR to the British in the war against Japan and how much SOE appreciated his personal support. After sorting out various personnel problems – Findlay Andrew was known to be 'extremely difficult to work with' and various SOE/British Military Mission wives notorious for their likes and dislikes in the small expatriate community in Chungking – he returned home carrying a piece of ancient Chinese manuscript as a reciprocal gift to Hambro.

On his return to London, Keswick became Regional Controller India, China, America, Africa, Australia and Russia with a seat on the SOE Council. However, it was not long before he was on the move again in September, this time to the staff of Admiral Lord Louis Mountbatten at SEAC in Kandy[101]. By October he was back in Chungking, still on the SOE payroll but attached to the FO as First Secretary. In January 1944, the FO agreed to his promotion as Counsellor.

After the war, he returned to Shanghai to rebuild the family business and moved to Hong Kong where he became a member of the Hong Kong Executive Council in 1952. Made a CMG in 1950, he later became Sir John Keswick KCMG.

*****

In their study *MI9: Escape and Evasion 1939-4*, the authors M.R.D. Foot and Tommy Langley asked: 'What indeed was China in 1942? It was an enormous, amorphous mess, nominally ruled by Generalissimo Chiang Kai-shek from

---

100 Formed in 1930, the company gave Lufthansa exclusive rights to the mail between Germany and China and also access to the Chinese market.
101 John Keswick was originally Chief Political Adviser but this was vetoed by the FO who put their own man in. Appointed in 1943, Esler Dening, who later became Britain's first post-war ambassador to Japan, never hit it off with the Supreme Commander and their relationship was at the best of times tetchy.

Chungking, where the apparatus of a central government – including a diplomatic corps – was maintained. In fact Chiang's authority did not often extend far. Several war-lords competed with each other, with the Japanese, and with the Chinese Communist party for control of South China; most of north east China was securely – for the time being – in Japanese hands; an embryo Communist state existed in north central China already'.

Killery had sent G. Findlay Andrew of Butterfield & Swire and author of *The Crescent in North West China*, who was an old China hand and friend of many of the key personalities, and J.A.T. Galvin, to keep the door open for SOE in Chungking. Findlay Andrew had originally gone out to China to join the Studd family[102] mission run by Norman Grubb. At one stage he was seconded to the powerful Soong family to assist in famine relief and in doing so came to know T.V. Soong and his three sisters. This gave him access to the highest level in business and politics, including the Generalissimo who was married to Soong May-ling.

It was Findlay Andrew who identified the Institute of International Relations, Chiang Kai-shek's Japanese intelligence arm, as a potential partner. Run by General Wang Ping-shen, the Generalissimo's principal expert on Japanese affairs and Director of the National Affairs Institute of the Chinese National Military Council, the British relationship with the IIR was to prove exceptionally valuable. Through a network of agents, many of who were in W/T contact with Chungking, the IIR gathered intelligence from all Japanese-occupied territories and from Japan proper. Wang turned out to be a very reliable partner who appreciated what the British were trying to do in the war against Japan.

In June 1943, Findlay Andrew decided to establish a sub-mission headquartered in Kunming, the SPIERS mission, to handle the insertion of Chinese guerrilla parties from China into Burma, Thailand and French Indo-China. Its first incursion was into Kokang, a Burmese border province of the Mandarin-speaking Han Chinese who had been there since the eighteenth century and currently governed by the Myosa of Kokang, Colonel Sao Yang Wen Pin, a descendant of the founding Yang dynasty. The aim of the mission was to set up an operational and training base for anti-Japanese activities in the Lashio-Bhamo area.

---

102 Educated at Eton and Trinity College Cambridge, Charles Studd was one of three sons of a wealthy retired planter, Edward Studd, who had made a fortune in India. Excelling at cricket – he played for England in 1885 in the original Ashes match – Charles was accepted by the China Inland Mission for missionary service in China where he spent the next ten years. Dressing in Chinese fashion, he began at once to learn the language and it was only ill-health that made him leave. On recovery, leaving his wife and four daughters in England, he sailed, contrary to medical advice, for the Belgian Congo in 1910, where he continued to work until his death in 1931.

Front row L to R: Chiang Kai-shek, Roosevelt, Churchill and Madame Kai-shek

Colonel Paul Munro-Faure, the MLO [India] attached to the British Consul General in Kunming, was selected to lead SPIERS. It was a good choice since Munro-Faure had served on the front line in the First World War, first with the Sherwood and Foresters in France and then with the King's African Rifles in Africa. From 1919, until being recalled to the colours in May 1941, he had worked for the Asiatic Petroleum Company in China and thus knew the people, the language and the territory exceptionally well. However, in October, after initially receiving permission from General Ho Ying-chin, CoS of the National Military Council, to go ahead, he was informed that he was not allowed to establish a SPIERS office in Kunming. As a result the first SPIERS party was dropped by parachute into Kokang in December 1943. Unfortunately they had to use a DZ at Meng P'eng inside China, so by the time they reached Kokang, the Chinese had had time to ensure that they were effectively prevented from operating. Munro-Faure himself arrived there on 26 February 1944 and rapidly came to the conclusion that the Chinese were hell bent on annexing the territory. He signalled Force 136 that 'the Chinese were acting as virtual rulers of the territory [which had been British since 1897]. They have attempted to suborn our interpreters; they spy on our movements and prevent our officers crossing the Salween without their permits'. Although he managed to arrange for the RAF to drop supplies[103] and agents from India and took command of the

---

103 357 Squadron dropped 27 containers in March 1944.

local Defence Force, Kokang was within the Chinese area of tactical responsibility and he had no choice other than to take orders from the Chinese Expeditionary Force.

Lieutenant Colonel Ronald Kaulback, the famous pre-war Tibetan explorer, botanist and geographer, took over from Munro-Faure, both as military commander and Civil Affairs Officer, the latter role not recognised by the Chinese. Soon the SPIERS mission was accused of raising an anti-Chinese force, and a visit in October 1944 by Brigadier Adam Wilson-Brand, the senior BLO to the Chinese Expeditionary Force, did not resolve the situation. Both Kaulback and Major Leitch of ISLD subsequently withdrew, with Kaulback ironically signalling that 'no British will be able to appear again in Kokang and achieve anything except the raising of a laugh'.

Writing a letter to A.G.N. Ogden of the British Consular Service in Calcutta, Monro-Faure fell foul of the censor for this paragraph:

'You will probably have heard of the unfortunate fate of the little operation I was mixed up with. Everything went wrong. I was disappointed when I got back to Kunming to find you had left. The backing there was then left to Samson and Clark, which of course was hopeless, and the people in my office in India who were administering the operation, quite rightly, had no adequate comprehension of the politics involved. I feel very sorry for the Myosa. I did not get the impression that he was really properly looked after when he arrived in India, but I may be wrong there – your namesake in the Burma Service was a good chap and did a lot of good ... '

L to R: Generals Wavell, Dennys and de Wiart

CHINA COUNTRY SECTION

By 1944, SOE had six units working in China.
- The IIR based in Chungking [also provided intelligence to SIS London and DMI India]. Codenamed the Resources Investigation Institute by the British, the IIR gave SOE access to a wealth of intelligence. But this was not what SOE was primarily about. Later, in 1945, when the activities of the IIR were transferred to General Cheng Kai-Min's International Intelligence Service [IIS], there was a window for SOE to contribute its sabotage and signals expertise but the war ended before IIS went into action in Japanese-occupied North China.
- A Liaison Mission in Chungking [and a member of the Sino-British-American Co-ordinating Council for clandestine activities] including W/T links to FIC, Kunming and Kweiyang.
- An Advanced Operational base in Kunming [attached to the Assistant Military Attaché's office].
- The China Coast Section based in Kweilin. The Section used the British Army Aid Group [BAAG] as its cover but had to wind up in late 1944 when the Japanese occupied Kweilin. It was reformed as Group C HQ at Kunming.
- Since 1942 SOE had loaned a number of officers to BAAG[104], the Hong Kong intelligence and escape organisation and in September 1944[105] was able to deploy them to assist the Chinese army in delaying the Japanese advance to Kweilin. Majors Teesdale, Cowie and Salinger all contributed to the demolition of roads and bridges, forcing the Japanese to abandon their frontal attack. Teesdale's party later withdrew to Kunming.
- Walter Fletcher's Operation REMORSE.

There were no operational commitments allocated to SOE by China Command.

Grand plans continued to be made by SOE planners to sabotage shipping all along the Chinese seaboard. Operation NONCHALANT was a plan to entice Chinese dock labourers to leave Hong Kong with offers of work in other countries [Eritrea] and then repatriation after the war end. In October 1944, fifty-two dock yard workers [out of a pool of 11,000] reached Waichow where twelve found work and BAAG had to look after the remainder, until the scheme was abandoned in March 1945 with an offer of three months' pay.

---

104 See Hong Kong.
105 In June that year an informal agreement was made between SOE and GHQ India whereby if SOE was authorised to work in China they could use BAAG as cover with the proviso that Ride agreed.

Operation OBLIVION, under Major Kendall, with Major D.R. Holmes as his 2 i/c, planned to infiltrate a group of Canadian Chinese into mainland China where they would link with the Communists and start operations in the Hong Kong area. A number of Chinese recruits from Canada were found and by December 1944, the party was ready to be deployed. Since the target area was not within SEAC boundaries, permission to go ahead had to be given by SWPA. General Wedermeyer pointed out that it was a wanton waste of SRD resources to launch it from Australia since China Command was quite capable of doing so itself. This argument merely masked the political reality: there was no question of Chiang Kai-shek approving any British operation that involved contact with the CCP nor were the Americans prepared to argue the case. However, over 150 of the Chinese who were trained at the STS in Canada were deployed by SOE in South East Asia before the end of the war, so all had not been in vain.

Likewise, Operation RESURRECTION, to reinsert the original members of Z Force into Hong Kong to attack the Japanese guns on Taimoshan Mountain never got off the ground.

MAJOR EDWARD TEESDALE, MC

Edward Teesdale

Edward Teesdale was born in Shanghai in 1915. After coming down from Oxford, he joined the Hong Kong Civil Service in 1937. 'A versatile and popular officer [with] a keen brain, strong character and confidence', he had been a member of Z Force in the early days and attended STS 101 in Singapore in August 1941. A fluent Cantonese speaker, he was recruited by John Keswick into SOE in February 1942 to stand by for operations with the China Commando Group. When this venture was disbanded, Teesdale served with V Force in India until December 1942 and then spent a year in India as an SOE instructor before being posted to the UK for another instructional post. It must have been a frustrating time for someone who yearned to operate in the Far East. Finally in September 1944 he was posted to China and attached to BAAG for Operation GAUNTLET. In a short time Teesdale won his spurs on the battlefields of China.

23 January 1946: Recommendation for MC

During the autumn of 1944, in order that the Allied airfields at Kweilin and Liuchow should be evacuated with minimum loss of stores and supplies, it was essential that the enemy advance be delayed north east Kweilin. In the absence of any Chinese units capable of undertaking demolition work, the BAAG offered the services of a demolition party to Marshal Chang Fa-kwei.

The preliminary reconnaissance and the operations were carried out over some hundreds of miles of roads, with inadequate transport and often with little or no protection; nor was it possible in the state of chaos existing then, to obtain in advance any accurate or reliable information concerning the many enemy columns operating in the adjacent hills. In spite of these difficulties and with commendable ingenuity and improvisation, the teams succeeded in demolishing all road bridges for forty miles north east of Kweilin and all villages and natural cover for MT accessible from the road; all the bridges in and around Kweilin were demolished and those on the Kweilin-Lipu-Liuchow road all mined. As a result, the fall of Kweilin and Liuchow were delayed for some weeks enabling the 14th USAAF to continue to employ their fighter aircraft with much success against the enemy columns, operations which would have been impossible had they not been able to use Liuchow as a forward base.

Major Teesdale's courage, technical skill and devotion to duty were leading factors in the success of these operations and his example a great inspiration to the Chinese forces with whom he established most cordial relations. The resulting restoration of British military prestige makes this the most important British military operation in South China and Major Teesdale's predominant part in it well merits the award now recommended.

Awarded

*****

When General Wedermeyer took over from Stilwell, one of his first priorities was to rationalise the various clandestine activities of the Allies in China. To this end, at a meeting on 24 January 1945 attended by the heads of the American, British and Chinese clandestine services, he stated that Generalissimo Chiang Kai-shek was happy with the existing arrangements as long as they came within the 'existing resources' available to the China Theatre and that they were aimed solely at prosecuting the war against Japan and had no internal significance. Given that the 'existing resources' i.e. the port facilities at Calcutta and the aircraft flying the Hump were operated by the Americans, this directive effectively shut SOE out of launching future operations in China. Furthermore, it soon became apparent that the twenty Chinese Commando Groups being armed and trained by the OSS were Wedermeyer's own idea.

The outcome of the meeting was far from satisfactory for it put Britain in the potentially awkward position of being seen by the Chinese to do nothing in expelling the Japanese from China. Lord Selborne, writing to the Prime Minister on 15 March 1945, warned that on current form Wedermeyer was not going to allot the British 'any role whatever' in China. Add to this General MacArthur's stated dislike of Special Forces in SWPA, and the future of SOE in the Far East looked bleak. If on the other hand SOE was given 'certain limited airlift', and thus able to conduct guerrilla operations successfully, British prestige among the Chinese would be enhanced and the recovery of Hong Kong and British Borneo might well be facilitated.

It was not to be. Britain did not have the resources to support a widespread guerrilla-based land campaign to evict the Japanese from China. Furthermore, the pact between Chiang Kai-shek and the CCP to jointly expel the Japanese was fast unravelling as the Americans were finding out to their alarm. None the less it was galling for SOE to sit on the sidelines and watch the OSS expand their operations. When Wedermeyer took over from Stilwell in October 1944, OSS strength in China numbered a mere 106 agents; by July 1945, it reached a peak of 1,891 spread across three Commands.

A final plan put together by Lieutenant Colonel Derek Gill-Davies, the GSO2 to the British Military Mission [BMM] to China, to raise 30,000 Chinese guerrillas commanded by British officers and supplied by a US air lift to liberate Hong Kong was endlessly debated but was always destined to failure since it would never receive the backing of the Americans. Hong Kong, after all, was a British colonial possession.

SOE's worries about the future of Hong Kong and their relations with the KMT came to an end when Japan abruptly surrendered after the Atomic bombs had been dropped on Hiroshima and Nagasaki. Deft footwork by Franklin Gimson, the interned Colonial Secretary of Hong Kong, in declaring himself acting Governor on 16 August, and the arrival of Admiral Harcourt on HMS *Swiftsure* in Victoria Harbour on 30 August secured the return of the island and the New Territories to Britain.

CHINA and HONG KONG

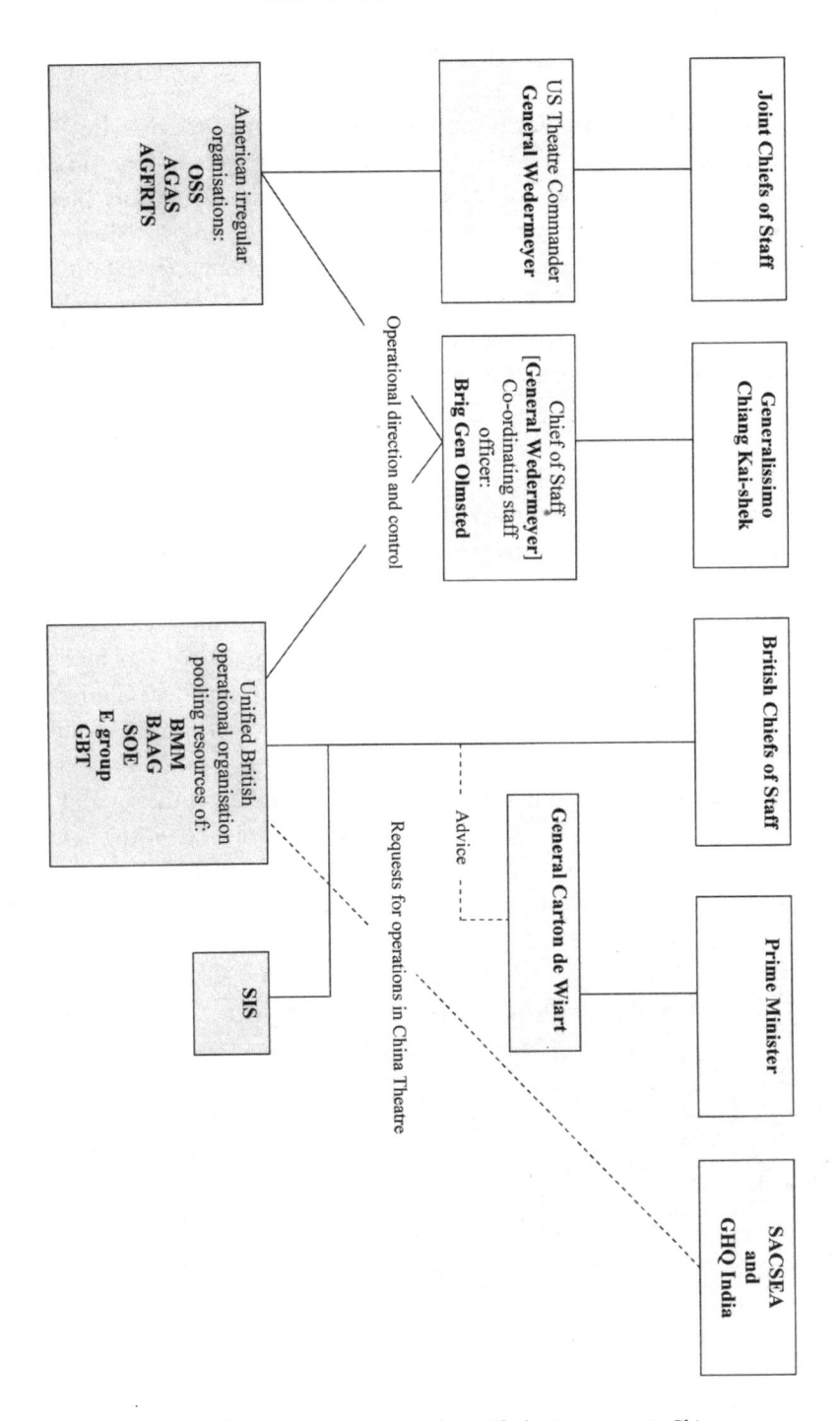

```
                                    ┌─────────────────────┐
                                    │ Joint Chiefs of Staff│
                                    └──────────┬──────────┘
                                               │
┌──────────────────┐      ┌──────────────────────────────┐
│ American irregular│──────│ US Theatre Commander          │
│ organisations:    │      │ General Wedermeyer            │
│   OSS             │      └──────────────┬───────────────┘
│   AGAS            │                     │
│   AGFRTS          │      ┌──────────────────────────────┐      ┌───────────────────┐
└──────┬───────────┘      │ Chief of Staff                │──────│ Generalissimo     │
       │                   │ [General Wedermeyer]          │      │ Chiang Kai-shek   │
       │ Operational       │ Co-ordinating staff           │      └───────────────────┘
       │ direction and     │ officer:                      │
       │ control           │ Brig Gen Olmsted              │
       │                   └──────────────────────────────┘
       │
┌──────────────────┐                                              ┌───────────────────┐
│ Unified British  │──────────────────────────────────────────────│ British Chiefs of │
│ operational      │                                              │ Staff             │
│ pooling          │                                              └───────────────────┘
│ organisation     │         ┌──────────────────────┐
│ resources of:    │ ─ ─ ─ ─ │ General Carton de Wiart│
│   BMM            │  Advice └──────────┬───────────┘
│   BAAG           │                    │
│   SOE            │                    │             ┌───────────────────┐
│   E group        │                    └─────────────│ Prime Minister    │
│   GBT            │                                  └───────────────────┘
└──────┬───────────┘
       │
  ┌────┴────┐       Requests for operations in China Theatre
  │  SIS    │ ─ ─ ─ ─ ─ ─ ─ ─ ─ ─ ─ ─ ─ ─ ─ ┐
  └─────────┘                                │
                                       ┌───────────────────┐
                                       │ SACSEA and        │
                                       │ GHQ India         │
                                       └───────────────────┘
```

SOE's 1945 proposal to work in tandem with the Americans in China

THE OSS IN CHINA

During its first three years in China, the OSS made little progress. In 1942, two OSS officers – Count Ilya Tolstoy and Captain Brooke Dolan – had set off from New Delhi to see the 7-year-old Dalai Lama in Lhasa. Ostensibly their quest was to establish whether a supply route from India to China via Tibet could be opened up. The British had expressed their doubts about the viability of this objective since the Tibetans regarded the Chinese as the equivalent of an occupying power and, in any case, the time lag of building a new road through Tibet made it an impractical strategy. Even a mule train needed six months to reach China.

Arriving there in December 1942, the two men delivered a letter from President Roosevelt to his Holiness and assured him that Tibet would qualify for independence under the post-war aegis of the United Nations. When news of this reached India, the Viceroy telegraphed the Secretary for State of India that he regarded 'with apprehension [the] amateur efforts of two Americans who have recently been in Lhasa...American enlightenment in matters may come in due course but I would judge it unsound that we from here should attempt to hasten its process'. The pair successfully reached Chungking in August 1943 after an eight-month journey. Little had been accomplished.

In Chungking, General Tai Li, head of the Chinese secret service, saw few advantages in co-operating with another American para-military and intelligence service when he was already intimately working with Lieutenant Commander Milton Miles's Naval Group China[106]. In this respect the OSS were in the same boat as SOE until General Donovan unexpectedly threw his lot in with the US Navy and appointed Miles the head of OSS in China. It was an opportunistic move which soon backfired when Miles became aware of Donovan's Dragon Plan to set up a secret intelligence [SI] network behind his back. The result of the OSS double dealing was the Sino-American Special Technical Co-operation

American Mission to Tibet

---

[106] Sponsored by Admiral King, C-in-C US Fleet, Miles's Project Friendship mission arrived in Chungking on 4 May 1942, a month after the CCG had been unceremoniously disbanded.

Organisation [SACO] signed in April 1943 whereby Tai Li became the head of Sino-American secret intelligence and special operations with Miles as his deputy. Now OSS had to toe the line.

When Mountbatten redefined British war aims in the Far East to focus on the reoccupation of colonial South East Asia, Stilwell, as commander CBI, likewise adjusted his aims with a view to attacking the Japanese in their 'inner zone' – East China, Manchuria, Formosa and Japan itself. This would necessitate direct contact with the CCP in Yenan who controlled much of the hinterland of northern China. After a false start when Ilya Tolstoy, the OSS SACO representative at Shanba, put together a secret mission without clearance, the OSS met up with the Chinese Communists by participating in the US Army Observation Group to the CCP HQ in Yenan in July 1944[107]. Five of the original eighteen members of this quasi diplomatic 'DIXIE Mission' were OSS. Despite an ambitious and in hindsight eminently sensible plan[108] to create four major bases across northern China from which to operate seventeen advanced teams to gather intelligence about the Japanese and indeed the Russians in Manchuria, nothing came of this initiative other than some sporadic training of CCP personnel.

It was only after General Wedermeyer had taken over CBI command in late 1944 and pushed Washington into creating an official OSS presence in Chungking independent of SACO that OSS in Europe was able to move resources, including trained operational groups, to the Far East[109]. The KMT grudgingly agreed in February 1945 to provide about 4,000 troops to form a force of some twenty OSS-trained commando units and by July three, each containing about 150 Chinese soldiers and twenty American advisers, were ready for the field. By the time the Japanese finally surrendered in August 1945, the commandos had acquitted themselves well and proved an effective fighting force.

To the end, SOE/OSS relations in China remained what could be politely described as competitive. On 5 August 1945, Mackenzie signalled London that he had heard from Colonel Ride of BAAG that 'psychological warfare officers calling themselves US 14th Air Force' were active with 'Reds' in Kwangtung [Guangdong] near the border with Hong Kong. These officers were in fact members of OSS who had been seconded by General Donovan to a bespoke

---

107 On arrival, they found that the Englishman Michael Lindsay had been working in Yenan as a 'technical radio adviser' since June 1941. Lindsay reported to Mr Harman, the SIS chief in Chungking.
108 The North China Intelligence Project.
109 When Wedermeyer took over from Stilwell in October 1944, there were 106 OSS 'agents' on the OSS strength. By July 1945, the tally came to 1,891.

unit termed the Air to Ground Forces Research and Technical Staff or AGFRTS, an OSS collaborative venture with General Chennault away from the prying eyes of Tai Li[110]. BAAG itself had long wanted to work with the CCP guerrillas but had been prevented by the British deference towards the KMT which forbade any contact. Mackenzie suggested that London should ask Donovan whether this was true and if so whether it was being done with General Wedermeyer's knowledge. If it was, then General Wedermeyer would be obliged to afford SOE similar freedom of action; if it had not been cleared by Wedermeyer, SOE had one over the OSS. At stake was the future security of Hong Kong, for Mackenzie was under no illusion about the weakness of the British position in regard to its recapture. It turned out that AGFRTS had been under Wedermeyer's direct control since February 1945, an example of just how patchy Anglo-American information sharing could be.

---

110 AGFRTS had in fact been operating under 14th Air Force since March 1944. On 7 February 1945, Wedermeyer made it an OSS unit and in April 1945 that it was placed under direct command of OSS under the name of Zhijiang Field Unit.

CHINA and HONG KONG

SIR WALTER FLETCHER, CBE

Walter Fletcher

Born Walter Fleischl von Marxon, the son of an Austrian-born wool broker, who became a naturalised British citizen in 1887, Walter was educated at Charterhouse and the University of Lausanne and began training as a manager in the rubber industry. On the outbreak of war in 1914 he was commissioned in the Royal Army Ordnance Corps and served in East Africa. By the end of the war, he had reached the rank of major and been awarded an OBE as well as being mentioned in dispatches.

In September 1919 he changed his name by deed poll to Walter Fletcher and returned to Africa where he managed a large number of rubber plantations. He then came back to England in 1924 where he subsequently became chairman and managing director of Hecht, Levis and Kahn, a major rubber and commodities company. On the outbreak of war, medically unfit to serve, he haunted the corridors of Whitehall looking for employment of his particular 'trading' talent.

The Japanese occupation of Malaya and the DEI had dramatically reduced the amount of rubber available to the Allies. The former adviser to the States of Kedah and Kelantan, A.C. Baker, proposed to the Combined Raw Materials Board a scheme whereby purchasing centres were established on islands close to Sumatra and producers encouraged to smuggle rubber past the Japanese authorities in exchange for handsome payments in silver. Oliver Lyttleton, the Minister of Production, approved it and Fletcher with his expertise in rubber trading was appointed by SOE to handle the project, now known as Operation MICKLEHAM. Described by Hugh Dalton as a 'thug with good commercial contacts', the nineteen-stone Fletcher left for Washington in July 1942 to discuss matters with Major L.W. Elliott, his US opposite number, and soon a plan had been agreed on. With £100,000 from HM Treasury and $100,000 from the US Board of Economic Warfare in his pocket, Fletcher headed east and arrived in India in October. On first meeting, Colin Mackenzie remembered him as 'being gloriously fat'.

After a number of attempts to implement the scheme, Fletcher concluded that little could be achieved in the immediate future for all sorts of reasons, not least the difficulties of building up a fleet to collect the smuggled rubber. Instead, despite the fact that he had not managed to recruit a single agent, he decided to expand the scheme to include other commodities such as agar-agar, cutch dye, benzoin oil, silk, mercury and quinine and put his case to the Minister of Production in February 1943. Given the abysmal performance of MICKLEHAM to date, it came as some surprise that his new plan was approved. With no time to lose, Fletcher, along with an old Dunlop China hand, Colonel Lionel Davis, flew to Chungking to put their proposal to Chiang Kai-shek to smuggle commodities out of Japanese occupied Territories into China.

Not only did the Chinese agree to it but they allowed Fletcher to set up a small company to handle the forthcoming transactions, of course with some participation by the Chinese themselves. Their first success was quinine, which was desperately needed by the Australians for their troops in New Guinea. Fletcher discovered that the International Red Cross had been sending it for years to China where, instead of distributing and using it, they had hoarded it. Soon a shipment arrived in Calcutta by air over The Hump but on inspection it was found to have been adulterated by the Chinese. A testing laboratory was quickly constructed and Fletcher instigated a strict payment system relating to proven quality. By June 1944, 25 million grains had been purchased by Fletcher and shipped to Australia.

However, in reality little had changed, for Fletcher still needed agents on the ground with good W/T communications and sea transport for the bulkier commodities, both of which would take a minimum of six months to set up. As an experienced trader, Fletcher's horizons were somewhat shorter and he returned to London post haste to table an altogether more ambitious and potentially rewarding plan.

At first, his visit went badly, with the Ministry of Production ruling that MICKLEHAM should be wound up without more ado; not one pound of rubber had reached Britain[111]. Fletcher was prepared for this and after advancing Colin Mackenzie's argument that the whole point of MICKLEHAM was really to provide cover for SOE agents, he delivered his own revised version. MICKLEHAM should be used to exploit the currency black market and thus enable the British to sidestep China's galloping inflation, for unlike the Americans who bribed the Chinese with the physical delivery of war materials[112], Britain was forbidden to trade in Lend-Lease equipment. If MICKLEHAM was disbanded, British government costs in China would soar as it was forced to source the Chinese national dollars [CNDs] they needed to pay for their military missions and businesses through the Central Bank of China. To prove his point, Fletcher executed his first black market sale of Indian rupees in exchange for Chinese National Dollars at a rate which showed a profit of 130 per cent. HM Treasury were suitably impressed and MICKLEHAM became the cover for another quite different operation, codename REMORSE.

A 1943 SOE report unequivocally states Fletcher's tasks as:
- Black market activities
- The obtaining of quinine [through Frank Shu and a Persian called Mogra]
- The procurement of intelligence for Director of P Division SEAC and DMI India

Now authorised to acquire CNDs 'through discrete banking and exchange transactions', in January 1944 Fletcher found himself at the centre of the biggest currency black market in history. Furthermore as a result of a Chinese warlord admiring a large diamond ring on his hand, he branched out into smuggling South African sourced diamonds and other high value 'portable' goods such as watches, pearls, cigarette papers and motorbikes for sale on the black market in China. With its headquarters run by Colonel Davis at 9 Hsin Chin Kai in Kunming, the terminus for the Hump flights from India, and hence perfectly suited for smuggling activities, the nascent organisation sprouted branches in Kweilin, Meng-tze and Chungking and CND bank accounts with the Chartered Bank and HSBC and sterling accounts in London.

In April 1944, SOE's finance officer, John Venner, had summoned Major Edward Wharton-Tigar from Madrid where he was SOE's number two to London to meet Fletcher. Recruited by Major Peter Boughey, Wharton-Tigar

---

111 In a letter to George Taylor in January 1945, Fletcher disarmingly recalled 'we were created to extract rubber from FIC, etc; we have never produced an ounce and Chungking knows it. Nevertheless, with their connivance, we have done a lot of other things'.
112 It was also rumoured that the Americans had the contract for printing Chinese banknotes, so they would help themselves from the printing press to whatever they needed.

had joined Peter Quenell in Gibraltar who had despatched him to Tangiers where he had excelled himself in blowing up No. 4 Rue de la Falaise, an isolated cliff-top villa owned by the Germans who had been using it to monitor with an infrared device all the shipping passing through the Straits of Gibraltar. Of more interest to Venner was Wharton-Tigar's successful money changing operation, buying vital low denomination notes for use by SOE agents in occupied Europe in exchange for a variety of financial instruments including gold sovereigns, postage stamps and precious stones. It had occurred to Venner that this currency trading experience in Tangier could be most useful in rolling out Operation REMORSE.

After being introduced to Fletcher, 'garrulous, old, impulsive, vague, obese – only by luck not known to the police', Wharton-Tigar set off to Kunming to join Colonel Lionel Davis who was already in situ. With a local Chinese businessman and former employee of BAT, Frank Shu, acting as fixer, and two English sisters, Jill and Lorna MacAlister, recruited as secretaries together with Davis's Chinese speaking nephews Arthur and Micky as general factotums, REMORSE was open for business.

Soon the sheer volume of transactions outgrew the capacity of Fletcher's original company, so a new enterprise known as Syndicate B was formed in conjunction with key Chinese political and commercial interests with a fifteenth of the profits going to General Tai Li's Chinese Secret Service to provide 'a necessary insurance against guerrillas and obstruction by Customs'. With his jaundiced commercial eye, Fletcher told George Taylor that 'these guerrillas and their men are all mercenaries and nothing else ... The only way to have any measure of control over a mercenary is to create a community of mercenary interest with him over as long a term basis as possible ... Joint trading in which we control the supply of vital goods and possibly arms for real trade protection, looks to me the best'.

Business boomed, including the diamonds for CNDs market, where the exchange rate was twenty times higher than the official rate. In July 1944, REMORSE smuggled in 200 gold Swiss watches[113] sourced by SOE in Berne. However although the value of goods sold on the black market exceeded 200 million CNDs, it was dwarfed by currency exchange transactions which brought in 14,000 million CNDs.

Davis and Wharton-Tigar also opened an office in Calcutta to liaise with the Indian Exchange Control. For the REMORSE team, prompted by Frank Shu, had come up with the idea of purchasing at knockdown prices Chinese investments in India, which had been frozen at the start of the Sino-Japanese War in

---

113 Rolexes, Omegas, Longines, Jaegers and other brands.

1937. The Indian banks — still operating under a British colonial government — would then unfreeze the monies for SOE. So a Chinese merchant with £100,000 worth of rupees locked up in Calcutta would be offered £22,000 in rupee notes in Kunming or anywhere else in China, with REMORSE pocketing the difference.

Another ploy was selling post-war credits to Chinese businessmen who planned to obtain goods or services in sterling after the war. Here the game was for the Chinese to deposit sterling at an outrageous exchange rate with British banks to be converted into credits when the war was over. John Keswick, as the *taipan* of the British trading house Jardine Matheson, was livid; SOE was eating his post-war lunch. Wharton-Tigar appealed to HM Treasury and nothing more was heard from Keswick.

At one point, the Kunming office received a cable from John Venner in London asking them to stop trading for a while: thanks to REMORSE, SOE had a worldwide operating surplus for the month and he was having trouble explaining the situation to the Chiefs of Staff. It has been estimated that during its lifetime, REMORSE gave the Allies additional spending power of over £77 million which today equates to approximately £2.5 billion[114]. The ever discreet Mackenzie referred to it as 'a very, very large sum'.

Characterised by a British government official as 'not exactly the person to be trusted with the private means of a widow or orphan', Fletcher became the clandestine banker to the Allies in China except for the Americans who made their own arrangements. Flush with money, he was able to finance Operation WALDORF to support the French troops fighting their way out of Indo-China into Yunnan, and also Operation NONCHALANT, a desultory attempt to entice the dockyard workforce away from Hong Kong. When the Chinese retaliated at a restriction on the import of textiles by the Government of India by banning the export of silkworms to Kashmir, REMORSE quietly arranged the purchase of eggs on the black market in China and smuggled them into India.

Success did not go unchallenged and the French made a number of attempts to circumvent REMORSE and play the market themselves. All ended in failure, and when the French Military Mission asked for 150 million CNDs in July 1945, Fletcher had the satisfaction of offering them a mere 17 million and at a

---

114 M.R.D. Foot estimated £900m in 1984 terms. Moreover, and unusually for a fighting service, SOE ended up with its accounts in the black. Its rear party, winding it up in the spring of 1946 – it had been disbanded on 15 January of that year – received a form letter from the Treasury in mid-March, reminding them that they were to return anything they had in their kitty to the Treasury on 3 April 1946, the last day of the financial year. SOE returned twenty-three million pounds, most of it in United States dollars.

rate of 250 compared to 575, the rate offered to the bank's other 'clients'. He was not a man to be messed with.

But there was much more to REMORSE than the in-house piggy bank of SOE. In the course of executing thousands of financial transactions, Fletcher and his team built up a huge 'favour' bank that could be leveraged for intelligence and operational requirements. In a note to Mackenzie and Taylor of 23 January 1945, Fletcher pointed out that it was impractical to report all his activities:

> 'We cannot very well put down in writing in a report – "we have transported the wife and child of so-and-so during the Kweilin panic and he will do anything for us"; or "Mr X, one of our Black Market agents, is the stooge of the Governor, or one of his family in Y, and we can, therefore, get certain privileges by seeing that on the next occasion we do some exchange, the rate is favourable to Mr X"; or again "while we are buying piastres, which is a purely financial transaction, we shall be in touch with certain groups working in and out of FIC"; or again "Mr Z, an agent of ours, arranges payments to missionaries in Northern territories; he has certain lines open that may be useful".'

The tentacles of REMORSE reached into every political and financial crevice in China, grasping the pockets of the Chinese while feeding the insatiable appetite of SOE with succulent intelligence. In early 1945, Fletcher proposed opening up a 'Northern Line' to Chengtu, an area traditionally hostile to the KMT, for 'spreading the sale of semi-blocked sterling'. By the use of a well placed contact, he anticipated being 'able to horn in on the big trade that is taking place now'.

After the war, Fletcher was made a Commander of the British Empire for his wartime services and elected as Member of Parliament for Bury in Lancashire in 1945. When that constituency was abolished for the 1950 election, he was returned for the new Bury and Radcliffe constituency, and held the seat until he retired from the House of Commons at the 1955 general election. In 1953 he was knighted. He died in London in 1956.

HONG KONG

In July 1939 General Grasett, the GOC Hong Kong, asked a Canadian mining engineer, Mike Kendall, to form Z Force in case the colony was occupied. After recruiting Major Ronald Holmes, Squadron Leader Robert Thompson, Lieutenant Eddie Teesdale, Captain Hugh Williamson and Captain Colin McEwan, Kendall attended the STS 101 in Singapore in July 1941. When Freddy Spencer Chapman arrived from Australia and took over as 2 i/c at the STS, Major Gavin went up to Hong Kong in October 1941 where he was well received by all parties. In the next few weeks, Z Force, now renamed The Reconnaissance Unit, was formed, six hideouts built in the New Territories and a secret training centre and covert HQ established.

Kendall was infiltrated into Japanese controlled Hainan Island and reported on the build-up of troops there. In the event the Japanese advance was so swift that, while the rest of the Reconnaissance Unit were out near the border blowing up trucks, Kendall with McEwan and Monia Talan ended up helping with the last-ditch defence of Hong Kong Island. They were closely involved in rounding up spies and fifth columnists in coordination with Admiral Chan Chak, Colonel Yee and the other Chinese KMT people in the Colony. On the 19 December, Talan and McEwan took a small boat out into the harbour and blew up a Japanese ship by attaching limpet mines to it. They then moved onto the motor torpedo boats [MTBs] at Aberdeen a few days before the surrender.

At first the plan was to try and make contact with the Chinese forces supposedly on their way to relieve the siege, but when it became clear it was all over, they were put in charge of ensuring Chan Chak and his colleagues got safely away. McEwan and Talan returned south to Nanao to collect the Lewis guns and stores after seeing off Kendall and his escape party as they left for Waichow.

After the arrival in China of Kendall's sixty-five men in Kukong, the next group of escapees from Hong Kong was headed by Lieutenant Colonel Lindsay Ride, Professor of Physiology at Hong Kong University, with two other university lecturers and Francis Lee, one of his Chinese students. Ride joined Harry Owen Hughes in the spare bedroom and it was there that the British Army Aid Group [BAAG] was born, whose principal objective was to organise escapes from the prison camps in Hong Kong and smuggle in food and medical supplies. General Yu Han Mou, the CinC of the VII War Zone, approved the name British Army Aid Group or 'Ying Kwan Fuk Mo T'uen' on 28 May; both Brigadier Grimsdale, the Military Attaché in Chungking, and SOE's John Keswick flew down to personally congratulate Ride. By then the existence and role of MI9 had become known to the BMM in Chungking and Ride was duly appointed its official representative on 16 May.

Although three SOE members from Z force – Ronald Holmes, Colin McEwan and Max Holroyd[115]- were members of its original team, BAAG was never part of SOE. Relations between the two organisations were excellent throughout the war, SOE benefiting from the excellent intelligence that Ride collected and then distributed to a small user group[116]. In return Ride could call on SOE for resources – for instance it handled all BAAG's signals traffic – and indeed when the Japanese launched their major attack in southern China in September 1944, his demolition section included Majors Cowie, Teesdale and Salinger of SOE under command of Lieutenant Colonel Gill-Davies.

Writing to Mackenzie in March 1946, Ride thanked him for his unstinting cooperation:

> 'You gave us some of our most valuable officers when I know that you could have used them to your own greater advantage elsewhere, and you helped us by commissioning officers when our War Establishment could not admit them; your W/T –and your help with supplies were invaluable; but above all these I would place the great help of your moral support in high places outside China.'

---

[115] Holroyd was not a member of SOE but after escaping from a POW two days after the surrender of Hong Kong had linked up with Holmes and McEwan.

[116] The weekly Waichow Intelligence Summary and after May 1943 The Kweilin Weekly Intelligence Summary.

CHINA and HONG KONG

LIEUTENANT COLONEL F.W. 'MIKE' KENDALL

Mike Kendall was a Canadian from Vancouver who had lived in Hong Kong since childhood, and spoke several local dialects fluently. He abandoned his mining business in China when the Japanese invaded and moved back to Hong Kong. There he worked for the Government organizing refugee relief, building and running the large camp at Kam Tin. Originally recruited by SIS to develop their intelligence gathering network along the coast of the South China Sea from Taiwan to Hainan, early in 1940 Kendall formed 'Z Force' in conjunction with SOE and together with his friend Eddie Teesdale travelled to Singapore to attend STS 101. On his return he organised a group of handpicked volunteers, who included a Russian born businessman named Monia Talan, and a PE instructor Colin McEwan.

Z Force met secretly each weekend at a camp near Kam Tin where they received training in cipher and intelligence work, weapons, wireless and explosives. They also spent a considerable amount of time walking across the hilly terrain of the New Territories, often in the dark, getting to know the trails and terrain in preparation for the day they would have to work behind Japanese lines. Weapons were stored in Kendall's bungalow near Shing Mun. They also set up hidden stores in the event of a prolonged campaign behind enemy lines. The Japanese later found the main store, in a cave about 1800 feet up on the south east slope of Tai Mo Shan. Another was in an old lead mine at Lim Ma hang, near the border at Sha Tau Kok. It was later pilfered by villagers, who had seen Indian soldiers carrying supplies there on mules.

On the outbreak of hostilities, Colonel Newham ordered Kendall and Talan to Lyemun Pass to fix limpet mines to a ship being used by the Japanese as an observation post. The remaining SOE men in the New Territories, led by Holmes and Teesdale, spent a month behind Japanese lines, crossing back and forth across the border, collecting intelligence and setting up contacts.

Kendall also travelled into the Chinese hinterland, setting up contacts and listening posts, including those installed by ISLD's Major Chauvin and Chinese intelligence.

After the surrender of Hong Kong on Christmas Eve 1941, Kendall escaped to South China on an MTB with seventy-five others, including Ronald Holmes. Over the next six weeks, they made their way north east, running into 'Doc' Ride in Kweilin when Kendall briefly worked for BAAG as a resistance organiser in northern Kwangtung Province before heading to India in June 1942.

Appointed an instructor at SOE's Eastern Warfare School at Poona, Kendall was then sent to Canada in November 1943 to negotiate the recruitment of Chinese-Canadians for clandestine operations with Force 136. His first recruit was the 29-year-old Cantonese-speaking Roger Cheng, the first Chinese-Canadian to be commissioned in the Royal Canadian Corps of Signals. He turned out to be an outstanding candidate and, along with twelve others, reported to a newly established SOE camp on Lake Okanagan. Here under Major Hugh Legg, they underwent intensive training for the next four months to prepare them for Operation OBLIVION, Kendall and Holmes's plan to insert them into China near to Hong Kong to train Communist guerrilla bands.

By December 1944, all training had been completed, a Royal navy submarine allocated and the party under Kendall, Holmes and Cheng assembled in Australia ready to embark. It was not to be for US General Wedermeyer, Chief of Staff to the Generalissimo and commander US Forces China Theatre[117], objected, first since there were OSS teams in Chungking who could be inserted more efficiently by air and second because he knew that the Generalissimo would never agree to British contact with Mao's Communists. A further reservation held by the Americans was that this operation was designed to recover Hong Kong as a colonial possession for Britain after the war. On 25 April 1945, OBLIVION was cancelled.

Kendall returned to SOE's Eastern Warfare School at Poona as 2 i/c.

COLONEL LINDSAY 'DOC' RIDE, CBE

Lindsay Ride was born on 10 October 1898 at Newstead, Victoria. After attending school in the countryside, Lindsay was awarded a scholarship to Scotch College, Melbourne, where he excelled in sport and won a senior government scholarship. Red-headed and nearly six feet, 'Ginger' Ride enlisted in the Australian Imperial Forces [AIF] in February 1917 and joined the 38th Battalion on the Western Front early in 1918. Twice wounded [once severely], he was invalided out of the army in April 1919.

Enrolling in medicine at the University of Melbourne, Ride took a commission [1921] in the Melbourne University Rifles and represented the university in athletics. Elected Victorian Rhodes Scholar in 1922, he went to New College, Oxford where he impressed the dons as 'a good Rhodes Scholar' and a 'first rate fellow'.

Entering Guy's Hospital, he qualified as a member of the Royal College of Surgeons and as a licentiate of the Royal College of Physicians. With a flair for

---

[117] In October 1944, the CBI was reorganised into two separate entities following the departure of General Stilwell. Wedermeyer became head of US Forces China Theatre [Chungking] and Chief of Staff to the Generalissimo; Lieutenant General Daniel I. Sultan assumed command of the US Forces India Burma Theatre [India, Ceylon, Burma, Thailand, the Malay States, and Sumatra] based in New Delhi.

medical research, in 1928 he was appointed Professor of Physiology at the University of Hong Kong, where he investigated blood groups of the peoples of the Pacific. Committing himself to life in the colony, Ride was commissioned in the Hong Kong Volunteer Defence Corps and appointed a JP.

Foreseeing war, Ride sent his wife and children to Australia in 1938. He commanded the Hong Kong Field Ambulance in 1941, but was taken prisoner by the Japanese in December. It was immediately apparent to him that the survival prospects for 600 British and Commonwealth officers and their 9,000 men who had been taken prisoner by the Japanese were far from rosy without adequate medical supplies. To that end he determined to escape and on 9 January 1942 he escaped from Sham Shui-po POW camp and made his way in a *sampan* to unoccupied China, a feat for which he was congratulated by FM Wavell and appointed OBE in 1942.

Once in China he founded, formed and commanded [as a colonel in the Indian Army[118]] the British Army Aid Group in Chungking which helped escapees from Hong Kong, provided medical and other assistance to POWs, and gathered intelligence. Operating in Kwangtung and Kwangsi provinces, BAAG gradually took on responsibility for medical services to the thousands of Chinese soldiers and their dependants living there, treating up to 30,000 patients a year and during the famine of 1943 feeding 6,000 people a day. 'Operating with great gallantry, skill and flair, [and] on a shoestring'[119], Ride was held in the highest esteem by SOE who co-operated with him throughout the war. The same could not be said for SIS who cavalierly ignored his authority or for the OSS, who more than once went behind his back to carry out their own forays. In the case of the latter there was a certain justification as the British refused to admit to the Americans that BAAG played a vital intelligence role.

Nicknamed 'The Smiling Tiger', Ride was elevated to CBE for his outstanding leadership.

---

118 Ride had the distinction of being commissioned a Second Lieutenant and promoted to Lieutenant Colonel on the same day.
119 Foot and Langley.

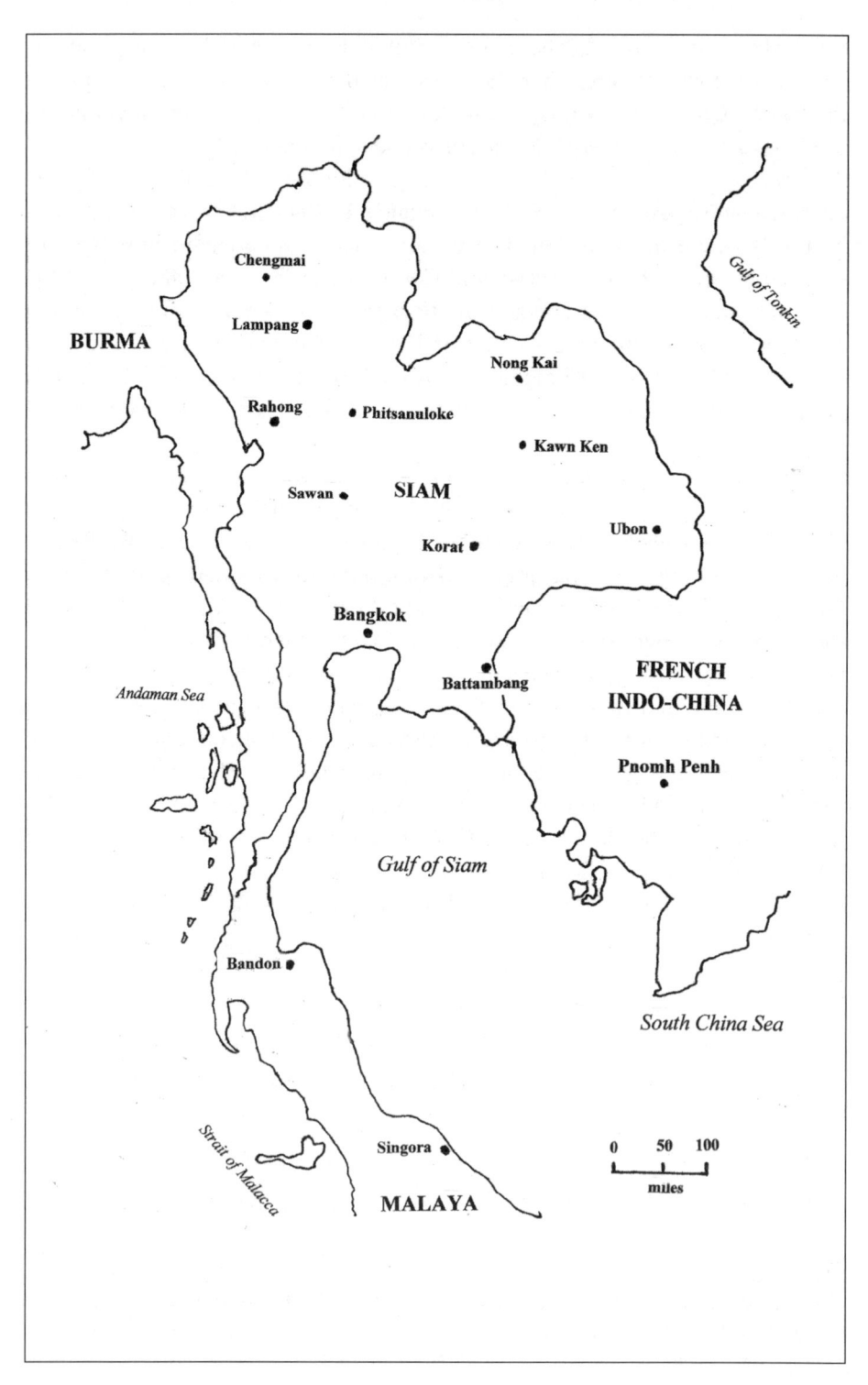

CHAPTER EIGHT

THAILAND [SIAM]

POLITICAL BACKGROUND

Despite European pressure, Thailand was the only South East Asian nation that was not colonised. This was due to deft footwork by its rulers who played off the rivalry between the French in Indo-China and the British in Burma and Malaya although they eventually had to concede the east side of the Mekong River to the French and waive the piecemeal takeover by Britain of the Malay Peninsula, including the loss of Penang and four predominantly ethnic-Malay southern provinces under the Anglo-Thai Treaty of 1909.

In 1932, a bloodless revolution carried out by The Promoters, a group of disgruntled military and civilian officials, resulted in King Prajadhipok granting the people of Thailand their first constitution, thereby ending nearly two centuries of absolute monarchy of the Chakri dynasty.

Although under strong British influence – in 1934 King Prajadhipok had gone to England of medical treatment and abdicated the following year in favour of his nephew still at school in Switzerland – the increasingly autocratic military government of Prime Minister Field Marshal Phibun toyed with the idea of throwing Thailand's lot in with Japan. This foreign policy of uneasy neutrality was accurately summarised by as 'watchful waiting'. Its first dividend was paid out in early 1941 when the Japanese helped Thailand acquire border territories from French Indo-China after a short war.

British plans to invade southern Thailand – Operation MATADOR – in order to deny the Kra Isthmus to the Japanese involved SOE officers making detailed cross-border recces, but without the consent of the US there was no chance of it going ahead for it would have violated Thai neutrality. When that consent finally came on 1 December 1941, it was too late.

On 8 December 1941, Japan invaded Thailand in order to gain access for its armies to invade Malaya and Burma. After a day's fighting, Phibun ordered an armistice. Shortly afterwards Japan was granted free passage and on 21 December 1941, Thailand and Japan signed a military alliance with a secret protocol wherein Tokyo agreed to help Thailand regain territories previously lost to the British and French.

Subsequently, Thailand declared war on the United States and Great Britain on 25 January 1942 and undertook to assist Japan in its war against the Allies.

In return, Thailand later acquired four states in northern Malaya as well as territory in the Shan States of northern Burma.

In a move that was to have a profound effect on relations between SOE and OSS, Washington chose to ignore the Thai declaration of war and treat it 'with the contempt it deserved', whereas the British responded in kind on 9 February 1942. As far as HMG was concerned, Thailand had taken the side of the Japanese and in due course it would be punished accordingly.

SOE IN THAILAND

During the ORIENTAL Mission, a two-pronged approach was developed, Operation ETONIAN which involved land-based raids to capture the Yala crossroads and to seize Phuket Island with its airfield, and Operation BETTY which featured a number of seaborne raids. To establish communications, two of Major Jack Knott's signal sergeants went infiltrated as 'mine managers'; both were later arrested by the Japanese. Phuket was successfully seized by the SOE Group and Victor Wemyss and his seaborne raiders on SS *Mata Hari* captured Tonkah, sank three Italian freighters and held it for four days before withdrawing. The Japanese took Yala with no resistance and there was no further role for SOE to play.

After the relentless Japanese advance had finally come to a halt in mid-1942, the challenge for SOE was to find a Thai resistance group to work with. Former Finance Minister and member of the Regency Council, Pridi Phanomyong, a bitter rival of Phibun, had been a staunch opponent of the Japanese alliance and after a number of discussions with those holding similar views the *Seri Thai*, or Free Thai movement, started up, with chapters opened in Washington by Seni Pramot and London by Mani Sanasen. Another anti-Phibun Thai, Chamkat Phalangkun, formed his own group *Ku Chat*, or Liberation, which then merged with *Seri Thai* to become the 'X-O Group'.

The priority of X-O was to contact the three principal Allied players, Britain, America and China. Pridi managed to contact Andrew Gilchrist, first secretary at the British Legation, and the HSBC manager before they were repatriated in August 1942 but it was imperative to get an emissary into China to solicit Chiang Kai-shek and General Stilwell. The man chosen for this all important task was Chamkat, the co-founder of the X-O Group.

Crossing into Indo-China on 4 March 1943, Chamkat met Lieutenant Colonel Doc Ride of BAAG in Kweilin who formed a favourable impression of him and sent a message to Major General Grimsdale, the British Military Attaché in Chungking, urging him to introduce Chamkat to British and American diplomats. Arriving in Chungking on 21 April, Chamkat urged the

British to bring Pridi out to India where he could set up a provisional government. This proposal was given short shrift by the FO for by now the tide had turned against the Japanese and there was little appetite to recognise a government-in-exile of what was still a belligerent state. Consequently Grimsdale was told to play down the Free Thai overtures, a policy which irked SOE. However since Chamkat was a guest of the Chinese KMT Government, there was nothing they could do. Chamkat fared better in his meeting with Chiang Kai-shek on 28 June and received an enthusiastic response to the ideas of a Free Thai army and government-in-exile in Chungking. Best of all he was given his own W/T link to Bangkok. A messenger was despatched to Bangkok carrying a microfilm of the Operation PRITCHARD plans for Pridi's extraction, but in the meantime Chamkat was diagnosed with cancer and died on 7 October.

The seeds of SOE's work in Thailand were meanwhile being sown in London when thirty-six young Thai students, who had voluntarily enlisted in the British army, came under SOE's control in 1942. Closely associated with Prince Suphasawat, the Queen of Thailand's brother, who had offered his services to HMG soon after Thailand's declaration of war, these young Thai were given the codename WHITE ELEPHANTS or WHITES for short. In parallel, but not coordinated, thirteen Thai students started training as a 'Free Thai' movement with the newly formed OSS on 13 June 1942. This group, increased to twenty, reached India in early June 1943.

THAILAND COUNTRY SECTION

Run out of Meerut by Major W.D. Reeve of the ORIENTAL Mission, the Thailand Country Section appointed Captain N.F. Nicholson [formerly Lever Bros in Thailand] and Major A.C. 'Peter' Pointon, a former forest manager of the Bombay Burmah Company in Thailand, in the spring of 1943 to take on the task of reinvigorating it. This was far from easy given the acute shortage of staff and it was only in November that Captain S.H.J. Read arrived as conducting officer and early in 1944 Captains Richard Bryce-Smith and Tom Hobbs were poached from the Burma section. Both had lived in Thailand and spoke the language. Captain F.H. Burdon arrived as IO and Captain John Balharry as admin officer around the same time.

Now with SOE, Prince Suphasawat had arrived in India in April 1943 as 'Major C. Arun' and was appointed chief adviser to Pointon on the subject of infiltrating operatives into Thailand and raising guerrilla forces there. He was also made conducting officer for the agents who had begun to assemble in India. Of the thirty-six WHITES who had arrived from the UK, twenty-two began their six-month training at Poona in July. Another group of twelve

Chinese recruited from the Chungking Military Academy and known as the REDS were also in training with the Thailand Country Section.

The planning for inserting the WHITES and REDS into Thailand was proving problematical, for although seaborne operations by submarine or Catalina in the Gulf of Siam were feasible, the distances were huge – the direct distance from Calcutta to Bangkok is 950 miles and the nearest dropping zone a 1,500 mile round trip – and, as ever, resources uncertain. A blind drop by Liberator looked too risky. So consideration was given to proving an overland route from Chungking through southern Yunnan. After obtaining permission from War Minister Ho Ying-chin, Captain Bryce-Smith set off alone in May 1943 and spent the next six months exploring the routes across the border area.

Major Edmund Grut, an ISLD officer on loan to SOE, was given a similar task but when he arrived in Chungking in July, his first action was to try and see Chamkat to put himself forward as the preferred candidate to cross into Thailand to meet with Pridi. Fobbed off by the Chinese who told him that Chamkat had no interest in meeting with the British as he was already totally committed to the American Free Thai Group, Grut went to see Captain Milton Miles[120] of the US Navy, the senior US intelligence officer in China and country head of the OSS. The outcome of the meeting confirmed the worst fears of the British, namely that the OSS had no intention of merging the respective groups of Free Thai soldiers and would run its own operations in Thailand without British knowledge or assistance.

This highly unsatisfactory state found a voice in the INDIA Mission's progress report of 4 August 1943 where the frustration experienced by SOE in dealing with the Americans in Thailand is palpable:

> 'Attempts to obtain co-operation from OSS for operations into Siam have not been successful. It is evident that under the influence of Colonel Kunjara, the Americans are not inclined to collaborate. The trouble is partly due to Siam politics: our man, Arun, is by birth a prince but is not a politician, whereas Colonel Kunjara is a supporter of the party that expelled the King some years ago. At the moment the Americans plan a series of disconnected sorties by air into Siam, in spite of the fact that their men are almost completely untrained in parachute jumping and SO work. These sorties are to engage in various demolitions which, so far as we know, have no bearing on military plans or on any known strategy. American representatives have denied that Siam is a no-man's

---

120 Miles's political opinions were considered by most SOE 'China hands' to be deeply flawed, since he was by his own admission an ardent disciple of Tai Li, the ubiquitous and anti-British KMT Secret Service chief.

THAILAND [SIAM]

land under the terms of the London Agreement, and have firmly refused to allow our representative to see Balankura, a Siamese who escaped into China some time ago and who is in possession of information which would be extremely valuable to us and our plans in Siam.'

The disenchantment rumbled on until November when Donovan announced he had halted all attempts to get agents into Thailand in the light of his forthcoming inspection visit to China.

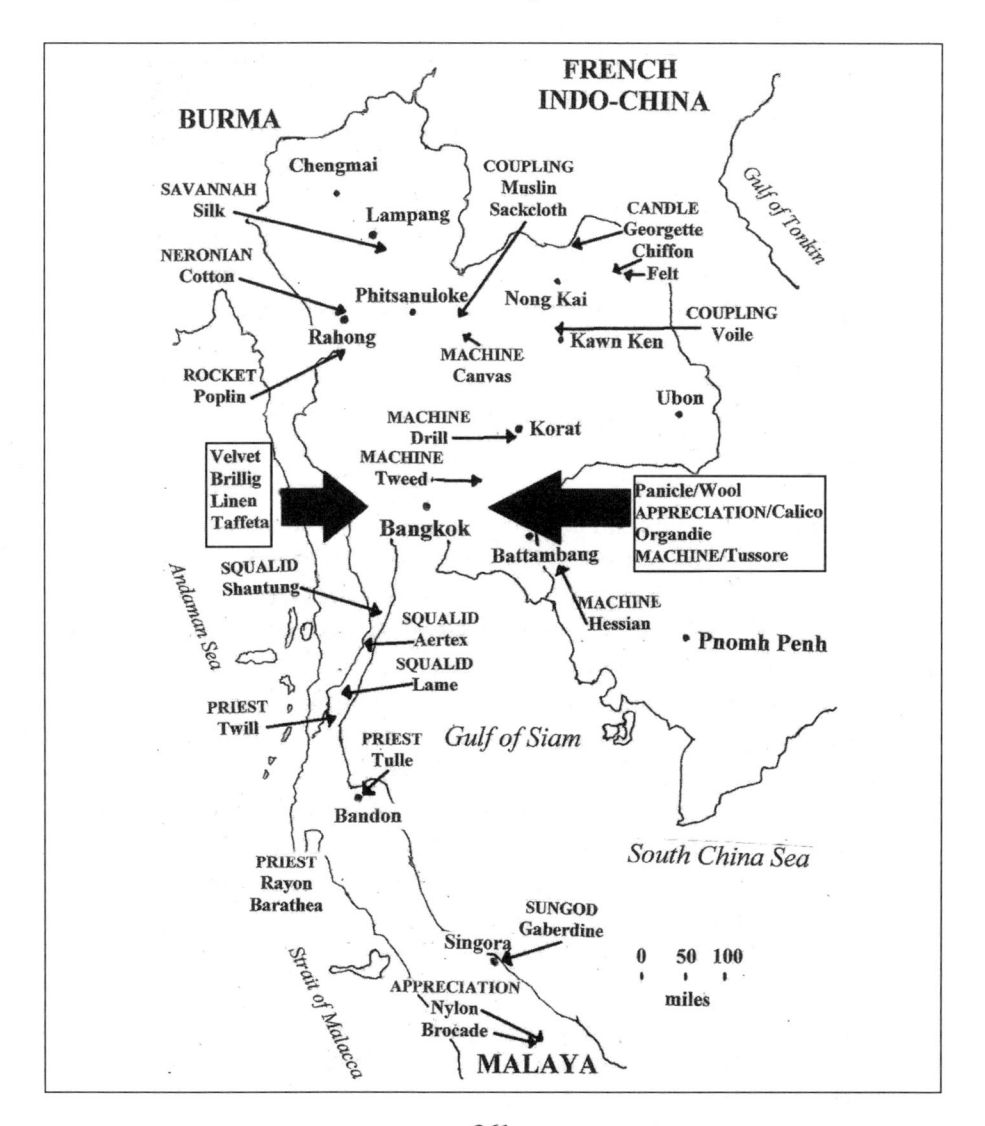

It was Prince Suphasawat who finally managed to obtain a meeting with Chamkat in August, albeit under the auspices of the Chinese. The two men instantly struck up a friendship and Suphasawat was able to persuade him that the British were best placed to bring Pridi out and that a government-in-exile in India was infinitely preferable to one in Chungking for the Chinese were not to be trusted[121]. In that respect, the Prince told him not to use the Chinese W/T station for traffic to Bangkok. SOE would make it a priority to get a W/T into the country as soon as possible.

As a result of the discussions between Chamkat and Suphasawat, SOE started to plan Operation PRICHARD for Pridi's extraction by submarine from the Andaman coast in December and also approved a financial package for the Free Thais in Chungking, including a large diamond ring with which to bribe a Chinese General to send secure messengers to and from Bangkok.

Although Thailand had been assigned to the China Theatre at the beginning of the war and hence under the strategic control of US General Stilwell, the Allied Conference at Quebec in late August 1943 gave it to Admiral Mountbatten's newly created SEAC. Chiang Kai-shek, who had not been consulted, was furious since it threatened his plan to raise a Sino-Thai army and it took all Mountbatten's considerable charm to smooth things over. The untimely death on 7 October of the by now avowedly pro-British Chamkat, officially from stomach cancer, gave rise to all sorts of rumours. One version doing the rounds was that he had been fed finely chopped pigs' bristles over a period of several weeks which had perforated his intestine and killed him. Major Grut pointed the finger at the Chinese and their history of preventing Chamkat meeting the British.

The much vaunted OSS Free Thai operations based in Chungking had finally started in March 1944 but all its operations had ended as dismal failures. By October, of the eleven agents who had left for the Thai border, two were dead, three were reported in the custody of the Thai Police, and the whereabouts of the others unknown. No W/T stations were on air. OSS Detachment 404 [Free Thais to be inserted from India] had meanwhile established itself in Ceylon under the umbrella of Captain Garnons-Williams's P Division.

On the assumption that Pridi had received a microfilm message despatched to him from Chungking, three WHITE Thai officers – Khem, Deng and Keng – with W/T sets were taken by the submarine HMS *Tactician* to an RV [Operation PRICHARD] near Ranong on west coast of Thailand. Despite a four hour recce ashore on the night of 12 December, they could find no sign of the recognition signals and, after seven days in the area, the submarine returned to Ceylon. It was clear that either Pridi had never received the message or that the

---

121 Relations between China and Thailand were fractious due to the influence of the large Chinese minority in the country. Thai educational laws and immigration issues were both contentious issues.

THAILAND [SIAM]

reception party had been waylaid or compromised. A blind drop by Liberator was then proposed. The first phase APPRECIATION I would involve three Thai agents, whose job was to establish W/T contact and then receive a larger party – RAZOR – which would include a British officer who would be the contact for Pridi. If APPRECIATION I did not make W/T contact, a further Mission, APPRECIATION II, would go in ahead of RAZOR.

On 14 March 1944 the three Thai officers of Operation APPRECIATION 1 dropped blind from a Liberator with a letter from Mountbatten to Pridi.
- Pridi was accepted as leader of Free Thai Movement [FTM]
- HMG would recognise an independent Thailand after war
- HMG were considering release of frozen Thai funds
- A Provisional Thai government would be allowed in India

Expecting to land in a remote valley north west of Bangkok, they came down instead near a village and were picked up by vigilantes and eventually arrested. However, Khem [Puai] did manage to hand over Mountbatten's letter to Pridi

On 4 April 1944 three Thai officers comprising the APPRECIATION 2 Mission dropped into Nakhon Sawan province with the same result. All were picked up and arrested. No less than six WHITES had been lost. Another attempt was made to drop a W/T set but was frustrated by the weather.

Although unconnected with APPRECIATION, the BILLOW Mission, consisting of four REDS, was inserted by Catalina on the south coast on 2 May to establish whether it was possible to move freely around the countryside and if so to proceed to the Bangkok area to await a British officer for D-Day. Captain Ngit Yin Kok was killed in a gun battle with Thai police and the other three captured. Add to these setbacks the failure of two ISLD parties in November 1943 and March 1944 [Operation SUN] and the picture looked glum. Furthermore the FO had yet to come up with a statement of HMG's post-war policy towards Thailand, a procrastination that merely served to advance the interests of the Americans and Chinese.

As it happened, American attempts to insert members of Detachment 404 into Thailand were also in trouble[122]. Two attempts to land two agents by submarine off the Andaman coast failed, and Operation ARISTOC, a plan to drop a three-man team into the mountains near Cheng Mai to arrange Pridi's escape, stalled when news came of a dramatic change in the Thai government. After submitting his resignation when two pieces of legislation were thrown out by the Assembly, Phibun had been outmanoeuvred by his opponents and was not named in the new cabinet. Furthermore, due to the resignation of the

---

[122] Two sabotage operations were also postponed: BOSOM to cut the Bangkok-Malaya railway in the Kra Isthmus and PEWIT to cut the Thailand-Burma railway in the north of the country.

co-Regent, Pridi found himself the sole representative of the King, in other words, head of state.

More good news was to follow when Pridi's brother, the *chargé d'affaires* at the Thai Delegation in Geneva, told the British that their WHITES in Bangkok were trying to contact them by W/T. On the same day a messenger arrived in Kunming with five messages from Puai, the commander of APPRECIATION 1, confirming that they were all alive and under the protection of the Thai police. By 27 August SOE was satisfied that the W/T traffic they now picked up from Bangkok was genuine and not under Japanese control. The mystery as to why it was transmitting out of Bangkok Jail was solved!

In response to these developments the BRILLIG Mission was quickly assembled. Two Thai officers – Krit and Prasoet – were dropped near Hua Hin on 6 September 1944 as suggested by Pridi's brother, and by 11 September had installed an independent W/T link between Pridi and SOE. They had also brought a letter for Pridi from Mountbatten, somewhat vaguer than the earlier one since there was still an FO reluctance to deal with a government that was seen to be collaborating with the Japanese[123]. Unknown to SOE, the OSS had dropped its own two-man HOTFOOT Mission [Free Thai officers Bunmak and Wimon] on the night of 8/9 September and after a slow start Wimon reached Bangkok on 21 September and the next night sat down to dinner with Police Chief Adun. That same night he met Pridi and urged the two men to cooperate as leaders of the Thai resistance movement. Ten days later, Bunmak turned up in Bangkok, and through a trusted intermediary also met with Pridi. A W/T link to the OSS listening station in Szemao opened on 5 October. The scene was now set for bitter rivalry between the two Allied Special Forces.

In talks with Pridi, SOE suggested that a high level Thai delegation should be brought to Kandy. However, when Pridi suggested sending former Foreign Minister Direk Chayanam, remembering the War Cabinet's caveat to restrict themselves to military matters only, SOE baulked at this proposal and Pridi dropped it. Instead he proposed that a senior Thai Section officer like Pointon or Gilchrist should be dropped to open up a formal consultative process. The risks were deemed unacceptable. Meanwhile, three more Missions went into Thailand. The OSS's ARISTOC dropped on the night of 1/2 November and, after evading intense Japanese patrol activity, reached Bangkok and the safety of police protection; DURIAN 2 which landed from HMS *Tally Ho* on 9 November on a small island in the Andaman Sea off the Kra Isthmus had an

---

123 It was fortunate that the War Cabinet approved on 25 September the sending in of agents on the proviso that SOE limited itself to the expulsion of the Japanese, two weeks after BRILLIG had dropped!

THAILAND [SIAM]

equally hard time and also ended up in Bangkok under police protection[124]. Neither achieved any of their objectives and, worse, it appeared that the Japanese had had prior warning about both missions. Pridi had not been consulted about either ARISTOC or DURIAN 2.

In contrast, three Thai agents, including Major Sena Ninkamhaeng [RAF], who knew all the senior officers in the Thai Air Force, successfully dropped with SOE's Operation COUPLING on 5 December and five days later they were conferring with Pridi and Arun in Bangkok. This spurred the Americans to send two senior OSS officers, Dick Greenlee and Major John Wester, to meet with Pridi [SIREN Mission] and they duly landed by Catalina on the night of 25/26 January near Kut Island, south of Trat. Greenlee was extracted by Catalina on 4 February in dangerous high waves and a week later was in Washington to report on Pridi's plans to support an Allied invasion and to establish some form of government-in-exile before the UN 1 March deadline expired, when prospective members were required to declare war against the Axis.

Captain Krit of the BRILLIG Mission had arranged a stores drop on 2 January to a close ally of Pridi, Tiang Sirikhan, at Hua Hin, which led to the development of a new base for training guerrillas in Sakon Nakhon in north east Thailand and the establishment of a W/T station there. A further arms drop – Operation CANDLE – was made on 27/28 January 1945 and, by mid-February, Tiang had 150 men in training in six separate camps. On 29 January Operation SAVANNA dropped three Thai officers near COUPLING's base at Phu Kradung to set up an additional W/T station. With its reserves of Thai manpower running low, SOE needed new recruits so, under Vic Wemyss and Ben Bathurst, Operation INFLUX was initiated, extracting suitable candidates from Thailand by Catalina, training them in Trincomalee and then reinserting them. The OSS adopted a similar system. INFLUX continued right up to August 1945 with students grouped as BUFFS, GREYS and INDIGOS.

Pridi's old plan to send Direk and a party to Ceylon was now revived, as the inclusion of Lieutenant General Chat Nakrop, the chief of staff of the Thai army, offered a priceless chance for SEAC to debrief a senior military officer. In Operation SEQUENCE, a Catalina picked up Direk, Chat, Thanat and two SOE Thai officers from near Tao Island in the Gulf of Siam and two days later, on 22 February 1945, they arrived in Trincomalee for a three-day visit. HMG used this opportunity to remind the Thais that they must 'work their passage home' – the same phrase that had been delivered to the Hungarians and

---

124 On the credit side, OSS established the BALMORAL Mission on the islands of Ko Surin Nua and Ko Surin Tai forty miles off the Thai coast in the Andaman Sea. By the end of January 1945 its strength was fourteen.

Romanians – and Mountbatten sent Pridi a message to the effect that the Free Thai movement could make 'a valuable contribution' to the Allied cause. All in all, SEQUENCE was regarded as a success and opened the way for SOE to up its game with increased supplies of arms and training cadres. General Chat's intelligence on Japanese troop dispositions was of the highest value.

In contrast, Operation ROGER, a reconnaissance of Phuket in late March, was a disaster. One man was killed, two captured by the Japanese and four arrested by the Thai authorities.

Dick Greenlee of the OSS SIREN Mission now returned to Thailand, arriving with Major Howard Palmer by Catalina on 23 March near Sattakut Island. He had little to tell Pridi for the Chiefs of Staff had not yet commented on Pridi's plan to assist an Allied invasion. What was apparent was that US bombing raids on Thailand with their inevitable collateral damage of civilian casualties, were becoming an issue for Pridi, particularly since the OSS were powerless to prevent them or even influence their targeting or frequency.

The PANICLE Mission, commanded by Colonel Victor Jaques [he had been a successful lawyer with Tilleke & Gibbins in Bangkok before the war and had been prised away from ME Command by SOE after a long search] with Major Tom Hobbs as 2 i/c and Prince Suphasawat[125] [Major Arun] was tasked to liaise with Pridi and other leading members of the Thai resistance in Bangkok and then establish a Force 136 HQ in the city to advise on the political and military position in Thailand. Landing safely by Catalina on the night of 27/28 April, the Mission was received by Direk. Over the next four days in meetings with Pridi, little was accomplished, for Jaques was unable to give any reassurances about the attitude of the British Government towards Thailand. Pridi volunteered that he had 5,000 trained guerrillas who were standing by to resist a Japanese takeover.

When Jaques and Hobbs left on 2 May, accompanying them was Puai, the leader of APPRECIATION 1. He had been tasked by Pridi to confront the British on a number of issues:

- Why had the British authorities failed to honour the undertakings they had originally given in the letter that Puai took with him in March 1944, namely a pledge on Thailand's post-war independence, the unfreezing of Thai assets in London for use by the resistance, and permission to establish a government-in-exile in India?

---

125 Mackenzie had originally wanted the Prince to work with Christopher Hudson near Tak on the Burmese border with the eventual aim of using his contacts with the Thai Army to provide a counterweight to Pridi. The Thai Section managed to get this decision reversed as Suphasawat himself was against it in that it would compromise his non-political status.

- Why had the SEQUENCE Mission been denied a meeting with Mountbatten?
- Finally, why were arms and supplies not being dropped at the anticipated level?

Five operations comprised of Sino-Thai personnel from the REDS were launched into Thailand from China via French Indo-China, ROTARY[126] in April 1944, BILLOW 1 in May 1944, BILLOW 2 in August 1944, BLANDINGS 1 in September 1944, and BLANDINGS 2in March 1945. All failed. Captain Lee, the Thai conducting officer who had gone in with BLANDINGS 2, attributed this lack of success to a wrong attitude – 'the party's behaviour and lack of guts were extremely bad at all times. They were all too keen on being well dressed and living an easy life'. For Major John Hill-Murray, the BLUES conducting officer, this lacklustre performance came as a disappointment[127].

On 22 May 1945 Pridi told Mountbatten that it was now time to act against the Japanese with whom Thai relations were becoming increasingly strained. Early action by the Thai resistance movement would hasten the surrender of the Japanese, whose forces in Thailand now numbered about 55,000 soldiers, of whom half were combat troops. Both the British and Americans viewed this proposal as unrealistic, for in their opinion the Japanese would quickly crush any insurrection and preparations for a long drawn out guerrilla war were far from complete. Furthermore, a premature uprising in Thailand would have little impact on Operation ZIPPER, the invasion of Malaya planned for September 1945. Far better to leave things be and to continue with intelligence gathering operations until November when sufficient supplies to sustain an effective uprising would have been dropped. Pridi's timing had been impeccable and as a result, he obtained British and American permissions to maintain relations with the Japanese while continuing to build up his resistance forces with OSS and SOE support. No one could accuse him of collaborating.

Jaques, now a Brigadier, returned to Bangkok on 1 June, this time with Captain Paul Ashwell[128] to set up a permanent Force 136 headquarters. Anxious to avoid confusion, he suggested forming a three-sided committee consisting of Pridi's representatives and SOE and OSS in-country heads. Predictably it was turned down by senior OSS officers. He also tried to coordinate the activities of

---

126 ROTARY members were actually BLUES.
127 Born in Peking in 1897, Hill-Murray had served with the Cameron Highlanders in the First World War and been wounded in 1917. After working in the Hong Kong and Shanghai Bank in China, he started his own import/export business and then returned to England to spend six years with the Civil Service. Fluent in Mandarin and Cantonese, Hill-Murray made an ideal conducting officer.
128 Jacques sent Ashwell out on 5 July to report to Kandy. He was replaced by Hobbs.

ISLD with those of SOE, for ISLD's two Thai agents from Operation OCCASION had both ended up in the hands of Police Chief Arun. Soon after, another ISLD Mission, OBSTACLE, also ended up in the custody of the Thai Police on the border with Malaya. With two further parties waiting to drop in July, Mackenzie asked SIS in London to refrain on the grounds that these unilateral actions upset Pridi and Arun who were trying to coordinate the training of the resistance. No undertakings were given. SOE itself was not above reproach for Operation TRUMPET, belonging to the Malayan Country Section, turned up in southern Thailand on the rather flimsy grounds that they were trying to keep on top of various Chinese contacts that had crossed the border in search of food.

Faced by a chronic shortage of aircraft, SOE had no option other than to trickle its agents and supplies into Thailand in marked contrast to the OSS who, thanks to the resources of the American 10th Air Force, had been able to deliver over 150 tons of supplies [Operation SALAD] by early July.

Concentrating on building up its guerrilla training bases, this time using experienced SOE officers and NCOs who had been released from the European theatre after VE Day, the Thailand Country Section organised the Free Thai areas as follows:

- Loei and Khon Kaen: Operation COUPLING [MUSLIN, SACKCLOTH – Major Peter Kemp; VOILE – Lieutenant Colonel Christopher Hudson and Major Christopher Blathwayt].
- Sakon Nakhon: Operation CANDLE [GEORGETTE – Captain Rowland Winn; CHIFFON – Major David Smiley and Major Tom Hobbs; and FELT – Sergeant Collins].
- Tak-Sukhothai: Operation NERONIAN [COTTON].
- Operation ROCKET [POPLIN].
- Operation SAVANNA [SILK].
- Phuket: Philip Oliver.
- Prachuap between Hua Hin and Chumphon: Operation SQUALID [SHANTUNG, AERTEX and LAME – Major Victor Wemyss and Lieutenant Small].
- Krabi, Phang Nha and Songkhla [Kra Isthmus]: Operation PRIEST [TULLE, RAYON and BARATHEA, each comprising three Thai operatives, covering intelligence and training]. A further Mission, TWILL, was tasked to contact POWs.
- Nakhon Si Thammarat [Malaya border]: Operation SUNGOD [GABBERDINE – Majors Scott, Moss and Hibberdine].
- Malaya/Thailand border: Operation APPRECIATION [CALICO and NINON, each comprising two Thai officers, dropped into the Yala area

THAILAND [SIAM]

on the Malaya/Thailand border and acted as reception on 6 August 1945 to BROCADE, Captains Charles and Dawson, a British party tasked to liaise with the Chinese Communist guerrillas on the Malayan side of the border and the Thai Resistance Movement on the Thai side].

- Operation MACHINE [CANVAS, DRILL, HESSIAN, TUSSORE and TWEED, the latter consisting of Majors Harrington and Read, Captain Gunn RAMC and Sergeant Hazelhurst who were dropped to Captain Redman, Scots Guards, to reinforce Operation BOILER, a POW contact and rescue mission designed to place W/T operators with the various Thai army headquarters to facilitate communications in the event of a Japanese move against Thailand.

*****

Operation SUNGOD

John Hibberdine [L] and Billy Moss [R]

Already a legend for his part in the kidnapping of General Kreipe in Crete, Stanley Moss arrived in Ceylon in May 1945 and after meeting up with old Balkan hands, John Hibberdine [Albania] and Ken Scott [Greece], he persuaded Peter Pointon, Head of Thailand Country Section, to let them drop as a team. After an uneventful drop near Bandon, they installed themselves in the bungalow of a disused tin mine where they patiently waited for their W/T set to arrive, for somehow it had been left off their drop list. After a fortnight, local Thai sources told them that the Japanese were planning to move 500 POWs from Bandon up to Bangkok, so Scott went to investigate. Their W/T set finally arrived five days later and Moss and Hibberdine set out for Narkhon on the old narrow-gauge railway. Here they met Scott who had little news of POWs in the area but had found out that the Japanese were mustering at the seaside town of Songkla. Just as they were readying themselves to go there, a signal arrived to 'stand fast and make no official contact with the Japanese until ordered'. Passing the time attending bullfights, cock fights and a Thai ball, the Mission eventually arranged the orderly surrender of Japanese forces in the area before retiring to the charms of Bangkok on 20 November and then home for Christmas.

*****

These increased levels of resistance activity – runways constructed, training camps built, roads improved, arms and equipment dropped – together with the waning fortunes of Tokyo combined to make the Japanese more nervous and

THAILAND [SIAM]

suspicious than usual. Senior Japanese commanders made it quite clear to Pridi that he needed to get his house in order. Furthermore, the two 'allies' would form a joint commission to investigate the location of secret airfields in Thailand. On 21 July, the Japanese persuaded the Thais to give them the northern border with Burma to defend and the city of Bangkok was designated a joint defensive responsibility as were other parts of the country.

With increased surveillance by the Kempeitai and unusually busy Japanese air activity sounding alarm bells, at the end of June Pridi asked SEAC to temporarily suspend all supply flights. Despite having over 1,100 tons of supplies earmarked for the Free Thais, Mountbatten acquiesced for he knew he would be unable to come to the assistance of Thailand if the Japanese took it over. SEAC planners had pencilled in February 1946 as the earliest date for an invasion of Thailand. If a period of inactivity was necessary to allay their suspicions, so be it. Meanwhile, the emphasis was switched back to the collection of intelligence, everything from troop movements, unit identification, defences, air and naval assets and locations [particularly runways] through to detailed information on the state of roads, bridges and enemy W/T installations.

When Pridi approved the resumption of night-time supply flights on 13 July, Mountbatten was relieved for the British had mounted a large scale deception campaign – Operation SCEPTICAL – to fool the Japanese into thinking that Thailand had precedence over Malaya as an Allied invasion target. The more troops retained by the Japanese in Thailand, the less the resistance would be to Operation ZIPPER in September. Force 136 delivered 450 tons and the OSS 100 tons of supplies to the Free Thai guerrillas in the last ten days of July to bring them up to strength for a full scale uprising at end of August. Personnel drops were also stepped up to meet ambitious targets. For instance, the OSS plan envisaged 214 American personnel organising twelve 500-strong battalions with sufficient arms and ammunition for 7,200 men. SOE plans for an 8,500-strong guerrilla force were similarly ambitious. Both were far from realised.

On 2 August, Jaques flew out to India, leaving Hobbs in sole charge in Bangkok. With the Japanese becoming edgier by the day, the reality of fighting a successful guerrilla war was still only a glimmer. When the Japanese surrendered after the atomic bombs had been dropped on Hiroshima and Nagasaki, Mackenzie opined that 'the end of the war took everyone by surprise'. In that respect, for SOE in Thailand it was a pleasant one as the prognostications of a long drawn out fight with the Japanese were not good.

Brigadier Jaques concluded that 'during the closing months of the war, the Japanese were definitely troubled by Force 136 activities and were compelled to deploy troops in various parts of Thailand, either in active efforts to locate guerrillas or impede the use of airstrips and DZs, or as a protective measure against possible Allied airborne operations. In addition, the Thais, encouraged by Allied parties being in the country, became more and more obstructive to Japanese requirements'.

After the Japanese surrender, two major Operations were launched by the allies to rescue POWs in South East Asia; BIRDCAGE, a leaflet information campaign, was followed by MASTIFF which delivered men and stores to the camps. In a brilliant display of bluff and bravado, 28- year-old Colonel Douglas Clague of E Force strode into the Japanese HQ in Bangkok on 27 August and demanded that his men be allowed immediate access to the camps. With the combined resources of SOE and its thirty-one W/T stations already deployed around Thailand and the OSS, Clague's Operation SWANSONG ensured that the majority of the 35,000 POWs received prompt medical and nutritional aid and were evacuated by the end of September.

THAILAND [SIAM]

LIEUTENANT COLONEL 'TOM' HOBBS, MC

Tom Hobbs

Before the outbreak of war, Tom Hobbs had been a banker with the Chartered Bank of India and spent five years in the branch in Bangkok. A member of the TA London Scottish, he had arrived in Burma in autumn 1941 and been 'engaged' by the ORIENTAL Mission on 31 October, spending time in the Chin Hills. Commissioned on 21 January 1942, Hobbs joined the Burma Country Desk where he was conducting officer of the FERRET party until transferring to Thailand Country Section in early 1944.

Recommendation for MC

Major Hobbs rendered exceptionally valuable and meritorious service in clandestine operations in that under the eyes of the enemy he entered into and lived under the greatest danger in Bangkok, the Thai capital, occupied in force by the Japanese. He did this on two occasions, first from 26 April to 3 May by seaplane [on the journey he was continuously airborne for thirty-nine hours except for an interval of less than an hour to change plane], second on 4 July when he was landed on a secret airstrip up country whence he was secretly conveyed to Bangkok. He remained there hidden and constantly at great risk until the Japanese surrender in late August. He was principal assistant to Brigadier Jaques and during the latter's absence from Bangkok on a visit to India in early August 1945 Major Hobbs remained alone in conditions of great strain and peril sending out information of the first importance. By his steady bearing, endurance and determination he contributed to the success of the clandestine mission set up in Bangkok. His services were of the highest value to his leader and to the Allied cause.

Awarded

MAJOR RICHARD BRYCE-SMITH, MBE

Born in Lancashire in 1903, Bryce-Smith worked as a Forest Assistant with the Borneo Company Ltd in Thailand. Based in the north of the country near Chengmai, he spoke Lao and Thai and was recruited by SOE in November 1941. Commissioned the following January, he carried out the very first recce of the Kengtung area and worked closely with the Thailand Country Section throughout the war.

14 December 1945: Recommendation for MBE

The officer has rendered distinguished and gallant service over a long period.

Recruited to Special Forces in April 1942, this officer was placed in command of a body of Karen levies at Mawchi, with instructions to withdraw them to the Karen Hills and discharge them there, after obstructing the Japanese pursuit. Having carried out this duty successfully, he made his way to Kunming in China, thus completing a march of over 1,000 miles.

In the rainy season of 1943, he made a reconnaissance journey on foot quite alone over a distance of 450 miles from Kunming, over routes to the west of Mount [?] to the Burma-China boundary and then some 150 miles west into the Wan States. Returning by different routes and tracks, still alone and on foot, the whole trip took six months, during which this officer had no contact with the outside world. He was the first British officer to make this journey after the withdrawal from Burma in 1942. Enemy dispositions were virtually unknown and no Allied aid could be given to him, which made his task dangerous, as well as arduous. He brought back reports and information of considerable value, the result of his fortitude, determination and courage.

On 26 July 1945, Major Bryce-Smith dropped into Thailand near Rahong to train an existing guerrilla force. The presence of a Japanese garrison which knew the area well, and had already compelled the abandonment of an airstrip and DZ, added to his risks. But despite their vigilance, he succeeded in arranging the safe reception by parachute of further personnel and stores in the short period before the Japanese surrender and in securing valuable intelligence of Japanese troop movement both into and out of Burma through the [Mae Sot] pass.

Awarded

THAILAND [SIAM]

LIEUTENANT COLONEL CHRISTOPHER 'SOAPY' HUDSON, DSO, OBE, Croix de Guerre

Christopher Hudson

Christopher Hudson joined SOE in January 1942. He was to become an outstanding officer. Born in 1910 in Tunbridge Wells, after finishing his education he became an industrial chemist and moved to Lausanne in Switzerland in 1935.

He enlisted in the Royal Fusiliers in May 1940 and was commissioned in 17th Battalion in February 1941.

His course reports give a hint of what was to come; 'Perhaps inspires me with the most confidence. Intelligent; unflustered and gives the impression that he is bound to succeed'; 'there is nothing but praise for this student who is a leader in whom all can have confidence. He has coolness, ability to weigh things up before he makes his clear decisions, yet quickness of brain when required and absolute sureness of touch. Philosophically minded, he is a man who through foresight avoids mistakes'; 'a sound and reliable officer'; 'quiet, unassuming, extremely efficient and very keen'.

On the night of September 24/25 1942, Hudson together with a French operative and W/T signaller dropped into the Clermont-Ferrand district, 'unfortunately ... in the wrong place and from too high'. One of the parachutes to which was attached a canister containing clothes, rucksacks and cover documents was never seen again. It was an inauspicious beginning but the team managed to find their contact in the centre of town and were taken to a safe house sixteen kilometres away. Here Hudson decided that although he would stay on himself, it was imperative to disperse the rest of his team. It was too late, for on 8 October, Hudson and his French hosts, the Werthers, were arrested. On 23 January 1943, Hudson and his hosts were moved to Prison St Paul in Lyons before being transferred to the Maison Centrale in Eysses. Although administered by the French, the prison inmates were nevertheless scrutinised by the Germans and Hudson knew he had to make plans to escape. On the evening of 3 January 1944, after making the necessary arrangements with their prison guards, fifty-four men 'walked quite openly to the door of the prison where they were let out by a friendly warder'. The Germans arrived at the prison by midnight but they were too late, the birds had flown. Hudson reached Albi by car and then went straight into the F section escape line and arrived at the British vice-consul in Barcelona after a strenuous trek over the Pyrenees, including two nights in a cave.

Three months later, on the night of April 8/9 1944, Hudson was dropped to the HEADMASTER circuit in the Sarthe, an area of considerable tactical importance to the Germans and hence keenly monitored by the Gestapo. Hampered by a lack of suitable DZs and an indifferent local populace, Hudson struggled to prepare the resistance for D-Day. He formed a large *maquis* in the Charnie Forest but on 15 June they were attacked and routed by the Germans, forcing Hudson to adopt new tactics of using small sections of five to six men on hit and run operations including cutting telephone lines and underground cables. In the day they could move openly about; at night, they went about their clandestine business. It proved a successful formula with 'telephones ... attacked over and over again, and though we were never able to completely isolate the town, the system was so reduced that it took two hours to telephone from Le Mans to Maners, a distance of forty-five kilometres by road'. Two ammunition trains were stopped by Hudson's sections and subsequently destroyed by Allied aircraft.

When the Americans overran Le Mans, Hudson placed his forces at their disposal and ran a number of intelligence missions for them from 10 August to 12 September 1944.

On 26 May 1945, Hudson parachuted into Konkhaen in north east Thailand on Operation PARTERRE and, after collecting as much intelligence about the enemy and information about the potential guerrillas as he could in a short period of time, he returned to India on 1 June. His conclusion was that:

'it is really wrong to consider the FSM as a Resistance Movement in any way comparable to those in Occupied Europe, except possibly the case of Yugoslavia. It is essential to realise that the whole country is being organised for future battle with the Japanese under the direction of the Government and using all the properly appointed officials and officers to do so. The entire resources of the country are at the disposal of the

THAILAND [SIAM]

Allies within the present limitations of security. On D-Day, these restrictions will disappear and it will be possible to mobilise all available men and material under the various local authorities. It is simply a question of providing the arms. What I have seen has convinced me of their determination. They feel that the Quisling Phibun government by its declaration of war on the Allies has put them, so to speak, beyond the pale of the rest of the world, and that they are bracketed with the Japanese whom they detest. They have a passionate wish to show that the Phibun Government was in no way representative and was merely a tool of the Japanese and by a national effort on D-Day to justify themselves and to show themselves capable of taking their place in the post war world by the side of the United nations.'

Having made firm plans, he went back to Thailand in June on Operation COUPLING/VOILE and set about raising and training a force of over 5,000 irregulars to fight the Japanese.

June 1945: Recommendation for DSO

Major Hudson whose task was to assist in the organisation of resistance groups was dropped by parachute in the Clermont-Ferrand area, but through no fault of his own, was caught within a fortnight of his arrival. After spending fifteen months in prison, he succeeded almost entirely by his own efforts in bringing to a successful outcome plans for the mass escape from the prison at Eysses. During his escape and the arduous journey across the Pyrenees to safety, this officer, by his coolness and selflessness, made a substantial contribution to the safe arrival of his twenty-seven comrades.

Despite his experience and the great danger of being recognised, he volunteered for immediate return to France to participate in the closing phases of the activities for which he had volunteered eighteen months before. After further training he was dropped again, in early 1944, to a new circuit in the Sarthe area in which the Gestapo were active. Despite many difficulties and hazards, Hudson built up an active organisation based on Le Mans. In their attacks on enemy communications to prevent the movement of troops against the Allied landing, his circuit effected considerable sabotage to roads, railways and other communications.

When his area was liberated Hudson offered his services to the Allied Forces, for whom he undertook twelve intelligence missions into enemy occupied territory. During one of these he was again taken prisoner but again succeeded in escaping.

For his perseverance and unfailing devotion to duty in the prosecution of attacks on the enemy, for his leadership and courage in many personal attacks and for the important results attained through his efforts, it is strongly recommended that he be appointed a Companion in the DSO.

Awarded

25 January 1946: Recommendation for OBE

Volunteered for service in the Far East, after long operational service in enemy occupied France. Parachuted into north east Thailand, south of Loey, on 26 May 1945, he carried out a most valuable recce in Japanese occupied areas of airfields and their dispositions, both on the ground at night and from the air in Thai aircraft. Returned to India after ten days with extensive and valuable information. While in Thailand he made preliminary contacts and plans with local guerrilla leaders.

He returned to the same area on 6 July 1945, landing at a secret airstrip, with the task of improving the organisation and effectiveness and increasing the strength of the guerrillas in the western part of north east Thailand. He carried out this duty with unflagging energy and conspicuous success without regard for his personal comfort or safety. By making use of Thai aircraft, he covered a large area personally. Advising and directing local guerrilla leaders, he won their complete confidence rapidly. Establishing a series of airstrips and DZs quickly, he was able to elude Japanese action and accept delivery of arms and stores sufficient to equip and partially train some 5,600 guerrillas by the time the war ended.

The Japanese were already active in their patrolling and through their spies, in trying to locate the scene of guerrillas preparations, the existence of which, and of Allied agents, they were well aware. They visited DZs and training places but Lieutenant Colonel Hudson's excellent training and organisation of warning posts foiled their fuller success.

Establishing a training school he had passed over 500 men through it before the surrender, trained as junior leaders.

After the surrender this officer rendered excellent service in aid of POWs. In Bangkok in September 1945, on his way home to be released, he volunteered at once to undertake an urgent mission to French Indo-China in the troublesome area of Pakse. By his ability and firmness he maintained control of law and order through a local council he set up until he handed over to French authorities a month later.

Awarded

CHAPTER NINE

OPERATION HAINTON/ HEAVY/WOLF

Set in the steep jungle-clad hills of northern Burma along the border with China, the HAINTON Mission epitomises the complexity of many SOE operations in the Far East. At a political level, there was underlying friction with the KMT in Free China and then by accident rather than design, with the Free Thai Movement; relationships with the US came under strain for so-called boundary transgressions; local politics threw up ethnic hatreds and financial and economic skulduggery; meanwhile the main target, the Japanese army and its Thai vexillations, proved elusive and devious when attacked. And throughout the duration of the mission, it was the mercurial weather that dictated its operational effectiveness.

When the Japanese and Thai armies invaded Kengtung, Michael Evans, of the Burma Forestry Service and Assistant Superintendant in Kengtung, raised levies on the Thailand/Kengtung State border. As the British withdrew, he was forced to retire to Nahsilek where he raised another group and later to Manna/ Namhku which he reached in June 1942. During that winter he managed to continue to offer sporadic resistance, which involved raiding across the border with a small group of Christian *Lahu* volunteers and then returning to Namhku. With no WT, no money, no uniforms and no modern weapons, the raising of an organised band was impossible; this was guerrilla warfare in the raw. The raiders were armed with shotguns, some captured Thai rifles, an old Lewis gun, and some revolvers. Evans himself used a sporting rifle. The *Lahus* south of the border gave him food and information and, after a raid, his *Lahus* levies would return to their villages and continue with their everyday lives. In April 1943, Captain Evans was killed while leading a successful raid on Mong Pawk, which was abandoned forever by its Thai garrison.

The primary objectives of the Mission were to establish overland contact with Operation CHARACTER parties in Burma – a forlorn hope as it turned out since they were a three week march away – and to explore the possibilities of operating behind enemy lines in Kengtung State by means of levies and guerrillas. Whereas the native Shan population was avowedly pro-British, perhaps not surprising given the deprivation inflicted on them by the war, the politics of Kengtung state,

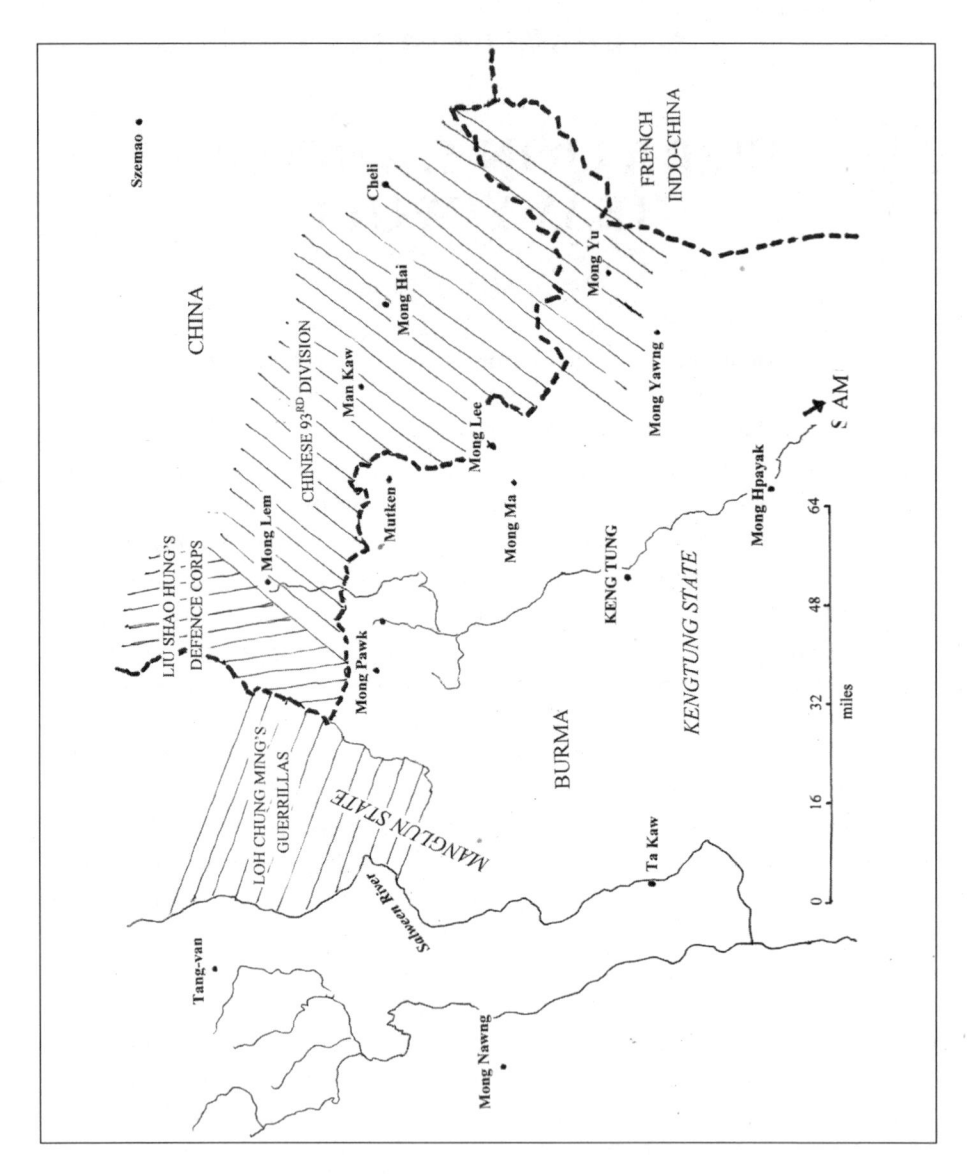

HEAVY/WOLF area of operations

the proposed area of operations, were far from straightforward. General Lu Han's Chinese 93rd Division, which had been deployed there to help the British in 1942, was still ensconced along the border from Mong Lee in the west to Menghai in the east, including the whole of the Hsipsang Fanna district. The Chinese troops had settled down to a comfortable life of trading in opium and selling Lend-Lease small arms and ammunition on the black market.

Also in the area were two bands of Chinese bandits who had thrived in the chaotic conditions which followed the British withdrawal. They had looted over forty villages and were now paid and armed by the 93rd Division as members of the official Defence Force. In reality, they were trading whatever came their way. Such was the lawlessness of the area, that a later report at the end of 1944 mentioned a third force of Chinese bandits arriving in the area, seizing the richest and most important officials and holding them to ransom.

Finally, and by far the trickiest factor confronting the Mission, Kengtung State had been given to the Thais by the Japanese in 1942 and was garrisoned by around 3,000 Thai troops who had captured Keng Tung on 27 May 1942. Badly equipped and ill-disciplined, these soldiers had to live off the countryside and, although not aggressive, their presence was loathed by the villagers who were British subjects. Although official British policy was to take a hard line with the Thai government, at the same time SOE were engaged on teasing them out of their alliance with Japan and enlisting their support for the FSM. Any attacks on Thai troops would be therefore construed by the FSM as bad faith on the part of the British. Here was the nub of the problem. There were some Japanese in the area, mainly to collect rice quotas, and relations with their Thai allies were reportedly poor.

Crucial to the success of the Mission were the services of two Chinese agents. Cheng Kai was one of General Cheng Kai-min's[129] men, who had gone with Major Bryce-Smith on the first recce of the Kengtung border area in 1943. He had so impressed SOE at the time that Findlay Andrew in Chungking specifically asked the Chinese to release him for HAINTON. Stephen Sim Kah Sun was a Singaporean Chinese born in 1918. He had gone to study medicine in Hong Kong, from where he managed to escape and reach French Indo-China. There he reported to Colonel Douglas Ride, his former lecturer in medicine, in May 1942, and was passed on to SOE.

HAINTON, or the Burmese Reconnaissance Group, was approved by General Ho Ying-chin[130], Chiang Kai-shek's Chief of Staff, on 17 March 1944[131]. Commanded by Major Jonah Jones, its insertion into Kengtung was planned in

---

129 Aka Zheng Jiemin who had been asked by Wavell to organise Chinese guerrilla forces in Singapore before its fall.
130 General Ho Ying-chin had visited British defences in Hong Kong, Burma and Singapore in the autumn of 1940. He was well acquainted with British special operations.
131 Unknown to SOE, an OSS Mission led by Captain Nicol Smith had visited General Lu Han at Meng Hai on 9 March. Four days later five OSS Thai agents and their Chinese conducting officer had crossed the border for Meng La. All five failed to infiltrate into Thailand and returned to the OSS forward operating base at Szemao.

three phases – HAINTON I consisting of Cheng Kai and Stephen Sim, HAINTON II comprised Jones, Major George Bridge, Lieutenant Joseph Byrne [to be dropped in September] and a party of six, HAINTON III – Captain George Pennell and two – was due to drop on 6 June. Attached to HAINTON II were two Chinese officers, Captain Wu Fen Chien, the Chinese LO, and Captain Chang Yih Cheng, a W/T operator.

Taking the mission's stores on mules, Kai and Sim left Mitu on 23 March for Szemao, where they met up with Jones's party a month later. The two group reached Mong Lem on 12 May where they set up their headquarters and made W/T contact. Soon after, having learnt of a 400- strong band of Chinese guerrillas in the vicinity, the Mission upsticked and relocated at Norfu[132]. On 6 June, HAINTON III dropped successfully [Captain Pennell, Lieutenant Kai Fa, and two Chin W/T operators] but the weather then closed in and no supplies of arms or equipment reached them until the end of July[133]. The Mission moved across the border into China where it set up its HQ at Manna. By August, in spite of the bad weather conditions, SOE had hopes that 'some 150 men will come forward when called upon.' It was wishful thinking for all the males in the area were now engaged on bringing in the harvest. There was another flaw in this projection for the Mission was convinced that there would never be a general uprising for 'the Shans cannot compare in toughness and virility with the Chins, Kachins or Karens ... patriotism is non-existent'.

By the end of September, augmented by Lieutenant Saw Johnny, a Burmese Rifles officer, Lieutenant Lore, intelligence officer, Major Davidson, OC Levies, and Captains Harrison and Byrne, HAINTON's tasks had split in two, Operation HEAVY and Operation WOLF. First, there was the original objective of raising levies to attack the Japanese lines of communication. However, based on experience to date, a second task had been identified, namely to penetrate disaffected Thai troops in the border area, for 'if north Thailand became a main Japanese line of communication for reinforcing Burma or withdrawing eastwards, a skilfully handled guerrilla force operating in the WA states coupled with a disaffected Thai army on the north of the Burma-Thailand border would present the enemy with a problem.' Two Free Thai officers were dropped – Arun Sorathet and Khamhaeng Phalangkun[134] – and in early October, the Mission moved its HQ to Loi Awng Lawng on the Burmese side of the border, about 6,000 feet on the side of a hill. Although it was easily defended and well sited for offensive operations, progress stalled when orders were received to

---

132 Mong Kai.
133 There is a discrepancy here between the Mission report and the SOE War Diary, the latter noting that Captain Murray, Arun Sorathesn and three other bodies were also dropped.
134 Chamrat's brother.

concentrate solely on intelligence gathering. Morale among the levies fell for what was the point in training for three months when there was no chance of action? Also, as one levy remarked, the camp was very cold compared to his family house a few miles away.

In November further supply problems were encountered, not helped by the antics of the local Chinese commander in Mong Lem who had ordered the villagers to desist from supplying the SOE Mission and had posted guards in the area of their camp. The Mission therefore returned to Namhku [Manna] at the beginning of December. Jones, by now a Lieutenant Colonel, reported on 20 December 1944 that 'lack of supplies and rations, changes of policy have somewhat appeared to us as careless and unnecessary mistakes, added to the difficulties incidental to work of this kind, might well have caused depression and a fraying of tempers. This has not been the case ... It is sufficient to state here that every man has given cheerfully and willingly of his best'. According to Pennell, the levies totalled a meagre 120.

By the beginning of January, matters had deteriorated when the Myosa of Wan Mutken was abducted and tied up for three days and two nights by Chinese troops. He was only released after paying a hefty ransom. At the same time a Chinese intelligence party crossed the border in the Mong Pawk area and set up a W/T station, in the process arresting the village headman and shooting a villager for 'failing to comply with orders'.

On 11 January 1945, an aircraft landed at Nanchiao airstrip to collect a Thai army deserter and to extract Major Bridge, Captain Harrison and others. What was a mere routine trip became a political hot potato overnight. The Chinese officially complained that SOE had failed to ask permission to land; the Americans likewise protested that the aircraft had intruded into their operational area without clearance. The incident typified the underlying tensions between the three Allies, whose only interest in common was the defeat of the Japanese. The Mission duly moved back across the border to Loi Awng Lawng. On 20 February, Lieutenant Colonel Dennis Herring, an experienced Chindit officer, Captain Sam Cope and sixteen ORs [Operation HEAVY/LYNX] were dropped at Loi and immediately began to recruit and train Kachins for guerrilla warfare. It was far from easy; on one occasion, a Kachin picked up a Sten gun and accidentally killed two of his comrades.

Major C.J. Davison took over from Jones who was extracted on 5 March and at the end of the month HEAVY/WOLF started offensive operations against Japanese and Thai forces[135]. By 4 April the enemy had been pushed back to the

---

135 Four raids on Thai army outposts between 21 and 31 March resulted in twenty-five enemy killed and sixteen wounded.

general area of Kengtung. Two weeks later a Chinese patrol of one officer and thirty men arrived to announce that their commander, General Wu, had ordered them to stay in the area until his advanced HQ arrived at Mong Yawng, once Force 136 had taken Keng Tung town. Persuaded to leave by Davison, the Chinese nonetheless reappeared in Mong Ma and after another stern admonition once again left. According to one Chinese officer's map, the border was incorrect; most of the Northern Shan States were well within China.

When this information reached SEAC, it prompted Mountbatten to signal General Carton de Wiart at Chiang Kai-shek's HQ with instructions to remind the Generalissimo that Kengtung was part of Burma and, whatever his fears, 'you will persuade him not to attack into British territory'. He pointed out that 'if Chinese forces create trouble in the area by attacking southwards, it is possible that the Japanese may react strongly and drive northwards towards China, which is precisely what is to be avoided'. Furthermore, could he please remind him that China was not at war with Thailand? As an aside, Mountbatten mused that the 93rd Division probably had in mind to spend the monsoon season in Kengtung because it was a 'relatively rich territory ... but whatever happens we do not wish them to beat up the Thai'.

Through May, 'jitter' raids were stepped up against Japanese and Thai posts. In June, it came to the notice of the Mission that the Chinese guerrillas in Pang-Yang had issued a proclamation that Manglun State had been returned to its rightful owners, the Chinese, and the people were now Chinese subjects and would be taxed accordingly. Chinese civilians from across the border were being encouraged to move in with promises of free land and other concessions. A vibrant trade in gold started up at absurdly low prices, as well as dealings in new Burmese 5 and 10 Rupee Treasury Notes.

The Mission, by now alarmed at the frequency of these incursions, noted that 'if the Chinese are allowed to get a footing in Kengtung State even for a short time, apart from the inevitable political "round the mulberry bush", and consequently delay in ejecting them, then the problems of relief, rehabilitation, war compensation, and a host of other headaches, is going to be enormous'. On 1 August, Davidson called for a battalion of regular army troops to be sent up as soon as possible; their appearance would undoubtedly resolve the issue by keeping the Chinese 93rd Division on its side of the border, reassuring the villagers and their headmen that their land was not up for grabs and, most importantly, releasing the greater part of HEAVY/WOLF for the role it was intended for, to fight the enemy.

The high hopes once held for HAINTON never materialised. Jones, the original operational commander, was none the less satisfied.

'Perhaps the most important work done by HEAVY was in denying entrance to the Chinese. The 93rd Divisional commander was most anxious to lead his troops back into Kengtung, as, having been driven from the State in 1942, he wished to recover "face". The fact that 93rd Division HQ had buried a lot of loot near Kengtung town shortly before their withdrawal may have had some bearing on this desire ... In connection with Chinese affairs, it should be mentioned that little help was received from HQ and the successive commanders of HEAVY were forced to deal with the Chinese on their own initiative and obtain results by a mixture of bluff, diplomacy and mysterious reference to being Personal Staff Officers of the Supreme Commander SEAC.'

Herring, who came out via Lashio on 2 July, was objective in his summation:

'All in all I did not find this operation very satisfactory in terms of solid achievements. No doubt we stirred up the countryside and occupied the attention of a number of Japs who might otherwise have been aggressively employed against us elsewhere. Certainly it seems we put the fear of God into the Thais to the extent that many deserted their posts and ran. There was too much marching around with too little results to pretend HAINTON was a notable success but Fourteenth Army seemed satisfied. As far as the levies themselves were concerned the Kachins were excellent, as usual, and also the Lahus under Pennell but the Shans were, by and large, a waste of time with few exceptions, notably GCOs and NCOs.'

He went on to pay tribute to the courage and toughness of the Kachins:

'Indeed it is most difficult to kill these hillmen. One of them was shot squarely in the right lung, through the jaw and again through the left hand, and was left for dead. He was, however, very far from dead, and walked up nearly 2,000 feet and three miles during the night to our Point Section where I found him. He eventually recovered.'

CHINA
TONKIN
HANOI
BURMA
GULF OF TONKIN
HAINAN
LUANG PRABANG
VIENTIANE
LAOS
SIAM
ANNAM
BANGKOK
CAMBODIA
PHNOM PENH
SAIGON
GULF OF SIAM
COCHINCHINA
SOUTH CHINA SEA
0
150
300
450
600
miles

CHAPTER TEN

FRENCH INDO-CHINA

POLITICAL BACKGROUND

French Indo-China was formed in October 1887 from Annam, Tonkin, Cochinchina [which together form modern Vietnam] and the Kingdom of Cambodia; Laos was added after the Franco-Thai War of 1893. In the four protectorates, the French formally left the local rulers in power, who were the Emperors of Vietnam, the Kings of Cambodia, and the Kings of Luang Prabang, but in fact all power was vested in French hands, the local rulers acting only as figureheads.

Nationalist sentiments intensified in Vietnam, especially during and after the First World War, but all uprisings and tentative efforts towards independence failed to obtain any concessions from the French. In February 1930, there was a rebellion by a small number of Vietnamese soldiers in the French Colonial Army's Yen Bai garrison in cahoots with the Vietnamese Nationalist Party [VNQDD]. Poorly planned and badly co-ordinated, it quickly petered out. However, the French response was disproportional. Over 500 prosecutions were brought against the suspected participants: of the eighty sentenced to death by guillotine, thirteen were top VNQDD leaders.

The mutiny was followed by a series of strikes which broke out at various spots in French Indo-China – at the Phu Rieng rubber plantation near Bien Hoa in Cochin China, at a match factory at Binh Thuy near Vinh in Central Vietnam, and at a textile plant at Nam Dinh in Tonkin. By midsummer the discontent had spread from outbreaks in the big industrial centres to the rural areas in Central and South Vietnam, where a series of major peasant revolts broke out against French colonial authority. As governmental authority in the Central provinces of Nghe An and Ha Tinh disintegrated, it was rapidly replaced by village peasant Soviets under Communist party leadership. The French responded ruthlessly to these 'Nghe-Tinh Soviets' but it was only several months later, in mid-1931, that order was restored.

From now on, the Indo-Chinese Communist Party took on the struggle for independence.

In 1940, Thailand's General Phibun took the opportunity of French weaknesses at home to reclaim previously lost territories, resulting in the French-Thai War between October 1940 and May 1941. In January 1941, Vichy French naval forces decisively defeated Thai naval forces at the Battle of Koh Chang, resulting in the loss of one large cruiser and the beaching of another. The war ended on 31 January at the instigation of the Japanese, and under the terms of the Treaty of Tokyo, in May the French ceded to Thailand the provinces of Batdambang, Siemreab, and parts of Kampong Thum and Stoeng Treng. Cambodia thus lost one-third of its territory and nearly half a million citizens.

In September 1940, Vichy France granted Japan's demands for military access to Tonkin. This allowed Japan better access to China in their war against Chiang Kai-shek. A year later, on 21 July 1941, the Vichy French government yielded yet again to Japanese demands and allowed her troops to occupy bases in southern Indo-China. At a stroke, Japan secured the use of the Camranh naval base 750 miles from Singapore and airfields 350 miles from Kota Bahru in Malaya. Furthermore, she now directly threatened Thailand.

SOE IN INDO-CHINA

After the Fall of France in May 1940, the Vichy government entered into a close political and economic association with Japan as a signatory of the Tripartite Pact. By August 1941[136] they had allowed 40,000 Japanese troops into the country which was now jointly administered by Japan and Vichy France. As the official SOE report on French Indo-China put it, 'the military situation was [thus] characterised by the co-existence of two armies, who, far from trying to contact each other, practically ignored one another, and generally lived in separate garrisons and camps'. The French army of 55,000, of whom 12,000 were Europeans, was headquartered at Tonkin and responsible for the defence of the northern frontier facing China; their 40,000 Japanese opposite numbers were based at Cochin, mainly en route to and from Thailand, Malaya and Burma.

HMG's immediate concern was to keep the French Far East fleet out of the war, so relations were maintained with Vice Admiral Jean Decoux, head of the French Indo-China administration[137] who reported to the Colonial Ministry at Vichy.

Somewhat out of step with the FO, SOE originally worked with Captain Baron Francois Girot de Langlade, head of the Belgian company SOCFIN and a committed Gaullist, and group of French rubber planters under Pierre Boulle.

---

136 On 29 July 1941, a protocol was signed by the Japanese ambassador at Vichy and Admiral Darlan in which a mutual promise of military co-operation for the joint defence of Indo-China was agreed, subject to special arrangements.
137 His predecessor General Georges Catroux had defected to the British in June 1940 and went on to join de Gaulle in London.

The two Frenchmen had set up a Committee for Free Malaya on 18 June 1941 to create a rallying point for Gaullists. One of their members was Lieutenant Colonel Emile Tutenges, later nominated by De Gaulle to head up the Mission Française Libre d'Extrême-Orient in Singapore in September. De Langlade met Colonel Alan Warren in Singapore and arranged for the first batch of students to attend the course at STS 101. De Langlade himself went to Saigon in July to establish links with the Free French in the city, including the Bureau de Statistiques de Hanoi [BSM] and the Bureau des Archives de Saigon [BAM].

On 19 October 1941, an SOE Mission was undertaken to:
- infiltrate two STS 101-trained agents into Indo-China.
- arrange for Professor Meyer May, de Gaulle's Far East propaganda chief and a former lecturer at the College of Medicine Hanoi, to confer with resistance leaders.

Major Freddy Spencer Chapman and Major Jackie Knott escorted the party of agents on board a Yangtze River steamer *Wuchang* and sailed for Indo-China; the landing was called off just as the party had put on rubber boots ready to go ashore. It returned to Singapore on 29 October 1941.

The reason for the last minute cancellation was that the CinC China Station, Admiral Layton, was at the time trying to persuade Admiral Decoux, as Governor General of Indo-China, to come over to the British side with the French fleet. The SOE-Gaullist operation nearly scuppered these delicate negotiations, although as it happened they did not succeed.

On 4 November 1941, Basil Goodfellow went to Saigon on a 'business trip'. To his dismay, he found that the authorities knew all about SOE's subversive organisation and that security was non-existent.

INDO-CHINA COUNTRY SECTION

In late 1941, the Free French decided that they needed representation with the KMT and accordingly dispatched a four-man Mission to Chungking in January 1942. Headed by Professor Jean Escarra with André Guibaut, the veteran Tibetan explorer, as his adjutant and Jacques Fischbacher as Press Attaché and Lieutenant Colonel Tutenges as Military Attaché [Mission Militaire française de Chine [MMF], it was soon joined in April by De Langlade and Boulle. Both using British passports, they set up their forward base at Mong Tzeu on the Thai-Yunnan border with the aim of running agents in and out French Indo-China, a parallel operation to what Tutenges was trying to do with the Service de Renseignement d'Extrême-Orient [SREO] out of Kunming. Little was achieved and when de Gaulle sent General Pechkoff[138] to China with responsibility for overall resistance to the Japanese, SOE took the opportunity to make de Langlade head of the Indo-China country section in July 1943. Boulle, who had crossed into Indo-China under the name Peter John Rule, was arrested by the Vichy French and court martialled for being a member of 'a foreign army'. A court in Hanoi sentenced him to hard labour for life in October 1942.

In October 1943 Commandant Jean Boucher de Crèvecoeur brought a small number of French officers[139] and Annamites from the Corps Leger d'Intervention [CLI] in Algiers to India for parachute and jungle warfare training and split them between the India Mission and the Pechkoff Mission in Chungking. The idea was to use them in small units all over Vietnam as the core of a larger resistance movement of around 15,000.

An overriding political problem was that President Roosevelt made it clear that he was determined that the French should never be allowed to regain power in South East Asia after the war on account of what the Americans considered was their poor colonial record. On return from the Teheran conference with Stalin and Churchill, on 16 December 1943 he summoned the Chinese and Turkish ambassadors, the Egyptian minister, and the Soviet and Persian first secretaries and informed them that he had been working hard to prevent Indo-China from being restored to France, suggesting that 'some UN trusteeship [would be needed] to govern these people'. The FO was stunned by this outburst and Sir Alexander Cadogan wryly noted that 'this is one of the President's most half-baked and most unfortunate *obiter dicta*'.

For SOE, the President's stance represented a serious setback, all the more so given the advanced state of FIC operational planning. It effectively prevented a Free French Military Mission being accredited to SEAC and hampered SOE's

---

138 Born Yeshua Zalman Sverdlov in Nizhny Novgorod, to evade Tsarist restrictions on Jews living in large cities, he was baptised into the Eastern Orthodox Church and officially changed his name to Pechkoff. On the outbreak of the First World War, he volunteered for the French Army. In May 1915, he was wounded and his right arm was amputated. After being decorated with the *Légion d'honneur* in 1917, Pechkoff worked with French diplomatic missions in Russia, Romania, China, Japan, and Georgia.
In the periods 1921-1926 and 1937-1940 he served in the French Foreign Legion; in between, he served in the Foreign Ministry in France and in the French Mandate of Lebanon. During the Second World War, Pechkoff fought in Morocco and Syria, then joined de Gaulle's Free French Forces in London, and was sent as the Free French ambassador to South Africa, where he organised arms shipments for the Allies. After his 1943 promotion to Brigadier General, he served as Free French ambassador to the Republic of China.
139 He was also accompanied by Professors Fabre and Mus who would later play a role in re-establishing French governance.

efforts in the field. Lord Selborne wrote to Churchill on 12 May 1944 pointing out that the absence of a French mission had 'serious repercussions on SOE work in the SEA theatre' and questioning why American permission needed to be obtained, given that the Dutch had a Mission attached to SEAC, 'the setting up of which was never referred to Washington'. After nine months of dithering, General Roger Blaizot was finally accredited to SEAC in October 1944 as head of *Free French Forces* in the Far East. Churchill did not inform Roosevelt, who was still pursuing his goal of keeping the French out of Indo-China.

Yet more time was wasted due to US reservations before the CLI, by now 1,200 specially recruited men, was ordered to the Far East[140]. Just as it was preparing to leave – it had renamed itself the 5th Colonial Infantry Regiment [5 RIC] – yet more political wrangling broke out, this time Sir Orme Sargent of the FO taking Major General Gubbins to task that SOE 'had not been frank' with him about the deployment of 5 RIC. Nearly a month after the Japanese coup of March 1945 had ended all hope of effective resistance in Indo-China, it was once again told to depart for the Far East. By the end of May, all of 5 RIC had arrived in India. It was eighteen months too late. As Mackenzie observed, 'they would have made all the difference in the world ... It would have made so much sense to deploy them, and it was ridiculous of the Americans to resist the idea. And once we had dealt with the Japanese they could have been used against the Viet Minh at a later date'.

Meanwhile the small number of French who had made it to SOE in India were aggregated into a separate unit, the Service d'Action [SA], which received official blessing from the Committee for National Defence on 5 August 1944[141], and, with the approval of Lord Mountbatten, were placed under the wing of SOE. Its establishment under Plan GUINNESS allowed for between 2,000 to 3,000 men. The RAF agreed to provide the SA air lift out of its Force 136 resources.

The first task in July 1944 was to send an exploratory Mission, Operation BELIEF 2 [conducting officer Captain R.A. Simpson] consisting of Commandant de Langlade, Major Milon and W/T operator Sergeant Chef Marong, aka Marmont[142]. Dropped by Liberator in the area of Lang-Son, they met up with General Eugène Mordant, the head of resistance in Hanoi, and handed over a letter from de Gaulle. This letter from an operational point of

---

140 The CLI was created on 4 November 1943 in Jijel, Kabylie [French Algeria] with 500 volunteer commandos under Lieutenant-Colonel Paul Huard. Its purpose was to reinforce the resistance in Japanese occupied French Indo-China.
141 On 15 March 1944 the French Indochina guerrillas numbered 1,349 [993 locals and 356 Europeans] including 242 in Laos [195 locals and 47 Europeans].
142 Originally planned for May, the first four attempts all failed due to bad weather or engine trouble.

view was considered invaluable as senior officers in the French army in FIC were unwillingly to be given orders or instructions by the comparatively junior Free French officers based in China and India. Mordant's reaction was initially lukewarm but on further meetings he promised full cooperation. After a complicated extraction, with de Langlade impersonating a downed British flier called 'Squadron Leader Barnes', the Mission crossed into China on 23 July and reached Kunming. Their W/T operator remained behind, thus establishing the first clandestine W/T link with French Indo-China since the Japanese invasion.

After returning to Meerut, de Langlade filed his report, which concluded that there was a definite resistance movement in French Indo-China with the potential to be on a much larger scale than mere guerrilla and sabotage activities. It would need nurturing with arms, food and personnel and, in his opinion, the deployment of the CLI would be essential. Subsequently further BELIEF/POLKA sorties were flown, dropping W/T stations and additional personnel and by the end of the year, of the twenty-three sets dropped, thirteen were on air.

A bad-tempered political row ensued after the US found out about de Gaulle's letter. Washington saw it as a deliberate attempt to undermine US policy. Both SOE and the FO were perplexed, for the letter had no political character at all and felt that the incident had been magnified out of all proportion. One senior SOE staff officer wrote 'I confess that I, myself, am becoming somewhat impatient of the pettiness of many senior officers and officials with whom we have to deal. I cannot conceive of anything more childish over which to make a fuss; it is almost as if someone has lost his nerve. It is beyond my comprehension that anyone should challenge De Gaulle's right to send a [handwritten] letter, more particularly a completely innocuous one of credentials, to French officers in French Indo-China.'

Nevertheless heads rolled. Brigadier Guinness, acting Head of the India Mission [Mackenzie had been in UK] was sacked on 14 November 1944 and replaced by Colonel John Anstey. At SEAC level, relations between Mountbatten and his US Deputy Chief of Staff General Wedermeyer deteriorated to the point where the Americans banned the RAF from using their airfield at Kunming to mount sorties to Indo-China. This prompted the British to launch supply drops from Burma without informing the Americans and the three RAF Liberators[143] of 358 Squadron, which went missing on the night of 22/23 January 1945, may

---

143 Two of the aircraft [KH-215 and KH-277] crashed ten miles apart in the Chin Hills in Burma. Only Flight KH-278 was never found. The source of speculation can be traced to remarks by Chennault to General Carton de Wiart, the British military representative in Chungking. Air Vice-Marshal Whitworth Jones conducted an inquiry but its results have never been published.

FRENCH INDO-CHINA

possibly have been shot down or damaged either by US Navy Wildcat fighters operating from a carrier in the South China Sea or by General Chennault's US 14th Air Force's P-41 night fighters based in China. However, on the night in question, the weather both to and over the target area was abominable and only two out of the eleven Liberator sorties [Operation BAZAAR] managed to drop their containers to the SOE reception parties.

Field Marshal Wilson met with Wedermeyer in Washington DC on 9 March 1945 to discuss special operations among other matters. Now Chief of Staff to the Generalissimo, Wedermeyer made it clear that his authority extended to full control of all clandestine organisations in China, British and American alike. When it came to Indo-China, he told Wilson that the French there were 'rotten to the core' and it was useless relying on them. There was no potential *Maquis* in the country and anything the British wanted done there, they would have to do themselves. That said, he insisted that Indo-China came within the China theatre and hence he had full control over all clandestine activities there, a claim that directly contradicted the verbal agreement between Mountbatten and the Generalissimo for SEAC to conduct pre-occupational activities in the country. To reinforce his argument, Wedermeyer used the story of the RAF Liberators to illustrate the 'fantastic' [unsatisfactory] state of affairs.

*****

Operation SATIRIST[144] was drawn up by Colonel Andre Dewavrin, aka 'Passy' [Head of the Bureau Central de Renseignements et d'Action [BCRA], the Gaullist equivalent to SOE]. Ten parties were to be infiltrated to work with Major General Sabattier[145], by now the leader of the resistance. After meeting de Gaulle in Paris, de Langlade flew to a clandestine airstrip near Dien Bien Phu [Operation RADICAL] and then went to Hanoi where he spent a month in discussions with Sabattier who had taken over from Mordant and the Governor General Admiral Decoux[146]. He returned to India on 13 December 1944,

---

144 Operations VOGUE, MEASURE, SATIRIST, DUSTY, CHALET, RADICAL 1-3, POLKA.
145 1940 Military Governor of Hanoi; 1942 General Officer Commanding Cochinchina Group; 1944 General Officer Commanding Tonkin Division.
146 Born in Bordeaux in 1884, in 1940 Decoux was named French governor of Indochina, succeeding General Georges Catroux. Like his predecessor, Decoux initially wanted to continue the fight against the Axis powers, but he swore allegiance to Pétain's regime after realizing that his armed forces were no match for the Japanese. Decoux worked to improve relations between French colonists and the Vietnamese, establishing a grand federal council containing twice as many Vietnamese as Frenchmen and installing Vietnamese in civil-service positions with equal pay to that of French civil servants. In 1945, the Japanese took direct control of the government and ousted Decoux.

satisfied that the revised plan for resistance was workable. In the intervening time, ten dropping zones were in use. On 1 January 1945, the following W/T stations were in regular contact with Calcutta: five in Tonkin, three in Laos, two in Annam, and one each in Saigon, Moi country [Ban-Me-Thuot] and Cambodia [Phnom-Penh]. By the end of February 1945 eighty-seven agents were in place. Large quantities of arms and explosives had been dropped to over fifty DZs and two Landing Grounds were in use.

Around this time, French members of the European 'Jedburghs' teams had begun to arrive in India to join the SA. Already with experience of operating behind enemy lines in France, they were given jungle warfare training and then the first two teams were dropped into Laos in January 1945, and Tonkin in February. By the end of 1946, forty-three had parachuted into Indo-China, fighting first against the Japanese, then against the Viet Minh and finally against the Chinese. Eight were killed.

FRENCH GUERRILLA ORGANISATIONS IN FRENCH INDO-CHINA AS AT 9 MARCH 1945

Organisation	Commander	Area
RIVIÈRE [Seven W/Ts]	Lt Col Vicarie, M. Isnardon	Tonkin
DONJON [Five W/Ts]	Comd Meyer, Comd Imfeld	Laos
MÉDÉRIC [One W/T]	Captain Peri, Comd Biseuil, M. Desprez	North Annam
PAVI	M. Giraud	Central Annam
SAVANNAKET [Four W/Ts]	Comd De Valathier	
LE GRAND [Three W/Ts]	Capt Pauwels, M. Nicoleau	Cochin-China
MANGIN [One W/T]	Col Bellin, M. Plasson	Cambodia

The advance of the Americans from their SWPA bases had focussed the minds of the Japanese High Command on the possibility of a US invasion of Indo-China. Consequently troop levels increased to around 60,000 and the coastal areas of Annam and Tonkin were reinforced. This forced the SA to change its supply strategy. Drops to coastal Missions were stopped and the emphasis switched to building up 'reserve' depots in the much safer hinterland dropping areas.

The question of whether the French army would remain loyal was resolved on 9 March 1945 when the Japanese Government seized key points all over the country and mercilessly dealt with all opposition, known and potential[147]. The French army was disarmed and interned. In some garrisons, the French were subjected to terrible atrocities: in Dong Dang and Lng Son eighty per cent of French military personnel were beheaded. Two French Jedburgh officers, Captain Maurice Stasse and Second Lieutenant Roger Villebois, were killed in action on 9 March; another, Lieutenant Pierre Roussett, was captured after dropping on 18 April and beheaded by the Japanese on 30 June. The timing could not have been worse for the French as the renewed offensive in Burma was using up all the resources of Force 136, especially aircraft and supplies.

It was as if the whole of Mackenzie's carefully nurtured FIC resistance movement had been wiped out overnight, especially in the south of the country. All twenty-one W/Ts temporarily went off the air. Decoux and Mordant were imprisoned.

Then, as news began to filter into Kandy, it was apparent that some 10,000 French troops were still fighting. SOE therefore decided to reinforce General Alessandri who was holding out with 4,000 men [including the formidable 5th Infantry Regiment of the French Foreign Legion] in the Black River sector of West Tonkin. They gave him thirteen W/T stations and dropped three actions groups – DAMPIERRE, GASSET and CORTADELLAS – together with arms and ammunition[148]. Fifty people including wounded men, women and children were evacuated from the airfields at Dien Bien Phu and Luang Namtha in northern Laos after F/O King parachuted in for a recce.

It was a race against time. Lord Selborne wrote to the Prime Minister on 15 March, advising him of the need to give 'our French Allies' the earliest possible support 'before it is too late'. To that end, he implored him to approach President Roosevelt as soon as possible to clarify the question of responsibility for operations in Indo-China as between SEAC and China Command.

After fifty-two days of bitter fighting and incessant marching, General Allesandri's 5,000 French troops reached China on 2 May where they received a cool welcome from both the Chinese and the Americans. The latter had initially refused to help, prompting Mackenzie to signal 'American name is mud, repeat mud, with French and British alike in this whole episode'. It had been, as he put it, 'a very poor show indeed'. Churchill had felt equally strongly, writing to Field Marshal Wilson that 'it will look very bad in history if we were to let the French force in Indo-China be cut to pieces by the Japanese through

---

147 Massacres of POWs and internees were reported at Long Son, Dinh Lap, Thakhek, Tan Qui, Dong Dang, Ha Giang and Tonkin.
148 The weather was appalling: between 9 March and 30 April, only twenty-seven out of seventy-two Liberator drops were successful.

shortage of ammunition[149], if there is anything we can do to save them'. It was only on 18 March that Roosevelt ordered US air forces in China to come to the aid of the French.

A number of guerrilla groups had survived the Japanese purge and were concentrated in the areas of Laos [Organisations FABRE and SERRES], Annam [Organisation PAVIE] and Cochin-China.

LOCATION AND NUMBERS OF FRENCH GUERRILLA FORCES ON 15 MARCH 1945

Group	Location	Personnel		
		European	Indo-Chinese	Total
Higher Laos				
TUAL	Vang Vieng/Muong Sing	10	40	50
SERRES	Xieng Khouang	18	20	38
FABRE MICHELIN	Paksane	19	135	154
Central Indo-China				
BILGER-DUMONET	Tchepone-Saravane	92	562	653
TEUNYNCK	West Hue	110	180	290
KERVAREC	West Vinh	11	-	11
Cochin-China				
GUILLAUME	Honquan	13	-	13
		273	937	1,210

Flight Lieutenant Kino dropped on 15 April 1945 at Nam Tha, 250 miles north of Hanoi, where he found the Vichy French army in retreat with poor morale. He recommended no further attempts to support them but to concentrate on SA operations.

The guerrilla groups of Higher Laos, by now consisting of about 200 Europeans and 1,100 local troops, reached the Chinese border on 19 May but their comrades in the BILGER and TEUNYNCK groups had been widely dispersed. Lieutenant Le Vallois's Jedburgh team was the only party still operating on the Annam coast. The monsoon made resupply to the surviving pockets of resistance even harder with only twenty out of forty-seven sorties succeeding between 15 April and 20 May. While some of the groups did manage to pull off individual acts of sabotage, this merely increased the urgency for the

---

149 Chennault's US 14th Air Force had accidentally bombed the French artillery depot. He later claimed that bad weather and lack of equipment prevented him from assisting the French.

Japanese to hunt them down and so they were ordered to restrict themselves to intelligence gathering.

The activities of the SA led by Lieutenant Colonel Cavalin had almost ground to a halt by the beginning of April. American opposition, shortage of transport aircraft, the priority accorded to Force 136 in Malaya and Thailand and the appalling weather all conspired to prevent the Free French from reforming and reinvigorating their clandestine forces in Indo-China. Sorties for the June/July moon period amounted to a paltry fourteen; in the meantime, incessant Japanese ambushes and attacks eroded the guerrilla groups, whose strength on 15 August was estimated at 319 Europeans and 200 natives.

Meanwhile, the American OSS was busy arming and training[150] Ho Chi Minh's Communist Viet Minh[151], in effect replicating what the British did with the MPLA in Malaya. Major Allison Thomas and the DEER Mission were parachuted in July 1945 into Tan Trao near Hanoi to train General Vo Nguyen Giap's 200 best Viet Minh guerrillas. Private Hoagland, an OSS medic, even cured Ho of a near fatal bout of malaria and dysentery. But there was a marked difference for the Asian lobby in the State Department saw the Viet Minh as Vietnam's post-war government. As Mackenzie later put it: 'We were in control of the Communists [the MPLA]. The OSS were not in control of the Viet Minh. I suspect they were taken in by Ho Chi Minh who was obviously a clever and able man.' There is a kernel of truth to this observation for Thomas later admitted that he had no idea that Ho Chi Minh – known to him as Mr C.M. Hoo – was a Soviet-trained Communist ideologue[152]. Some commentators hold that the hoodwinking of Thomas and Captain Archimedes Patti, head of the OSS base at Kunming, and later Hanoi, constituted an intelligence shortcoming that smoothed the way for Ho's emergence as a national leader and, in the end, an enemy of the United States.

Paradoxically, the rise of Ho Chi Minh was to some extent a by-product of a row between a British sponsored intelligence network and the OSS. Laurence Gordon, a Canadian with British citizenship, who had spent some of the interwar years in Indochina working for Texaco, had taken his family to California in 1940 after the arrival of the Japanese in Vietnam. Texaco were anxious for him to return to South East Asia to protect the company's interests, and after the attack on Pearl Harbour arrangements were made with Sir William Stephenson of the BSCO to infiltrate him back into Indo-China. Now

---

150 The OSS had already been funding the Viet Minh to the tune of $100,000 a month since October 1943. Most of these funds had been used to buy arms for the coming war of liberation against the French.
151 Viet Nam Doc Lap Dong Minh Hoi or the League for the Independence of Vietnam.
152 General Giap styled himself 'Mr Van'.

a Captain in the Intelligence Corps reporting to Brigadier Cawthorne, DMI India, who funded and equipped him with W/T sets, Gordon set up shop first in Chungking and then in Kwangsi Province. In effect, he created his own private intelligence organisation in Indo-China, while at the same time keeping an eye of Texaco assets and personnel. Acting as a freelance oil agent, he travelled freely through Tonkin, Annam and Cochin-China, purchasing oil and other commodities for the Chinese black market. Joined by two former colleagues, Harry Bernard and Frankie Tan, both US citizens, Gordon's network – GBT – provided first class intelligence to General Chennault's 14th Air Force and came to the attention of the OSS who attached a former Associated Press war correspondent, Major Charles Fenn[153], to it as LO.

When General Wedermeyer became the commander of the China Theatre in November 1944, he viewed Indo-China as his patch and put the GBT network under the control of Colonel Heppner, the OSS chief in Chungking. Gordon, thoroughly alarmed by what he viewed as American high-handedness, resisted. In February 1945, he went to Washington in an attempt to retain his independence and in the meantime a compromise was worked out whereby GBT reported to AGAS, the US Air Ground Aid Services responsible for recovering downed pilots, liaising with POWs and general intelligence collection.

Driven out of Indo-China in March 1945 by the Japanese, GBT regrouped in Kunming. They had lost all their French agents, so pragmatically decided to recruit indigenous Vietnamese nationalists, many of whom were well known to Gordon. For instance, together with Austin Glass of the Standard Oil Company, he had been in contact with the Viet Minh since 1941 and in January 1942 had overseen the shipment of 600 rifles to them for a 'war of liberation' against the Japanese. On the recommendation of the American Office of War Information, Fenn recruited Ho Chi Minh, code-name LUCIUS, for the OSS. Although warned by both KMT and French intelligence agencies that Ho was 'tricky' and a dyed-in-the-wool Communist, GHQ ordered Fenn to carry on regardless and he met him twice in March 1945, the second time fixing up a visit to General Chennault's HQ. The die was cast, and from relative obscurity Ho rapidly advanced to be the head of a revolutionary party that was to be America's nemesis twenty-five years later, a far cry from the 'awfully sweet guy ... sitting on his hill in the jungle ... with the quality ... [of] gentleness'.[154]

---

[153] Born in London in 1907, Fenn later became a US citizen and joined the OSS in 1942 as a propagandist. A self-professed leftist, Fenn was later investigated by the FBI during the McCarthy era.

[154] Lieutenant Phelan of AGAS who dropped to Ho's jungle base to supervise drops of W/T sets, medical supplies and weapons.

FRENCH INDO-CHINA

Throughout the war, SOE never read the French Country section radio traffic[155]. It sufficed that Mackenzie found them 'very cooperative', not forgetting de Gaulle's proviso that the British were not to share French-generated intelligence material with the Americans.

The official SOE historian Guy Cruikshank concluded that 'Force 136's efforts in Indo-China were totally wasted', a somewhat bleak assessment in the light of Esler Dening's observation to the FO's Far East mandarin, Sir John Sterndale-Bennett, that 'Force 136 have been the guiding light and but for them the French ... would have been unable to get going.'

For the French, their worst fears were confirmed when, on 25 August, the Viet Minh installed a government in Hanoi under Ho Chi Minh and widespread unrest broke out across the remainder of the country. On 9 September, Son Ngoc Thanh's Cambodian government established an independence committee, while at the same time Chinese and Viet Minh forces began to create disorder in Laos. All this disruption and political ferment made the transition from Japanese occupation to French civil administration both difficult and dangerous. Charged with establishing a normal working administration, the French sent in various SA missions from India, including some with E group, but it was only after the arrival in Saigon of the British 20th Division under General Gracey in September that the situation stabilised.

Relations with the OSS did not improve. In order to facilitate the release and repatriation of Allied POWs[156] in Vietnam, Lieutenant Peter Dewey of the OSS [Project EMBANKMENT] had made contact with the Viet Minh-established Committee of the South, who looked to America, China, and Russia to prevent a French colonial restoration. Simultaneously, Allied military decision-makers had ordered French General Jean Cedile to occupy all major buildings in Saigon, while arming previously interned French troops, and instructed General Gracey's division to disarm the Japanese in accordance with the Potsdam Agreement of July 1945. Sensing a pro-French agenda, Dewey lodged an official complaint with Gracey, who responded by declaring him *persona non grata* and ordered him out of the country. Returning from the airport in his jeep owing to a delay in the arrival of his aircraft, Dewey was shot dead in a Viet Minh ambush on the airport perimeter. He had been mistaken for a Frenchman.

---

155 Force 136 codes were used for all interior main line communications in India and Ceylon. It was only between Calcutta, SA's advanced base, and Kunming and clandestine field W/T stations that French codes were used. French diplomatic codes were used for internal communications within Force 136.
156 Dewey arranged the repatriation of 4,549 Allied POWs, including 240 Americans, from two Japanese camps near Saigon.

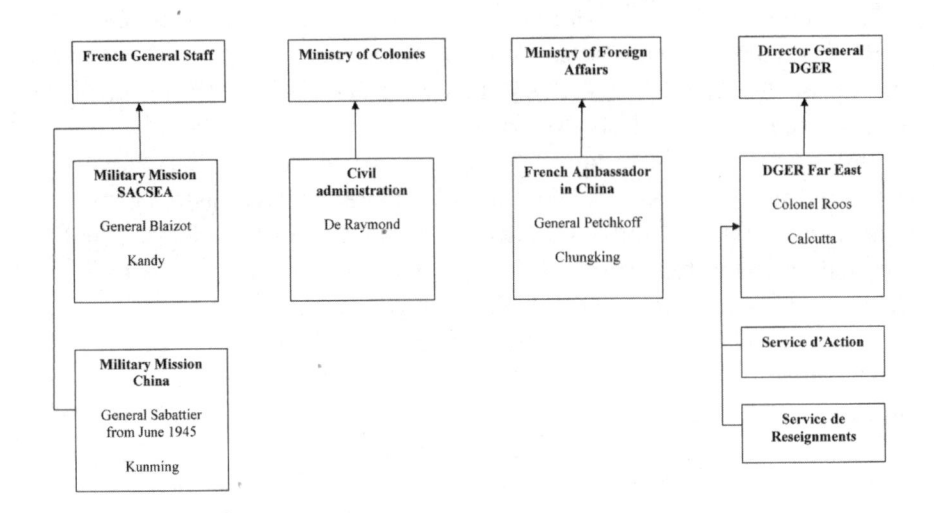

```
┌─────────────────┐   ┌─────────────────┐   ┌─────────────────┐   ┌─────────────────┐
│ French General  │   │ Ministry of     │   │ Ministry of     │   │ Director General│
│ Staff           │   │ Colonies        │   │ Foreign Affairs │   │ DGER            │
└────────┬────────┘   └────────┬────────┘   └────────┬────────┘   └────────┬────────┘
         ▲                     ▲                     ▲                     ▲
┌────────┴────────┐   ┌────────┴────────┐   ┌────────┴────────┐   ┌────────┴────────┐
│ Military Mission│   │ Civil           │   │ French Ambassador│  │ DGER Far East   │
│ SACSEA          │   │ administration  │   │ in China        │   │                 │
│ General Blaizot │   │ De Raymond      │   │ General Petchkoff│  │ Colonel Roos    │
│ Kandy           │   │                 │   │ Chungking       │   │ Calcutta        │
└────────┬────────┘   └─────────────────┘   └─────────────────┘   └────────┬────────┘
         │                                                                 │
         │                                                        ┌────────┴────────┐
         │                                                        │ Service d'Action│
         │                                                        └─────────────────┘
┌────────┴────────┐
│ Military Mission│                                               ┌─────────────────┐
│ China           │                                               │ Service de      │
│ General Sabattier│                                              │ Reseignments    │
│ from June 1945  │                                               └─────────────────┘
│ Kunming         │
└─────────────────┘
```

Structure of Free French Operations in Indo-China in August 1945

To the north in Laos, similar friction existed between the newly returned French and the OSS RAVEN Mission which had parachuted into the country on 16 September 1945. As far as the French were concerned, OSS officers were not only opposed to them but actually supported pro-independence groups including Prince Phetsarath, the Laotian nationalist leader. Events reached a climax on 27 September when Major Peter Kemp's ALFPMO party crossed the Mekong from its base at Nakhon Phanom in north east Thailand with medical supplies for Lieutenant Tavernier of the DGER who was based near Thakhet. Surrounded by an armed Viet Minh patrol, Kemp was forced to hand over his French colleague Lieutenant François Klotz who was summarily shot at close quarters. Dragging the Frenchman's body back to the river, Kemp could scarcely believe the conduct of his OSS team member who had lamely claimed neutrality[157] and had refused to intervene. When news reached them of this

---

[157] As commander of the OSS team at Thakhet, Major Aaron Blot in his 1986 autobiography *From OSS to Green Berets* has a different recollection of events. He states that it was a Laotian patrol which opened fire and that the OSS helped Kemp carry Klotz's body back to the launch. Blot was incensed that the French were conducting operations in territory north of the 16th Parallel which had been allocated to General Wedermeyer's China Command and the KMT and saw it as a blatant attempt to reassert colonialism by force of arms. A week before the incident, Blot had met Ho Chi Minh in Hanoi who told him: 'You are not colonisers like the Europeans. You have given Cuba its independence and you've pledged to do the same for the Philippines next year. Therefore I trust you and hope for your economic, financial, and military aid in establishing our independence. We have been milked and exploited by the French who have occupied our country as a colony for the past seventy-five years'. Blot was impressed.

cold-blooded execution, both Mountbatten and Mackenzie were outraged but not surprised, for it merely once again confirmed their suspicions of American intentions towards the French in Indo-China. Given that most of Laos including the capital at Vientiane lay to the north of the 16th parallel, the terms of the Potsdam Agreement clearly stated that it was China Command's patch and it was the task of the KMT to disarm the Japanese, not SEAC's. However, this ruling did not deter several SOE officers based in Thailand, including Rowland Winn and David Smiley, from rescuing a number of French civilians, including women and children, from the rapidly deteriorating security situation in Laos.

This was by no means an isolated incident. On 7 September 1945, Colonel Jean Sassi found his three Jedburgh teams attacked on the Laos-Annam border by 'a horde of Japanese and Annamites, assisted by two Americans clad in light coloured uniforms of paratroops'. After several assaults, the enemy withdrew but not before killing a French officer and six Laotians and wounding another nine including a Jedburgh team leader. The following day, a new attack was launched, again directed by the two Americans, conspicuous in their dress. Lieutenant Jean-Marie Herenguel was killed as he carried a wounded guerrilla to safety.

Events in Indo-China marked a sad ending to inter-Allied Special Forces co-operation which had proved so effective in Europe in the run up to D-Day and the advance to the Rhine. The war against Japan and Germany was over. The politics of opposing ideologies and divergent self-interests replaced the mutual advantages of close military collaboration in defeating a common enemy.

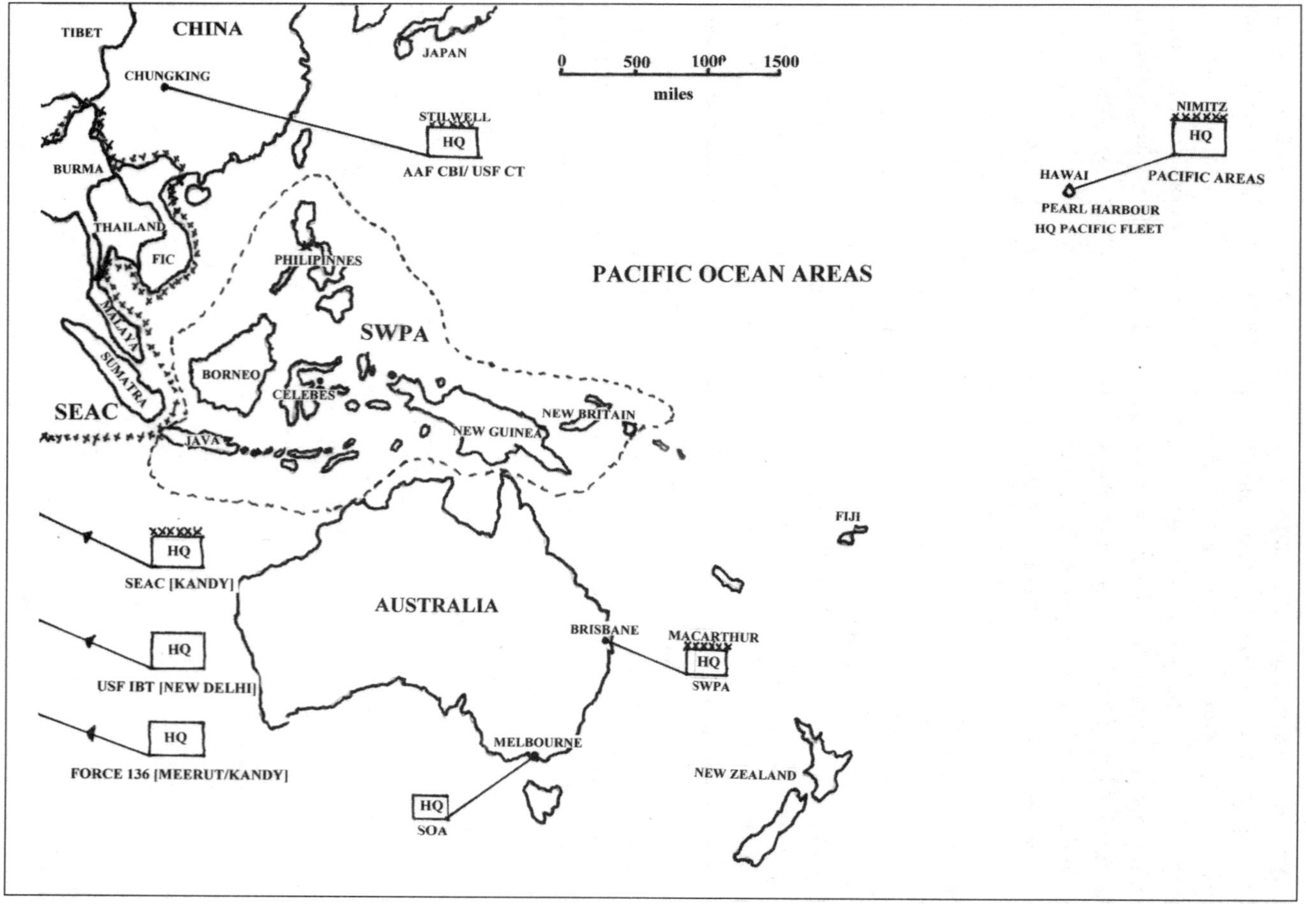
TIBET
CHINA
JAPAN
CHUNGKING
0 500 1000 1500
miles
STILWELL
HQ
AAF CBI/ USF CT
NIMITZ
HQ
HAWAI
PACIFIC AREAS
PEARL HARBOUR
HQ PACIFIC FLEET
BURMA
THAILAND
FIC
PHILIPINNES
PACIFIC OCEAN AREAS
MALAYA
SWPA
SUMATRA
BORNEO
CELEBES
SEAC
NEW BRITAIN
NEW GUINEA
JAVA
FIJI
HQ
SEAC [KANDY]
AUSTRALIA
BRISBANE
MACARTHUR
HQ
SWPA
HQ
USF IBT [NEW DELHI]
HQ
FORCE 136 [MEERUT/KANDY]
MELBOURNE
NEW ZEALAND
HQ
SOA

PART TWO

SOE IN SOUTH WEST PACIFIC AREA

CHAPTER ELEVEN

SOE in AUSTRALIA

SOE had arrived in Australia in the person of Colonel Egerton Mott, who had flown to Java with General Wavell from where he escaped in a fishing boat and headed towards Australia. Rescued by a Royal Australian Navy [RAN] corvette, he disembarked at Freemantle on 10 March 1942 and after informing London, proceeded to Melbourne where he opened SOE's first Australia office under the name of the Inter Allied Services Department [ISD], having first obtained permission from General Thomas Blamey, the Australian commander of Allied Land Forces South West Pacific Area [SWPA]. Its brief was to 'weaken the enemy by sabotage and destruction of morale and to lend aid and assistance to local effort to the same end in enemy-occupied territories'.

There, assisted by the Australian DNI Commander R.B.M. Long and Colonel A.G. Oldham of Royal Australian Army [RAA], he began to rebuild SOE's operational capability. In February 1941, No. 104 BMM[158] from Lochailort centre had arrived in Australia[159] and set up the Independent Companies Training Centre[160] at Foster on Wilson's Promontory, the extreme south point of Victoria. Mott and his colleagues soon realised that the climatic conditions on Wilson's Promontory, particularly the extended periods of cold wet weather, were unsuitable for men straight from the tropics, so a further Special Training School known as Z Experimental Station [ZES] was established at Cairns in northern Queensland in July 1942.

On 6 July 1942, ISD and all its outstations including Z Special Unit, the operational arm of the Anglo-Australian arrangement, came under the command of US General MacArthur, who had taken over SWPC in April. MacArthur and Admiral Nimitz, Commander of the Pacific Areas, had both shut the OSS out of the Philippines, the former furious about an OSS report[161] filed by Warren Clear which had referred to his 'incompetence'. MacArthur in

---

[158] CO – Lt Col J.C. Mawhood; demolitions – Capt Mike Calvert RE; fieldcraft – Capt Freddy Spencer Chapman; weapons training – WO2 Peter Stafford; signals – WO2 Frank Misselbrook.

[159] SOE's first cover name in Australia was the Inter-Allied Services Department [ISD] and although under Australian operational control it was allowed its own cipher communications to London where it was known as Force 137.

[160] Renamed the Guerrilla Warfare School in January 1942.

[161] The CLEAR Mission April 1942.

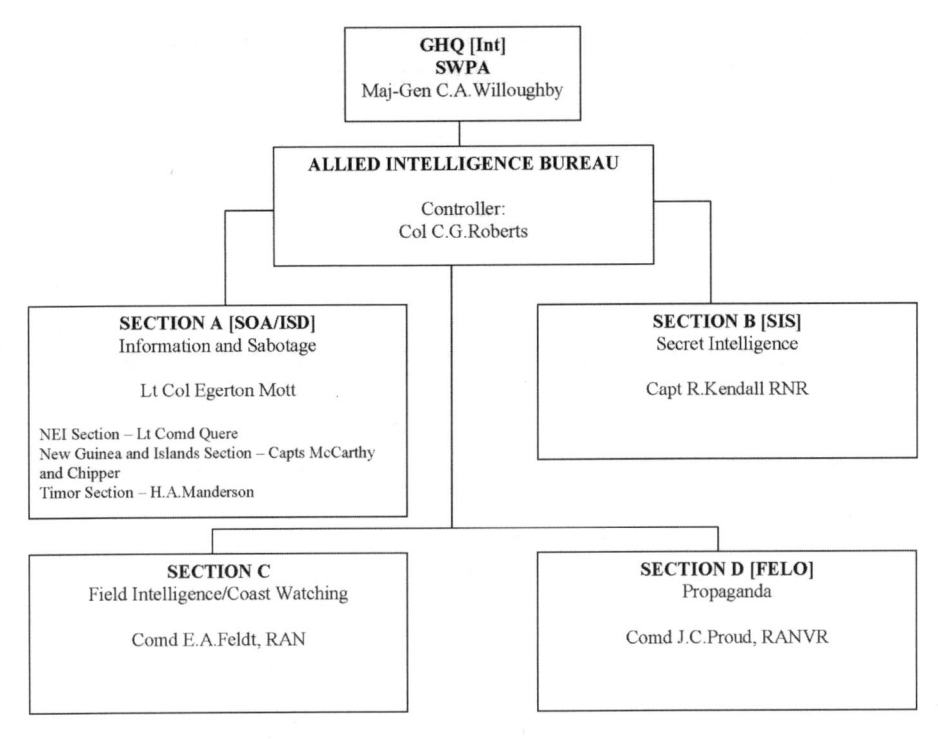

```
                    ┌─────────────────────────┐
                    │      GHQ [Int]          │
                    │        SWPA             │
                    │ Maj-Gen C.A. Willoughby │
                    └───────────┬─────────────┘
                                │
                    ┌───────────┴─────────────┐
                    │ ALLIED INTELLIGENCE BUREAU │
                    │      Controller:        │
                    │     Col C.G. Roberts    │
                    └─────────────────────────┘
```

SECTION A [SOA/ISD]	SECTION B [SIS]
Information and Sabotage	Secret Intelligence
Lt Col Egerton Mott	Capt R. Kendall RNR
NEI Section – Lt Comd Quere	
New Guinea and Islands Section – Capts McCarthy and Chipper	
Timor Section – H.A. Manderson	

SECTION C	SECTION D [FELO]
Field Intelligence/Coast Watching	Propaganda
Comd E.A. Feldt, RAN	Comd J.C. Proud, RANVR

ISD after its reorganisation under AIB in June 1942

particular was adamant that it was his headquarters which would determine which guerrilla groups would receive official sanction, including payment, supplies, and a place at the post-war political top table.

Almost immediately difficulties and disagreements arose. Mott was furious that he could not commission three ex-superintendents of the Malaya Police who were working for him behind enemy lines and almost apoplectic when one of them, Ian Wylie, was summoned to GHQ after returning from Timor for a dressing down, virtually accused of defeatism and intentionally misreading orders.

In December 1942, the principal ISD activities in the field were:

- Three parties had been introduced into New Guinea and two to Papua with the object of influencing native support and later operating against the enemy's coastal installations. Valuable information had been obtained to such a degree that the Allied Intelligence Bureau [AIB] had taken control of them.
- The ISD's party in Timor had collected useful intelligence and maintained communications in difficult conditions. It had met with unexpected success in arming and promoting resistance.

- The parties sent to Java and the Aru Islands had both been recovered and had been able to provide good intelligence. A further party had been inserted in the Aru Islands.

In April 1943, the ISD was reorganised and its name changed to Special Operations Australia [SOA] which in turn used the cover name of Services Reconnaissance Department [SRD]. In a letter to Major General Gubbins in London, Lieutenant General Smart of the AIF wrote:

'I have received a personal signal from General Sir Thomas Blamey, of which the following is a paraphrase:-

1. SOA has been set up by me as a joint British Australian organisation for two purposes:
    - ii. Advising and co-operating with GHQ in the conduct of special operations inside the SWPA.
    - iii. Conducting special operations outside SWPA but based in Australia.
2. The provision and cost of the following will be met by the Australian army:
    - i. All Australian personnel who may be required for service within SOA.
    - ii. All stores which can be provided from service sources in Australia.
    - iii. Accommodation, travelling and administrative services which can be provided by service sources in Australia.
3. The Director of SOA must be directly responsible to me but will have complete freedom to consult and co-operate with SOE as they or he may require and I propose that SOE should participate in the operation of SOA by providing:
    - i. An SOE officer as Director of SOA [Lieutenant Colonel Chapman-Walker has already been placed at my disposal].
    - ii. Such additional SOE officers as may from time to time be required by the Director with my approval.
    - iii. In this connection, I should like the following placed at my disposal for SOA: Major H.A. Campbell, Captains I. Tremlett, D.K. Broadhurst, I.S. Wylie, I. Lyon, F.G.L. Chester.
    - iv. Such special stores, advice and technical information as may be required by SOA and training facilities in England for any Australian officer of SOA who may be selected for that purpose.

v. Cash requirements of SOA for administrative purposes in Australia and operations outside SWPA will be borne by GHQ, SWPC.

vi. Salaries and allowances of British officers will be paid by SOE.

Replying on behalf of SOE in London, Tony Keswick, Director of Far East and Australia, wrote that he was 'very glad to say that we can comply with all the requests contained in General Blamey's signal' and that apart from a caveat in respect of the ready supply of British SOE officers at any one time, 'we look forward to fruitful co-operation with SOA and desire to express our appreciation of the part played by General Blamey in its establishment'.

Under these new arrangements, Mott returned to England in April 1943 and Lieutenant Colonel John Chapman-Walker[162], a Conservative politician and Bond Street solicitor in peacetime, took on the new role of Director SOA, dealing with a myriad of interests, British, American, Australian, Dutch, Portuguese and French. To conform to General Blamey's wishes, all British officers previously serving with ISD, while retaining their commissions in the British army, were formally assigned to the Australian army.

For SRD operations in the SWPA Chapman-Walker reported to General Blamey with the proviso that all operations had to be approved by MacArthur; within SEAC, he was responsible to Mountbatten, Supreme Allied Commander SEAC, yet he could not undertake any special operations without the approval of SOE London, who in turn had to consult on all military ones with the Chiefs of Staff. All this without a dedicated W/T link to SOE in London or New Delhi. He scarcely put a foot wrong and presided over a highly effective office that soothed ruffled feathers on countless occasions and delivered a number of remarkable successes in the field despite, on occasions, in the teeth of American opposition. He was awarded a well deserved OBE in 1946.

In an internal February 1944 memo, Colonel George Taylor summarised the position as this:

'SOA is not an SOE Group or Mission at all but is primarily an Australian organisation, to which certain British personnel are loaned, including the Commander, Colonel Chapman-Walker, and to which SOE gives direction, advice and financial and material assistance.

In practice, however, in view of the fact that the Commander is an SOE officer and that the Australian authorities are anxious to strengthen the connection with Great Britain and the British SOE, SOA can to a

---

162 Chapman-Walker had previously run SOE's USA and South American desks.

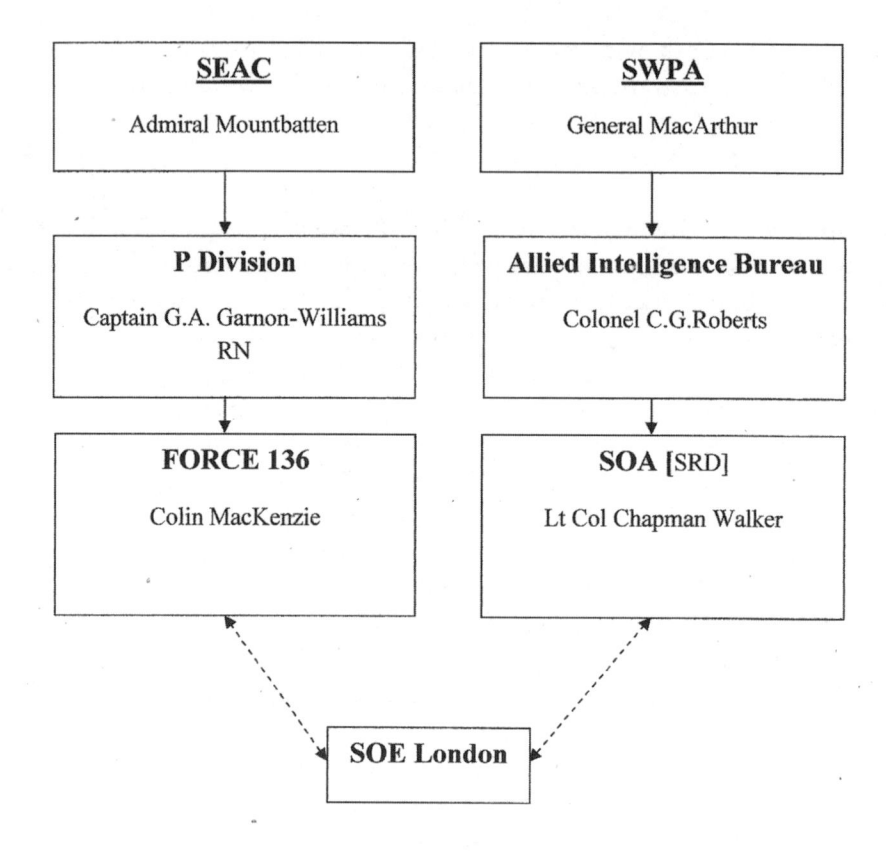

```
┌─────────────────────────┐      ┌─────────────────────────┐
│         SEAC            │      │         SWPA            │
│  Admiral Mountbatten    │      │   General MacArthur     │
└───────────┬─────────────┘      └───────────┬─────────────┘
            │                                 │
┌───────────▼─────────────┐      ┌───────────▼─────────────┐
│      P Division         │      │ Allied Intelligence Bureau │
│ Captain G.A. Garnon-    │      │   Colonel C.G. Roberts  │
│      Williams RN        │      │                         │
└───────────┬─────────────┘      └───────────┬─────────────┘
            │                                 │
┌───────────▼─────────────┐      ┌───────────▼─────────────┐
│       FORCE 136         │      │       SOA [SRD]         │
│    Colin MacKenzie      │      │  Lt Col Chapman Walker  │
└─────────────────────────┘      └─────────────────────────┘
             ▲                                 ▲
              ╲                               ╱
               ╲      ┌──────────────┐      ╱
                ◀─────│  SOE London  │─────▶
                      └──────────────┘
```

The relationship between SOA and Force 136

large extent be regarded as part of the SOE organisation.

As regards SOA's responsibility to local military authority, the position is that Colonel Chapman-Walker is responsible solely to General Blamey for the organisation and conduct of SOA within Australia and for its activities as a base.

In regard, however, to any operations which it undertakes in the SWP theatre it is entirely under the ultimate authority and control of SAC, SWPA, and his GHQ in Brisbane, although General Blamey continues to have some interest in its operations in his capacity as CinC Land Forces in SWPA.

In all operations to be carried out in the SWP theatre approval of GHQ must be obtained through AIB, a body set up to co-ordinate the activities of irregular organisations.

For operation outside SWPA no authority is required from GHQ, SWPA, but for operations to be carried out by SOA using Australia as a base, in the SEAC area, the necessary authority can be obtained from SACSEA [Supreme Allied Commander South East Asia]. In regard to operations in areas covered by neither the SWPA nor SEAC commands, the position regarding authorisation is obscure.'

By the end of the war, SRD [Z Special] had grown to a force of 1,500 officers and OR's [mainly Australian but including many British, New Zealand, Canadian and South African operatives]. Operating behind enemy lines in practically every area from New Guinea to Borneo and the Chinese and Malayan coasts, it raised and trained some 6,000 native guerrillas and inflicted some 1,700 casualties on the Japanese.

THE OFFICIAL HISTORY OF *AUSTRALIA IN THE WAR AGAINST JAPAN* RECORDS:

Organisation	Total operations	Party killed/captured	Unsuccessful
SRD	73	6	12
SIA	15	5	1
NEFIS	32	14	2
NEA	244	10	nil

*****

When an evaluation report on SOA was called for by SOE London after the war, it was fitting that the task fell to Lieutenant Colonel Ambrose Trappes-Lomax who had been one of the first to join it in March 1942. He had seen the organisation develop from 'a cumbersome system' bogged down in inflexible country sections whereby 'owing to the scarcity of SO officers and operations it was often only possible to build up in a selected area by contraction in other areas'. The situation improved when the four operational groups – New Guinea and the Islands, the Moluccas, Borneo and the China Seas, the South Nei [the Sundas] – were set up in 1944 for they related to the operational commitments. Even so, 'due regard was not paid to the resources available'.

Not afraid to mince his words, Trappes-Lomax was scathing about 'the ill will and incompetence' of GHQ SWPA, 'the only Allied Supreme HQ which was in no way allied. It was purely American. Such diplomatic qualities as a broadminded and urban outlook, tolerance and sense of compromise are rare outside a few carefully selected and highly trained public servants and statesmen. Military commanders and staff officers are in general somewhat nationalistic, narrow and bigoted ... the average American [officer] sees such qualities of tolerance and compromise only as forms of trickery and as such, signs of fundamental weakness.'

He identified the weak representation of the UK at SWPC as the biggest single factor mitigating against SOA, 'particularly among Americans', with their 'ignorance and mistrust of special operations'. The UK's good intentions [trade, self-determination of peoples, etc] were suspected, 'for the SWPA was a theatre of war in which politics played a more important part than strategy in setting priorities. The Americans sought not only victory but full credit for it. They also determined on a huge diversion to re-occupy the Philippines and on no other diversion. The average American staff officer was thoroughly suspicious of special operations and had grave suspicions of British "intrigue"[163].'

In hindsight, Trappes-Lomax advocated the need for two 'entirely different types of senior officers' to run effective special operations in the Far East. 'The Diplomat, shrewd, informed, intellectual, tactful and capable of compromise, and the Soldier, direct, methodical and ruthless ... control should alternate between the two men'. It was almost a perfect picture of a Colin Mackenzie and General Gubbins double act. He ended his report with a heartfelt plea: 'In future it is recommended that under NO circumstances should separate British Commonwealth organisations be controlled by any foreign or partly foreign co-ordinating authority.'

---

163 US Army Colonel Miers, deputy director of the AIB, was on record as saying that 'there can be no doubt that British [UK] organisations acted against GHQ policy on orders of 'London'. He further remarked 'we put the brake on things we don't understand'.

LIEUTENANT COLONEL EGERTON MOTT,
Officer of the Order of Orange-Nassau with swords

Egerton Mott

Grey Egerton Thornley Mott had started his career in 1914 as a regular soldier in the King's Dragoon Guards, serving in France, Palestine, India and Afghanistan. In 1922, he left and became a partner in Maclaine Watson & Co, a Far East trading house and shipping company established in the early nineteenth century, working in the DEI, Malaya and China with a six month stint in Japan. As an inveterate traveller, he also knew Korea, Manchuria and the Philippines well. He kept his hand in with the military by commanding The Shanghai Light Horse [Volunteers] from 1934 to 1937. Fluent in Dutch and Malay, he was an obvious candidate for Val Killery's ORIENTAL Mission, and he joined him in 1941.

His first brief was to plan and organise the SBPs in Malaya but as he later wrote 'owing to the stubborn refusal of the civil and military authorities to accept the scheme or to acknowledge the necessity for such work, nothing was done until it was too late. At the last moment, at the urgent request of the authorities, partially trained and poorly equipped parties were introduced, but they had little chance of success and resulted in the loss of valuable personnel and equipment.'

He then went up to Burma in December 1941 with Peter Lindsay to organise the SOE Mission there, with the dual task of establishing SOE in the country and to supervise stores for the China Mission. 'Fair progress was made but again we were far too late' and Mott was then sent to Java with General Wavell in February 1942. Here he desperately tried to arrange for the British to make an official approach to the Dutch to deploy SOE in the DEI but to no avail, although he finally succeeded in 'sowing some seeds' in the mind of Captain Lovink, the intelligence adviser to the Dutch Governor General. As a result, three British agents were selected as the nucleus of a skeleton organisation and sent to Singapore for training [Special Mission 43]. When Mott returned to Java in February 1942, it was too chaotic to achieve anything other than to arrange for a few secret W/T sets to be cached.

Mott managed to escape by boat to Australia where he arrived on 17 March 1942 and became the principal adviser to the Australian Director of Military Operations on Special Operations matters. In the next month, the Australians convened a number of meetings, which resulted in the establishment of Special Operations in Australia to be known as the Inter-Allied Services Department [ISD] with the blessing of General McArthur, Supreme Commander, South West Pacific Area [SWPA]. Mott was told to set it up from scratch. It was far from easy, Mott having to rely on funds he had brought with him from Java. Not being familiar with the Australian armed services was another handicap. Nevertheless, by 17 May, Mott had set up in South Yarra in Melbourne with Trappes-Lomax as his 2 i/c, Lieutenant J.J. Quéré as head of DEI section and four other staff officers together with three secretaries.

Rapid progress was made and soon ISD had its own training facility at Cairns in northern Queensland – Z Experimental Station – and a special top secret outfit, Z Special Unit, which belonged exclusively to ISD. Then, in June 1942, MacArthur's HQ took control of ISD by imposing on top of it the Allied Intelligence Bureau, an umbrella organisation encompassing the activities of ISD, SIS and other intelligence agencies. If the lines of demarcation were vague, at least its funding structure was clear, with the US, Australia and DEI as equal partners.

More difficulties then emerged, for GHQ saw ISD as an intelligence gathering tool rather than Special Operations, and transferred its New Guinea operations to Combined Field Intelligence. After serious allegations made against him by the NEFIS[164] – Naval Lieutenant Quéré[165] to be precise – that through bad security and lack of training, valuable Dutch personnel had been

---

[164] The Netherlands Forces Intelligence Service [NEFIS] was established in Melbourne under the commanded of Lieutenant Commander G.B. Salm. Its task was to collect intelligence about the occupied DEI and Japanese activities there. Naval Lieutenant J.J. Quéré and his Section III [Special Intelligence and Operations] trained and led intelligence parties deployed to the DEI. By war's end, NEFIS had deployed a total of thirty-seven such intelligence parties.

[165] An SOE file states that from October 1942 onwards Quéré got involved in very serious domestic complications which had a devastating effect on his work and the work of the section as a whole.

sacrificed and lost[166], Mott's position as Director of ISD and adviser to AIB on Special Operations became untenable, and he returned to London in May 1943. Before he sailed, he penned several robust letters in his own defence, including to Blamey, Willoughby and CD in London. There is also a suggestion that the mock attack on the harbour at Townsville by Captain Sam Carey, which Mott had sanctioned left him exposed to bitter in-fighting. There were certainly several red faces desperately trying to explain away how a party of canoeists had entered the harbour and stuck dummy limpet mines on two destroyers and seven cargo ships.

Arriving back in London, Mott found himself figuratively in the dock, having to defend himself against all sorts of allegations and ill-informed comment. As he wryly recorded in his SOE record of service, 'June 1943 to January 1944 "in the dog house"'. Fortunately, senior SOE officers had 'great confidence in him as an intelligent, capable and reliable officer' and from May 1944 to September 1945 he served as Far East branch Regional Head in London. The SOE War Diary also recognised that 'Mott had done excellently in establishing in only six months a most thorough organisation and in securing the respect and co-ordination of Australian HQ'.

Following a meeting between HRH Prince Bernhard of the Netherlands and Major General Gubbins about the future of SOE in the DEI, in September 1945 Mott was appointed Force 136 LO to the Java Task Force and returned to Batavia. Once again, he managed to become embroiled in another monster row with the Dutch and came in for severe criticisms as he followed orders from Kandy to wind down Force 136 operations. This involved withdrawing all Dutch personnel serving in the Anglo-Dutch Country Section and handing them over to NEFIS. Wires were crossed and Mott was worsted.

---

166 There was no substance to these allegations. The operations referred to in New Guinea, Ceram, Java, Celebes and Aroe Islands had little or no input by ISD.

MAJOR AMBROSE TRAPPES-LOMAX

Ambrose Trappes-Lomax

Born in London in 1910, Ambrose Trappes-Lomax was brought up after the death of his father by his uncles and aunt at Salesbury Hall, an Elizabethan house rear Ribchester in Lancashire, and educated at Stonyhurst College. Commissioned in the Border Regiment in 1932, Major General Theo Birkbeck, a contemporary, remembered: 'Second Lieutenants were rare birds in those days when in the 1st Battalion the CO 'Sandy' Sanderman was in his mid-fifties, there were only two Majors and the Senior Subaltern had nineteen years service!' After a year in England, he went to India with the 2nd Battalion, where he had a varied career as a young officer, including a stint as IO for 3 Jelum Infantry Brigade in Waziristan on the North West Frontier in 1938, and a month in Tibet where he travelled to Gyantse for the British Agency to deliver ciphers to the British embassy.

It was his first taste of the exotic world of intelligence and he wrote to his aunt [and godmother]: 'The Rim Pochi [the Regent] of Shigatse who I had lunch with at the Agency at Gyantse is at present the biggest man in Tibet as the Dalai Lama has not yet been found ... I met the Germans on the way through to Sikkim, the leader Dr Schafer was at Gangtok ... he appeared to me to be nearly a nervous wreck, they were all black guards, and they won't get into Tibet again for they were stoned by the monks for trying to stop a religious dance in order

Germans in Tibet: The Great Game, this time with the Third Reich

to take photographs[167] ... The Tibetan officials and noblemen are very pleasant and the women very pretty. They all wore their provincial headdresses'. Trappes-Lomax bought a Tibetan fox cub called Charlie which bit him three times when he picked him up but, after a week in a sack on his saddle bag, became 'quite tame'. He gave him to a Staff Officer in Jalapahore whose children at the time of writing 'had not been bitten yet'. Presciently, he finished his letter 'I must say it looks like war.'

In 1940, when serving as a Company Commander at an Infantry Training Centre, he volunteered for parachute training and was accepted for No. 10 Commando and attended the guerrilla warfare school at Lochailort, followed by a parachute course at Ringway.

He joined SOE in February 1941 as a W/T and tactics instructor at STS 101 in Singapore, where he went on to become Chief Instructor and briefly Commandant. In September and October 1941 he was sent to Burma to draw up a plan for Special Operations in conjunction with Philip Fogarty, the Commissioner of the Shan States, and the GOC, Major General Donald

---

[167] He is referring to the quasi-scientific/military intelligence German Expedition to Tibet 1938-39, sponsored by Himmler and the SS.

McLeod. When the Japanese invaded Malaya, Trappes-Lomax trained a number of Chinese and European SBPs, although he expressed severe doubts about sending them into the jungle without adequate W/T equipment. When Singapore was surrounded, he gathered up the remnants of the STS training team and sailed for Burma, only to be diverted to Batavia where he was relieved as Officer Commanding by Lieutenant Colonel Jim Gavin. He stayed on in Java to join the new HQ General Wavell was in the process of setting up. His task was to establish SBPs in the interior of Java. Once again the Japanese arrived before any of his plans could be put into practice and he managed to escape on the last refugee ship to Australia where he helped Lieutenant Colonel Egerton Mott raise the ISD. He then became Commandant of the ISD training school at Cairns in Northern Queensland, known as Z Experimental Station. It was here under his guidance that Major Ivan Lyon's Operation JAYWICK crews trained until they had perfected their folboat and limpet mine techniques.

Trappes-Lomax played a key role in the planning of MOSSTROOPS forces in the Sepik Valley of New Guinea. The requirement was to protect forward SRD observation parties from being bumped by Japanese patrols protecting the air bases on the north of the islands. Working with Major Townshend of FELO, a former District Officer of Sepik, and Major Farlow, AIF, Trappes-Lomax proposed using the martial natives of the middle Sepik tribes as a local guerrilla force under European officers and NCOs. From August through to November 1943, a number of patrols were inserted, but aggressive action by Japanese forces restricted their movement and the operation was wound up.

After becoming GSO2 SRD Melbourne for a year, and then LO with FELO, the Australian Political and Propaganda warfare organisation, in March 1945 Trappes-Lomax formed SRD B group in Morotai in the Halmahera Islands. At that time the Moluccas were still occupied by the Japanese with a division deployed across the many islands and the best part of a brigade still ensconced on Morotai. Under Trappes-Lomax's bold and imaginative leadership, Group B completed fourteen operations in which thirty-three enemy soldiers were killed, two POWs taken, two large *prahus* seized, 102 people rescued including the Sultan of Ternate [Operation OPOSSUM] and four European children. A Sangarese guerrilla force of 250 was fully trained.

Operation GIRAFFE, a nine man mission led by Trappes-Lomax, was inserted by Catalina flying boat on 17 March at Tagoelandang in the Sangihe group, some forty miles from the north east tip of the Celebes. One of their number was 65-year-old 'R.K.' Hardwick, an Englishman who had 'gone native' as a young man in Borneo and learnt to kill his own food using a *Dayak*

The irrepressible 'R.K.'

blowpipe[168]. His knowledge of native dialects across South East Asia was encyclopaedic, including Sangirese. Its mission was fourfold: to deny the enemy use of native boats by removing them to Morotai; to collect all available documents; to recover sensitive equipment from a downed US Ventura bomber and then to destroy what was left of it; and finally to search for the missing children[169] of Dr and Mrs Cseszko, two Hungarian missionaries who had lived in Tahoena in the North Celebes. The mission was recovered by two Catalinas twenty-four hours later after having successfully achieved all its objectives.

A week later, Trappes-Lomax led Operation GIRAFFE 2 to assist in extracting some native people from Majoe Island. Once more inserted by Catalina, the mission soon found the party of sixteen natives, including women and children, but the extraction went wrong when the Catalina sank trying to take off in a three-metre swell. All reached the shore safely and were taken off a day later by a US army Crash Boat.

---

168 Hardwick was Assistant District Officer of the Labuk and Sugut District in 1908 in British North Borneo. In the course of arresting a Moro murderer, the top of his head was sliced open like a boiled egg. He survived and in 1913 when he was the manager of the Membakut Rubber Estate [and associated crocodile farms], he accepted the post of Secretary of the Planters Association of the West Coast. In 1947, he was mentioned in despatches for his work with SRD.

169 Emma 13, Eva 10, Djoela 7 and Jozef 5. They were found by Major Hardwick but tragically their mother had been tortured and then beheaded by the Japanese and their father later killed in an Allied air raid.

In June, Trappes-Lomax escorted the eleven-strong Operation MAGPIE 3 on its mission to recce Siaoe, Tagoelandang and Biaro Islands and to gather as much intelligence as they could. The shore party was warned that the Japanese knew they were in the vicinity, and as they made their way back to Trappes-Lomax on the Command PT boat, they came under sustained enemy fire. As soon as they were on board, the PT boat, now joined by two others, attacked shore targets with all their weapons and after pummelling the flimsy shore defences, returned to Morotai.

Lieutenant Colonel Jock Finlay described Trappes as 'a memorable leader, ever ready for anything whatever the risk involved; he liked to think of himself as a Catholic gentleman, as indeed he was undoubtedly of ancient Lancastrian lineage. He was a man of principle attaching over-riding importance to the qualities of integrity and humility. As a Pom well of the norm he came to be both loved and trusted by the tough characters he gathered around him and asked to follow him on such dangerous missions'.

Trappes-Lomax did not receive any recommendation for an honour or award other than a Mention in Despatches. It is an inexplicable oversight for one of the original members of the ORIENTAL Mission and a founding father of SRD and Z Experimental force.

CHAPTER TWELVE

JAYWICK and RIMAU

'When the deed is so heroic, its sublime spirit must be respected, and its success or failure becomes a secondary matter.'
Proceedings of a Japanese Military Court 1944

Japanese troops celebrate their arrival in Singapore

LIEUTENANT COLONEL IVAN LYON, DSO, MBE

Ivan Lyon

Born on 17 August 1915, the son of Brigadier-General Francis Lyon, CB, CMG, CVO, DSO, Ivan Lyon was educated at Harrow and from there went to the RMAS and was commissioned into The Gordon Highlanders in 1935. After an uneventful year with the 1st Battalion in Redford Barracks in Edinburgh, he asked for a posting to the 2nd Battalion in Singapore and sailed east on TS *Dorchester* in the winter of 1936.

On arrival, Lyon was seconded to a counter-intelligence unit run by Lieutenant Colonel Francis Haley Bell who had been appointed Defence Security Officer by Major General Dobbie, the British commander in Malaya, with a brief to counter the rampant activities of the Japanese intelligence services. Hayley Bell's team soon penetrated the Japanese networks and established that, in the event of war, the Japanese army planned to invade Thailand and northern Malaya using Indo-China as a springboard. Far from galvanizing the British political and military establishment into making pre-emptive plans, this intelligence was dismissed as irrelevant as the combination of the monsoon and impenetrable jungle ruled out any such threat.

Determined to familiarise himself with the seas and straits around Singapore and further up the Malayan coast, Lyon spent much of his time cruising between the islands and coasts in the South China Sea in a three-ton ocean-going yacht, *Vinette*, he shared with Francis Moir-Byres, a fellow Gordon Highlander. Although these were more or less holiday cruises, he once returned to Singapore with a report which convinced his commanding officer that a lot more should be done for the defence of the North Malayan territory.

Like most young officers, Lyon was a regular 'customer' in all the well-known bars in Singapore. On one occasion, when he got terribly drunk on Tiger beer, he went into the nearest tattoo bar, and came out with a large red, blue and yellow tiger's head on his chest, which made him famous overnight among the European community. Tattooed officers were rare but not unknown in the Far East: Admiral Lord Charles Beresford had himself adorned in Japan with a full hunting scene on his back, with riders and hounds pursuing, in a north to south direction, the fox, which was going to earth.

During a cruise on *Vinette* in August 1938, Lyon met and fell in love with Gabrielle Bouvier, the beautiful daughter of Commandant Bouvier, the French governor of Poulo Condore prison island off the south coast of French Indo-China. It was no accidental meeting for fame of Gabrielle's chestnut hair and blue eyes had travelled far and wide. They married on 27 July 1939 in Saigon and then set up home in a married quarter in Singapore, where Gabrielle found a job as secretary to the head of the Free French organisation.

Over time, Hayley Bell's robust and unorthodox methods, which included the targeted assassination of Japanese agents, had upset both the Governor of Singapore, Sir Shenton Thomas, and the new commander of Malaya, Major General Lionel Bond, possibly egged on by Major Kenneth Morgan, the head of Special Branch, who held a longstanding grudge against Bell. The outcome was his recall to London in May 1939 and the unit was disbanded.

The Hin Lee heads for Ceylon

In May 1941, Major Alan Warren RM of MI[R] opened the office of SOE's ORIENTAL Mission in Singapore and he promptly recruited Lyon to assist him. The brief was extensive, covering sabotage, stay behind parties, intelligence gathering, and propaganda in all enemy-occupied territories. Lyon threw himself into his new role with his customary energy and infectious sense of humour. No avenue was left unexplored, including the provision of intelligence by his father-in-law whose prison island now lay well behind enemy lines[170].

When the Japanese attacked Malaya in December 1941, Warren ordered Lyon to establish a series of supply bases along an escape route from Singapore to Dutch-held Sumatra and report to Major H.A. 'Jock' Campbell of the KOSB. The two officers cruised the Riau Archipelago in a small coastal trader, the *Hong Chuan*, cajoling and bribing village headmen into helping refugees. It was on one such trip, after several near 'meetings' with Japanese destroyers, that he met a tall Australian, Bill Reynolds, on his ship, the *Kofuku Maru*, a motorised Japanese fishing boat. They immediately became friends[171].

The route set up by Warren and Lyon proved to be a lifeline for hundreds of refugees as they made their way by sea to the east coast of Sumatra, then up the Indragiri River to Rengat and across the mountains to Padang, where there was a chance of finding a ship for India or Ceylon. Lyon was ordered by Warren to sail with other key SOE personnel[172] to India in a native *prahu*, a coastal junk called the *Hin Lee*[173], and, after an epic voyage during which Lyon directed the navigation, they reached landfall after thirty days. As a former member of the ORIENTAL Mission, Lyon was quickly absorbed into the INDIA Mission.

OPERATION JAYWICK

The irrepressible young Gordon Highlander met up with Bill Reynolds who had also made it safely across the Bay of Bengal, and the two of them hatched a daring plan, Operation JAYWICK, derived from the deodoriser that removed unpleasant smells from Singapore colonial homes. Conceived by

---

170 Commandant Bouvier was arrested by the Vichy French and died of ill-treatment received at their hands. His wife was beaten up and died of her injuries in hospital. Both were posthumously awarded La Croix de la Libération by General de Gaulle.

171 Bill Reynolds didn't survive the war. He started to work for the US Intelligence Service in Australia and was dropped by US submarine *Tuna* on Lacet Island to collect intelligence information. Three days later he was betrayed by natives and captured by Japanese soldiers. He was sent first to Balikpapan Gaol and later transferred to the notorious Soerabaja Gaol, where he was, several months later, beheaded together with several other Indonesians and US airmen.

172 Lieutenant Brian Passmore RNVR, Major Campbell, Dick Broome and John Davis. Total crew and passengers came to eighteen.

173 Renamed *Siderhana Johannis*.

Lyon, who intimately knew the waters of the Rhio and Lingga Archipelagos near Singapore, the idea was to infiltrate a party of canoeists into Singapore by transporting them into the area on a local fishing boat from which they would paddle into the harbour and blow up shipping by attaching limpet mines. Madcap or not, SOE chief in India Colin Mackenzie approved it on the proviso it was launched from Australia where a new SOE capability was being set up alongside the Australian armed forces. The operation was based in Australia for additional security. Through an old sailing friend, Lyon managed to arrange a meeting with General Wavell, now CinC India, who, after hearing him out, gave him a glowing letter of introduction and sent him on his way to Australia.

His French wife, Gabrielle, and small son had managed to get away from Singapore to Perth before the surrender. When he reached India, Lyon cabled her to join him but as fate would have it, he found himself en route to Australia after she had sailed on the SS *Nankin* in May. Her ship was attacked by the German raider *Thor* and its passengers sent to Japan, where she spent the war with her son, Clive, in Fukushima internment camp, 200 miles north of Tokyo. Lyon arrived in Perth on 6 July 1942; he would never see his family again.

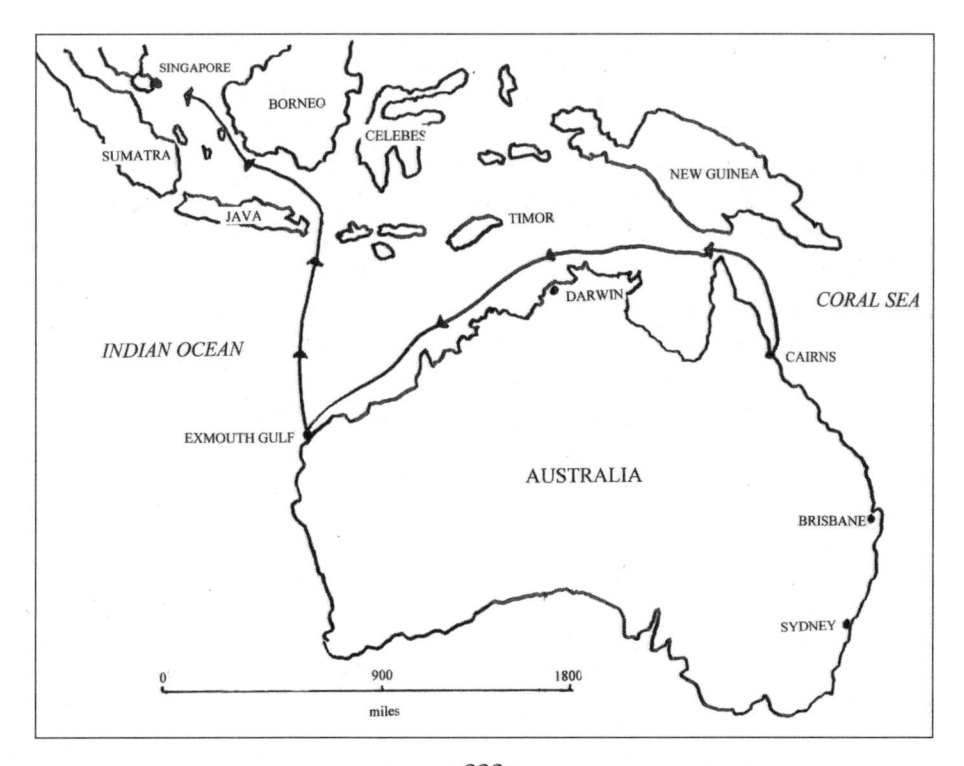

The JAYWICK Team
- Major Ivan Lyon, DSO, MBE
- Lieutenant Duncan Davidson, RNVR, DSO
- Lieutenant R.C. Page, AIF, DSO
- Lieutenant H.E. Carse, RANVR, MID
- Leading Stoker J.P. McDowell, RN, DSM
- Leading Telegraphist H.S. Young, RANR, MID
- Acting Leading Seaman K.P. Cain, RANR, MID
- Acting Able Seaman W.G. Falls, RANR, DSM
- Acting Able Seaman A.M.W. Jones, RANR, DSM
- Acting Able Seaman A.W. Huston, RANR, DSM
- Acting Able Seaman F.W. Marsh, RANR, MID
- Acting Able Seaman M.M. Berryman, RANR, MID
- Corporal R.G. Morris, RAMC, BEM, MM
- Corporal A. Crilley, AIF, MM

The local fishing boat that Lyon had selected was the MV *Krait*, originally called the *Kofuku Maru*, once operated by a Japanese firm in Singapore. The *Krait* which was tied up in Bombay where Bill Reynolds[174] had sailed her after the fall of Singapore, was shipped[175] as deck cargo to Darwin to be fitted out for the operation. She arrived in November 1942.

After a period of intensive training in Refuge Bay, Australia, in July 1943 SOE London gave its approval for Operation JAYWICK to go ahead, and on 2 September MV *Krait* sailed from Exmouth Gulf on the north west corner of Australia[176] with Lyon as commander and Lieutenant H.E. Carse RANVR as navigator, for Bill Reynolds had been posted elsewhere. The few vessels they encountered took the *Krait* for the fishing vessel she used to be.

On 17 September, having decided that Durian Island the original dropping-point was too dangerous to use as a raiding base, Lyon opted for Pandjang Island in the Rhio archipelago and by 04.00 hrs the next day the shore party of six landed at Otter Bay with their three folboats and all their gear including nine limpet mines per folboat[177]. Lyon made another change to the plan and told the *Krait* to RV with them further south at the heavily wooded Pompong

---

174 Reynolds had reached Ceylon under his own steam from Padang with a Chinese crew.
175 She had made two attempts to sail to Australia but engine breakdown forced her to return to India both times.
176 Krait had sailed from Refuge Bay in January but her engine had again broken down and had to be replaced with a new Gardiner Diesel 6 cylinder engine, a process which took nearly six months.
177 The nine mines weighed 100 lbs.

MV Krait

Island in Lingga archipelago. Pandjang, he concluded, was too close to Singapore.

The three heavily laden folboats now set off on their first leg which took them to the uninhabited island of Bulan. Here they were nearly spotted by a patrolling Japanese *sampan* but luck was on their side and after a night paddle

A life on the ocean waves [Lyon in foreground]

to the mangrove swamps of Bulan Island, they harboured up until setting off to complete their crossing of the Bulan Strait and reached Dongas Island, just eight miles from Singapore.

Lyon, who with Huston had been on watch, returned to the lying up point [LUP] with news of a sighting of thirteen ships – three were oil tankers – anchored in The Roads. At 20.00 hrs on 25 September, the raiders headed off in their folboats for Singapore. Defeated by the strong current, Lyon signalled the team to abort the mission and return to Dongas. All made it back, although Lyon and his No. 2 made a different landfall and only found the others the following morning.

It was clear that Dongas was too far away and that any passage from it was at the mercy of the strong tides and currents, so the raiders paddled off to Subar Island, seven miles to the West of Dongas, and as first light broke on the morning of 26 September, the exhausted raiding party fell asleep after crudely camouflaging their folboats.

Davidson climbed to the top of the island to spy the ground and on return to the makeshift camp allocated the tasks:

- He and Falls would make for Keppel Harbour protected by a boom. If it proved impossible to get inside it or if there were no suitable ships to target, they would head for The Roads to find opportunity targets there.
- Lyon and Houston would attack targets in The Examination Anchorage.
- Page and Jones would attack shipping in Pulau Bukum.

By 02.00 hrs on 27 September, Page and Jones had placed limpets on three ships, timed to go off at 05.00 hrs, and were on their way back to Dongas. Lyon and Houston had no luck after two hours in the dark reaches of the Examination Anchorage, but fortuitously located a tanker in the vicinity of Blakang Mati Island and attached all three chains of nine limpets on it. Meanwhile Davidson and Falls, although successfully circumventing the Keppel Harbour boom, had not found any suitable targets and had therefore headed for the Roads where they found rich pickings.

For once all went according to plan. Page and Jones and Lyon and Houston all made it back to Dongas in time to hear a series of explosions as the limpets detonated. Later reports confirmed seven ships sunk or damaged, a total of 46,000 tons of shipping. Soon there was evidence of a major search operation by the Japanese; over twelve planes had been scrambled by 06.30 hrs and were in the air almost all day; naval patrol vessels and fast *sampans* scurried between the islands.

Davidson and Falls, as the fastest and most experienced canoeists, had gone ahead and reached Pompong Island at 01.00 hrs on 1 October after a couple of overnight stops. Their task was to RV with the *Krait* and hold it until the other two groups of canoeists arrived. Conscious that the longer the *Krait* waited at the RV, the greater the chance of discovery, Lyon made another tactical change to the plan – the two folboats would make a daylight crossing from Pandjang to Pompong. After eighteen hours of paddling, at around 03.00 hrs on 2 October, they reached what they thought was the pick-up point.

The *Krait* had made the first RV well in time and collected Davidson and Falls who estimated that the others were about a day behind them. On 3 October they found them, and by 19 October the *Krait* was safely back in Exmouth Gulf, after a narrow escape when a Japanese destroyer had taken what threatened to be more than a passing interest in her.

Operation JAYWICK remains unique in the annals of British military history. The sheer bravado to carry off the raid, the distances covered – over 5,000 miles – and the thirty-three days spent in enemy controlled waters, the relentless physical and mental stress experienced by the raiding party – burst boils, blisters, fatigue, adverse weather conditions of torrential rain and high seas, all combined to make JAYWICK the very stuff of legends. Above all, the three Sisters of Fate were benign. Call it good luck or absence of bad luck, JAYWICK led a charmed life.

JAYWICK, like many SOE and commando operations, triggered a violent reaction and many innocent people found themselves hapless victims of the

The heroes of Jaywick

frenzied Japanese hunt for culprits. The Kempeitai, unable to find any traces of an Allied raiding party, assumed it was the work of fifth columnists and rounded up scores of suspects, including internees in Changi Jail. Hundreds of Malays and Chinese and more than twenty Europeans died or were executed after signing nonsensical confessions wrung out of them under torture.

Major Ivan Lyon, MBE: Citation for DSO

Major Lyon was in command of a party of fourteen naval military officers and other ranks who sailed from Australia in MV *Krait* on 2 September 1943, on a hazardous expedition to destroy enemy shipping at Singapore.

Passing between Bali and Lombok and steering along the south west coast of Borneo the vessel arrived off the Bulan Strait some twenty-one miles south of Singapore at nightfall on 16 September. After six members of the expedition, who were to take part in the actual operations, had been landed on the island of Panjang with their canoes and stores, the MV *Krait* sailed for Borneo.

A week later the operational party had concealed themselves on a small uninhabited island, only eight miles south of Singapore roads, from which observation was kept on Japanese shipping for five days.

Major Lyon and one naval rating set out in their canoe on the night of 26/27 September, and entering the anchorage and paddling alongside the stern of an oil tanker, they fixed two limpets on the engine room and one on a propeller shaft.

Another canoe after penetrating the boom and entering Keppel harbour attacked three large cargo vessels lying in Singapore roads while the third canoe also damaged three freighters.

As a result of this daring night attack on the great port of Singapore, serious damage was inflicted on nearly 40,000 tons of Japanese shipping. Seven separate explosions were heard in the early hours of the morning of 27 September and several ships are believed to have been sunk. Within a quarter of an hour of the first explosion the whole of Singapore was blacked out and subsequent enemy air activity made accurate observation of the results difficult.

The three canoe parties were picked early in October at an agreed rendezvous by MV *Krait*, which after a close scrutiny by a Japanese patrol vessel managed to pass through the Lombok Strait on the return journey and arrived back in Australia on 19 October 1943, after a cruise of 4,000 miles in enemy waters lasting forty-eight days.

The remarkable bravery and outstanding leadership shown by Major Lyon, throughout what can only be described as one of the most hazardous undertakings of the war, contributed more than any other factors to the success of the expedition, which returned to its base without suffering any casualties and which apart to the damage done to Japanese shipping brought back most valuable information regarding enemy dispositions.

Awarded

OPERATION HORNBILL/RIMAU

Flush with success and recommended for a VC by the Australian Prime Minister[178], Lyon travelled to London to sell Baker Street Operation HORNBILL, an ambitious plan devised by him in conjunction with the INDIA Mission to set up a major base on Natuna Island 300 miles north east of Singapore from which to launch commando-style operations into Malaya, Thailand [Bangkok] and Indo-China [Saigon]. Six replicas of Japanese motorised *sampans* ['Country Craft'] would be built to carry stores and then serve as raiding vessels, with a final projection of sixty such vessels. Both Selborne and Gubbins agreed to HORNBILL in principle but realised that they would have to sell it on to the Americans. Meanwhile, Lyon set to work with Major Walter Chapman RE to evaluate the new one-man submersible canoes [Sleeping Beauties or SBs] pioneered by Major Blondie Hasler of the Royal Marines.

The American sale proved far from easy. After Lyon had passed through Delhi en route to London, P Division had put through a routine request to the Americans for a submarine to be released from patrol duties to take a recce party to Natuna Island. Colonel Chapman-Walker of SOA suddenly found himself embroiled in the sharp end of Allied politicking. McCollom, the chief of the American Naval Intelligence Staff, told him: 'The strategy in the Japanese war has been clearly laid down and provides for no action by SEAC other than promotion of supplies to China. SEAC has no business to undertake operations of any kind in the South China Sea and GHQ is [consequently] unwilling to provide transport for anything which does not contribute directly to general strategy'. The dispute never reached MacArthur but is revealing of not just the

---

178 The British ruled that 'his action although an extremely gallant one did not quite reach the very high standard of outstanding gallantry required for the award of a VC'. [*Telegram from Secretary of State for Dominion Affairs to Governor General Australia, 28 October 1944*]. Lord Selborne as Head of MEW wrote to Lyon's parents stating he had done everything he could to get Lyon a VC and that he was 'absolutely fearless'. Both Gubbins and Admiral Miles of the RAN supported the award of a VC as well.

inherent sensitivity between the Allies but also of the inter-service rivalries that lurked constantly under the surface of harmony.

At the beginning of April 1943, Lyon was invited to meet the CIGS, Field Marshal Sir Alan Brooke, in London, a most unusual accolade for a young officer. By the middle of the month, SOE and Combined Operations had given their blessing to HORNBILL and approved the allocation of fifteen SBs and the Navy's largest submarine, the minelayer HMS *Porpoise*, which sailed from the Clyde almost immediately. The SBs were ferried to Australia as deck cargo.

However, HORNBILL was destined not to be, for the Americans failed to produce a submarine for the KOOKABURRA Mission and its crucial recce of the Natuna Islands. Furthermore technical problems had arisen at the production line of the Country Craft. On 17 July, Lyon circulated a modified plan, essentially reducing HORNBILL down to RIMAU, a second attack on Singapore shipping.

THE RIMAU TEAM	
Lt Col Ivan Lyon, DSO, MBE*	Killed in action
Lt Comdr Donald Davidson, DSO, RNVR*	Died of wounds
Capt Bob Page, DSO*	Captured and executed
Lt Robert Ross	Killed in action
Lt Bruno Reymond	Drowned at sea after being assaulted
Lt Blondie Sargent	Captured and executed
Sub Lt Gregor Riggs, RNVR	Killed in action
Maj Reginald Ingleton, RM	Captured and executed
WO Jeff Willersdorf	Died from ill treatment in prison
WO Alfred Warren	Captured and executed
Sgt David Gooley	Captured and executed
Sgt Colin Cameron	Killed in action
Able Seaman 'Poppa' Falls, DSM*	Captured and executed
Able Seaman 'Boofhead' Marsh, MID*	Died from ill treatment in prison
Able Seaman 'Happy' Huston, DSM*	Drowned at sea
Cpl Pat Campbell	Died of wounds
Cpl Clair Mack Stewart	Captured and executed
Cpl Colin Craft	Drowned at sea after being assaulted
Cpl Roland Fletcher	Captured and executed
L/Cpl John Hardy	Captured and executed
L/Cpl Hugo Pace	Died from ill treatment in prison
Pte Doug Warne	Died from ill treatment in prison

Conducting officer: Maj Walter Chapman	Returned to Freemantle. Committed suicide 1964
Officer i/c Base Party: Lt Sam Carey	Captured and executed
Conducting NCO: Cpl Croton	Returned to Freemantle
HMS *Porpoise*: Lt Comdr HAL Marsham, OBE, RN	Retired
HMS *Tantalus*: Lt Comdr 'Rufus' MacKenzie, DSO, DSC, RN	Retired in 1969 as Vice-Admiral Sir Hugh Mackenzie, KCB, DSO and bar, DSC

*JAYWICK Mission veterans

It was a highly complex plan involving the new SB technology as opposed to the tried and trusted though cumbersome folboats used in JAYWICK, and an intricate transportation formula into the target area. The whole plan revolved on the capture of a passing junk on the high seas as the SBs had a limited range of fifty kilometres which ruled out direct insertion by submarine.

On 30 August, the containers with the fifteen SBs arrived at Freemantle and after a lot of unnecessary aggravation between Commander Branson, head of the SRD Naval department, and Major Chapman about last minute modifications to the stowage of the SBs, Operation RIMAU departed on HMS *Porpoise* on 11 September 1944 with twenty-two members of the operation and two conducting officers on board, together with fourteen and a half tons of stores. Whether Lyon had with him the list of the forty-two Catalina pick-up points in the DEI established by the Allies to rescue downed fliers remains an unknown, as does the fact that the Mission's signals codebook was found on the bed in Lyon's Melbourne quarters after the submarine had sailed. Without it, RIMAU's call sign, Alfa Charlie Foxtrot, could not talk to Darwin on a secure net.

HMS *Porpoise* reached Merapas Island at the eastern extremity of the Riau Archipelago on 23 September and enough stores were taken ashore on folboats to establish a rear base. Lieutenant Carey was left to guard them. Now to find a junk, and on 28 September *Porpoise* spotted the *Mustika*, a forty-ton Indonesian *tonkan* about thirty miles off Pontianak, Borneo. The nine-strong Malay crew offered no resistance to the boarding party and both vessels then made for Pedjantan Island where over the next two days the SBs and other equipment were transferred to the junk. *Porpoise* then headed for Freemantle which she reached on 11 October, intending to return to Merapas to pick-up the party on 8 November or at any time during the following four weeks.

It later transpired that *Mustika* had returned to Merapas Island and dropped off three men – WO Warren, Sergeant Cameron and signaller Corporal Craft – to support Carey. The pick-up plan was simple. The raiders would return to

MALAYA
SINGAPORE ISLAND
SINGAPORE
SOUTH CHINA SEA
SINGAPORE STRAITS
PHILLIP CHANNEL
MAIN STRAIT
DONGAS IS.
SUBAR IS.
LABAN IS.
BATAM IS.
BINTAN IS.
KEPALA JERNITH
BULAN IS.
MAPOR IS.
MERAPAS IS.
CHAMBOL STRAIT
REMPANG IS.
SOREH IS.
SOLE IS.
LINA IS.
SUJI IS.
SUJI STRAIT
KUNDUR IS.
PANGKIL IS.
GALANG IS.
TAPAI IS.
KURUS IS.
MANTANG IS.
NUMBING IS.
DEMPU STRAIT
POMPONG IS.
TEMIANG IS.
BOEAJA IS.
TJEMPA IS.
SEBANKA IS.
BAKUNG IS.
SUMATRA
LINGGA IS.
SELAJAR IS.
SINGKEP IS.
0
35
70
miles

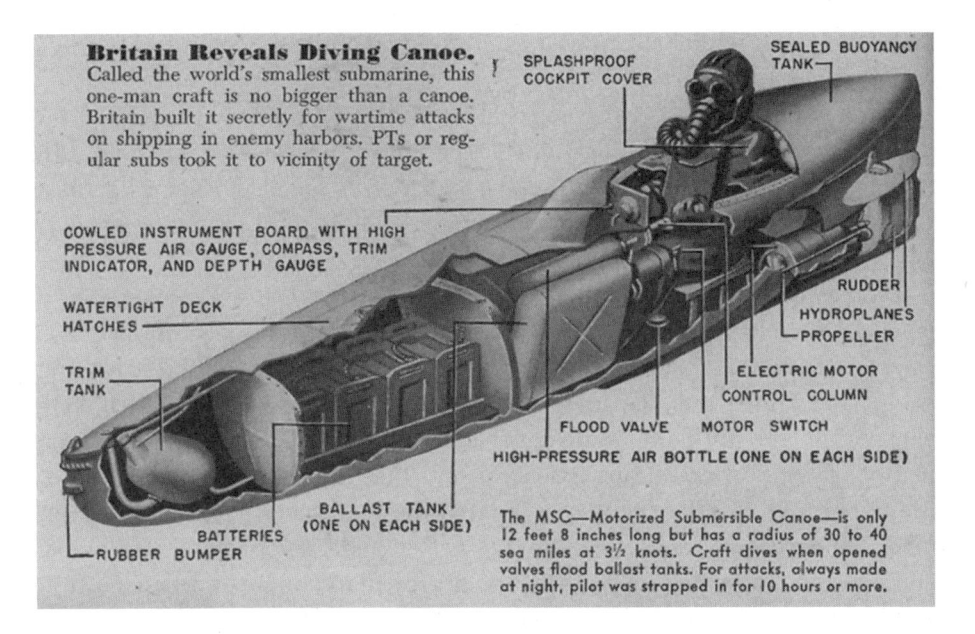

Britain Reveals Diving Canoe.
Called the world's smallest submarine, this one-man craft is no bigger than a canoe. Britain built it secretly for wartime attacks on shipping in enemy harbors. PTs or regular subs took it to vicinity of target.

The MSC—Motorized Submersible Canoe—is only 12 feet 8 inches long but has a radius of 30 to 40 sea miles at 3½ knots. Craft dives when opened valves flood ballast tanks. For attacks, always made at night, pilot was strapped in for 10 hours or more.

A sleeping beauty

Merapas after the strike and would be recovered by *Porpoise* on the night of 7/8 November.

Mustika then made for Laban Island via the Temiang and Sugi Straits and dropped off two recce parties; the first folboat paddled to Laban and returned to report it was suitable for unloading the SBs while the second went on to the Subar Islands to establish an OP to spy out shipping targets. Lyon moved the *tonkan* to a group of small islands off Batam Island but on 10 October, when lying in the Rhio Straits, it was sighted by a Police observation post on Caroe Island. An inspection vessel was subsequently despatched by Batang police station with an inspector, Bin Shiapel, and four other Malays. Under the impression that it was a Japanese launch, the RIMAU party opened fire and killed three of the occupants of the launch. Two, however, got away and realising that the operation was now totally comprised, Lyon gave the order to scuttle the *Mustika* with all the SBs after the crew had transferred their equipment including the limpet mines into the rubber boat. A new plan had taken shape: Lyon, Davidson, Campbell, Warne and Stewart would paddle the rubber boat to Subar Island where Ross and Huston had their OP. Three of the folboats would then continue the operation, slipping into the harbour before the alarm could be raised, and, after mining their targets, regroup on Pangkil Island in the Riau group. The remaining twelve raiders under Captain Bob Page were to make their way by folboat to Merapas Island where they would join Carey's four-man caretaker party.

Some military historians have concluded that in all likelihood Lyon and his raiding party did make it through into the target area and blew up three ships with their limpet mines. What is not disputed is that on 14 October, some white men were spotted by a Malay informant on Pangkil Island and the information was duly logged by the Japanese [their signals were subsequently intercepted].

Lyon died on the tiny island of Soreh on 16 October 1944. Discovered by a Japanese search party, Lyon – together with Stewart, Ross, Campbell and Davidson – sprang a snap ambush inflicting heavy casualties on the advancing troops and killing their Japanese officer. Both Davidson and Campbell were wounded in the fire fight. Knowing that the Japanese would come back in a matter of hours with reinforcements – and that there was no possibility of island-hopping to safety with two injured and exhausted comrades – Lyon made the decision to dose the injured Davidson and Campbell with morphine, and sent them on their way towards the nearby island of Tapai, where Huston and Warne were known to be holed up.

Lyon set about creating rudimentary defences, taking into account the position of a Malay household. The danger of accidentally involving the occupants of the shack in the forthcoming battle led Lyon to switch the position of his defences away from this location, a formidable task given that the tiny island was bereft of any significant cover, and almost entirely indefensible in daylight. Lyon and Ross climbed a large Ru tree, having first equipped themselves with as many magazines and grenades they could carry. Corporal Stewart was positioned in a stone-lined ditch, about thirty metres to their left, together with a cache of grenades and ammunition for the Silent Stens that all three carried.

The Japanese renewed their attack about two hours later at around 20.00 hrs after another barge with fifty reinforcements had arrived on Soreh. For the next five hours, shooting continued and it was at dawn the next day, when the Japanese cautiously advanced, that they found the bodies of Lyon and Ross, both killed by a hand grenade. They had accounted for over sixty dead and wounded Japanese. Stewart remained undiscovered on the island, but as his folboat had been taken by the Japanese, he was effectively marooned and, caught three days later, was taken, after a series of different island jails, to Singapore.

In spite of their injuries, Davidson and Campbell had managed to paddle the eight kilometres to Tapai Island which they reached around 15.00 hrs on 16 October. Shortly after daybreak the next day, their bodies were discovered by a

Japanese patrol. They had both died of their wounds[179]. The remaining members of the raiding party continued paddling from island to island in their folboats and reached Merapas in good time for the RV with the submarine. The RIMAU detachment was now eighteen strong.

When HMS *Porpoise* had arrived back in Freemantle on 11 October, its commander Captain Marsham had asked to be relieved of his duties for he was on the edge of a breakdown. So the retrieval of RIMAU was entrusted to HMS *Tantalus* under the command of Lieutenant Commander Hugh MacKenzie RN which sailed on 16 October with Major Chapman as the SOE conducting officer.

On 4 November the Japanese, acting on a tip-off, sent a party to Merapas and after a fire fight that evening in which a Japanese officer was killed, the RIMAU contingent split into two groups. Captain Page and nine others escaped by folboat to Mapor Island while the remainder under Lieutenant Sargent headed for Pompong Island in two stolen sailing *koleks*. Riggs and Cameron remained behind to engage with the Japanese: both were killed.

On the night of 7/8 November, Page sent two men over to Merapas from Mapor to wait for the signal from HMS *Porpoise*, for in the absence of W/T communications, no one was aware of any change to the pick-up plan. In fact, HMS *Tantalus* was nowhere near the area, for her captain had decided to extend his uneventful patrol for another fourteen days in the hope of sinking enemy shipping. He finally arrived off Merapas on 21 November but when Chapman and Corporal Croton went ashore, they could find no sign of any survivors, although there was evidence of camps, including eight one-man shelters. The pick-up party returned to the submarine and no further attempt was made to look for any RIMAU survivors.

In fact, Page and the survivors had been waiting patiently on Mapor, sending over a picket each night to man the RV at the Hammock Tree. Once the 7 December deadline had past, it appears that Page's surviving raiders had split themselves into three boat parties: Page, Falls, Gooley and Fletcher; Ingleton, Hardy, Marsh, Huston, Carey and Warren; Sargent, Craft and Reymond with Willersdorf, Pace and Warne headed south in two native *koleks*.

On 15 December, Page and his party were compromised on Selajar; Falls was shot and wounded but the others escaped, only to be captured a few days later. Ingleton's party ran into a Kempeitai and Heibo force between Pompong and Boeaja on 16 December and in the encounter Marsh and Huston's folboat sank, with the result that Huston drowned. Marsh, who had hidden with Carey and Warren, was captured with them on 27 December. Meanwhile Sargent,

---

179 One report states that they had both eaten their cyanide capsules and were found propped up back to back.

Craft and Reymond had managed to locate a junk with a Chinese/Malay crew and been taken aboard, in hindsight a fatal error, since all three were viciously assaulted and Reymond and Craft drowned after being thrown overboard. Sargent was luckier. He clung to a log for ten hours until he drifted into Cape Satai where local fishermen handed him over to the Japanese. Ingleton and Hardy were rumbled on Gentung Island on 18 December, and, after a brief exchange of fire, during which time Hardy was wounded, they were both captured.

The second *kolek* of Willersdorf, Pace and Warne was still at liberty and headed south until Warne became delirious and his companions had no option other than to leave him on Kadapongan Island. They continued their journey, eventually reaching Romang Island on 17 January 1945, only 400 miles from Darwin. Betrayed by a local village chief, they were captured two days later and taken to Dili where they were tortured and left to die of their wounds in their cells. Warne, who had recovered from his delirium on Kadapongan, managed to commandeer a small native boat and evaded Japanese patrols until he was tracked down in March on the coast of Borneo. He died in a prison one month later after being brutally interrogated and tortured.

The ten captives were held in isolation in Outram Road jail on grounds that they were 'war criminals' who had acted 'in violation of international law and the conventions of warfare'. This was an absurd indictment by a nation that was not a signatory to the Geneva Agreement and at that very time was engaged in subjecting 2,000 Australian POWs to a forced march in Borneo, at the end of which six remained alive. On 3 July 1945, the ten POWs stood trial on charges of 'perfidy and espionage'. Found guilty, they were taken to a rough execution ground and beheaded on 7 July, and then thrown into three graves, one on top of the other.

The RIMAU raiders received no posthumous honours other than one Mention in Despatches.

LIEUTENANT COMMANDER DONALD DAVIDSON, RNVR, DSO

Donald Davidson

Donald Davidson was the son of the Reverend Gerard Davidson, the vicar of Woodford Kettering in Northamptonshire. After finishing his studies at Cheltenham, he travelled to Australia where he spent five years as a jackaroo in Queensland. Returning to England, he joined the Bombay Burmah Trading Corporation and was posted to the teak forests of northern Thailand and then Burma.

Davidson loved the outdoor life and thrived on physical challenges; he once canoed almost the full length of the Chindwin River. He thrived on danger and was never happy unless in a tight spot. He once shot an old tiger at point-blank range with birdshot. Yet there was another quieter and more studious side to Davidson as epitomised by his avid bird and insect watching and superb butterfly collection.

One the outbreak of war, Davidson was refused leave by his company to join the army but nonetheless obtained a commission in the Burma Frontier Force. When the government announced that, as part of their engagement, officers needed a job to return to at the end of the war, Davidson decided to outflank such blatant bureaucracy and headed to Australia to join up. It was while he was waiting for a ship in Singapore that the Navy offered him a commission which he happily accepted.

His wife Nancy[180] and 4-month-old daughter Caroline – they had married in Penang in 1935 – were evacuated to Australia in December 1941 and Davidson managed to get away with the Singapore Naval base staff to the DEI before the island surrendered. He eventually escaped by small boat from Sandakan in Borneo and finally reached Melbourne in March 1942 where he was given a post at the Navy Office.

It was in July that he received a call to meet Lyon and from then became 2 i/c Jock Force. He and Lyon made for a formidable partnership, both equally tough and determined, with Lyon's creativity complemented by Davidson's assiduous powers of attention to detail.

Davidson, along with other members of Operation RIMAU, is remembered at the Kranji Commonwealth War Graves Cemetery in Singapore.

---

180 She later wrote *Winning Hazard*, the story of the sabotage raids, under the pen name of Noel Wynyard.

LIEUTENANT BOBBY ROSS

Bobby Ross

The son of an Indian Medical Service [IMS] officer, Harold Ross was born in Madras, India, in September 1917 and educated at Wellington College and then Cambridge [Trinity Hall] where he read Anthropology and Zoology. In 1936 he spent two months in Germany, studying the language in the Cologne-Mainz area and in 1938 went to Iceland for eight weeks, 'exploring and planning a self-contained expedition'. In August 1939, he became a Probationer in the Colonial Service and in September 1940 graduated to Cadet in the Malayan Civil Service.

In his SOE application form, Ross described his experiences there: ' ... during my eighteen months in Malaya, my interests were with the people and the countryside. I was therefore accustomed to finding my way about alone, and was in the habit of staying with Malays in their own villages. I also used to spend weekends on shooting expeditions in the jungle, again in sole company of Malays. The fact that I am interested in primitive tribes led me several times into the forests of Palang-Negri Sembilan area. As a result my Malay speech was of a serviceable and colloquial kind, not best suited to passing examinations, but nevertheless of some value in making my way about the less visited parts of the country.'

Ross had been a keen member of the OTC both at Wellington and Cambridge, so straight away he joined the FMS Volunteer Force from which he later transferred to a RA Light Battery as a gunner, and saw active service from December 1941 to February 1942, when he escaped after the surrender of Singapore. Although he joined the Indian Army as a cadet in March 1942, he was discharged in June and re-employed by the Colonial Service, this time being sent to the Nigerian Administrative Service in July 1942. 'In Nigeria I spent my tour in isolated districts of the coastal area and consequently I am accustomed to finding my way by river or bush-path through overgrown, and in some cases unmapped country, with a not always very helpful population.' As an Assistant District Officer [ADO], he spent sixteen months in Nigeria before being released to SOE.

Bobby Ross's greatest wish was to be a fighting soldier and when it was finally granted, he upheld the finest traditions of the British army, engaging the enemy against all odds until his comrades had reached safety.

Posthumous Mention in Despatches

Lieutenant Ross, a member of a party which left Freemantle by submarine in an attempt to carry out a second attack on enemy shipping in Singapore Harbour, volunteered to remain behind with Lieutenant Colonel Lyon on Asore Island when the party was apprehended by the enemy.

Lieutenant Ross with Colonel Lyon fought a very gallant delaying action by which all other members of the party managed to effect their escape from the island. During the engagement casualties were inflicted on the enemy and the fight was carried on until Colonel Lyon and Lieutenant Ross were killed. It is recommended that Lieutenant Ross should receive a Mention in Despatches.

Mentioned

CHAPTER THIRTEEN

DUTCH EAST INDIES

POLITICAL BACKGROUND

From the arrival of the first Dutch ships in the late sixteenth century, it was not until the nineteenth century that Dutch dominance was extended by force of arms across what was to become the territory of modern-day Indonesia.

The Dutch subjugated most of Sumatra in the Padri War [1821-38] and Java in the War of 1825-30. The Banjarmasin War [1859-1863] in response to an uprising brought eastern and southern Kalimantan [Borneo] under permanent Dutch control. The most prolonged military expedition by the Dutch was the invasion in 1873 of the Sultanate of Aceh in northern Sumatra. It met with fierce resistance – the Dutch commander General Kohler was shot dead by an Acehnese sniper – and the territory was only pacified forty years later when the Acehnese surrendered in 1912. The island of Lombok, ruled by the Balinese, came under Dutch control in 1894.

Direct colonial rule was extended throughout the rest of the archipelago from 1901 to 1910 and control taken from the remaining independent local rulers; south western Sulawesi was occupied in 1905-6, the island of Bali subjugated by military conquests in 1906 and 1908, as were the remaining independent kingdoms in Maluku, Sumatra, Kalimantan, and Nusa Tenggara.

The Bird's Head Peninsula [Western New Guinea] which had been formally recognised as Dutch in 1872 – the rest of the island divided between the Germans and the British – was designated in the 1920s as an area to resettle Dutch Eurasians, a social experiment that never came off as the climatic conditions were too harsh for the settlers, many of whom were office workers.

From the beginning of the twentieth century, the DEI gradually developed as a state distinct from Holland itself with treasury functions separated in 1903. Public loans were raised by the colony from 1913 onwards, and quasi-diplomatic ties were established with Arabia to manage the Hajj pilgrimage. In 1922 the colony was placed on an equal footing with the Netherlands in the Dutch constitution, while remaining under the aegis of the Ministry of Colonies.

The population of the DEI consisted of three groups: 'Europeans', 'Natives' [Indonesians] and 'Foreign Orientals' [Chinese, Arabs, Malays, British Indians, etc]. In 1940 there were approximately 68 million 'Natives', of whom 47 million lived on Java and Madura, and over one and a quarter million 'Foreign Orientals', including some 1,250,000 Chinese, 50,000 Arabs, and 20,000 Malays.

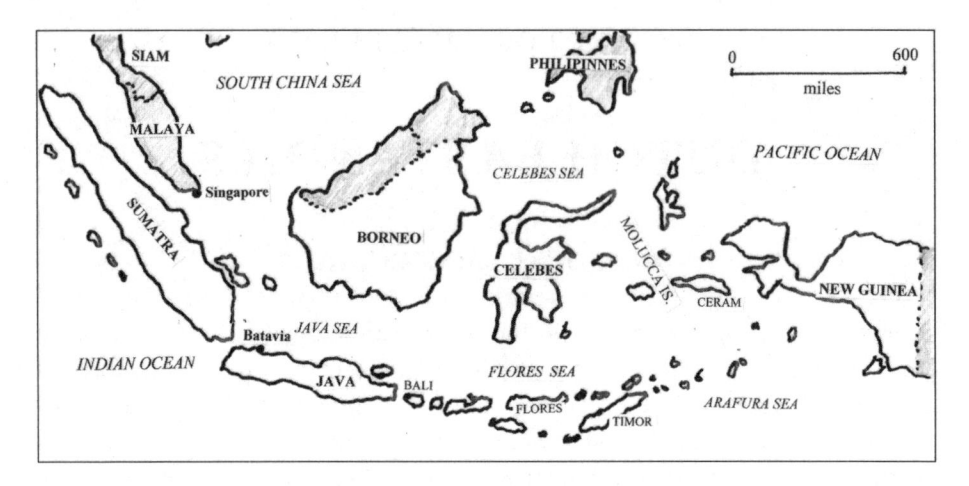

The 'Europeans' – most of them Dutch nationals – consisted of the *trekkers* who only worked in the DEI for a limited period of time, and the *blijvers*, those who had settled in the colony permanently, many over several generations. From 1892 onwards the descendants of European fathers and native mothers were given Dutch nationality, on the condition that they had been acknowledged by their father, and automatically classified as 'European'. An estimated 80,000 Dutch nationals from the Netherlands and over 200,000 Dutch nationals born in the East Indies, lived in the DEI at the time of the Japanese invasion.

The general government of the DEI was entrusted by the Dutch parliament to a Governor-General, who was appointed for a period of five years. He was the commanding officer of both the Royal Netherlands Navy in the East Indies and the Royal Netherlands East Indies Army. Organised into Provinces [run by a Governor, Resident or Assistant Resident], in turn broken down into Divisions and Sub-Divisions [run by an Assistant Resident/Civil Administrator with a Controller], the DEI was administered by the *Binnenlands Bestuur* or European Provincial Government staffed by Dutch members of the Netherlands East India Civil Service who had all been trained at Leiden or Utrecht University.

Recognising that the 'Native' population should ideally come under the direct rule of their own chiefs, each Division had a 'Native' Regent appointed by the Governor-General, Districts 'Wedanas', and Sections 'Assistant Wedanas'. These 'Native' civil servants were trained in Java. In large population centres, municipalities governed by their own councils were established and some Provinces had self-governing councils as well. Native villages were maintained in their traditional forms across the DEI with their chiefs more or less 'acting' as civil servants.

This system of colonial government in parallel with indigenous tribes was epitomised by the *Volksraad*, a People's Council comprised of 30 'Native' members, 25 'European' and 5 from 'Foreign Orientals'. Although in 1925 it was made a semi-legislative body, its role was in effect advisory, with the Governor-General expected to consult it on major issues. In reality, decisions were still made by the Dutch government and in that respect, the system was intrinsically flawed, for below the surface of consent and co-operation simmered militant nationalism fuelled by Marxist-Leninist ideology.

Discontent with Dutch colonial rule resurfaced in the early twentieth century with the founding of the Marxist Indies Social Democratic Association [ISDV] by two Dutch socialist parties, SDAP and SDP, in the DEI. The October 1917 Revolution in Russia sparked off a revolt at the major naval base of Surabaya, which was quickly suppressed, with the Dutch leaders of ISDV being sent back to the Netherlands. However, the ISDV continued to function and at its congress on 23 May 1920 in Semarang, it changed its name to the Communist Union of the Indies [PKH] and became the first Asian Communist party to join the Comintern.

Four years later, after creating the Union of Indonesian Labour Organizations, the party changed its name to Communist Party of Indonesia [PKI]. This signalled greater militancy and in May 1925, at a conference in Prambanan [Central Java], the PKI-controlled trade unions decided to start a general strike with the aim of bringing down the colonial government and replacing it with the PKI. Although a security clampdown at the beginning of 1926 led to the arrests of many PKI members, on 12 November a limited revolt in Batavia [Jakarta] broke out, with similar unrest in Padang, Bantam and Surabaya. In Batavia, the revolt was crushed within a day or two, and after a few weeks it had been comprehensively defeated throughout the country. As a result of the failed 'revolution', 13,000 people were arrested, 4,500 imprisoned, 1,308 interned, and 823 exiled to the Digul River valley in Dutch New Guinea. Many non-Communist political activists were also targeted by the colonial authorities under the pretext of suppressing the Communist rebellion. The PKI, outlawed by the Dutch East Indies government in 1927, went underground.

The sugar, tin, copra and coffee trade on which the DEI had been built continued to thrive, and together with rubber, tobacco, tea and oil, became the principal exports, offering rich economic pickings to Japan[181]. Oil was the jewel in this crown of commodities, for Japan imported ninety per cent of its oil. Even though it had stockpiled about 42.7 million barrels of oil by 1941, it knew

---

181 In 1941, the DEI produced 20% of the world's tea and coffee, 25% of the world's cacao and coconut supply, 35% of the world's rubber and most of the world's supply of quinine.

that to keep its fleet at sea, its armies in the field and its factories working, it would need at least 35.9 million barrels a year. The DEI fields produced 65 million barrels of oil in 1940[182], a rate which would be more than adequate for Japan's import needs.

The problem for the DEI government was who was going to defend them. Mother Holland simply did not have the military resources and therefore successive Governor-Generals had banked on the notion that the Japanese would be so severely constrained by their occupation commitments in China and Manchuria that they would be unable to launch a decisive attack. If they did, then the more powerful British and Americans would come to their defence. Such calculations were thrown into awry when Germany invaded Holland in the spring of 1940. More than ever before the DEI looked vulnerable.

On 17 June 1940, an Australian newspaper reported that 'the Netherlands East Indies parliament has conferred wide powers on the Governor General [Jonkheer van Starkenborch Stachouwer] for the preservation of the Integrity of the Netherlands East Indies. He said he was doing his utmost to aid the Allies without infringing the interests of America and Japan. He confidently expected the democracies to win. Holland's capitulation had resulted in a reduction of DEI exports by twenty-five per cent, which, it is expected, will be counterbalanced by an increased demand from the Allies, America, and Japan'.

This was not wishful thinking, for the Japanese had been quite open about their interest in DEI oil. In September 1940, a large delegation headed by the Minister of Trade and Industry, Ichizo Kobayashi, had arrived in Batavia with a request that the DEI government increased their exports to Tokyo from the existing 570,000 tons to 3.75 million tons, in other words around 50 per cent of DEI production. Although they agreed to an increase to 1.8 million tons, the Dutch failed to assuage the Japanese of their thirst for oil, and in December another delegation arrived led by former Foreign Minister Yoshizawa, with a new demand, this time for 3.8 million tons. Seven months later, after the US and Britain had announced an embargo on all oil exports to Japan and frozen all bank transfers, the authorities in Batavia followed suit and on 28 July 1941 all trade with and payments to Japan ceased. Now the oil die was irrevocably cast. Cut off from US oil, Japan only had one course of action open to it – to take the oil resources of the DEI by force. The alternative, to withdraw from China and FIC, meant the end of her imperial ambitions; it was never going to happen, for as Liddell Hart later pointed out, 'no government, least of all the Japanese, could be expected to follow such humiliating conditions, and utter loss of face'.

---

182 Compared to the USA's 1.35 billion barrels a year in 1940, 63% of world production.

At the start of the Pacific War in December 1941, Dutch forces in Indonesia numbered around 85,000 troops, a combination of European and mainly *Ambonese* regular soldiers[183], locally organised militia, territorial guard units[184] and civilian volunteers. After the Japanese conquest of the DEI, unlike the British in Malaya, the Dutch government-in-exile in London was reluctant to play the Communist resistance card, instead opting for limited reconnaissance and commando raids.

Although they never seriously supported Indonesian independence until late 1944 when the Pacific War was at a turning point, the Japanese facilitated the politicisation of Indonesians down to village level, particularly in Java, and to a lesser extent, Sumatra, where they educated, trained and armed many young Indonesians and gave their nationalist leaders a political voice. Thus, through dismantling the Dutch colonial regime and at the same time empowering Indonesian nationalism, the Japanese occupation created extremely adverse conditions for raising guerrilla forces which depended on local support. On a practical level, the Kempeitai took over the DEI Police Information Service [PID] with its network of agents and spies covering every corner of the DEI.

By war end, 26,233 Dutch nationals had been killed by the Japanese during their occupation of DEI, a figure that palls in comparison to the estimated 4 million civilian deaths of the indigenous population from famine and slave labour, and the 200,000 women and girls forced to work in Japanese army brothels. Although they lost the support and sympathy of most Indonesians through their brutal treatment and the poverty and starvation that subsequently engulfed the islands, the Japanese were never confronted by any meaningful organised armed resistance movement.

SOE IN THE DEI

The sprawling archipelagos that characterised the geography of the DEI fell within the SWPC area with the exception of Sumatra which was within the SEAC Theatre of operations [see Chapter Six].

From the beginning, special operations in the DEI were fraught with difficulties. The DEI government had made no plans for post-occupation resistance and thus there was no skeletal organisation on the ground, even though there were large Christian and Moslem communities loyal to the Dutch. NEFIS was too small and under-equipped to cover the whole of the DEI and, by closely

---

183 On the eve of the Japanese invasion in December 1941, Dutch regular troops in the East Indies comprised about 1,000 officers and 34,000 men, of whom 28,000 were indigenous.

184 In 1922 a Home guard or *Landstorm* was created for European conscripts older than thirty-two.

allying itself to the American-controlled AIB, was restricted to intelligence gathering patrols.

So, exactly as in Borneo, SOE's involvement was limited to supporting ISD/SRD operations originated and directed by NEFIS and sanctioned by the AIB. This support usually took the form of the secondment of qualified British officers and training of key personnel. Having lost all their Far East possessions, the Dutch were particularly sensitive to British ideas of partisan warfare as they suspected London's motives were more to do with self-interest rather than altruism. In some circles, it was even mooted that the UK had designs on acquiring Dutch territories after the war.

In fact, the problem for the Dutch as with the French lay in Washington. Joseph Grew, the Acting US Secretary of State, received a visit on 13 July 1945 from the Dutch Ambassador, who bemoaned the fact that no Dutch troops were being sent for training in Australia to prepare for the re-occupation of the DEI. Speaking with 'great emphasis and emotion and indicating his profound regret, even indignation,' the Ambassador said that if the invasion of the DEI was undertaken by American and Australian forces with no Dutch content it would constitute such a loss of face in the opinion of the natives that Holland would never recover. But the US Chiefs of Staff had made it clear, that same month, that it was impossible for Dutch armed forces to play a major role in Far Eastern operations, and any accepted for operations would be under the complete control of the Allied CinC concerned, and their use would 'depend solely on military considerations'. In short, American anti-colonialism was calling the shots from now on as Europe's oriental empires emerged from the yoke of Japanese oppression.

When, in the spring of 1945, General MacArthur proposed liberating the entire Indonesian archipelago using US troops, President Truman turned his offer down, wary of using US lives to recover European colonial possessions. Instead it was the British and SEAC who took on the task of reoccupation, including the repatriation of over 300,000 Japanese troops and the rehabilitation of Allied Prisoners of War and internees [RAPWI]. In his report to the Chiefs of Staff, Mountbatten later wrote that, having taken over the DEI from SWPC without any Intelligence reports[185], he had been given no hint of the political situation in Java. In a meeting with the Lieutenant-Governor-General of the DEI on 1 September, he had 'no reason to suppose that the reoccupation of Java would present any operational problem beyond that of rounding up the Japanese.'

---

185 This is an extraordinary omission. An SOE memo of 9 October complains of several OSS parties in Java – 'it is not known how they were introduced' – and adds that SOE had no idea where they were or what they were doing.

Almost immediately British commanders were faced with the prickly problem of dealing with rampant Indonesian nationalism – independence had been declared on 18 August – and found themselves engaged in an undeclared anti-guerrilla war. The 49 Indian Brigade Group, which arrived in Central Java on 25 October, soon found itself deployed in a full-on battle against indigenous Indonesian militias. Over a three day period in November, the port of Surabaya saw fierce house-to-house fighting that claimed 600 casualties among the Indian Army troops and many thousands of Indonesian lives. Among the casualties were the brigade commander, Brigadier Aubertin Mallaby, and his brigade major. This was the antithesis of the humanitarian and RAPWI mission that SEAC had come to do.

SOE found itself caught up in the chaos that erupted in Java. Although Force 136 had nine parties in Sumatra and four in Java monitoring the various nationalist movements, Brigadier John Anstey, Mackenzie's Chief of Staff, had to implement the SEAC ruling that no Dutch troops were to take an active part in the Theatre, on the grounds that their deployment would only serve to inflame the situation. Therefore all Dutch members of the Anglo-Dutch Country Section were withdrawn from the field and returned to the CinC DEI, Admiral Helfrich, 'for use as he directed'. While this suited Helfrich who was intent on starting his own intelligence service in Sumatra along the lines of NEFIS in Java, it impacted on the effectiveness of Force 136's intelligence gathering activities. Nor did it take into account 'the considerable anti-British feeling' among the Dutch internees which Lieutenant Colonel Egerton Mott, the SOE LO to XV Corps, noted in his intelligence summaries to Commander Group B in Kandy.

Mackenzie wrote to Helfrich on 12 November, expressing his personal disappointment that:

> 'current conditions have not made it possible to maintain the scheme of running mixed parties, primarily Dutch, under the control of our Anglo-Dutch Section. As you are aware the Military Authorities have ruled against this and again in accordance with military instructions we have prepared a limited number of British parties ... We have insisted that this must be considered a short term policy only and that the long term policy should remain as it was before, namely that mixed parties of primarily Dutch personnel should be used as soon as possible, the British element being eliminated as soon as British military responsibilities in DEI come to an end'.

Meanwhile, Force 136 itself began to be disbanded – the Anglo-Dutch Country Section was scheduled for liquidation by 31 December – opening up a potentially serious gap in SEAC's capability to acquire vital DEI intelligence. Mackenzie's solution to transfer a limited number of British parties to the Ops 4 Section of ALFSEA [Lieutenant Colonel R.V. Johnston-Smith] was implemented. Reporting directly to the GOC XV Corps in Batavia, a Base Liaison Team [Major Carew and Captain Marchant] and four Mobile Patrols [Captain Jeffries and Lieutenant D'Astugues; Captain Macdonald and Captain Prescott; Major Pierce and Lieutenant Cunningham; Captain Houseman and Captain West], were deployed out of Singapore. Dutch elements of the Anglo-Dutch Country Section regrouped in Batavia.

In the end it was a combination of Dutch manpower and US arms that took to the field in 1947 to re-establish Dutch sovereignty. It was to no avail and Indonesian independence came of age in December 1949.

CHAPTER FOURTEEN

BORNEO

OVERVIEW

The British Official History of the War against Japan describes 'the island of Borneo as a land of primeval jungle. The coasts are fringed with mangrove and swamp, and over nine-tenths of the interior is covered with thick evergreen forests. In 1941 the population was small – that of the whole island was estimated at less than three million – and there were less than a dozen settlements large enough to be called towns. There were few roads and only one short railway; communication was by the many waterways or by narrow jungle paths. Much of the interior was unexplored, or very inadequately known. It was rich in oil and other raw materials'.

The main Japanese strategic objectives in Borneo were the oil fields. Those in British Borneo lay in two groups: one at Miri [2.1 million barrels], close to the northern boundary of Sarawak, and the other [3.2 million barrels a year] thirty-two miles north, at Seria in the State of Brunei. The crude oil was pumped from both fields to a refinery at Lutong on the coast, from which loading lines ran out to sea. In Dutch Borneo, the main Royal Dutch Shell oilfields were on Tarakan Island with a production of about 5.1 million barrels per year from two fields near the centre of the island, and at Balikpapan on the south east coast of Borneo with production of 7.4 million barrels a year, together with a refinery and a newly constructed port with enough facilities to load tankers. There was a well developed road following an oil pipeline to Samarinda that also provided access to the interior oil fields.

The conquest of Borneo was completed in eight weeks in a series of sea launched assaults and parachute drops.
- 16 December 1941: Japanese troops landed on British Borneo at 05.00 hrs and captured the oil fields at Miritonk and Seria and the oil refinery at Lutong. British and Dutch authorities began to issue orders to destroy other oil-related facilities.
- 24 December 1941: Japanese troops captured the town of Kuching, Sarawak at 16.00 hrs after heavy fighting against troops of the Indian 15th Punjab Regiment.
- 11 January 1942: Japanese troops began the campaign against the Dutch East Indies by landing on Tarakan Island off Borneo. In the face of

superior forces, Dutch commanders at Tarakan decided to destroy the 700 oil wells on Tarakan.
- 24 January 1942: After sundown, 5,500 Japanese troops landed unopposed at two sites north and east of Balikpapan.
- 13 February 1942: Japanese troops captured Bandjermasin, the capital of Dutch Borneo, unopposed.

In terms of military significance, Borneo was somewhat of a backwater as its geographical position shielded it from the main battlefields of Burma, China and the Philippines, and Papua New Guinea. Singapore and Saigon controlled the entrance to the South China Sea.

SOE IN BORNEO

As Borneo fell within the operational area of General MacArthur's SWPC, SOE's involvement was limited to assisting ISD/SRD in Australia with personnel and equipment. Furthermore, Dutch Borneo remained under the jurisdiction of the Dutch government-in-exile to which its intelligence agencies such as NEFIS were politically accountable.

SRD operations on the Borneo landmass took place on both British and Dutch territory; the former covered the States of North Borneo, Brunei, Labuan Island [part of the Straits Settlement], Sarawak [ruled by the Brook family], and the latter the remaining and largest part of the island, Dutch Borneo.

Run out of Australia, the SRD Directing staff, Colonel Jack Finlay, Director of Plans, his GSO2 Jumbo Courtney and GSO3 George Crowther, formerly an oil-fields surveyor in Borneo, reported via the AIB to General MacArthur's Pacific Command rather than to SEAC, whose boundary ended in Malaya and Sumatra.

According to Dr Ooi Keat Gin, as early as December 1941, there was a proposal for a scheme utilising guerrilla tactics in Sarawak 'to make periodic raids on the oilfields [namely at Miri] from the interior and prevent the Japanese from making effective use of them'. Second Lieutenant P.M. Synge of the Intelligence Corps proposed that 'a force of 500 men or more if necessary, skilled in forest-craft, could be raised from the Long Houses of the Baram, Tinfar [Tinjar] and Niah rivers and organised into an effective guerrilla force'. Benefiting from his participation in the Oxford Sarawak Expedition of 1932, Synge had knowledge of the terrain and of the inhabitants of north eastern Sarawak. He admitted, however, that such a force was 'unlikely to be able to effect recapture of or to hold the oilfields'; nonetheless, the continuous commando-style raids would 'do much destructive work'.

BRITISH NORTH BORNEO

Operation PYTHON 1 and 2

Major Frank Chester, a former rubber planter, and Captain Dougie Broadhurst were infiltrated into North Borneo on 6 October 1943. Their objective was to identify and then mobilise opposition to the Japanese occupation from various communities – Overseas Chinese, *Dusuns* [farmers], *Muruts* [hunters], *Bajaus* [coastal peoples], *Sulus* and *Dayaks* [Sarawak].

Lieutenant Albert Kwok at the head of the 2,000-strong Kinabalu Guerrilla Defence Force attacked Japanese forces at Menggatal on 9 October 1943.

Assisted by Charles Peter and Jules Stephen, he then captured Jesselton before retreating back into the jungle. The Japanese responded to what they thought was a full scale revolt by indiscriminate bombing and machine-gunning of villages from the air. They extracted appalling revenge: all males on the Suluk Islands were reportedly killed.

With the capture of Kwok on 19 December, resistance petered out. Ex-Chief Inspector Duallsi continued to fight on with the *Muruts*. However, with the fate of Kwok unknown to SRD, a second party under Major Jinkins landed on 20 January 1944 with guns, explosives and medical supplies for the Kinabalu Guerrilla Defence Force.

All members of PYTHON were recovered by 21 June, with the exception of Sergeant Brandis, who had disappeared into the jungle shortly after landing with Jinkins and was never seen again.

Operation AGAS [Sandfly]
On 3 March 1945, Major Chester, together with Captain Sutcliffe and four ORs, landed by submarine on the west coast of North Borneo. Their mission was to revitalise the resistance which had been crushed in 1943 and to gather intelligence for the invasion of Borneo by the Australians.

Augmented by AGAS 2 – Major Combe, Captain May, Sergeant Watts and Corporal Maaruff bin Ali – who were dropped by long-range Liberators on 3 May, Chester was redeployed to Kimanis Bay north of Labuan Island and remained there till 9 June.

On 21 June, AGAS 3 – Flight Lieutenant Ripley and Sergeant Hywood – went into Ranau to rescue POWs. It later transpired that only six out of 2,400 Allied prisoners had survived the infamous Borneo death march, when POWs and Indonesian slave labourers were forced to walk 160 miles through the marshes and jungle from Sandakan to Ranau.

AGAS 4, commanded by Major Rex Blow, who had won a DSO fighting with Filipino-American guerrillas on Tawi-Tawi and Mindanao, landed on Semporna peninsula in a heavily armed launch supported by Catalina flying boats. Their brief was to collect intelligence and to recruit, train and arm indigenous guerrillas to harass the enemy in inland areas.

AGAS 5 commanded by Major J. MacLaren arrived in Lahad Datu on 27 July.

All personnel from the AGAS Missions were extracted by 11 October 1945.

DUTCH BORNEO

Lieutenant Davijd of the Royal Netherlands East Indies Army formed a guerrilla group including three European NCOs in Putussibau in March 1942 for three months. The Japanese despatched a force of 200 men to find them. Davijd with seven men and two women crossed a mountain range and reached the coast after a punishing trip of 270 miles. When they reached Mahakam River, they heard that Samarithe had fallen to the Japanese. There was no option other than to move to upper reaches of the Kaupus River when they were attacked and killed by Punan *dayaks*. It was not an untypical story of the hazards Europeans faced in these inhospitable climes.

In December 1944, Operation APPLE commanded by Flight Lieutenant Dryber with seven ORs was inserted by submarine south of Kali Tanah Koeningand River. After working in the Tarakan area, it was recovered on 26 January 1945

SARAWAK

Operation SEMUT [Ant]

Major Tom Harrisson, who had taken part in university expeditions to the New Hebrides and Sarawak, dropped by parachute with Operation SEMUT 1[Staff Sergeants Sanderson and Bower, Sergeant Barry and second stick, Captain Edmeades NZF, Sergeant Hallam, Staff Sergeant Tredea and WO Cusack] into the Plain of Bah on 25 March 1945.

Harrison had been welcomed by Penghulu Lawai Bisarai and soon made contact with two outstanding indigenous leaders – Penghulu Badak, chief of the people living in the upper reaches of Limbang River and Lasong Piri, chief of Bawang people.

He was soon reinforced by Operation SEMUT 2, Major Toby Carter, a veteran of the New Guinea campaign who knew the Baram-Tinjar river area well, and Major Bill Sochon, a former policeman under the Third Rajah Brooke.

Carter took over the country west of Tamabo and Sochon the area between the Baram and Rajang river systems [SEMUT 3].

By July 1945, the combined SEMUT Missions represented a major investment in personnel and resources. Fifty out of seventy had been dropped by parachute and over eighty per cent of stores dropped in difficult jungle terrain were recovered.

Mission	Officer i/c	Other officers	ORs	Total
SEMUT 1	Harrisson	8	27	36
SEMUT 2	Carter	4	14	19
SEMUT 3	Sochon	5	9	15
Grand total	3	17	50	70 all ranks

HARRISON was later joined by Lieutenant Westley with SEMUT 4.

LIEUTENANT COLONEL FRANK CHESTER, DSO, OBE

Front, second from right: Frank Chester

Born in South Africa in 1899 and later educated at King's School Canterbury[186], Frank 'Gort' Chester had been resident in North Borneo since 1927, where he had a small estate of his own and also worked for The Borneo and Manila Hemp Company. Well known to many of the native chiefs and the Chinese community, he moved to South Africa in 1940, where he was commissioned in The King's African Rifles and served in the Abyssinian campaign. Recruited into SOE by Gavin Stewart in May 1942, he joined the INDIA Mission.

In September 1943, Chester went to Australia to join the JAYWICK Mission but instead, in October, he was selected to lead the six-strong party PYTHON Mission, the first SRD Mission into British North Borneo. Their task was to contact the locals and to obtain as much intelligence as they could about enemy troop disposition, installations and shipping movements. Infiltrated by US submarine *Kingfish*, they landed on a small beach near Labian Point and slowly made their way inland. It took five weeks before they finally completed hauling all their equipment and stores upriver, and on 7 November W/T contact was made with Darwin.

Joined by Captain Hamner, an American operating in the Sulu Archipelago, and two others at the end of November, Chester set about recruiting agents on Sitankay and Tumindao Islands, and then left for Tawi-Tawi via Manuk-Manuk

---
186 Some sources state that Chester then went to RMAS and was commissioned in 1917 in King Edward's Horse [The King's Overseas Dominions Regiment] but this is not on his SOE record.

and Simunul islands where he contacted Lieutenant Colonel Suarez, commander of the US sponsored partisans. Suarez agreed to second Lieutenant Valera, the former District Forest Officer at Sandakan and an old friend of Chester, to the PYTHON Mission. His help in recruiting agents and setting up coast watching parties was invaluable.

In early October 1943, news reached Chester of Lieutenant Kwok's planned raid on Jesselton on the west coast of Borneo, and Valera brought his 2 i/c, Lim Keng Fatt, to see him at Python Bay. Chester urged him to tell Kwok to stand down as it was far too early to take up arms against the Japanese. That said, he was prepared to support them and gave him 2,400 gold sovereigns. Unknown to Lim, Kwok's rebellion had been savagely quashed and Lim himself was murdered on his return and all his money stolen.

*****

The Double Tenth Uprising

New Year's Day 1942 saw the unopposed landing of Japanese troops on Labuan Island off the coast of northern Borneo. Two day later they reached Beaufort on the mainland and the process of occupation began. On 16 May, all Europeans were summoned to the hotel in Jesselton for internment, their positions in the territory's administration from then on filled by members of the Asian community. From the beginning, the promise of co-prosperity proffered by the Japanese wore thin: fifty per cent of food was requisitioned, forced labour on airfield construction compulsory, craven subservience in public obligatory, the Japanese paper currency an object of ridicule[187] and increased taxation on the Chinese.

Resistance was not immediate. As Maxwell Hall, author of *Kinabalu Guerrillas*, observed, 'to the native mind, patriotism is rather a love of their own part of the country, but not of the whole of it, for they are only dimly aware of its size. They love the area or district which is their homeland, and whoever, as ruler, allows them to live there receives immediate recognition. It need only be said that these inland tribes [Dusuns and Muruts] showed a customary subservience and obeyed the commands of the ruling power whoever it might be. Their warlike spirit was not quickened until others had set an example.' The 'others' turned out to be the overseas Chinese.

---

[187] In 1945, the Australians found a train in Jesselton with five tons of Japanese paper currency on it. No one had touched it.

Albert Kwok had been born in Kuching [Sarawak] where his father was a dentist. Sent to Shanghai to be educated, he escaped from the city when the Japanese seized it and travelled extensively around China studying Chinese medicine and assisting the Chinese Red Cross, during which time he developed an expertise in treating haemorrhoids. It was said that at one point he treated the Generalissimo himself. In all probability he was recruited as an intelligence officer by the KMT and sent back to Borneo where he arrived in late 1940 and practised as a *tsin-sien* [physician] in Jesselton until his dispensary stocks ran out. In February 1942, as the Japanese took over North Borneo, Kwok set out to try and contact a group of European civilians and soldiers at Longnawan, 400 miles to the south of Jesselton in Dutch Borneo, but Japanese patrols on the rivers prevented him from reaching his destination and he returned in July. It transpired that the Longnawan group were all murdered shortly after[188].

News travels in the South West Pacific by boat, and by the beginning of 1943, Kwok and his contacts were heartened by tales of the US victory at the Battle of the Coral Sea and the step by step successes in the struggle for the north coast of New Guinea. Given the speed of the Japanese advances in 1941-42, there was an expectation that their eviction could be equally quick. A nascent resistance movement was founded – the Overseas Chinese Defence Organisation [OCDA] – with the initial objective of upping the tempo of passive resistance to the Japanese occupation forces. Lim Kenh-fatt, one of the most active members, managed to make contact with Imam Marajukim, a representative of Lieutenant Colonel Alejandro Suarez's resistance movement in Tawi-Tawi, an island to the east of Borneo, and the idea of pooling their resources began to take shape.

Accompanying Marajukim, whose congregation were concentrated in the Sulu Islands, Kwok arrived in Tawi-Tawi and met up with Suarez, the CO of 125th Infantry Regiment of the US Armed Forces in the Philippines and also Provincial Governor of the Sulu Islands. After establishing his credentials, Kwok returned to Jesselton in May 1943 with orders to collect intelligence on Japanese troop and shipping movements. Concurrently, he began to collect funds and stockpile clothing and medical supplies in preparation for an uprising, and it was while engaged in this that the Japanese got wind of his plans and he had to go underground. The raising of a guerrilla force now became a priority for the OCDA and Kwok once again sailed to Tawi-Tawi, taking with him the money and clothes collected in Borneo.

At this stage, the Japanese launched an assault from their base at Sandakan against Tawi-Tawi and fierce fighting took place over three days and nights

---

188 Major Oldham [SRD] Longnawan atrocity report 1945.

Albert Kwok

before they withdrew. Kwok had been involved and made such a good impression on Suarez that he was gazetted Third Lieutenant in the Reserve Force of the US Forces in the Philippines and designated Leader of Special Operations Group [SOG] Borneo. Now officially assigned to Borneo as a Military Intelligence Officer, he returned to Jesselton with Imam Marajukim, both with cover stories as sugar traders. Assisted by Bajaus, Binadans and Sulus, the two immediately set to work in September, raising funds and devising a price list for Japanese heads, with rewards ranging from $200 to $400 for each skull taken. Finding recruits in the interior was problematical as the tribes remained somewhat aloof; nevertheless, the impetus gathered pace.

Major Frank Chester, who was operating with the PYTHON mission on the eastern coast of British North Borneo and, having already met with Suarez, was well aware of the OCDA's activities, urged Lim Keng-fatt to pass on to Kwok that the timing of the proposed insurrection was premature and it should be postponed until more favourable conditions prevailed. This message did indeed get through, but by this stage Kwok was faced with an intractable problem. The Japanese were planning to conscript 3,000 Chinese youths for their own garrison requirements; if this levy went ahead, the OCDA would not have any guerrillas with which to fight the enemy. The die was cast and Kwok moved to Menggatal in the foothills of Mount Kinabalu to set up his HQ. Orders were issued for the revolt to start on the night of Saturday 9 October with the aim of occupying the district between Jesselton and Tuaran and raising the Allied flags. It was to be a three-pronged attack with a seaborne assault on the docks, coinciding with the arrival of a motorised column under Kwok and a flanking attack by a foot party.

Armed with a few Lee-Enfield rifles, some shot guns, *parangs*, spears and heavy clubs, some in suits, others wearing just loincloths, the guerrillas captured the police station at Tuaran, seized some more rifles and ammunition and then headed down the road for Jesselton in three trucks. A bugle call signalled the start of the attack on the town at 22.00 hrs. The Sulus swarmed over the sea wall and set fire to the wharf, the main body rushed into the town centre in their trucks and the foot party entered from the opposite direction. After capturing the police station and military post office, Kwok issued a proclamation on behalf of the North Borneo Overseas Chinese Defence Force under his assumed name Wong Fah-min. It castigated the Japanese for their maladministration, for reducing the inhabitants to poverty and for their ill-treatment of women. With the support of the British and the Americans, Kwok announced that he would drive the Japanese out. At midnight another bugle call sounded the retreat and the guerrillas withdrew in good order, after accounting for the death of a number of enemy troops and collaborators[189].

The next few days saw more guerrilla activity in the Tuaran area and in Kota Belud, and although the number of recruits had risen to nearly 300, Kwok's men were still desperately short of arms and ammunition and it was this that forced him to remain near the coast to await promised supplies form Suarez in Tawi-Tawi rather than retire into the safe haven of the Borneo jungle, the correct move for any guerrilla band. By November there was still no sign of resupply. With food supplies running low and Japanese air and ground searches intensifying, Kwok discharged all those who wanted to return to their homes and headed off to Kiangsam only to be interdicted by the Japanese there and forced to move to the Penambang area about four miles outside of Jesselton. Here they were surrounded on 19 December and reluctantly surrendered in response to a Japanese threat to kill all the villagers in the area. Ten days later Lim Keng-fatt[190] and the long awaited boatload of American arms and ammunition arrived from Tawi-Tawi. After being interrogated and tortured, Kwok was executed on 21 January 1944.

The insurrection, which in effect had petered out after two days, provoked the Japanese into taking massive retaliation. Over the next six months, towns and villages were indiscriminately bombed and strafed, houses burnt, both Overseas Chinese and native villagers arrested and tortured with many shot or beheaded, including the massacre of 176 prisoners at Petagas on 21 January 1944. The full fury of the Japanese was visited on the Sulus and Binadans from the Mantanani group of islands who had provided the seaborne assault force

---

189 Japanese sources put the death toll at sixty; the OCDA estimated about 100.
190 Leng was murdered off the mouth of the Tuaran River by Bajaus acting on the instructions of the Japanese.

for the attack on Jesselton. Of the 114 people living on Suluk Island, fifty-four were killed and twenty-five later died from malnutrition and ill-treatment[191]. Similar massacres took place on the islands of Udar and Danawan.

The flame of resistance passed to ex-Chief Inspector Duallis, a Murut who had distinguished himself in the Armed Constabulary before the war. The Muruts, head-hunters armed with parangs and blowpipes, exacted a terrible revenge on the Japanese in the last days of the war, long after the official surrender in October. As Japanese troops began their long march from Pensiangan to surrender to the Australians in the north, the muruts were lying in wait for them. No one will ever know how many perished along the way but it was for the Japanese to prove their very own death march.

Kwok's untimely uprising did serve to prevent the Japanese going ahead with their conscription of 3,000 young Chinese. It could also be argued that it influenced the Japanese to keep some 25,000 troops in Borneo and move their HQ from Sarawak to British North Borneo. But it was also a costly reminder, very similar to uprisings in Italy in 1944, that unless closely coordinated with advancing Allied armies, such actions by guerrilla troops invariably fail and provoke indiscriminate and harsh retaliation on the civilian population.

****

Now securely established, Chester's Mission was reinforced on 20 January 1944 by PYTHON 2, an all AIF team of six under command of Major W.T.L. Jinkins. Their task was to organise guerrilla warfare in the area, but no sooner had they landed by submarine when one of their party, Sergeant Brandis, got lost in the jungle and was never found. It soon became clear that the Japanese were onto them and they moved camp to the Tenagian Kechil River further north. After a series of aborted pick-ups, three of PYTHON'S officers were taken off by a US submarine but Lieutenant Rudwick and Sergeant McKenzie were both captured and subsequently executed by the Japanese as spies. Between 30 March and 6 June, four attempts were made to bring off the remaining members of PYTHON, the submarine USS *Harder* finally succeeding, in the process sinking four Japanese destroyers.

PYTHON had been behind enemy lines for 243 days. Despite being continually harassed by the Japanese for the last three months of their stay, the Mission had succeeded in setting up a comprehensive intelligence organisation with the capability of signalling urgent operational matters direct to Darwin. Over

---

191 When the British landed on Suluk Island in 1945, they discovered that every adult male had been exterminated.

eighty-eight enemy shipping movements were notified during this period. The survivors, who had evaded crocodiles and water buffaloes as well as the enemy, were exhausted, Chester himself wracked with regular and violent attacks of malaria. After a period to recover, Chester went to London in October 1944 where he briefed the Far East desk on some of the command and administrative shortcomings he had experienced on PYTHON. Apart from one instance when he had been sent 7,000 lbs instead of 5,000 lbs of stores and the resultant headache of caching unwanted materials, his main bugbear was how he had been ordered to go to an RV which he knew to be dangerous and when he had signalled his reservations, he had been told 'to get on with it' or be relieved.

In February 1945, Chester once again set off to British North Borneo as commander of AGAS 1, an eight-man Mission to establish an intelligence network on the east coast prior to the reoccupation of British North Borneo by I Australia Corps. The first attempt to land was called off due to the presence of 'radio' masts in the area, and a second attempt, this time with a slightly different Mission membership, successfully went ashore from US submarine *Tuna* on 3 March and, after paddling upriver for three miles, pitched camp between Labuk Bay and Cape Tagahan. By 10 April, Chester, travelling by folboat, had reached Jambongan Island making friendly contact with natives along the way. He now organised air drops at Jambongan and Lokopas, the latter being the drop zone for AGAS 2 headed by Chester's old friend, Bob Combe, the former Kudat District Officer. Extracted by Catalina on 21 May, Chester reported to the AIB in Morotai and was subsequently tasked to return to the Beaufort-Jesselton area to collect further intelligence.

At dusk on 29 May, Chester and three men [Operation STALLION 4] were inserted by Catalina into Kimanis Bay for a close reconnaissance. Two days later they contacted some Chinese who Chester knew, but found them reluctant to co-operate in taking the fight to the Japanese, no doubt on account of the all too recent memories of the reprisals taken by the Japanese against Kwok and his band of Chinese and Malay rebels. For a time off the air as the sound of the generator would have attracted the attention of the large number of Japanese troops who were in close proximity, the Mission got through on 5 June and asked to be extracted. A punishing march to the Catalina RV, wading through swamps up to their necks and at times almost disappearing under water due to the loads they were carrying, saw then safely through and after a successful extraction, all three Europeans were hospitalised, Chester with jungle sores, Sue with dysentery and Hywood with tropical ulcers.

Chester returned to his HQ in Borneo in July and continued to prosecute the war against the enemy. Intelligence supplied by AGAS 1 resulted in the destruction by air action of approximately 850 Japanese. In the period June to

August, AGAS 1 guerrilla forces killed over 100 enemy for a loss of one guerrilla killed and one wounded. A very extensive medical service was established – in the month of August 1945, over 15,000 patients were treated in SRD posts in the AGAS territories.

Chester returned to Borneo after the war and died of blackwater fever in 1946. His grave, when located in 1999 at the Old Christian Cemetery, Kota Kinabalu, Sabah, was in a state of neglect. However, with the help of local people, it was restored, along with the cemetery generally. Later, the historian Lynette Ramsay Silver was able to prove that Chester's death in 1946 was due to a war-related condition. This resulted in not only his grave being recognised as a 'war grave' but also his 'elevation' to Lieutenant-Colonel, his temporary rank at the time of his death.

The inscription on his grave includes the words 'a pioneer of victory and a most lovable man.'

Frank Chester remains for many the most outstanding SOE officer of the war in the Far East.

21 October 1944: Recommendation for DSO by PM of Australia [for Operation PYTHON]

On 21 October 1944, the Governor General of Australia forwarded the Australian Prime Minister's recommendation to the Under-Secretary of State, Dominions Office, that Chester should be awarded a DSO 'in recognition of services rendered in highly dangerous operations in enemy held territory and while aboard with SOA Party PYTHON. The Military Secretary replied on 4 December that 'I am to point out that while valuable services which this party rendered are fully appreciated, it is not considered that gallantry decorations and medals are the appropriate form of award, as from the report on this operation it does not appear that they ever came under enemy fire'.

Never can the gap between military officialdom and the reality of life behind enemy lines have been so apparent.

Awarded OBE on the grounds that no shots were fired.

1947: Recommendation for DSO

From 3 March 1945 to 16 August 1945, this officer displayed leadership, gallantry and cold-blooded courage of the highest order. On 3 March 1945 this officer leading a small party of three officers and three NCOs re-entered British North Borneo, well knowing:

a. that there was a large price on his head as a result of his previous mission into the area [Enemy posters were found bearing his portrait and offering a reward of 15,000 dollars for him, dead or alive].

b. that having left the submarine there was no chance of withdrawal.

c. that the coast was strongly held by the enemy and continuously patrolled by land and sea.

The landing was made midway between two enemy posts at Tahahan and Pura Pura three miles apart. Owing to the hostility of the natives, Lieutenant Colonel Chester travelled 250 miles by canoe at night before finding a friendly contact enabling him to lead his party inland. Once inland Lieutenant Colonel Chester established his HQ from which he successfully:

a. obtained military intelligence for future operations.

b. raised a guerrilla force among the local inhabitants to harass the enemy and destroy his resources.

c. organised the native population to deny the enemy essential native food and labour.

d. spread pro-Allied propaganda thus ensuring a friendly and co-operative people to welcome the Allies when the time for invasion of the country came.

On 24 May this officer was extracted by Catalina for interrogation by I Australian Corps and when further information was required on behalf of 9th Australian Division he volunteered to re-enter Borneo for the third time.

On 29 May 1945 with two ORs and a native, Lieutenant Colonel Chester was inserted by Catalina into the strongly held area near Brunei Bay. After a reconnaissance of the situation on 31 May, this officer discovered that the railway station master at Bongawan was a Chinese named A. Lee. This station master was extracted in broad daylight from the station, which was staffed and guarded by Japanese, and interrogated by this officer. During the next eight days, this officer checked the information passed by A. Lee and at great personal risk watched hundreds of Japanese moving down the railway line towards Bongawan. The intelligence thus obtained and passed on was of the highest importance to 9th Australian Division and subsequently his estimate of strength was proved accurate.

From 29 May to 7 June this small party operated in the heart of the most strongly defended area in British North Borneo, necessarily on the alert twenty-four hours a day. On 7 June, Lieutenant Colonel Chester and his party were extracted by Catalina and a few weeks later he returned to his HQ in the interior where he continued his work so successfully that, at the time of the enemy surrender, two-thirds of British North Borneo was under his control.

Awarded

MAJOR R.G.P. COMBE, OBE, MC

Bob Coombe

Born in London in 1907 and educated at Rugby School, after reading law at Cambridge and taking silk at Lincoln's Inn, Bob Combe joined the British North Borneo [Chartered] Company in 1930 as a civil servant in the Administrative Service. He was promoted to District Officer and served in Kota Belud, Kudat, Tawau and the Interior. Half the month was spent in travelling to the outstations, where his responsibilities included sitting as a magistrate, acting as inspector of schools, catching smugglers, supervising public works, presiding over the marriage of Christians and registering midwives.

He was in England on leave when war broke out in 1939, and immediately joined the Royal Norfolk Regiment as a private. In 1940, he was granted an Emergency Commission and transferred to the Royal Artillery. After service in Persia, Lebanon, Syria, Egypt, Sicily and Italy, it was felt that his knowledge of Malay, Dusun and Bajau, and experience could be put to better use in the Far East and he was transferred to the SRD in March 1944.

Originally scheduled to drop with Chester on AGAS 1 in British North Borneo, Combe led the AGAS 2 mission to establish a base on the west coast in the Kudat area from which it could organise a guerrilla force and create an efficient intelligence network to support the 9th Australian Division landings in June 1945. On 3 May 1945, the five-man AGAS 2 team dropped by Liberator into the Lokopas area where they were welcomed by Chester and Combes' old friend, Datu Mustapha. After reinforcements of W/T operators and commando trained operatives, Combe established bases at Lokopas, Melobong, Pitas and Kudat from where the mission could contact Chinese guerrillas and friendly pro-British headmen and natives. Soon an intelligence network covering all of British North Borneo was operational.

During June 1945, Combe led attacks on Banguey Island and on enemy troops deployed around Marudu Bay. In August, Captain McLean and five sections attacked Japanese posts near Kudat, killing twenty-four and wounding four enemy soldiers. After taking the Japanese surrender at Kota Belud in September, Combe helped the British Borneo Civil Affairs Unit to assume control, disarming and paying off the guerrillas and transferring all their stores, warlike and medical, to BBCAU officials. By the end of October, AGAS 2 had all left.

After the liberation of Borneo, he was appointed Senior Civil Affairs Officer for North Borneo and Brunei, with the task of restoring order and government under the British Military Administration.

BORNEO

LIEUTENANT COLONEL TOM HARRISSON, DSO, OBE

Tom Harrisson [L]

Tom Harrisson was born in Argentina in 1911 where his father had gone to make his fortune after the Boer War. His mother, a Liverpool heiress, had had an eccentric upbringing, cycling all over France and Italy with her sister and widowed father, bird-watching and butterfly collecting. On the outbreak of war, his parents sailed back to England with their two sons and his father rejoined the colours, finishing the war as an acting Brigadier-General with a CMG, DSO, Order of the Crown of Belgium, the Belgian Croix de Guerre and five Mentions in Despatches. The General, as he was now referred to, decided to return to Argentina with his wife, and the boys were left in the care of a French nanny in Hampshire before going to boarding school in 1919. Holidays were spent as paying guests in impoverished vicarages with an assortment of Danes and Swedes and 'other grass orphans'.

In 1922, the General came to collect Tom and his brother, who had just had his appendix removed and after a month long journey they arrived in Concordia on the middle reaches of the Uruguay River which was where the headquarters of the General's railway company were. The next year was spent riding, shooting, playing tennis, canoeing and swimming, every 12-year-old's idea of heaven. Harrisson developed his lifelong interest in birds during these carefree days which came to an end in 1923 when the boys returned to their prep school and two years later went to Harrow. Here he was lucky to have a housemaster who shared the same unorthodox and rebellious traits as some of his charges and he emerged as a determined and unconventional young man, still passionate about birds and with an aptitude for the natural sciences. It was due to this combination that he was invited by the scientist Charles Elton to join the Oxford University Expedition to Lapland in 1930 while still a schoolboy, although he had been offered a place at Pembroke College, Cambridge.

As the expedition's ornithologist, Harrisson studied the food and habits of the birds in the region and after his first year at Cambridge had come to an end, he was off again on another expedition, this time the Oxford-Cambridge Expedition to St Kilda, a group of islands teeming with bird life in the Outer Hebrides. In the autumn of 1931, the fiercely independent Harrisson disillusioned by the male heartiness of Pembroke decided to leave without finishing his degree. The General, who himself had cut short his own university degree to go off to the Boer War, was not amused and the relationship between father and son went downhill from there on. Help, however, was at hand, for Charles Elton, impressed by Harrisson's performance in Lapland, sought him out and asked him to organise an Oxford University expedition in 1932 to the interior of Sarawak in Borneo to explore its flora and fauna. In the next ten months, the 20-year-old Harrisson raised funds[192], assembled equipment and chose the members of the expedition who included later luminaries like Air Marshal Sir Christopher 'Cub' Hartley, and Lord [Eddie] Shackleton, son of the Antarctic explorer Sir Ernest Shackleton, and later leader of the House of Lords in the Wilson Government.

After a six week journey via the Suez Canal, Penang and Singapore, the expedition reached Sarawak and by late July 1932 they were guests in a longhouse on the Tinjar River, a tributary of the Baram. Welcomed by the local tribes, they spent the next four months on field trips, penetrating into areas where the Sarawak expats had never ever been. Arriving in Kuching in December, the exuberant and cocky young Englishmen raised a few hackles of the Sarawak Club members which were later consolidated in a litany of complaints by E. Banks, the Oxford alumnus and curator of the Sarawak Museum, who had been the titular head of the expedition. If Banks considered that Harrisson was 'lacking normal manners', it certainly did not impact on Charles Elton's next offer to him to be the ornithologist in an Oxford Expedition to the New Hebrides in the South West Pacific. After writing up his Sarawak notes and giving a lecture about the expedition to the Royal Geographical Society in London, he set off to the East once more and arrived at Hog Harbour on the island of Santo on 2 September 1933.

---

192 Over £140,000 in today's terms.

Life in the New Hebrides proved challenging in more ways than one, for the 22-year-old Harrisson was having a passionate affair with Zita Baker, the wife of the zoologist and expedition leader and ten years his senior. Baker turned a blind eye and allowed the two of them to spend three weeks alone on Gaua, an island sixty miles by sea from Santo. When it was time to collect them, the weather had disrupted the shipping arrangements and it was not until a month later that Zita's husband finally recovered them. Given that Zita had left their two children behind in Oxford, Baker was greatly relieved and they both left for England in February 1934.

Harrisson continued his expedition studies in the New Hebrides, spending time with the Sakau people until there was a tribal war with the Yekuls which confined him and the new expedition member, a young Australian called Jock Marshall, to their camp in Hog Harbour. Both men went down with fever [Harrisson had malaria] but recovered in time to explore the extremities of the north west peninsula including climbing the mountain there. Marshall then went down with fever again and after nursing him back to health, Harrisson left Santo in the last week of July 1934 to continue his adventures on his own.

Not yet twenty-three, he persuaded some natives to take him from Hog Harbour to Malekula, the territory of the Big Nambas, the New Hebrides's best known cannibals. Soon after he arrived, he received an invitation from Ewan Colette, a scholarly copra planter of some thirty years residence on the island who had married a local girl from the Ambae. Described by an Australian travel writer staying with Colette as 'a cross between John the Baptist and a beachcomber', Harrisson methodically carried out a census of Malekula, including details of its inhabitants' sex lives, totems and the like, and in the course of it came to know the people of the island better than any other outsider. Then, on the whim of the British district agent who was about to go on leave to recover from blackwater fever, Harrisson was appointed the Governor of the Northern Isles of the Anglo-French New Hebrides Condominium, a position which not only allowed him to continue with his field work but also one which remunerated him.

One day in May 1935, literally out of the Pacific blue, a magnificent yacht, the *Caroline*, arrived and dropped anchor in Bushman's Bay. On board was Douglas Fairbanks Senior, who much taken by the engaging young Englishman, commissioned him to make a film about the Big Nambas, so called for the large size of their distinctive penis wrappers or *nambas*. Sensing this was an offer he could not refuse, Harrisson completed the film with the help of Chuck Lewis, Fairbank's cinematic Man Friday, and now in funds way beyond his meagre Governor's pay and allowances, resigned his post and after sending Jock

Campbell £80 for his fare home, sailed to Tahiti with Lewis in the *Caroline* which had been sent to fetch them.

Ill once more with malaria, Harrisson stayed put in Papete for three months before embarking on the seven week voyage back to Europe via the Panama Canal. It was the end of the first chapter of an extraordinary life. Few if any 23-year-old Englishmen could boast of two serious jungle expeditions and making a film about cannibals. In the process, Harrisson had developed his self-confidence and self-reliance and from the beginning had adopted an open-minded attitude to native peoples who he refused to patronise or stereotype. Tough, resourceful and ambitious with a determination to get what he wanted, there was a sort of manipulative ruthlessness about him which many found intimidating.

Back in England in early 1937, Harrisson found himself practically penniless and with no academic degree, of doubtful value to the scientific community. All the capital he possessed was a partly finished book about the New Hebrides but there was no prospective publisher. Zita Baker, with whom he was still in love, had left her husband for an Oxford don, Richard Crossman, and Douglas Fairbanks had failed to reply to Harrisson's request to fund a four year expedition to New Guinea. Suddenly, with a well attended talk at the RGS on 'Living with the people of Malekula' and an advance by Victor Gollanz for *Savage Civilization*, Harrisson found himself in the mainstream of British academia. As John Layard, the foremost expert of the New Hebrides, wrote: '[He] went out to the New Hebrides as an ornithologist, knowing nothing about ethnology. He comes back knowing more about the natives than many ethnologists'.

In a typical mercurial act of impulse, Harrisson suddenly changed course and took a job in a cotton mill in Bolton in order to familiarise himself with the conditions of the English working man, much the same as George Orwell in *The Road to Wigan Pier*. His employment as mill worker changed to lorry driver, then ice cream vendor and finally shop assistant. The ever restless Harrisson then answered an advertisement in *The New Statesman* and met up with Charles Madge and Humphrey Jenning to co-found Mass Observation [M-O], the first attempt to apply the methodology of anthropological field work to a developed nation, 'a sounding of the English collective unconscious'. It was the start of a remarkable sociological experiment, studying the English at work and play rather than the natives of remote islands in the Celebes and in 1938, Harrisson and Madge published the results of their first studies, *First Year's Work*.

The Munich crisis provided M-O with the opportunity to undertake political polling, and in January 1939 Harrisson and Madge published *Britain by Mass Observation*, an instant best-seller that provided 'the first comprehensive and sophisticated account of British public opinion in rapid flux.' When war was declared, M-O busied itself with taking sounding of civilian morale on behalf of the Ministry of Information. Another source of work was polling opinion in naval dockyards on behalf of the Director of Naval Intelligence. Both assignments kept Harrisson out of the war until April 1942 when all able bodied members of M-O were called up. By August, he was a King's Royal Rifleman and then, somewhat to his annoyance, was sent the following year to the War Office Selection Board, and by winter 1943 he was awarded an emergency commission in 161 Reconnaissance Regiment, formerly The Green Howards.

For Harrisson, life in a former infantry regiment in Northern Ireland was about as stifling as socialising with the expat community in the South West Pacific and it was with alacrity that he accepted an offer by SOE's Colonel Egerton Mott to join 'a few men to go back into Borneo ... ' In June 1944, he gave a memorable farewell party at his house in Ladbroke Grove and then set off to fight the Japanese. It had been yet another remarkable metamorphosis for this rebellious, brilliant iconoclast, this time from market researcher to a highly trained SOE operative. The question which had not yet been asked was how Harrisson would respond to orders in the field.

In March 1945, Harrisson and his seven-strong team waited patiently on Mindoro Island in the Philippines for the thick cloud over Borneo to clear. Their deployment was to support the imminent landing of the AIF's 9th Australian Division on Tarakan and Labuan Islands and the subsequent capture of north west Borneo, thereby denying the Japanese the crucial oil fields of Brunei and Sarawak. Harrisson's Mission, Operation SEMUT, was to drop into the mountains of north central Borneo and gain as much intelligence as it could about Japanese troop dispositions and movements.

As a part of the Mission's preparations, Harrisson, uneasy about the chances of a successful coastal landing and convinced that the most sensible strategy was to work from the interior outwards, had gathered as much pre-war research about the proposed area of operations as he could and had come upon a report filed by a Shell engineer, Swiss-national Dr Schneeberger, in which he described a series of plains hidden in the mountains of Dutch Borneo some forty miles to the east of the Plain of Bah in Sarawak. Elated by this discovery, he hitched a ride in a Liberator and was able to identify – just – a suitable dropping ground, thereby reversing at a stroke the Z Special Force doctrine of landing Missions exclusively by submarine. As a bonus, Dr Schneeberger was spirited to Australia from the US and was able to advise in person about the nature of the terrain and its people, including the use of needles and fish hooks for currency. By a lucky coincidence, a flight of heavy-lift long range Liberator aircraft became available at the same time.

At 07.19 hrs on 25 March, Harrisson jumped out of a Liberator[193] into the damp cloud and drifted nervously down into the unknown terrain, followed by Sergeants Sanderson, Bower [W/T] and Barrie. The second stick under the NZ Captain Edmeades dropped from a second Liberator and both parties met up at midday at a nearby Kelabit longhouse after recovering their stores. It transpired that the Japanese had not bothered these former head-hunters living on the Plain of Bah since 1942 and they had easily reverted to their traditional culture of self-sufficiency. The arrival of SEMUT 1 caused consternation and soon young men flocked to the longhouse to inspect the warriors who had fallen from the sky. Anxious to progress the Mission, Harrisson made a tour of all the longhouses on the Plain of Bah and then crossed into Dutch Borneo onto the Barang Plain where he was warmly welcomed by the Lun Bawang people, cousins of the pagan Kelabit, who had not long ago been converted by American Evangelical Missionaries. From them he heard news of downed US fliers in the locality and therefore decided it made good sense to move his HQ from Sarawak into Dutch Borneo. This decision was also in line with the advice to disregard the colonial borders that Schneeberger had given him for they were not observed by the indigenous peoples.

A contrarian by inclination, 'Tuan Mayur' Harrisson did nothing by the book. SEMUT 1 operatives were forbidden to wear boots or shoes in or near longhouses, despite the risks of hookworm, tropical ulcers and snake bite. For food, they were encouraged to eat the same as the local people wherever they were rather than carry rations drawn down from SEMUT HQ. Both these strictures were based on common sense to safeguard operational security and to enhance the team's chances of survival in an unforgiving environment. With these rules in place, Harrisson's modus operandi was to send his operatives in units of one or two men with local guides and porters on long detailed patrols. He later wrote: 'all of us [had] to become proficient in languages and quick movement in this difficult country, and to learn every possible trick from living off it, independent of extra porterage and personal stores'. This ensured that members of SEMUT were rarely in any one place long enough to be discovered or betrayed by enemy agents, and secondly they learned how to live and work effectively with the indigenous people of northern Borneo, replicating in many ways Harrisson's experiences as a young man in Sarawak and the New Hebrides. There was, as in everything he did, method in his madness and soon SEMUT 1 assembled a detailed and up to date picture of the military and economic

---

193 On the return journey, it crashed on East Timor, killing all thirteen crew members.

situation in North Borneo, including valuable targets for pin-point bombing. And despite what many considered to be unnecessary hardships and deprivations imposed on them by their eccentric commander, all forty-two Z Special Force operatives who worked for SEMUT 1 survived the war.

Harrisson's leadership style was a mix of intuition, manipulation and impatience. He never courted popularity, in fact he eschewed it, tended to rate his men on the basis of their achievements and capabilities rather than rank, for he found it hard to tolerate fools.

On 16 April, Major Toby Carter and Major Bill Sochon arrived with SEMUT 2. By now the Mission was so large and covered such a wide area that Z Force HQ decided that the three SEMUT Missions should remain autonomous and report direct to Morotai. So while Harrisson moved his HQ to the east just across the Sarawak-Dutch Borneo border, Carter stayed on the Barang River with SEMUT 2, and Sochon and Sergeant Barrie headed to the Rejang valley to set up SEMUT 3. In May, Harrisson moved again, this time to Penghulu Lasong Pin's longhouse at Belawit as part of his strategy to keep extending the radius of SEMUT's influence until it became tangential with Japanese occupied areas. At the end of May news came that the Australians had captured the airfield at Tarakan which meant that SEMUT 1 was now within range of Auster light aircraft. Within days, Harrisson had constructed with the help of the Lun Bawang, Kelabits and Ibans the world's first bamboo airstrip which received two Austers on 7 June. It transpired that the strip was too short for take-off, so its length was doubled overnight and the next morning Harrisson took off for Tarakan Island for a meeting with Brigadier Torpy Whitehead.

D-Day took place on the coast of British North Borneo on 10 June when 30,000 Allied soldiers and airmen landed in Brunei Bay, the majority on Labuan Island. Harrisson flew back from Morotai the next day to Belawit where the runway was now 250 yards long. The tempo of the Mission's activities dramatically increased, with daily engagements with the enemy and the capture of documents. Sergeant Sanderson ['Tuan Sunday'] and Driver Hendry now had a band of 100 Ibans who enthusiastically revived their headhunting skills. The idea was to disrupt enemy lines of communication and 'to put the fear of God into the Japanese'. Unfortunately, poor co-ordination between the SEMUT Missions and the 9th Australian Division led to mistrust and friction: it was extraordinary that Z Force LOs had not been attached to AIF formations down to brigade level, although Colonel David Leach did his best at divisional level.

20 Brigade found 'SRD information [on Japanese troop movements] was often too old to be acted upon as it generally reached this brigade by native courier some of whom travelled several days on foot and by canoe to deliver their messages. It is considered that a sound military training including

knowledge of how to deal with military information is as necessary for those engaged in guerrilla warfare as for regular troops'.

To try and mitigate the effects of this lack of communication, Harrisson ordered his men to avoid AIF regular forces and spent the next three weeks at divisional HQ trying to iron out the problems.

While the Allied invasion forces were in the process of winding down having achieved their objectives – the capture of the oil fields, ports and rubber plantations on the coastal strip – in early August, Harrisson concentrated on how to deal with the considerable numbers of Japanese still at large in the interior. He knew that there were an estimated 2,000 enemy soldiers at the Sapong Estate and another 2,000 to 3,000 at Ranau and that, with the experienced guerrilla bands now at his disposal [in SEMUT 1's area more than 1,000 enemy soldiers had been killed or captured by them], he was in a good position to take the fight to them. But when news of the Japanese surrender was received on 15 August, Harrisson was summoned to Morotai to explain the existence of British and Australian personnel on Dutch sovereign territory to the Netherlands Indies Civil Affairs representatives.

Not satisfied by his explanation that they were there in lieu of Dutch Special Forces, he was told to report to Colonel Spoor of Dutch Special Operations in Brisbane who, after keeping him waiting for three days, asked him to disarm all his irregulars and hand over authority to a DEI official. There was no meeting of the minds and by September, Harrisson was back in Borneo, ready to drop into the Bahau-Kayan valley to see whether the Japanese were trying to infiltrate into the centre of the island. The area was inhabited by the riverine Kenyah people and on 1 October he reached their great settlement at Long Nawang from where he went on to visit nineteen longhouse villages, travelling in dug-out canoes. The expected force of Japanese did not materialise but other SEMUT 1 units were still engaged, with Lieutenant Middleton signalling on 23 September, forty days after the Japanese surrender, that he had engaged the renegade Japanese Fujino Tai unit and killed fifty-five of them on the Limbang River.

With permission from 9th Australian Division to negotiate the surrender of Fujino Tai, Harrisson proceeded with Major Rex Blow, W/T operator Sergeant Nibbs, a 9th Australian Division LO and a captured Japanese officer up the Trusan River to Lawas and eventually persuaded the 340-strong column to lay down its arms on 28 October 1945.

SEMUT 1 and Harrisson's war was over. In 1947, he was awarded a DSO.

BORNEO

MAJOR 'TOBY' CARTER, DSO

Toby Carter [R]

Born in New Zealand of British parentage in 1910, Toby Carter was employed in 1935 as a surveyor in Miri, Sarawak, by the Sarawak Oilfields Ltd. In 1940, he joined Shell [Queensland] Development Pty Ltd in Brisbane as their Chief Surveyor. He joined the AIF in August 1942, first serving with the RAE and then the Australian Intelligence Corps before transferring to the British army with a General Service commission for service with SRD in Borneo. As well as the usual SRD menu of intelligence gathering and organizing guerrilla forces and identifying the locations of POWs, Carter was also charged with investigating the 'internal political situation [in Borneo] and [to] ascertain the feelings of the natives towards the pre-war government and the possible return of the Rajah and/or the British Government' in the post-war reconstruction phase. It was an extensive brief and initially the idea was for Carter to take control of the whole SEMUT Mission's resources to fulfil it. However, such a notion proved impossible when Harrisson made it abundantly clear that he was not playing second fiddle, so when Carter and Captain Sochon and six team members of SEMUT 2 dropped by parachute into Borneo on 16 April 1945, they prepared to cross into Sarawak over the 5,000 feet Tama Abo range and establish independent sub-missions.

It proved more practical to travel by river and a four day march and paddle took SEMUT 2 to Long Akah which it set up its headquarters in the old Sarawak

Government fort. Five weeks after first landing, they received a resupply drop and two additional team members, one of whom landed in a crocodile infested river. By now, after securing the support of Penghulu Tama Wing Ajang, the Kenyah great chief, Carter had began to build an accurate picture of what life in the interior was like and found that 'there was no clothing, medicine or any of the simple necessities of life. There was no government; the persuasion of the sword and the rifle butt prevailed ... This once pleasant and peaceful land, where trouble was the exception and not the rule, had become a region of terror.' It was hardly surprising therefore that the local tribes like the Kenyah and Kelabits, even the shy jungle dwelling Punan, all gravitated to the Mission to join the colours. Soon Carter's men were in action against the Japanese and his long range patrols resupplied by Catalinas began to exact revenge.

Recommendation for DSO

Major Carter has been associated with SRD operations into Sarawak from the recruiting and planning stage until he was withdrawn from his operational area on 11 August 1945 to embark on a special mission for relief of POWs in Kuching.

During the preliminary planning, he organised and trained the original party and kept morale and enthusiasm at a high level during long periods of unavoidable delay in transport prior to insertion. On 16 April 1945 he parachuted with five white personnel and two Asiatics into the Bawang Valley base on the Kalibit Plateau in Central Borneo. From there he moved down the Akah River organizing native strong points and W/T stations en route. He raised and trained a guerrilla force of 500 natives and ultimately penetrated as far as the mouth of the Baram River on the west coast of Sarawak. He established complete control and cleared all Japanese over an area of 6,000 square miles and organised native relief and medical aid throughout.

His intelligence network and efficient W/T organisation was responsible for much valuable information on enemy movements reaching 9th Australian Division prior to Operation OBOE 6. During his period of occupation, Major Carter's forces killed 258 Japanese and captured two. His full strength of white personnel was seventeen. His own casualties were five guerrillas killed. The excellent results reported above were obtained mainly by Major Carter's enthusiasm, ability and self-sacrifice. His service and bearing throughout was a fine example and encouragement to every member of his party. On several occasions this officer personally led his guerrilla bands into attacks which inflicted heavy casualties upon the enemy.

Awarded

MAJOR BILL SOCHON, DSO

Second from left: Bill Sochon

Bill Sochon was born in London in 1904 and became an Assistant Housemaster at the Borstal Institution at Rochester, Kent in 1927. In 1929, he took up the position of Assistant Superintendent of Police and Prisons in Sarawak where he remained until 1938 when he contracted malaria. Returning to England, he rejoined the Borstal Institute and served in the Home Guard until recruited by SOE in 1944.

On 6 April 1945, Sochon dropped to Harrisson at Bario with WO Horsnell and Sergeant Kassim. Within a day, they set out to Long Lelang, a SEMUT 1 outpost five days journey away. With seventy pound packs, they traversed the 5,000 feet Tamabo mountains. Sochon later wrote to Harrisson: 'Which causes the most exertion I do not know, either climbing up step by step, or sliding down the other side. The following day's journey was one of the most depressing I have ever made – dense jungle, endless brown fallen leaves, the awful smell of dankness, and [what appeared to be on every leaf] a leech of some inches long, sitting up and just waiting to get his bloody suckers on to you...'

When they reached the Akah River, they followed it downstream until they met up with Sergeants Barrie and Hallam. Hallam was ill with malaria and both were suffering from malnutrition thanks to Harrisson's 'live off the land' directive. Joined by Major Toby Carter, at that stage the titular commander of Operation SEMUT, the SOE mission set off for Fort Long Akah which they reached on 1 May. They soon discovered that their main W/T set was damaged and it was only by relaying messages to Harrisson on their small back up W/T set that they managed to arrange a drop of stores and a new set on 19 May.

On 22 May, Carter and Sochon decided that they should split SEMUT 2 and Sochon set off with Sergeant Barrie and Sergeant Abu Kassim down the Baram, through the remote jungle area populated by the shy Punan tribe until they reached Belaga on 1 June. It had been an extremely difficult trip, along rivers and over mountains and impossible to keep dry for six days. Setting up a small base in the mangrove swamps at the point where the Pila River joins the Rejang, Sochon settled down to wait for resupply by Catalina. It was to be a long wait. Three weeks later, a Catalina landed on the river with stores and reinforcements [Captain David Kearney, Lieutenant Pip Hume and W/T operator Sergeant Spurling]. Sochon's motley band of guerrillas, who had been beginning to waiver, now took heart as arms and ammunition were handed out. The Tuans really did mean business. Two days later, Captain Astill and Lieutenant Baker arrived by Catalina together with Harrisson who wanted to take over Sochon's operation. He received a flat 'No'.

Bill Sochon went on to raise a potent force of 450 guerrillas which he unleashed on the Japanese. On one expedition, Sergeant Barrie returned ashen-faced, his hair having turned white overnight. He had found the headless corpses of thirty Japanese soldiers on a riverbank. However, Barrie soon recovered his composure and went on to create his own force of 'Sumpiteers', Dayaks armed with blowpipes or 'sumpits'. On another occasions, a Japanese patrol was enticed to a dinner in a longhouse and then set upon by *parang* wielding Ibans. One village even used naked young women splashing about in the river to lure Japanese soldiers into the area, when the tribal warriors then descended on them and decapitated them.

After a brilliant ruse when he tricked the Japanese garrison in Sibu into surrendering without a shot being fired, Sochon finally withdrew from the area on 17 September and most of SEMUT 3, which now totalled nearly fifty men[194], was finally extracted by Catalina from Sibu on 15 October.

Recommendation for DSO

Extract: Major Sochon parachuted into Central Borneo on 6 April 1945. His assignment was to penetrate the Rejang River area and establish an intelligence network and to commence guerrilla activities against the Japanese in this area. Major Sochon, with a sergeant and one Asiatic corporal, set out on [xx] April 1945 to reach the headwaters of the Rejang River, travelling over wide and hostile country. By 6 June a point was reached sixty miles down the

---

194 Including Major Ray Wooler, an ex-Sarawak civil servant, and Roger Cheng, the Chinese–Canadian officer who had been originally earmarked for Operation OBLIVION.

river which was suitable for Catalina aircraft landings. He established W/T contact with SRD after great difficulty owing to the high mountainous nature of the country and a Catalina successfully landed on 23 June with reinforcements and supplies. The party had undergone severe physical strain and privation in extremely hostile territory for four weeks. Major Sochon then quickly, by contact with native chiefs known to him in pre-war days, established himself on the ground setting up a base at Belaga. He raised and trained a guerrilla force and moved down the Rejang River to Kanowit. By 15 August he had forced the Japanese to evacuate the whole of the Rejang River valley, exclusive of Sibu, and had restored law and order throughout some 15,000 square miles of Sarawak territory. He cut the escape route from Balikpapan via Central Borneo and the Rejang and successfully transmitted much regular and valuable enemy movement information to 9th Australian Division and I RAF. During these operations, Major Sochon's force killed 227 Japanese and captured five.

Major Sochon displayed great courage and initiative.

Awarded

CHAPTER FIFTEEN

JAVA, LOMBOK, CELEBES and MOLUCCA ISLANDS

- 28 February 1942: Japanese troops landed at Bantam Bay and Eretan Wetan, west and east of Batavia, respectively; another force landed 100 miles east of Surabaya.
- 1 March 1942: More Japanese troops landed on Java and immediately began marching for Batavia, with the Japanese 2nd Division capturing Serang and the 230th Infantry Regiment capturing Kalidjati airfield at Soebang en route.
- 5 March 1942: Japanese 2nd Division captured Batavia.
- 8 March 1942: All Dutch forces on Java surrendered to Japanese General Hitoshi Imamura.
- 12 March 1942: British General Sitwell, Australian Brigadier Blackburn, and US Colonel Searle formally surrendered to General Maruyama at Bandung.

After the Japanese invasion of East Java, some 400 Australian, Dutch, British and American troops took to the hills to wage guerrilla warfare rather than capitulate. By the end of April, they had all been captured and incarcerated by the Kempeitai, who then stuffed them into small bamboo pig baskets [approx. 100 cm long by 50 cm across] and threw them into the sea as food for the sharks.

The difficulties of establishing a viable resistance movement on Java were more or less identical to those faced by SOE in Sumatra, namely the distance from Ceylon, the initial Japanese stance of freeing the islanders from the colonial yoke, strained relations with the Dutch in Ceylon and London and the Dutch preference for commando raids.

Early operations carried out by the Dutch Section involved inserting small teams to spy out the land and make tentative contacts with villagers.

- 14-15 September 1942: Operation MACKEREL. Captain van Arcken and two operatives inserted by submarine *Radjek Winbay*. After a dire landing when their boat turned over injuring Van Arcken and swamping their W/T equipment, contact was made with villagers and the party safely withdrew by submarine the following night.
- 30 November 1942: Operation TIGER 1. Lieutenant Beregsma and two men inserted by submarine at Prigi bay. Captured and shot [?].

JAVA, LOMBOK, CELEBES and MOLUCCA ISLANDS

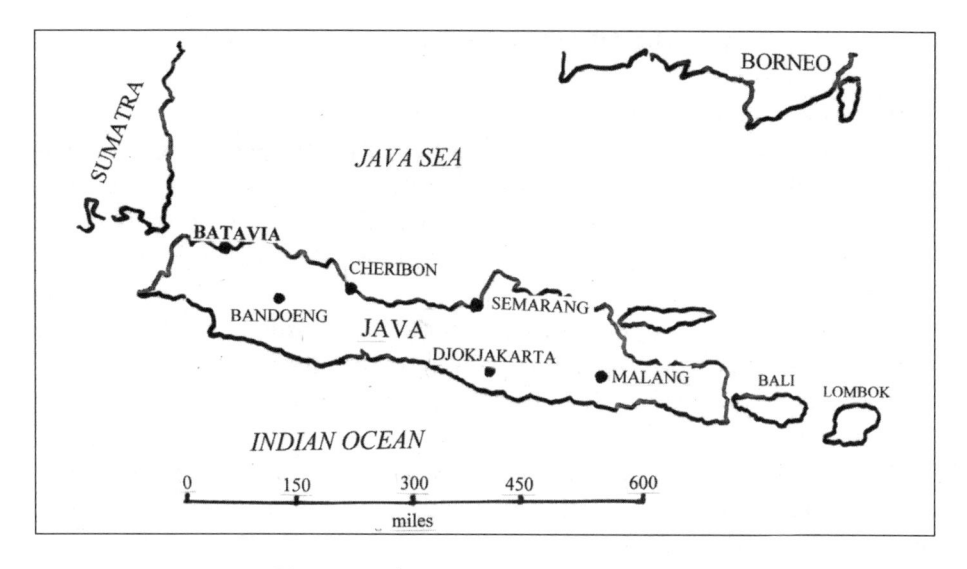

- Operation TIGER 2 under Lieutenant Brox with two men landed at Searng Bay. All were captured.
- 9 February 1943: Operation TIGER 3. No news after landing.
- 3 May 1943:Operation TIGER 4. Corporal Soejitno landed at Pang Pang Bay. No news after landing.
- 4 May 1943: Operation TIGER 5. Seaman Oentoeng landed at Pang Pang Bay. No news after landing.
- 21 August 1943. Operation TIGER 6. Corporal Papilaja landed at Pang Pang Bay. Captured.

With such dire results, operations were suspended until 1945 when:
- 6-7 June 1945: Operation PARSNIP. Lieutenant Abimanjo and two W/T operators landed at Pang Pang Bay.
- 7 May 1945: Operation POTATO. Sergeant Brouwer and two NCOs were inserted by submarine at Kemirian. Brouwer later showed up in Balikpapan in Dutch Borneo in September 1945.
- June 1945: Operation GOLDFISH 1 and 2. Lieutenant de Haas and eight Indonesians inserted by submarine on the Great Paternoster Islands. They travelled by *prahu* to East Java where Hass was killed. Mission went on to collect intelligence on Java, Lombok, Sumbawa, Flores, Celebes and Satengah Islands. GOLDFISH 2 then landed on Satengah Islands and collected intelligence about Madura, Java, Bali, Lombok and Makassar.
- September 1945: Operation MOSQUITO/HOOK dropped on Batavia Airfield prior to Allied landings.

SUMMARY OF SOE IN SUMATRA AND JAVA

Little was accomplished. Colin Mackenzie described SOE activity in DEI as 'very weak' and 'only a fraction of what we had in other places'. He cited the problem of the Acehnese who although nearest to Ceylon were the most anti-Dutch and thus made operations by the Anglo-Dutch Section only viable in force, i.e. eight men plus, putting a strain on limited resources both in terms of personnel and transportation.

However, Mackenzie understated the contribution made by the DEI section to the success of 26th Indian Division landings. The official history noted that 'whatever value may be put on Force 136 activities in the DEI by responsible authorities at a later stage, it is irrevocably true that without the intelligence supplied by these parties during the period between the Japanese surrender and the Allied landings there would have been practically nothing known about the state of affairs prevailing in these territories'.

LOMBOK

Operation STARFISH was planned by SRD to put out of action three six-inch Japanese gun batteries high up on the cliffs of Cape Padanan overlooking the Lombok Strait, a passage regularly used by Allied submarines going to and from the Java Sea. The operation was designed in two phases, a recce, to be followed by the main demolition party. On 14 March 1945, the recce group consisting of Lieutenant Lawrie Black, Lieutenant Malcolm Gillies [British], Lieutenant James Crofton-Moss [British] and Sergeant Alex Hoffie made a preliminary landing at 22.00 hrs from the submarine USS *Rock* on the western end of Pengantap Bay to cache their emergency supplies in the event they had to withdraw east along the south coast of the island. It was a far from easy landing as their ten-man rubber boat was swamped by the high surf, smashing the outboard motor and their W/T set. With no means of communicating to the USS *Rock*, the party paddled through a thick sea-fog to where they hoped the RV was. There was no sign of the submarine and as they were about to head back to the shore, what appeared to be a patrol boat came through the mist. Fortunately it was the USS *Rock* which had picked them up on her radar.

Born in Birtley in County Durham, 36-year-old James Crofton-Moss had been lent by SOE to the SRD as he was a fluent Malay speaker. He had had a varied career, first as a W/T operator in the merchant navy and then as a rubber planter from 1929-32 and from 1937-41 with a mysterious five year gap. In Malaya, he had joined the FMSVF and been with their signals company in

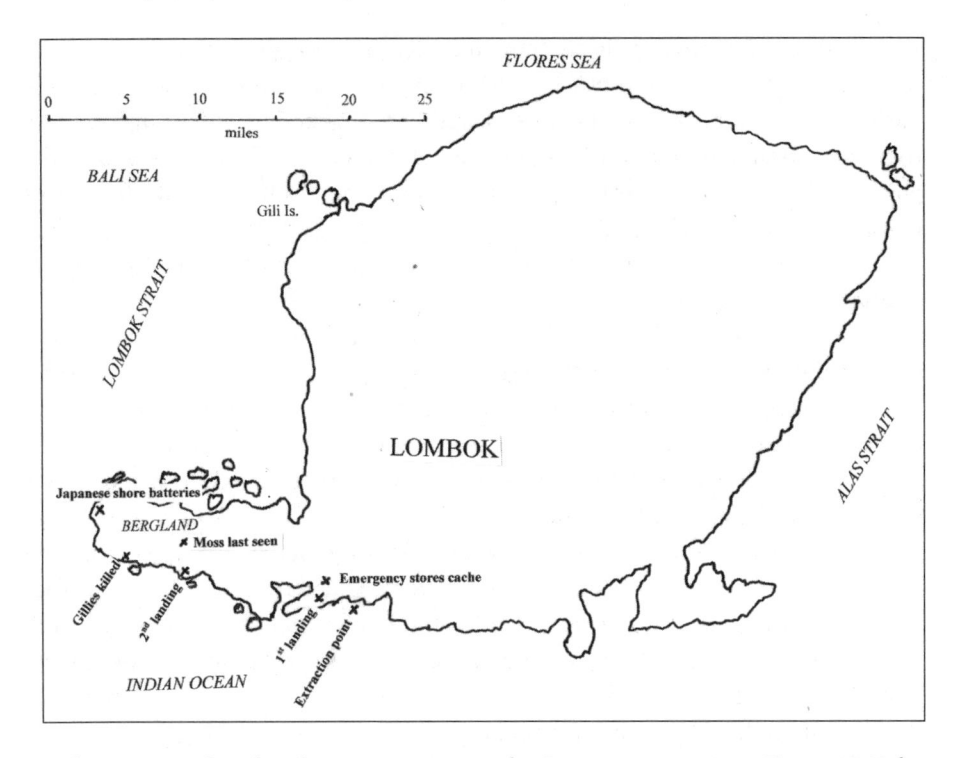

Kuala Lumpur for the three years up to the Japanese invasion. From 1942 he was once again a W/T operator at sea, this time on SS *Darvel*, a vessel belonging to the Straits Steam Ship Company[195]. On 18 August 1944, he was commissioned as a Second Lieutenant.

The following night, the group was put ashore about six miles to the east of Cape Batoengendang. Once again it was far from easy as a riptide carried them well to the east of the planned landing site and hurled their dingy against rocks at the base of an 800-foot cliff. Luckily they managed to pull the boat and their stores to safety having found a small cave about twelve feet above the crashing surf. Here they cached the rubber boat and its outboard engine and fuel. That night, they hauled their equipment up the steep cliffs and located a suitable site for a base camp in the thick undergrowth. From there they scouted inland and in a coastal valley four hours walk away, set up a forward outpost.

On the night of 14 April, under the cover of a bombing raid on the Japanese gun batteries, a Liberator dropped supplies to STARFISH. This was observed by two native fishermen who returned two days later with their chief and with eggs and fruit. Crofton-Moss spoke to them in Malay and although they were

---

[195] SS *Darvel* acted as a troop, munitions and stores ship transporting all three between Australia and the Islands as the Allies advanced north towards Japan.

very frightened of the Japanese, they did not appear to present a threat to the mission's security. On the morning of 18 April, Black and Hoffie, with some native guides made a recce north of Cape Batoengendang, intending to work their way along the coast to the gun emplacements on Cape Padanan. The going on the steep seaward slopes proved extremely difficult and after three days, the two men returned to the forward outpost for more supplies. When they reached the camp on 22 April, they found Gillies but there was no sign of Crofton-Moss.

It transpired that Gillies and Crofton-Moss had decided to move some of the stores from the forward outpost to the base camp as they were fearful of being betrayed by the natives and wanted to ensure that they were well prepared for a quick escape. On one of their trips to the main base, the two men became lost and unable to agree on which route to take went their separate ways. Gillies arrived at the base in half an hour and, after waiting for Crofton-Moss for two hours, returned to the forward outpost. Black immediately organised a search party but after two days without success, it became apparent to STARFISH that they were now in grave danger. In all likelihood, without a compass or pistol, Crofton-Moss had probably wandered into a Japanese lumber camp to the north and on his person were the patrol's code books. On the evening of 24 April, Black radioed HQ and was told to await further instructions.

The next morning, as they were eating breakfast, a twenty-strong Japanese patrol swept through the outpost. Gillies was shot and wounded; Black and Hoffie escaped and made it back to base camp in less than an hour and a half. Here they hid until dusk and then, loaded with supplies and equipment, climbed down to the cave where they had hidden their rubber boat. Silently paddling away from the shore, Black started the outboard and headed towards the western end of Pengantap Bay where their emergency stores were cached. After scuttling the rubber boat outside the reef, the two men lay down to get some sleep before day broke. By using the boat, they reckoned to be about three days ahead of a search party although they assumed that all Japanese troops on the island would have been alerted of their presence.

Daybreak revealed that they were in a heavily populated agricultural area and local villagers warned them that a Japanese deputation was due at any moment to assess the rice harvest. Remaining concealed in the scrub, they watched the Japanese come and go and that evening reached the emergency cache where they found the W/T set in working order. Over the next two days, keeping on the move to avoid the Japanese patrols which were now looking for them, they tried but failed to get through to base. A villager came and told them that eight villagers had been beheaded for failing to give information as to the whereabouts of two Australians. Hoffie then went down with blackwater fever and it was with huge relief that Black got through to HQ on the afternoon of 29 April to arrange a pick by Catalina on 2 May.

Spotted by two enemy soldiers the next day, who had come to within five yards of them, Black and Hoffie smashed the W/T set and grabbing the codebooks and two days supplies of water and food, made for the RV. Dodging Japanese patrols, they lay up on the cliff overlooking the evacuation beach. A large enemy force was spotted moving east down the coast towards a large village where they had evidently established a search HQ. At 04.30 hrs on 2 May, the two STARFISH survivors moved cautiously down to the shore and laid out their rescue signal on the beach. At 06.00 hrs, they spotted the Catalina and lit the signal fires but, sighting another aircraft approaching from the west, they assumed it was Japanese and doused their fires. As it circled over them it revealed itself to be a Liberator, enabling the men to relight their fires.

A heavy swell was running as the Catalina landed and disgorged the ferry party who started to paddle to shore. Black and Hoffie, to save time, swam out to a reef about 400 yards offshore but just as the rescue boat reached them it capsized, tossing its three occupants into the water. Somehow they all managed to right it and climb aboard and, as they paddled furiously back to the Catalina, they heard the sound of firing from the shore. With the rescue party now safely aboard the aircraft, the captain made a daring take-off along the ridge of a huge wave and, once airborne, flew low over the beach to strafe the Japanese patrol. The circling Liberator joined in and after a ten hour flight to Darwin, Black and Hoffie stepped onto home ground.

After the end of the war, a SEAC POW Contact and Enquiry Unit led by Captain Ken Beattie discovered the bodies of Gillies and Crofton-Moss buried in a shallow grave in the Muslim portion of Praja cemetery [rather than the Christian cemetery at Mataram]. The unit established that native informers had betrayed the whereabouts of Crofton-Moss to the Japanese. At first light on 25 April, a patrol led by a Japanese Naval WO, Yoshihiro Yamamoto, who was dressed as a native in a shirt and sarong, had opened fire on the figure of a sleeping man on a *bali-bali* in a hut in Dessar Tampah. The body riddled with small arms fire was identified as that of Crofton-Moss wearing British army uniform. It also transpired that the Japanese, who had become aware of the presence of STARFISH as early as 16 April, had mobilised the entire local population, including school children, to comb the southern part of Lombok in search of European soldiers. In the opinion of Beattie, the manner of Crofton-Moss's death constituted a War Crime.

The fate of Gillies was also established. After being wounded during the Japanese attack on the forward outpost, he was called upon to surrender. This he refused to do and continued to fire his weapon until he was finally killed. In the course of resisting, he shot dead a Japanese soldier. The islanders remembered this heroic action of the man they called 'the white soldier'.

CELEBES and MOLUCCA ISLANDS

Control of the Moluccas Islands, the original 'spice islands' of cloves, nutmeg and cinnamon, was vigorously contested by the major European colonial powers, until the Dutch finally established supremacy in the seventeenth century. On the back of this lucrative trade, huge fortunes were amassed in Holland. But by the beginning of the twentieth century, the islands had become agricultural backwaters. Nevertheless, their strategic position as air strips and anchorages was not lost on the Japanese, soon to be their conquerors.

On 11 January 1942, Japanese troops landed on the Menado Peninsula in the north of the island of Celebes. Two weeks later, the Japanese Eastern Force took control of Kendari, along with its air base, which would allow the Japanese to control the skies between Java and Australia. On 9 February, Japanese troops captured Makassar.

To the east, on 6 January 1942, Japanese aircraft began bombarding the major Dutch military base on the island of Ambon. The invasion began on 30 January when 1,000 Japanese Special Naval Landing Force and army troops landed at Hitu-lama on the northern coast and on the Laitimor Peninsula on the southern coast. Batugong was captured the following day and the town of Passo fell by that afternoon, signalling the end of the main Dutch resistance. On 3 February, the main Australian resistance surrendered at Kudamati and, after a lull, the Japanese captured Aru, Babar, Kai, and Tanimbar islands by late July 1942.

Although the Celebes and Moluccas fell within the remit of SWPC and from SOE's point of view were under command of SOA, Force 136's Major Ambrose Trappes-Lomax played a significant role and his operations are shown within the context of overall SOA activities. The Japanese left the Moluccas in August 1944, unable to withstand Allied air power.

- 24 June 1942: Operation LION. Lieutenant Van Hees and two others left Darwin by *prahu 'Samoa'*, intending to land on Wotoe, sixty kilometres west of Malili. No news of them was heard thereafter.
- January 1945: Operation APRICOT. Sergeant Manopo and four others were inserted by submarine. Manopo was captured but remainder reached Australia.

JAVA, LOMBOK, CELEBES and MOLUCCA ISLANDS

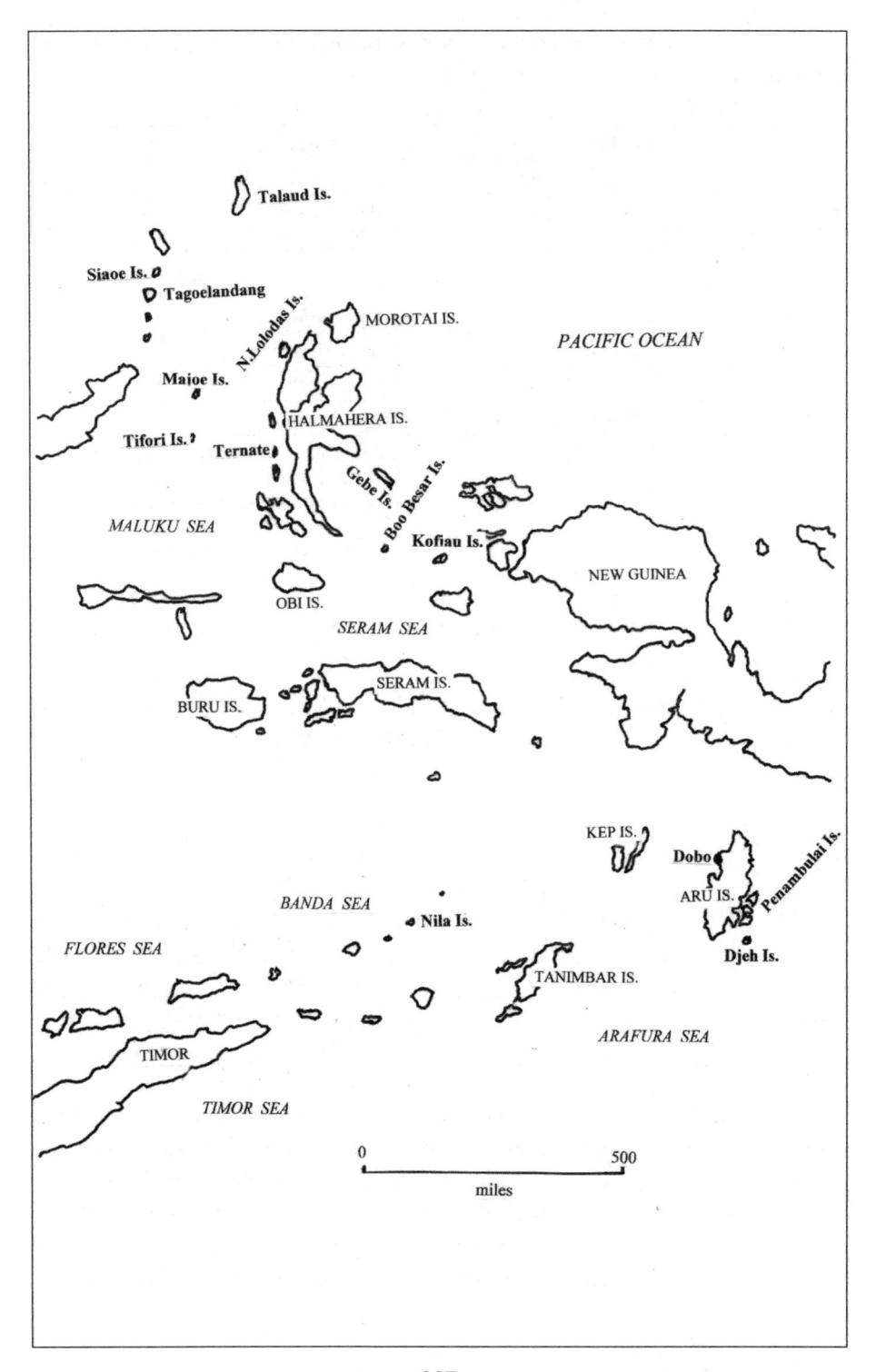

SRD Group B under Major Trappes-Lomax [British SOE] conducted a number of intelligence gathering operations in the Celebes:

Operation	1945	Target area
GIRAFFE 1	17 to 18 March	Tagoelandang Island
GIRAFFE 2	24 to 26 March	Majoe Island
GIRAFFE 3	27 to 29 March	Majoe and Tifore Islands
CRANE 1	14 to 15 May	Batoe Daka and Togian Island
SHRILL	19 May	Talaud Island
CRANE 2	24 May	Togian Island
MAGPIE 1	11 to 12 June	Majoe Island
MAGPIE 3	11 June to 13 June	Siaoe Island
RAVEN	12 to 20 June	West Celebes. This had been requested by 13th USAF to search for survivors of a missing Catalina. Three members of SRD were killed and no crew members recovered, prompting Trappes-Lomax to note 'very wasteful and not our job'.
MAGPIE 2	29 June to 3 July	Majoe and Tifore Islands

A second group of operations, run by the Commanding Officer of NICA [Netherlands Indies Civil Administration] but planned and commanded by SRD Group B, concerned the defence of the base at Morotai.

Operation	1945	Target area
OPOSSUM	8 to 11 April	Ternate and Hiri Islands
SWALLOW	7 April	North Loloda Island
SWIFT	14 to 18 May	North and South Loloda Islands
FINCH 1	7 to 8 July	Tifore and Halmahera to Obi Island
FINCH 2	4 to 10 July	Ternate Island
FINCH 3	14 July	Boo Besar and Gebe Islands
FINCH 4	21 July	Kofiau Island

Of these operations, OPOSSUM is particularly worthy of note. The aim of the operation was to extract Iskander Muhammad Jabir Syah, the Sultan of Ternate, and his family from under the noses of the Japanese. A small group of *Ternatans* had rowed the 200 kilometres to Morotai in February 1945 to warn the Allies that the Sultan's life was at risk as he had refused to kow-tow to the Japanese administration. The plan had been approved by no less than General MacArthur himself since the Sultan had been earmarked by the Dutch to play an important part in post-war plans for the DEI.

The eleven-strong party commanded by Captain Kroll of the NEFIS left Morotai by PT boat on 8 April and landed at Kg Saki on the north coast of Hiri that night. Kroll despatched a messenger to the Sultan who was in hiding at Boekee Bandera on Ternate Island. The next morning, Kroll taking seven men with him walked around the east coast of Hiri to Kg Togolobe where, after retrieving seven native 'traitors' from Dorari 'Isa, they met up with the remainder of their party, who had travelled from Saki by *prahu*.

On the evening of 9 April, a reply came back from the Sultan saying he would try to cross from Ternate that night but he was far from confident of the loyalty of those around him. Japanese spies were everywhere. After a six hour trek to the coastal village of Kulaba, he did in fact make the crossing by *prahu* the next day and arrived at Togolobe at 10.00 hrs. Major 'R.K.' Hardwick, a British citizen working as an IO for NEFIS at the time, wrote in *The Straits Times* two years later that 'the landing of the Sultan was one of the most dramatic scenes I have ever witnessed in these lands ... Hundreds poured down the slopes of the hills to the beach to greet their ruler. They squatted, with one raised knee, with hands pressed against their faces in an attitude of prayer and remained so until dismissed by a nod from the Sultan'.

After maintaining a strict watch during the night of 10/11 April, a native brought word that the Japanese were on their way from Ternate in pursuit of the Sultan. So OPOSSUM moved to Trafraka on the southern tip of Hiri, only to find Japanese troops already on the beach engaged with native fighters. A *prahu* was engaged by Bren gun fire and two of its crew killed. The nine Japanese who had landed at Trafraka were all killed as they tried to swim back to Ternate but at a cost of two SRD dead – Lieutenant Bosworth was shot in the head by a wounded Japanese soldier, and Private Higginbottom, shot by a native in mistake for the enemy, died of his wounds.

When the fighting had died down, OPOSSUM returned to Togolobe where with top cover provided by three Spitfires, it was collected by PT boat and safely arrived in Morotai by 16.45 hrs that afternoon.

ARU ISLANDS

- 7 July 1942: Operation WALNUT 1. Captain Sheldon and one civilian [Monsted] sailed by schooner to Dobo where they arrived on 7 July. Both returned to Australia in September.
- 15 February 1943: Operation WALNUT 2. Captain Sheldon, Lieutenant Feetun and Sergeant McCandlish inserted by Catalina on Penambulai Island. Possibly captured on 12 August 1943, their fate still remains unknown.
- 12 July 1943: Operation WALNUT 3. Monsted and nine others landed from the lugger *'Express'* on Djeh Island. Their last contact with HQ was on 25 July; their fate remains unknown.

SERAM

- 30 December 1942: Operation FLOUNDER. Lt Nygh Ran and seven other NEFIS operatives inserted into Seram. All were captured and executed at Ambon.
- 1944: Operation FIRTREE. Lieutenant Julius Tahya and nine others landed at Medio. Safely recovered.

HALMAHERA

- 1945 Operation OPOSSUM [see Trappes-Lomax p.329]

LOLODA ISLANDS

Off west coast of Halmahera
- 7 April 1945: Operation SWALLOW. Lieutenant Van Wyk [NICA], Lieutenant Bettington and four others inserted. Extracted on 9 April.
- 15 May 1945: Operation SWIFT. Lieutenant Brunnings, Lieutenant Bettington and four others inserted. Returned on 18 May.

MAJOE ISLAND

Between Halmahera and Celebes.
- September 1943: Operation PINE NEEDLE. Sergeant-Major de Bruyn and four others inserted by submarine. Evacuated by Catalina on 20 January 1945.

DAMAR ISLANDS

- 26 March 1944: Operation TURNIP 1. Sergeant Pejoh and one inserted by Catalina in Boerner Bay. Pejoh drowned.
- July 1944: Operation TURNIP 2. WO van Haren and eight others inserted by submarine. Operated around Nila Island. Evacuated on 21 August 1945.
- June 1945: Operation SALMON 1. Inserted by Catalina at Damar.

CHAPTER SIXTEEN

NEW GUINEA

DUTCH NEW GUINEA

On 12 April 1942, the Japanese arrived at Doré Baai in Manokwari, situated to the north of the Vogelkop area. There were only about 150 Dutch military stationed here under command of Captain J.B.H Willemsz Geeroms. Realising that they were outnumbered, he decided to sink their only ship by setting it on fire, thereby keeping it out of the hands of the enemy. After several bombing raids on Manakwari, the port fell and the Japanese established a strong military presence at this location. All the Europeans were taken off and interned on Ambon.

However, some of the Dutch infantry [KNIL], sixty-two Dutch soldiers and seventeen indigenous Papuans [Meja-Arfakkers], withdrew into the jungle, and for the remainder of the war they organised guerrilla warfare against the Japanese. On 1 April 1943 the Japanese attacked the headquarters of the guerrilla fighters and captured their commander Willemsz Geerom, who was later executed in Manokwari. Sergeant Mauritz Christiaan Kokkelink and Sergeant Major P.P. de Kock took over the leadership, and on 18 April 1944 the guerrilla group, by then consisting of only thirty-five men, attacked the Japanese base in Manokwari. Just about every one present was killed. When the American counter-attack started on 9 May 1944, Manokwari was destroyed and its Japanese defenders fled into the jungle, where most of them were killed off by the Papuans. Only fourteen of Willemsz Geeroms's sixty-two Dutch soldiers survived.

Apart from Willemsz Geeroms's group, the other groups involved in action were: the resistance group led by Dr J.V.de Bruyn in the Wissel lake area, the Australian CRAYFISH and OAKTREE parties, and a group led by the former Police Commissioner of Dutch New Guinea, Jan van Eechoud, who collected information for the Americans and whose work was known as Operation BULLDOZER. Not much is known about the history of these groups.

- 30 January 1943: Operation WHITING. Lieutenant Staverman and four NEI personnel inserted Hollandia area. All killed or captured except Corporal Topman.
- 29 September 1943: Operation TROUT 1. Lieutenant Tol and eight. Left from Mappipost on Begul River 29 September 1943; returned 30 October 1944.

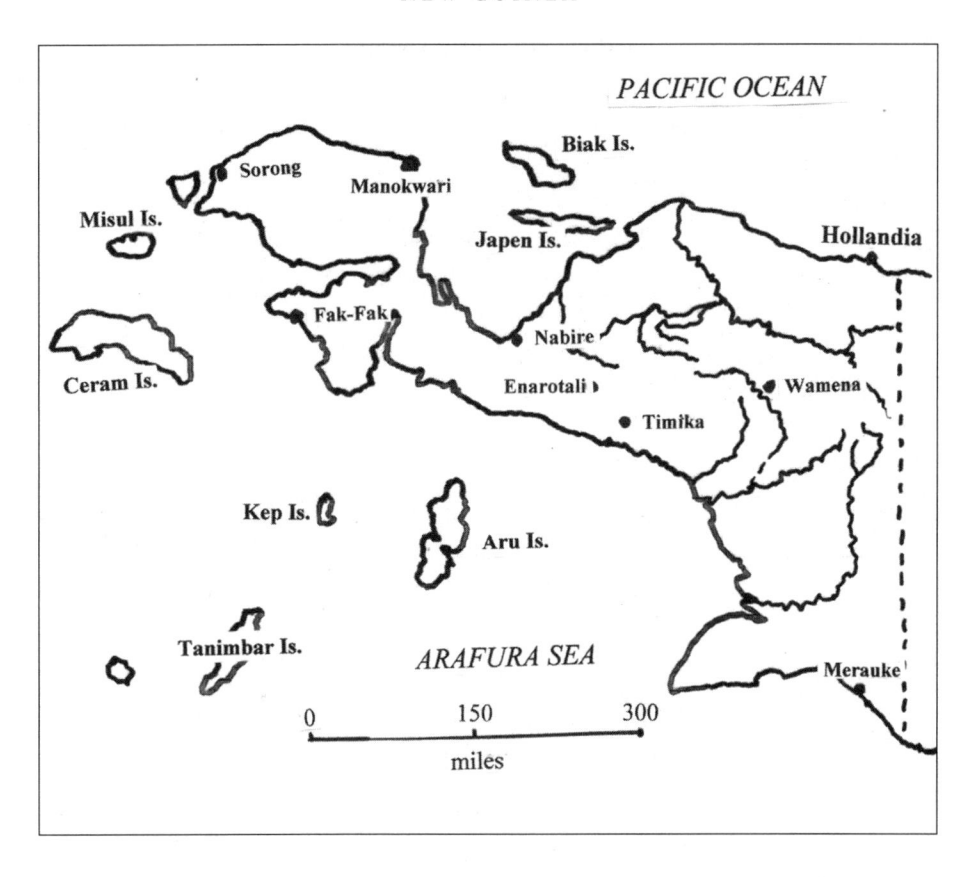

- 12 February 1943-26 May 1943: Operation TROUT 2. Lieutenant Tol and seven inserted on south west coast of New Guinea.
- 18 July-28 October 1943: Operation ASPARAGUS. Sergeant Swart and nine conducted fact-finding mission in Tanah Merah area.
- May 1944: Operation SHARK. Lieutenant Swart and seventeen inserted by Catalina at Camp Bernhard on Idenburg River. Operation CARROT, Lieutenant de Bruine and sixteen, joined Operation SHARK to collect intelligence on Wakde.
- August 1944: Operation RADISH. Lieutenant Razak and seven dropped on Kebar Plateau on Birds Head peninsular. Rescued wounded from Sergeant Kokkelink's guerrilla group.
- 20 June 1944: Operation MENZIES. Lieutenant Prentice and five others landed on Batanta Island where they spent the next 100 days. All recovered in good health.
- 13 August 1944: Operation PERCH. Captain Lees and three others inserted near Sawis. All extracted on 25 September.

BRITISH NEW GUINEA

ISLD Operations

Operations	Date	Target area
COCKROACH	October-November 1942	Markham Valley
BEETLE	September-November 1942	Waria River
LADYBIRD	October-November 1942	Madang

SRD Operations

Operations	Date	Target area
GOLD	April 1945	Wewak
COPPER	April 1945	Muschu Island
VOKEO	April-May 1945	Vokeo

CHAPTER SEVENTEEN

TIMOR

POLITICAL BACKGROUND

The Portuguese had arrived in Timor in 1515, the Dutch East India Company a hundred years later. Over the next centuries, the two European states jostled for ownership and finally laid claims to the island which were ratified in the Treaty of Lisbon in 1859 with the agreement of a border. This was followed by a formal division of the island territory in 1913.

Relations between the colonial powers and the islanders proved vexed. An attempt by the Portuguese to extract greater wealth from East Timor resulted in a rebellion in 1912 which was quashed after Portugal brought in troops from its colonies in Mozambique and Macau, resulting in the deaths of 3,000 East Timorese. The Dutch, who had changed their policy of non-interference to one of proactively imposing *rust en orde* [peace and order] on the indigenous tribes in the early 1900s[196], attracted some opprobrium when they fell out with Raja Bil Nope of Amanuban, an altercation which ended with the heroic death of the Raja and his wives as he ordered his palace at Niki Niki to be set ablaze.

The island of Timor as a whole is 290 miles long and up to 62 miles wide. Mountains, highly dissected and extremely rugged, occupy most of the interior and rise to 9,000 feet. The north eastern part of the island is dominated by them but much of the south west is open country, which in 1941 could be easily traversed on foot or on Timorese ponies, the small sturdy horses that were the basic form of island transport.

The area of Dutch Timor, comprising the south western portion of the island, was some 5,500 square miles. Koepang, the capital and principal port, about 670 miles from Java, looked out on Koepang Bay where there were sea plane and shipping anchorages. The main airfield was six miles south east of the town at Penfui. The population in Dutch Timor was around 400,000 Timorese and 4,000 to 5,000 Dutch, Chinese and Arabs.

The eastern part of the island, and a small enclave called Ocussi on the north west coast, were under Portuguese control. This colony had an area of some 7,700 square miles and a population of about 300 Portuguese, 500,000 Timorese, 2,000 Chinese and a few Japanese and Arabs. Its capital, Dili,

---

196 This policy was applied to all the territories of the DEI.

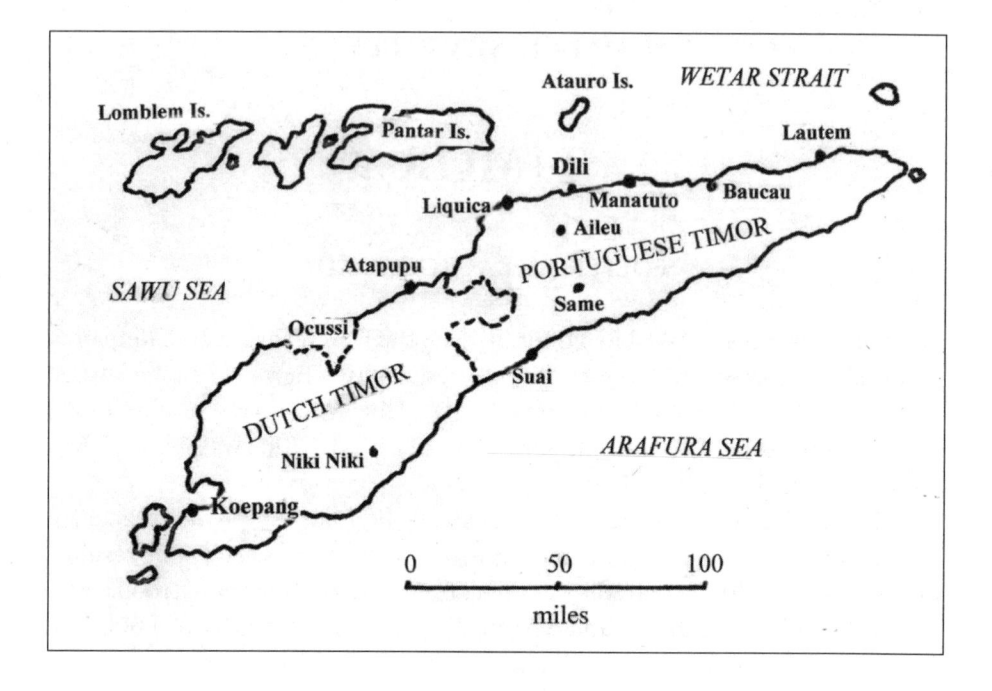

situated on the north coast of the island had an airfield a mile to the west of the town, and shipping and sea plane anchorages. The colony was administered by a Governor and divided into provinces each with its own administrator, and each province subsequently divided into *'postos'* under junior officials.

ISD/SRD IN EAST TIMOR [PORTUGUESE]

When the Pacific War broke out, an expedition of Australian and Dutch troops was on its way to Timor to provide assistance in the event of a Japanese attack. It landed at Dili, the capital of Portuguese Timor, on 12 December 1941 but lost contact with HQ until 19 April 1942, some two months after the island had been taken by the Japanese on 23 February 1942. SPARROW force reported that it was holding out in the mountains of Bobonaro in Fronteira Province. ISD sent LIZARD in early 1942 to make contact. SPARROW later became LANCER.

By the time all surviving Allied troops had been taken off the island in February 1943, the Australians had caused some 2,000 Japanese casualties at a cost of forty of their own side killed[197]. Importantly, they had proved that it was

---

[197] The Australians lost 40 men, Portugal 75 and Japan 1,500. By contrast, estimates of casualties among the local population indicate that between 45,000 and 70,000 East Timorese were killed during this period, 10-15% of the pre-war population, estimated at 450,000.

possible to operate behind enemy lines in a rugged environment where concealment was possible. However, equally importantly, they had already demonstrated that without the support of a large section of the native population, it was impossible to maintain security and forage for supplies. Due to Japanese intimidation and a degree of anti-colonialism, most of the native Timorese population was either no longer friendly or was actively hostile towards them. Curiously an SOE report on Australian operations as of November 1943 bemoans the fact that, despite 'the natives being good guerrilla material', '...such activity is not permitted by GHQ [SWPA], ostensibly because they do not consider that the island could contribute to the general strategic plan, but in reality because they are frightened of having to supply the guerrillas and they wish to demonstrate to the world that only under the American auspices will native populations rise and fight for democracy'.

ISD/SRD OPERATIONS

- 17 July 1942: Operation LIZARD 1, commanded by Captain Ian Wylie with Captain Dougie Broadhurst as his 2 i/c, both former Malayan Police Force officers, established a base on the east end of the island with help from the Portuguese administrator, Senhor Pires. The party left by Catalina on 17 August with some of the wounded from SPARROW in order to re-equip in Darwin before returning to the island. A quick turn-around was achieved and LIZARD 2 landed by motor launch at Beasso on 2 September. Wylie, who was seriously ill with malaria, handed over command to Broadhurst and was evacuated by sea on 23 October. Three weeks later the four-man LIZARD 3 team arrived to reinforce Broadhurst. Due to the increasingly dangerous security environment and deteriorating health conditions, all LIZARD and LANCER personnel were recovered by US submarine *Gudgeon* on 10 February 1943. On 3 August 1943, a further group, PORTOLIZARD, consisting of eighty-seven Portuguese, Timorese and Chinese evacuees including women and children, were picked up by RAN HDMLs [Harbour Defence Motor Launch] at the mouth of the Dilor River.
- 2 July 1943: The Operation LAGARTO party of Portuguese Lieutenant Pires and three others landed by submarine at the mouth of the Luca River on the night of 1/2 July. Its primary mission was to establish a secret intelligence network covering the eastern part of the island and report on all enemy activities. Joined on 3 August by Sergeant Ellwood, an experienced signaller from LANCER, the party made heavy weather of moving into position due to the presence of pro-Japanese natives and

aggressive patrolling by the Japanese themselves. Ellwood was captured on 29 September 1943 and his W/T set 'turned' by the Japanese, who continued to communicate as LAGARTO with Darwin right up until VJ Day

- 29 January 1944: Operation COBRA commanded by Captain Cashman landed at Dara Bei River on the south coast of Portuguese Timor. Met by a native guide, it was led into an ambush where all five men were captured. The Japanese maintained the pretence of COBRA being 'free' until 12 August 1945, although in fact SRD realised that it was compromised on 28 February 1944. Two members of the party, Cashman and Sancho da Silva, survived the war as POWs.
- 21 August 1944: Operation ADDER consisting of Captain Grimson, Sergeant Gregg and three others landed at Cape Ile Hoi. All were captured within four hours of landing. Later the Japanese announced that Grimson and Gregg had been killed in action. It is a reasonable deduction that ADDER had been compromised by references to its arrival in signals traffic to LAGARTO, the W/T station controlled by the Japanese.

In June 1945, another series of intelligence gathering operations was launched in Portuguese East Timor and the Lesser Sundas under the code name SUN FISH.

- 26 April 1945: Operation SUNCHARLIE: Sergeant Marshall and eight others carried out recce in Roti Island area. Successfully extracted.
- 17 May 1945: Captain A.F. Wilkins and three others were all killed when their aircraft went missing on a recce of their Flores Island drop zone for Operation SUNBAKER.
- 27 June 1945: Operation SUNABLE [Captain D.M. Williams and three sergeants] was dropped in the Cape Batoemerah area in the Ocussi Province of Portuguese East Timor to set up OPs to observe coastal and road traffic. Williams was killed in a gun battle with Japanese troops on 5 July, and the remainder captured.
- June 1945: Operation STARLING/SUNDOG: Landing in East Timor abandoned.
- 29 June 1945: Operation BLACKBIRD/SUNLAG [Captain Stevenson, Sergeant Dawson and Celestino dos Anjos] dropped into the Laleia River area south east of Manatuto on East Timor to relieve Ellwood [LAGARTO] and to establish the strength and disposition of Japanese forces. Dropped two days earlier than the time given to LAGARTO, Stevenson was able to observe the Japanese reception committee on the DZ with a white man who he identified as Ellwood. After signalling his

concerns to Australia, with only eight days rations, Stevenson quickly realised that they were being hunted by the Japanese, and after a tense and punishing period on the run, SUNLAG was finally extracted on 4/5 August by sea. Sergeant Lawson later died of an illness contracted on the island. In all probability SUNLAG was compromised on account of its communications with LAGARTO.

- 2 July 1945: Operation PIGEON/SUNCOB [Captain W.P. Wynne and Corporal Lawrence] was dropped by parachute into the Seical River area to check out the COBRA Mission. Separated after jumping from 1,000 feet in a 30 mph wind, both were independently captured. As they had done with LAGARTO and COBRA, the Japanese subsequently controlled SUNCOB communications with SRD.

LIEUTENANT COLONEL IAN WYLIE, OBE, MBE

Ian Wylie

Ian Wylie was born in Calcutta in 1910 and educated at Radley and then Bedford College. He became an Assistant Superintendant in the Malayan Police Service, mastering the Malay language and studying Chinese for a year in Hong Kong in 1931. Commissioned as a temporary Captain in August 1942, he attended the guerrilla warfare course at Foster, Victoria, in May and June and by the beginning of July was inserted into Timor on Operation LIZARD 1.

When the Pacific War broke out, the British Government made an agreement with Portugal whereby the Government of Portuguese Timor was to invite Australian assistance if a Japanese attack seemed imminent, or would acquiesce in the dispatch of such assistance if there were not sufficient time to invite it. However, when an expedition comprising Australian and Dutch troops landed at Koepang and then Dili in December 1941, the Portuguese had a change of mind and requested the withdrawal of all Allied troops, once their own force of 700 Portuguese troops had arrived to defend the island. A Japanese landing on 20 February 1942 put paid to this idea and so the combined units of Australians and Dutch held out in the mountains of Bobonaro in the Fronteira Province. Without air cover and with perilous lines of communication, this force was tenuously tasked with locating possible aerodrome sites on the south coast, harassing and sabotage, collecting intelligence, preparing for counter-offensive operations, containing the enemy, and reoccupying Dili if strength permitted, unlikely given that enemy strength was about 6,000, while the Australians had less than 600.

Early in 1942, ISD made preparations to introduce an SO party into Portuguese Timor with a view to keeping the Portuguese and natives in active sympathy with the Allies, or at least, in non-co-operation with the Japanese and to select OPs for reporting enemy shipping through the Wetar Strait. Commanded by Wylie, with fellow Malaya Police Service officer Captain Broadhurst as his 2 i/c, Operation LIZARD I travelled to Timor by the launch *Kuru* and with 3,000 lbs of stores landed at Suai on 17 July. After landing, the party proceeded to SPARROW HQ at Mape where it settled in with Force HQ pending the arrival of Lieutenant Greaves, a former Australian stockman who knew the area and its personalities well. Contact was made with Senor Antonio de Souza Santos, Administrator of Fronteira Province, and Dr Carlos Brandau, the most influential of the '*deportados*', and opportunity was taken of visiting Bobonaro, the provincial capital and other places in the vicinity.

In early August, a Japanese warship appeared off the south coast of Timor near Beco, together with two small transports, and it appeared that an attempt was to be made to dislodge SPARROW Force from its mountain position by a rear attack, and to cut off its L of C to Australia. Consequently, it was decided to abandon Force HQ at Mape, and LIZARD, lacking local knowledge, was compelled to follow suit. The party moved away by a circuitous route from Mape through Bobonaro, Atsabe, Hatu Builico, Maubisse to Same, about 20 miles east of Mape.

On 16 August 1942, a Catalina landed at Betano to evacuate SPARROW wounded. After consultation with SPARROW commander, Wylie decided to take the opportunity of evacuation offered by the Catalina and to cross to Darwin to refit the party prior to returning to Timor.

Operation LIZARD 2 under command of Wylie and comprised of the same team, this time including Greaves, was inserted by Motor Launch on 2 September, and after setting up a temporary HQ at Loi Uno, the Mission worked towards the central ranges, burying its stores at various points, and made contact with the Chef de Poste at Ossu. LIZARD 2 then contacted Senhor Pires, Administrator of the province, whose HQ was at Baucau. They found him to be staunchly pro-Allied. With his advice and assistance, and that of loyal native telephone attendants at several north coast '*Postos*', and by secret runners, effective communications were set up in Dili.

About a week after LIZARD 2 landed, the Japanese made a patrol down the Baucau road and remained for some days in the Viqueque district, making enquiries as to the whereabouts of the party. On 20 September, the Japanese left the district, announcing that they would be back within a fortnight. LIZARD 2 was then able to arrange through Senhor Pires for the release of a Chinese infantry captain and five Chinese soldiers who had been interned in

Macao and later sent to Timor. The party also aided Pilot Officer Wadey, an Australian airman, who had been shot down in a raid and was lying wounded in Ossu goal. He was carried across country into the SPARROW area, and eventually evacuated to Australia. The Chinese together with a sick Portuguese volunteer saboteur were also evacuated. Through LIZARD 2's secret information services, ISD learned that the Japanese were dominating the Dili Administration, and that it was merely a matter of time before Portuguese authority entirely disintegrated.

GHQ concurred and the arms were run into Timor at the emergency point of Aliambata on the night of 13 October 1942. The usual landing place at Beasso was at that time unsafe as the Japanese had returned down the Baucau road.

Native chief Don Paulo furnished transport service from the beach for the rifles and from that time was of inestimable assistance to the party. Under LIZARD 2's guidance and control, a schedule of training for Paulo's followers was started. Native OPs were established, resulting in information concerning enemy movements along the north coast between Manatuto and Lautem being passed back. A chain consisting of Paulo's family connections was a valuable factor in gaining intelligence of the enemy's intention to occupy all the north and south coast anchorages and of his activities generally.

On 1 October, three Portuguese officials, four NCOs and twenty soldiers were massacred at Aileu, twenty-five miles from Dili, by natives of Dutch Timor, as part of an enemy scheme to terrorise the Portuguese into consenting to be concentrated at two 'protective' points, Liquica and Mubara, small towns to the west of Dili. LIZARD 2 discovered that the Governor planned to evacuate his nationals to Mozambique and that he proposed to submit the plan to Lisbon via Japanese radio. ISD reported this action to GHQ and to SOE, London. Nothing further was heard of the Mozambique scheme and soon afterwards Senhor Pires learned that the Governor wished to contact Lisbon through LIZARD 2 and Australia. Later in the month, he did this on two occasions, the cipher telegrams being passed on to GHQ for transmission.

By the middle of October 1942, except in Sao Domingos, Portuguese authority in Timor had almost ceased to exist. Senhor Pires made an urgent request to LIZARD 2 for 100 Winchester .44s to replace weapons which had been taken from the Portuguese by the Japanese. The administration also asked that the party hold a stock of 100 rifles for emergency use by the Portuguese against roving bands of hostile Dutch Timor natives, some of whom had been imported from the neighbouring islands of Alor and Kisar.

On 19 October 1942, Wylie was seriously ill with malaria and four days later was evacuated by HMAS *Vigilant* and control of the party passed to Captain

Broadhurst. Reinforced in November by LIZARD 3, the ISD team finally left Timor by US submarine in February 1943.

Wylie went on to serve in various staff jobs in Australia until May 1945, when he was posted to Ceylon and joined the Malaya Country Section. When Martin was killed, Wylie took over Operation CARPENTER and after the surrender became Group Liaison Officer to the 5th Regiment AJA in Perak.

20 December 1945: Recommendation for OBE

Operation CARPENTER under the leadership of Major Martin has landed and established itself on the east coast of Johore in October 1944 but owing to the considerable Japanese activity in that area and to the fact that Major Martin was killed on a DZ, the operation was unable to expand to the centre of Johore. Lieutenant Colonel Wylie was chosen to take over command and dropped into a reception near Kulaj on 23 June 1945. He realised the vital importance of arming and organising the 4th Regiment of the AJA and placing them astride the north and south communications through Johore. The Japanese, however, almost immediately became aware of his presence and for the next month and a half Lieutenant Colonel Wylie and his party were continually harassed, so much so, that on occasions they were driven from the DZ when about to receive a drop, and aircraft bringing vital stores and reinforcements personnel were turned back. Lieutenant Colonel Wylie, however, managed to keep his men together and maintain contact with base under the most trying conditions. At the time of the surrender he had approximately 500 guerrillas at his disposal and was in a position to cut the road and railway north of Johore Bahru which would have been vital to the Japanese in repelling the British invasion.

After the surrender Lieutenant Colonel Wylie was posted to Perak where he took over the duties of Group Liaison officer to the 5th Regiment of AJA although he had no previous experience of this regiment. He quickly established excellent relationships with the Chinese leaders during the difficult period between the surrender and the disbandment, which was carried out with complete success.

Awarded

CHAPTER EIGHTEEN

EPILOGUE

Peter Goss, who served as a 20-year-old 'tearaway' in a Force 136 unit in Burma, volunteered in later life, when he addressed the members of the Special Forces Club, that his knowledge and understanding of the range of Force 136 operations and strategic implications was limited. His contacts with senior commanders was restricted to an uncomfortable interview with Gavin Stewart, the Commander Group A, whose Jeep he had unwisely borrowed in order to fetch additional supplies of drink to fuel a rather good party at the FANY Mess in Calcutta.

Bearing in mind his typical modesty as symbolic of his generation, his conclusions about the role and effectiveness of SOE in the Far East are both perspicacious and accurate.

> Force 136 initially found itself saddled with a European-oriented charter [subversive political activity, sabotage and subversive propaganda], which did not respond to the operational requirements of the Far East Theatre for clandestine tasks. These emerged as intelligence collection and the raising and training of guerrilla forces. There was a pragmatic adaptation to these requirements over a period of time. At all times Force 136 functioned within a military chain of command.
>
> There were serious doubts in the minds of British military leaders [in the Far East] as to the cost-effectiveness of Special Force operations – expensive in quality manpower and special equipment, a problem posed in parallel by assessing the place and value of Wingate's operations vis-a-vis the strategic priorities of the Burma Campaign.
>
> The very considerable problems of distances, terrain and climate rendered the mounting and support of operations extremely complex and hazardous. Moreover, many operations took place in an environment in which the sympathies of the local population could not be relied upon [an environment which Japanese counter-intelligence was also able to exploit].
>
> Only in Burma was the effectiveness of Force 136 operations really successful [as the end game played out]. There is no doubt that they made a positive contribution to Fourteenth Army's liberation of the

country, as recognised by General Slim. The guerrilla infrastructure established in Malaya was never put to the test, but there is every reason to believe that it would have provided significant support to Operation ZIPPER and subsequent operations to liberate Malaya [A similar proposition can be advanced in the case of the invasion of Thailand].

The official *Australian History of the War against Japan* concludes that by the end of the war AIB had justified its existence. Its comments, it could be argued, apply equally to Force 136:

> 'Some of the difficulties encountered by AIB stemmed from the fact that it had to coordinate four separate national groups with differing aims and allegiances; some, undoubtedly, from the fact that the kind of organisation it controlled tends to attract men who are not only adventurous but imaginative, individualistic and temperamental to an unusual degree. Such men also tend to be enthusiasts, who see their own chosen activity, whether it be propaganda, sabotage, or irregular warfare, as exerting a far greater effect on the progress of the war than it actually did.
>
> After enduring a series of crises, the AIB belatedly acquired a form of control that could not probably have been bettered, at least in principle: the grouping of headquarters, the channelling of proposals through the senior Operational intelligence officer to the senior operations officer, and tactical control by the field commander of any operations in his area.
>
> The operations of the AIB as a whole undoubtedly justified the expenditure of blood and effort, but that is not to say that each of its components justified itself or that every type of project it undertook was wise. Practically all the effective work done by AIB seems to have been achieved by two sorts of parties: intelligence groups stationed in areas where they could gather information of direct interest to the commanders, and guerrilla groups operating under the only conditions which justify the initiation of guerrilla warfare, namely, that it be among a friendly population and in rugged or otherwise difficult country. A glowing example of the first type of activity was provided by the coast watchers; the second was seen at its best in Bougainville, New Britain and in the mainland of Australian New Guinea, in the Philippines, and in the mountains of Borneo.'

ANNEX A

NIXON'S MOST SECRET MEMO OF JANUARY 1941 TO COLONEL GEORGE TAYLOR IN LONDON RE HIS DISCUSSIONS WITH GENERAL DEWING IN INDIA [Extract].

A. Dewing agrees that:
1. There is obvious scope for SO2 activities in Far East.
2. He is anxious that as soon as possible we commence laying foundations of organisation.
3. We must proceed with extreme caution in view of delicate political situation in various countries concerned.
4. I must concentrate first on building up my cover.
5. But at the same time I must not delay formulating plans concerning both activities and personnel.
6. Soon after arrival I am to see Naval CinC who is stationed Singapore.

B. It is understood we shall not proceed with any type of SO2 activity in any of the various countries without first obtaining agreement in principle of CinC and/or CinC Far East.

C. I outline possible activities as follows:
   a. Preparations in neutral countries to delay advance of enemy.
   b. Attacks upon supplies bound for enemy with special reference to para-naval activity.
   c. Assistance to China working from outside China.
   d. Propaganda.

D. In order of importance Dewing will want our organisation to aim at being ready to attack following objectives at appropriate times.
   a. Thailand and especially West Thailand. Firstly aerodromes including planes, fuel and bomb dumps; secondly railway running south Malaya and communications generally; thirdly para-naval activity of toughest variety against Japanese fishing boats on West Thailand coast between Burma and Malaya, this to supplement existing Police Patrol between Rangoon and South Burma boundary.
   b. Dutch East Indies. As we cannot rely upon NEI Government resisting attack or alternatively being able to prevent country being overrun in event of attack we need to lay foundations of organisation to deal with situation after successful invasion, with special attention to aerodromes.

ANNEX A

c. French Indo-China. Due to extreme complexity of present political situation this for further discussion at Singapore when political situation may be entirely different.

d. China. This to be discussed at Singapore with our other representative. Our activities will probably have to be based on Shanghai and possibly Hong Kong also. They will be quite independent of activities already underway from Chungking to supply materials and educate Chinese in their use.

e. Malaya. Army is handling operations to delay enemy advance but our part will be to form organisation to deal with situation if and after territory occupied by enemy.

f. Oil. Some preparations throughout Far East have been made and are being improved to deny oil to invaders, firstly by a slow denial scheme based on 48 hours warning which Dewing estimates would put refineries out of operation for possibly six months and secondly a quick denial scheme which he estimates might stop supplies for about two months. Our part will be to deal with the situation if these schemes fail or after invader has made repairs but I shall discuss this again at Singapore. Possibly additional plans should be made for attacks on wells as distinct from refineries and pipe lines.

g. Philippines. This is for discussion in Singapore

h. Propaganda. Firstly dissemination of true pro-British news through underground channels. Dewing says that MOI Far East representative Scott has already done a certain amount but that he is absent and will not be back in Singapore for three months. He cannot possibly have done much. Secondly unclean propaganda. To be effective propaganda must obviously be handled by an expert and I asked Dewing whether he thought there was scope for such a person if we could find one. He answered yes providing the man really is expert. Therefore if you have a man available I suggest you send him to contact me in Singapore. But I cannot overemphasise the extreme care in choosing the man from point of view first of not compromising my cover and second his ability. Recommend that as long as we remain at peace with Japan you do not, repeat not, send any personnel from Mideast because in my opinion our activities and possibly our personnel also are known to the enemy.

ANNEX B

NATURAL RESOURCES IN JAPANESE OCCUPIED AREAS 1937-1945

Occupied Chinese Mainland
From 1937, during the Japanese military occupation of territories in China, they controlled mineral deposits of tungsten, tin and manganese. In Chekiang, coal reserves were 101 million tonnes and extraction came to 250,000 tonnes in 1934.

South China area
- Fukien: coal reserves of 500 million tonnes in 1934.
- Kwangtung [Canton]: 421 million tonnes of coal reserves, and production of 338,000 tonnes in 1934. Iron reserves in Hainan, with 400 million tonnes of iron of high grade in 1934.
- Kwangsi: coal reserves of 300 million tonnes, and production of 30,000 tonnes in 1940. There were some sources of tungsten, manganese [production of 1,246 tonnes in 1940] and tin production of 417,000 tonnes.
- Hunan: coal reserves of 1,793 million tonnes and extraction of 1,050,000 tonnes in 1940. Some deposits of tungsten, mercury, antimony [Hsikwangshan mine], manganese and gold.
- Kweichow: coal reserves of 1,549 million tonnes, and extraction of 360,750 tonnes in 1940. Deposits of mercury, copper, antimony, and sulphur.

ANNEX B

South East Asia

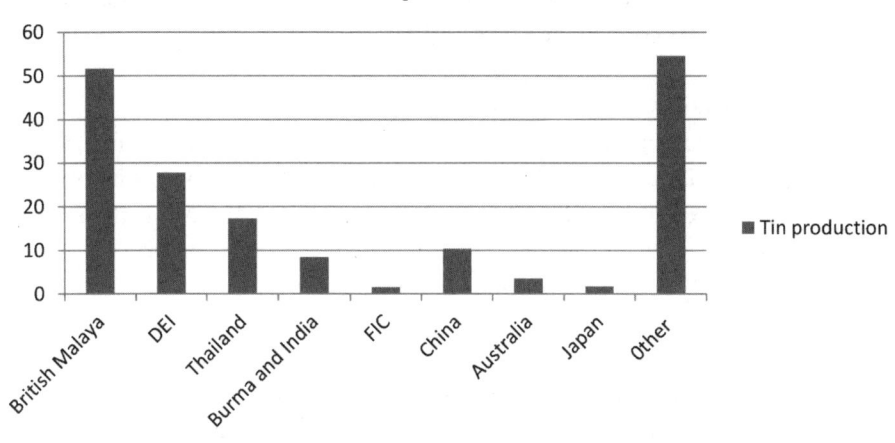

World Tin production 1939

[Bar chart showing tin production by region: British Malaya ~52, DEI ~28, Thailand ~17, Burma and India ~8, FIC ~1, China ~10, Australia ~3, Japan ~1, Other ~54]

Note: World Smelter Production 1935-39: British Malaya 45.2%, DEI 6.9%, UK 20%, Netherlands 12.2%, Rest of World 15.7%

Burma
- In the Irrawaddy river zone, there were the Yenangyaung and Chauk oil fields, 300 miles north of Rangoon. The Burmah Oil Company produced 6.56 million barrels in 1936 with exports to the US of $35 million in 1940.
- Amber and jade [nefrite stone], lapis lazuli, lazurite, rubies, sapphires, etc. in Shan Mesete.
- There was a major mine in Bawdwin, producing silver, lead, zinc, nickel and copper. This deposit produced 72,000 tonnes of ore in 1933, with mineral content twenty per cent of lead and zinc.
- In Mergui and Tavoy [Tenasserin area] mines produced tungsten and tin from 1910.
- Seventy five per cent of world teak.

Malaya
- Tin extraction was mainly in the hands of the Chinese; production in 1939 was 55,950 tonnes or nearly twenty-eight per cent of world production.
- There were tin smelters in Singapore and Penang for processing local extractions, and those of Thailand, Burma and Indo-China.

- The Kelantan, Trengganu and Johore iron mineral extractions represented 1,944,701 tonnes in 1939.
- Rubber production on Malayan plantations equated to over forty-one per cent of world production. Johore on its own exported $86.3 million in 1937 [2007 equivalent $1.28 billion].

Dutch East Indies
- The oil fields in the Palembang [Sumatra], Djambi, Medan and Borneo fields in Balikpapan and Tarakan produced 7,938,000 tonnes in 1940.
- Coal was extracted in Sumatra and Borneo, with 1,456,647 tonnes mined in 1940.
- Additionally there were sulphur and manganese mines in Java, and nickel in Celebes.
- Tin came from Banka, Bintang Island and the Billington Islands. DEI produced seventeen and a half per cent of world production.
- Rubber plantations accounted for thirty-three per cent of world production.
- Sugar was Java's principal export followed by rubber and petroleum.
- Other exports included timber including kapok and ebony, tea, tobacco, tapioca, spices[198], coffee, palm oil, copra, rattans, shells and fibres.

British Borneo
- In 1937, Brunei exports totalled $5.5 million and Sarawak's $32.7 million, mainly oil and associated products.

Philippines
- Gold extraction in 1941 represented 1,109,000 troy oz [34,500 kg], five times more than in 1931, and silver associated with gold ore at the same level. These extractions were mostly from the Benget district in Baguio Province, Luzon.
- Iron deposits were rapidly developed and during 1941. 1,191,641 tonnes was exported to Japan. Iron sources were located in North Camarines [Luzon], Samar Island and Surigao in Mindanao island. In the last of these, the iron reserves were estimated as 500 million tonnes.
- Chromium was not discovered until 1935. By 1939 the Philippines produced 164,000 tonnes and had fifth place, or eleven per cent of world production. Sources were in Zambales [Luzon] with its extraction of 10 million tonnes of chrome oxide with a fifty per cent of chrome content.

---

198 Nutmeg, cloves, mace, cassia fistula, sesame seeds.

ANNEX B

- Manganese was abundant but of medium quality, and was sent to the USA from 1935; local production was 58,038 tonnes in 1940.
- There were also copper, lead, zinc and coal deposits.

But whatever the Far East prizes were, Japan was doomed from the very beginning:

Table 79 Annual Allied and Axis Coal Production 1939-45* (m. metric tons)

DATE	USA	USSR	UK	CANADA	TOTAL	GERMANY	ITALY	HUNGARY	RUMANIA	JAPAN	TOTAL
1939	—	—	231.3	13.3	244.6	332.8	—	—	—	—	332.8
1940	—	—	224.3	14.9	239.2	364.8	4.4	1.2	0.3	—	370.7
1941	—	151.4	206.3	15.3	373.0	402.8	4.4	1.3	0.2	—	408.8
1942	528.5	75.5	204.9	15.9	824.8	407.8	4.8	1.3	0.3	61.3	475.4
1943	535.3	93.1	198.9	14.7	842.0	429.0	3.3	1.4	0.3	60.5	494.5
1944	562.0	121.5	192.7	14.2	890.4	432.8	—	1.4	0.2	51.7	486.2
1945	523.9	149.3	182.8	13.6	869.6	50.3	—	?	?	11.0	61.5
TOTAL	2,149.7	590.8	1,441.2	101.9	4,283.6	2,420.3	16.9	6.6	1.6	184.5	2,629.9

Table 80 Annual Allied and Axis Iron Ore Production 1939-45 (m. metric tons)

DATE	USA	USSR	UK	CANADA	TOTAL	GERMANY	ITALY	HUNGARY	RUMANIA	JAPAN	TOTAL
1939	—	—	14.5	0.1	14.6	18.5	—	—	—	—	18.5
1940	—	—	17.7	0.4	18.1	29.5	1.2	1.9	2.1	—	34.7
1941	—	24.7	19.0	0.5	44.2	53.3	1.3	2.4	2.4	—	59.4
1942	107.6	9.7	19.9	0.5	137.7	50.6	1.1	2.5	3.0	7.4	64.6
1943	103.1	9.3	18.5	0.6	131.5	56.2	0.8	2.6	3.3	6.7	69.6
1944	96.0	11.7	15.5	0.5	123.7	32.6	—	4.7	?	6.0	43.3
1945	90.2	15.9	14.2	1.0	121.3	?	—	?	?	0.9	?
TOTAL	396.9	71.3	119.3	3.6	591.1	240.7	4.4	14.1	10.8	21.0	291.0

Table 81 Annual Allied and Axis Crude Oil Production 1939-45 (m. metric tons)

DATE	USA	USSR	UK	CANADA	TOTAL	GERMANY†	Germany synthetic oil only	ITALY	HUNGARY	RUMANIA	JAPAN	TOTAL
1939	—	—	?	1.0	?	3.1	2.2	—	—	—	—	3.1
1940	—	—	11.9	1.1	13.0	4.8	3.2	0.01	0.3	5.0	—	10.1
1941	—	33.0	13.9	1.3	48.2	5.7	3.9	0.12	0.4	5.5	—	11.7
1942	183.9	22.0	11.2	1.3	218.4	6.6	4.6	0.01	0.7	5.7	1.8	14.8
1943	199.6	18.0	15.8	1.3	234.7	7.6	5.6	0.01	0.8	5.3	2.3	16.0
1944	222.5	18.2	21.4	1.3	263.4	5.6	3.9	—	1.0	3.5	1.0	11.1
1945	227.2	19.4	16.6	1.1	264.3	?‡	?‡	—	?	?	0.1	?
TOTAL	833.2	110.6	90.8	8.4	1,043.0	33.4	23.4	0.17	3.2	25.0	5.2	67.0

Source: John Ellis's *World War II Data Book*

ANNEX C

TROPICAL DISEASES TO WHICH SOE PERSONNEL WERE EXPOSED

Disease/affliction	Diagnosis/Symptoms	Cause	Treatment [1941-45]
Tertiary benign malaria	Headaches, muscular pain, fever, chills and sweating	Mosquito borne disease	Quinine or atabrine
Cerebral malaria	Convulsions followed by periods of unconsciousness	Mosquito borne	Quinine or atabrine
Malignant tertian malaria		Mosquito borne	Quinine or atabrine
Beriberi	Lethargy and fatigue	Lack of vitamin B1	Improved diet
Jungle ulcers, also known as *Naga* sores	Painful open sores that won't heal	Scratches and grazes from undergrowth/obstacles or insect bites	M&B 760 powder
Blackwater fever	Chills, with rigor, high fever, jaundice, vomiting, progressive anaemia, and dark red or black urine, leading to death in the majority of cases	A serious complication of malaria in which red blood cells burst in the bloodstream, frequently leading to kidney failure	Quinine or atabrine
Pneumonia	Cough, fever, sweats, shivers, breathlessness. A sharp pain in the chest may develop if the infection involves the pleura	Cold and wet Complication of other diseases	
Snakebite	Various	Poisonous snake	
Leptospirosis	Flu-like symptoms, possibly jaundice and diarrhoea	Ingestion of water infected by animal urine	Penicillin
Liver fluke	Nausea, vomiting, fever, fatigue, hives	Parasite ingested by eating uncooked fish	
Tick typhus	Rashes, headaches and fever	Ticks	
Murine typhus	Headaches, fever, chills, nausea	Fleas from rats	

ANNEX C

Heat stroke	Dizziness/irrational behaviour	Dehydration	Rehydration
Dental deterioration	Gum disease, abscesses, rotting teeth	Lack of dental hygiene/gum disorders	
Leech bites	Can lead to blood poisoning, secondary infections	Leeches [Tiger leech the largest]	
Exposure	Dizziness/irrational behaviour	Cold and wet climatic conditions causing drop in internal body temperature	
Typhoid	Muscle weakness, a characteristic rash, and decreased heart rate	Ingestion of food or water contaminated with the faeces of an infected person, which contain the bacterium *Salmonella typhi*, serotype Typhi	
Dengue fever [Breakbone]	Fever, headaches, muscle pain	Mosquito borne	Rehydration
Cholera	Diarrhoea, vomiting and muscle cramps	Ingestion of food or water infected with the *vibrio cholera* bacterium	
Amoebic dysentery	Diarrhoea, abdominal pain, fatigue	Parasites found in contaminated food or drink	Mild – two doses bacteriophage Medium – liquid extract of kurchi Severe – M&B 693 and 760
Sandfly	Small scab which can develop into jungle sore	Insect bite	
Head lice and nits	Scratching	Infestation by bugs	
Asian giant hornet	Shortness of breath, nausea, paralysis and pronounced swelling of affected area, faintness	Insect bite	
Jungle flies	Cause infection in open sores/wounds	Insect bite	
Dim-dam fly	Swollen legs	Insect bite	

413

Scabies	Itching	The mite *Sarcoptes scabiei*, which burrows under the host's skin, causing intense allergic itching; usually passed from person to person by touch	
Schistosomiasis [Bilharzia]	Abdominal pain, fever, diarrhoea, fatigue	Infectious blood fluke ingested through infected water	Tartar emetic
Pallagra	Skin lesions	Chronic lack of niacin [vitamin B3] in diet	
Hook worm [Ankylostomiasis]	Diarrhoea, nausea and vomiting; anaemia	Contracted by walking barefoot in soil that is contaminated with the faeces of an infected person. Hookworm larvae enter through the skin, typically on the foot, and travel up through the bloodstream into the lungs	Thymol and oil of chenopodium

ANNEX D

COLIN MACKENZIE'S 1945 REPORT ON FORCE 136

11 September 1945
To: Head of P Division
From: Commander, Force 136

1. Herewith is a note on Force 136 operations split up into the same periods as I understand will be used for the SAC's Despatches.
2. In this connection I attach a SHAEF[199] note on the value of SOE operations in the Supreme Commander's Sphere. I understand that this paper prepared by SHAEF will probably form an eventual annexe to SHAEF Despatches. I think you will find this of considerable value in writing your own note.
3. It is clear, of course, that in Europe SOE carried on a considerable number of activities which were never possible in this theatre e.g. passive industrial resistance, the dropping of forged ration cards [one of the most successful operations of this kind against Germany], various types of industrial sabotage. Further, as in Europe the invasion went very much further before capitulation than it did in this theatre; there were opportunities for anti-scorch earth etc, which we might have had if the campaign had developed further here.
4. General Eisenhower's letter to CD is also attached as a matter of interest.

REPORT OF FORCE 136 ACTIVITIES

August 1943 to February 1944

During this period much preparatory work was going on and before the end of 1943 initial contacts were established with resistance elements in Burma and Malaya. In the case of Malaya contact was regained with elements recruited and trained before the fall of Singapore. In both countries however W/T contact was broken from time to time and progress in organisation was consequently slow.

Parties had also been infiltrated into the Andaman Islands primarily for intelligence purposes and a W/T station was set up in the Mergui Archipelago primarily for relay purposes.

---

[199] Supreme Headquarters Allied Expeditionary Force.

February 1944 to June 1944

Burma
In the north we successfully cooperated in the Mogaung-Katha-Bhamo area with the operations of the 3rd Indian Division.

Our party in Kokang had difficulty in maintaining itself against local opposition, but gradually succeeded in extending its activities and obtaining useful intelligence from west of the Salween.

In the Karenni Hills we suffered a severe setback as the Japanese killed two of our officers and scattered their parties while their persecution of the Karenni villagers decided Major Seagrim to surrender himself in the hope of preventing further atrocities. Evidence seems to show that Major Seagrim was finally executed by the Japanese in Rangoon in September 1944.

Our Forward Propaganda Units did useful work both in Arakan and later Imphal. They were instrumental in obtaining a few prisoners, issued the divisional news-sheet for 17th Indian Division and IV Corps and for the 20th Division when that Division was in the Box on the Imphal-Tamu Road. Useful intelligence was also obtained through the establishing of mobile markets for villagers on the flanks of our troops.

Other
During this period repeated efforts were made to re-establish contact with Malaya, while initial parties were put into Thailand and French Indo-China.

Two special operations were carried out to Sumatra to obtain information regarding landing strips. These were successfully accomplished by a mixed British and Dutch party but two British officers were killed.

June 1944 to March 1945

Burma
By the end of 1944 we were in a position to carry out operations:
- In the southern Kachin area, Mogaung-Katha-Bhamo
- In the Shan States
- In Karenni
- Through the Anti-Fascist Organisation [AFO] in Central Burma
- In Arakan

ANNEX D

The South Kachin area first came into action but we were for some time restricted by China National Aviation Corporation[200] to an intelligence role so that the movement did not develop on the scale it otherwise might have done.

In Arakan active operations began in January 1945. These clearly showed that Jedburgh teams on the European model of two officers and one W/T operator – particularly if they were supplied with one reliable native contact – could work very successfully even though they had no knowledge of local eastern conditions or language. Our Arakan operations were on a small scale but were most successful. We not only supplied XV Corps with the bulk of its intelligence and provided twenty-three direct observation air targets of importance to the RAF but killed seventy-eight Japanese and impeded the Japanese retreat by the destruction of a number of boats.

In Karenni and Central Burma we were authorised to raise guerrillas on the basis of 100 arms to be issued per King's Commissioned Officer infiltrated by us. By the end of March we had over forty officers in Karenni but it was only at the end of this period that the northern end of Karenni was authorised to take the offensive. In the meantime several AFO parties south of Mandalay had also been authorised to go into action.

Thailand

Contact had by now been successfully established with the Regent of Thailand and the Resistance Movement there. A Mission of leading Thai was successfully brought out of Bangkok and returned. A considerable amount of valuable intelligence was brought by the Mission and on the basis of information supplied by them plans were drawn up to assist both the Thai resistance movement, and, providing political clearance was obtained, for supplying essential equipment to the Thai army.

French Indo-China

In French Indo-China we had through the French set up a number of resistance groups particularly in the north of the country where conditions were more favourable. When the Japanese took over the control of the country on 9 March 1945 these groups went into action, but were for some time involved in the purely military resistance of the military columns which were gradually driven back over the Chinese border. Several groups were, however, able to maintain

---

200 After the Burma Road fell into enemy hands, Pan American Airways' subsidiary China National Aviation Corporation [CNAC] was charged with the mission of flying supplies over the 'Hump' into occupied China. This company, which employed many disbanded Flying Tiger P-40 pilots, had been awarded the US Army contract to fly supplies for the American Military Commission in China.

themselves and through them we were able to start building up again the intelligence network which had been completely wiped out by the Japanese action on 9 March.

Malaya

In Malaya we finally re-established contact with Perak and by establishing parties also in Johore we were able to obtain a fairly reliable picture of the widespread resistance movement organised as the Malayan Peoples Anti-Japanese Union and Forces [AJUF] throughout most of Malaya. We also succeeded in making satisfactory arrangement with this resistance movement which allowed for the attachment of BLOs and by which the AJUF undertook to carry out SACSEA instructions. In the north our officers succeeded in initiating a purely Malay resistance movement as well.

March 1945 to September 1945

Burma

During this period the guerrilla movement in Karenni came up to full strength. About 10,000 men were put under arms and we had about ninety officers in the area. These lightly armed forces succeeded in holding up the 15th Japanese Division from reaching Toungoo sufficiently to ensure its previous capture by Fourteenth Army. Subsequently guerrilla forces were established either south of Moulmein or eastward out of Burma. Between 1 January and 1 September 1945 the Karenni have accounted for 11,874 Japanese killed, 644 wounded and 119 prisoners.

Contact having been established in December 1944 with the Headquarters of the Anti-Fascist Organisation and in March 1945 with the Headquarters of the Burma National Army [now the Patriot Burma Force] on 28 March, these elements became fully active on both sides of the Irrawaddy and the Delta.

Both in the southern Kachin area and in the Northern Shan States activities were increased and the total casualties inflicted by Force 136 controlled forces are set out in Appendix A.

In January 1945 Force 136 was also given the role of operational intelligence in the Battle Area. This resulted in a large increase in the number of intelligence reports submitted by us and this is set out statistically for Burma and other areas in Appendix B.

Malaya

In Malaya a great effort was made to build up the necessary guerrilla forces by the end of August 1945 instead of by the end of October 1956 which had been the previous target date. Although the full programme was not achieved, considerable progress had been made and at the time of the Japanese capitulation we had ninety-seven officers with fifty-two W/T sets working, we had also introduced six of the twelve Ghurkha Groups specially organised to protect DZs and to stiffen local resistance. Here also we were given operational intelligence as our primary role and the figures showing the number of reports submitted appears in Appendix B. Evaluation of these reports shows that the quality as well as the quantity was steadily improving.

Thailand
In Thailand we were handicapped by the fact that first priority in air supply had to be given to Malaya with the result that the number of sorties which could be flown to Thailand was relatively small. Further there was the over-riding necessity not to provoke the Japanese to take over the country, and this resulted in a further restriction of air sorties from time to time. In spite of this, however, firm foundations had been laid for guerrilla activity in several areas and at the time of the capitulation we had ten British officers, besides twenty-three Thai officers with British commissions and twenty-one W/T stations.

Throughout the period close contact was maintained through our senior liaison officer with the Regent and the resistance movement headquarters. Intelligence derived through these channels was of varying but sometimes of considerable value. It included among other things the complete Japanese Order of battle in South East Asia.

Sumatra
After many delays and failures a start was made to penetrate Sumatra in June 1945 and at the time of the capitulation we had four British and Dutch officers and five W/T stations. These were immediately available to deal with POW camps.

General remarks
It must be appreciated that clandestine effort in this theatre presented peculiarly difficulties. First, the number of potentially high calibre and trustworthy native agents who could be found outside their respective countries was very limited. Secondly, the very large distances involved, particularly in the case of Malaya, where aircraft were flying at extreme range and Liberator sorties were usually over 3,000 miles for the round trip, taking twenty-three hours and forty minutes. Thirdly, monsoon conditions made flying and the picking up of DZs extremely difficult during a substantial part of the year, while on the ground the very high humidity required the special packing of arms and

supplies, particularly foodstuffs, and the tropicalisation of W/T sets. The clandestine effort was further limited by the fact that the number of aircraft which would be allocated to this purpose was often far smaller than desirable in view of the fact that preparatory work was required contemporaneously over such an enormous area. In spite of these disabilities, however, a very considerable amount of supplies was despatched to the field. The bulk of these supplies had to be despatched by air and this is set out in statistical form at Appendix D.

The political implications of arming resistance elements who tended to be extremist in character and by no means necessarily pro-British had to be continually kept in mind and the relative advantages and disadvantages reviewed. Although it was only in Karenni and one or two other areas in Burma that opportunity could be given to Force 136 to show what they could do in their primary role in inspiring and organising resistance, apart from intelligence produced by the organisation, the extent and efficiency of Force 136 parties and their communications have now been tested and not found wanting in connection with the first contact with, and initial relief of, POW.

Kandy
10 September 1945.

ANNEX E

NOTES ON INTELLIGENCE COLLECTED BY FORCE 136 IN ENEMY OCCUPIED AREAS IN SOUTH EAST ASIA

General
Until November 1944 Force 136 was considered to be a purely operational body and the collection of intelligence was more of an incidental nature.

However, as the number of parties infiltrated into Burma, Thailand, Malaya and French Indo-China increased, material collected by them proved to be of such value that, in certain instances, the policy was reverse and a number of parties were sent with directives to concentrate on the collection of intelligence until the moment when they could be ordered to pass on to the offensive. In general, the collection of intelligence became since 1945 the second principal assignment of all operational parties in the entire theatre.

Methods of collecting intelligence
General conditions being widely dissimilar in different areas of South East Asia theatre, methods employed for the collection of intelligence were consequently at great variance. Following is a tentative list of those methods:
- Visual Observation Points, Permanent
- Visual Observation Points, Temporary
- Fighting patrols
- Native agents
- Interrogations
- Co-operation of leaders of resistance movements
- Co-operation of friendly native administrations
- Co-operation of French colonial administration
- Creation of joint allied intelligence organisations.

Results achieved: Burma

Visual observation points
Temporary observation points have been established from time to time on main Japanese lines of communication.

Intelligence obtained by this method proved to be very valuable from both tactical and strategic point of view as it provided exact and continuous data on enemy troop and supply movements.

It should be noted that as Japanese troop movements usually took place at night and that in day time they remained in widely scattered and well camouflaged camps or hidden in the jungle, it was impossible to detect such movements by Aerial Reconnaissance.

Visual observation patrols
Most of the information collected from their battle zone was obtained by such patrols and transmitted by Force 136 W/T links either to Fourteenth Army formations, to Eastern Air Command, or to E Group, with copies to ISLD for dissemination among higher headquarters. To illustrate the amount of information transmitted and give an indication as to its nature, following are some exact figures:

INFORMATION SENT TO LOs WITH ARMY FORMATIONS [WITH COPIES TO BGS [1], ALFSEA, AND ISLD] DURING THE PERIOD 28 JANUARY-23 MAY 1954

Subject	Number of reports	Total
Strength, dispositions and activities		
Troop dispositions	72	
Troop concentrations	174	
A/T concentrations	7	
Arty concentrations	26	
M/L concentrations	10	
Strengths	14	
Location of HQs	33	
Location of OPs	13	
Patrols	6	
Reinforcements	3	
Areas clear of troops	1	
Hospitals	5	
Morale	3	
Miscellaneous	2	
Total		369
Identifications		
Detailed identifications	3	
Total		3
Defences and dumps		
Defences, areas and positions	28	

ANNEX E

Dumps inc MT parks	127	
Minefields	4	159
Total		
Communications		
Road, railway and river movements	235	
Transit and staging posts	16	
Road and railway conditions	22	
W/T, telephones and telegraph	11	
Movement by water	4	
Bridges	9	
Lines of retreat	2	
Total		299
Bombing results		48
Aircraft and airfields		6
Targets		13
PW reports		5
Appreciation of situation and intentions		6
Answers to detailed questionnaires		1
Political		6
Economic		4
Grand total		919

The above figures by no means give a complete picture; hundreds of reports on fleeting targets etc have been transmitted by field stations to LOs with Fourteenth Army formations without being recorded by this headquarters.

Tactical intelligence sent to Eastern Air Command [with copies to ISLD for further dissemination]

Following figures are quoted from a report by the Eastern Air Command regarding information they received from Force 136 during the period 1 January-28 February 1945.

Total number of messages indicating targets received by EAC formations and units	415
Number of messages on which action has been taken by 221 Group, 224 Group and 10th USAAF	127 [30.6%]
Total messages classed as reliable	318 [76.7%]

Total messages classed as semi-reliable	97 [23.4%]
Total messages asking for air support	22 [5.5%]
Total messages asking for air support acted upon	5 [1.2%]
Success of resulting attacks on targets: Good 50% Poor 12% Not observed 34% [mostly obscured by foliage] Unable to locate target 4%	

The above figures are so illustrative that they do not require further comment.

Fighting patrols
Fighting patrols went into action only during the later stages of the Burma campaign, when a general rebellion against the Japanese had taken place.

In general, as all fighting had to be of a 'hit and run' type, there were seldom opportunities for searching bodies for identity discs, documents etc.

However, on the few occasions when conditions proved to be favourable, extremely valuable documents were captured and exfiltrated by daring pick-up operations e.g. the capture on two occasions of a number of documents by DILWYN in NCAC sector, the killing of a Japanese intelligence officer in Central Burma by HYENA when some very revealing documents were obtained and the killing of a Japanese divisional commander by one of NATION's parties which provided valuable identifications.

Native agents
The employment of native agents proved to be, on the whole, rather disappointing, the reasons being the lack of training, and general propensity of Orientals to exaggeration.

Interrogations
Only intelligence of doubtful value has been obtained through interrogation of natives and none of their reports have been transmitted unless verified by British officers.

Co-operation of leaders of resistance movements
The whole-hearted co-operation of most BDA leaders provided this Force with a large network of listening posts and observation points.

ANNEX E

Information collected through this agency proved to be very valuable from political and economic aspects but purely military intelligence proved of doubtful value owing to the inability of the natives to distinguish between rumours and information.

However, it is due to this co-operation that this Force achieved one of the most spectacular results. This was brought off by LANCELOT when he went to Rangoon in December 1943 where he saw the Minister of Agriculture and returned with bagfuls of official documents which proved to be of the greatest value to the Government of Burma and the Secretary of State for India.

Results achieved: Malaya

Permanent observations points
A permanent observation point was established by CARPENTER/MINT [a joint Force 136/ISLD operation[201]] near Singapore. The observation point provided continuous and complete information on Japanese shipping entering and leaving Singapore for a period of almost one year. The value of this information to the East Indies Fleet and to the Air Force is evident and needs no comment.

Co-operation of AJUF
The collection of intelligence in the interior of Malaya was made possible principally by the co-operation of the AJUF leaders.

Information collected in Malaya covered a variety of subjects such as political situation, economic conditions, enemy defences, conditions of roads, railways, waterways, beaches etc. It has been estimated that eighty per cent of information from clandestine sources available to ALFSEA for planning future operations in Malaya was originated by the Force.

Considerable volume of information was provided on enemy airfields, targets, dumps, bombing results, crashes of own planes, and location of PW camps. It must be stated however that hardly any identifications of Japanese formations have been obtained in this area.

---

201 Hembry as a former member of SOE did his best to keep Force 136 informed of ISLD activities. Operation MULLET failed in February 1944 when Hembry's party was compromised on Langkawi Island; Operation EVIDENCE 1 and 2 in January 1945 when a six-strong party dropped near Sungei Siput with orders to keep an eye out for GUSTAVUS. At one stage Hembry had six parties in the field excluding MINT, all in W/T with Calcutta.

Results achieved: Thailand

Almost all intelligence from Thailand was due to the underhand co-operation of Thai Government authorities who have actually opened all their cards and supplied exhaustive data on the following subjects:
- Order of Battle and dispositions of the Thai Army
- Japanese strengths, dispositions in Thailand
- Japanese Order of Battle in Thailand
- Industrial capacity of Thai arsenals and factories
- Available stocks of rice
- Location of Japanese dumps
- Manifests of ordinary and military trains plying between Bangkok and French Indo-China
- Names of Japanese commanders
- Topographical maps
- Thai Army, weapons and ammunition
- List of airfields used by the Japanese, Thai or both, giving length and nature of runways
- PW camps, locations, conditions etc
- Economic survey
- Thai internal political situation
- Strength Thai Navy

The value of this information was such that this Force received on 14 March 1945 personal congratulations from the Supreme Allied Commander for 'the very valuable intelligence which your organisation has obtained as a result of Operation SEQUENCE'.

Results achieved: French Indo-China

A number of French military and civil officials, although openly collaborating with the Japanese as members of Admiral Decoux's Vichy administration, have been recruited by the Anglo-French section [FICCS] of Force 136 for service to the Allies.

Until 9 March 1945, the date when the Japanese took over the administration of the colony, this Force collected much precise and valuable intelligence covering every aspect of the military, naval and economic situation.

Particularly valuable results were obtained from observation points established along the French Indo-China coast so that the movements of Japanese ships and convoys were observed and tallied for a period of about a year.

Furthermore, the same source supplied description and location of some radar stations which proved of great interest to the RCM section of SACSEA.

After 9 March 1945 most of the sources of information were lost through enemy action and, until the re-organisation and introduction of new parties, the value of military intelligence greatly declined. However, close contact with the retreating French units was maintained and proved to be the only channel through which intelligence from the interior of French Indo-China reached SEAC headquarters.

After the Japanese surrender, Force 136 parties re-organised and, reinforced, continued to be practically the only source of information on the political situation principally in Laos, Cambodia and to a lesser extent in Tonkin and Annam.

Results achieved: Netherlands East Indies

Owing to a number of complex problems it was impossible to establish an intelligence network in Netherlands East Indies until a month before the Japanese surrender.

After the surrender, operations were greatly intensified and, until the first landings by ALFSEAs formations, Force 136 was the only source of information from this vast area.

The success of this operation can best be illustrated by mentioning SACSEA's request to introduce a large additional number of parties in Dutch overseas possessions which were formerly part of the SWP theatre.

Results achieved: China

Occupied China

The establishment of listening and observation posts in occupied China proved to be an extremely delicate task as it could not properly function with the knowledge and co-operation of the Chungking Government.

A solution was therefore reached whereby the Chinese established a network of agents in China and in Manchuria, financed and equipped by Force 136 who also provided the W/T sets.

In spite of many handicaps, this organisation provided a great volume of information which proved to be particularly valuable in its following aspects.
- Broad picture of Japanese movements in China and Manchuria
- Shrewd Chinese appreciations of Japanese policy and intentions and political situation
- Internal political and economic situation in occupied zones

- Indications of Russian policy in Far East
- Insight into Chinese Government's policy, propaganda and intentions.

Furthermore, after the Japanese surrender, this organisation obtained a number of important documents pertaining to the organisation and methods of the Japanese army, sitemaps, geographical maps etc.

Free China

Excellent results have been obtained in Kwangsi-Kwangtung-Hong Kong area by a joint E group/Force 136 operation headed by Colonel Ride. His well scrutinised illuminating reports gave a full picture of the military situation in the Kwangsi battle zone, while from Hong Kong he obtained a continuous tally of Japanese shipping and reported on all developments of military, political and economic nature.

Summary and conclusions

Information collected by Force 136 contributed considerably to the final success of Allied armies in SEA theatre by facilitating the following tasks:

Ground operations – by supplying 'hot' intelligence from behind the enemy lines in the battle zone, disclosing enemy's tactics, strength, movements and intentions.

Air operations – by indicating both fleeting and permanent targets, reporting on damage caused by strafing and bombing sorties and by saving Photo Recce sorties. Also by indicating AA positions and location of radars.

Tactical planning – by giving precise topographical information in road, rail, and waterway reports, assessing Japanese logistical problems and indicating location of defensive positions.

Strategic planning – by providing a broad picture of the situation in all Japanese occupied zones in SEA viewed from all possible angles.

Diplomatic planning – by keeping a close watch on the political developments in occupied zones and assessing the feelings and trends of local populations and Governments.

E group operations – by supplying considerable data on the locations and conditions of PW camps, indicating methods of escape etc. It is greatly due to the preparatory intelligence work of this Force that E Group and RAPWI had the opportunity of performing a tremendous task efficiently and without undue delays.

Kandy
30 October 1945

ANNEX F

SUMMARY OF FORCE 136 CASUALTIES in BURMA
1 JANUARY TO 12 SEPTEMBER 1945[202]

Operation	Casualties Enemy Killed	Wounded	POW	Own Killed	Wounded
NATION					
TERRIER	43	1	-	-	-
PANDA	250	-	1	-	-
CHIMP	980	-	56	-	-
REINDEER	1205	111	84	3	13
GIRAFFE and COW	58	5	-	-	-
DOG	9	-	-	-	-
HART	-	-	-	5 [203]	-
ZEBRA and JACKAL	816	84	15	5	11
RABBIT	20	-	-	-	-
CHARACTER					
OTTER and FERRET	2814	422	4	6	4
HYENA	5279	78	113	7	2
WALRUS and SKUNK	2551	62	1	6	22
MONGOOSE	1830	82	1	3	1
DILWYN					
MONKEY and CHEETAH	128	31	-	3	2
BEAR	9	-	-	-	-
SQUIRREL	77	23	-	4	8
BADGER	25	5	-	-	1
LABEL					
RAT	3	-	-	4 [204]	-
HEAVY					
LYNX	20	1	4	1	-
WOLF	250	73	-	1	-

---

202 Excludes 1944 casualties of Major Seagrim, Major Nimmo, Captain McCrindle and Lieutenant Ba Gyaw.
203 Plane crash.
204 Possibly POWs: Major J.B. Smythe and Captain R.J. Meredith.

CALF	256	-	-	-	-
MANUAL					
CAMEL and MOUSE	133	-	5	1	-
RAMROSE/FUTURE					
RHINO and BISON	58	1	-	1	1
FOX	-	-	-	1	-
GRAIN					
ELEPHANT	19	4	1	2	1
NUTSHELL					
TIGER	46	12	-	-	-
Total	16,879	995	285	53	66

Source: HQ GROUP A/ FORCE 136 [Int]/ 3 October 1945

ANNEX G

FORCE 136 MILITARY ESTABLISHMENT, RECONCILIATION AND POSTED STRENGTH [OFFICERS] 1 AUGUST 1945

RANK	NAME/INITIALS	REGIMENT
Colonels		
	Jacques W.H.	R.Sussex
	Davis J.L.H.	Gen. List
Lieutenant Colonels		
	Seelleur A.J.le	RE
	Critchley R.A.	RAC
	Crosby M.G.M.	Gordons
	Peacock E.H.W	RA
	Cromarty-Tullock J.	RE
	Chapman F.S.	Seaforth Highlanders
	Howell H.W.	IAC
	Bennett G.	R.Sigs
	Bridge H.V.	LF
	Wylie I.S.	Gen. List [BS]
	Arun C.	Gen. List [BS]
	Broadhurst D.K.	Gen. List
	Campbell-Miles A.C.	10/15 Punjab
	Hannah J.P.	RAPC
	Dobrée P.G.J.	3 GR
	Fenner C.H.	Int Corps [IA]
	Davison C.J.	RA
Majors		
	Hare A.V	LG
	Landes R.	Gen. List
	McLean N.L.D	Greys
	Smiley D.	RHG
	Maze S.B.	
	Scott K.F.	RE
	Fielding A.W.F.	Int Corps
	Cope S.A.	Burif
	Gibson J.A	RA

	Lovett-Campbell P.B.	RA
	Burne C.L.	ABRO
	Abbey I.E.	Innisks
	Boal A.M.	W.Yorks
	Boiteux R.R.	Gen. List
	Charlesworth F.V.	RA
	Chasse P.	RCEME
	Clowes J.E.	RAC
	Denning A. du Pre	Hamps
	Harington J.T.	RB
	Herring D.C.	Burif
	Hood E.H.M.	Som LI
	James H.M.	Cyprus
	Lewes P.V.	RA Sigs
	McAdam M.G.	RAC
	McCoull D.M.	RTR
	Milner F.S.	Dorset
	Nevill I.S.	Int Corps
	Poles W. E.	NRR
	Shaw J.K.H.	RUR
	Turrall R.G.	Int. Corps
	Bryce-Smith R.B.	ABRO
	Hobbs A.T.	ABRO
	Broome N.	Gen. List
	Richardson J.D.	Gen. List
	Latham W.	Gen. List
	Olsen A.S.	Gen. List
	Tovey J.H.	RE
	Harrison F.P.W.	5 RGR
	Hislop J.A.	5 RGR
	Leonard G.R.	AIF
	Sime D.	2/4 Aus. Cav. Commando Sqn
	Shaw C.M.A.	15 Punjab
	Cockle A.T.	ABRO
	Blathwayt C.C.W.	KRRC
	Headley D.	Gen. List

ANNEX G

	Hedley J.D.H.	Burif
	Pennell G.E.	RA
	Read S.H.J.	10 Baluch
	Saw Butler MC	Kacnin Levies
	Ungphakorn Puey	Gen. List
	Foster – Clark H.	RWK
	Cox J.H.	RA
	Ford D.D.	BW
	Wilson R.W.	RWF
	Lucas J.P.	RIASC
	Rubinstein R.A.	RA
	Smallwood J.St C.	RAC [9L]
	Abbott A.J.	6 RAJ Rif
	Hunter A.J.	19 Hybad
	Carew T.A.	RA
Lt Cdr	Hall R.	RNVR
Lt Cdr	Jackson H.	RNVR
	Young G.S	RE
	Deening W.	RASC
	Woodcock E.J.	RASC
	Howe W.A.	ABRO
	Stanes D.M.	MX
	Franklin A.H.B.	5 Mahrattas
	Reid R.W.	ABRO
	Wright F.P.	RAC [DWR]
	Warren I.R.	RA
	Watson J.	Surreys
	Metcalfe J.M.	RA
	Zau June L.	ABRO
	Weymss V.L.H.	ECIA
	Wilson T.A.	RAC
	Phillips B.G.	2 Punjab
	Owen S.F.	Gen. List [BS]
	Lodge E.F.	RTR
	Maxwell C.F.	RE
	Thompson-Walker R.T.	RE
	Kemp P.M.M.	Int. Corps
	Beaumont-Nesbitt	Gren Gds

	Grieg C.L.	RA
	Samson A.H.	Welch
	Oliver J.P.F.	KRRC
	Hudson C.S.	RF
	Scott R.C.	Gen. List
	MacPherson J.A.E.	Burif
	Hill H.H.	RF
	Olsen F.A.	Gen. List
	Courtney G.E.	RWK
	Bromley-Davenport A.R.	FFR
	Alexander D.R.W.	FFR
	Hasler G.A.	Raf Rif
	Somerville D.A.	Gen. List
	Kemball J.P.G.	RAC
	Pierce R.F.	RWF
	Mackenzie I.F.	6 Raj Rif
	Cambell A.P.	Gen. List
	Eckford C.V.	IAOC
	Maddox P.R.	ABRO
	Milton O.M.B.	ABRO
	Holmes D.R.	Gen. List
	Kyaw Thu	RASC
	Tengnu Manyldeen	Gen. List
Lt Cdr	Lewis H.G.	RNVR
Lt Cdr	Booker A.G.	RNVR
	Nimmo W.	A & SH
	Benoit J.H.A.	CAN ARMY
	Lea R.V.	RA [FD]
Captains		
	Byrne J.M	ABRO
	Calvin O.C.	Burma Reg
	Kumji Tawng Wa	BA Sigs
	Maitland A.R.	Gen. List
	Burron R.J.	Gordons
	Beamish J.M.	Raj. Rif
	Bourne H.E.	E.Yorks
	Brown B.	RA
	Bullman J.M.	KRRC

ANNEX G

	Clark L.W.	Buffs
	Coomber A.W.R.	RAC
	Craster O.E.	Oxf Bucks
	Guthrie D.D.	DCLI
	Hall H.	RAC
	Dumonth A.A.	RA
	Houseman J.W.	Bays
	Livingston G.R.	RE
	Lockie D. Mc. N.	Y & L
	MacLeod J.	Seaforth
	Marchant J.J.	Wilts
	Meunier P.C.M.	Fusiliers de Montreal
	Allen-Mirehouse J.N.S.	Welch
	Sell C.H.	RA
	Steele W.O.	LF
	Taschereau L.J.	R de Chaud Can. Army
	Thibault P.E.	Can. Gen. List
	Troward T.J.	RTR
	Wakelin H.M.	RA
	Waller J. deW	RB
	Williams J.P.	Welch
	Wilson F.W.	RAC
F/Lt	Green A.V.	RAF
	Lee J.S.	2 GR
	Camp K.F.	2 GR
	Evans G.E.	ABRO
	Ashwell P.C.	ABRO
	Browning D.	Gen. List
	Melliar-Smith P.L.	Gen. List
	Foss C.E.	Oxf. Bucks
	Gabb C.L.	E.Yorks
	Tatham M.R.	B.W.
	Clifford J.P.M.	16 Punjab
	Dorrity J.D.	2 Punjab
	Bhaskaran P.	Madras
	Trofimov A.A.	RA
	White L.V.C.	RE
	McCalam A.F.	KAR

	Donald A.T.	RE
	Locke P.F.C.R.	R. Sigs
	West D.D.	RAC
	Farrant R.W.	R.Sussex
	Phillips M.A.	4th Bombay
	Kirby I.L.	ECIA
Lt	Wallin O.O.	RNNR
Lt	Sture J.E.	RNNR
	Stegmann G.F.C.	RE
	Unger W.	ABRO
	White V.G.L	9 Jat Regt
	Davidson J.	RAC
	Dring E.A.	Lincolns
	Sturges E.M.	RM
	Sayers W.J.	R.Sigs
	Bailey A.N.L.	Wilts
	Buchanan D.R.	KOYLI
	Rawes B.C.	8 Punjab
	Taylor R.H.R.	RE
	Nairac C.L.	Gen. List
	Charter A.G.	RA
	Hicks M.	RAC
	Gill R.W.	RAOC
	Razair M.J.S.	ECIA
	Davies C.	RA
	Riley T.A.	S.Lancs
	Kelsey J.O.	LF
	Fraser H.	RAC
	Kennard N.G.	Camerons
	Ellam P.J.	RA
	Leng C.A.W.	RAC
	Dickson M.C.	Norfolks
Lt	Cumming A.M.	RNVR
	Godwin R.D.	RAC
	Williams F.W.	Bedfs Herts
	Sneddon J.R.	2 GR
	Barton H.J.	Gurkha Regt
	D'Astugues A.R.	Gen. List

		McFarlaine J.	
		Quinn P.E.	ECIA
		Heine K.R.R.	RE
		Hussain K.	Madras
		Saw Ohn Pe	ABRO
	F/O	Cameron C.M.	WAAF
	F/Lt	Kino D.G.	RAFVR
		Sherington E.R.	RIASC
		McDonald I.A.	FFR
		Naismith W.N.	IAOC
		Chapman J.L.	AIF
		Morrison J.R.	AIF
		Trevaldwyn D.E.	AIF
		Edgar W.	AIF
	F/Lt	Bird I.	RAAF
	Lt	[Sp]Verity T.	RNVR
		Charles T.A.W.	Gen. List
		Davies S.J.	IGR
		Philpott A.J.	RE
		Hon. Winn R.D.G.	8 H
		Burr D.H.	RUR
		Vivian G.H.	Gen. List
		Hubart A.	Gen. List
		Hunter C.B.	RA
		Gordon J.R.	2 L
		Blake H.J.	Madras
		Planel J.P.M.	Gen. List
		Baldev Singh	Dogra
		Johnson J.R.C.	RE
		Lilleyman D.	RA
		Grant A.P.	17/21 L
		Williams W.A.W.	Gen. List
		Wight T.A.	IE
		Quayle F.T.	Gen. List
		Ansell W.F.H.	Burif
		Briant J.E.	Burif
		Prem Buri	Gen. List
		Prantan Pramekamol	Gen. List

	Samram Varubriksha	Gen. List
	Rachit Buri	Gen. List
	Thana Poshyananda	Gen. List
	Kris Tosayananda	Gen. List
	Kamhaeng Balahkura	Gen. List
	Snoh Nilkamhaeng	Gen. List
	Praphed Paurohitya	Gen. List
	Deb Semtnite	Gen. List
	Boonsong Phungsoondarg	Gen. List
	Prapit Na Nagara	Gen. List
	Chungkeng Rinthakul	Gen. List
	Padama Patmastana	Gen. List
	Jiyavare Wattana	Gen. List
	Karawik Chakrabandhu	Gen. List
	Chiridanai Kitiyakara	Gen. List
	Tos Pantumasen	Gen. List
	Despaigne H.M.	DCLI
	Foot J.P.	Dorset
	Lahpai Knun Nawng	Gen List
	Ross J.	LAOC
	Hyde G.A.	Burif
	Francis D.S.	ICIA
	Moseling E.W.J.	RA
	Montague J.C.	RTR
	Dendy P.	RWK
	Liddle J.N.	Som. LI
	Massey B.E.	
	Ferrier R.G.	Norfolk
	Sanderson A.O.	DWR
	McClair A.R.	Essex
	Dunne E.C.	RE
	Newell C.L.D.	RAC
	Hibberdine J.G.	Camerons
	Ross I.D.	Camerons
	Wright H.H.	RUR
	Hanbury-Tracy N.J.F.	ECIA
	Wilkinson G.C.	DRI
	Stafford W.F.	Gen. List [BS]

ANNEX G

	Wheeler D.H.	RE
	Moss I.W.S.	CCS
	Fordyce A.W.	GR
	Davies R.S.	Manch. Regt
	Dawson H.J.	RE
	Small H.	RA
	Allan J.A.B.	S.Staffords
	Prescott J.C.M.	1 GR
	Audley W.H.	1 GR
	Goffin P.E.	Gen.List
F/Lt	Brown-Bartrolli A.J.	RAF
	Battle A.F.	Punjab
	Platt R.	Gen.List [IA]
	Fournier J.E.	Can R.Sigs
	Grant A.B.	Gordons
	Winyard F.W.	IE
F/Lt	King G.D.	RAF
	Reddish N.G	AIF
	Trevaldwyn D.E.	AIF
	Robinson N.B.	AIF
	Rogers J.H.	E.Yorks
Lieutenants		
	Knott G.L	R.Sigs
	Van Kett E.H.	Gen.List [IA]
	Woolf I.J.	Gen. List
2/Lt	Marlam J.	Gen. List [IA]
2/Lt	Renny H.B.	Gen. List [IA]
2/Lt	Renny T.W.	Gen. List
Sub Lt	Moore H.M.	RNVR
	Creer J.K.	
	Crystal H.	
F/O	Robertson J.	RAAF
Sub Lt	Mohdain Bin Hussain	RNVR
	Huttermier H.H.	AIF
	Caza R.M.	Can. R. Sigs
	Hanna J.E.	CIC [GL]
	Ritson J.B.	Gen. List
2/Lt	Osman T.	Gen. List [BS]

2/Lt	Tonnison J.A.	Gen. List [BS]
	Frank G.N.	17 Dogra
	Petrie S.E.	REME
	Brophy P.M.M.	RAC
	Arnold G.	Gen. List [BS]
	Levy M.G.	Gen. List [BS]
	St. John A.P.	ABRO
	Harding J.J.	Gen. List [Can]
	Easterby S.H.	Gen. List
	Chambers P.B.	Hants
	Vickers [Voetzky] A.R	Int. Corps
2/Lt	Thibaut G.J.	Gen.List
	Barclay S.L.	RE
	Prosser J.R.	RE
F/O	Nicholson J.E.H.	RAF
2/Lt	Beatson W.	Gen.List [IA]
	Langley C.P.	RSF
Sub Lt	Hilltout A.W.	RNVR
Sub Lt	Powers	RNVR
Sub Lt	Fowler E.J.	RNVR
F/O	Stein P.	RAFVR
	Lucas E.	RAC
	McCloy A.C.	RA
	Merry H.W.	RE
	Munro H.A.C.M	Gordons
	Whyte G.E.A.	RAC
2/Lt	Curry J.A.	2 GR
Sub Lt	Kanwar H.I.S.	RINVR
	Knight-Hall I.	Oxfs. Bucks
	Bacon D.B.	RE
	Dillon E.H.S.	2 GR
	MacIntyre W.J.	A&SH
2/Lt	Sabarwal Amar Singh	Dogra Regt
	Saw Po Hla	ABRO
2/Lt	Tha Gyaw	ECIA
	Saw Sankey	Buri
	Svasti Srisukh	Gen.List
	Adam M.M.E.	Gen.List

ANNEX G

Non British Army		
Capt	Stephen H.R.	Canadian Army
Lt	Erickson A.C.	Canadian Army
Lt	Davis D.M.	Canadian Army
Lt	Flarsham R.F.	Canadian Army
Capt	Harvey G.L.	Canadian Army
Lt	Johnson E.M.	Canadian Army
Capt	Swinton G.H.G.	Canadian Army
Medical staff		
Major	Felton W.F.	RAMC
Major	Dumoulin J.G.	RAMC
Sgn/Lt Cdr	McPhail D.S.	RNVR
Major	Dafoe C.S.	RAMC
Major	Rogers L.S.	RAMC
Major	Mukerji S.N.	IAMC
Capt	Heptinstall R.H.	RAMC
Capt	Donaldson D.B.	RAMC
Capt	Gunn D.R.	RAMC
Capt	Ray R.L.	RAMC
Capt	McDougall J.R.	RAMC
Capt	Rapaport A.	RAMC
Capt	Rapaport M.	RAMC
Capt	Dewanjea B.C.	ABRO [MED]
Lt	Price J.E.L.	RAMC

ANNEX H

SOE NOTES ON THE USE OF JEDBURGHS

1. Definition of a JEDBURGH Team
A JEDBURGH team consists of a small group of officers and NCOs whose primary objective is to provide liaison and communication between resistance groups behind enemy lines and GHQ. In the European theatre of operations each team was made up of two officers and one NCO. They are, however, trained and equipped to carry out any, or all, of the following tasks:
1. Development of resistance potential.
2. Leadership as and when required.
3. Individual acts of sabotage on specified targets.
4. Provision of Intelligence.
5. The preparation and laying out of landing fields for aircraft.
6. Organisation of reception committees.
7. Instruction in guerrilla warfare and the use of all weapons appertaining thereto.
8. Flank protection for an advancing army.

2. Areas of Operation
[a] Tactical. Operational areas are considered to be tactical when the activities of the JEDBURGHS have a direct bearing on operations being carried out by regular forces, i.e.:
1. Destruction of railways, roads and bridges in order to interfere or completely stop the flow of enemy reinforcements towards the front line.
2. Ambushing enemy convoys.
3. Destruction of intercommunications such as telegraph lines and cables, etc.
4. Destruction of forward petrol dumps.
5. The preservation of all the above in order to facilitate a breakthrough by our own troops.
6. The protection of our own flanks immediately after a breakthrough.
7. The provision of guides and intelligence for our forward troops.

[b] Strategical. An operational area is considered to be strategical, when it has no direct bearing on operations being carried out by regular forces. In such areas the function of a JEDBURGH team is as follows:
1. To build up, organise and equip resistance groups.

ANNEX H

2. To form a base from which formations can carry out operations against the enemy with the utmost safety.
3. To build up the potential threat of a large armed force which the enemy cannot afford to ignore, thus diverting enemy troops away from tactical areas.

3. Planning

[a] In planning JEDBURGH operations, the question of supply and airlift should be very carefully considered in order that it fully embraces tactical and strategical areas. If these points are not fully covered it will be found that the urgency of supplying tactical areas is inclined to starve strategical areas, the result being that valuable resistance potential is dispersed or destroyed before it is armed or equipped.

[b] The question of timing must also be considered and careful thought given to the following points:
  1. The desirability of putting in a JEDBURGH team before large scale operations commence.
  2. The possibility of this being done with sufficient security to avoid the development of enemy action against the area.
  3. If a JEDBURGH team cannot be put in early enough before D-Day owing to security, it is essential that they are given the maximum time to carry out the highly important organisation required.
  4. Although it is highly desirable to have a great deal of previous knowledge of the area of operations and also contacts in the field, the possibility of the 'blind dropping' of a team into an area which is comparatively underdeveloped must not be overlooked if the tactical situation demands such a course of action.
  5. The question of security differs largely according to the local circumstances, but in general, it can be said that security has to be closely guarded in tactical areas, but in certain cases in strategical areas it can be completely dispensed with and daylight drops carried out without impairing the chances of success of operations.
  6. The attitude of the people residing in the area to be developed must be carefully considered. In some cases, areas in which it would be impossible to work before D-Day, may be found to contain a valuable potential after large scale operations have commenced. In other areas the population may be willing to give plenty of support months before D-Day, but care must be taken not to destroy this state of affairs by bringing reprisals upon the area at an early date. Development in an area of this kind should

not be brought to a head until enemy forces are being fully occupied elsewhere.

4. Intercommunication

To obtain the maximum results from resistance groups in the field JEDBURGHS must remain in constant contact with their base in order that the directive of the Army Commander can be passed to them. This means that not only must the JEDBURGHS and the Home Station be highly trained from the technical point of view, but there must be sufficient staff to deal with the flow of telegrams from the field so that the answers to vital questions and the passing of instructions can be carried out with the minimum delay.

In certain cases it may be considered desirable to set up lateral W/T communications between groups in the field.

5. Conclusion

It will be seen that the above notes are of general nature, applicable to the use of JEDBURGHS in any theatre of war.

ANNEX I

SUCCESS RECORD OF ACTUAL SUPPLY SORTIES TO Operation HAINTON: MAY 1944 – FEBRUARY 1945

Note: Several flights were cancelled before take-off due to weather conditions at departure airfield or en route, mechanical faults etc and are not listed.

Date	Dep Airfield	Aircraft	Load	Outcome
5.6.44	Dum Dum	Hudson	Stores	Unsuccessful – fog over DZ
6.6.44	Fenny	Hudson	3 agents 4 packages	Successful
7.6.44	Digri	Liberator	7 containers	Unsuccessful – 10/10 cloud
6.6.44	Digri	Liberator	12 containers	Unsuccessful – engine trouble in flight
8.6.44	Fenny	Hudson	7 packages	Unsuccessful – extremely bad weather
8.6.44	Fenny	Hudson	9 containers	Unsuccessful – extremely bad weather
8.6.44	Digri	Liberator	12 containers	Unsuccessful – engine trouble in flight
8.6.44	Digri	Liberator	12 containers	Unsuccessful – thick cloud
10.6.44	Digri	Liberator	12 containers	Unsuccessful – 10/10 cloud over DZ
10.6.44	Fenny	Hudson	9 containers	Dropped to SPIERS Mission
11.6.44	Fenny	Hudson	4 containers	Unsuccessful – 10/10 cloud
6.7.44	Fenny	Hudson	8 containers	Unsuccessful – extremely bad weather
7.7.44	Chittagong	Hudson	8 containers	Unsuccessful – 10/10 cloud
25.7.44	Sylhet	Liberator	12 containers 10 packages	Successful
4.9.44	Sylhet	Liberator	1 agent 12 containers 5 packages	Successful
4.9.44	Sylhet	Liberator	12 containers	Successful
28.9.44	Jessore	Liberator	3 agents 6 containers	Successful

29.10.44	Jessore	Liberator	Containers	Unsuccessful – very hazy over DZ
29.10.44	Jessore	Hudson	Containers	Unsuccessful – very hazy over DZ
1.11.44	n/a	Liberator	3 agents 11 containers	Successful
1.11.44	n/a	Liberator	n/a	Aircraft crashed
1.11.44	Jessore	Liberator	n/a	Unsuccessful – 10/10 cloud and rain
4.11.44	Jessore	Hudson	n/a	Unsuccessful – ground visibility nil
4.11.44	Jessore	Hudson	n/a	Unsuccessful – ground visibility nil
26.11.44	Jessore	Liberator	9 containers	Successful
26.11.44	Jessore	Liberator	n/a	Unsuccessful
26.11.44	Jessore	Liberator	n/a	Unsuccessful
27.11.44	Jessore	Liberator	n/a	Unsuccessful – no ground signals
29.11.44	Jessore	Liberator	n/a	Unsuccessful – low on fuel
30.11.44	Jessore	Liberator	n/a	Unsuccessful – no ground signals
2.12.44	Jessore	Liberator	n/a	Unsuccessful
4.12.44	Jessore	Liberator	n/a	Unsuccessful – no ground signals
24.12.44	Jessore	Liberator	3 containers 5 packages	Successful
25.12.44	Jessore	Liberator	9 containers 3 packages	Successful
1.1.45	Jessore	Liberator	35 packages	Unsuccessful – low cloud
2.1.45	Jessore	Liberator	35 packages	Successful
15.1.45	Mengse airstrip		Pick up 8 passengers	Successful
27.1.45	Jessore	Liberator	10 containers	Successful
29.1.45	Jessore	Liberator	7 containers 3 packages	Successful
29.1.44	Jessore	Liberator	7 containers 5 packages	Successful
22.2.45	Jessore	Dakota	3 containers 9 packages	Successful
26.2.45	Jessore	Liberator	11 containers 7 packages	Successful

ANNEX J

V FORCE

When the Japanese drove the British from Burma and seemed likely to invade India, General Sir Archibald Wavell, in April 1942, ordered the creation of a secret guerrilla organisation called V Force. It was to operate along the 800 mile mountainous eastern frontier of India running from the Himalayas in the north to the Bay of Bengal in the south. When the Japanese invasion took place, V Force was to remain behind enemy lines to harass their lines of communication, carry out post-occupational sabotage and provide post-occupational intelligence.

The frontier was organised into areas corresponding to those of the civil administration. Raised from the Assam Rifles [five military police battalions maintained by the Assam Government and composed of Ghurkhas commanded by British officers seconded from the Indian Army], V Force officers were recruited locally. By May 1942 area commanders had all been appointed and patrols sent into Burma to collect stragglers and help refugees fleeing to India.

To improve its intelligence network, V Force enlisted local tribes – the *Nagas* in the Naga and Cachar Hills, the *Kukis* in the hills around Imphal, the *Chins* south of Manipur and the *Lushais* in the Mizo Hills, part of the Patkai range which extend south into Arakan. Each area was split into smaller areas with an officer and a small force of Assam Rifles stationed at a secure base from which patrols operated forward to gather information.

When the Japanese invasion of India did not materialise, V Force's role was changed to intelligence gathering. It moved forward through the hills and established outposts in enemy territory in the area of the Chindwin River as far as Kalewa and then across northern Arakan.

In December 1943, V Force was split into two zones – Assam Zone, which included Ledo, Kohima, Manipur State, the Lushai and Cachar Hills, and Arakan Zone, consisting of the Arakan and what remained of the Tripura State area.

The caches of food, which V Force had built up, had been allowed to run down during the summer and autumn of 1943. This had serious repercussions in 1944 when several V Force areas were overrun by invading Japanese, leaving personnel no choice but to make their way back to Imphal and Kohima through the Japanese lines.

With Fourteenth Army's advance into Burma, V Force took on a different but prominent role of short-range intelligence gathering similar to the role of Z force with which it was merged. Officers and men of V Force were trained to parachute into Burma to collect and transmit back operational intelligence 80-100 miles forward of the leading formations. This also included establishing contacts with local populations, but did not include undertaking sabotage, guerrilla activities or leading fighting patrols.

With thanks to Pauline Hayton

ANNEX K

GSI[z]/Z FORCE

When the British had completed their withdrawal from Burma to India in 1942 it was apparent that no arrangements had been made to collect post-occupational Intelligence.

Fourteenth Army through GSI[z] took steps to remedy this by recruiting officers with specialised knowledge of forest areas who were able to live in the jungle and had friends and acquaintances among the local population.

Set up by SOE's Lieutenant Colonel Jack Shelley, their clandestine role was:
- To collect and transmit intelligence by W/T back to GHQ.
- To recruit local people [Chins, Kachins and Karens] of sufficient education, ability and courage to operate their own sets.

Each patrol consisted of two officers [to lend 'moral support' to each other and in case of casualties] and ten ORs. Equipped with lightweight automatics and semi-automatics [Stens and carbines] meant a high rate of fire could be laid down to effect a getaway when in difficulties.

Patrol officers	Background	Area
Robin Stewart	BBTC [205]	Sittaung, Sinlamaung, Kabaw Valley
Dickie Wood	BBTC	
'Red' Parker	BBTC	Sittaung, Sinlamaung, Kabaw Valley
Jimmy Middleton	BBTC	
J.K. Parry	Foucar Bros	Chin Hills
Micky Merton	Foucar bros	
Sammy Newland	DFO Burma Forest Dept	Chin Hills
Denis Rae	DFO Burma Forest Dept	
Bertie Castens	DFO Burma Forest Dept	Homalin and Katha
Freddie Webster	DFO Burma Forest Dept	

The patrol commander was responsible for every detail of his patrol's equipment, rations, etc., and how it functioned. This system was workable when there were only five patrols in the field but when GSI[z] was reorganised to expand into Z Force, Standard Operating Procedures for all patrols were introduced.

---

205 Bombay Burmah Trading Corporation.

In August 1942, the first five patrols moved on foot to positions inside Burma. Without air drops, resupply was a major problem which seriously curtailed their range and ability to remain behind enemy lines for long periods of time. It was a testament to the courage of Z force that the patrols returned two or three times to their tactical areas behind enemy lines. By May 1943, all five patrols had returned to Delhi and when the monsoon had finished, seven set out, this time resupplied by air.

In all, twenty-six patrols went out behind enemy lines between August 1942 and May 1944.

Track discipline and concealment were crucial to the survival of Z patrols. Some of their precautions included:
- Each man took great care how he trod so as never to leave a footprint in a soft spot. The last man in the patrol was an officer with a piece of brushwood who 'swept' out any tracks left.
- When halting for a smoke, cigarette ends and matchsticks were put in pockets or a stone lifted and replaced over them. Even cigarette ash was hidden, as the enemy were quite likely to halt at the same place and spot it.
- Dry bamboo was used for cooking as it was smokeless. As far as possible cooking was done before dawn and after dark.
- Remains of a fire and blackened stones were thrown into rivers.
- When the grass was crushed where a patrol had been sleeping, it was pulled up in the morning and dead leaves sprinkled about to leave no sign of a 'bed'.
- When going through long grass where it was impossible not to leave a trail, single file was strictly adhered to so it looked like the track of an animal.
- Officers avoided exposing their white bodies in day time.
- No old tins or other rubbish were ever left lying about.

ANNEX L

PETER FLEMING'S MI[R] NOTES ON THE POSSIBILITIES OF BRITISH MILITARY ACTION IN CHINA

1. If a state of war existed – with or without[206] a declaration of war – between Great Britain and Japan, British politico-military objectives would be to a great extent identical to those of China.
2. Chinese objectives are implicit in the policy on which she embarked, after some hesitation, in late July 1937. She has since followed that policy with complete consistency and with more success than was at first apprehended.
3. China's intention is to break, rather than to defeat, Japan. Her method is attrition. If we were involved in war against Japan [and assuming that our principal land forces were engaged, or at any rate contained elsewhere] our logical course would be to accelerate and intensify the process of attrition.
4. These processes, in so far as they are military, have been found to depend largely on what is loosely-termed guerrilla warfare[207]. The value and function of the guerrillas was not recognised by the Chinese until after the fall of Nanking in December 1937. Since then considerable attention has been paid, not without success, to increasing their sticking-power and effectiveness.
5. Lawrence could not have won his war without Allenby: Allenby could not have won his war without Lawrence. Chinese high strategy recognises that guerrillas can only represent a subsidiary military effort; but that strategy is coloured by the tacit admission that China, however

---

[206] The Japanese are, collectively, a cautious and conservative people. This does not apply to the personnel of either subordinate or high commands in China, whose record during the past two years has been one of spasmodic, often dangerous, but usually successful impetuosity in dealing with the local interests of Western powers. In the event of a major crisis in Europe, whether or not it leads at last to hostilities, it is more than possible that a period of weeks or even months will supervene during which the Japanese armed forces in China will commit isolated acts of war against Great Britain without any formal declaration of war by the Japanese Government.

[207] True guerrillas should, ex-officio, claim and retain the initiative. In some, though not by any means all, sectors in China, the initiative is claimed and exploited by the Japanese garrisons, whose sorties from the walled cities in which they are loosely beleaguered represent the only positive military action normally taken in those particular areas. The reverse [it is only fair to say] is sometimes true; but not often enough.

numerous her Lawrences, has nothing equivalent to Allenby – has, in fact, no offensive power capable of producing decisive results in the field.
6. In the Chinese conception, Allenby's role is filled by Time. This is logical and up to a point realistic; but the theory coincides with and justifies much that is ineffective in Chinese military practice. The almost pathological reluctance of the Chinese to take the offensive: their tendency to procrastinate: and their dislike of finality in any form – all these failings are condoned by a conception of high strategy which is, by implication, passive and which largely leaves it to the enemy to destroy himself.
7. The result is an avoidable declaration of the process of attrition. It seems probable that any British military effort in China would most profitably be directed towards eliminating this factor.
8. It also seems probable that this could best be achieved by concentrating at least as much on the fringes as on the centre of the Chinese military organisation. The German Military Mission, before it was recalled in 1938, enjoyed the confidence of Chiang Kai-shek and had undoubtedly done good work in training his regular troops before war broke out. The Germans appeared, nevertheless, to sacrifice effectiveness by being concentrated overmuch at Headquarters, where they remained – and were sometimes deliberately kept – out of touch with realities in the war areas. A British Mission would, of course, need to have a well-manned and influential stronghold at Chiang Kai-shek's Headquarters; but to supply even the best strategic advice and the best technical aid would be of far less practical value than to supply local tactical initiative in as many sectors as possible.
9. Pending the results of a preliminary reconnaissance in China, it is possible to visualise a scheme of intervention developing, very broadly, along the following general lines:
    a. Establishment of Mission headquarters at Chungking, probably with a liaison and line of communication branch at Kunming, disposing of 3 or 4 aircraft [as well as some lorries, etc.] for transportation of stores and personnel.
    b. Propaganda. This should not be neglected and should be laid on at an early stage. The Chinese will be very responsive to the idea of British co-operation and propaganda, even of the simplest kind, will greatly improve the Mission's chances of getting results out of junior officers and men.

ANNEX L

    c. The dispatch, probably via Chungking, of small parties of officers, with a limited number of technical personnel[208] to the Headquarters of the various 'War Areas', which at present number 5 [?].

    d. These sub-missions might operate along [roughly] the following lines:

        i. The senior officer, together with a minimum personnel for liaison, signals and intelligence, would remain at the Headquarters of his War Area, where he would endeavour to advise and stimulate the local Chinese command both directly and [through contact with British headquarters at Chungking] indirectly.

        ii. His junior officers would make their way, singly or in pairs, to different sectors either of the 'front' or of the 'occupied' areas. Their function would be to organise and, where possible, to lead personally local offensive action against the enemy, particularly in the more stagnant sectors.

    e. The value of even a very small number of British officers going into action [e.g. on night patrols or raiding parties] with, if not at the head of, Chinese troops might be expected to be twofold. It would have a considerable effect [which our propaganda could exploit] on the Chinese rank and file, who would be pleasurably surprised to find foreign officers coming with them under fire; and it would be the surest way to overcome the obstacles of pride, jealousy and 'face' which will be encountered in local commands. The average Chinese general will not take kindly to foreign direction or control, however tactfully imposed on him; but he will view with gratitude, respect and astonishment a foreign officer who undertakes in person, and with success, the distasteful task of fighting.

    f. On the more technical forms which co-operation with the Chinese might usefully take, the present writer is not competent to give an opinion. But we could probably help them and ourselves by teaching them up-to-date methods of demolition, by building bridges for them, and by training a certain number

---

208 It might be worth considering providing each officer with a minimum personal bodyguards, for reasons of 'face' and convenience. These details [not more than 4 men, including one driver, per officer] might consist of British-trained Chinese troops, or of Indian troops, or of [non-Burmese] troops from Upper Burma.

of their young officers in Burma. It is assumed that co-operation in the air will not be available on a scale large enough to make it economic.

10. The following points are implicit or explicit in the foregoing appreciation:
    a. In the present circumstances, should the Far East become a British theatre of war, our best way of striking at Japanese on land is by accelerating and intensifying the processes of attrition to which she is being subjected by the Chinese regular and irregular forces.
    b. This can best be achieved by providing the Chinese with leadership, initiative and the will to attack. Lack of these attributes represents their most serious military weakness. Given these attributes, there is nothing wrong with the fighting qualities of the rank and file.
    c. The method here proposed is the infiltration of a small number of picked British officers into the Chinese forces, not merely advisers at Headquarters, but as fighting guerrilla leaders. In this connexion, liaison with the central Chinese authorities and propaganda directed at the Chinese people as a whole, are matters of considerable importance.
11. In conclusion it may be noted that the obstacles in the path of effective Anglo-Chinese co-operation in the field, however great the goodwill on both sides, will be formidable, various and complex. Given the right men, however, there is no reason why they should not be overcome.
12. The attitude of the Russians towards British military intervention in China would probably require watching.

August 1939

NOTES ON PERSONNEL
1. The best material from British sources in China would probably come from such firms as Jardine Matheson, Butterfield and Swire, the BAT, the APC and the ICI. The banks would be unlikely to produce men with the best kind of qualifications, since their employees have, in the nature of things, very little experience of the interior. It should not be forgotten that the above firms dispose of the services of a certain number of resourceful and relatively trustworthy Chinese, some of whom would be

ANNEX L

of considerable value for purposes of liaison and intelligence work under British officers.

2. It might be worth considering the possibility, if the organisation envisaged is either relatively large at the outset or needs to be capable of swift expansion, of using individual firms as the basis on which to create cadres. Commercial yeomanry might not be a bad substitute for territorial yeomanry, where the latter cannot exist; and such a scheme would offer obvious, though perhaps not very important, advantages from the point of view of organisation, and morale.

3. The following individuals occur to me as completely trustworthy men whose services would be of value, if necessary at an early stage

   a. W.J.KESWICK. [Jardines; wife and child in Shanghai; circa 36] Member of Shanghai Municipal Council. Very good man. His contacts and ability as a negotiator would be most valuable at Chiang Kai-shek's HQ.

   b. A.J.KESWICK. [Jardines; unattached; circa 32] Like his brother, is liked and trusted by most of the important Chinese, and, in addition, would make an excellent local leader or adviser.

   c. Both Keswicks are at present based on Shanghai.

   d. Michael LINDSAY. [Yenching University, Peking; son of the Master of Balliol; unattached [?]; circa 32] During the last 18 months has made 3 or 4 fairly extensive trips with guerrillas in the north and has written about them [for *The Times*] with shrewdness and discrimination. I know nothing of his military qualities, but his first hand experience and his local contacts would clearly be of value. The fact that he has avoided getting into trouble with the Japanese speaks well for his discretion.

   e. C.M.MCDONALD. [*The Times* correspondent in Shanghai; wife and child in Shanghai [I think]; circa 40] A thorough and reliable man who understands the Chinese and gets on well with them. When bombed on the 'Panay' showed great gallantry and resource, but this and other war experiences may have affected him in such a way as to make him more valuable at the centre rather than the fringes.

   f. Roger HOLLIS. [MI5; married; circa 34] Did several years in China with BAT. Though he has not been there recently, his judgment of Far Eastern affairs has always impressed me as unusually realistic. His co-operation, or even his comments, might be valuable at an early stage, particularly as he is available in London.

g. Richard FLEMING. [Lieutenant Lovat Scouts; married; circa 29] I have put down my brother's name, because, although he has no experience of China, he is the best potential leader of irregular troops I know.

4. The following names occur to me as 'possibles', not necessarily to be brought in at an early stage.

   a. F. Anson FIRTH. [Ex-Indian Army; ex BAT; married; circa 37; now works in England] Wild but ingenious and enterprising, and has 'pull' with the Chinese. Good colloquial knowledge of Cantonese and knows the South and Southerners well. Might do excellent work locally, for he has [or had] a creative touch in matters of organisation.

   b. Ian MORRISON. [Lately private secretary to Sir R. Craigie, now assistant *Times* correspondent in Shanghai; son of the famous *Times* Peking correspondent; unattached; circa 28] Outwardly a little soft, but has enterprise and might be valuable for his understanding of the Japanese mentality and, I believe, language.

   c. Sir Anthony JENKINSON. [Freelance journalist; now [believed] in England; unattached; circa 29] Slightly mad but has an original mind and in 1938 showed enterprise as a war correspondent in Central China. A good chap, but I cannot answer with certainty for his discretion.

   d. Dr Robert MacCLURE. [Canadian medical missionary; now in China; circa 50] His habit of persistently bicycling through both the Chinese and Japanese lines has given him a considerable insight into the conduct of the war. An irrepressible man of immense energy, who would be an asset to our wartime organisation, whatever form it took.

   e. Rewi ALLEY. [New Zealander; formerly connected with the Shanghai Municipal Administration, now organising Co-operative movements in the interior.] Have never met him, but from all I hear he sounds a useful man.

Note   It should be remembered that these observations are based on a fleeting and picaresque experience of the foreign communities in China. The lists of names at [3] and [4] should be regarded as suggestions for an anthology rather than a definitive edition. There are plenty of other candidates of whom I either know nothing or not enough.   P.F.

ANNEX M

ALLIED INTELLIGENCE AGENCIES

AIB The Allied Intelligence Bureau was a joint United States, Australian, Dutch and British intelligence and special operations agency in SWPC, responsible for operating parties of agents and commandos behind Japanese lines in order to collect intelligence and conduct guerrilla warfare.

BAAG The British Army Aid Group, Kweilin-based organisation for Hong Kong POWs.

BURINT The Burma Intelligence Corps was formed to provide liaison personnel, interpreters and guides with the Indian Army facing the Japanese in Burma. By October 1943, Burint was organised with a Central HQ, 10 Platoons [BAF] and two Platoons of Burma/Indian personnel of the Burma Regiment.

D Division D for deception; originally GSI[d] reporting to GHQ India, 'D' was SEAC's counter-intelligence/propaganda unit run by Colonel Peter Fleming.

DGER Direction générale d'Études et Recherches; French escape and evasion organisation.

E Group MI9's advanced base in New Delhi, E group was responsible for escape and evasion in Burma and Malaya and worked closely with MIS-X in other FE countries including China, Thailand and French Indo-China.

FELO The Australian Political and Propaganda warfare organisation.

ISLD Inter Service Liaison Department, a cover name for SIS in the Far East.

MI9 Officially established in December 1939, MI9's mission was to facilitate British evaders whose aircraft were downed in enemy occupied territory and to assist British prisoners of war in escaping from German POW camps.

MI[R] Military intelligence Research, an organisation set up in June 1939 in the War Office for the conduct of para-military activities.

MIS-X Established on 6 October 1942, MIS-X was a branch of the Military Intelligence Service of the US War Department with a mandate for escape and evasion activities.

NEFIS Netherlands East Indies Forces Intelligence Service/Section was a Dutch intelligence service set up in Melbourne, Australia after the conquest of the DEI by the Japanese. It was not involved in carrying out secret intelligence operations until the ISD had merged with the AIB. In May 1943 NEFIS III was given the task of sending secret agents into occupied territory by submarine or plane to gather intelligence on the local political and military situation. NEFIS III, and its predecessor, the Dutch section of ISD, sent a total of 36 teams into enemy territory. Over 250 agents were involved in these operations; 39 lost their lives.

OSS The Office of Strategic Services [OSS] was the approximate US counterpart of Britain's SIS and SOE with which it co-operated throughout the Second World War and its immediate aftermath. The OSS was created by Presidential Military Order on 13 June 1942 and it functioned as the principal US intelligence organisation in all operational theatres. Its primary function was to obtain information about enemy nations and to sabotage their war potential and morale.

P Division P for Priority; an SEAC staff function created by Admiral Mountbatten to co-ordinate the planning and execution of all special operations including those of SOE, ISLD and OSS.

Section D	Formed in 1938, Section D was an integral though distinct branch of SIS, under the command of Major Laurence Grand RE. Tasked to cause trouble in German-occupied Europe, it was later merged with SO2 of SOE.
SIS	Founded in 1909 as a joint initiative of the Admiralty and the War Office to control secret intelligence operations in the UK and overseas, during the 1920s SIS established a close operational relationship with the FO through providing 'Passport Control Officers' within embassies, based on a system developed during the First World War by British army intelligence. This provided its operatives with a degree of cover and diplomatic immunity. SOE operations were overtly offensive in the occupied countries, which clashed with the more discreet approach of SIS, leading to a significant level of friction between the two services. Despite these difficulties SIS nevertheless conducted substantial and successful operations in both occupied Europe and in the Middle East and Far East where it operated under the cover name 'Interservice Liaison Department' [ISLD].
SOE	The Special Operations Executive was formed in 1940 out of a collection of other agencies such as MI[R], a branch of the War Office's Military Intelligence Directorate, Section D of SIS, The Independent Companies [later Commandos] and the propaganda section at Electra House. Responsible for propaganda [SO1] and subversion [SO2], SOE reported initially to Dr. Hugh Dalton, Minister of Economic Warfare, and then Lord Selborne.
V Force	see Annex J.
Z Force	see Annex K.

ABBREVIATIONS

ABRO	The Army in Burma Reserve Officers, a formation of volunteer officers formed c.1937 who were distributed across a number of formations including SOE
ADO	Assistant District Officer
AFO	Anti-Fascist Organisation
AFPFL	Anti-Fascist People's Freedom League
AGFRTS	Air and Ground Forces Resources and Technical Staff
AIB	Allied Intelligence Bureau
AIF	Australian Imperial Forces
AJA	Anti-Japanese Army
AJUF	Anti-Japanese Union and Forces Malaya
Aka	also known as
ALFPMO	Allied Land Forces Paramilitary Organisation
AMF	Australian Military Forces
BAT	British-American Tobacco
BBCAU	British Borneo Civil Affairs Unit
BCP	Communist Party of Great Britain
BDA	Burma Defence Army
BIA	Burmese Independent Army
BLO	British Liaison Officer
BMM	British Military Mission
BNA	Burmese National Army
CASB	Civil Affairs Service Burma
CBE	Commander of the Most Excellent Order of the British Empire
CBI	China, Burma, India Theatre, a US command area
CCG	China Commando Group
CCP	Chinese Communist Party
CD	Symbol of executive director of SOE
CinC	Commander in Chief
CND	Chinese national dollar
CO	Commanding Officer
CoS	Chief of Staff
CPB	Communist Party of Burma
CPM	Communist Party of Malaya
CQMS	Company Quarter Master Sergeant
DC	District Commissioner
DCM	Distinguished Conduct Medal
DEI	Dutch East Indies
DMI	Director Military Intelligence
DNI	Director of Naval Intelligence
DSO	Companion of the Distinguished Service Order
DZ	Dropping zone
FANY	First Aid Nursing Yeomanry
FIC	French Indo-China
FMS	Federated Malay States
FMSVR	Federated Malay States Volunteer Reserve
FO	the British Foreign Office
Force 136	title of SOE in South East Asia

FSM	Free Siam Movement
FTM	Free Thailand Movement
GC	the George Cross
GLU	General Labour Union [Malaya]
GOC	General Officer Commanding
GSO	General Staff Officer [there are three grades, 1 being the most senior]
HDML	Harbour Defence Motor Launch
HMG	His Britannic Majesty's Government [British Government]
HMS	His Majesty's Ship
HQ	Headquarters
ICP	Indian Communist Party
IMS	Indian Medical Service
INA	Indian National Army
IO	Intelligence Officer
ISD	Inter Allied Services Department
ISDV	Indies Social Democratic Association
ISLD	see SIS
101 Detachment	see OSS
KMA	Kailan Mining Administration
KMT	Kuomintang or Chinese Nationalist party established by Sun Yat-sen in Peking in 1912
LO	Liaison Officer
LUP	Lying up point
MB	Motor boat
MBE	Member of the Most Excellent Order of the British Empire [Military Division]
MC	Military Cross
MEW	Ministry of Economic Warfare, official cover for SOE
MI[R]	Military Intelligence [Research]
ML	Motor Launch
MLO	Military Liaison Officer
MPAJA	Malayan People's Anti-Japanese Army
MTB	Motor torpedo boat
NEA	North Eastern Area of SWPC
NEFIS	Netherlands Forces Intelligence Service
OBE	Officer of the Most Excellent Order of the British Empire [Military Division]
OCDA	Overseas Chinese Defence Organisation
OCPD	Officer commanding Police District
ORs	Other Ranks i.e. all those other than commissioned officers
OTC	Officer training corps
PA	Personal Assistant
PKH	Communist Union of the Indies
PKI	Communist Party of Indonesia
PM	Prime Minister
POW	Prisoner of War
Psc	Passed Staff College
PWE	Political Warfare Executive
RA	Royal Artillery
RAA	Royal Australian Army

ABBREVIATIONS

RAF	Royal Air Force
RAMC	Royal Army Medical Corps
RAN	Royal Australian Navy
RANR	Royal Australian Navy Reserve
RANVR	Royal Australian Navy Volunteer Reserve
RAPWI	Rehabilitation of Allied Prisoners of War and Internees
RASC	Royal Army Service Corps
RE	Royal Engineers
RM	Royal Marines
RMAS	Royal Military Academy, Sandhurst
RN	Royal Navy
RNVR	Royal Naval Volunteer Reserve
SACO	Sino-American Special Technical Cooperative Organization
SACSEA	Supreme Allied Commander South East Asia
SBO	Senior British Officer
SBP	Stay behind party
SEAC	South East Asia Command
SHAEF	Supreme Headquarters Allied Expeditionary Force
SO	Special operations
SOA	Special Operations Australia
SOG	Special Operations Group
SRD	Services Reconnaissance Department
STS	Special Training Schools run by SOE to teach sabotage and guerrilla warfare
SWPA	South West Pacific Area
SWPC	South West Pacific Command
WO	War Office; when used as prefix to surname, Warrant Officer
W/T	Wireless telegraphy [transmitter and receiver]
2 i/c	Second in command

GLOSSARY

MILITARY

Catalina	long-range flying boat used to insert and extract covert parties.
Folboat	light collapsible craft just over sixteen feet in length; rubberised fabric on bamboo frame; weight some seventy lbs; capable of carrying 800 lbs of personnel and stores.
Liberator	long range US bomber converted for dropping men and supplies behind enemy lines.
Limpet	type of naval mine attached to a target by magnets.
Lysander	small army liaison aircraft capable of using very short jungle airstrips to insert an agent or a small container behind enemy lines.
STEN	9mm light weight sub-machine gun with a maximum effective range of 60 metres; 32 round box magazine.
Storepedo	cylindrical storage container with an attached parachute used to air-drop supplies to SOE parties in the jungle.

CIVIL

Atap hut	wood or bamboo framed hut with overlapping palm fronds as thatch.
Basha	bamboo hut.
Beri Beri	Vitamin B deficiency disease.
Borak	fermented drink made from rice or tapioca root.
Burman	tribe living in Burma; over 50 per cent of population.
Chapatte	type of Indian bread.
Chaung	small river or stream.
Elephant grass	bamboo-like grass up to twelve feet tall.
Headman	official rank given by Government to leading member of village.
Hine	tuskless elephant species.
Junk	ocean-going, cargo-carrying Chinese sailing vessel. Also used for deep-sea fishing.
Kampong	native village [Borneo and Malaya].
Kepala	head.
Kolek	small fishing boat.
Kuala	mouth or estuary of a river.
Kukri	sharp curved knife.
Ladang	jungle clearing for dry cultivation.
Lalang	sharp pointed grass about three feet high that takes over abandoned cultivated land.
Levies	for more than 200 years, the British ruled India with indigenous 'levies', conscripted Indian soldiers led by British officers and supported by British units. The same system was used in Burma to raise guerrilla forces to fight the Japanese.
Longyi	sheet of cloth worn round the waist running to the feet [Burma].
Maidan	flat open space.
Maughs	Arakanese Buddhists who inhabit southern half of Arakan.
Moulovi	Muslim priest.
Nibong	palm tree with edible growing point.

GLOSSARY

Orang Asli	an aborigine.
Padang	village green.
Parang	jungle knife.
Penghulu	headman of small district.
Prahu	Malaysian or Indonesian sailing boat, typically having a large triangular sail and an outrigger.
Pulau	an island.
Sakai	aboriginal tribes.
Sampan	flat-bottomed Chinese wooden boat from 3.5m to 4.5m used on inshore waters or rivers.
Sungei	rver or stream.
Taipan	term commonly used to refer to senior business executives in China, specifically the heads of the Jardine Matheson and Swire trading houses.
Thugyi	Burmese headman.
Tongkaung	light wooden boat for carrying goods upriver.
Tuan	Lord or Master, a title of respect formerly accorded to Europeans.
Ubi Kayu	tapioca root of poor nutritional value.
Ulu	jungle.

SELECTED BIBLIOGRAPHY

Aldrich, Richard: *Intelligence and the War against Japan*, CUP, 2000
Allen, Louis: *Burma: the Longest War*, J.M. Dent and Sons, 1984
Australia in the War of 1939–1945 Vols 4-7, Official History
Bailey, Roderick: *Forgotten Voices of the Secret War*, Ebury Press, 2008
Bank, Aaron: *From OSS to Green Berets – the Birth of Special Forces*, Presidio Press, 1986
Barker, Ralph: *One Man's Jungle, biography of Freddy Spencer Chapman*, Chatto & Windus, 1975
Bayley, Chris and Harper, Tim: *Forgotten Armies – Britain's Asian Empire and the War with Asia*, Penguin Allen Lane, 2004
Beamish, John: *Burma Drop*, Elek, 1958
Boulle, Pierre: *The Source of the River Kwai*, Trans Xan Fielding, Secker & Warburg, 1967
Bowen, John aka Gebhard: *Undercover in the Jungle [V force]*, William Kimber, 1978
Callahan, Raymond, *Burma 1942-1945*, Davis-Poynter, 1978
Chan, Sui-jeung: *Resistance in Hong Kong; the East River Column*, Royal Asiatic Society, 2009
Christie, Maurice A.: *Mission Scapula: Special Operations Executive in the Far East*, London, 2004
Cookridge, E.H.: *Inside SOE*, Arthur Barker, 1966
Courtney, G.B.: *Silent Feet – the History of Z Special Operations 1942-5*, McPherson's, 1993
Cox, Howard: *The Global Cigarette, the Origins and Evolution of BAT*, OUP, 2000
Crevècoeur, General Jean Boucher de: *La Liberation du Laos 1945-46*, Service Historique de l'Armée de Terre, Vincennes, 1985
Cromarty Tulloch, 'Pop': *In the Wake of Taw-Mei-Pa*, unpublished MSS IWM.
Crosby, M.G.M.: *Irregular Soldier*, XB Publications, 1993
Cross, John: *Red Jungle*, Robert Hale, 1957
Cruikshank, Charles: *SOE in the Far East*, OUP, 1983
Currey, Cecil: *Victory at any cost; the Genius of Vietnam's General Vo Nguyen Giap*, Potomac Books
Dear, Ian: *Sabotage and Subversion: SOE and OSS at War*, Phoenix, 1999
Dewavrin, Andre: *Memoires du Chef des Services Secrets de La France Libre.*
Dewavrin, Andre: *Souvenirs 1 – 2e Bureau Londres*, Solar, 1947
Dewavrin, Andre: *Souvenirs II – 10 Duke Street [BCRA]*
Dobrée, Peter: *Hot rain means danger – my war against Japan*, unpublished IWM, 1993
Dunlop, Richard: *Behind Japanese Lines: With the OSS in Burma*, Rand McNally, 1979
Dunn, Peter: *The First Vietnam War*, Hurst & Co, 1985
Evans, Sir Geoffrey: *The Johnnies*, Cassell, 1964
Fellowes-Gordon, Ian: *Amiable Assassins – the story of Kachin guerrillas in North Burma*, Robert Hale, 1957
Felton, Mark: *Japan's Gestapo: Murder, Mayhem and Torture in Wartime Asia*, Pen & Sword Books, 2009
Fenn, Charles: *At the Dragon's Gate, with the OSS in the Far East*, Naval Institute Press, 2004
Foot, M.R.D.: *SOE*, BBC Publications, 1984
Ford, Douglas: *Britain's Secret War against Japan 1937-48*, Routledge, 2006
Feuer A.B.: *Australian Commandos: Their Secret War against the Japanese in WWII*, Stackpole Books, 2006

SELECTED BIBLIOGRAPHY

Fleury, Georges: *La Guerre en Indochine 1945-1954*, Perrin, 1994
Gilchrist, Sir Andrew: *Bangkok Top Secret*, Hutchinson, 1970
Gilchrist, Sir Andrew: *South of Three Pagodas*, Robert Hale, 1987
Gin, Ooi Keat: *The Japanese Occupation of Borneo 1941-45*, Routledge, 2011
Gough, Richard: *SOE Singapore*, William Kimber, 1985
Gowda, Franes: *American Visions of NEI/Indonesia*, Amsterdam University Press, 2002
Griffiths-Marsh, Roland: *Sixpenny Soldier*, Angus Robertson, 1990
Guthrie, Duncan: *Jungle Diary*, MacMillan, 1946
Hall, Maxwell: *Kinabalu Guerrillas*, Opuys, 2009
Hammer, Ellen J.: *The Struggle for Indo-China 1940-1955: Vietnam and the French Experience*, Stanford University Press, 1966
Hammond, Robert: *A Fearful Freedom*, Leo Cooper, 1984
Harper, Tim.: *End of Empire and the Making of Malaya*, CUP, 1999
Harrisson, Tom: *World Within; a Borneo story*, The Cresset Press, 1959
Hedley, John: *Jungle Fighter: Infantry Officer, Chindit and S.O.E. Agent in Burma, 1941-45*, Tom Donovan Publishing Ltd, 1996
Heimann, Judith: *The Most Offending Soul Alive – Tom Harrisson and his remarkable life*, Aurum, 2002
Hembry, Boris: *Malayan Spymaster*, Monsoon, 2011
Hickling, Hugh: *Crimson Sun over Borneo*, Pelanduk, 1997
Holland, Mabel and John: *El Tigre, Frank Holland, Commando, Coastwatcher*, Oceans Enterprises
Holman, Dennis: *The Green Torture – The Ordeal of Robert Chrystal*, Robert Hale, 1962
Holt, Thaddeus: *The Deceivers, Allied Military Deception in the Second World War*, Phoenix, 2005
Horton, Dick: *Ring of Fire*, Leo Cooper, 1983
Howarth, Patrick: *Undercover*, Routledge and Kegan Paul, 1980
Ind, Allison: *Spy Ring Pacific*, Weidenfeld and Nicolson, 1958
Irwin, Anthony: *Burmese Outpost*, Collins, 1945
Jeffery, Keith: *MI6, the History of the Secret Intelligence Service 1909-49*, Bloomsbury, 2010
Jones, J.D.F.: *Storyteller, the Many Lives of Laurens van der Post*, John Murray, 2001
Kemp, Peter: *The Thorns of Memory*, Sinclair-Stevenson, 1990
Keswick, Maggie and Weatherall, Clara: *The Thistle and the Jade*, Francis Lincoln, 2008
Kings College Foyle Special Collection PAsMPH Box D 810.S7 ATH [Louise Atherton] *SOE Operations in the Far East*
Kirby, Maj-Gen Woodburn: *The War against Japan*, HMSO, 1965
Laffin, John: *Special and Secret [Australians at war]*, Time Life, 1990
Latimer, Jon : *Burma: The Forgotten War*, John Murray, 2004
Leasor, James: *Singapore, the Battle that Changed the World*, Hodder & Stoughton, 1968
Leasor, James: *Boarding Party*, Heinemann, 1978
Lindsay, Hsiao Li: *Bold Plum*, lulu.com
Lindsay, Michael: *The Unknown War – North China 1937-45*, Bergstrom & Boyle, 1975
Lindsay, Oliver: *At the Going down of the Sun*, Nelson, 1981
Liu, F.F.: *A Military History of Modern China: 1924-1949*, Princeton University Press, 1956
Lomax, Sir John: *The Diplomatic Smuggler*, Arthur Barker, 1965
Long, Bob: *Z Special Unit's Secret War – Operation SEMUT 1*, Transpereon, 1989
MacLaren, Roy: *Canadians behind Enemy Lines 1939-45*, UBCP, 1981
MacPherson, Sir William: *The Secret History of SOE*, St Ermin's Press, 2000
Marr, David: *Vietnam 1945 – the Quest for Power*, University of California Press, 1995

McDonald, Gabrielle: *New Zealand's Secret Heroes*, Reed Books, 1991
McKie, Ronald: *The Heroes [Ivan Lyons]*, Angus and Robertson, 1968
Moffit, Athol: *Project Kingfisher*, ABC Books, 1995
Morrison, Ian: *Grandfather Longlegs: the life and gallant death of Major HP Seagrim, GC, DSO, OBE*, Faber & Faber, 1947
Moss, Stanley: *A War of Shadows*, Boardman & Co, 1952
Moynahan, Brian: *Jungle Soldier [Freddy Spencer Chapman]*, Quercus, 2009
Neville, Peter: *Britain in Vietnam, Prelude to Disaster*, Routledge, 2007
Noonan, William: *The Surprising Battalion, Australian Commandos in China*, NSW Bookstall Co., 1945
Noone, Richard: *Rape of the Dream People*, Hutchinson & Co, 1972
O'Brien, Terence: *The Moonlight War*, Collins, 1987
Ooi Keat Gin: *The Japanese Occupation of Borneo, 1941-45*, Routledge, 2010
Patti, Archimedes: *Why Vietnam? Prelude to America's Albatross*, University of California Press
Parker, Geoffrey: *Black Scalpel*, William Kimber, 1968
Peacock, Geraldine: *The Life of a Jungle Walla*, Arthur Stockwell, 1958
Peers, William and Brelis, Dean: *Behind the Burma Road*, Little, Brown & Co, 1963
Petro, W: *Triple Commission*, John Murray, 1968
Powell, Alan: *War by Stealth: Australians and the Allied Intelligence Bureau*, Melbourne University Press, 1996
Reynolds, E. Bruce: *Thailand's Secret War – OSS, SOE and the Free Thai Underground in World War II*, CUP, 2004
Ride, Edwin: *BAAG [British Army Aid group]: Hong Kong Resistance 1942-45*, OUP Hong Kong, 1981
Roosevelt, Kermit: *OSS War report*
Rose, Angus: *Who dies fighting*, Jonathan Cape, 1944
Ross, Sheila: *And Tomorrow Freedom [Australian Guerrillas in the Philippines]*, Allen and Unwin, 1989
Rowland, Sir John: *Diaries*, British Library.
Sabattier, General: *Le Destin de l'Indochine: Souvenirs et documents*, 1952
Sacquety, Troy: *The OSS in Burma: Jungle War against the Japanese*, University Press of Kansas, 2013
Seaman, Mark: *Special Operations Executive: A New Instrument of War*, Taylor and Francis, 2005
Sheenan, Margaret: *Our Man in Malaya: John Davis, CBE, DSO, Force 136 SOE and Postwar Counter-insurgency*, The History Press, 2007
Skidmore, Ian: *Escape from the Rising Sun*, Leo Cooper, 1973
Slim, Viscount: *Defeat into Victory*, Cassell, 1956
Smiley, David: *Irregular Regular*, Michael Russell, 1994
Smith, Martin: *Burma – Insurgency and the Politics of Ethnicity*, Zed Books, 1991
Spencer Chapman, Freddy: *The Jungle is neutral*, Chatto & Windus, 1949
Stafford, David: *Camp X, SOE and the American Connection*, Viking, 1987
Sweet-Escott, Bickham: *Baker Street Irregular*, Methuen & Co, 1965
Tan Chong Tee: *Force 136, Story of a WWII resistance fighter*, Asiapac Publications, Singapore, 1995
Taylor, Robert: *View Larger ImageMarxism and Resistance in Burma, 1942-1945: Thein Pe Myint's Wartime Traveler*, Ohio Universoty Press, 1984

SELECTED BIBLIOGRAPHY

Trenowden, Ian: *Operations Most Secret SOE in the Malayan theatre*, William Kimber, 1978
Tyson, Geoffrey: *Forgotten Frontier*, WH Targett, Calcutta, 1945
Yu, Maochun: *OSS in China: Prelude to Cold War*, Yale University Press, 1966
Van der Post, Sir Laurens: *The Night of the New Moon*, Hogarth, 1960
Van der Ven, Hans: *War and Nationalism in China 1925-45*, Routledge, 2012
Verlander, Harry: *My War in the SOE: Behind Enemy Lines in France and Burma with the Special Operations Executive*, Independent Books, 2010
Wakeman, Frederic: *Spymaster, Dai Li and the Chinese Secret Service*, University of California Press, 2003
Wasserstein, Bernard: *Secret War in Shanghai*, Profile Books, 1998
Wharton-Tigar, Edward: *Burning Bright*, Metals Bulletin, 1987
West, Nigel: *Secret War*, Hodder and Stoughton, 1992
Williams, J.H.: *Elephant Bill*, Rupert Hart-Davis, 1950
Wong, Marjorie: *The Dragon and the Maple Leaf*, Pirie, 1994
Wylie, Neville: *The Politics and Strategy of Clandestine War, SOE 1940-1946*, Routledge, 2006
Wynyard, Noel: *Winning Hazard*, Sampson Low, Marston & Co, 1946

INDEX

ADDER, 398
Afghanistan, 63, 64
AGAS, 352, 361, 365-6
Alessandri, Gen, 295
Alexander, Comd Alex, 49
Alexander, Gen, 16, 89
Allen, Sgt, 84
Allied Intelligence Bureau, 305, 312-3, 346
Amery, Leo, 63
Andaman Islands, 84-5
Andrew, Findlay, 231-3, 281
Annan, Capt W.R., 209
Anstey, Brig John, 75, 78, 347
Anti-Fascist Organisation, 100
APPLE, 353
APPRECIATION, 262-3, 268
APRICOT, 386
ARISTOC, 263
Aru Islands, 390
Arun, Maj C., see Suphasawat, Prince
Ashwell, Capt Paul, 267
ASPARAGUS, 393
Assam Tea Planters Association, 53

Bacon, Capt, 106
BADGER, 101
BALDHEAD, 84-5
Balharry, Capt John, 259
BALMORAL, 265
Barlow, 2/Lt Morley, 153
Barnard, Maj Jack, 95
Barrie, Sgt, 378
Barry, Maj James, see Cauvin
Barry, Sgt, 354
Bathurst, Ben, 265
BAZAAR, 293
BEACON, 159
Beevor, Col John, 78
BELIEF, 291
Benson, Sgt, 54
Berwick, 2/Lt Edward, 153
BETTY, 258
Beyts, Col, 84
BILLOW, 263, 267
BIRDCAGE, 272

Bishop, Adrian, 74
BISON, 102, 137
Black, Lt Lawrie, 382-6
BLACKBIRD/SUNLAG, 398
Blackburn, Sir Arthur, 216
BLADET, 123
Blain, Maj, 123
Blaizot, Gen Roger, 291
Blamey, Gen, 304-8
BLANDINGS, 267
Blantan Agreement, 186
Blathwayt, Maj C.C., 103, 268
Blow, Maj Rex, 352, 374
BOILER, 269
Borneo, 349-79
Boulle, Pierre, 288
Bourne, Capt H.E., 134
Bower, S/Sgt, 354
Boyt, Noel, 52-3, 59, 89, 113, 144
Brandis, Sgt, 352, 360
Bridge, Maj George, 282
Brierley, Sgt, 139-41
BRILLIG, 264
British American Tobacco, 35-6, 248
British Army Aid Group, 236, 238, 243-4, 251-3, 255, 258
Britton, Capt David, 139
Broadhurst, Lt Col D.K., 160, 201-2, 306, 351, 397
Brockman, 2/Lt George, 154
Broke-Popham, ACM Sir Robert, 14, 38, 42
Broome, Col Dick, 42, 150, 155-6, 158, 160, 171-2, 174, 181-90, 322
Brown, 2/Lt F.G., 154
Brown, 2/Lt Leslie, 153
Brown, 2/Lt R.H., 154
Brown, Capt, 104
Brown, Sgt Ken, 144
Bryce-Smith, Capt Richard, 259-60, 274, 281
BUCCANEER, 84
Bullard, Sir Reader, 75
BULLDOZER, 392
BUNKUM, 84-5
Burdon, Capt F.H., 259
Burma Defence Army, 88, 100,
Burma Independence Army, 88, 99, 113-14

INDEX

Burma, 86-143
Bush, Maj John, 65
Butler, A.B., 36
Butt, Maj, 18
Byrne, Lt Joseph, 282

Cadogan, Sir Alexander, 36-7, 290
CAIRNGORN, 159
Calvert, Brig Mike, 89, 123, 167, 224, 304
CAMEL, 103
Cameron, Sgt Colin, 330-6
Campbell, Cpl Pat, 330-6
Campbell, Maj Jock, 40, 42, 49, 306, 322
Campbell-Miles, Maj A.C., 150, 160
CANDLE, 265, 268
Carew, Maj T.A., 103-4, 348
Carey, Lt Sam, 331-6
CARPENTER, 158, 189, 403
CARRIAGE, 210-11
CARROT, 393
Carse, Lt H.E., 324-8
Carter, Maj Toby, 354, 373, 375-6
Cashman, Capt, 398
Cauvin, Maj Louis, 42, 153
Cavalin, Lt Col, 297
Cawthorne, Maj Gen R., 74, 298
Cedile, Gen Jean, 299
Celebes and Molucca Islands, 386-9
Chak, Adm Chan, 251
Chapman, Capt Leslie, 159
Chapman, Lt Col Freddy Spencer, 37, 38, 40, 44, 46, 49, 150, 156, 161, 163-74, 194
Chapman, Maj Walter, 329
Chapman-Walker, Col John, 306-7, 329
CHARACTER, 106-9, 279
CHEETAH, 101, 142
Cheng, Roger, 254
Chennault, Gen Claire, 218, 244, 298
Chester, Maj Frank, 306, 351-2, 355-64
CHIMP, 104, 144
China and Hong Kong, 212-55, 451-6
China Commando Group, 41, 48, 225-6, 242
Chinese Communist Party, 18-19, 213, 222-3, 233, 237, 240, 243-4
Chins, 2, 88-9, 282, 447, 449
Chrystal, Robert, 150, 152, 167, 179, 194-200

Churchill, Winston, 7-8, 19, 209, 230, 290-1, 295
Civil Affairs Bureau [Burma], 103
Clague, Col Douglas, 272
Clark Kerr, Sir Archibald, 41, 216, 221, 224
Clark, Capt, 134
Clarke, Col Brien, 12, 32
Clarke, H.G., 223
COBRA, 398-99
Cockran, Lt, 38
Collins, Sgt, 268
Combe, Maj Dick, 352, 361, 365-6
Communist Party of Malaya, 42, 148, 155, 196
Communist Union of the Indies, 343
Connolly, Sgt, 178
CONWAY, 226
Cooper, Duff, 37, 230
Cope, Capt Sam, 283
CORONET, 70
Corps Leger d'Intervention, 290-2
CORTADELLAS, 295
Cotterill, J.M., 154, 170
COUPLING, 265, 277
Courtney, Maj Jumbo, 351
COW, 105
Cowie, Maj, 236
Cox, Maj, 104
Craft, Cpl Colin, 330-6
Craigie, Sir Robert, 37
CRANE, 388
Crawford, 2/Lt H.R., 154
CRAYFISH, 392
Creer, John, 179, 195-7
Critchley, Lt Col Ronald, 74, 107, 130-5
Crofton-Moss, Lt James, 382-6
Croley, Maj T.V., 85
Cromarty Tulloch, Col 'Pop', 107, 111
Crosby, Lt Col Bing, 101-2
Crosby, Sir Josiah, 37
Cross, CQMS John, 25, 42, 153
Cubitt, 2/Lt Thomas, 153
Cumming, 2/Lt James, 154
Cumming, Lt Col Steve, 37-8, 46, 54, 58-9
Cunningham, Lt, 348
Cusack, WO, 354

D'Astugues, Lt, 348
DAHFORCE, 98, 131-2

DALFORCE, 98
Dallow, Sgt, 134
Dalton, Hugh, 8, 246
Damar Islands, 391
DAMPIERRE, 295
Darby, 2/Lt Oliver, 152
Darlington, Saw, 113
David, Col Lionel, 246
Davidson, Lt Duncan, 162, 324-40
Davijd, Lt, 353
Davis, Col John, 42, 155, 158, 167, 171, 181-90
Davison, Maj C.J., 283-4
Dawson, Sgt, 398
De Crèvecoeur, Comdt Jean, 290
De Langlade, Baron Francois, 288-293
De Wiart, Gen Carton, 284, 292
Decoux, Adm, 288, 293
DEER, 20, 297
Dennys, Maj Gen L.E., 224
Detachment 204, 224-8
Dewavrin, Col Andre, 293
Dewey, Lt Peter, 299
Dickens, Sgt, 84
Digay, Saw, 113
DILWYN, 98-9 101, 424
DIXIE, 223, 243
Dobrée, Lt Col P.G., 158-9, 161, 191-3, 198
Dolan, Capt Brooke, 242
Dolly, Cyril, 15
DONKEY, 100
Dorman-Smith, Sir Reginald, 41, 89, 99, 113
Double Tenth Uprising, 356-60
Dryber, Fl Lt, 353
Duallsi, Insp, 352, 360
Dunlop, Lt Col Weary, 51
DURIAN, 264
Dutch East Indies, 341-8

Edmeades, Capt, 354
Eifler, Maj Carl, 90-1
ELEPHANT, 102
ELK, 104
Elkin, 2/Lt Edward, 152, 169
Ellwood, Sgt, 397-8
EMBANKMENT, 299
Escarra, Prof Jean, 289
ETONIAN, 258

Evans, Michael, 279
Eve, W.D.R., 41
EYEMOUTH, 100

FABRE, 296
Falconar, Capt K.J., 84
Falls, A/S W.G., 324-6, 330-6
Fatt, Lim Keng, 356
Fellowes-Gordon, Maj Ian, 19
Fenn, Maj Charles, 298-300
Fenner, Maj Claude, 17, 155-6, 158, 160, 186-7
Fergusson-Warren, Lt Col Alan, see Warren
FERRET, 273
Field, Brig, 38, 43
FIGHTER, 159
FINCH, 388
Finlay, Lt Col Jock, 318, 351
FIRST CULVERIN, 209
FIRTREE, 390
Fischbacher, Jacques, 289
Fleming, Lt Col Peter, 159, 204, 220
Fletcher, Cpl Roland, 330-6
Fletcher, Walter, 69, 236, 245-50
FLIMWELL, 98
FLOUNDER, 390
Forrester, Maj R.E., 96
Francis, Lt, 94
Fraser, Capt, 56
Freer, J.K., 150
French Indo-China, 287-301
FUNNEL, 158

GALAHAD, 94
Galvin, John, 36, 233
Gamble, Col, 91
Gande, W.J., 41, 223
Garden, Pat, 152, 167, 194
Gardiner, Lt Col Ritchie, 53, 56, 60, 109-10
Garnons-Williams, Capt G.A., 14, 69, 262
GASSET, 295
GAUNTLET, 238
Gavin, Maj Gen Jim, 38, 41, 45-6, 48, 89, 167, 223, 251
Geeroms, Capt B.H. Willemsz, 392
Giap, Gen Vo Nguyen, 297
Gilchrist, Andrew, 258
Gill-Davies, Lt Col Derek, 240

INDEX

Gillies, Lt Malcolm, 382-6
GIRAFFE, 316-7, 388
Glen, Sandy, 68
Goa, 76-7
GOLDFISH, 381
Golley, Sgt David, 330-6
Goodfellow, Maj Basil, 32, 38, 41-2, 46, 155, 182-5, 289
Gordon, Laurence, 297-8
Goss, Capt Peter, 106, 404
Gracey, Gen, 299
Graham, Roland, 40, 151, 167, 183, 194
Green, Conor, 63
Green, Maj Jimmy, 182
Gregg, Sgt, 398
Greig, Maj C.L., 84
GRENVILLE, 78
Grew, Joseph, 346
Grimsdale, Maj Gen, 251, 258
Grimson, Capt, 398
Grut, Maj Edmund, 260, 262
GSI[k] – see INDIA Mission
Gubbins, Maj Gen Sir Colin, 48, 69, 83, 291, 313
Guibaut, Andre, 289
GUINNESS, 291
Guinness, Brig Bobby, 75, 292
Gupta, Sunil Datta, 96
GUSTAVUS, 155-6, 186
Guthrie, Capt Duncan, 114
Gyaw, Lt Ba, 98

HAINTON, 98, 279-85, 445-6
Hallam, Sgt, 354
Halliwell, Comd Davis, 20
Halmahera, 390
Hambro, Sir Charles, 10, 69, 77, 231-2
Hannah, Maj Jim, 156, 158, 161, 186
Hardwick, R.K., 316-17, 389
Hardy, 2/Lt William, 153
Hardy, L/Cpl John, 330-6
HARLINGTON, 98, 114
Harmon, Walter, 221
Harrington, Maj, 105, 269
Harrison, Maj, 156
Harrisson, Lt Col Tom, 354, 367-74
Hart, Maj J.V., 159
Harvey, Bill, 151

Harvey, Lt Ronald, 89
Hasler, Maj G.A., 159, 198
HATCH, 85
Haywood, 2/Lt Clark, 152, 168-9, 194
Headley, Maj Derek, 160
Heath, Lt, 38, 89
HEAVY/LYNX, 283
HEBRIDES, 159, 161, 189, 19, 198-9
Hedley, Maj 'Bath', 136-8
Helfrich, Adm, 208, 347
Hembry, Boris, 40-2, 151, 167, 194, 198
Heppner, Col, 298
Herenguel, Lt Jean-Marie, 301
Herring, Lt Col Dennis, 99, 132, 283-5
Hibberdine, Maj John, 268, 270
Hill-Murray, Maj John, 267
Hislop, Maj J.R., 161
Hla, Saw Po
Hoagland, Pte, 297
Hobbs, Maj Tom, 259, 266, 268, 273
Hoffie, Sgt Alex, 382-6
Hollis, Roger, 455
Holmes, Maj D.R., 237, 251-2
Holroyd, Max, 252
Hood, Maj Hugo, 101, 105, 142-3
HORNBILL, see RIMAU
HOTFOOT, 264
HOUND, 102
Houseman, Capt, 348
Howe, Maj William, 56, 101, 144
Hudson, Col Christopher, 12, 67, 155, 208
Hudson, Lt Col Christopher 'Soapy', 268, 275-8
Hung, Chang, 156
Huston, A/S A.W., 324-6, 330-6
HYENA, 107, 132
Hywood, Sgt, 352

INDIA Mission, 63-85
Indian Communist Party, 64
INFLUX, 265
Ingham-Clark, Maj George, 65
Ingleton, Maj Reg, 330-6
Institute of International Relations, 233, 236
Inter-Allied Services Department, 304-6, 311, 351
Inter Service Liaison Department, 5, 14, 17, 18, 27, 37, 42, 46, 75, 98, 101, 100, 119, 151, 153, 155, 172, 182, 198, 208, 235, 253, 260, 263,

471

268, 394, 422, 425 also see SIS
Ismail, Capt Ibrahim bin, 159, 203-5
Ivory, Lt Col Basil, 74

JACKAL, 105
Jaques, Brig Victor, 266-7, 271
Jardine, Capt, 53, 56
Java, 380-82
JAYWICK, 69, 162, 186, 319-29
Jeffries, Capt, 348
Jinkins, Maj, 352, 360
Johnston-Smith, Lt Col R.V., 348
Jones, A.E., 32, 223
Jones, A.M.W., 324
Jones, Major C.B. Jonah, 98, 140, 281
Joyce, Col, 63
JUKEBOX, 158
Jupp, S.D., 99

Kachins, 2, 19, 61, 88-92, 94-6, 98, 111, 113, 132, 137, 144, 282-3, 285, 449
Kai, Cheng, 281
Kai-shek, Generalissimo Chiang, 3, 34, 36-7, 41, 78, 90, 99, 214, 216, 220, 224-6, 231-4. 237, 239-40, 246, 258-9, 262, 281, 284, 288, 452, 455
Karens, 2, 52, 86, 88-90, 98, 106-20, 123, 127-8, 132, 134, 274, 282, 449
Kaulback, Lt Col Ronnie, 110, 235
Kemball, Maj J.P.G., 103
Kemp, Maj Peter, 268, 300-1
Kempeitai, 7, 21, 51, 98, 115-18, 187, 192, 204-5, 271, 328, 335, 345, 380
Kendall, Lt Col Mike, 225, 237, 253-4
Keswick, Col David, 229
Keswick, John, 10, 11, 41, 77, 220, 225-6, 231-2, 238, 249, 251, 455
Keswick, Tony, 69, 229-31, 307, 455
Keyes, Adm Sir Roger, 48
Killery, Val, 10, 14, 32-4, 39, 41, 43, 48, 89
Kino, Fl Lt, 296
Klotz, Lt Francois, 300
KMT, 78
Knott, Maj Jack, 38, 258
KOOKABURRA, 330
Kroll, Capt, 389
Kroon, Lt, 40
Kwok, Albert, 351, 356-60

LAGARTO, 397-8
Lamb, Sgt, 41
LANCER, 396-7
Lawrence, Cpl, 399
Le Selleur, Maj Alfred, 38, 64
Le Vallois, Lt, 296
Leach, Maj Edmund, 91
Leese, Gen Sir Oliver, 103
Leitch, Maj, 235
Leith-Ross, Sir Frederick, 41, 214
Leney, Sgt Roger, 109
Leonard, Maj George, 159, 161
Leyden, John, 54
Li, Gen Tai, 222, 224-5, 231, 242-4, 248, 260
LIKEWISE, 159
Lindsay, Lt Col Peter, 52-62, 89
Lindsay, Michael, 220-3, 455
Linlithgow, Marquess of, 63
LION, 102, 386
Livingston, Capt Dick, 144
LIZARD, 201, 396-7, 401-3
Lodge, Maj Ernest, 210-11
Loloda Islands, 390
Lomax, Sir John, 10, 38
Lombok, 382-6
Lone, Maj Shan, 98, 101
Long, Comd, 304
Lovett-Campbell, Maj Percy, 99
Lovink, Capt, 312
Low, Capt Michael, 38, 46
Lowe, Capt Donald, 209
Lucas, Maj, 134
Lyon, Maj Ivan, 42, 49, 69, 306, 319-40
Lyons, Brig, 48

Macadam, Maj, 105
MacAlister, Jill and Lorna, 248
MacArthur, Gen, 3, 18, 20, 201, 240, 304, 307, 312, 329, 346, 351, 388
Macdonald, Capt, 348
MACHINE, 269
Mackay, Lt Thomas, 154
Mackenzie, Colin, 10, 13-14, 20, 52, 63, 72-81, 89, 103-4, 243, 246, 291, 295, 297, 299, 301, 323, 329, 382, 347, 415-20
MACKEREL, 380
Mackrell, Gyles, 57-62

INDEX

MacLaren, Maj J, 352
Maddox, Lt Col 'Red', 92-4
MAGPIE, 318, 388
Magruder, Brig Gen John, 219
MAHOUT, 96
Majoe Island, 391
Malaya, 146-206
MANUAL, 102
Marchant, Capt, 348
Marsh, A/S 'Boofhead', 330-6
Marshall, Gen George, 219
Marshall, Sgt, 398
Martin, Maj 'Paddy', 158, 189
Masters, Maj John, 136-7
MASTIFF, 272
MATADOR, 257
MATADOR, 38
Matheson, 2/Lt James, 154
Mathews, Lt Dudley, 154
MATRIARCH, 208
Maw, Dr Ba, 86, 88, 99
May, Capt, 352
May, Prof Meyer, 289
McCarthey, Maj Denis, 84
McCoull, Maj, 105
McCrindle, Capt E.J., 53, 98, 114, 116-17
McEwan, Capt Colin, 251-2
McGarry, Lt, 38, 46
McGlashon, 2/Lt Ernest, 154
McGowan, Sir Harry, 33
McKenzie, Sgt, 360
McLeod, Lt Gen D.K., 41, 89
MENZIES, 393
Merrill, Col, 94
Meunier, Capt Pierre, 105
MICKLEHAM, 246
Miles, Comd Milton, 242-4, 260
Millar, G.D.L., 54
Milon, Maj, 291
Milton, Capt Oliver, 95
Minh, Ho Chi, 148, 297-301
Miskin, S.C., 36
Mollinger, Maj, 208
Molucca Islands, see Celebes
MONGOOSE, 107-9, 134, 142
MONKEY, 101
Mordant, Gen Eugene, 291

Morgan, Capt, 42
Morrison, 2/Lt Leonard, 153
Morter, Sgt Doug, 42, 153
MOSQUITO/HOOK, 381
Moss, Maj Stanley, 268, 270
Moss, Sir George, 43
MOSSTROOPS, 316
Mott, Lt Col Egerton, 36, 41, 304-5, 311-13, 316, 347
Mountbatten, Adm Lord Louis, 3, 14, 69, 77, 80, 82-3, 103, 111, 116, 186, 232, 243, 262-4 266-7, 271, 284, 291-3, 301, 307, 346
MOUSE, 103
MULTIPLE, 160
Munro-Faure, Col Paul, 234
Murphy, Peter, 77, 82-3
Musgrove, Col R., 161

NATION, 104-6
Nawng, Capt Hkun, 101
Neil, Charles, 74
Nelson, Sir Frank, 10, 32, 34, 68
NERONIAN, 268
Nethersole, Michael, 74
New Guinea, 392-4
Nicholl, C., 36
Nicholson, Capt N.F., 259
Nimitz, Adm, 20, 304
Nimmo, Maj Jimmy, 98, 114, 116-17
Nixon, F.H.B., 32, 406-7
NONCHALANT, 236, 249
Noone, Pat, 2, 150, 156, 170-1, 175-80, 185, 188, 191, 195-7, 199
Nyholm, Erik, 41, 225

O'Dwyer, Maj A.B., 12, 39
OAKTREE, 392
OATMEAL, 159, 203-5
OBLIVION, 237, 254
OBSTACLE, 268
OCCASION, 268
Ogden, A.G.N., 235
Oldham, Col A.G., 304
Oliver, Philip, 268
OPOSSUM, 316, 388-9
ORIENTAL Mission, 5, 10, 13, 32-64, 66, 89-90, 92, 96, 167, 182-3, 195, 201, 223-4, 226, 258-9,

273, 311, 318, 322
OSS, 14, 18-22, 78, 90-6, 100, 158-9, 209, 221, 239-40, 242-4, 254-5, 258-60, 262, 264-8, 271-2, 281, 297-301, 304, 346
OTTER, 107, 126

Pace, L/Cpl Hugo, 330-6
Page, Capt Bob, 330-6
Page, Lt R.C., 324
Pang-tzo, Gen Mao, 218
PANICLE, 266
Park, Col Robert, 21
PARSNIP, 381
PARTERRE, 276
Passmore, Lt, 38, 42, 46
PAVIE, 296
Pe, Thein, 99-100
Peacock, Lt Col Edgar, 107, 125-9
Pearson, 2/Lt Cyril, 152, 169
Pechkoff, Gen, 290
Pel, Capt H.G.C., 208
Pelton, 2/Lt Foster, 153
Pennell, Maj George, 18, 282
PERCH, 393
Percival, Lt Gen Arthur, 11, 38
Phalangkun, Chamkat, 258-62
Phanomyong, Pridi, 17, 258-60 262-8, 271
Phibun, FM, 257-8, 263, 277, 287
Pierce, Maj, 348
PIG, 104
Pilditch, Denys, 74
PINE NEEDLE, 391
Peng, Chin, 156, 171, 185-6, 188-90
Ping-shen, Gen Wang, 99, 232-3
Pointon, Maj Peter, 259, 264, 270
Poles, Capt Bill, 127
PONTOON, 159
POTATO, 381
Pramot, Seni, 258
Pratt, Sgt, 56
Pratt, Sir John, 217
Prescott, Capt, 348
PRIEST, 268
PRITCHARD, 259, 262
PYTHON, 201, 351-2, 355-6, 358, 360-2

Quayle, Frank, 150, 152, 169, 187, 194
Quéré, Lt J.J., 312

RADISH, 393
RAF, 28-30
Rand, 2/Lt Guy, 152
RAVEN, 300, 388
RAZOR, 263
Read, Maj S.H.J., 259, 269
Reddish, Maj Neville, 158, 206
Redman, Capt, 269
Reeve, L.D., 36
Reeve, Maj W.D., 259
Reid, 2/Lt John, 153
REINDEER, 104, 139-40, 144
REMARKABLE, 158, 187, 191
REMORSE, 69, 236, 247
RESIDENCY, 209
RESURRECTION, 237
RETALIATE, 209
Reymond, Lt Bruno, 330-6
Richardson, Maj J.A., 160
Ride, Col Lindsay, 236, 243, 251, 254-5, 258, 281, 428
Riggs, Sub Lt Gregor, 330-6
RIMAU, 329-40
Ripley, Fl Lt, 352
Robertson, William, 150
Robinson, 2/Lt William, 152, 167, 179, 194
Robinson, Capt Noel, 159
ROCKET, 268
ROGER, 266
Roosevelt, Franklin D., 7-8, 20, 218-19, 242, 290-1, 295-6
Rose, Archibald, 35
Rose, Maj Angus, 33, 40, 49
Rosher, Maj, 46, 182
Ross, Lt Robert, 330-6, 339-40
Rossiter, E.W., 53-60
ROTARY, 267
Roussett, Lt Pierre, 295
Rowland, Sir John, 53-61
Rowley-Conwy, Maj Geoffrey, 51
Rubinstein, Maj, 101, 104, 144-5
Rudwick, Lt, 360

INDEX

Sabattier, Maj Gen, 293
Salinger, Maj, 236
SALMON, 391
San, Aung, 88, 99
Sanasen, Mani, 258
Sanderson, S/Sgt, 354, 373
Sansom, Sir George, 36
Sarawak, 354
Sargent, Lt Blondie, 330-6
Sargent, Sir Orme, 291
Sartin, Sgt John, 46, 151, 168
Sassi, Col Jean, 301
SATIRIST, 293
SAVANNA, 265
Saw, Willie Saw, 113
Sawyer, Cpl, 56, 89
Saya San Rebellion, 86
SCAPULA, 38
SCEPTICAL, 271
Scheepens, Lt Jan, 208-10
Scott, Maj Ken, 268, 270
Scott-Skovso, Lt A.E., 153
Seagrim, Maj Hugh, 89-90, 98, 112-121
Selborne, Lord, 76, 239, 291, 295, 329
SEMUT, 354
SEMUT, 372-3, 375, 377-8
Seng, Lo Bo, 156, 184
SEQUENCE, 265
Seram, 390
SERRES, 296
Service d'Action, 291, 294, 297
Services Reconnaissance Department, 161, 306
SHARK, 393
Sharpe, Sgt, 104
Shebbeare, E.O., 177
SHRILL, 388
Shu, Frank, 248
Shwe, Tin, 99
Sime, Maj Durward, 158, 206
Simpson, Capt R.A., 291
SIREN, 265
SIREN, 266
SIS, 4, 8, 16-18, 35, 39, 43, 69, 78, 221, 223, 236, 253, 255, 268, 312; also see Inter Service Liaison Department
Slim, Gen William, 16, 79, 100, 103, 106-7, 405
Small, Lt, 268

Smiley, Maj David, 268, 301
Smith, Cecil, 52, 89
Smith, J.W., 154
Smith, Maj Nicol, 20
Smyllie, Capt Tom, 153
Sochon, Maj Bill, 354, 373, 377-9
Soong, T.V., 218, 233
SPARROW, 396, 401
Special Operations Australia, 10, 306-9, 312
SPIERS, 233-5
Spoor, Col, 374
SQUALID, 268
SQUIRREL, 101
STARFISH, 382-6
STARLING/SUNDOG, 398
Stasse, Capt Maurice, 295
STATUS/BUTTON, 210
STEEL/GLOVE, 210-11
Steer, Maj George, 106
Stephenson, Sir William, 297
Stevenson, Capt, 398
Stevenson, Maj Noel, 52-3, 89, 92, 113
Stewart, Cpl Clair, 330-6
Stewart, Gavin, 10, 73
Stilwell, Gen Joe, 3, 90-1, 96, 239-40, 243, 254, 258
STS, 37-9, 41, 46, 49, 64-5, 89, 151, 167, 182, 185, 194, 223-4, 237-8, 251, 289, 315
Stubbington, Lt Bill, 152, 167
SUGARLOAF, 209
Sumatra, 207-11
Sun, Stephen Sim Kah, 281
SUNABLE, 398
SUNBAKER, 398
SUNCHARLIE, 398
SUNFISH, 398
SUNGOD, 268
SUNLAG, 398
Suphasawat, Prince, 259, 261-2, 266
Supheert, Capt, 40
Sutcliffe, Capt, 352
Suzuki, Col, 88
SWALLOW, 388, 390
SWANSONG, 272
SWEEP/STUD, 210
Sweet-Escott, Col Bickham, 20, 43, 75, 78
SWIFT, 388, 390
Synge, 2/Lt P.M., 351

Tallant, 2/Lt Fred, 154
Taung, Capt Kumje, 98
Tavernier, Lt, 300
Taylor, 2/Lt Leslie, 153
Taylor, Col George, 68-9, 78, 307
Teesdale, Lt Eddie, 251
Teesdale, Maj Edward, 236, 238-9
Tek, Lai, 171, 182
TERRIER, 104
TETHER, 210
Thailand, 20, 257-78
Thomas, Maj Alison, 297
Thompson, 2/Lt David, 154
Thompson, 2/Lt Roland, 154
Thompson, Lt, 89
Thompson, Sqn Ldr Robert, 251
THURSDAY, 123, 132
TIDEWAY, 150
TIGER, 380-1
Timor, 395-9
Tolstoy, Count Ilya, 242
Trappes-Lomax, Lt Col Ambrose, 5, 18, 38, 41, 46, 309-10, 312, 314-8, 386, 388, 390
Tredea, S/Sgt, 354
Tremlett, Maj Innes, 10, 67, 155, 158, 161, 185, 306
Trofimov, Capt, 132
TROUT, 392
TRUMPET, 268
Tun, Capt Sein, 100
Tun, Than, 104
TURNIP, 391
Turrall, May Guy, 107, 122-4
Tutenges, Col Emile, 289
Tyson, B.F., 154, 170

Upton, Brig Norman, 92

V Force, 447-8
V Force, 66, 447-8
Van der Post, Capt Laurens, 39
Van Kett, Lt, 134
Vanrenan, Frank, 40, 151, 167, 183
Venner, John, 247
Villebois, 2/Lt Roger, 295
Villiers, 2/Lt Harold, 154

Wagstaff, Sgt Fred, 42, 153
WALDORF, 249
Waller, Capt Jock, 139
WALNUT, 390
WALRUS, 107
Walsh, Maj Gen, 100
Warne, Pte Doug, 330-6
Warren, Lt Col Alan, 32, 40, 46, 47-51, 167, 182, 289, 322
Warren, WO Alfred, 330-6
Watts, Sgt, 352
Wavell, Gen, 14, 38, 76, 230, 311, 323
WEASEL, 104
Wedell-Wedellsborg, Baron, 74
Wedermeyer, Gen, 237, 239-40, 243-4, 254, 292-3, 298, 300
Weilong, Gen Zhou, 225
Wei-lung, Gen Chow, 41
Wemyss, Victor, 258, 265, 268
West, Capt, 348
Wharton-Tigar, Edward, 247
WHITING, 392
Wilkins, Capt A.F., 398
Wilkinson, Gerald, 18
Willersdorf, WO Jeff, 330-6
Williams, Capt D.M., 398
Williams, Capt, 134
Williams, Col Bill, 89
Williamson, 38
Williamson, Capt Hugh, 251
Wilson, 2/Lt James, 153
Wilson, FM, 293
Wilson-Brand, Brig Adam, 235
Windle, Maj Oliver, 65
Wingate, Brig Orde, 98, 123
Winn, Capt Rowland, 268, 301
Wint, G., 36
Woolf, Capt, 134
Wren, P.R.C., 36
Wright, Capt A.F.S., 209
Wright, Jim, 26
Wylie, Lt Col Ian, 160, 305-6, 397, 400-3
Wynne, 2/Lt Alfred, 153
Wynne, Capt W.P., 399

X-O Group, 258

INDEX

Ying-chin, Gen Ho, 234

Z Experimental Station, 304, 312
Z Force [Hong Kong], 225
Z Force, 100, 449-50
Zau Rip, Lt, 18
ZEBRA, 104, 142
ZIPPER, 160-1, 172, 189, 205, 267, 271, 405

More *SOE Heroes* book by Alan Ogden

A SPUR CALLED COURAGE

The little known exploits of seventeen courageous SOE officers in Italy are vividly recounted by Alan Ogden in this riveting new study of SOE and the Italian Resistance.

Through their gallantry, ingenuity and determination, a small handful of SOE missions were able to arm and inspire thousands of Italians to fight the occupying German army from 1943 onwards and in the process give invaluable support to the advancing Allied armies as they pushed north towards Austria.

The author has been in contact with many of the families of these SOE heroes and has had access to hitherto unpublished letters, photographs and diaries. The picture that emerges is one of a heroic struggle not only against a ruthless and experienced enemy but also against the elements, hunger and harsh landscapes of the Italian Alps and Apennine Mountains.

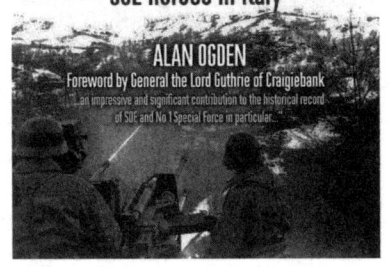

These extraordinary stories of individual SOE officers illustrate the many and varied tasks of SOE missions throughout the different regions of Italy from 1943-45 and thus provide a fascinating collage of the history of SOE during the prolonged and difficult Italian campaign.

"*A Spur Called Courage is a well-written, meticulously-researched and highly-inspirational book about a courageous group of Second World War heroes. I congratulate Alan Ogden on using a magnificent series of profiles to provide such a fascinating insight into the achievements of British and Commonwealth SOE officers in Italy from 1942-5. His splendid book is a welcome contribution to the greater understanding of a largely unsung group of men whose dangerous and secretive work is only now, quite rightly, being more widely acclaimed.*"

Lord Ashcroft, KCMG, author of *Special Forces Heroes, George Cross Heroes, and Victoria Cross Heroes*

Hardback
ISBN: 978-1-903071-35-9
Price: £25.00

SONS OF ODYSSEUS

In this follow-up to his acclaimed *A Spur Called Courage*, military historian Alan Ogden repeats the formula of picking exceptional SOE heroes – this time nineteen who operated behind enemy lines in Greece during World War II.

Sons of Odysseus highlights many of the extraordinary acts of sabotage carried out by SOE personnel against German occupation forces and examines the difficulties SOE Missions experienced in working with a resistance torn apart by irreconcilable political divisions. Unexpected stories emerge of humanitarian aid dispensed to starving children in the Peloponnese and of the struggle to safeguard 11,000 Italian POWs after their surrender in 1943.

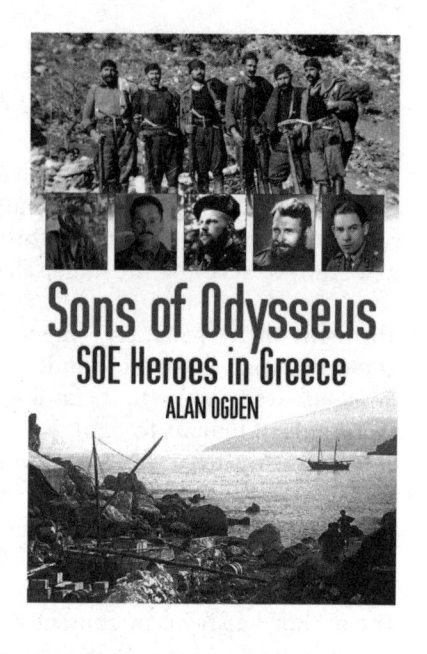

Much of the research for these profiles has been from original unseen sources as are many of the accompanying photographs.

"Thorough research has produced a marvelous book...Brimming with anecdote and full of character...very readable...[the author] is to be congratulated on producing a superb book that is a fitting tribute to those who fought with SOE in Greece"

Guards Magazine

Hardback
ISBN: 978-1-903071-44-1
Price: £25.00